MANAGEMENT: MAKING ORGANIZATIONS PERFORM

MANAGEMENT

MAKING ORGANIZATIONS PERFORM

H. R. Smith
Archie B. Carroll
Asterios G. Kefalas
Hugh J. Watson

College of Business Administration
University of Georgia

Macmillan Publishing Co., Inc.
New York
Collier Macmillan Publishers
London

Printed in the United States of America

Macmillan Publishing Co., Inc.
866 Third Avenue, New York, New York 10022

Collier Macmillan Canada, Ltd.

Library of Congress Cataloging in Publication Data

Main entry under title:

Management, making organizations perform.
Includes bibliographies and index.
1. Management. 2. Organization. I. Smith, Howard Ross.
HD31.M2929 1980 658.4 79-18340
ISBN 0-02-412500-8

Printing: 12345678 Year: 0123456

PREFACE

If advances in science and technology increase human potential, they also increase the complexity of their effective application and the fulfillment of that increased potential. Through organizations we master that complexity. Future historians may well conclude that one of the most significant developments of the twentieth century was the proliferation, maturation, and institutionalization of human collective effort in the form of the organization. It is also probable that those same historians will attribute at least part of the successes and failures of humanity to successes and failures in the management of these organizations: to how well management met the needs and desires of society in perceiving the roles of the organizations, establishing objectives for them, and following strategies through them. In our own time we acknowledge the importance of organizations in the large and growing body of research and theory concerning their nature, purpose, and management.

Management: Making Organizations Perform is about organizations and their management. It is written for introductory management courses, and although its content addresses colleges of business administration primarily, it also serves other disciplines that include management offerings, e.g., public administration. Topics covered in the book are selected for their interest, relevance, and currency. They satisfy accreditation requirements for AACSB members.

In some business schools the introduction to management course takes a specific orientation along one of the conventional lines of management theory, such as a behavioral, process, or quantitative orientation. But many schools prefer to expose their introductory students to all aspects of management, and it is according to this preference that *Management: Making Organizations Perform* divides its emphasis almost equally among the four prevailing schools of management theory—namely, systems, process, behavior, and management science. The treatment of each school of thought is thorough yet concise enough to admit supplementation according to the wishes of the instructor or reader. The integration of the four schools, however, best incorporates what managers need to know to make organizations function effectively, and it is with a proper, balanced integration as our object that we organize this book. Our rationale is as follows:

1. Increasingly, the *systems approach* with an emphasis on the environment is affecting decision-making within organizations.
2. The traditional *process* approach is still the major conceptual foundation for explaining and understanding what managers do.
3. Organizational *behavior* is providing significant insights into how to make employee performance more harmonious and effective.
4. Emerging *decision technology* is making it possible to analyze complex systems in a more scientific manner.

We perceive management to be the art and science of organizing human and natural resources for the purpose of setting and accomplishing organizational objectives effectively, efficiently, and ethically. The manager is seen as the agent whose purpose is to assess the organization's external environment and devise the internal structure and behavior that will lead to the greatest success. It is only through this careful assessment of the potential of the external environment that a manager can, by using the latest decision technology, make sound decisions regarding corporate objectives and strategies.

The book is divided into five major parts. Part I, the introduction provides an overview (Chapter 1) and a brief historical perspective of the origins and developments of management (Chapter 2). In Part II, "Systems and Environments," the systems approach is examined, and its application to the management of organizations is assessed (Chapter 3). Furthermore the interface between the organization and its external environment is carefully investigated (Chapter 4). With that background established the book tackles three of the main functions of the management process (Part III). Thus, the subjects of planning and controlling are treated jointly in Chapter 5, while the organizing and decision-making functions are the subjects of Chapters 6 and 7, respectively.

One of the most troublesome tasks of contemporary management is to deal with the human element of an organization. This task is the concern of Part IV of the book. A person's behavioral characteristics, motivational aspects (Chapter 8), power and authority needs (Chapter 9), leadership qualities (Chapter 10), and communicative skills and capabilities (Chapter 11) are of paramount importance. It is primarily the manager's duty to provide the appropriate organizational structure and climate that elicit the appropriate communicative and leadership skills that will, in turn, through careful use of power and authority instruments (Chapter 11), stimulate the necessary motivation for continuous organizational development (Chapter 12).

The second half of the twentieth century ushered in a new decision technology that created the greatest changes in the manager's job since the Industrial Revolution of the previous century. This decision technology augments the manager's cognitive capacity. In other words, decision technology enables the manager to acquire, process, evaluate and use information better for the purpose of making better decisions. The application of decision technology by management requires the use of management science methods and, frequently, the computer. Thus Part V begins in Chapter 13 with an introduction to management science modeling. Subsequently, it focuses on two types of models—planning (Chapter 14) and controlling models (Chapter 15)—and ends with a brief exposure to the role of computers in organizations.

The last chapter of the book (Chapter 17) addresses itself to the future and the managerial methods of dealing with it. Increasingly managers are beginning to recognize that they must attempt to relate today's actions to tomorrow's consequences. If this practical feat appears impossible, it seems so because we are accustomed to looking at the future mistily and mystically through a crystal ball. Today there are numerous legitimate future-assessing methods that a manager can use to develop an appreciation of the future impact of today's decisions.

Managing an organization is a complex and difficult task. A host of activities performed by many people and much equipment must be integrated through a network of complicated methods and approaches. Not one person but a group of persons must perform the numerous functions of management. It is also obvious that writing about how managers manage can best be done through a group effort. In such a group, each writer applies his or her specialized knowledge to the appropriate particular aspect of management. We have taken advantage of diverse expertise in writing this book. Four authors collaborated in researching the writings each perceived as pertinent to the subject of his interest and cast them into a framework upon which each hung his own experience and insights. *Executive Commentaries* were added to enhance the student's understanding of the practical significance of management. For each topic, a practicing executive offers his thoughts concerning his own experiences and shares his insights on the subject.

To further enhance this diversity and flexibility the book has been enriched with (a) discussion questions, (b) short cases at the end of each chapter, (c) longer cases at the end of the parts, and (d) a reader entitled *Readings in Management: Making Organizations Perform.* To facilitate the use of the text we offer a *Study Guide* by Professor T. Edwin Boling. These supplements provide a complete package and an excellent tool for an educational experience.

The authors would like to acknowledge the contributions of their students who as usual provide the first tests of new and half-baked ideas before those musings can reach the publishing stage. Numerous colleagues and graduate students have contributed during the different stages of writing this work. Particular mention must be made of Professor James Lahiff for his contribution of the entire chapter on communication. Our thanks also go to the administration of the College of Business Administration of the University of Georgia for its continuous support and encouragement, without which this work would not have been possible. Our appreciation of Mrs. Cindy Lloyd, head of our Word Processing Center, is more than she has thus far been able to ascertain. Finally, to the secretarial staff, in particular Mrs. Nancy Parks, Mrs. Jackie Ogletree, Mrs. Pat Bryant, and Mrs. Betty Brewer who struggled with the various drafts of our manuscripts, we extend the highest honor for courage for taking their chances when in doubt about certain words and for their other efforts as well.

H.R.S.
A.B.C.
A.G.K.
H.J.W.

CONTENTS

EPILOGUE

1

INTRODUCTION

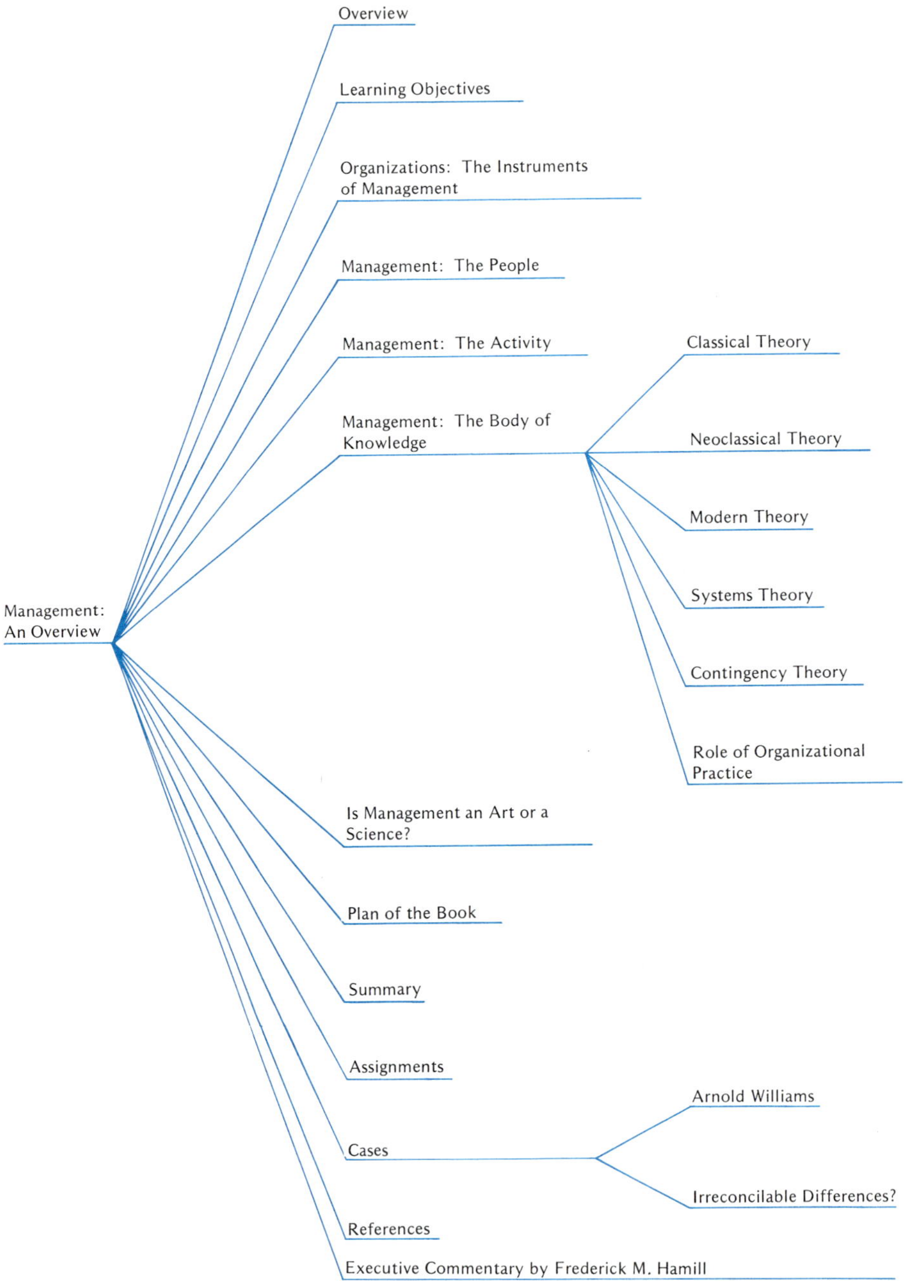

Management: An Overview
Overview
Learning Objectives
Organizations: The Instruments of Management
Management: The People
Management: The Activity
Management: The Body of Knowledge
Classical Theory
Neoclassical Theory
Modern Theory
Systems Theory
Contingency Theory
Role of Organizational Practice
Is Management an Art or a Science?
Plan of the Book
Summary
Assignments
Cases
Arnold Williams
Irreconcilable Differences?
References
Executive Commentary by Frederick M. Hamill

1

MANAGEMENT: AN OVERVIEW

OVERVIEW

One of the most straightforward ways of summarizing what management is all about is to restate the title of this book—*Management: Making Organizations Perform.* Management *is* concerned with making organizations perform. The eminent management expert Peter F. Drucker recently affirmed this view with his assertion, "The first job of the manager is to make his organization perform."[1] We must move beyond such succinct expressions of management's task, however, if we are to fully understand and appreciate the essentials that constitute contemporary management practice.

To begin with, we should acknowledge that there is some lack of agreement among management practitioners, scholars, and theorists as to what management really is. Or, perhaps it would be more accurate to say that although we recognize management to be many different things, some choose to stress or emphasize one aspect of it over another. This is so because, as with most other fields of study, there are a number of schools of thought concerning the best way to approach the subject.

For example, there are the management process school, the behavioral school, the systems school, and the management science school, just to mention several major streams of thought. Each of these schools represents a view or a *perspective* that addresses important facets of management. It is for this reason that we have chosen to draw upon each of four major perspectives in conceptualizing the

[1] Peter F. Drucker, "We Have Become a Society of Organizations," *Wall Street Journal*, Jan. 9, 1978, p. 12.

structure of this book. The perspectives we have chosen are dominant ones. First, we have selected knowledge about systems and the environment and combined them together into an *environmental* component or perspective. Second, we explore management as a *process*. Third, we address *behavioral* issues, and finally, we present *decision technology*. We will discuss each of these more fully at the end of the chapter.

In this chapter we intend to provide an overview of management. To do this, we will first discuss *organizations*—what they are, their characteristics, and various types. Second, we will examine *three major understandings* of the concept of management. Third, we address the important question of whether management is an *art or a science*. Last, we will more fully develop and discuss the *plan of the book*.

LEARNING OBJECTIVES

This chapter is especially intended to help the student:

1. **Gain an appreciation of organizations as instruments of management.**
2. **Comprehend the various facets of management—the people, the activity, and the body of knowledge.**
3. **Understand, in a broad way, the evolution of management theory.**
4. **Discern the art versus the science aspects of management.**
5. **Grasp the overall structure and plan of the book.**
6. **Learn, especially in the context of thinking about management, the meaning of the following concepts:**

   management
   types of organizations
   classical theory
   neoclassical theory
   modern theory
   systems theory
   management as art and science

ORGANIZATIONS: THE INSTRUMENTS OF MANAGEMENT

Organizations are pervasive in our society. Indeed, it may be said that we are "a society of organizations."[2] Organizations are the instruments by which management achieves its objectives. Although at one time society was able to achieve its objectives through instruments such as the family, the home, the farm, and the shop, these tasks are today achieved primarily through larger, more formalized structures.

[2]Drucker, ibid., p. 12.

Organizations, as we will study them, can be defined as goal-oriented, collective groups of individuals who band together in a system of formal relationships. Thus a *group* of individuals is involved; this group has come together with *goals* in mind, and the group *formalizes* itself by specifying role relationships. Of course, if our major focus were on *informal* organizations, we would have to relax our last requirement of formalization; however, our major focus here will be on *formal* organizations.

Why Organize?

The reason [that] men organize is always the same: to ensure that *individual efforts are directed toward a common purpose and that they support each other.* The latter is largely a question of timing, the timing of individual efforts. Each form of human collaboration, from two persons to two million, is like an orchestra. It only works really well if the individual players "keep time," so that their efforts support each other and are in accord with "the score." If a single player (instrumentalist) fails to "keep time," the whole effect may be ruined. That is why orchestras have "conductors" and *business undertakings have managers.* [Emphasis added.]

Lt. Col. L. F. Urwick, "That Word 'Organization,'" *Academy of Management Review,* Vol. 1, No. 1, January, 1976, p. 90.

Organizations today are much larger and much more complex than those of many years ago. Just as our economy has experienced tremendous growth, particularly since World War II, the instruments of business and government—organizations—have likewise grown at a faster pace. Complexity is another characteristic of modern organizations. The rate of change in the social, political, technological, and economic spheres has been at a pace heretofore unseen in our society. This turbulence has created a need to modify the rather traditional structures of the past, and to move toward more flexible, responsive, adaptive and, hence, more complex forms of organization.

As the title of this book suggests, management has the responsibility for making organizations perform. To do this, managers must know a great deal about organizations—how they function, the role of people in them, and their internal dynamics. Organizations provide the context within which managerial activity takes place. As a consequence, organizations are, indeed, instruments of management. As we shall see, management can create them, design them, and make them more or less effective for their purposes.

There are many different types of organizations—business, governmental, educational, military, hospitals, and so on. Although our focus will be on business organizations for the most part, it should be kept in mind that much of what is said could also apply to these other types of organizations as well. There are differences between these organizational types, however, so care must be exercised when assuming that everything said is applicable to every organizational type.

A number of different typologies of organizations have been developed for purposes of classifying organizations into broad categories. Within each of these broad categories we might more realistically assume that the organizations operate similarly. However, organizations are different from one category to the next. One typology that clearly illustrates the differences classifies organizations as being coercive, utilitarian, or normative, depending on the type of power that is predominantly used to achieve results.

The *coercive* organization is one that attempts to control behavior through *punishment* and the *fear* of reward deprivation. Examples of coercive organizations would be prisons, prison-of-war camps, and custodial mental hospitals. The *utilitarian* organization controls behavior by using *extrinsic* rewards in exchange for task performance. These rewards might include wages, retirement programs, and status symbols (offices, secretaries, names on doors). There are times, of course, when certain forms of deprivation may be used—demotions, withholding of pay raises, and so on. Examples of utilitarian organizations would be business firms, peacetime military organizations, and most governmental organizations. The *normative* organization attempts to control behavior primarily by using *intrinsic* rewards. Intrinsic rewards are those that are valued in their own right and might include the feelings of self-accomplishment, mastery, or commitment to the work that one is doing. Examples of organizations that emphasize normative controls are churches, colleges and universities, ideologically based political organizations or parties, voluntary associations, and professional associations. Extrinsic rewards are used here, too, but are not the primary emphasis as in a business organization.[3]

It should be evident after examining these three types of organizations that the differences may in many instances dictate different structures and managerial styles. For this reason, care must be exercised in making broad statements about organizational similarities. One must be well aware of what types of organizations are being referred to in any given instance. Within the broad class of utilitarian organizations in which we are most interested, however, we shall primarily look for similarities.

Now that we have provided a brief overview of what organizations are all about, it is appropriate to discuss in more detail what is meant by *management.* It has three major facets: people, activities, and a body of knowledge. Each of these deserves special attention.

[3] Amitai Etzioni, *Modern Organizations* (Englewood Cliffs, N.J.: Prentice-Hall, 1964). See also Amitai Etzioni, *A Comparative Analysis of Complex Organizations* (New York: The Free Press, 1961).

MANAGEMENT: THE PEOPLE

Management is either a person or a group of persons within a formal organization. Management refers to those who have the official authority and responsibility for the achievement of the organization's objectives. The organization's objectives, of course, are really the objectives of the owners in the case of a business organization, or the objectives of the governing body in the case of a government organization or, perhaps, an educational institution. Because we are concerned primarily with business organizations, we will focus our main attention on them. It should be kept in mind, however, that organizations of all types have managers. The main distinction lies in the source of authority for appointing or designating the management group—whether they be owners, taxpayers, elected officials, or some other type of governing body.

A management group usually has a number of managers. A *manager* is a person within an organization who has been appointed or designated by its owners or a higher authority to take a leadership role in guiding the organization toward its objectives. In the case of a business, the major objective might be to make a product or to provide a service for a profit. In the case of a governmental unit (local or state, for example), the objective may be to provide a public service efficiently.

Managers occupy various levels of authority within the organization and have responsibility for a variety of different people and functions. A typical organization has several levels or layers of authority and, hence, of managers. Because there are usually fewer managers at the top of the organization than at the bottom, the typical organization is pyramidal in shape. Figure 1-1 depicts how a business organization appears in the abstract.

Although many large organizations such as General Motors, Dupont, or Burlington Industries have more levels of management than three, we typically speak of there being three levels of management—top, middle, and lower. In the large

FIGURE 1-1. A Typical Organization.

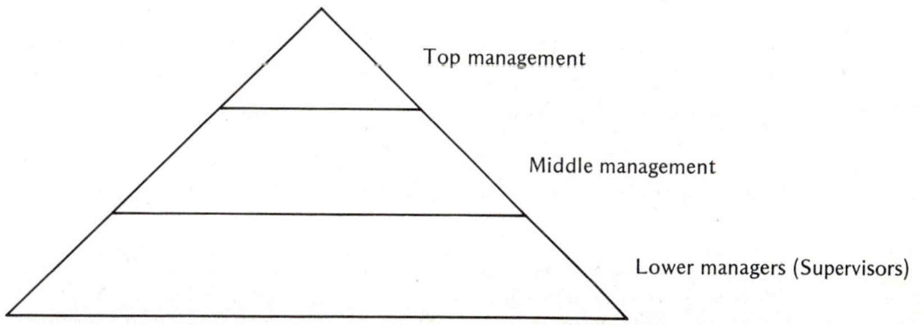

organization, therefore, each of these levels would include perhaps several layers of managers.

The managers at the various levels in the organization frequently have a different scope of responsibility and time orientation. At the lowest level, managers are frequently referred to as *supervisors.* Lower management, or supervisors, have the immediate task of overseeing the first-line employees who carry out the daily tasks of the organization. In the typical firm, the supervisor is the lowest-level manager in that organization. As a consequence, the supervisor is truly the link between the employees and the rest of management. That is why the supervisor has frequently been said to be the "man in the middle," or today, the "person" in the middle. Not only is that literally true, but it has important implications for the supervisory management role. Supervisors, thus, are the members of management that employees come into contact with on the most regular basis—probably every day.[4]

Middle managers are just that—managers between top management and the lower-level supervisors. Perhaps their most distinguishing characteristic is that they are "managers of managers." They frequently have a number of lower-level supervisors reporting to them. Whereas supervisors are usually oriented toward the short run (a week or a month), middle managers are more medium range in their outlook. Their job is to act as translator of top management's overall organizational strategy into operational policies, procedures, and methods of work.

The Middle manager

As the responsibilities of these specialists (middle managers) expand, amoeba-fashion, to engulf practically every aspect of running a huge corporation, their collective influence becomes apparent. Middle managers are making most of the day-to-day operating decisions and also are making nearly all of the specialized studies and recommendations on which top management is basing its long-range decisions. As a result, "sometimes it appears that middle management is practically running the company . . ."

"The Managers," *Wall Street Journal,* April 18, 1977, p. 1.

Top management in most business firms is made up of the president along with high-level vice-presidents. Some consider the board of directors to be a part of top management. Top management shapes the organization's overall direction, mission, or strategy. The top management group provides specific answers to such crucial questions as: What business are we in? What course of action shall we

[4]For an elaboration on supervisors as managers, see Archie B. Carroll and Ted F. Anthony, "An Overview of the Supervisor's Job," *Personnel Journal,* May, 1976, pp. 228–231; 249. See also Ted F. Anthony and Archie B. Carroll, "Preventing Supervision From Becoming an End- of-the-Line Job," *Personnel Journal,* June, 1977, pp. 295–297.

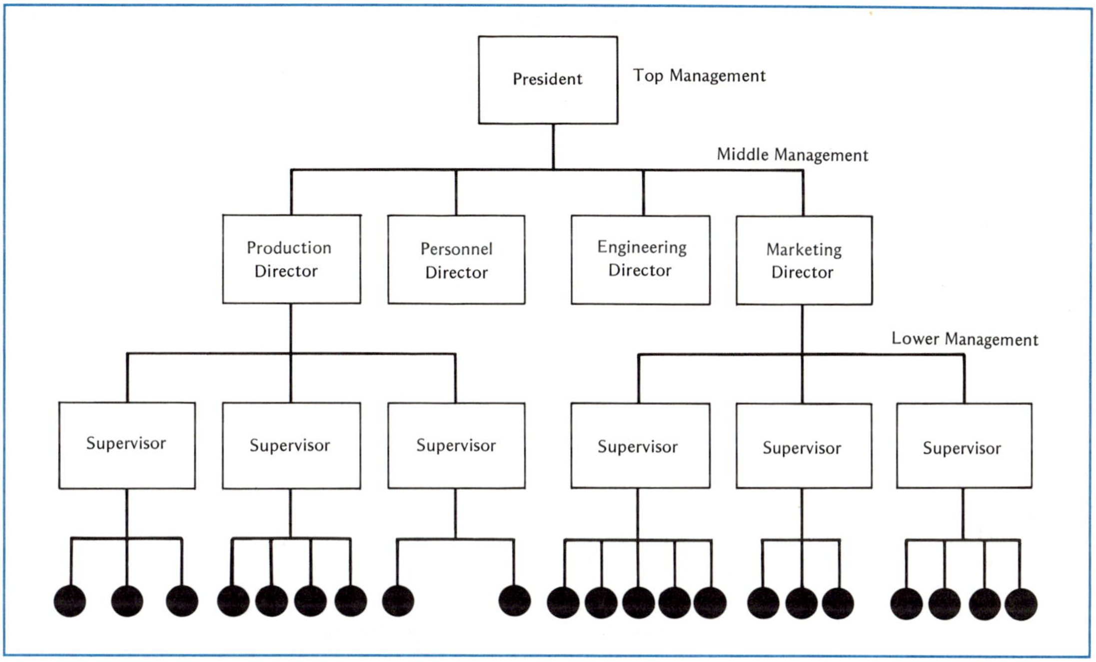

FIGURE 1-2. A Typical Organization Chart.

pursue? How should resources be acquired and used? What major market opportunities are most compatible with our goals? What is the optimal organization-environment "fit"? Top management's orientation is toward the long run and toward the organization's role in the economy and the larger society. A *Business Week* article of several years ago called the chief executive "Mr. Outside" because of this external orientation.[5]

Thus we see that whereas management is a group of people assigned the overall task of moving the organization toward its objectives, it is necessary to specify clearly to which manager or managerial level we are referring so as to fully understand what these people do within the organization. Figure 1-2 illustrates these various management levels in a typical organization chart.

MANAGEMENT: THE ACTIVITY

Management as an *activity* represents the *action phase* of what management—the people—do. Perhaps this sounds a bit obvious but it nevertheless does provide an additional perspective on what management is all about.

[5]"The Top Man Becomes Mr. Outside," *Business Week,* May 4, 1974, pp. 38–42.

Management—the activity—is a collective term describing all of the behavior in which managers engage as they attempt to achieve the organization's objectives. Using this understanding, when we talk about management, we are referring to such action-oriented activites as planning, organizing, leading, coordinating, motivating, delegating, communicating, decision making, handling crises, and so on.

There has been considerable debate about which activities or set of activites most nearly capture the essence of what managers do, but we will not enter that debate here. Suffice it to say that the manager engages in a widely diversified set of activities.

MANAGEMENT: THE BODY OF KNOWLEDGE

Management is also a field of study—a discipline—a *body of knowledge.* As such it is a collective term describing the state of knowledge about managing people and organizations. Management is an eclectic body of knowledge. It draws heavily from other disciplines. The role of other disciplines in providing knowledge that is useful in managing organizations—in making organizations perform—has changed over time. And it would be extremely difficult to pinpoint on a time line when various other fields of study came to bear on the state of management knowledge in a significant way.

We can, however, indicate what some of these other fields of knowledge are. Knowledge about management has come from the behavioral sciences (psychology), from the social sciences (sociology and economics), and from the quantitative disciplines (engineering, mathematics, and statistics). Each of these fields of study has contributed both theoretical and practical insights into the task of making organizations perform.

It is also useful to examine briefly how the management body of knowledge has evolved over time. Although in Chapter 2 we will look at management in historical perspective in closer detail, a cursory overview of the evolution of management theory will aid in our understanding of the management body of knowledge.

William G. Scott provides a helpful classification of the evolutionary development of management or organization theory. He has classified theory development into four parts: classical theory, neoclassical theory, modern theory, and systems theory.[6] We will then look briefly at what is known as contingency theory of management.

Classical Theory

Classical theory focuses almost exclusively on the *anatomy of formal organization.* The theory deals with management and organization by emphasizing

[6] William G. Scott, "Organization Theory: An Overview and an Appraisal," *Academy of Management Journal* (April 1961), pp. 7–26.

various attributes of the organization's *structure*. Scott argues that classical theory is built around four key pillars, each of which pertains to the formal structure of the organization. We will examine these key pillars in Chapter 6.

The most conspicuous characteristic of classical theory is its lack of concern for the human element in organization. The focus on structure is so intense that one gets the impression that the early thinkers viewed organizations as not having people in them. The classical theorists largely ignored problems stemming from interpersonal conflict, informal groups, and individual personality. In addition, they made no effort to incorporate contributions of the emerging behavioral sciences into their doctrine. In sum, though classical theory did provide a number of insights into the nature of organizations, its omission of behavioral elements limited its usefulness as a comprehensive theory of management and organization.

Neoclassical Theory

Neoclassical theory's point of departure was the observation that in the classical organization/management theory the human element was either oversimplified or ignored. Thus, neoclassical theory made the human dimension of managing the focal point, as contrasted with the impersonality of classical theory, and thus built beyond the emphasis on efficiency and productivity that so absorbed the classicists. For this reason, the movement initiated by this school was termed the *human relations* movement. Neoclassical theory accepts the basic postulates of the classical theory but modifies them by superimposing changes in operating methods and structure appropriate to individual behavior and the influence of the informal group. Thus, individual and group behavior became the center of focus.

Modern Theory

Modern theory is characterized by three parallel developments: (1) the extension of earlier classical and neoclassical theory, (2) the emergence of behavioral science research; and (3) the emergence of decision technology. The extension of classical and neoclassical theories was inspired by the work of Chester Barnard. Although his book, *The Functions of the Executive,* appeared in 1938, his ideas were not current until Herbert Simon popularized them a quarter of a century later. Barnard-Simon's conceptualization of organizations and their emphasis on decision making and communication can be regarded as the beginning of systems theory.

Systems Theory

What differentiates systems theory from the previous theories of organization/management is its emphasis on the integration of all facets of the organization and its management into a coherent whole (wholeness), and also its conception of an organization as an open system that is in a continuous interaction with its external environment. The application of systems theory to the management of organizations is referred to as the systems approach, and it is covered in detail in Chapter 3.

Despite the frequent use of the term *systems* by management, academicians, and practitioners, there is little agreement with respect to one accepted meaning of the term. As accountants talk about accounting systems, production specialists about production systems, data processing personnel about electronic data processing systems, marketing people about market systems, behavioral scientists about reward and motivation systems, the student of management is understandably confused. We hope that the fuller discussion later aids in clarifying systems concepts and systems theory.

Contingency Theory

One can quite readily see that the search for management universals can be quite frustrating. Practicing managers were perhaps the first to note that it is not accurate to speak of management principles as though there were a set of guidelines that could provide universal direction. Researchers, too, noted that management theory was situational. For example, Joan Woodward in her research into relationships between organization structure and human relationships found the existing technology of the organization to be an influential situational factor. Later research into organization structure, design, and leadership style supported the finding that the specific situation or circumstances at hand dictated significantly how management had to deal with it.

The situational approach, or contingency theory as it is contemporarily called, is summarized well by Fremont Kast and James Rosenzweig:

> *It [contingency theory] emphasizes the multivariate nature of organizations and attempts to understand how organizations operate under varying conditions and in specific circumstances. Contingency views are ultimately directed toward suggesting organizational designs and managerial practices most appropriate for specific situations.*[7]

The attractiveness of contingency theory is immediately seen: it all depends on the *situation* as to whether a particular management approach will work or not. Contingency theory tries to move beyond the simple dictum that "it all depends," however, to spell out the specific attributes of situations and environments in which various management approaches will be most successful. Contingency theory of necessity, then, pulls the best of the other approaches together and integrates them into a contingency perspective.

[7]Fremont E. Kast and James E. Rosenzweig, *Contingency Views of Organization and Management* (Chicago: Science Research Associates, Inc., 1973), p. ix.

	Classical Theory	Neoclassical Theory	Modern Theory	Systems Theory	Contingency Theory
Emphasis of theory	Efficiency	Human Relations	Behavioral Research	Wholeness/ Integration	Situation
	Productivity	Satisfaction	Decision Technology	Openness to Environment	Managerial Approach

FIGURE 1-3. A Summary of Five Management Theories

Figure 1-3 summarizes some of the major characteristics or emphases of the five management theories presented. It should be kept in mind that each subsequent theory is built upon previous theories and that the five are not thought to be independent of one another. And, as you shall see as you move through the book, efforts to categorize management knowledge or approaches can all too easily result in oversimplified conceptual schemes. It is our aim, however, to create some order that will be useful.

The Role of Organizational Practice

Actual organizational practice in a variety of different types of organizations is also a significant contributor to the development of management knowledge. Managerial practice represents attempts on the part of practicing managers to put into effect knowledge gained from numerous sources—theory, practical experience, judgment, intuition, and philosophy.

Figure 1-4 illustrates the iterative process by which exchange is made between the theoretical world (the world of ideas, some tested, some untested) and the real world in which managers attempt to make organizations perform. Note the inputs from the various bodies of knowledge in the theoretical world and the practical experience of organizations of all kinds in the real world. In an evolutionary process, then, management knowledge develops.

There are other ways of viewing management than those we have examined—the *people,* the *activity,* and the *body of knowledge.* We believe, however, that an examination of these major facets provides a reasonably representative understanding of the ways in which management is viewed today. All of the elements are there: (1) those who are doing the managing, (2) the activities they engage in, and, (3) the body of knowledge (ideas, approaches, techniques) they employ. Someone might ask, What about the people and the organization that are being managed? To be sure, they are part of the total configuration, but neither the people nor the organization are management; rather, they are components of the larger management scene. Figure 1-5 depicts how all of these components fit together.

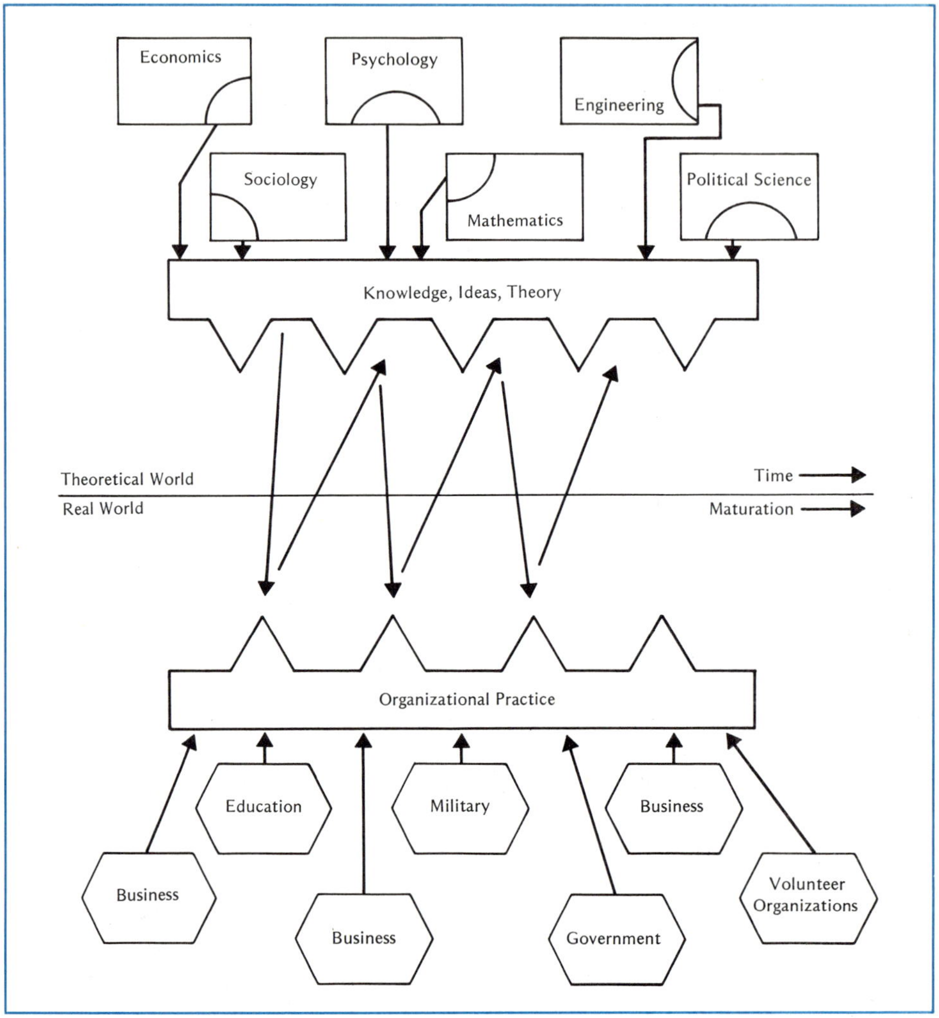

FIGURE 1-4. The Evolution of Management Knowledge.

IS MANAGEMENT AN ART OR A SCIENCE?

One question that frequently puzzles students is whether management is an *art* or a *science*. Actually, it is both, but some elaboration may be useful. When we talk about whether management is an art or a science, we are usually referring to the degree to which the knowledge has been systematized and is capable of being stated as definitive principles, laws, or theories. Perhaps definitions of art and of science would be helpful in understanding this distinction.

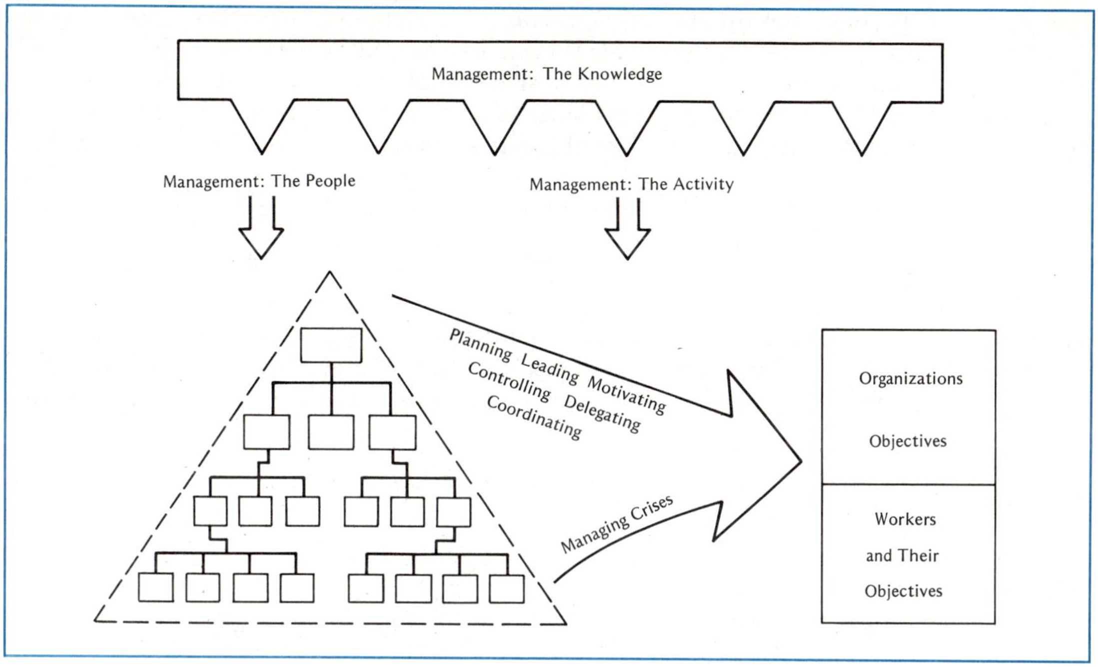

FIGURE 1-5. The Management Configuration.

Louis A. Allen, in discussing this issue, has defined a science as "a unified and systematically arranged body of knowledge dealing with facts or truths and showing the operation of general laws or principles."[8] It is clear, using this definition, that management is not yet a science, a *true* science as rigidly defined. It is also true, however, based upon this definition, that management as a field of study does have some scientific characteristics; that is, it is becoming more science-like. Without question, the management body of knowledge is moving in the direction of achieving scientific status and great strides have been made over the past 70 years in this direction.

It is doubtful that we will ever reach a point, however, at which anyone would argue that management has achieved full scientific status. As long as human beings are a part of the total management process—and every indication is that this will always be the case—the field can develop no more quickly than our knowledge of psychology and sociology. It is fairly safe to say, too, that management will never become a science in the sense that chemistry or physics is a science in which one deals with elements that have known and constant properties.

Management over time is becoming more scientific in that great strides are

[8]Louis A. Allen, *The Management Profession* (New York: McGraw-Hill, 1964), p. 86.

being made toward developing codification schemes to assist us in classifying the knowledge we do possess. Recent years, too, have also seen both academicians and practitioners engaging in empirical research at an increasing rate to test our tentative or speculative knowledge of management theory. The application of measurement techniques—mathematics and statistics—has led the way in these efforts to become more scientific.

A recent study has been conducted to determine the ways in which published management articles reflect an emphasis on conceptual (less scientific) knowledge or empirical (more scientific) knowledge over the last 30 years.[9] The findings of this study suggest a tremendous upturn in the quantity of more scientific research and a decline in the quantity of less scientific research. Figure 1-6 summarizes the findings of this study. Note the clear-cut trend toward more scientific publishing. There is some correspondence between research, writing,

[9]Robert D. Gatewood, James Lahiff, and Archie B. Carroll, "Management Publication Trends: A Thirty Year Perspective." A paper presented at the Southern Management Association meeting, New Orleans, 1978.

FIGURE 1-6. Trends Toward More Science in Management Publishing.

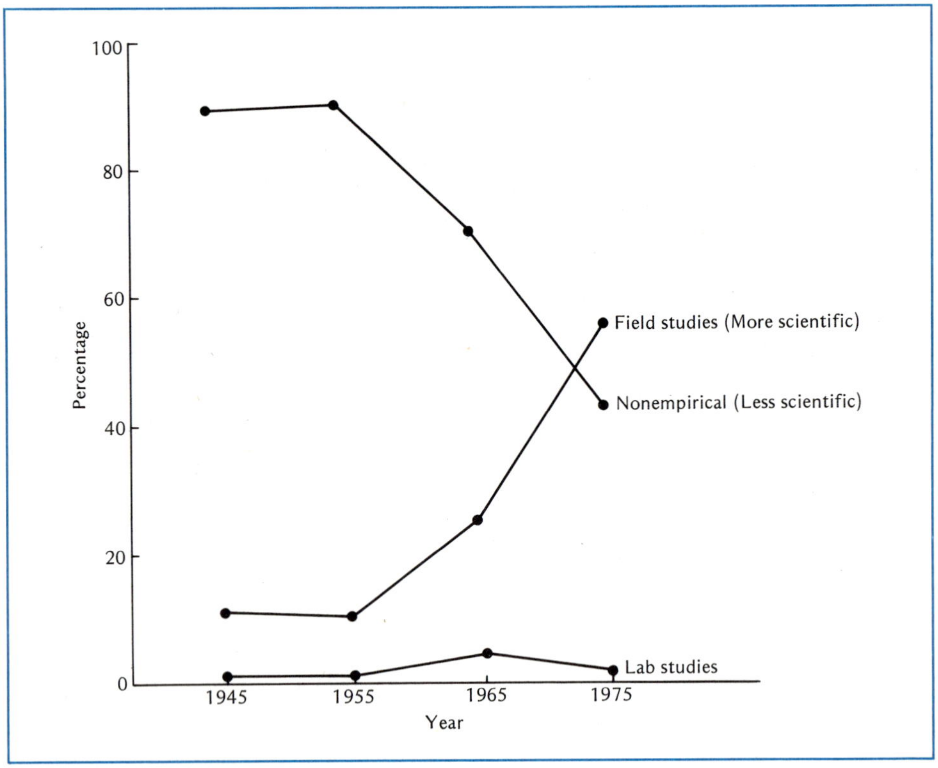

and management practice; therefore, this chart helps to document what is happening in management practice.

Let us turn our attention to management as an art for a moment. Allen defines an art as "a skill exercised in terms of the individual personality of the practitioner."[10] Using this definition, we would have to agree that management has an art component to it. We have long known that the individual's skill—the practicing manager's skill—has been a key variable in the success of management practice. Experience shows that managers develop over time their own special bundle of skills that interact very directly with their knowledge to bring about goal accomplishment and effectiveness.

Another definition lends additional perspective to the art of management. Harold Koontz asserts that "art is the application of knowledge to reality with a view to accomplishing some concrete results, ordinarily with compromise, blend, or design to set the best total results."[11] Here we see the special role played by the individual manager employing specialized skills such as compromise to achieve results. Other specialized skills or attributes that might legitimately be included in the art component of management include intuition, judgment, and instinct. In addition to these, craft, vision, and communication have been held to be indispensable aspects of management as an art.[12]

Explicit in Koontz's definition of art is that the manager is *applying* knowledge. It should be clear then that to the extent the individual has available a store of categorized knowledge, a greater facility to manage appropriately should result. Koontz carries this point further:

> *The best art arises where the artist possesses a store of organized and applicable knowledge and understands how to apply it to reality. Thus, engineers have long understood that the best designers are those who are well grounded in the underlying sciences. . . .*
>
> *The same can be said of the task of managing. As an art, there is every reason to believe that it will succeed best if the practitioner has a store of applicable and organized knowledge to serve him.*[13]

Thus we see the vital roles that both the science and the art of management assume in the total process. Although management is becoming more scientific, we will always need its art aspects in order to make organizations perform effectively. Even the casual observer of organizations knows that this is true. Different managers, all operating from the same knowledge base, frequently end up with varied results. The art of management partially explains this occur-

[10]Louis A. Allen, op. cit., p. 86.

[11]Harold Koontz, "A Model for Analyzing the Universality and Transferability of Management," *Academy of Management Journal,* Vol. 12, No. 4, (Dec., 1969), p. 420.

[12]Henry M. Boettinger, "Is Management Really An Art?" *Harvard Business Review,* Vol. 53, No. 1, (Jan.–Feb., 1975), pp. 54–64.

[13]Koontz, op. cit., p. 420.

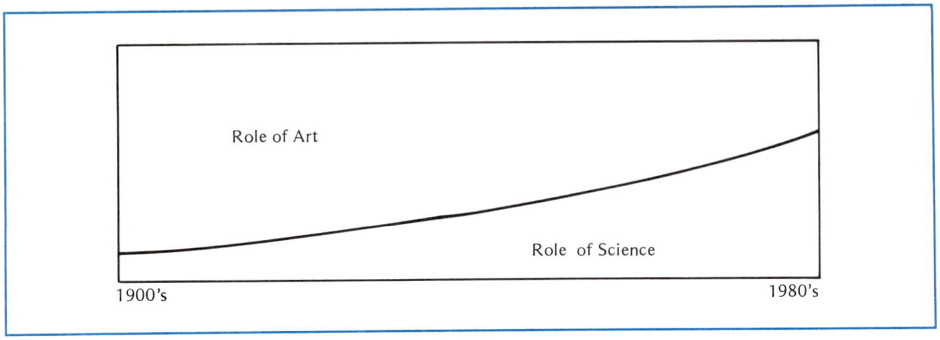

FIGURE 1-7. Art Versus Science in Management over Time.

rence.[14] Figure 1-7 suggests the changing proportions of art versus science in management since the early 1900s.

A word of caution is needed concerning management as a science. In the literature of management, you will encounter the expressions *scientific management* and *management science.* Both of these terms have very specialized meanings that set them somewhat apart from the meaning conveyed in the foregoing discussion. Scientific management was a term that came to be identified with the early 1900s and particularly with the efforts of the pioneer Frederick W. Taylor, who attempted to apply principles of science and engineering to the improvement of work methods. Taylor's efforts were admittedly toward making management more scientific, but the special term *scientific management* is usually limited to those 1900–1930 efforts and, therefore, does not include what has subsequently occurred in the efforts to make management more of a science. The expression *management science* is a contemporary one. It is a term that has come to be used for the body of knowledge which applies quantitative methods to the solution of business problems. Although it, too, is related to our discussion, the phrase has a more limited and specific usage of its own.

PLAN OF THE BOOK

There are many ways an introductory management book might be structured. We have chosen our structure because it represents what we think to be the major thrusts that ought to be covered in an introductory course in management. There are five major parts of the book, covering the following: Introduction, Systems

[14]For an interesting discussion of cognitive styles of managing, see James L. McKenney and Peter G. W. Keen, "How Managers' Minds Work," *Harvard Business Review,* Vol. 52, No. 3, May–June, 1974, pp. 79–90.

and Environment, Process, Behavior, and Decision Technology. We close the book with an Epilogue.

In Part I, the Introduction, we have two overriding focuses. First, we present an introductory overview of management. Second, we present a chapter on management in historical perspective. With these two chapters as background, we then proceed to present four management emphases in Parts II through V.

Part II is entitled "Systems and Environment." First, we present a chapter on the systems approach and then we present a chapter on the organization and its environment. In the systems chapter we develop concepts and a way of thinking about organizations and management. The next chapter deals in less theoretical terms with the interrelationships that exist between the organization and its environment and employs a number of the concepts developed in the systems chapter.

In Part III we present process-oriented management theory. This approach conceptualizes management as several major processes (or functions) in which managers engage. The process school of thought sees management as a process of achieving goals through the planning, organizing, and controlling of the work. Also, we present a chapter on decision making, which is perhaps the most pervasive of the management functions. Decision making is intricately intermingled with the processes of planning, organizing, and controlling, and in this chapter we show how decision making overlaps other managerial tasks.

The emphasis in Part IV is on behavior. A chapter on behavior and motivation fundamentals introduces the subject. Another chapter presents concepts of authority, power, and influence. Leadership is the subject of another chapter. A fourth chapter covers communication and group dynamics. Finally, the last chapter in this section introduces concepts of organization development. This topic is especially important because of the recent concern that large, complex organizations will not be flexible enough or sufficiently adaptive to the dynamic environments they live within. This chapter will discuss the struggle toward building into organizations the inner resources to remain viable amid the anticipated turmoil that we believe will characterize our world in the foreseeable future.

In Part V, the decision technology chapters present an overview of how management science models and computer-based information systems have become useful to managers. A chapter on the nature, role, and use of management science models opens the section. Next, a chapter on planning models focuses on models that support management's planning function. Closely related to this is a chapter on controlling models and techniques. Finally, the chapter on computer-based information systems examines the role and impact of computers and information systems upon organizations and management. As a whole, Part IV attempts to help the student gain an appreciation of the role and the importance of emerging management science technology and the variety of models that can be employed to support decision making, as well as the evolution of computer-based information systems.

The epilogue of the book is a chapter on the future of the organization. This chapter focuses on answers to the question, What does the future hold for the organization as we know it today? It will summarize the work of two schools of thought that are concerned with the future of mankind—the neomalthusian or pessimistic school, primarily the reports commissioned by the Club of Rome, and the post industrial society or optimist school, specifically Herman Kahn's work on *The Next 200 Years.* The epilogue will conclude with managerial implications for management philosophy, process, behavior, and decision technology.

Taken together, the book's five parts, along with the cases, assignments, and executive commentaries, give the introductory student of management the essentials needed to embark upon a more specialized study of management, an ability to relate concepts of organizations to the other business disciplines, and a firm grounding upon which to delve into the action or experience phase of practicing management in organizations of the 1980s and beyond.

SUMMARY

Management is concerned with making organizations perform. Organizations, thus, are the instruments of management. Organizations are more complex and dynamic today than in the past, and there are different types of organizations. Coercive organizations attempt to control behavior through punishment or reward deprivation. Utilitarian organizations emphasize the use of extrinsic reward in exchange for performing tasks. Business organizations fall primarily into that category. Normative organizations attempt to use intrinsic rewards to shape and channel behavior. Our primary, though not exclusive, focus in this book is on utilitarian organizations.

Management may be viewed as having three facets: people, activities, and a body of knowledge. An understanding of each of these facets is essential to fully comprehending management's role in society. Of particular note as we attempt to understand the body of management knowledge is the helpful classification scheme of classical, neoclassical, modern, systems, and contingency theories. The role of management or organizational practice should be stressed too. The actual experience of managers is also a significant contributor to the development of management knowledge.

Management may also be usefully conceptualized as being both an art and a science. Although management is becoming more scientific, we will always need the art aspects in order to effectively make organizations perform.

The plan of the book involves five major parts (1) introduction, (2) systems and environment, (3) process, (4) behavior, and (5) decision technology. The book ends with an epilogue. Taken together, these emphases provide the reader with the essentials that are needed to study management in more depth, relate organizational concepts to other disciplines, and to delve into the practice of management both now in the future.

Assignments

1-1. What is an organization? Why are organizations formed?

1-2. Differentiate between coercive, utilitarian, and normative organizations. What type of organization is a bank? a chamber of commerce? a credit union? a fraternity?

1-3. What are the primary differences between top, middle, and lower managers? Are the functions of management the same for each of these levels?

1-4. Why are supervisors frequently referred to as the "person in the middle"? Should not middle managers be referred to in this way also?

1-5. Top managers have been called "Mr. Outside" by *Business Week* magazine. Discuss why this title is appropriate and/or inappropriate.

1-6. Differentiate between classical theory and neoclassical theory. Which do you feel best describes management as it should be?

1-7. Differentiate between modern theory, systems theory, and contingency theory. How does each build upon the prior?

1-8. Describe the iterative process by which exchange is made between the theoretical world and the real world in which managers operate.

1-9. Is management an art or a science? Discuss.

1-10. Differentiate between the phrases *management as a science, scientific management*, and *management science.*

CASES FOR PART I

Case 1-1

ARNOLD WILLIAMS

Arnold Williams, a recent business administration graduate from a large university in the Southeast, was looking forward to his first job interview for a management position with a large electronics firm based in Atlanta. Arnold had made excellent grades in college, but was especially proud of the performance he had displayed in his management courses. As a consequence, Arnold was quite confident as he prepared to be interviewed by Miss Martha Hollowell from the firm.

"Good morning, Arnold," the interviewer greeted him as he took a seat in the interview room. "What were your favorite courses at the business school?" "I guess management and marketing were my favorite courses, though accounting was also very stimulating, too." "Good, Arnold, let me know, then, your reaction to this definition of management: 'Management is a series of interruptions interrupted by interruptions.'"

Arnold was quite shaken by this statement of Miss Hollowell's. It did not sound like any definition of management he had ever heard before. He decided to think for a moment before responding.

1. Based upon what you have learned about what management is, to this point, how would you respond in Arnold's situation?

Case 1-2

IRRECONCILABLE DIFFERENCES?

Jonathan Wesley, president of Wesley Enterprises, a company with annual sales of $20 million, was not accustomed to entering into debates with lower-level managers in the company. However, on one occasion he found himself doing precisely that. It seems that an instructor in a supervisory development program had recently been discussing whether management was an art or a science.

Wesley entered the employees' lounge one spring day and overheard a heated discussion among the supervisors regarding the art versus science issue. As he entered the room, he heard one of his most experienced supervisors exclaim, "There is no question about it. Management is nine-tenths art and one-tenth science!"

Wesley was quite taken by this because he had just left a top-level planning session where many of his staff middle managers had been arguing quite articulately that the management task can be made scientific and systematic and all that was necessary was to apply a little brainpower to the task. Wesley agreed with their arguments and thus was visibly shaken by his supervisor's comment. Wesley's immediate response to the supervisor's comment was, "Well, it's obvious you have a lot to learn about management!"

1. What is your appraisal of the positions taken by the supervisor and Mr. Wesley? What about the middle managers?
2. Which of the positions is more nearly right?
3. Is it possible that they could both be right? If so, relate your answer to the pertinent variables or factors that would make it possible.

References

BOWMAN, JAMES S. "The Meaning of Work and the Middle Manager." *California Management Review* (Spring 1977), pp. 63–70.

CARROLL, ARCHIE B. "Making Sense of Management Theory." *Management Quarterly* (Winter 1973–74), pp. 25–29.

CULBERT, SAMUEL A. "The Real World and the Management Classroom." *California Management Review* (Summer 1977), pp. 65–78.

DAVIS, RALPH C. *The Fundamentals of Top Management.* New York: Harper & Row, Publishers, 1951.

DUNCAN, W. JACK. "Management Theory and the Practice of Management." *Business Horizons* (Oct. 1974), pp. 48–52.

FOLLETT, MARY PARKER. "Management as a Profession." Chapter IV, Henry C. Metcalf (ed.) *Business Management As a Profession.* Chicago: A. W. Shaw Co., 1927, pp. 72–87.

LUTHANS, FRED. "The Contingency Theory of Management." *Business Horizons* (June 1973), pp. 67–72.

MINTZBERG, HENRY. *The Nature of Managerial Work.* New York: Harper and Row, Publishers, 1973.

ROSS, JOEL E., AND ROBERT G. MURDICK, "What Are the Principles of 'Principles of Management?'" *Academy of Management Review* (Jan. 1977), pp. 143–146.

RYAN, WILLIAM G. "Management Practice and Research—Poles Apart." *Business Horizons* (June 1977), pp. 23–29.

SUMMER, CHARLES E., AND JEREMIAH J. O'CONNELL. *The Managerial Mind.* Homewood, Illinois: Richard D. Irwin, Inc., 1964.

WEINWURM, GEORGE. "The Practical Endowment of Management." *California Management Review* (Spring 1971), pp. 25–31.

FREDERICK M. HAMMILL
Planning/Control Superintendent,
E. I. du Pont de Nemours & Company

Frederick M. Hammill has held various positions in Process Development, Manufacturing, Control, and Planning at plants of the Textile Fibers Department of E. I. du Pont de Nemours & Company. He is currently Planning/ Control Superintendent at a du Pont plant in Athens, Georgia.

Executive Commentary
Beginning to Study Management

The long-term success of any management group depends on the realization that management is a means, not an end. It is critically important that management should maintain a reasonable balance in meeting the needs of the employees, the customers, and the stockholders (and more recently, "all the people" as represented by government), if it is to perform its function properly. If it is not doing so, it should change its management objective or its mode of management before it is either replaced by other management or forced to liquidate the business.

Balance is probably one of the key words in management. If management focuses entirely on each new problem or each new opportunity, it will find an organization that responds well to the new direction but loses its capability in areas which are not currently being emphasized. A good manager will realize that he must not lose that which he has already achieved while he is attempting to make progress in a particular phase of the business. This boils down to being both consistent and predictable. Continue to expect what you have been expecting and to perform as you have been performing in all aspects of the business that are performing acceptably. Augment this consistency with clear communication of changes so that your particular desired deviation from a past consistency will not be misconstrued as a signal to de-emphasize other aspects of the business.

As you will see in this book, the practice of management has been changing rather dynamically in recent decades and will change more dynamically during the span of your work life. There has been an evolution of theories and a revolution of changing needs. However, some theories have been applied almost singlemindedly as fads, without recognition of deviation from the environment in which they were first successful. It is probably wisest to alter your present management mode to accommodate the latest management theories rather than to suddenly abandon past modes of management to singlemindedly adopt a new mode.

A good manager learns all he can and never stops learning. This should not be confined to his own specific job or business, but should be as broad as he can find the time and interest to do so. You will be amazed as you progress through different management assignments and levels that you will make practical use of the majority of the fields of knowledge or bits of knowledge you have acquired. Some will help you make good decisions, some will help you avoid bad decisions, and some will unlock a two-way communication with a person whom you may never have understood without this bit of "ice breaker" information.

In sum, management is a means and not an end, and its viability and success hinge on its ability to strike a proper balance in meeting the expectations of the various claimant groups on the organization. Additionally, the management group must maintain consistently high expectations with respect to each phase of the business, especially when particular problems or areas are being emphasized over others. In spite of the dynamic environment, it is possible for managers to adapt with the changing times and, indeed, to make change happen when it appears to be in the best interests of the organization. Good management, therefore, requires individuals who not only accumulate knowledge but are willing and able to make practical use of it as the situation demands. The potentially successful manager, thus, not only begins to study management as a discipline, but continues to study and practice it throughout his life.

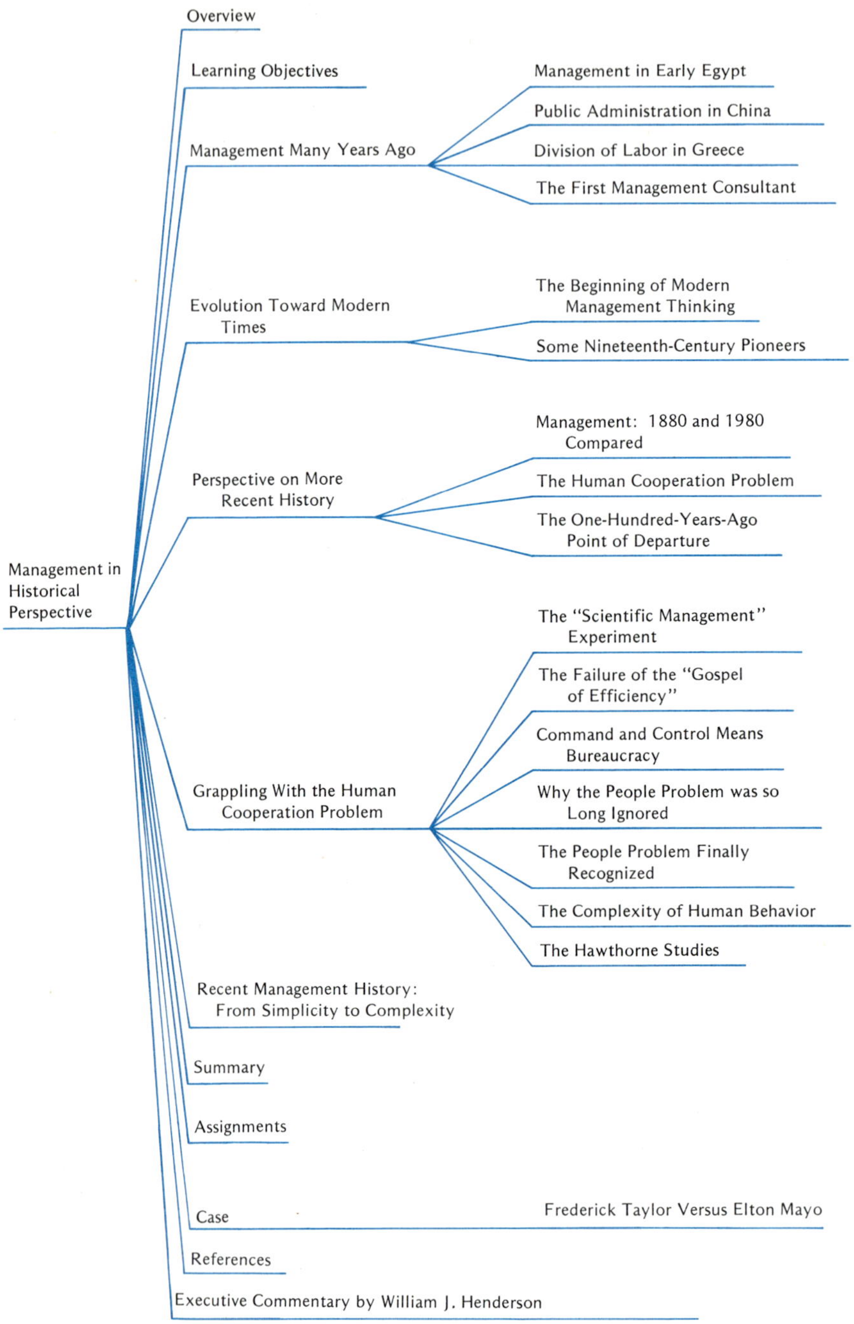
Management in Historical Perspective
Overview
Learning Objectives
Management Many Years Ago
Management in Early Egypt
Public Administration in China
Division of Labor in Greece
The First Management Consultant
Evolution Toward Modern Times
The Beginning of Modern Management Thinking
Some Nineteenth-Century Pioneers
Perspective on More Recent History
Management: 1880 and 1980 Compared
The Human Cooperation Problem
The One-Hundred-Years-Ago Point of Departure
Grappling With the Human Cooperation Problem
The "Scientific Management" Experiment
The Failure of the "Gospel of Efficiency"
Command and Control Means Bureaucracy
Why the People Problem was so Long Ignored
The People Problem Finally Recognized
The Complexity of Human Behavior
The Hawthorne Studies
Recent Management History: From Simplicity to Complexity
Summary
Assignments
Case
Frederick Taylor Versus Elton Mayo
References
Executive Commentary by William J. Henderson

2

MANAGEMENT IN HISTORICAL PERSPECTIVE

OVERVIEW

It will be the purpose of this chapter to look back at the history of management. This look will first note that management has been an important activity for a very long time. It will then summarize where management was in its evolution 100 years ago. Finally, this historical overview will look closely at some of the more dramatic developments in the evolution of management during this century. In later chapters, particularly in connection with our discussion of motivation, the same closer scrutiny will be given to more recent evolution.

Management 100 years ago was practiced in a context of laissez faire, a public policy outlook which gave businessmen a great deal of freedom. In particular, the late nineteenth-century situation gave organizations much freedom to deal with employees as seemed best from the standpoint of the interests of business organizations and their owners. A great deal of recent management history has centered on tension between management and employees, as the latter have achieved more of a say about what happens to them in organizations.

The need to take workers' needs more into account is one reason why the recent history of management can be described as an evolution from relative simplicity to a much greater complexity. There are two other reasons. One is the complications being introduced into both organizations and the technology they are using. The other is the abandonment of laissez faire, with the result that complex government bureaucracies have become active partners in the making of a wide variety of important organizational decisions.

LEARNING OBJECTIVES

This chapter is especially intended to help the student:

1. **Understand the pervasiveness of management throughout history.**
2. **See the beginning of a much more intensive thinking about management in recent times.**
3. **Compare the task of management today with that of 100 years ago.**
4. **Understand the problem and the hopes that undergirded the scientific management experiment.**
5. **Trace the events and circumstances that brought a much greater emphasis on managing human resources.**
6. **Learn, especially in the context of thinking about management, the meaning of the following concepts:**

laissez faire	**the human cooperation problem**
specialization	**traditional management**
human resources	**scientific management**
professional managers	**bureaucracy**
"natural harmony"	**the "speed-up"**

MANAGEMENT MANY YEARS AGO

There have always been *managers.* That is because civilization is first, last, and always *organizations*—and organizations must necessarily be managed. Of course, too, because managers have been with us for a very long time, the study of *management* is very old.

Management in Early Egypt

Management was very important in ancient Egypt more than 6,000 years ago. One can imagine the immense management task of building one of Egypt's many pyramids. It would contain more than 2,000,000 stones, each weighing $2\frac{1}{2}$ tons. Every one of these stones had to be cut in a quarry and moved long distances to the construction site. There, with the use of crude equipment and mostly human power, these huge stones would have to be raised into position—up to hundreds of feet above level. One of these pyramids would require coordinating the work of 100,000 men for as long as 20 years. Understandably, Egyptian "how-to-do-it" writings on management, now more than 3,000 years old, were used as text materials in schools in those early times.[1]

[1] Claude George, *The History of Management Thought* (Englewood Cliffs, N.J.: Prentice-Hall, 1972), p. 4.

Public Administration in China

The Egyptians, with a large geographical area to hold and govern, also developed some of the principles of managing government activities, now called *public administration.* Nevertheless, the building of The Great Wall of China is surely the most massive government production project ever undertaken. Thus, the Chinese, with an even larger empire to manage, were more advanced in their thinking about management. In fact, so thoroughly developed had one principle of management become by the eighteenth century B.C. that an emperor who persistently ignored the advice of his counselors was deposed for three years by his prime minister. That principle is the need to bring to decision making the understanding of whatever specialists know most about what is being decided.

Division of Labor in Greece

It is commonly supposed that Adam Smith in 1776 in his famous book, *The Wealth of Nations,* invented the concept of *division of labor.* That principle of organizing a society's work is that production will be more efficient if workers are required to master one skill rather than many. Interestingly enough, however, the great philosopher Plato, some 2,000 years earlier, had already penned some lines about this that sound surprisingly like Smith's classic paragraph on *specialization.*

> *Which would be better—that each should ply several trades, or that he should confine himself to his own? He should confine himself to his own. More is done, and better and more easily when one man does one thing according to his capacity and at the right moment. We must not be surprised to find that articles are made better in big cities than in small. In small cities the same workman makes a bed, a door, a plough, a table. . . . In big cities, on the other hand . . . a man can live by one single trade. . . . One makes men's shoes, another women's, one lives entirely by the stitching of the shoe, another by cutting the leather. . . . A man whose work is confined to such a limited task must necessarily excel at it.*[2]

In fact, the Greeks even piped music into workplaces to keep work from being so dull, an idea that has only recently appeared in modern management practice.

The First Management Consultant

The ancient Hebrews were also very much caught up in the management process and, therefore, in developing the skills and understandings essential to that work. The Bible nicely captures for us an event that has half seriously come to be thought of as the birth of *management consulting.* After the Hebrews left the Egyptians' *administrative system,* they, of course, had to develop a management program of their own. Understandably, at first, Moses carried this load by himself. On the occasion of a visit by Jethro, his father-in-law, however, he was

[2]Francis Cornford, *The Republic of Plato* (New York: Oxford University Press, 1959), pp. 165–67.

strongly advised that he must systematize what he was doing by *delegating*, making use of more of the administrative talent around him.

The First Management Consultant

The next day Moses sat as usual to hear the people's complaints against each other, from morning to evening.

When Moses' father-in-law saw how much time this was taking, he said, "Why are you trying to do all this alone, with people standing here all day long to get your help?"

"Well, because the people come to me with their disputes, to ask for God's decisions," Moses told him . . .

"It's not right!" his father-in-law exclaimed. "You're going to wear yourself out—and if you do, what will happen to the people? Moses, this job is too heavy a burden for you to try to handle all by yourself.

"Now listen, and let me give you a word of advice. . . .

"Find some capable, godly, honest men who hate bribes, and appoint them as judges, one judge for each 1,000 people; he in turn will have ten judges under him, each in charge of 100, and under each of them will be two judges, each responsible for the affairs of 50 people; and each of these will have five judges beneath him, each counseling 10 persons. Let these men be responsible to serve the people with justice at all times. Anything that is too important or complicated can be brought to you. But the smaller matters they can take care of themselves. That way will be easier for you because you will share the burden with them."

The Living Bible, "Exodus" (Wheaton: Tyndale House, 1971), p. 64.

EVOLUTION TOWARD MODERN TIMES

The great empires of Babylonia and Persia also had to have managers. The Roman Empire at its largest extent controlled a territory extending from England to Asia. In our part of the world, the Aztec Indians developed skilled managers to direct and coordinate the work of many citizens toward the accomplishments of that civilization.

It is important to emphasize, however, that the mastery of management understandings and skills, though essential to the civilization enterprise, does not guarantee that civilization will thereby be maintained. Thus, the glory that was Greece fell victim to the Roman Empire, and the grandeur of that establishment in turn was overrun by barbarians.

Western civilization now had to build itself anew. Again, managers and management had to be developed, building from that point forward more specifically toward the world in which we now live. Much of this building was accomplished by the Catholic Church and the Holy Roman Empire. As conditions became more settled, the Holy Roman Empire as a management unit gave way to city-states and then to nation-states. Within both of these, smaller organizations—as, for example, many *private enterprises* operating for *profit*—took over much of the work of economic development.

The Beginning of Modern Management Thinking

Only quite recently has a great deal about management been written for publication. One obvious reason was that the printing press was not perfected until 1456. Another was that most organizations were so much less complex than pyramid-building and the Great Wall of China. Other reasons were that then, as now, managers rarely wrote about their affairs, and there were no professors of management. A number of things began to happen, however, that would one day make thinking about management a much more important matter.

Niccolo Machiavelli

Not quite a contributor to *modern management thought,* though an important thinker about these kinds of things, was Machiavelli. A product of the intensely chronic conflict among Italian city-states, his concern was how a "prince" might most effectively get and make use of *power.* Because he wished through his writings to gain influence with one or another of the "princes" of his day, he was very candidly realistic about the techniques for most successfully living with power and the powerful. Indeed, Machiavelli is not thought of as a significant contributor to modern management thought primarily because that thinking has mostly ignored Machiavelli's emphasis on power. Probably this has been in substantial part because, until very recently, the availability of power to the leader could so much more nearly be taken for granted within the economic organization than within the much larger and more complex political organization.

Writing in the early 1500s, Machiavelli set forth his most important ideas in *The Prince,* James D. Atkinson, Translator (Indianapolis: Bobbs-Merrill, 1976) and *The Discourses,* Leslie J. Walker, Translator (London: Routledge and Kegan Paul, 1975).

One of these developments was the Commercial Revolution, an explosive expansion of trade between Europe and much of the rest of the world, and the accumulation of wealth thereby made possible. Another was the rapid introduction of a much higher level of *rationality* into warfare, much more sophistication about how an enemy might be destroyed. This resulted in greater attention to the organization and management of armies. Another factor was the Reformation, a breakup of organized religion into smaller sects, which occasioned a searching examination about how church organizations might best serve member beliefs. Still another reason that thinking about management became much more important was the emergence of the *limited-liability* private enterprise concern. With that development, persons could invest in a company and be liable only for the amount of their investment, rather than risking all of their assets.

Perhaps, however, none of these developments was as important as the Industrial Revolution. Among other things, that marked the beginning of a much more rapid introduction of *new technology* into the production process. This made it possible to supplement muscle power with machine power. More generally, however, the Industrial Revolution began to bring much more rationality, *science,* into organizations. To be sure, this was physical science, the beginning of a systematic application of engineering to organizations. A substantial organization interest in social science, *human behavior,* would have to wait another century and a half. But it is well worth keeping in mind when a little later our attention turns to what is "officially" called *scientific management* that management's interest in science did not begin in the late nineteenth century.

The "Father of *Laissez Faire*"

Side by side with developments within management came now, too, a major break-through from the standpoint of how managers should be handled by governments. Prior to this time, important affairs had been thought to be primarily government's responsibility. But why not, men began to wonder, let *private entrepreneurs* take their own risks and reap their own rewards by making their own business decisions. The landmark writing expounding this view was Adam Smith's *Wealth of Nations.** Smith was a Scotsman, writing for England's situation as of the last half of the eighteenth century. His basic argument was that businessmen in the process of working toward their own best interests would rapidly accomplish the economic development which was becoming the preoccupation of *public policy.* As more and more citizens began to think this way, particularly in England and the United States, a prodigious amount of growth and expansion were accomplished under the name *laissez faire*—an approach to public policy which gave businessmen a great deal of freedom to decide for themselves what and how they would do.

*The full title of Smith's work, published in 1776 was *An Inquiry Into The Nature and Causes of the Wealth of Nations,* ed. by Edwin Cannan (London: Methuen, 1961).

Some Nineteenth-Century Pioneers

It is often characteristic of great changes that they are foreshadowed before they really begin. In particular, it is of special note in the history of management that at several points approaches to managing that much later would become very important saw very small beginnings in the early nineteenth century.

First, almost a century before Frederick Taylor's scientific management movement, James Watt, Jr., and Mathew Robinson Boulton were systematically using a highly rationalized approach to managing. Taking over the operation of a foundry established by their fathers, they pioneered a list of management techniques that sounds like a modern business administration study curriculum. These techniques included market research and forecasting, the planning of machine layouts in terms of work-flow requirements, production-process standards, standardization of product components, production planning, cost control systems, worker and executive training programs, work study, compensation by results, and a worker health program.

Second, there has recently developed a vigorous concern about the *human factor* in management. But again, a century before that concern became important, another pioneer decisively pointed toward that emphasis. This man was Robert Owen, who carried on an unprecedented experiment in textile mills, first in Scotland, and later in the United States. Often now referred to as the "father of personnel management," he handled his employees on the premise that if the employer does better by them, they will do better by their employer. This approach would be in sharp contrast to most business practice for many years. Owen stated his philosophy as follows:

> *Many of you have long experienced in your manufacturing operations the advantages of substantial, well-executed machinery. If, then, due care as to the state of your inanimate machines can produce beneficial results, what may not be expected if you devote equal attention to your vital machines which are far more wonderfully constructed.*[3]

Third, yet another emphasis already mentioned in Chapter 1, *management science,* has even more recently come into management thinking and practice. One key dimension of this emphasis is the use of computers in the making of management decisions. In 1822, Charles Babbage, often these days called the "father of the computer," invented a mechanical calculator he called a "difference machine." Its basic principles were employed in accounting machines 100 or so years later, and it made use of many of the principal elements found in today's computers.[4]

PERSPECTIVE ON MORE RECENT HISTORY

Understandably, we shall want to look more closely at recent developments in the management field. As a beginning, let us contrast manager concerns of a century ago with those of today.

Management: 1880 and 1980 Compared

Management today differs from management in the 1880s in five primary ways. First, the central focus of manager attention 100 years ago was on how "things" could most effectively (meaning, typically, most profitably) be converted into

[3]Quoted in L. Urwick, *The Golden Book of Management* (London: Newman Neame, 1956), p. 7.
[4]Babbage's insightful thinking, on a wide range of management topics, is best reported in his book *On the Economy of Machinery and Manufactures* (Philadelphia: Carey and Lea, 1832).

goods and services. In those days, however, "things" included *human resources*, the energy and skill of human beings, to a much greater extent than is the case today.

A second large difference is that management has become much more demanding over the past century. In part, this is because human beings must now be handled so much differently than other resources. But in large part, also, this much greater challenge confronting managers is because both the technologies used in organizations and *organization structure* have become much more complex.

Third, and this is in substantial part the other side of the first two, there is now a much altered environment within which managers must work. A century ago entrepreneurs were enjoying America's laissez-faire years, when public policy was first and foremost dedicated to seeing to it that businessmen were not interfered with as they brought economic development to North America. Now, however, public policy takes no such leave-them-alone stance. In a multitude of ways— from fair trade to unfair labor practices, from antitrust to environmental protection— legislation has made the public an active partner in much that managers are doing. In still another way, in other words, manager work has become much more demanding.

It might be useful to emphasize the social responsibility challenge to managers further. So marked is this transformation of the conditions within which businessmen function that the public policy implications of what organizations do has become central to a wide range of manager decisions. That is one of the principal reasons that a major focus of this book explores the impact of the environment on the management of organizations.

Also, there is a great difference in the kind of person in charge of our economic organizations now as compared with a century ago. Earlier, in part because of our laissez-faire philosophy, these men were entrepreneur-owners, often called captains of industry. Included in this group were men such as John D. Rockefeller, James B. Duke, Henry Clay Frick, Andrew Carnegie, Cornelius Vanderbilt, and J. P. Morgan.

A "Captain of Industry"

Indicative of the laissez-faire spirit, while at the same time illustrative of the characteristics of your true "rugged individualist," is this story attributed to one point in the career of Cornelius Vanderbilt. An associate who had, he thought, "bilked" him said defiantly, "sue me." Vanderbilt is said to have retorted, "No, the law is too slow. I'll ruin you."

Today, in part because public policy has become so large a factor in organizational operations, in part because of the *separation of ownership from control* in large private enterprise concerns,[5] and in part because management has become

[5] A. A. Berle and Gardiner C. Means, *The Modern Corporation and Private Property* (New York: Macmillan, 1932).

"That's what I like about you, Fenton. It takes a big man to admit my mistakes are his."

A Commentary on the Professional Manager. **(Saturday Review © *1975.*)**

so much more complex, there are many more *professional managers* than "captains of industry." This difference might usefully be summarized by emphasizing that "rugged individualists" worked primarily for their own profit, whereas professional managers are tied to a much wider band of interests.

And finally, there is the rapidity with which the environment that organizations operate within is changing now as compared with 100 years ago. To be sure, there is probably some element of illusion here, highlighted by our nearness to our own understandings. Certainly, the economic organization "landscape" was changing very rapidly in the days of the "rugged individualists," too, by comparison, for example, with the rapidity with which things were changing in medieval times. But students of our years, side by side with conditions a century back, have no difficulty concluding that rapid change is a significantly larger factor for today's managers.

These differences are summarized in Table 2-1:

The Human Cooperation Problem

The most dramatic developments in the history of the management realm over the past century have focused on the problem of handling people in organizations.

TABLE 2-1
Management: 1880 and 1980 Compared

1. Human resources must be handled much more carefully.
2. Organization structure and technology have become much more complex.
3. Government as a partner of business has been substituted for laissez faire as public policy.
4. Professional managers have largely replaced captains of industry.
5. The organization's external environment is now changing much more rapidly.

For that reason and one other, let us here especially highlight some 70 years of that history. The other reason is the possibility that solving this problem may be the greatest test our civilization will encounter in the years ahead.

The *people problem* in organizations is so fundamental because we live surrounded by *scarcity.* That is, most of us want more of the good things of this life than are available. Granted, we live these days in what we popularly term an *affluent* society. But in point of fact, we do *not;* scarcity continues to live intimately with us. To be sure, we are now producing much more on a man-hour basis than we once were. Thus far in man's history, however, human wants have expanded at least as rapidly as productivity. This leaves us with much the same relative scarcity as before.

In addition to scarcity, living together in society forces us to come to terms with *individual differences.* Out in the real world, individual differences in the form of such things as family background, education, and motivation become *inequality;* that is, a few come to be much better able to get what most people want than can the majority. Another way of saying this is that everywhere one looks in civilization, past or present, there are some who are more equal than others and who therefore receive a larger share of what everyone helps produce.

The One Commandment

The animal farm had for many years been operated on the basis of the Seven Commandments. A change in management resulted in a marked shift in the *rules.* All of the old lists were torn down, and in their place was put this substitute:

ALL ANIMALS ARE EQUAL
But some animals are more equal than others

From George Orwell's study of inequality in an allegorical context. *Animal Farm* (New York: Harcourt Brace Jovanovich, 1946), p. 123.

These are the basics of the people problem, the *human cooperation problem.* Given scarcity and inequality, there must be competition and even conflict over who will get how much of what is produced. We see this in organizations, for example, in competition for *leadership* positions, and in tensions between management and workers. Of course, from the standpoint of productivity, organizational affairs must be conducted so that those who are being rewarded most meagerly will nevertheless be willing to shoulder "their share" of the burden. "Their share," then, becomes central to the people problem—for who is to say with convincing objectivity what any group's "fair share" is of either the work to be done or the rewards to be received for doing it.

The One-Hundred-Years-Ago Point of Departure

Let us select 1876 as a beginning point for our historical highlighting. That was the mid-point of our first 200 years as a nation. It was also approximately 100 years since the Industrial Revolution. And that point in our history fairly clearly marks the beginning in the United States of a sizable human cooperation problem that is still not fully resolved.

More specifically, you will recall that American managers preferred to deal with human resources as if they were "things." Actually, from time immemorial it had been taken for granted that those who are "more equal than others" should receive unquestioning obedience from those who are "less equal." Obviously, this is a more comfortable approach for leaders. To be sure, by the 1870s we were well beyond the medieval version of that understanding, the "divine right of kings" idea that rulers had a mandate to rule from heaven. But we had substituted through laissez faire a "divine right of property" way of retaining much of that outlook. In other words, it was taken for granted that the task of managers was to *command,* to *control* resources, to move assets, including, of course, workers, from place to place on the organizational chessboard as seemed to be indicated in the interest of productivity and profits. To say these things a little more technically, *traditional management*—often referred to as the Classical School—was built around a basically unilateral relationship between managers and the resources they use.

Granted there were hints on the horizon that this "conventional wisdom" about workers *vis a vis* organization leaders might not always be true. Ever since before the beginning of the United States as a nation, the idea that government should be by *consent of the governed* had been more and more securely taking root. Workers, beginning to believe that this must surely apply to organizations as well as to the larger political community, had been struggling to develop organizations of their own capable of protecting them against "greedy capitalists."

Not much had yet been accomplished on this front, however, and it was not until much later that the nation's industrial leadership realized that these movements would one day amount to something. Meanwhile, the first two years of our second century as a nation were traumatic ones from the standpoint of worker-manager frictions. The most violent labor uprising that had ever been launched in this country against the conditions industrialization was imposing on workers, in the form of a bitter railroad strike, was disastrously defeated.[6]

Managers, focusing on the defeat rather than the fury of that uprising, quite understandably saw little cause for concern. Even in 1886 when the American

[6] Howard R. Smith, *Economic History of the United States* (New York: Ronald Press, 1955), pp. 343–46.

Federation of Labor was formed, no one could know that workers had finally found an enduring formula for *labor union* viability. Significantly, that formula was called *business unionism,* meaning working within the capitalist system rather than seeking to destroy it.

If these things did not then seem significant, some other developments on the management front were much more apparent. Organizations, and especially industrial organizations, were rapidly coming of age. With a speed that was almost breathtaking, big organizations were beginning to dot the economic landscape. Often these large organizations "gobbled up" small organizations in the process of becoming large. This was, in other words, one of the great *trust*-building eras in our history. Side by side with this burgeoning size had come also a much greater complexity. Both the technology used in the production process and the organizational relationships required to make full use of an elaborate technology were rapidly becoming much more complicated. Not at all surprisingly, these developments were already beginning to replace the "swashbuckling" entrepreneur of earlier years with the forerunners of today's professional managers.

A So-Called "Robber Baron"

On the matter of making a few big organizations out of many little ones, John D. Rockefeller once said, "After all, the magnificent American Beauty Rose is made by carefully pinching off all of the buds that want to form lower down, so that all of the ensuing splendor can be concentrated in one bloom at the top.

GRAPPLING WITH THE HUMAN COOPERATION PROBLEM

In the hustle and bustle of these events our human cooperation problem did not yet seem large, but some indications that this might not be the case for long were visible. A major new management effort, one nicely reflecting trends toward larger size, greater complexity, and a growing managerial professionalism, was launched to solve this problem before it could get a secure foothold. The next 50 years would see this effort become a major missionary endeavor built around traditional thinking before it gave way to the dramatically new emphasis on how human resources might productively be handled quite differently.

The "Scientific Management" Experiment

In 1878 Frederick W. Taylor became keenly interested in a difficulty that would be his primary concern for the remainder of his life.[7] As he looked about him,

[7] Sudhir Kakar, *Frederick Taylor; A Study in Personality and Innovation* (Cambridge, Mass.: M.I.T. Press, 1970).

studying efficiency in organizations, he saw workers producing significantly less than they easily could. Moreover, this evidently was not an occasional happening; it seemed rather to be a distressingly general phenomenon. Others were also becoming concerned about what appeared to be an emerging threat to the economic foundations of our living.

One of the principal conclusions Taylor reached was closely in keeping with the assumption that those who are "less equal" should give unquestioning obedience to those who are "more equal"—even though that assumption could not yet be explicitly examined. The *soldiering* (so named to reflect the need/effort within a peacetime army to seem much more fully occupied than was in fact the case) he saw surely, the management understanding current at that time concluded, could not be caused by any willful indifference on the part of workers. The cause must rather be the ineffective exercise of manager control. Efficiency within organizations, in other words, must be increased by centering attention on the efficiency of management rather than the *motivation* of workers. And improved management efficiency was precisely what an engineer of that time might think he could do something about. Not casually, in other words, did Taylor come to be widely known as the "father of scientific management."

Now let us be very clear about one aspect of *scientific management*. From the standpoint of what would always be seen as its enduring contribution, it was most timely. Increasing complexity in organizations, especially the greater and greater intricacy of technology, coupled with a rapid evolution toward professional management, made a much more systematic application of science to management a greatly needed emphasis. Beyond this urgency and the "Taylorites'" great creativity toward it, however, scientific management also became a "movement." And it was this movement dimension that entered dramatically into the history of attempts to solve the cooperation problem in American organizations.

Looking back at the movement Taylor began, one is particularly struck by two things. First, he and his followers saw in soldiering the human cooperation problem and essentially denied that they had seen it. Second, to an extent it would be difficult to exaggerate, scientific management became a missionary endeavor, coming thus very seriously to be called "The Gospel of Efficiency."

Some "Taylorite Missionaries"

Carl Barth has been said to be Taylor's most orthodox "disciple," and he was very proud of that designation. Taylor's most unorthodox "disciple" was Henry Laurence Gantt, who was perhaps more influential for that reason. And of course there was that remarkable woman, Lillian Gilbreth, of *Cheaper By The Dozen* fame.

To be sure, there is no real surprise here. Of course, leaders in that day and time would want to believe that nothing had happened to *worker discipline*. Surely the willingness of workers to do "their part" in turning out the goods and services wanted could not be in question. What better way to deny this possibility than to assume, if management would "put its own house in order," the productivity problem many were seeing would be readily solved?

More specifically, Taylor and "Taylorites" believed that a central difficulty within management was organizational leaders' lack of understanding of what constituted a *fair day's work* for a *fair day's pay.* If only, therefore, how workers shall work were "scientifically" defined, surely that would resolve the "soldiering" difficulty. On the one hand, managers could then "bear down" in their control function with a clear conscience, because they would be assured that their demands were reasonable. On the other hand, there could be no tension with workers over this approach. According to the "unquestioning obedience" hypothesis, workers only wanted to be shown "the way" in a context of goodwill and fairness.

It is difficult today to recapture how basic finding "the way" became as the route to greater productivity.[8] But surely—it was supposed—it is the responsibility of modern science to determine, down to the last detail, the *one best way* to do whatever job is to be done. It is then, just as surely, the task of managers, as supervisors, to select the best employees for a particular task, and to meticulously train them in effectively using the "one best way." Finally, and equally obviously, it is up to the workers thus selected and guided to put "the one best way" to work turning out the world's goods and services.

The Failure of the "Gospel of Efficiency"

In summary, several points need especially to be noted about the scientific management approach to the problem Taylor and others were seeing. First, the program they delineated, true to long-standing traditions in the world of management, continued to center attention on control. Work within organizations was essentially to be divided into two kinds: *planning* and *doing*. The former would be done by managers, the latter by workers: "Just do as you are told; you're not paid to do any thinking around here."

Also, the scientific management emphasis approached the productivity problem essentially as if there were no cooperation problem. It was as if all that is required to get enough work done is for managers to decide what they want workers and machines to do and to command them accordingly. As we will have occasion to stress later, the underlying presupposition here was that workers did not (quite) have a will of their own—that worker motivation could be taken for granted.[9]

Third, scientific management "missionaries" were not at all cynically indifferent to workers as human beings. Rather, they were convinced that they were

[8] Cyril C. Ling, *The Management of Personnel Relations: History and Origins* (Homewood, Ill.: Irwin, 1965).

[9] Alvin Gouldner, *Patterns of Industrial Bureaucracy* (New York: Free Press, 1954), p. 223.

fulfilling an important "mission" here on earth. Thus, these leaders were quite certain they were using their gifts in substantial part for the benefit of the less gifted. And this seemed so self-evident because they saw workers and managers as caught up together in a truly God-given "natural harmony" in which what was good was good for all. As Taylor once said to a Congressional committee:

> *The great revolution that takes place in the mental attitude of the two parties under scientific management is that both sides take their eyes off the division of the surplus as the all-important matter, and together turn their attention toward increasing the size of the surplus until the size of this surplus becomes so large that it is unnecessary to quarrel over how it shall be divided.*[10]

This was why managers had no need to feel inhumane or indifferent when they presumed that workers could not make significant contributions to the thinking needing to be done. It was also why managers could in good conscience concentrate almost solely on controlling and coordinating organizations that were so rapidly becoming much more complex.

Fourth, if the scientific management theorists had their "hearts in the right place," something had to give when the time came to actually apply scientific management thinking in organizations. Thus, the theory said that workers who master and perform according to "the one best way" are to be rewarded accordingly, up to and including compensating handsomely those who produce outstandingly. It was assumed that workers—who are really *economic men,* moved primarily by their pocketbooks—would work more effectively for a share of the fruits of what they were producing. What, however, is to be done in situations in which *incentive payouts* exceed what seems to be the supply-demand value of the workers involved? Here, in other words, is the matter of how practicing managers would understand and utilize what management "missionaries" were prescribing.

History is clear about what did happen on this front. Frequently, when workers succeeded in earning outstanding rewards under prevailing rules, management would find a way to defeat those promises—by re-engineering either the job or its technology. The net effect of this came to be called *the speed-up,* as workers then found themselves producing more but taking little, if any, more money home. In other words, the invitation to be much more productive was converted by way of broken promises into a harder work life with relatively little compensation to show for it. The response of workers to this could easily be predicted. They quickly concluded that it was pointless to play hard at a game that was "stacked" so winning was virtually impossible. Consequently, much that it was hoped would be accomplished by the "scientific" way of managing became quite out of the question.[11] From that point forward, much work restriction would in fact be

[10] *Hearings before Special Committee of the House of Representatives to Investigate the Taylor and other Systems of Shop Management under Authority of House Resolution 90* (Washington: Government Printing Office, 1912), pp. 1388–89.

[11] R. F. Hoxie, *Scientific Management and Labor* (New York: Appleton Century-Crofts, 1915).

TABLE 2-2
Why the "Gospel of Efficiency" Turned Out Not to Be a "Gospel" After All

1. Continued to focus almost exclusively on control.
2. All but denied the human cooperation problem.
3. Assumed a "natural harmony" between managers and workers.
4. "Stacked the deck" against high producers.

a response to the way managers were managing the incentive pay systems that scientific management had pioneered with so much hope.

Table 2-2 summarizes why scientific management in practice did not live up to the high hopes of its most enthusiastic proponents:

Command and Control Means Bureaucracy

We will take up this history again a little later in connection with our discussion of the Hawthorne Studies. Next, however, let us note how thoroughly entrenched the command and control approach to management had become by the time scientific management reached its heyday. Let us do that by looking at Max Weber's thinking about organizations. Just as F. W. Taylor is understood to be the father of scientific management, Weber is often recognized as the "father of bureaucracy." He systematically described the "ideal" way of fashioning complex organizations most efficiently. That "ideal," furthermore, was primarily preoccupied with logically, "scientifically" maneuvering resources on the organizational chessboard—with little "in principle" concern for the preferences of the people being maneuvered.

The Father of Bureaucracy

Max Weber, one of the founders of modern social science, had very widely studied large bureaucracies of all kinds. Writing during the first part of the twentieth century, his ideas about organizing were only a small part of a much larger study of all aspects of society. His conclusions about bureaucracy were an outgrowth of his thinking about the historical and social factors which led to the development of much more complex organizations.

Weber's description of bureaucracy entails, most basically, three principles. First, sizable organizations must be operated by competent *specialists*, everyone thereby trading off knowing more about what he is supposed to do against knowing less about the work of others: "A place for everyone, and everyone in his place." Second, authority relationships must be hierarchically interrelated so that each organizational participant will have one and only one immediate superior. Here is the once sacred *chain of command*, "one man, one boss," principle. Third, the organization's business must be conducted on the basis of *formal*, impersonal

TABLE 2-3
The Basics of Bureaucracy

1. An elaborate division of labor.
2. A "one man, one boss" chain of command.
3. Formal, impersonal rules and discipline.

rules and discipline. Everyone, in other words, would be treated according to his/her task responsibilities, rather than in terms of the personal characteristics or the personal preferences of either boss or subordinate.

Table 2-3 summarizes Weber's key elements.

Again, as with scientific management, it is important to emphasize the fundamental validity of Weber's principles—as far as they go. Thus, he set for himself the task of delineating a set of basics, as a sort of checklist, which would help fashion organizations that would function more efficiently. Of course, workers who know their own work fully, even though they know much less about the work of fellow employees, represent one of the foundations on which modern civilization rests. Of course, too, there are great advantages in having every worker guided by and reporting to only one supervisor when that is possible. And there is no argument about the danger to organizational efficiency posed by favoritism when friendships rather than arms-length relationships are encouraged.

Nevertheless, bureaucracy in this overview of historical developments—and here, too, just as scientific management—is especially noteworthy as a continuation of traditional thinking. Its outlook did not really comprehend the much greater complexities into which we were so rapidly moving. Thus, it did not suggest the challenge that would become a part of the managing of organizations should relationships between managers and their employees become bilateral. Weber's classic deception of bureaucracy continued to take worker motivation for granted.

Why the People Problem Was So Long Ignored

Why, one might wonder in retrospect, was the command and control way of thinking so exclusively adhered to? Why, for example, when it seemed to be encountering difficulty inside real organizations, such as the widespread problem Frederick Taylor and his followers endeavored to solve, was it still assumed that this difficulty was only poor management—with no substantial element of deliberate withdrawal of worker willingness? Why in the day-to-day operation of scientific management programs was worker motivation so decisively taken for granted by, for example, re-engineering jobs and/or technology as soon as workers began to "cash in" on incentive pay promises? Why, in short, was the worker cooperation problem so persistently ignored?

Perhaps a number of factors explain what superficially seems like a head-in-the-sand blindness. One of these was that the belief in "natural harmony" was deeply sincere; it seemed quite obvious to many people that the competent few would make decisions that would benefit everyone. Another was that traditional ways are never easily given up. Indeed, this can happen only after the old ways have clearly been demonstrated to be ineffective.

A third important factor is that there are inherent "necessities" embedded in the control and structure approach to management. One of these is that a sizable organization that is even fairly complex cannot function effectively without a high degree of both structure and control. Structure is required so that the necessary coordination can be built out of highly dependable expectations about the behavior of workers whose tasks interlock. Moreover, we all find much of our personal security in the dependability of the relationships affecting us. The other side of the structure that organizations and people must have is the constraints and controls that are required to maintain this dependability.

The other "necessity" here has to do with the inescapability of scarcity and inequality. Is it not a predictable "necessity" that those who are "more equal than others" will work to arrange matters to their liking? Of course, too, that approach might at some point find itself on a collision course with the outlooks of large numbers of people who do lower-level work in organizations. If both of these pushes were to become simultaneously powerful, would that not take on some of the characteristics of "an immovable object" encountering "an irresistible force?" In the history of western civilization, specifically in the United States, it can poignantly be suggested that we were vigorously bringing just such a tension into the evolution of management.

On the one hand, the "natural harmony" understanding, coupled with equally optimistic notions that "every day, in every way, things are getting better and better,"[12] helped people feel that there were no near limits to the fruits of production that might come to them. What else, after all, could it mean to live in an affluent society? On the other hand, we had for several hundred years been endeavoring to teach people that society's institutions exist for the benefit of all of the people. By now, aspirations about the fruits of affluence had made contact with expectations about managing the nation's affairs much more democratically. That would necessarily set the stage for worker insistence on "more," side by side with the similar preferences leaders have always had. Indeed, just such a confrontation outside organizations, in the larger political community, was rapidly replacing laissez-faire freedom for businessmen.

The People Problem Finally Recognized

It is quite understandable that the stage was now set for some dramatic developments. Clearly, scientific management was not going to turn out to be the "Gospel of Efficiency" so many had hoped. This does not mean, however, that scientific management was now to sink without leaving a trace. Because organizations and production technology were becoming more and more complex, it

[12] J. B. Bury, *The Idea of Progress* (New York: Macmillan, 1932).

was most appropriate that a systematically scientific approach to management was coming into being. Only the feeling that fundamental solutions had been found for basic problems would have to be given up.

Henri Fayol

Perhaps the outstanding early systematizer of management thinking was a French industrialist who is often called the "father of management theory." Fayol's most enduring contribution to thinking about management was identifying its primary elements—planning, organization, command, coordination, and control. Also, however, he delineated a number of "principles" of management which are still the point of departure for much thinking in the field.

Henri Fayol, *General And Industrial Management* (London: Pitman & Sons, 1949). First published in 1925.

That all was not well on the cooperation front was quite dramatically revealed as the 1920s merged into the 1930s. It was coming to be popularly thought that worker restriction of output—and, remember, that is the problem scientific management had set out to resolve—was quite likely to be a consequence of labor union activities. Of course, men steeped in the laissez faire-private property traditions of the nineteenth century would not easily come to the idea that workers who had not been led astray by "foreign socialist ideologies" would sabotage "sacred" institutions within their own country.

In the late 1920s, a labor relations researcher decided to inquire into the truth of this proposition.[13] The findings in this study must have been thoroughly discouraging to all who had been significantly carried away by the possibilities scientific management had seemed to offer. For what Professor S. B. Mathewson discovered was that it was for all practical purposes impossible to find a nonunion production operation in which workers were not quite deliberately restricting output. Of course, no one would have supposed that this was not also true in unionized plants. Overall, therefore, this was a grim picture in the thinking of people who had come to feel that the way to a longer-term management future had pretty well been charted.

The Complexity of Human Behavior

Some other research was also going forward that would one day powerfully reinforce Mathewson's findings. Specifically, it was being discovered that the human being is a much more intricate mechanism than the traditional view of management had assumed. The time was coming, moreover, when all of this research would enter into the manager-employee relationship in a quite decisive way.

[13] S. B. Mathewson, *Restriction of Output Among Unorganized Workers* (New York: Viking, 1931).

This reinforcing research had its beginnings during World War I in England. Questions had arisen whether the British Air Force was losing fighter pilots as a consequence of fatigue, and whether such losses might not be substantially reduced if fatigue were better understood. Accordingly, a team of scientists, which included a psychologist, a medical doctor, and a sociologist, was assembled to find out much more precisely what fatigue is. Interestingly, to this day we know little more about the answer to that question than was known when the British Fatigue Laboratory was created. The trouble was that every time these scientists thought they might be within hailing distance of an understanding, complicated humanness would intervene. In this research, they would succeed in getting one of their research subjects thoroughly tired by the end of a working day. However, this very fatigued person upon leaving the laboratory would experience what every one of us has also probably experienced many times. At home, with family or friends, doing things we enjoy, by 7 or 8 P.M., we have completely forgotten how tired we were at 5 o'clock. And of course, what is fatigue, if it behaves like the light in a refrigerator?

Even though the fatigue researchers did not accomplish their mission, that episode is important for a quite different reason. One of these men, the medical doctor named Elton Mayo, came to the United States and vigorously entered into some fundamental industrial relations research that was just then beginning to get underway here. Because Mayo had lived through the frustrations of the earlier fatigue research, he was in a special way prepared to cope with some later results that were just as puzzling.[14]

Let us note at the outset a key presupposition, which until later would dominate this kind of studying. Taking its point of departure from the "harder" natural sciences, and thereby implicitly denying more complicated humanness, workers-in-organizations research set itself to look for direct, simple, causal relationships. And, what is most significant here, this "hard science" analogy closely parallelled the command and control conception of their task so universally held by managers. At its inception, the fatigue inquiry had been thus oriented: "If only we can find out what is going wrong, we can reach in and fix it."

The Hawthorne Studies

Shortly before Mayo became involved in social science research in this country, just such a research project had been conducted at the Hawthorne Works of the Western Electric Company. Officials there had determined to find out what light intensity on a workbench would most effectively yield maximum output. Observe the relatively simple cause-effect assumptions that guided these investigations.

It was the fatigue research situation all over again. Production, as was expected,

[14]Elton Mayo, *The Human Problems of an Industrial Civilization* (New York: Macmillan, 1933).

increased when illumination went up. Even more interestingly, however, production also went up when illumination went down—when the researchers told the workers that illumination was to be increased. Still worse, from the standpoint of the cause-effect, command-control thinking that might have been reinforced by this research, production increased also in the control group that had experienced no changes in the workplace light level.

The "Hawthorne Effect"

Ever since these "Hawthorne" studies, social science researchers have been plagued by fear of the "Hawthorne Effect." This problem is that human beings under investigation will respond to the fact that they are being studied—as much as, or more than, the deliberate research manipulation of variables. When that does happen, and it is not easy to know whether or not it has, researchers do not know what they are learning from their control of specific variables.

It was at this point that Elton Mayo became a part of what was going on at Hawthorne. He and Professor F. J. Roethlisberger put together what may even now be the most elaborate piece of social science research ever conducted.[15] As only one measure of this, the records kept weighed 14 tons by the time the study was completed.

The central purpose of their research was to see what relationship might be found between output and various workday and work-week configurations. Accordingly, experimentation was conducted with various kinds of morning and afternoon rest breaks, with workdays shortened by one hour, and with a five-day rather than a six-day work week. The results were the fatigue and illumination studies once more. Production went up during all phases of these changes. And this even included a period at the end when all of the "easier" configurations were abandoned and work conditions returned to the situation at "point zero."

However, in large part because of Mayo's Fatigue Laboratory experience, this research was no longer looking for relatively simple cause-effect results. Therefore, other changes had been introduced that overlapped the workday-work-week experimentation. Improved work methods and an incentive pay plan were introduced, and relationships between supervisors and workers were markedly altered. These researchers were by now more nearly looking for "total system" relationships than expecting human beings to be almost as simplistic in their behavior as tables and chairs.[16]

Given this abandonment of "hard science" assumptions, what was to be concluded from this research? This question necessarily generated much soul searching. The researchers had initially made several hypotheses about what

[15] F. J. Roethlisberger and W. J. Dickson, *Management and the Worker* (Cambridge, Mass.: Harvard University Press, 1939).

[16] F. J. Roethlisberger, *Management and Morale* (Cambridge, Mass.: Harvard University Press, 1941).

might improve productivity. After they had puzzled long and hard over what had happened, their conclusion was that only two of these—wage incentives and supervision methods—were worth pursuing further.

An investigation to test the effect of wage incentives proved nothing, although that finding may say something about why incentive pay plans such as the "Gospel of Efficiency" movement had fallen so far short of the hopes many had held out for them. Productivity did increase, and, therefore, worker income, but the study was terminated after nine weeks because workers who were still on the regular wage plan were building up so much resentment.

Nor was the Hawthorne research on the productivity implications of different approaches to supervision any more conclusive. The study of a group of workers already on an incentive pay plan, an experimentation with worker-oriented as distinguished from production-oriented supervision, seemed at first to be helpful. But that research was complicated by the Great Depression of the 1930s; because many other things relating to work and compensation were so fundamentally changing, it was decided that nothing was really being learned about the variable singled out for special study.

It would be after World War II before this history could resume under non-depression and nonwar conditions. As we conclude this overview for now, therefore, let us make a few overall observations. First, the battle was by now clearly joined; from here forward, worker motivation would be seriously taken into account. Second, the problem scientific management had first begun to wrestle with in the 1870s would continue to exist without visible abatement. Third, to this point, research about an issue that could only become larger had thus far only begun to learn some things about how not to go about this endeavor. Fourth, much research on the challenge of motivation would from now on be much less simplistic in its assumptions about human behavior than had thus far been the case.

RECENT MANAGEMENT HISTORY: FROM SIMPLICITY TO COMPLEXITY

We will have occasion in other chapters, especially Chapters 8 and 9, to look much more closely at the *management history* that has been and is being made since the Hawthorne investigations. Here it will be enough to do some summarizing—looking from what was happening then toward what has been happening more recently.

Perhaps one summary observation in three parts will best describe the situation in which management now finds itself by comparison with 40 years ago. These especially emphasize that in every way the job of managers in our society has become much more difficult.

A first dimension of this is behavioral science, where the discovery of the human cooperation problem has immeasurably complicated the *internal environment* to which managers must respond. Much has happened since Frederick Taylor and his followers first proclaimed a victory that turned out not to be that. Not only are we now living with residues from other proclaimed solutions that in fact solved very little, but we are also living with other current innovations. Among these are *job enrichment*, making work more interesting for those asked to do it, and *participative management*, giving workers a voice in making the organizational decisions that affect them. These in turn may be not much more helpful. When we look now at our productivity situation, it is not at all certain that the underlying cooperation problem is not pinching us more painfully than it was half a century ago.

The second dimension of today's much greater complexity has to do with the many and ever-greater complications being introduced into both our organizations and the technology they are using. In the realm of organizational relationships, we are currently wrestling with a number of nontraditional approaches designed to help us manage complexity more effectively—such as *project and matrix management*, ways of letting the chain of command be less sacred without losing all of its advantages. There is, furthermore, an uncomfortable irony in the increasing intricacy in organizations with which we must somehow live. Almost by definition, greater size coupled with greater complexity make it all the more difficult for managers and workers to interact as productively with one another as is wanted.

Technology complicates managing, especially by way of the requirements and techniques of problem solving. In part, because of the number of variables that must often be examined simultaneously; in part, because the sheer quantity of data are so immense; and in part, because problem-solving techniques have been so greatly modernized, a fundamentally new branch of management called *management science* has come into existence. In a sense, management science is today's version of scientific management, although no longer presuming to be *the* solution to labor-management problems. A problem for management science is to resist the temptation to ignore the human element in implementing highly rational decisions.

Third, not only must managers struggle with greater and greater complexities of both of these kinds. They must also contend with difficulties created by a much different kind of partnership these days with public policy. Earlier, businessmen enjoyed a high degree of freedom in making business decisions. Today, a very different spirit rules. Government (and, for example, labor unions powerfully supported by legislation) has become an active partner in virtually everything managers do. From antitrust regulations to fair trade laws, from consumerism to preserving the environment, from safety legislation to unfair labor practices, public policy must have an often frustratingly detailed and sometimes quite confusing say in what goes on.

Government decisions are particularly entering into the way managers must deal with employees these days. Specifically, public policy decision making is substantially overlapping enterprise decisions bearing on worker motivation. This is done directly by way of various kinds of "welfare," which help many people achieve a minimum income without regard to their work contribution. It is done indirectly by specifying the terms and conditions under which managers may not withhold rewards from workers, again regardless of their work contribution. Examples of this include civil service protection for government employees and public policy support for labor unions that similarly protect private sector workers through equal employment opportunity legislation, unfair labor practices constraints, and minimum wage guarantees.

SUMMARY

Although management is as old as civilization, management today reflects particularly the last 100 years of its history in western civilization. In that context, the key fact about recent management history is how much more complex and therefore challenging it has become.

The most basic stages in that evolution moved us away from laissez faire, a public policy approach permitting captains of industry to have mostly their own way. That approach was replaced by a *mixed economy,* in which professional managers have become partners of government in the making of many important organizational decisions.

Side by side with that evolution, the most dramatic events focused on manager-worker relationships. Laissez faire, "leave businessmen alone," had by definition included allowing economic organizations to deal with their workers much as if they were "things." Beginning in the very heyday of laissez faire, workers began successfully to erode that status,

The manager-worker side of this history began with F. W. Taylor and scientific management. He noticed that workers were producing systematically less than they easily could and concluded that managers were not managing as efficiently as they should be. Accordingly, he and his followers worked out an elaborate program for systematizing work and the rewards for working so that organizations would be more efficient.

The scientific management experiment did not turn out to be the "Gospel of Efficiency" its missionary proponents were so sure it would become. This was primarily because these people focused so exclusively on manager deficiencies, thereby ignoring worker reluctance. They did not recognize that there is in civilization a human cooperation problem—that high output from workers in large, complex organizations cannot be taken for granted.

Because scientific management enthusiasts did not attack one of the major problems, the command and control approach to management continued to be pre-eminent. Understandably, therefore, the problem Taylor had devoted his life to solving turned out as of the 1930s to be as far from a solution as ever. However, there was beginning to appear a way of looking at workers in organizations that seemed to promise more on the motivation front than scientific management had accomplished.

Specifically, research directed toward the human cooperation problem was beginning to see human beings as more nearly the intricate mechanisms they are. The research that especially began to reveal that truth was conducted in the Hawthorne Works of the Western Electric Company. What was being so decisively learned was that simple assumptions about causal relationships are less likely to describe significant truth in social science than in the natural sciences. At that point, thinking about the human cooperation problem was interrputed by World War II.

Figure 2-1 summarizes the emergence of new ways of thinking about management in modern times. The heavy lining in the Figure refers to periods during which particular emphases were a major preoccupation of those who were thinking about management. Thus, although scientific management became a focus of attention before 1900 and continued to be important after 1925, during that quarter of a century it was a dominant emphasis. Similarly, although the turn in attention toward the human cooperation problem began before the 1930s, it was not until then that it became a pre-eminent concern.

FIGURE 2-1. Management in Historical Perspective.

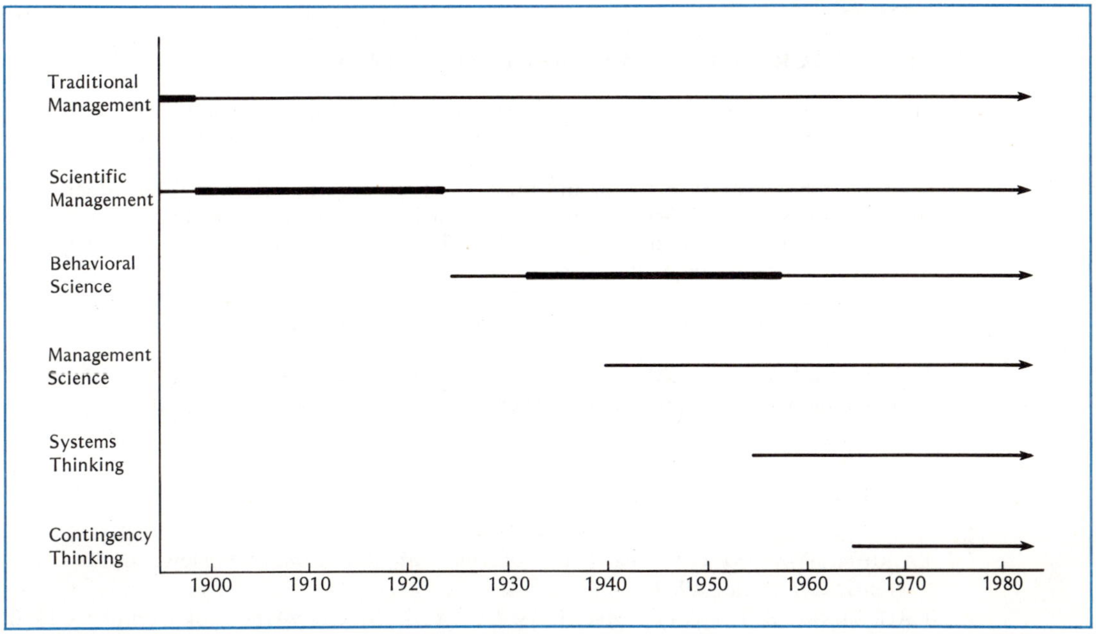

Assignments

2-1. How would the management problems of building a Great Wall of China differ from the management problems of building a massive pyramid in Egypt?

2-2. What would be the advantages and disadvantages to Moses of following his father-in-law's advice?

2-3. Why do you suppose thinking about management has focused on the problems and possibilities of power so much less than Machiavelli did?

2-4. Why would a nation follow a laissez-faire public policy for quite a long time and then systematically abandon that policy?

2-5. In terms of the "human cooperation problem," why are those who are rewarded most meagerly nevertheless willing to shoulder a large share of the burden of producing the goods and services we require?

2-6. Explain why the "Gospel of Efficiency" was not really a gospel.

2-7. How far do you agree with Weber's conception of bureaucracies as having little room in them for close friendships?

2-8. Why was it so much easier to believe in a "natural harmony" of interests in the nineteenth century than in the twentieth?

2-9. What factors especially led to the recognition of the human cooperation problem?

2-10. Why is human behavior thought of as a "soft" rather than a "hard" science?

Case 2-1

FREDERICK TAYLOR VERSUS ELTON MAYO

Taylor and Mayo were not only not colleagues. They were not really even contemporaries. Taylor died in 1915, and Mayo did not come to this country to begin his work here until 1922.

Suppose, however, that Taylor and Mayo, both men in the prime of their careers, had discussed management with one another at some length. Suppose, further, that they came together for this discussion just after both of them had read Mathewson's *Restriction of Output Among Unorganized Workers.*

1. How would each of these men present his thinking to the other in the middle of the 1930s?
2. How would each describe the "people problem" as evidenced in Mathewson's study?
3. What managerial approach to workers would each suggest for the future?

References

BAUGHMAN, JAMES P. (ed.) *The History of American Management.* Englewood Cliffs, N.J.: Prentice-Hall, Inc., 1969.

DALE, ERNEST E. *The Great Organizers.* New York: McGraw-Hill Book Company, 1960.

FILLIPETTI, GEORGE. *Industrial Management in Transition.* Homewood, Ill.: Richard D. Irwin, Inc., 1949.

GRAY, A. *The Development of Economic Doctrine.* New York: Longman, Inc., 1931.

KOONTZ, HAROLD (ed.) *Toward A Unified Theory of Management.* New York: McGraw-Hill Book Company, 1964.

MCGUIRE, JOSEPH W. (ed.) *Contemporary Management: Issues and Viewpoints.* Englewood Cliffs, N.J.: Prentice-Hall, Inc., 1974.

MEE, JOHN F. *Management Thought in a Dynamic Economy.* New York: New York University Press, 1963.

MERRILL, HARWOOD F. (ed.) *Classics in Management.* New York: American Management Association, 1960.

SMITH, ADAM. *The Wealth of Nations.* New York: Modern Library, 1917.

PUGH, HICKSON, AND HENINGS. *Writers on Organizations.* Middlesex, England: Penguin Books, 1974.

URWICK, L. *The Golden Book of Management.* London: Newman Neame, 1956.

WORTMAN, MAX S., JR., AND FRED LUTHANS (eds.) *Emerging Concepts in Management.* Second Edition. New York: Macmillan Publishing Co., Inc., 1975.

WREN, DANIEL A. *The Evolution of Management Thought.* New York: The Ronald Press Company, 1972.

WILLIAM J. HENDERSON
President, International Consumer Credit Association

Before joining ICCA, William J. Henderson was vice president of Associated Credit Bureaus, Inc., Houston, Texas. With ACB, Inc., he directed the activities of the association's districts and Canadian provinces. Later as its executive vice president, he organized and administered regional activities for 13 states and two Canadian provinces.

In 1972, he joined ACB's national staff as the director of state programs, coordinating all association field programs in 50 states and Canadian provinces, and also handled ACB's education activities including ACB's Institutes at Indiana University, University of Kansas, and the University of Georgia.

Prior to his affiliation with ACB, Inc., he was director of public relations and economic education for the Associated Industries of Missouri; was personnel director and public relations director for the George Evans Corporation; and was an administrative assistant for the Associated Industries of the Quad Cities.

In addition to holding a Certified Association Executive (CAE) certificate from the American Society of Association Executives, Washington, D.C., where he is a board member and currently chairman of its education section, he is a member of the Public Relations Society of America; the American Society of Training and Development; the St. Louis Society of Association Executives; the National Speakers Institute; and the U.S. Chamber of Commerce. Henderson also serves on the banking, monetary, and fiscal affairs committee of the U.S. Chamber. He is the holder of three Freedom Foundation Awards and the U.S. Chamber of Commerce Award for creative writing in the area of the American economic system.

Bill Henderson becomes only the fourth chief executive in the 66-year history of the ICCA.

Executive Commentary

A Short Perspective on Contemporary Management

Each new generation of managers leaving academia and joining the march or climb up the corporate ladder brings with him (and it is hoped adds to the business community) his management learning and/or his research. It may be a while before he is noticed and allowed to input much of his knowledge, but the influences of even *one* adds to the weight of others to change and update the art and science of management.

Research in management—and teaching in management—far exceeds what is going on in management. Just talk to the managers and find out. The exception might be managers in the large corporate structure, but in such places as small retail stores or small manufacturing industries or local trucking firms (where more than 80% of managers are found), old-style, dictatorial management is the name of the game. And maybe it needs to be. If you haven't heard of theory *y*—and a crisis is at hand—theory *x* works very well. Let's just use crisis management as an example.

In my own field of activity where an association executive is responsible for meetings and conventions, lack of sophisticated planning and organization can occur and often does. Nothing in the management world will work as does crisis management. This by its very nature is dictatorial management that is not often taught but always learned in a small business battlefield. "Do this" and "do that" replaces "let's sit down and talk about it." Often it is not smooth. Often it is offensive and abrasive. But it gets the job done, depending on the skill and persuasion of the manager and the receptiveness and cooperativeness of the employee. Some managers haven't cracked a business book in years and are not prepared for any other style of management than crisis management—Monday through Friday. It will always be that way. The majority of American business is small business, and the man who opens up a hot dog stand on Monday or a hardware store on Friday probably knows more about hot dogs and hardware than about management.

The management researchers and management experiments go on and on from pre-Taylor to post-Hawthorne and so do the hot dog and hardware owners. Unless or until small business managers have an opportunity to sit quietly and contemplate management techniques, they will always manage as they always have.

I think the new student of management must look carefully at management fads. If you have sufficient rear view vision, you'll see the management road, down which we've come, lettered with management fads. There are some management fad candidates for nomination for the junk pile. As a management pragmatist, I'm not sure about the real contribution of sensitivity training or transactional analysis, or whether biofeedback has any relevancy in the management process at all. Stress analysis is in many management programs today and it will, I am sure, soon be replaced by something else.

As in the world of popular music, it is sometimes difficult to decide which compositions will be popular for just a while and then fall quickly off the charts and which will become standards and stay to become part of everyone's repertoire.

Managing by objectives has been around for a long time; yet, judging human characteristics by body shape (mesomorph, endomorph, and ectomorph) may not be remembered by many. A management professor reminded me recently that the stable of management sciences contains economics, marketing, personal development, accounting, and the like, and they will be around for a long time. But not the fads. I would suggest that a young manager know about all of the fads, use all or part of them, and be prepared to drop them quickly in favor of more solid management subjects.

The Hawthorne studies left us something to read and ponder, and sometimes I wonder who is to say whether they have added more significantly to the management process than biofeedback. The social psychologist must be having a picnic. I'm also aware that management consultants are making a fortune, racing back and forth across the country, receiving high honorariums to discuss every single last idea that has been developed, packaged, and sold to others as the answer to dealing with people. In the main, the man who sits at the desk at the head of a company must spend more time in the areas of finance, law, sales, and research than he does in the area of the different techniques of dealing with human beings. He will leave that to the training directors and the junior management men who have come from the universities having been supplied with historical proof that the technique of management has constantly improved the quality and the value of the product. Maybe the president of the company should listen longer and more intently, but in the real world priorities soon take over. In the real world, I'm afraid the analogy that best suits the example is the native with the wooden plow turning over the soil in a cleared area in Africa, trying desperately to survive on what he can raise. Somehow he is able to look skyward and see three men walking on the surface of the moon, aided by all their technology and planning, money, and support teams. The disparity is frightening, but it is there in the world of business, too. Two delusions fostered by higher education are that what is taught corresponds to what is learned and that it will somehow pay off in money. There is some credence to the thought that each generation of managers equates to the decade in which he was born.

If managers grew up in the 1920s, their viewpoint and judgment about the management process and how all the interactions should occur is different than if they grew up in the 1930s, 1940s, 1950s, and 1960s. Think about the teenagers of the 1950s and 1960s and the social crisis through which they went (on and off college campuses), surrounded by wars, rebellions, Watergate, marshal law, and marijuana. Another generation grew up in a depression, and something their parents taught them related to the Protestant ethic for hard work and early rising being the magic key to success. How do each of these groups handle the management of men? In the business world—I know, quite differently.

Our wants and needs in the business world are similar to our wants and needs as an individual. What we need in business is a well-organized system that includes but does not end with money, material, manpower, management, and marketing, all orchestrated to produce the finest product at the lowest cost. What we want is for a crisis to go away, for an advocate to sit down, for a legislator to do nothing, for a federal agency to regulate someone else, and for a competitor to have a bad business year.

In our context of management and the management process, what kind we want and what kind we need are clearly defined in the accounting department.

II

SYSTEMS AND ENVIRONMENT

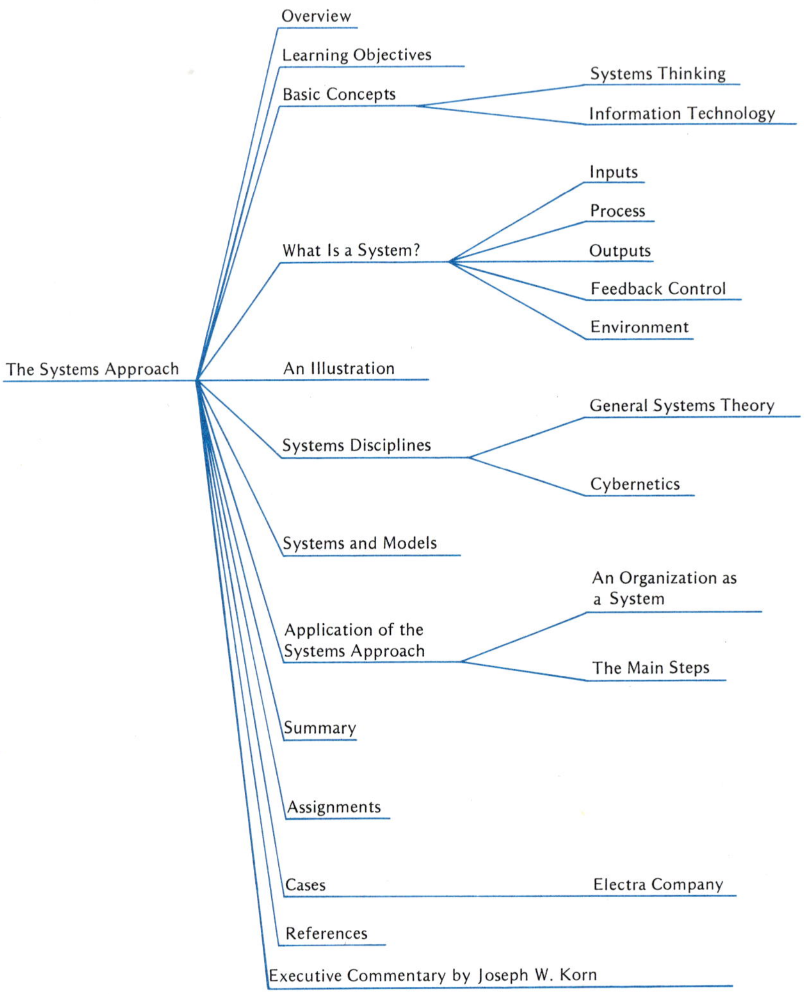
The Systems Approach
Overview
Learning Objectives
Basic Concepts
Systems Thinking
Information Technology
What Is a System?
Inputs
Process
Outputs
Feedback Control
Environment
An Illustration
Systems Disciplines
General Systems Theory
Cybernetics
Systems and Models
Application of the Systems Approach
An Organization as a System
The Main Steps
Summary
Assignments
Cases
Electra Company
References
Executive Commentary by Joseph W. Korn

3

THE SYSTEMS APPROACH

OVERVIEW

The purpose of this chapter is to familiarize the student with the systems approach and its application to the management of organizations. The terms *systems approach* and *systems* are used in the management literature with different connotations. For this reason, this chapter begins with an explanation of the meaning and evolution of the systems approach, both as a way of thinking (systems thinking) and as a specific technology (information technology).

With this clarification in mind, we subsequently turn to a major focus of this chapter, which is the meaning of the term *system*. Under the heading, "What is a System?" we discuss the main elements of a system as well as the systems environment. Then in "An Illustration," a description of two actual systems is presented to enhance the understanding of the systems elements and their environment.

The third major focus of this chapter centers around the concepts of general system theory and cybernetics. The section entitled "Systems Disciplines" provides a brief explanation of the origins and development of general systems theory and cybernetics.

Finally, in the last sections, the chapter focuses on the application of the systems approach to the management of organizations. After a brief explanation of the organization as a system, we present the application of the systems approach as a three-step process that incorporates the following three interrelated steps:

1. *Conceptualization,* which deals with the identification of the main concepts and their relationships.

2. *Measurement,* which involves the assignment of numerical values to the concepts and relationships identified under 1.
3. *Computerization,* or the utilization of computers for the purpose of both assessing the present state of a system as well as analyzing future developments.

LEARNING OBJECTIVES

This chapter is especially intended to help the student:

1. **Sharpen and further develop his or her conceptual skills.**
2. **Understand the nature and importance of the systems approach.**
3. **Learn what a system is: its main elements and its environment.**
4. **Familiarize oneself with the way a manager who uses the systems approach builds a model of a real life phenomenon or situation and how from this model the manager designs a system.**
5. **Gain knowledge about the basic steps of the application of the systems approach to organizational situations.**
6. **Learn, especially in the context of thinking about management, the meaning of the following concepts:**

systems approach	**general systems theory**
systems thinking	**cybernetics**
information technology	**conceptualization**
system	**measurement**
inputs, process, outputs, feedbacks	**computerization**
systems environment	

THE BASIC CONCEPTS

Despite the frequent use of the term *systems* by management, academicians, and others, there is little agreement with respect to one accepted meaning of the term. While accountants talk about accounting systems, production specialists about production systems, data processing personnel about electronic data processing systems, behavioral scientists about reward and motivation systems, the student of management is confused in the midst of nebulous and, at times, seemingly contradicting terminology.

The *systems approach* is primarily a framework within which to organize one's thinking so that one can more easily understand the complexity of a real world phenomenon. The systems approach consists of two main parts:

1. Systems thinking.
2. Information technology.

The former (systems thinking) provides the knowledge for developing a theory of systems, whereas the latter (information technology) supplies the tools for testing and improving the theory. The relationship between the two is complementary. Advances in theory lead to the development of better technology, and improvement in technology makes theory development easier and more reliable.

Systems Thinking

There are three main characteristics of systems thinking that must be understood at the outset:

1. Systems thinking is a viewpoint of the world.
2. Systems thinking is interdisciplinary.
3. Systems thinking conceives of real-world phenomena as systems and stresses interrelationships and interactions.

First, systems thinking represents a *viewpoint* of the world and man's role within it. It is, in other words, one's own conceptual scheme by which one organizes his own thoughts and actions with respect to reality. Every human being is subject to what Kenneth Boulding calls the "iron law of perception."[1] According to this law, every human being has his own view of the world about him. Man then uses this image to interpret his observations about events that happen in the world. Managers of private and public organizations have a certain image or idea of what the organization is and how he or she fits into the picture.

The second characteristic of systems thinking is that it is *interdisciplinary.* That is to say it represents an attempt to build a general viewpoint by borrowing from several seemingly diverse disciplines. It represents an attempt to reverse conventional thinking away from its emphasis on division and isolation and to direct it toward a synthesis that began in the life sciences (biology) and spread into the social sciences. In the management profession, this shift is marked by such terms as *integrated systems* and *total systems.*

The third characteristic of systems thinking is that it conceives of the empirical world as *configurations of interrelated activities.* It focuses attention on the *interactions or interfaces among the entities* generating these activities rather than on the entities themselves. The systems-oriented investigator conceives of real-world phenomena as systems, or sets of objects together with the relationships between the objects and their attributes. Each system is connected to another one in a serial, random, or feedback fashion. In this image of the world, systems do not exist in isolation but are rather parts of a whole, namely, the universe. Thus, one studies systems-within-systems-within-systems. . . .

In sum, then, this is the meaning of systems thinking. As the term implies, it

[1] Kenneth Boulding, *The Image: Knowledge in Life and Society* (Ann Arbor, Mich.: The University of Michigan Press, 1961), pp. 3–18.

represents conceptual frameworks which conceive of real-world phenomena as systems. This includes physical phenomena, as well as social phenomena, such as organizations. These conceptual frameworks are constructed in an interdisciplinary fashion by borrowing the theories and interpretations of empirical findings from a variety of disciplines. Thus, while the contemporary economist may be talking about economic ecology, his colleague the ecologist may be talking about ecology economics. This emphasis of the systems approach on integration is of paramount importance for management. In the words of Robinson F. Barker, chairman and chief executive officer of PPG Industries, "I believe that the most successful executive in the period ahead will be the well-rounded men and women who understand the various *interrelated* functions of professional management and who can *integrate* the available resources needed to achieve their goals. They will indeed be men and women for all seasons."[2]

Information Technology

The second component of the systems approach, information technology, will be dealt with in greater detail in Part IV of this book when the subject of Decision Technology will be scrutinized. Here, a brief general overview will suffice.

A common thought running through the writing of systems thinkers is the idea that all phenomena, if viewed as systems, "feed" on information. Just as the physical scientist's maxim is, "Life feeds on energy," so the systems thinker's maxim "Systems feed on information" is of a paramount importance. What ties all systems (biological, physical, social) together is the fact that their function and evolution can be studied as inflows, processes, and outflows of information. The biologist, for instance, studies a cell or an organism by observing what it does (its function) and what it becomes (its evolution) as a result of supplying or withholding certain "information" from the organism's environment. The economist and the stock market analyst study the behavior of the economy by tracing the results or impacts of certain kinds of information.

A firm is an organic system; it, too, feeds on information. The production of certain items begins and ceases upon receipt of certain information contained in daily reports about the availability or lack of needed inputs. Thus, the functioning and evolving of a firm, or an organization in general, depends upon the existence of an efficient information system. The information system scans the internal and external environment of the firm or organization for the purpose of acquiring data. The data are processed into meaningful information. The information system then transmits this information to persons needing to make decisions that result in certain actions necessary for the managing of the enterprise.

[2]Quoted in *Industry Week*, Feb. 20, 1978, p. 105.

WHAT IS A SYSTEM?

The systems concept was borrowed by the social scientist from the exact sciences, specifically from physics, which deals with matter, energy, motion, and force. All of these items lend themselves to exact measurement and obey certain laws. In science, a system can be defined in very precise terms and in mathematical equations that describes certain relationships between variables. This type of definition, however, is of little use to the social scientist and the practicing manager.

The following definition is a verbal, operational one, which although nonmathematical, is appropriate for our purposes. A system is here defined as:[3]

> *a set of* elements *together with* relationships *between the elements connected or related to each other and to their* environment *in such manner as to form an* entirety *or a* whole.

This definition has a dual property: it is extensive enough to allow for wide applicability and, at the same time, it is intensive enough to include all elements necessary for the detection and identification of a system. To further reduce the vagueness inherent in the terms, the key concepts, such as elements, boundary, and environment, will first be theoretically explained, and then illustrated by describing real systems.

Figure 3-1 depicts a diagrammatical representation of a system that is in constant interaction with its external environment. The first thing that one should notice when looking at Figure 3-1 is that the input to one system is the output of another system. The output of that system becomes the input to another system, and so on.

Also, one should notice that the line separating the system from its environment, (that is, the system boundary) is not solid. There are two reasons for this. Such a line indicates that there is a continuous interchange of information between the system and its environment. This kind of a boundary serves the same purpose as the cell membrane: it connects the exterior to the interior. The broken line indicates that the boundary's actual position is more or less arbitrarily determined by the designer, investigator, or observer of the system. He or she tentatively assigns a boundary, examines what is happening inside the system, and accordingly readjusts the boundary.

In this diagrammatical presentation of a system, the control component usually positioned over the output or process box in conventional diagrams has been deleted. Instead, the control function has been incorporated into the feedback component for reasons that will become clear when the science of control and communication (cybernetics) will be further discussed. Finally, it should be

[3]For a more detailed treatment, see Peter P. Schoderbek, Asterios G. Kefalas, and Charles G. Schoderbek, *Management Systems: Conceptual Considerations* (Dallas, Texas: Business Publications, Inc., 1975), Chapter 2.

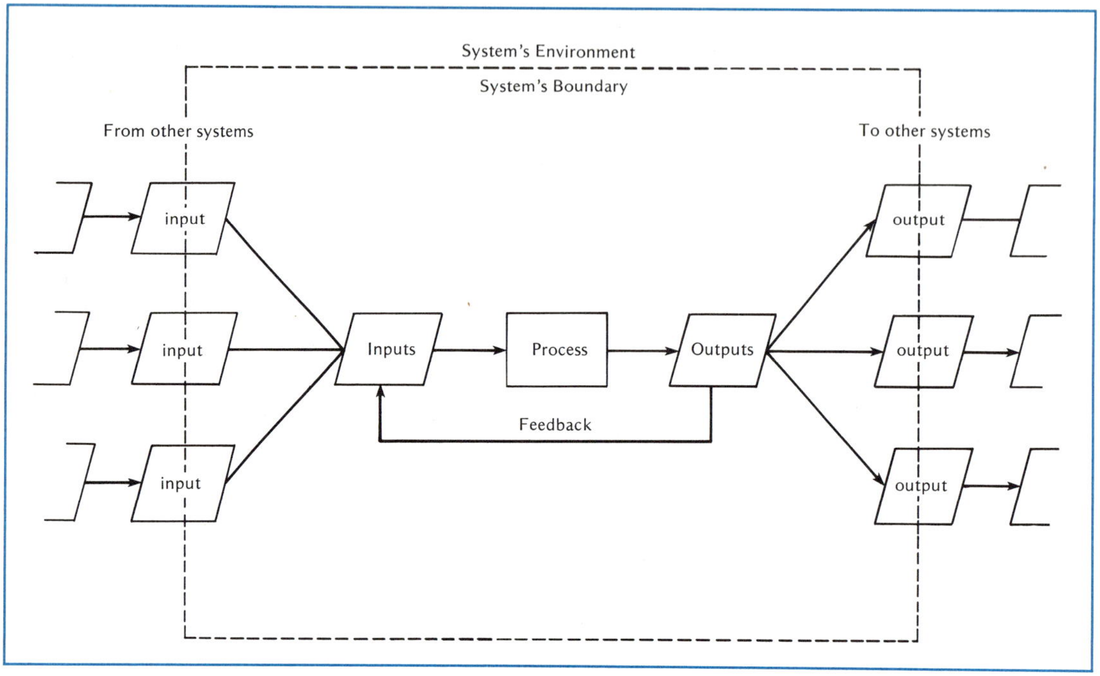

FIGURE 3-1. A Diagrammatical Presentation of a System.

noticed that the lines connecting the system's elements to each other as well as the system to its environment represent the systems' relationships. Let us turn to an elaboration of the major terms of the foregoing definition.

Elements are the components of a system. From the static viewpoint, the elements of a system would be the various parts comprising the system. From the functional viewpoint, however, a system's elements are responsible for the basic functions performed by the system. Thus, the elements of a system are: (1) the input(s); (2) the process(es); (3) the output(s); and (4) the feedback control.

Inputs

An *input* is the energizing force that provides the system with its operating necessities. A system can have a number of inputs. Each input to a system is the output of another system. Inputs can take the form of energy, material, information, or, of course, a combination of all three. A human system, for example, needs all three inputs to function. A computer, a household, a factory, a city, a nation, and so on all need these three basic inputs.

Process

Process refers to the manner of combining the inputs so that the system will achieve a certain result (output). To the observer, investigator, or manager of a system, process represents a great number of problems. Except in a very simple system, the combination of inputs and the generation of outputs is a probabilistic phenomenon with great uncertainty. When one does not know with absolute certainty all the details involved in transforming inputs into outputs, this process is called a *black box*. When one knows how inputs are transformed into the outputs, the process is known as a *white box*.

A process may represent an assembly whereby an array of inputs is transformed into one output (for example, a car assembly line), or it may represent a disassembly (a meatpacking plant) where one input is converted into many outputs.

Outputs

Output is the result of the process, or, alternatively, the purpose for which the system exists. In either case one should realize that every system's output is actually the aggregate of three kinds of outputs: (1) other-consumable, (2) self-consumable, and (3) nonconsumable. The first kind of output is, of course, the *marketable* output. Under normal circumstances, this is the largest portion of the output. The second kind of output is that which does not meet the standards of a marketable output, such as rejects that can be either better or worse than the standard. This output is usually reprocessed by the system or given to another system that uses it is as an input. And finally, the last portion of the output is what is usually called waste. One of a system's objectives is to minimize waste.

Feedback Control

As the word implies, a *feedback* is information about a portion of the system's output that is re-introduced or fed back as an input into the system. It must be kept in mind that whereas the inputs discussed earlier came to the system from other systems, feedback inputs are outputs of the *same* system. In discussing the output of the system, it was pointed out that one of the outputs was called self-consumable and it was defined as that portion of the output that does not meet a standard and must be reprocessed. This reprocessing is the result of feedback. The nature of the feedback, however, is less important than the function it serves. The main purpose of feeding back a portion of the system's output is to inform the system of the degree of accomplishment of its goal. In feeding back information from the output to the input, the system closes the loop, thereby forming a *closed-looped system*, as shown in Figure 3-1.

The significance of the existence of this closed loop in the system is paramount for the practicing manager. The closed loop ensures that the system's deviations from a goal will always be communicated back to the manager for evaluation and corrective action. This is the main function of a control system, as will be seen in later chapters. Systems that do not possess feedback loops are called open-loop systems. These systems require an external agent to keep them under control. The quality control department serves a loop-closing function that guarantees a certain quality of a firm's output. Firms without quality control functions are open-loop systems and depend on an external agent such as the public or the government to tell them when their output is or is not of an acceptable quality.

Environment

The term *environment* is a troublesome one. Usually it is defined as "everything which lies outside of the system." This definition presupposes that the system designer or manager has already drawn the boundary of the system. In other words, the individual already has knowledge about what is inside the system and what is outside. In reality, however, the problem of determining what is part of the system and what belongs to the environment is a primary task of the manager. The manager needs a set of criteria that can be used to sort out the real phenomenon under investigation into those elements that belong to the system (the system resources) and into those factors that are part of the environment. The system's environment is composed of all variables, factors, or events that meet the following criteria: (1) relative relevancy and (2) relative uncontrollability.

Relevancy refers to the relative degree of impact of a variable, factor, sector, or event upon the system's operation and/or performance. *Relative controllability* refers to the degree of influence that the system can exercise upon the behavior or a variable, factor, sector, or event. Using these two criteria, the system manager classifies variables, factors, sectors, or events into those that are relevant and under the control of the system (the system's objects). He also classifies those that are relevant but over which the system has relatively little control (the system's environment).

This distinction will become considerably clearer when the subject of the organization as a system is dealt with later in this chapter and in the next chapter.

AN ILLUSTRATION

Let us now illustrate the theoretical description of a system, provided in the previous section, by explaining the major elements and functions of two systems with which everyone is familiar. The purpose of describing these two systems is to enhance understanding of systems *in general* rather than to give a full description of the details of these two systems.

The first example is a description of a rather simple system, and the second deals with a much more complex system. *Simplicity* and *complexity* in systems are terms that refer to (1) *the number of objects* in a system (the larger the number, the more complex the system), and (2) *the degree of predictability* of system behavior (the more predictable a system's outcome, the simpler the system). A system can have a large number of objects but can be very simple because all objects behave in a predetermined manner. For example, a large number of cars on a one-way divided highway equipped with an effective traffic system is less complex than a five-car system in a shopping center parking lot, because it is more predictable.

Figure 3-2 provides a diagrammatical presentation of a simple system, a house heating system. The main inputs to the system are gas, air, and electricity. The process involves burning the incoming gas and heating the incoming air. The process is essentially a white box process. The outputs of the system are hot air, (which becomes an input to the system/house), heat (which disseminates into the environment), and possible undersirable fumes. Because this is a fairly simple system with a white box process, the undesirable outputs are almost nonexistent.

The system's immediate environment is the house of which it is a subsystem. The house's environment is, of course, its external world: the yard, trees, and so on. The walls of the house serve as the boundary of the system. As it was pointed out earlier, the boundary doesn't completely isolate the system from its environment; rather, it insulates the system.

The system's purpose, goal, or objective is to maintain a given temperature chosen by yet another subsystem, the human element. The chosen goal reflects the homeowner's values and desires. The mechanism that guarantees the main-

FIGURE 3-2. A Simple System: House Heating System.

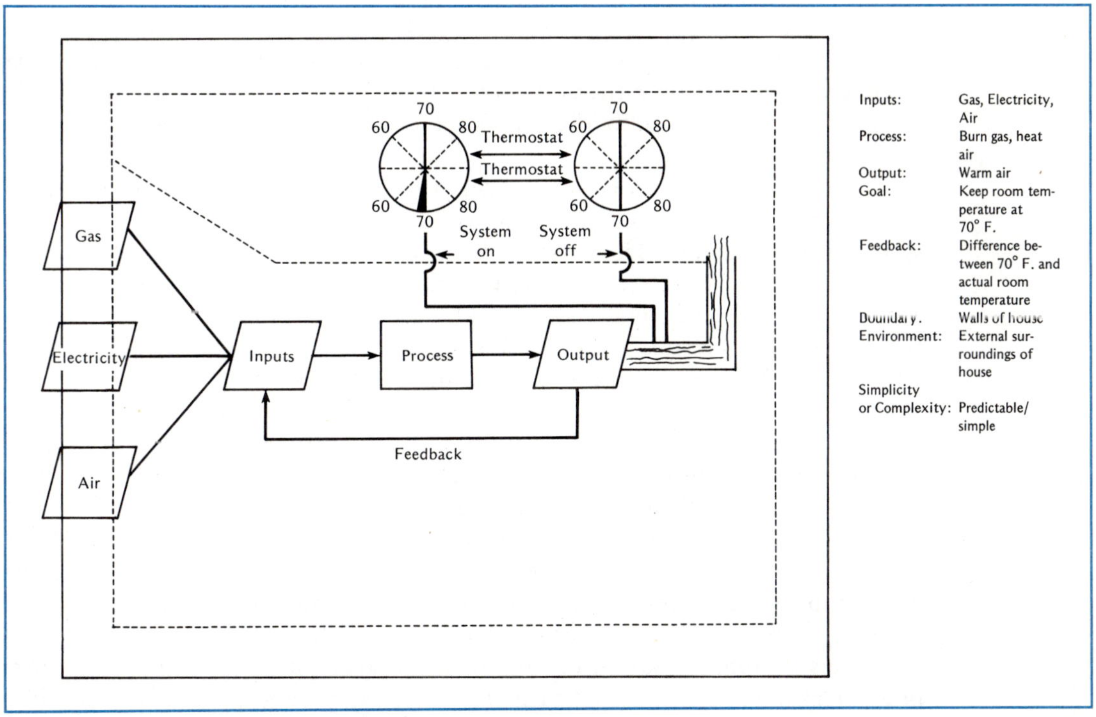

tenance of that temperature (goal accomplishment) is the feedback. This mechanism compares the chosen temperature (goal) with the room temperature (actual performance of the system) and *orders* the furnace to turn on and off. When the actual room temperature is below the desired level, the feedback mechanism turns the furnace (process) on. When the actual room temperature reaches the desired level, the feedback orders the system to turn itself off. Because the feedback always counteracts the system's present behavior, it is a negative feedback. There is no positive feedback in this simple system.

Finally, barring technical malfunction in the system, its outcome is predictable with complete certainty. For this reason, the system is a *simple* system. At any given point in time, the actual room temperature (the system's performance) will be close to the desired temperature (the system's goal), regardless of the external environmental conditions. The human body temperature maintenance system functions in the same manner. The principle is known in physiology as *homeostasis.*

With that understanding of a simple system, let us now turn our attention to a more complex system. The example chosen to illustrate the basic elements and functions of a system is that of a university. Within that system the focus will be directed toward a particular subsystem, the University Computer Center (UCC). Because the focus is placed on the UCC, that system will be termed the *focal system,* whereas the university at large will be called the *system.* Finally, the system that encompasses the university and its relationship to the external world (the city, state, the nation, and the world) will be referred to as the *suprasystem.* It must be pointed out at the outset that the degree of complexity increases considerably as the investigation moves from the focal system (UCC) to the system (the university) to the suprasystem (the university and its external environment).

Figure 3-3 depicts the complex system of the University Computer Center and its relationship to the larger systems of which it is a part. It was said earlier that no system can be considered in isolation. It can be understood only as a subsystem of a larger system for which it serves a particular function or need. Thus, the UCC is a subsystem of the university system. The university, in turn, is a subsystem of the city, which is a subsystem of the state, which is a subsystem of the nation, and so on. This is precisely the meaning of the phrase "systems-within-systems-within-systems. . . ."

Having thus established the relationship between the focal system, the UCC, and the environment within which it functions, let us now turn to a description of its main elements and functions. Again, the main inputs to the focal system, the UCC, are electricity, material and equipment, and projects from students, faculty, and the university administration (budget, class lists, billing, payroll). These inputs are processed inside the UCC by computer systems (IBM, CDC, Univac, Burroughs, and so on). The outputs of the UCC system are reports (solutions to problems submitted by students and faculty, student lists, class lists, bills, checks) waste (mutilated cards and paper, nonusable film, tapes), and heat produced by the equipment.

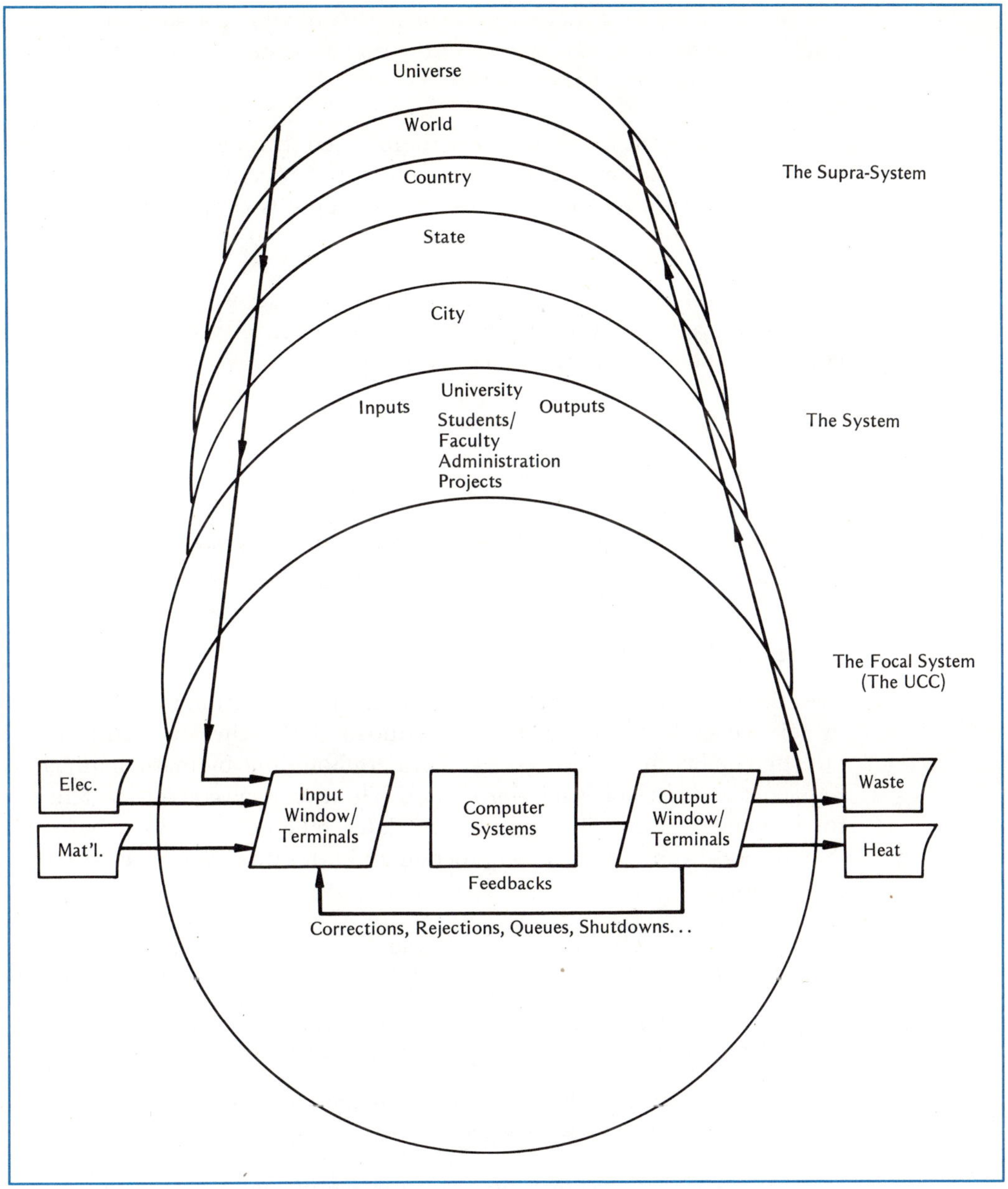

FIGURE 3-3. A Complex System: The University Computer Center.

From the preceding theoretical explanation of what a system is and the subsequent illustrations, it can be concluded that all systems of interest to a manager share two common characteristics:

1. They are *open systems;* that is, there is a continuous interchange of material and information between the system and its environment.
2. They are *closed-loop systems;* that is, there is continuous feeding back of information between the system's outputs and the system's inputs.

Before going into yet another illustration of these two main characteristics of systems, a brief overview of the attempts to organize systems knowledge into a coherent whole, or discipline, is necessary.

SYSTEMS DISCIPLINES

The systems approach is characterized by the development of two independent movements: general systems theory (GST) and cybernetics.[4]

General Systems Theory

At the 1954 annual meeting of the American Association for the Advancement of Science (AAAS), a society was founded under the leadership of biologist Ludwig Von Bertalanffy, economist Kenneth Boulding, biomathematician Anatol Rapoport, and physiologist Ralph Gerard. This society was given the name Society for General Systems Theory and was later renamed the Society for General Systems Research. The original program and intention of the society were stated as follows:

> *The Society for General Systems Research was organized in 1954 to further the development of theoretical systems which are applicable to more than one of the traditional departments of knowledge. Major functions are to (1) investigate the isomorphy of concepts, laws, and models in various fields, and to help in useful transfers from one field to another; (2) encourage the development of adequate theoretical models in the fields which lack them; (3) minimize the duplication of theoretical effort in different fields; (4) promote the unity of science through improving communication among specialists.*[5]

What are general systems theory's antecedents and how does it operate? GST has its roots in the organismic conception in biology, developed by Bertalanffy.

[4]Schoderbek, Kefalas, and Schoderbek, ibid., Chapter 1.

[5]Ludwig Von Bertalanffy, "General Systems Theory—A Critical Review," in W. Buckley, ed., *Modern Systems Research for the Behavioral Scientist* (Chicago, Ill.: Main Publishing Co., 1968), p. 11.

Organismic conception (or, as it is more frequently called, organismic revolution) is stated by Bertalanffy as follows:

> *In contrast to physical phenomena like gravity and electricity, the phenomena of life are found only in individual entities called organisms. Any organism is a system, that is, a dynamic ordering of parts and processes standing in mutual interaction.*[6]

Guided by the philosophy of organicism, GST can employ either one of the two following approaches suggested by Kenneth Boulding:

> *The first approach is to look over the empirical universe and pick out certain phenomena which are found in many different disciplines, and seek to build up general theoretical models relevant to these phenomena. The second approach is to arrange the empirical fields in a hierarchy of complexity of organization of their basic "individual" or unit of behavior, and to try to develop a level of abstraction appropriate to each.*[7]

The second approach has been dealt with in Boulding's classic article, entitled "General Systems Theory: A Skeleton of Science." In the next few pages we will explain the first approach to the development of a GST viewpoint.

General systems theory draws heavily on biology, mathematics, physiology, and economics. Its main area of study, its domain so to speak, is the phenomena of growth and evolution. Its main assumption is that the process of growth and its intermediate and final state (evolution) follows the same pattern whether it is the growth of a single organism, a group of organisms (such as a human organization), or of society.

A general system theory-oriented economist, for example, desiring to explain and predict the process of growth of a firm or of the economy at large would "look over the empirical universe." He or she would see that biologists, for instance, have been studying growth phenomena of organisms and groups of organisms for a long time. The economist can "borrow" the knowledge accumulated by the biologist to explain and predict phenomena of economic growth. Is he justified in doing so, or is he merely attempting to gain from the prestige of a well-established science? The answer, of course, is that he is fully justified, and for the following reason: both biologists and economists are seriously interested in explaining and predicting phenomena of "balanced growth." These phenomena are supposed to come about through a variety of small growth processes ranging from simple straight-line growth to exponential growth. Furthermore, they are interested in setting the conditions for the avoidance of "unbalanced" growth (such as overpopulation versus underpopulation, or galloping inflation versus stagnation or depression).

In addition to that "logic," the mathematics, (the language used to talk about

[6] Von Bertalanffy, ibid., p. 5.

[7] Kenneth Boulding, "General Systems Theory—A Skeleton of Science," in P. P. Schoderbek, ed., *Management Systems*, 2nd ed. (New York: John Wiley & Sons, Inc., 1971), p. 22.

the phenomenon of growth) is the same. Consider, for example, the growth process that is called exponential growth (a quantity increases by a constant *percentage* of the whole in a constant time period). The formula for computing the doubling time of the growth process is the same whether one is a demographer, concerning oneself with the growth of population, or a miser concerning oneself with the question of whether to hide accumulated savings under the mattress or to invest it in a bank.

In summary, this approach to GST operates as follows. A scientist or a researcher of any kind who is interested in the phenomena of growth and evolution would scan the diverse science of nonliving matters, living organisms, and social institutions with the objectives of (1) identifying similarities in these phenomena; (2) constructing a model based upon these similarities that would be applicable to at least two different disciplines; and (3) suggesting a way of explaining and predicting growth phenomena in general.

Cybernetics

Historically, cybernetics dates from the time of Plato, who in his *Republic* used the term *kybernetike* (a Greek term meaning *the art of steermanship*), both in the literal sense of piloting a vessel and in the metaphorical sense of piloting the ship of state. From this Greek root was derived the Latin word *gubernator.* It, too, possessed the dual interpretation, although its predominent meaning was that of a political pilot. From the Latin, the English word *governor* is derived. It was not until Watt termed his mechanical regulator a governor that the metaphorical sense gave way to the literal mechanical sense. It was this evolution that in 1947 provided the motivation for Norbert Wiener to coin the term *cybernetics* to designate a field of studies that would have universal application. With this, the term has come full circle, and we can now say that *cybernetics is the science of control and communication in the animal and the machine.*[8] There are general observations that must be made about the definition of cybernetics with respect to the following areas: (1) control and communication and (2) animal and machine.

Control and Communication. Professor Wiener deliberately joined the terms *control* and *communication* when he defined cybernetics because he wanted to make clear that in cybernetics control is achieved as a result of communication, or transmission of messages. More specifically, the system maintains a critical variable, let's say, its output, within certain predetermined limits (control). Through the transmission of a message (communication), a deviation between a certain desired level (goal) and an actual performance (output) is indicated. This message contains what is known as feedback information that forces the system to change its current course of action. Because the

[8]Norbert Wiener, *Cybernetics,* (Cambridge, Mass.: MIT Press, 1948), p. 248.

result of this introduction of information is a reversal of the current situation, this feedback information is called *negative* feedback. The control and communication process will be explained in more detail later on.

Animal and Machine. The reason that these two concepts are used together in the definition of cybernetics is that Professor Wiener wanted to emphasize the universality of the phenomenon of control. He maintained that the process of keeping a given variable of the system's preformance within certain predetermined limits (control) through the introduction of negative feedback information (communication) is the same in both living systems (a human body) and in mechanical systems (a heat thermostat). There was no intention in Professor Wiener's theory to equate man with a machine. However, in the 1940s when the science of cybernetics was formulated this was the erroneous conception of the time.

SYSTEMS AND MODELS

The terms *system* and *model* are sometimes used interchangeably with perhaps little harm done. However, it is convenient and more useful from the educational viewpoint to distinguish between the two.

Models and systems are man's ways of dealing with the real world. The real world is considerably more complex than the human mind can comprehend. Therefore, man first constructs a picture that contains a number of the real-world characteristics great enough to give him an understanding of what is involved. *This picture, which is an abstraction of reality and which contains the most important elements of reality, is called a model.* The purpose of constructing a model is to *understand reality* by organizing it and simplifying it. The model *represents* reality but it *is not* reality.

If the model is an organized abstraction of reality, the system is organized reality. Real-world phenomena, such as organizations, are exceedingly complex. As a rule they are not organized in a manner that will conform with man's pursued goals. For this reason, man creates real-world systems. Because it is an abstraction of reality, the model is always less complex than the real phenomena. Because the system is a tool for dealing with reality, it must be as complex as the real phenomenon.

Thus, the relationship between the model and the system is of the following nature. Because man's cognitive capacities are limited, real-world phenomena are first reduced to models. From these models man designs real systems to deal with them. Figure 3-4 explains this relationship in more detail.

The systems-oriented manager who looks at phenomena from the holistic viewpoint perceives them as an orderly summary of those features of the physical and/or social world that may affect his behavior. Thus, the box labeled "The

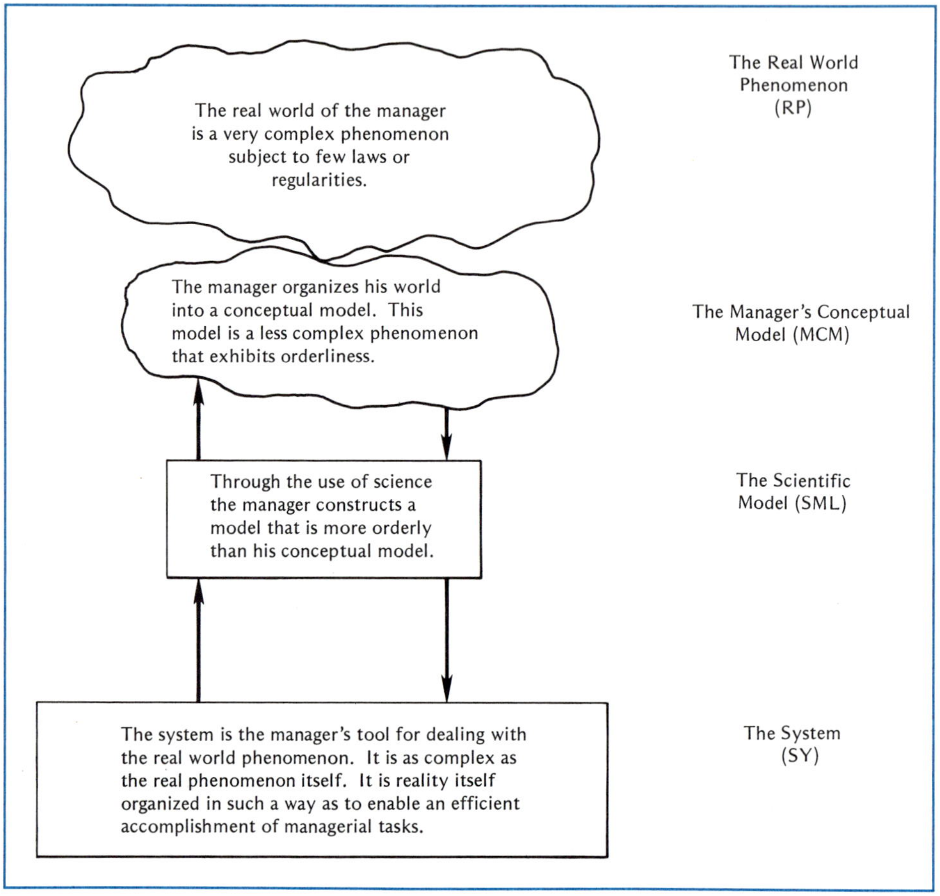

FIGURE 3-4. The Real World, the Model, and the System.

Manager's Conceptual Model" (MCM) represents the manager's interpretation of "what is really out there." The Real-World Phenomenon is his own "reality," of course. He at a later time may modify the real phenomenon to accommodate changes resulting from fresh evidence or new data. Another observer, given the same or similar background, may entertain a different "picture" of the real phenomenon. In short, the conceptual model represents the ultimate outcome of the manager's sequence of mental activities (observation plus conceptualization) and not the outcome of the sensor system alone.

As previously stated, the systems-oriented manager of real phenomena will treat them as systems. If he were to study the real phenomena (RP) as a system, he would soon discover its impossibility if for no other reason than its sheer complexity. Hence, he actually models the RP: first, conceptually; then, scientifically. The model (SML) is a representation of the RP but with much less detail than the RP itself. Again, it should be recalled that the systems thinker is most of all interested in acquiring an adequate knowledge of the RP. Hence, the models, both conceptual and scientific, include only those factors or elements that are absolutely necessary for a rough description of the RP. The modeling process is not a once-and-for-all exercise. Rather, it should be conceived of as consisting of several provisionary models that adequately but roughly describe the manager's conception of the RP.

In summing up the four main parts of Figure 3-4, the real world perceived as the real phenomena (RP) is studied as a system by first being converted into a manager's conceptual model (MCM). By working between the RP and MCM, the systems-oriented manager constructs a scientific model (SML) from which he will eventually arrive at a system (SY) that will be as complex as the real phenomena (RP) itself. This last point cannot be overstated. Systems thinking does not advocate conceptual simplicity. The apparent simplicity involved in the modeling process is only of a temporary nature. It is used as a means of comprehending the complexity inherent in the RP. The ultimate system that will be used to deal with the real world situation must be as complex as the real phenomena (SY = RP). That is, of course, dictated by the universal law of requisite variety: one deals with complexity through complexity.

Let us consider an example to illustrate this relationship between a model and a system. Suppose an engineer desires to build a pipeline to carry oil from the northern part of a geographical area to the southern part. He first constructs a model by drawing a map of the area and then he draws a line across this terrain (a conceptual model). He will continue this modeling process until a physical model of the pipeline is constructed (a scientific model). Upon completion of this model, he will then assemble equipment, men, material, money, and so on and begin building the pipeline. The end result will be an oil transportation system (pipeline), which will be as complex as the terrain itself. It will not only follow the exact characteristics of the real world but it also will be able to adapt to changes in environmental conditions.

APPLICATION OF THE SYSTEMS APPROACH

The first prerequisite for a successful application of the systems approach by managers is that the manager must be convinced of the importance of looking at an organization as an open system. This viewpoint implies that there is a continuous interaction or interface between the organization and it environment. Once the manager is convinced of the validity and usefulness of this viewpoint, then the application of the systems approach is simply a matter of going through the three main steps.

The Organization As a System

There are numerous ways of looking at an organization. Depending on the manager's educational background, his position, the role he or she plays within the organization, and the issues at hand, he or she can adopt several viewpoints and focus on several key concepts. In this section, a brief description of an organization from the systems viewpoint is presented. A more detailed treatment will be given in the next chapter.

As was pointed out earlier in this chapter, with the systems viewpoint, emphasis is placed on the relationship between the organization and its external environment. In managing this relationship, the manager must identify the main inputs, processes, outputs, and feedbacks. Figure 3-5 depicts an organization as an open system. In this system, inputs are drawn from the external environment, are processed, and the resulting outputs are sent to the environment.

There are three main inputs to any organization: people, materials and equipment, and money. These three inputs are processed in accordance with certain economic principles (such as least cost combination). The results of this processing are three outputs: products, waste, and pollution. All three of these functions (input, process, output) are coordinated by the management through such

FIGURE 3-5. The Organization As a System.

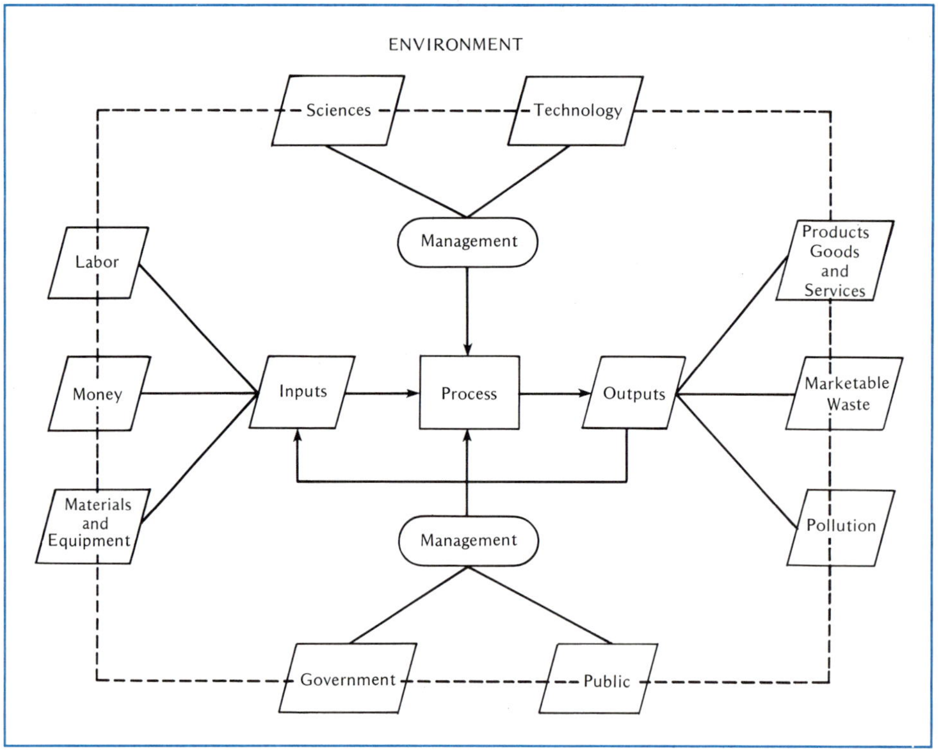

functions as goal setting, decision making, and controlling. Management, in carrying out this combination of the input, process, and output functions, receives inputs from the external environment regarding scientific and technological development and governmental and public attitudes and policies.

The dotted line around the system represents its boundary. As was already stated, the boundary delineates the system from its external environment. The environment represents the totality of factors that have a marked impact on the organization's function but are beyond its immediate control. For example, as can be seen from Figure 3-5, the organization has considerable more control over the input variables labor and money than it has over material and equipment. On the output side, the same situation can be observed with respect to products (goods and services) and waste (reprocessable) on the one hand and pollution on the other.

The next chapter will provide a fuller description of an organization as a system and will clarify this viewpoint with some examples from the real world of organizations. The intention here has been to offer a preliminary picture in order to facilitate the following discussion with respect to the application of the systems approach to the management of organizations.

The Main Steps

Operationally, the application of the systems approach to management is a sequential process that involves the following three interrelated steps:

1. Conceptualization.
2. Measurement/quantification.
3. Computerization.

Step 1. Conceptualization. Conceptualization refers to the process of organizing one's thoughts for the purpose of understanding the phenomenon under scrutiny. This process involves the following two steps: (1) identification and definition of the main *concepts*, and (2) identification and definition of the main *relationships* that tie these concepts together. These two steps will enable the systems designer to develop a framework that will help him to look at the phenomenon in a practical manner.

The phenomenon under investigation in this work is the organization and its management. Let us then develop a conceptual framework for the phenomenon. It has already been said that from the systems viewpoint we are concerned with the relationship between the organization and its environment. Thus, the management of an organization can for all practical purposes be equated with the management of that particular relationship. As was said previously, conceptualization begins with the identification and definition of the main concepts and continues with the identification and definition of the main relationships among the concepts.

In Figure 3-6, three levels of conceptualization are suggested. The first level

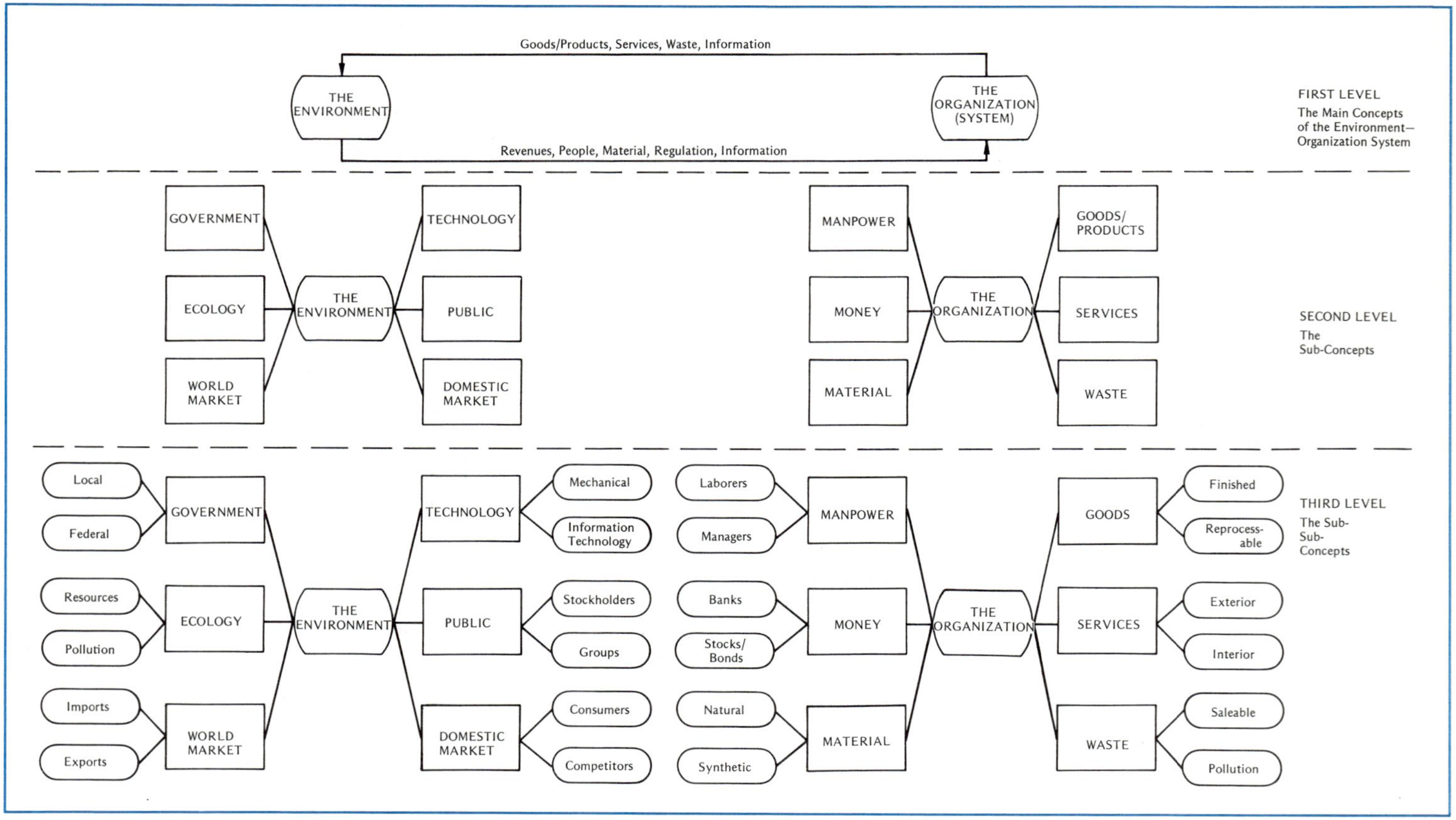

FIGURE 3-6. Applying the Systems Approach to Management.

involves the identification of the two main concepts: (1) *the environment,* that is, the sum total of all variables, factors, and events that have a marked impact upon the organization's performance and that at the same time are beyond the immediate control of the organization; and (2) *the organization,* that is, its inputs, processes, outputs, and feedback controls.

The second level represents a more detailed identification and definition of the subconcepts that comprise the two main concepts. Finally, at the third level, the degree of detail increases considerably. At this level, the concepts that are necessary for defining the subconcepts are identified.

Looking at the same figure, one could identify and define numerous relationships. About those relationships one would want to know the following: (a) the nature of the relationship; (b) the origin of the relationship at a particular moment of time (such as, is it originated by the organization or the environment?); and (c) expression—how does one talk about the relationship? In general, relationships can be expressed in either of the following three ways: (1) in monetary terms; (2) in terms of physical quantities (number of people, tons of resources or output); or (3) in abstract terms (superior-subordinate, regulatory, threats, opportunities, and so on).

Step 2. Measurement/Quantification. It is fairly obvious from this brief description of the conceptualization process that at some time one must end this essentially diagrammatical presentation and begin thinking about assigning some unit of measurement to the relationships identified and defined through the conceptualization process.

Measuring has been man's preoccupation from the beginning of time. In organizations, measuring inputs (material) and outputs (products) has been one of the earliest applications of science to the management of organization known as accounting and/or finance. Stafford Beer seems to think that "the origins of a scientific approach to management were connected with the measurement process."[9] One cannot but agree that measuring changes in the firm's internal and external states is as old as organizations themselves.

Thus far, we have been using the terms *measurement* and *quantification* more or less interchangeably. The reason for this is that *measurement* is frequently defined as the assignment of numerals to elements or objects according to certain rules.[10] From such a definition, one can easily get the impression that measuring means quantifying and, consequently, one might conclude that whatever cannot be quantified cannot be measured; or to carry the logic a step

[9]Stafford Beer, *Management Science: The Business Use of Operations Research* (Garden City, N.J.: Doubleday, 1967), p. 65.

[10]For a more detailed treatment of the subject of measurement, see: C. West Churchman and P. Ratoosh (eds.), *Measurement: Definitions and Theories* (New York: John Wiley & Sons, Inc., 1959); also C. W. Churchmen, "Why Measure?" in *Management Systems,* P. P. Schoderbek (ed.), 2nd ed. (New York: John Wiley & Sons, Inc., 1971); also R. W. Shepard, "An Appraisal of Some of the Problems of Measurement in Operation Research," in P. P. Schoderbek (ed.), *Management Systems.*

further, what cannot be measured cannot be of any consequence for management. Practicing managers and administrators, however, know better. They know that quantification is only one way of measuring. Another way of measuring, known as qualitative measurements, does exist and is as meaningful, and under certain conditions, as useful, if not more so, than quantitative measurement.

Again, as with the case of conceptualization, the measurement/quantification step is a multilevel process. Here, as in the case of conceptualization, the same process of disaggregation of aggregate relationships among the main concepts is involved.

A further elaboration on measurement and the measuring process would carry us beyond the intended scope of this chapter. For our purposes, it will suffice to restate that (1) the function of measurement is to develop a method for generating a class of information that will be useful in a wide variety of problems and situations. This method may involve either a qualitative assignment of objects to classes or the assignment of numbers to events and objects; in most instances, both quantitative and qualitative measuring processes will be employed; and (2) the process of measurement is facilitated by rigorous conceptualization along the three levels depicted in Figure 3-6. The quality of measurement/quantification will definitely help or hinder the descent to the next level of computerization.

> Today we preach that science is not science unless it is quantitative. We substitute correlation for causal studies, and physical equations for organic reasoning. measurements and equations are supposed to sharpen thinking, but . . . they more often tend to make the thinking non-causal and fuzzy. They tend to become the object of scientific manipulation instead of auxiliary tests of crucial inferences.
>
> Many—perhaps most—of the great issues of science are qualitative, not quantitative, even in physics and chemistry. Equations and measurements are useful when and only when they are related to proof; but proof or disproof comes first and is in fact strongest when it is absolutely convincing without any quantitative measurement.
>
> Or to say it another way, you can catch phenomena in a logical box or in a mathematical box. The logical box is coarse but strong. The mathematical box is fine grained but flimsy. The mathematical box is a beautiful way of wrapping up a problem, but it will not hold the phenomena unless they have been caught in a logical box to begin with.
>
> John R. Platt, "Strong Inference." *Science*, No. 3642, (1964).

Step 3. Computerization. Sometimes, the end result of Step 2 is a mathematical model. This model is then most likely computerized—Step 3 in the application of the systems approach. With a computerized model, the manager is better equipped to deal with the complexity of the real-world system. It may be, however, that the comparison of the behavior of the real-world system with the mathematical model reveals a need to either reconceptualize (back to Step 1) or to remeasurement and quantification (back to Step 2) or to both. After any of these steps have been reperformed, a computerized model is once again created.

To recapitulate, it is imperative that the system-oriented manager proceeds from conceptualization to computerization and not vice versa. A better grasp of the problem along the lines of Step 1 will enable the manager to develop a better measurement method and a better computer model. To move in the opposite direction, a bottom-up approach will mean that the manager is attempting to force the problem into a preconceived model—a tactic definitely doomed to failure. to failure.

Table 3-1 provides a summary of the three steps involved in applying the

TABLE 3-1
Applying the Systems Approach to Management: A Summary

Conceptualization	1st Level Identify and define main concepts and relationships of the generic phenomenon (the environment-organization interface). 2nd Level Identify and define the subconcepts for each of the main concepts and the relationship among them and to the generic phenomenon. 3rd Level Identify and define the subconcepts of the concepts and relationships defined in the previous level. *Result:* A CONCEPTUAL FRAMEWORK
Measurement Qualification*	1st Level Define the main variables and determine their relationships—agree on the degree of quantification. Determine qualitive criteria for intangibles. 2nd Level Define the subvariables and determine their relationships. Agree on the degree of quantification. Determine qualitive criteria for intangibles. 3rd Level Same as 2nd Level, with more details. *Result:* A MATHEMATICAL MODEL
Computerization*	1st Level Convert the mathematical model into a computer-readable language. Main program. 2nd Level Determine subroutines. 3rd Level Determine subsubroutines/operate. *Result:* A COMPUTER MODEL

*More detailed presentation is in Part V: *Decision Technology* (Chapters 13, 14, 15, and 16).

systems approach to managerial problems: conceptualize first, measure and quantify second, and computerize third. This is, of course, an ideal situation that may or may not be realized in all occasions. There might, in other words, be managerial problems for which conceptualization alone will be sufficient or adequate. On the other hand, there might be managerial problems whose solution requires quantification and computerization with little attention needed for conceptualization.

The explanation of the systems approach offered in this chapter is unusual to the extent that it is conceived as a unified three-step process that is not confined merely to one of the three steps. Most management scholars define the systems approach as a way of looking at an organization (our conceptualization). On the other hand, most practicing managers equate the systems approach with either the use of mathematics and statistics (our measurement and quantification) or computer systems (our computerization).

Because of this diversity of perception as to what the systems approach is, its acceptance by the management community has not been of the magnitude we would like to see. Nevertheless, the integrative quality of our three-step approach merits serious consideration by management students and practitioners.

SUMMARY

The systems approach is a way of looking at an organization and managing it as an open system. General system theory and cybernetics are two main thrusts of the systems approach. Both of these disciplines have, over the last three decades, developed a set of concepts concerning the structure and behavior of open, complex, and probabilistic systems that have consistently enhanced our understanding of our relationship to the physical and man-made world.

Contemporary organizations are exceedingly complex open systems. Their functions are daily being scrutinized more and more by their external environment. Our society is becoming ever more critical of organizational goal setting and managerial motives. This ever-increasing openness and the accompanying complexity require an equally complex approach for dealing with them. The three-step systems approach that has been explained in the last portion of this chapter is highly recommended for dealing with such complexity.

In this chapter the focus has primarily been on the first step of the systems approach, conceptualization. The second step (measurement/quantification) and the third step (computerization) will be discussed in greater detail in Part IV of this book.

Assignments

3-1. What is the systems approach? Explain the two main parts of it.
3-2. What are the three pillars of systems thinking?
3-3. Briefly trace the development of general systems theory and cybernetics.
3-4. What is a system? Give a diagrammatical presentation of a system and identify and explain the system parameters or objects.
3-5. How does one go about determining what a system's environment is?
3-6. Show the connection between the real-world phenomenon, the model, and the system.
3-7. What are the three steps in applying the systems approach?
3-8. Select a manufacturing company in your community and study it as a system. Begin by identifying the main inputs, processes, outputs, feedbacks, and, of course, its environment.
3-9. Select a service organization, such as a bank, insurance company, a hospital, or your university and study it as a system.
3-10. Apply the systems approach to a specific problem of your university or your community.

Case 3-1

ELECTRA COMPANY

Electra Company was founded in the mid-1950s by a group of young engineers and accountants. Over the last two decades the company has been very successful. During the last five years alone Electra grew at an average annual rate of some 10%. Over the same period a number of new departments and divisions were created.

Last year Electra hired Systemics, Inc., a large consulting firm, to take a look into the company's present operation and future plans. Systemics, Inc., spent about six months studying Electra's documents and interviewing top managers. The general impressions and specific recommendations of Systemics were put forth in a report that was sent to Electra's president.

The *Executive Digest,* a one-page summary highlighting Systemic's main recommendations concluded: "There appears to be a lack of understanding by the company's personnel in general and by most of the top managers in particular regarding the main goals and objectives pursued by Electra. Specifically, most executives do not see how their particular job affects the duties of the others and vice versa. In addition, nobody seems to know what the external environment of the company is and how it is affected by what the company does and how the environment affects the operations of the company. We, therefore, highly recommend that Electra Company adopt the *systems approach.*"

After reading this last paragraph, the president of Electra Company called a meeting for the next day with all top executives. The president opened the meeting with the following statement: "I trust that all of you have a copy of Systemic's report and that you have had the opportunity to take a look at it. Well, I don't know what you got out of it, but it seems to me it all boils down to our using the systems approach. Now, I was an engineer for quite a long time and I think I know something about engineering systems. In any case, what's wrong with our engineering department?"

"Well, sir," said Bill Billings, the young vice-president for corporate affairs, "I wish it were that simple. With all due respect to you, sir, I don't think you've interpreted Systemic's recommendations correctly. Because of the nature of my job, I spent a lot of time with these young gentlemen from Systemics. I think I am correct in saying, sir, that the systems approach that is recommended by Systemics has little to do with engineering systems. It rather has . . ."

Billings was interrupted by Joe Smith, the vice-president for marketing, who said, "Bill has got a point, sir, if I may interrupt for just a second. I just returned from an executive development program where we had a two-day workshop on the systems approach. Well, I don't want to put you through the entire ordeal I went through, but what I think Systemics wants us to do is to set up a new department and then buy a large computer, and that will take care of us."

The president noticed that Billings was a bit skeptical. He turned to him and said, "Well, Bill, you don't seem to be in complete agreement with Joe. What's on your mind?" Billings thought for a while and then said, "You're right, sir. See, Joe is partially right, but only partially. Computers and computer systems are a part of the systems approach, but only a part. And to be honest with you, sir, that's the last thing we have to consider at this point. I tell you what we ought to do. I think we ought to do some homework. In other words, we ought to do some reading on the systems approach, talk to our friends who might have had some experience with it, and so on, and then have another meeting some time next week. I'll volunteer to present an introductory paper to get us started."

"That sounds like an excellent idea," said the president. "Thank you for volunteering, Bill. You're on a week from today. Good luck to all of you. Do some homework. I myself am going to skip my usual weekend fishing and dig out some of my old books on engineering and systems. Good day, gentlemen."

[A week later]. The president entered the meeting room smiling and full of excitement. "Good morning, gentlemen," he said. "This is going to be a lot of fun. This systems thing is really very exciting. It makes a lot of sense to me. I don't understand why we couldn't have come up with something like Systemics did. It's mostly common sense . . . but let Bill tell us all about it."

Billings got up, turned on the overhead projector and then turned it off. "I just wanted to test this thing," he said. "Good morning gentlemen. Today I'll give you, as I promised, a brief talk on what the systems approach is all about. In a later meeting I'll show you how we, as a manufacturing company, can begin implementing it."

"Let me first point out that the systems approach is a way of looking at an organization. In other words, it is a viewpoint . . ."

Continue Mr. Billings' presentation.

How would you conceptualize Electra as a system? What are Electra's main inputs? Explain to Electra's management how every manager must develop a way of thinking of Electra as an open system.

References

ASHBY, W. ROSS. *Introduction to Cybernetics.* New York: John Wiley & Sons, Inc., 1956.

BECKETT, JOHN. *Management Dynamic: The New Synthesis.* New York: McGraw-Hill Book Company, 1972.

BEER, STAFFORD. *Management Science: The Business Use of Operations Research.* New York: Doubleday & Company, Inc., 1967.

BERTALANFFY, LUDWIG VON. *General Systems Theory*. New York: George Braziller, 1968.
BOULDING, KENNETH. "General Systems Theory—The Skeleton of Science," in *Management Systems:* P. P. Schoderbek (ed.) New York: John Wiley & Sons, Inc., 1971.
CHURCHMAN, C. WEST. *The Systems Approach*. New York: Delacorte Press, 1968.
CLELAND, DAVID I., AND WILLIAM R. KING. *Management: A Systems Approach*. New York: McGraw-Hill Book Company, 1972.
EMERY, FRED E. (ed.) *Systems Thinking*. Middlesex, England: Penguin Books, 1969.
LASZLO, ERVIN. *The Relevance of General Systems Theory*. New York: George Braziller, Inc., 1972.
LOW, ALBERT. *Zen and Creative Management*. New York: Anchor Press/Doubleday & Company, Inc., 1976.
SCHODERBEK, PETER P., ASTERIOS G. KEFALAS, AND CHARLES G. SCHODERBEK. *Management Systems: Conceptual Considerations*. Dallas, Texas: Business Publications, Inc., 1975.
SHRODE, WILLIAM, AND DON VOICH, JR. *Organizations and Management: Basic Systems Concepts*. Homewood, Ill.: Richard D. Irwin, Inc., 1974.
WEINBERG, GERALD, M. *An Introduction to General Systems Thinking*. New York: John Wiley & Sons, Inc., 1975.
WIENER, NORBERT. *Cybernetics: On Control and Communicaton in the Animal and the Machine*. Cambridge, Mass.: The MIT Press, 1948.

JOSEPH W. KORN
Executive Vice-President,
Parts Warehouse Company, Inc.

Joseph W. Korn is presently employed as Executive Vice-President of Parts Warehouse Company, Inc., a wholesale distributor of automotive parts in Augusta, Georgia. In 1976, Mr. Korn began the computerization of Parts Warehouse Company's operations. This project included the company's inventory, payroll, cost accounting and sales forecasting systems.

Executive Commentary
The Systems Approach to Management

I believe the key in systems is to view the system as a whole. No system can be considered in isolation. It must be viewed as a subsystem of a larger system for which it serves a particular function or need. The outputs from each and every system are the inputs to other system. The systems thinker does not break the whole down into its constituent parts and then study each part in isolation. He must secure an adequate knowledge of the whole relevant system before pursuing an accurate knowledge of the working of the parts.

The real world of the practicing manager is very complex and subject to few laws or regularities. He begins his search for the system determinants with the construction of a conceptual model. The model then becomes the link between the real phenomenon and the manager's system. It is less complex but exhibits orderliness. He then applies science to construct a model that is more orderly than his conceptual model. The ultimate system derived from this process must be as complex as the real world.

After conceptualization, the manager must begin to assign some unit of measurement to the relationships previously identified and defined. I would like to pause here to express a word of caution to the student of the systems approach to management. One must not get bogged down in the detail of quantitative measurement. That is a hazardous pitfall for many practicing managers. It is easy to get so involved in scientific measurement that one forgets about viewing his system holistically. This pit is easy to fall into, as I myself have done. For example, let's look at the problem of rising expenses. The manager may spend a great deal of time quantitatively analyzing the various expenses. He knows they are too high, so he analyzes them to determine where his largest problems are. He then decides to cut these expenses by a certain percentage. He can get so wrapped up in the quantitative analysis of the expenses that he tends to forget to qualitatively determine what is causing these excess expenses in the first place.

It is imperative that the manager proceeds from conceptualization to quantification and then to computerization, and not vice versa. I cannot emphasize this point strongly enough. As is stated in this chapter, to move in the opposite direction, a bottom-up approach, will mean that the manager is attempting to force the problem into a preconceived computer program. From personal experience I can fully appreciate the fact that this tactic is definitely doomed to failure. One may not have to go through all three steps; however, they *must* be followed in the correct order.

For example, our inventory had grown to a point where we could no longer continue to control it manually. We should have followed the steps of conceptualization, measurement, and computerization years before. It appeared to us that we needed to jump directly into computerization, bypassing the preliminary processes. After a year's time, we were forced to start over once again, this time beginning with conceptualization, then proceeding to measurement, and finially computerization. I might add that we have been quite successful the second time around.

I would like to reiterate the importance of viewing any and all systems holistically. The systems approach to management can be a useful and extremely effective tool in improving any organization. However, we must remember that there are many other approaches to management. Each of us must decide which path we wish to take to reach our desired goals.

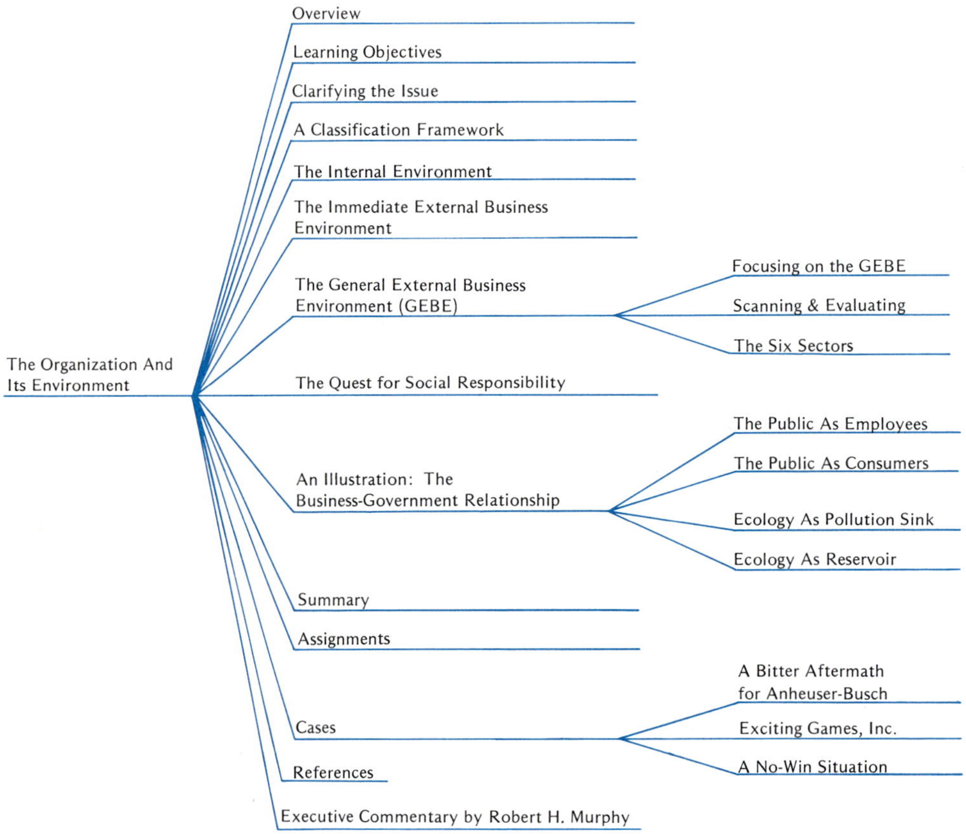
The Organization And Its Environment
Overview
Learning Objectives
Clarifying the Issue
A Classification Framework
The Internal Environment
The Immediate External Business Environment
The General External Business Environment (GEBE)
Focusing on the GEBE
Scanning & Evaluating
The Six Sectors
The Quest for Social Responsibility
An Illustration: The Business-Government Relationship
The Public As Employees
The Public As Consumers
Ecology As Pollution Sink
Ecology As Reservoir
Summary
Assignments
Cases
A Bitter Aftermath for Anheuser-Busch
Exciting Games, Inc.
A No-Win Situation
References
Executive Commentary by Robert H. Murphy

4

THE ORGANIZATION AND ITS ENVIRONMENT

OVERVIEW

Chapter 3 provided an explanation of the systems approach, which was defined as a way of looking at an organization and managing it as an open system. In utilizing this approach, the manager focuses on the relationship between the organization and its environment. The term *environment* was defined as the factors or events that have a marked impact upon the organization's performance and are beyond the immediate or complete control of the organization. Figure 3-6 of Chapter 3 provided a diagrammatical presentation of the interface between the organization and its environment.

This chapter is exclusively devoted to the subject of the organization's environment. The term *environment* has been subject to many interpretations, which have resulted in considerable confusion on the part of academicians and practitioners alike. For this reason the chapter begins with a clarification of the misconceptions surrounding the term. This is the subject of the first section, entitled "Clarifying the Issue." A major portion of this chapter deals with the classification of numerous environmental factors into a coherent framework and identification of six basic categories that are the primary concern of the contemporary manager. These factors are the public, the government, domestic markets, world markets, technology, and ecology. The last section of this chapter, in an effort to illustrate the significance of the environment for the manager, discusses the latest institutionalizations of environmental factors that have and will have far-reaching implications for management. This is the subject of the government-business relationship. Governmental intervention has been heralded by the public-at-large as the most significant event of the 1970s and at the same time is considered by the business community as the most sophisticated attempt by society to intervene in the internal working of the organization. The purpose of this discussion is not to settle the question of desirability and/or effectiveness of the government's intervention; rather, the intention is to illustrate the importance of the external environment for the contemporary manager.

LEARNING OBJECTIVES

This chapter is especially intended to help the student:

1. **Clarify the issue of the business external environment because this term has had many connotations.**
2. **Learn the difference between the immediate or operating external business environment and the general external business environment.**
3. **Appreciate how general events that appear to have no relation to an organization become part of that organization's environment with potentially detrimental consequences.**
4. **Enable him or her to trace the developments in the various sectors of the general external business environment and to draw inferences or speculate as to the significance of these developments for a given organization or industry.**
5. **Familiarize him or her with the rationale and the latest developments of governmental regulation of business and other organizational activities or sectors.**
6. **Learn, especially in the context of thinking about management, the meaning of the following concepts:**
   - **environment**
   - **business environment**
   - **immediate external business environment**
   - **general external business environment**
   - **social responsibility**
   - **government regulation**
   - **EEOC, OSHA, ERISA, EPA**

CLARIFYING THE ISSUE

Traditionally, the study of organizations and their management focused on the internal working of the organization, that is, its structure, function, people, and so on. The rationale behind this emphasis on the internal organization was based on the belief that a well-organized and equally well-managed firm would perform well under any conditions or circumstances. This assumption could perhaps prove to be true as long as the world surrounding the organization is both *stable* (does not change too frequently and too drastically) and *benevolent* (sympathetic with or in agreement with the organization's main objectives and activities). Until recently, there did not seem to be any reason to doubt the validity of that assumption. Most concerned scholars would agree that there was a congruence between the organization's objectives and purposes and the external world's desires and aspirations. As a matter of fact, the organization was considered to be the most effective mechanism for achieving societal desires and aspirations.

Although evidence of some kind of environmental concern can be found earlier, it can be safely stated that the 1960s marked the appearance of the first scholarly interest in the impact of the external world on organizational performance and success. Researchers began to realize that organizational performance depended just as much, if not more, on a set of circumstances that were beyond the immediate control of the organization as it did on a sound internal structure and management. This set of circumstances that are beyond the control of the organization's management but have considerable influence on organizational performance are referred to as the *environmental forces, factors,* or just as *the business environment.*

The need for developing an understanding of the business environment was recognized very early by such management writers as Davis and Blomstrom who opened the preface of their book *Business and Its Environment* with the following statement: "The notion that just because we live in a business environment we understand it is a myth."[1] Although more than a dozen years have elapsed since this statement was made, there still exists considerable diversity in the approaches seeking to dispell this myth. This diversity or lack of uniformity in dealing with a definition of the business environment and how it affects and is affected by the organization reflects the variety and complexity of the issue.

A CLASSIFICATION FRAMEWORK

Traditionally, management literature defined the business environment as *social, technological, economic, and political (STEP) influences or conditions that have a potential or real impact upon the organization.* Starting with this definition, considerable scholarly effort has been expended in systematizing those influences or conditions into a coherent scheme. Some writers classify the business environment into two major categories: (1) the internal environment and (2) the external environment. Others concentrate on the nature of the environmental

[1] Keith Davis and Robert L. Blomstrom, *Business and Its Environment* (New York: McGraw-Hill, 1966) p. vii. Actually, the first foundations of the importance of the environment for management were laid by Chester Barnard and his followers who later popularized his ideas. See Chester Barnard, *The Functions of the Executive* (Cambridge, Mass.: Harvard University Press, 1938); Herbert A. Simon, *Administrative Behavior* (New York: Macmillan, 1957); also *Models of Man* (New York: John Wiley & Sons, 1957); Richard Cyert and James March, *The Behavioral Theory of the Firm* (Englewood Cliffs, N.J.: Prentice-Hall, 1963); James March and Herbert A. Simon, *Organizations* (New York: John Wiley & Sons, 1958).

Input \ Output	Organization	Environment
Organization	Internal Business Environment (IBE)	Immediate External Business Environment (IEBE)
Environment	General External Business Environment (GEBE)	External Environment (EE)

FIGURE 4-1. The Organization-Environment Interface.

forces and desire to know whether they represent (1) a problem, (2) a threat, or (3) an opportunity, whereas others, interested in the volatility of the environmental forces, attempt to classify them (in accordance with the degree of the rate of change) into (1) stable, (2) dynamic, and (3) turbulent environment. The framework proposed in this chapter represents an attempt to combine all the relevant approaches of classifying the business environment. As such, it gives a panoramic view of the situation managers face.

As it was pointed out in Chapter 3, the relationship between the system (organization) and its environment is a two-way interaction process. Certain actions taken by the organization will have an impact upon the environment, and certain environmental actions will affect the organization. Some of these two-way interactions may be the result of an action (such as a response) by one party, or they may be spontaneous. For example, society may desire to control organizational behavior because of certain negative consequences it may have upon society. As it will be seen later, the entire issue of environmental protection falls into this category. It is being interpreted as society's response to environmental deterioration brought about by business and other organizations. On the other hand, advertisement by a business firm concerning a newly introduced product or service is a spontaneous interaction and not a response. The entire complexity of these two-way interactions between the organization and its environment can be arranged as presented in Figure 4-1.

THE INTERNAL BUSINESS ENVIRONMENT

The term internal business environment appears in the literature as a synonym for "psychological climate," "work climate," "organizational personality," "organizational or company culture," "working conditions," and, most often, "organizational climate." Regardless of the nomenclature used, the term refers to the totality of things in a work situation that are beyond the immediate or complete control of the jobholder (individual) and that are determined by the organization or, alternatively, are within the organization's official jurisdiction. These may range from the most obvious physical surroundings of the workplace (site of the office or work station, noise, cleanliness, safety) to general and more abstract attributes of the social atmosphere of the workplace.

Over the years society (through legislation) has specified the necessary conditions for a safe, healthy, and to some extent pleasant physical working environment. Despite these efforts, numerous instances of unhealthy and/or unsafe physical environments have occurred, either because of insufficient legislative coverage or because of noncompliance with the law. As a result, more unified, more intensive, and extensive legislative efforts have recently been introduced. These efforts are exemplified in the Occupational Safety and Health Act (OSHA) of 1970. Because of the importance of the government's role in this, the subject will be treated later when the governmental sector of the external environment will be discussed.

An overwhelming majority of contemporary management literature concentrates on the social atmosphere portion of the internal environment. The most commonly used term is *organizational climate,* which is defined as "a set of measurable properties of the work environment, perceived directly or indirectly by the people who live and work in this environment and assumed to influence their motivation and behavior."[2] This definition refers to *employee perception* of general conditions that are set up by the organization. In this sense, the term organizational climate describes a subjective interpretation of the quality of the work environment. Thus, it is very likely that of two employees working in the same environment, one might describe it as extremely frustrating, but the other might find it very pleasant. This is the same experience one might have listening to two people talking about Plainview as a place to live and work. One might describe it enthusiastically as a "very nice place" and the other could call it a "God-forsaken place."

In summary, it should not be forgotten that organizational climate refers to employee *perceptions* about certain factors of the work environment. It is therefore likely that whereas certain individuals will judge a small organization with a rather passive image and a centralized structure as having a favorable climate, others will prefer a large, aggressive, and decentralized organization. By

[2]George H. Litwin and Robert A. Stringer, Jr. *Motivation and Organizational Climate* (Boston: Harvard University Press, 1968), p. 1.

the same token, some jobholders would find responsible, risk-taking, and independent subordinates a good climate in which to work, but others would consider it an unfavorable climate.

THE IMMEDIATE EXTERNAL BUSINESS ENVIRONMENT

The discussion on the classification framework of the business environment started by dividing the entire environment into two main categories: (1) the internal business environment and (2) the external business environment. The previous section dealt with the internal business environment (physical, social, or organizational climate). The remainder of this chapter will be exclusively devoted to the *external* business environment. This is defined as the totality of environmental influences or conditioning that are outside the systems boundary.

This portion of the business environment is divided into two main categories: (1) the immediate, operating, or task environment and (2) the general external environment. Figure 4-2 presents yet another way of depicting the relationship among the three categories or levels of the business environment and the relationships among them: the one internal and the two external environments (the operating and the general environment).[3] While there is no complete agreement in the literature as to what those parts of the external environment are that can be considered as the task environment, the following are found to be most frequently used: (1) stockholders (2) creditors (3) suppliers (4) competitors (5) unions.

Stockholders or shareholders are persons (individuals) or groups of persons (institutions) who have exchanged a certain amount of money for a claim on

FIGURE 4-2. Another Perspective on the Organization-Environment Interface.

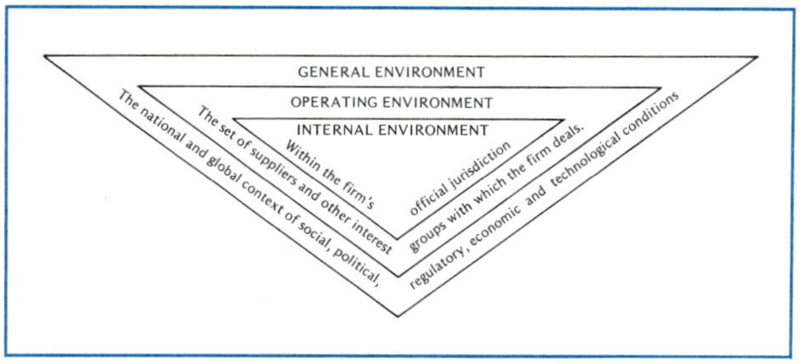

[3]Philip S. Thomas, "Environmental Analysis for Corporate Planning," *Business Horizons,* October 1974, pp. 27–38.

future earnings. The stockholder receives a certificate indicating a claim on the company, expressed in terms of a share of the company's wealth. The stockholder can considerably influence the organization's management *indirectly* by trading the stock in the stock market. Or, the stockholder can *directly* influence the organization by appearing at the annual stockholders' meeting to render or withdraw support for management.

This environmental factor is gaining increasing importance for the management of an organization. In the past, stockholders were thought of as a rather passive group of people who were primarily interested in receiving the quarterly, semi-annual, or annual dividend check, leaving management completely free to carry out the actual running of the organization. Recently, however, there has been considerable change in the role of the stockholders. They are becoming more and more interested in the actual running of the organization as well as the composition of the top management team and the board of directors which oversees management. The most vivid example that illustrates this change is represented by a 1974 action taken by the stockholders of the General Motors Corporation which forced top management and the board of directors to make certain changes in the composition of the board to allow for participation by minority groups.[4]

Creditors are usually institutions that supply a certain amount of funds needed by the organization which cannot be raised through internal sources or the stock issuing process. Banks, savings and loan associations, and other commercial credit institutions are the most important creditors of any organization. The relationship between the organization and its creditors is thought of as being one of mutual benefit. The organization is enjoying the use of certain amounts of the creditor's assets (money) and the creditor is expected to receive a certain amount of money in the form of interest, fees, and other payments.

Recently, there has been considerable discussion on the amount of control a creditor can exercise over the debtor's (the organization's) ways of managing the concern. In addition, there seems to be an increasing interest in creditor representation on board membership. Finally, the recent increase in the number of failed banks (banking institutions that closed), such as Franklin National Bank, New York (1974); U.S. National Bank, San Diego (1973); and Hamilton National Bank, Chattanooga (1976), just to name the three largest bank failures, makes this relationship more and more complex.[5]

Suppliers are individuals or organizations who provide the necessary material and nonmaterial inputs to an organization. Such inputs include raw material and semi-finished products, energy, water, maintenance, equipment, office supplies, services, and everything else that is needed by the organization to carry out its

[4]Earl C. Gottschalk, Jr., "The Annual Trial by Stockholders Is About To Begin," *Wall Street Journal* (July 2, 1977), p. 12.

[5]Joseph F. Sinkey, Jr., "Problem and Failed Banks: Examining the Issue," testimony before the United States Senate Committee on Banking, Housing and Urban Affairs, exerpted in *Georgia Business* (Sept.–Oct., 1977), pp. 5–11.

daily activities. Some of these suppliers will have a permanent relationship with the organization to the extent that there will be only one supplier who will provide a specific input. For example, gas and electricity in most cases will be provided by the only utility company in the area. Water is usually provided by the city or county within which the organization operates. For the majority of suppliers, an organization will usually have a pool of potential sources from which to draw its needed supplies. For example, an organization that desires a new computer system for its electronic data processing (EDP) department can choose a system from companies such as IBM, CDC, Honeywell, Burroughs, NCR, and so on.

Because of recent perceived or real scarcities in a number of vital resources, the relationship between suppliers and the organization has taken a new dimension. During the 1973 oil embargo, for example, a number of manufacturing organizations were faced with severe problems in securing the gas and oil to run their factories. Taking another example, as a result of extreme drought in the western part of the United States during 1977, a number of organizations considered deferment of new investment in those areas because of a fear of not having adequate water.

Competitors are organizations that belong to the same industry by virtue of the fact they produce and sell a similar or the same product or service. Although some industries consist of a small number of organizations, the majority is composed of a large number of concerns. The automobile industry in most parts of the world is a typical example of an industry with a small number of competitors, usually between four to six firms. On the other hand, banks and insurance companies belong to an industry with a large number of individual establishments.

Traditionally, society has encouraged increasing the number of competitors in a given industry because it is believed that this strategy leads to lower prices and facilitates *new entry*, thereby encouraging entrepreneurship. Most recently there seems to be a concerted effort to further encourage competition by attempting to break up firms in industries that have evolved into highly concentrated industries. Currently, the United States Congress is attempting to break up or discourage further vertical or horizontal concentration of the so-called Seven Sisters, the seven largest oil companies (Exxon, Mobil, Gulf, Texaco, Shell, SoCal, and BP).

Unions represent employee organizations whose purpose was originally to provide a channel of communication between workers and managers. Today, unionism has spread over to other job categories and professions. The Netherlands even has a unionized army. The history of unionism in the United States is well known. Immediately after the Great Depression, in 1935, the United States Congress passed the National Labor Relations Act, usually referred to as the Wagner Act. This act declared that employees "shall have the right to self-organization, to form, join, or assist labor organizations, and to bargain collectively through representation of their own choosing." The subsequent amendments of this act, known as the Taft-Hartly Act (1947), and the Landrum-Griffin act (1959), have further strengthened the right to union representation and/or union formations.

After several decades of a relatively happy marriage between unions and management, the relationship has recently begun to deteriorate. Whereas business and other organizations claim to be "too union-dominated," the unions attempt to demonstrate that management pursues policies aimed at erosion in union power. It is not uncommon nowadays to see industry seminars on "how to keep unions out of your business." Recent scandals regarding congressional hearings on union misuse of membership pension funds have not helped the cause of unionism.

In summarizing the brief discussion of this portion of the external environment, which was labeled *immediate, operating,* or *task environment,* it has been demonstrated that these environmental influences refer to more or less long-standing relationships between the organization and its external environment. Stockholders, creditors, suppliers, competitors, and unions are industry-related environmental factors, as opposed to the internal environment which consists of organization-related environmental factors. In other words, whereas each organization will have a certain special internal environment, it also will have a more or less common task environment. For example, certain developments in banking and financial institutions (such as the increase in interest rates for long-term financing) will affect equally every single firm in, let's say, the construction industry. On the other hand, a change in the employee perception of a given organization's internal environment (such as its leadership) will affect immediately only that particular organization.

THE GENERAL EXTERNAL BUSINESS ENVIRONMENT

To this point we have discussed two categories of the business environment: (1) the internal business environment or organizational climate (IBE) (employees' perceptions of certain factors that influence their task performance and that are within the jurisdiction of the firm), and (2) the immediate external or task environment (IEBE) (certain external environmental influences pertaining to industry-related factors representing long-standing relationships between the organization and its external environment). The remainder of this chapter focuses on the rest of the external business environment, which is superordinate to the immediate or task environment (See Figure 4-1).

The general external business environment (GEBE) is usually defined very loosely as "persuasive background factors such as social, political (or regulatory), economic, and technological conditions."[6] The intention in the literature is to point out to the manager that whatever is happening in the external environment-at-large, appearing to have little or no effect upon managerial decision

[6]Philip S. Thomas, *op. cit.,* p. 28.

making, must be taken into consideration when the present or future organizational strategy is contemplated. This was succinctly dramatized by C. Jackson Grayson, a former Wage and Price Commission official who is said to have remarked, "The chief executive has to watch out for the killing variable in the external world. The new law, the currency devaluation—that can change everything for his company."[7]

The next section of this chapter focuses on (1) an explanation of how these general external environmental factors evolve so as to become relevant for the organization, and (2) grouping some of the most important ones into six basic categories (public, government, technology, domestic market, world market and ecology) to facilitate sensing and evaluating of the GEBE.

Focusing on the General External Business Environment (GEBE)

As a rule, general external environmental influences (EE, Figure 4-1) become part of the general external business environment (GEBE, Figure 4-1) through a well-defined but ill-understood process. This process begins with the emergence of a social issue. Starting from that point, a process of "building-up of social energy" begins.[8] This process of building up of social energy is illustrated in Figure 4-3.

FIGURE 4-3. The Build-up of Social Energy.

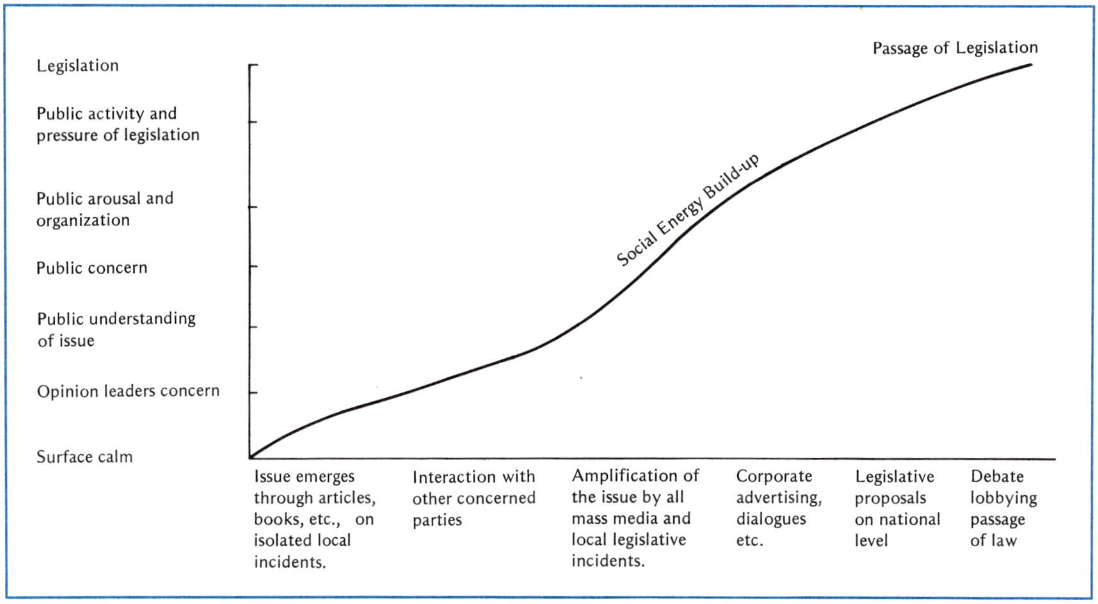

[7]Ibid., p. 29.

[8]Hazel Henderson, "How to Cope With Organizational Future Shock," *Management Review* (July 1976), pp. 19–28.

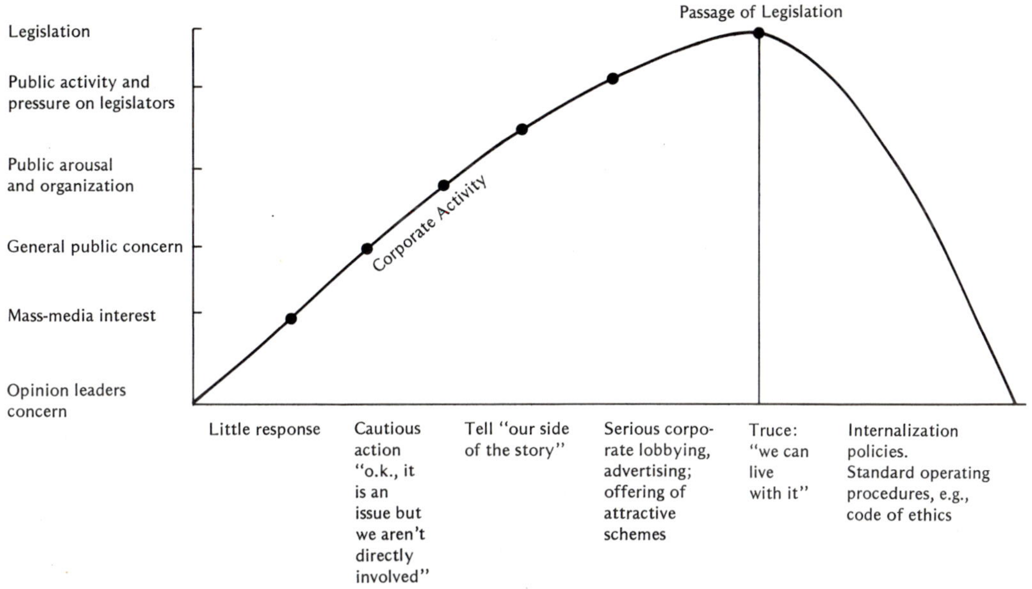

FIGURE 4-4. Corporate Response Patterns to Public Issue Development.

The process begins with articles in printed media such as magazines, books, and so on. At this stage of issue development, opinion leaders begin to emerge. By expressing their opinions, they motivate interaction with other opinion leaders. This interaction stimulates further amplification of the issue through public mass media, which develop specials (such as CBS's 60 Minutes). This amplification leads first to an enhancement in public understanding, and then to the formulation of public interest groups, sometimes called pressure groups, such as Common Cause, Nader's Center for Study of Responsive Law, and the Sierra Club. At this stage local governmental leaders become interested and begin a preliminary investigative process, which makes the national news, which, in turn, arouses formulation of public interest groups such as federal congressmen and government interest. This can lead to specific legislative proposals, introduced in the Congress as bills, which end up in specific legislation.

Corporate response follows the same pattern. Figure 4-4 illustrates the building up of corporate activity. This process begins with a "not getting involved" type of response. For example, "it is not our policy to take sides in social issues." The process moves into cautious statements of the importance of the issue in public speeches by corporate executives. However, careful qualifications of "not wanting to rock the boat" are frequently made. As social energy build-up reaches the third stage of amplification by the public mass media and local legislation interest arousal, corporate activity changes to "let's tell our side of the story," and moves into serious national lobbying and corporate advertising. With the passage of legislation (sixth stage in the social energy build-up process) adverse corporate activity ceases, a truce is declared, the new law is praised, and finally the statement, "we can live with it," is issued. The process of corporate response to social energy build-up about a social issue ends with internalization of the legislation and complete adaptation and compliance with the law.

Figure 4-5 summarizes the process of internalization of the external environmental influences. The external environmental factors (EE) first become part of the general external business environment (GEBE), then the immediate external business environment (IEBE), and finally enter the internal business environment ment (IBE). All important external environmental issues that will be discussed in the next section followed this process. For example, the entire issue of consumerism started with Nader's concern about automobile safety and ended up as a law. Environmental protection, minority concerns, product safety, the Occupational Safety and Health Act (OSHA), all of these followed the same pattern of (1) social issue, (2) interest group formulation, (3) local legislation, and (4) national and international legislation.

Scanning and Evaluating the General External Business Environment (GEBE).

The preceding discussion of the dynamics of the appearance and evolution of an external environmental factor demonstrated that this process seems to be straightforward. What complicates it, however, is that a multitude of environmental factors are undergoing this process more or less simultaneously. For this reason, the manager is literally overwhelmed with the complexity of these simultaneous happenings and therefore finds it difficult to focus on any specific or single process. As Judson Gooding from *Fortune* correctly observed, "It's no easy trick to be the well-informed executive."[9]

For the purpose of this chapter, the entire general external business environment can be conceptualized as consisting of six interrelated and, to some extent, overlapping sectors, namely, the public, government, technology, domestic market, world market and the ecology sectors. The manager who is interested in assessing the events in these sectors must develop a set of criteria that can be used to define and evaluate the meaning of events for the organization. Two such criteria are suggested in this chapter. The first is associated with the *volatility* of each sector, and the second deals with the *nature* or *significance* of these events for the organization.

Figure 4-6 presents a matrix-type of arrangement of these six sectors of the GEBE along with the two characteristics of volatility and nature. *Volatility* refers to two attributes of the external environment: the degree of change, and frequency of change. An external environmental sector that changes infrequently and is of

[9]Judson Gooding, "It's No Easy Trick To Be the Well-Informed Executive," *Fortune* (January 1973), pp. 85–89.

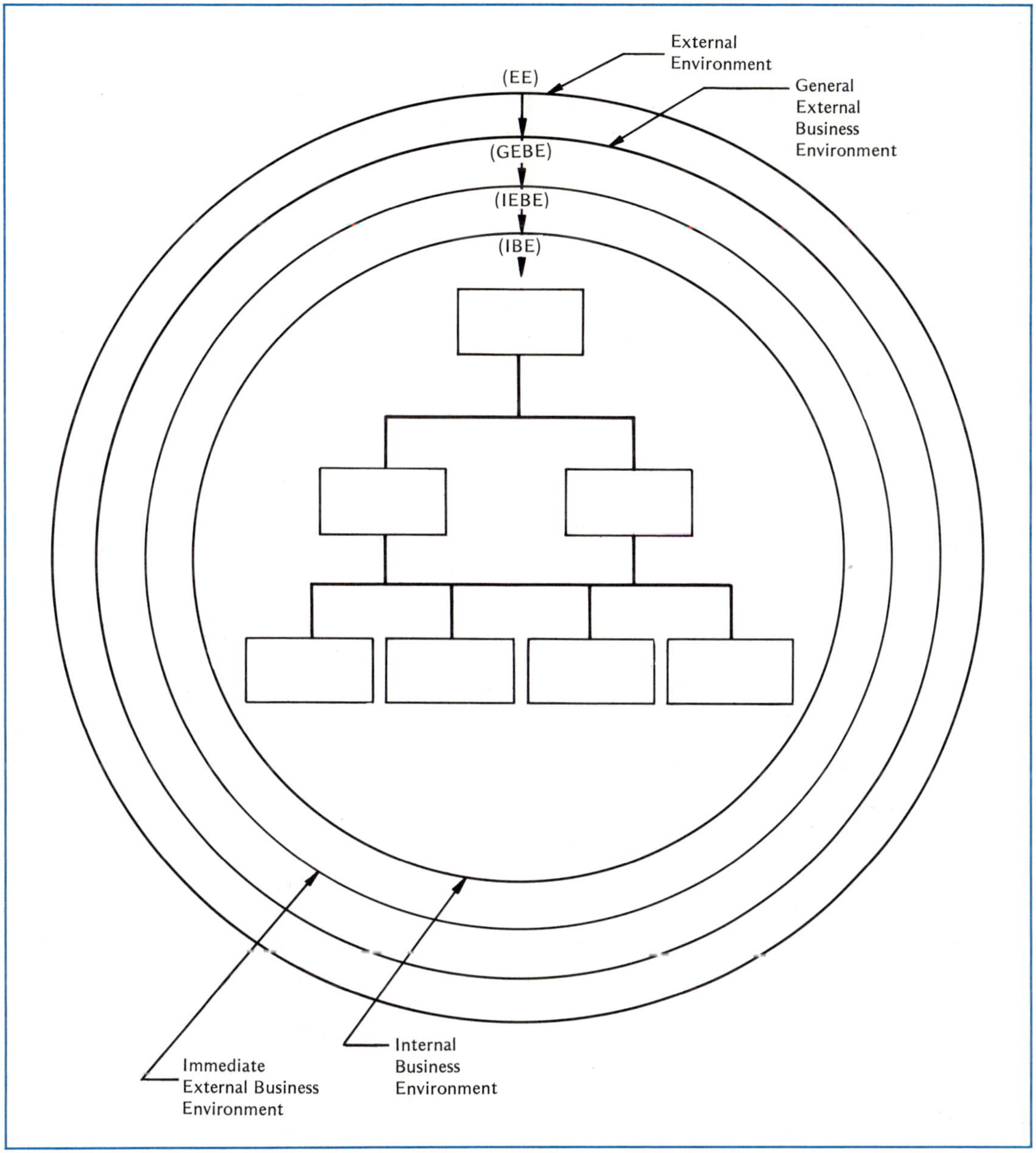

FIGURE 4-5. The Organization-Environment Interface: Formalization-Internalization of External Environmental Events.

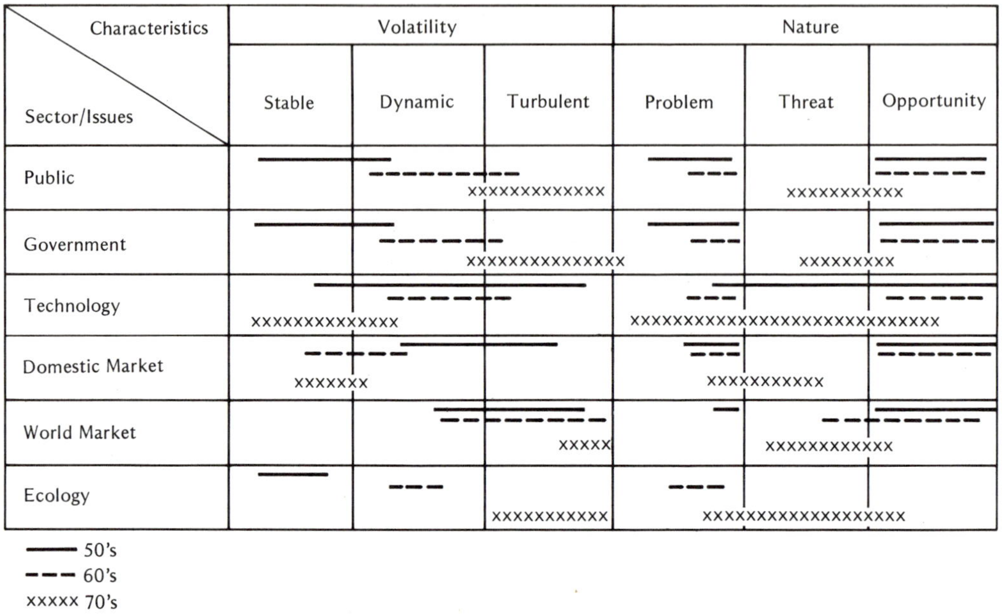

FIGURE 4-6. The General External Business Environment: A Demonstration of Changes Over the Last Three Decades.

small magnitude allows for quite a lot of prediction to the extent that the manager of an organization can forecast the time and magnitude of the next change by simple extrapolation techniques. These circumstances or conditions characterize a *stable environment.* A *dynamic environment,* on the other hand, is characterized by frequent changes of a rather substantial magnitude, both of which increase the complexity of that environment and make it less predictable. Forecasting techniques must then be more sophisticated.

Finally, a *turbulent environment* is characterized by accelerating frequency of change of exceptionally high magnitude and of an unexpected nature, creating a situation of extreme complexity that is beyond any kind of prediction. In this kind of environment, normal, historical, and conventional patterns, or trends and expectations are broken or disappear and new ones begin to emerge. Because of this discontinuity and novelty, formalized forecasting techniques are ineffective. This is the kind of environment that one describes with such a phrase as "completely out of the blue."

After making an accurate assessment of the volatility of the GEBE sector, the manager must ask the question, "what does it mean to the organization?" This is a question of assessing the potential impact of an external environmental factor upon the organization's functioning. This impact can be arranged along a continuum, ranging from a problem to an opportunity, with a threat as an intermediate point. A *problem* is a question raised for inquiry, consideration, or solution. It usually involves a discrepancy between a desired state (a goal or a standard) and an actual state (the actual situation or performance). A *threat,* on the other hand, is an expression of intention to inflict evil, injury, or danger. It again involves a difference between a goal and an actual performance. In both cases the actual performance is considered unsatisfactory. The difference between a problem and a threat is essentially the amount of time allowed for finding a solution. Usually under a threat situation the amount of time allowed for reaction is considerably smaller than it is under a problem instance. Finally, an *opportunity* is defined as good chance for advancement or progress. Here the actual performance exceeds expectations, thereby indicating an underestimation of potentialities.[10]

The Six Sectors of the General External Business Environment

In order to illustrate the workability of this scheme for scanning and evaluating the GEBE, the next few pages provide a close look into the six sectors of the GEBE, which are the public, government, technology, domestic markets, world markets, and ecology.

The Public. This sector of the external business environment refers to sentiments and attitudes of the general populace towards the aims of the organization and the means it employs in achieving them. Theoretically, an organization represents a sector of the public organized for the purpose of accomplishing a particular objective that could not be achieved by the individual alone or by a group of individuals working informally. This being the case, one would expect a rather strong congruence between the intentions and activities of an organization and the public's perceptions and attitudes.

Figure 4-6 illustrates the characteristics of the six external environmental sectors over the last three decades since World War II. During the 1950s a typical organization was operating within a rather stable to dynamic public environment. Most people during that era were "behind" the organization, so to speak. Both governmental and private organizations enjoyed high prestige in the eyes and the minds of the public. The adage "What's good for General Motors is good for the country" (and one could add "and for the public") summarized fairly accurately

[10]For more detailed explanations of these characteristics of the environment see James D. Thompson, *Organizations in Action* (New York: McGraw-Hill Book Company, 1967); Paul R. Lawrence and Jay W. Lorsch, *Organization and Environment* (Homewood, Ill.: Richard D. Irwin, 1964); Fred Emery and E. L. Trist, "The Casual Texture of Organizational Environments," *Human Relations* (March 1965); Shirley Terreberry, "The Evolution of Organizational Environments," *Administrative Science Quarterly* (March 1968), pp. 590–613; and Fremont E. Kast and James E. Rosenzweig, (eds.) *Contingency Views of Organization and Management* (Chicago, Ill.: SRI, Inc., 1973).

the situation. For this reason, the environment offered plenty of opportunities and virtually no problems or threats of any significance.

The 1960s saw the beginning of the era of questioning the motives and intentions of the organization. At the beginning of this disenchantment process, large business corporations became the center of attention, then organized labor, the government, educational institutions, the military, and so on. By the end of the 1960s, about 50% of the public assigned a "great deal of confidence" to the major companies as compared to 73% for medicine, 62% for military, and 22% for organized labor.[11] The entire sector of the public can be characterized for this era as dynamic to turbulent, presenting some problems and threats but still plenty of opportunities.

In the 1970s the process of questioning the motives of organizations that was ushered in during the 1960s began to accelerate. A Harris Associates survey in March 1976 reported a tremendous deterioration in the public's attitude toward organizations. Only 16% of the population sampled (1,512 adults nationally) assigned a great deal of confidence to the major companies (55% in 1966) as compared to 42% for medicine (73% in 1966), 31% for higher education (61% in 1966), 23% for the military (62% in 1966), and finally 10% for organized labor (22% in 1966).[12] In summary, the external environmental sector (the public) of the 1970s is characterized as dynamic to turbulent, presenting severe problems and threats. The opportunities seem to have dwindled considerably.

Government. This sector of the GEBE refers to the organization, mechanism, or agency through which a political unit exercises authority and performs functions. This exercise of authority and performance of functions is done at both local (city and state) and federal, or national, levels. This sector by virtue of the authority vested in it is becoming increasingly important for any organization, especially for business corporations. For this reason, this chapter will conclude with an in-depth discussion of the relationship between the government and the business corporation. Here, a brief treatment of this relationship is provided.

As can be seen from Figure 4-6, this sector of the GEBE was more or less stable to dynamic during the 1950s. In other words, there was a rather harmonious relationship between the government and most organizations to the extent that governmental attitudes toward organizations were favorable and changed very little. When changes did occur, they were fairly predictable. Little turbulence was present and government actions were creating more opportunities for all organizations, domestically and abroad.

The 1960s ushered in a few turbulences in the governmental sector. Changes in public attitude toward organizations in general and business corporations in particular triggered some governmental intervention that led to more legislation

[11] *The Harris Survey*, March 1976, p. 18.
[12] Ibid., p. 20.

and regulation. From 1962 to 1969, 18 regulatory laws were enacted covering six major areas, namely, consumer products, discrimination in employment, traffic safety, consumer finance, job safety, and environment and resources.[13] Although this new turbulence in the governmental sector of the GEBE created problems and a few threats, it still provided for plenty of opportunities.

The 1970s experienced more government intervention in the internal decision making of organizations. Although business corporations received the lion's share of government regulations, other organizations such as municipalities, institutions of higher education, and even government received a lot of attention. Again, this added turbulence should be interpreted as the end result of the turbulence in the public sector rather than as a spontaneous action by the government. This turbulence seems to be creating many problems and sizeable threats for organizations. At the same time, it is perceived as crowding out a lot of private organizational initiative for searching and exploiting opportunities.

Technology. This part of the GEBE represents the application of scientific knowledge to practical and commercial uses. Organizations depend for their survival on technology for it makes them develop a better combination between man and machine. For this reason organizations must keep a close eye on scientific developments that occur in a society's scientific institutions such as universities, laboratories, foundations, and private organizations that specialize in technological innovations.

During the 1950s, the technological environment was truly dynamic and turbulent. Most of the Western world was going through the last phase of the First Industrial Revolution (mechanical technology involving the substitution of machine power for muscle power), which started some 200 years before in England. At the same time there began to emerge a new technological revolution, which is known as Information Technology, or the Second Industrial Revolution. Unlike the First Revolution, information technology represents an extension of man's cognitive (thinking) power through electronic power in the form of computers. Whereas the First Revolution freed man from tedious and back-breaking labor, such as ditchdigging, lifting, and so on, the Second Revolution was designed to free man from the equally tedious task of endless computations and record keeping. The dynamism and turbulence of the technological environment during that period, although it presented some problems and threats, overall created numerous opportunities.

The turbulence of the 1950s continued into the 1960s. At the same time a portion of the technological environment—mechanical technology—appeared to stabilize. Automated assembly lines and automated chemical production processes reached a stage of near perfection. Most of the turbulence was created by the introduction of new, faster, smaller, and less expensive data processing systems.

[13]Murray L. Weidenbaum, *Business, Government and the Public,* (Englewood Cliffs, N.J.: Prentice-Hall, 1977), pp. 6–8.

Although some organizations experienced some problems and threats, overall the environment continued to create numerous opportunities.

The technological environment of the 1970s can best be characterized as paradoxical. There exists an apparent stability mixed with a great deal of turbulence. Although both mechanical and information technology seem to have reached an apex, society appears to be much more concerned with the by-products of technology, which are considered to be rather undesirable and to some extent dangerous, rather than with encouraging further developments in technology. The rationale behind this skepticism seems to be that the technology that developed during the two previous decades is causing a dehumanization of man and a deterioration in the physical environment. Critics, for example, have accused the Detroit asembly line production process of turning blue-collar workers into mindless robots. Computer-based data processing systems are looked upon as electronic substitutes for human reasoning. The end result of this new attitude is a push for societal control of new technology. In the United States, the government has introduced a new machinery for regulation of new technology, the Office of Technological Assessment. In addition to responding to the concern for less technology, the Congress has created the Office of Appropriate Technology to assist individuals and public groups such as cities and communities to develop their own small-scale technology for small, labor-intensive purposes. All this development creates considerable problems and some threats to organizations but at the same time provides numerous opportunities.

Domestic Market. The market is the place where suppliers of goods and services come to exchange them with their consumers or users. In the preindustrial era, the market was a geographic place within a community, usually the center of the community, but today, with the advent of communication devices, the market is mostly a coincidence of intention to buy or sell. In any case, the market as a general external environmental factor incorporates not only the absolute numbers of suppliers and consumers of goods and services but also a number of attributes such as their spendable income, desires, needs, aspirations, attitudes toward innovation, and a host of other characteristics of a whole human being or an institution.

During the 1950s, most organizations that operated within the industrialized or developed world experienced an extremely dynamic and turbulent environment. In the United States, organizations were called upon to satisfy a tremendous demand coming from consumer needs that were deferred during the World War II period. This satisfaction of consumer needs led to a tremendous expansion in investment for manufacturing facilities, machines, buildings, offices, and such. Hundreds of new organizations were created daily. Although a few organizations might have had some problems in changing from a low-consumer production or war-oriented production to high-consumer and nonwar-related production, overall the environment could be characterized as offering opportunities and virtually no threats.

The market boom that started during the 1950s accelerated more rapidly during the 1960s. The dynamism of the previous decade continued and, at the same time, turbulence subsided, primarily because both producers and consumers of goods and services became familiar with one another's needs and aspirations. Neither of the two parties experienced any great problems or sizeable threats. Opportunities seemed to develop daily. Virtually every new need was satisfied and every new idea for a product or service was destined to catch on. Toward the end of that decade there seemed to be an apparent shift in organizational activity toward service and away from farming and manufacturing.

In the 1970s the market for consumer goods appears to have stabilized itself, either because of a relative satisfaction of consumer needs or because of a slowdown in economic activity. In any case, this decade ushered in the beginning of the end of the "go-go" market environment of the previous two decades. This stability of the market sector, however, disguises considerable turbulence. As will be seen in the next section, government's intervention in the free market mechanism creates considerable uncertainty and, at times, confusion. Coupled with that, the 1970s saw the rise of a new awareness about the physical environment both as resource supplier and as pollution absorber. This stable/turbulent market environment is currently creating numerous problems and threats for most organizations. The opportunities of the previous two decade have dwindled considerably.

World Market. Few organizations operate solely within a domestic market. Most organizations depend on the world market for either their resources or for selling their products and services. Natural resources are not equally distributed in the world, and some countries do not have certain resources. Whereas some countries depend exclusively on the world market for a certain resource (for instance, Japan imports all of its oil), others do not have a resource in sufficient quantity and quality to satisfy its needs (the United States imports some 50% of its oil). On the output side, some countries' domestic markets cannot absorb all the goods and services produced by its organizations (for example, Japan and West Germany export most of their cars, refrigerators, and television sets to the world market just as the United States does with agricultural products, military equipment, and consulting services).

The United States' world market during the 1950s was one of phenomenal dynamism. Because World War II left much of Europe and Japan in destruction, organizations in the United States were called upon to assist in the recovery and reconstruction process. A well-conceived and equally ingeniously executed plan—the Marshall Plan—created a boom for American products and services. Thus, during that era, the external environment of the world market can be characterized as extremely dynamic with virtually no turbulence, because both the recipient and the giver of goods and services were able to estimate their needs fairly accurately. For this reason, no problems or threats were present and the opportunities were all obvious.

During the 1960s, the dynamic processes continued to accelerate and at the same time began to change slightly. By the middle of that decade, the first foreign products began to find their way to markets in the United States. Slowly but surely, the first Japanese transistor radios, Italian shoes, and West German Volkswagens were displayed in American establishments. At the same time many American goods were displaced in the world markets. The tremendous expenditures for the war in Vietnam caused a further deterioration in the United States' balance of payments, which started with the slowdown of exports and acceleration of imports. More turbulence was added when the United States government attempted to discourage further investment by American corporations abroad in order to reverse the outflow of capital and to strengthen the dollar. All of these developments presented some problems and even threats for some organizations. Overall, however, the environment was still full of opportunities.

The turbulence of the 1960s gained more momentum in the 1970s as the United States involvement in the Vietnam war continued and as more American products and services were displaced in both domestic and foreign markets by Japanese, German, and even Korean producers. In August 1971, the American dollar reached its lowest point in the international money markets to that date. The same month, the Nixon administration devalued the dollar in an effort to make American products in the international markets less expensive and foreign imports more expensive for American customers. As a result of these moves, foreign producers who exported to the United States market found it more difficult to do so and began setting up factories in the United States. This process, usually referred to as *investment-in-reverse,* is indeed an extraordinary event. In addition, the resource-producing nations of the world began to organize themselves into cartels to enhance their bargaining power. In 1973, the Organization for Petroleum Exporting Countries (OPEC) quadrupled the price of oil and imposed an oil embargo. All these developments created numerous problems and some threats for most organizations in much of the developed world. The vast opportunities available in the world markets of the two previous decades seem to have dwindled considerably.

Ecology. The ecology sector of the general external business environment encompasses the totality of relationships between organisms and their environment. As it is used here, the term refers to the physical world surrounding an organization. A manager of an organization is concerned with ecology insofar as the organization depends on the physical environment for needed resources and/or for disposing of waste generated as a by-product of the organization's operations. In Chapter 3, Figure 3-1 depicted the organization as an open system. It was pointed out then that every organization derives all of its material and energy inputs from the physical environment and disposes of most of its nonmarketable waste into the physical environment—into the air, the rivers, the lakes, the ocean, and the land. Because of this double dependence on the physical environment, this sector of the GEBE is of paramount importance for the contemporary manager.

During the 1950s an organization's physical environment was very stable. There appeared to be a rather harmonious relationship between the organization and its physical surroundings. On the input side, the physical environment represented a vast depository of natural resources awaiting to be exploited by man's organized effort. On the output side, the physical environment was conceived of as a huge sink into which all nonmarketable output (that is, pollution) could literally be dumped. The apparent lack of scarcity of resources and dumping places provided great opportunities and no problems or threats of any significant magnitude. The few instances of excessive exploitation of resources and pollution were viewed as local, isolated phenomena of a rather temporary nature.

The 1960s experienced a tremendous public awareness of the importance of the physical environment for human survival. The few isolated incidents of excessive pollution of the 1950s began to increase in number and magnitude. News media developed special reports on pollution in large cities, primarily in the Los Angeles and the Gary–Hammond–Chicago industrial complexes. Students in liberal universities organized the first ecology sit-ins, which reached a climax with the so-called E-Day in the last year of the decade. Legislative bodies at the city and state levels began to contemplate legislation, and some legislation for water and air quality was enacted. The legislative momentum continued to accelerate and reached its climax with the passage of the National Environmental Policy Act (NEPA) at the end of 1969. This new dynamism of the ecological sector of the GEBE, although it presented few problems for some organizations, left the general impression of an opportunity-rich environment completely intact.

Two related developments characterized the 1970s: continuous acceleration of the ecological awareness of the previous decade during which the main emphasis was on pollution, and a new environmental awareness concerning the finiteness of material resources contained in the physical environment. The NEPA marked the completion of the legislative process concerning pollution of land, water, and air because it brought total responsibility for coordinating and to some extent replacing city and state laws under one federal agency, the Environmental Protection Agency (EPA). The first turbulence began to appear around the end of 1972, the target date for compliance with the new law. The second development of this decade, the awareness about finiteness of resources, began with the publication of a report of the Club of Rome, submitted by a group of systems dynamics experts at Massachusetts Institute of Technology (MIT). The report, entitled *The Limits to Growth,*[14] revived an old and somehow forgotten issue advanced two centuries ago by Thomas Malthus regarding the relationship between increases in population and the inability of the physical environment (nature) to provide the means for survival of that population. These issues will be dealt with later in this chapter and in the last chapter of the book when the "Future of the Corporation" will be scrutinized. It should suffice to say here that

[14]Donella H. Meadows, and others, *The Limits to Growth* (Washington, D.C.: Potomac Associates, 1972).

this sector of the GEBE presented the first true threats to a large portion of organizations in most of the industrialized world. Most of the opportunities of the two previous decades seem to have completely disappeared.

THE QUEST FOR SOCIAL RESPONSIBILITY

The preceding discussion on the past and present developments of the six sectors of the GEBE lead to the inevitable conclusion that the GEBE factors are slowly but surely becoming the decisive elements in organizational success. The rather brief description of the historical developments in these six sectors must have helped in forming the reader's opinion that a fresh wind of public, governmental, technological, market, international, and ecological happenings is blowing that hints at society's intentions of writing a new "social contract" to govern organizational-societal relationships. For the contemporary and future managers of organizations, a bottom-line interpretation of this contract is that organizations must become more socially responsible and even socially responsive.

Discussions on organizational and business social responsibility have in the last decade increased virtually exponentially.[15] No attempt will be made here to even summarize the main arguments advanced pro and con. Rather, a brief overview of the issue will be offered in the hope that it will enhance the reader's understanding of the importance of the GEBE. In a nutshell, the issue of social responsibility involves the expectation by society that organizations reduce and even eliminate undersirable or negative effects of their activities upon society. An organization will respond well to this request by not only "doing good" (supporting the arts, sciences, the youth, the old, and the underprivileged) but also by *not* "doing harm" to the physical world (by not exploiting resources and not polluting the environment; in one phrase, by respecting Mother Nature and unborn generations' right to enjoy nature).

It will be helpful in understanding this rather complicated and at present extremely controversial subject to accept Sethi's conceptualization of it as a three-stage process.[16] The first stage, *social obligation*, may be defined as society's request that an organization provide for all goods and services (consumption) as well as provide the opportunities for everyone so desiring to gainfully participate in organizational activities (employment). It is safe to associate this stage with the time span ending with the beginning of the 1960s.

[15] See, for example, Archie B. Carroll, *Managing Corporate Social Responsibility* (Boston, Mass.: Little, Brown and Company, 1977); George A. Steiner, *Business and Society*, 2nd ed. (New York: Random House, 1975); Neil H. Jacoby, *Corporate Power and Social Responsibility* (New York: Macmillan, 1973); Richard M. Hodgetts, *The Business Enterprise; Social Challenge, Social Response* (Philadelphia, Pa.: W. B. Saunders Company, 1977).

[16] Prakash Sethi, *Advocacy Advertising and Large Corporations* (Lexington, Mass.: Lexington Books, 1977).

(© *Charles G. Sauers, 1977, first published in* The Wall Street Journal.)

The second stage, *social responsibility,* began with societal demands for considerable benevolence by the organization. This benevolence, sometimes referred to as handouts, giveaways, charitable contributions, donations, and community involvement, is designed to project the organization's image as a good corporate citizen. In other words, the organization is telling society that it is concerned with and is actively participating in the solution of societal problems. During the 1960s organizations contributed heavily toward the solution of some of society's problems by supporting the arts, poor neighborhoods, the handicapped, veterans, educational institutions, victims of natural and man-made disasters, and so on. Some people criticized organizations for engaging in activities that did not seem to be in the best interest of their stockholders.

The 1970s ushered in a new and slightly different wave of societal demands. Whereas thus far the organization had been expected to satisfy certain societal needs *after* they appeared or arose, now there seems to be a desire for the organization to *anticipate* potential occasions for contributions. This third stage of social responsibility is referred to as *social responsiveness.* An organization is socially responsive when it not only complies with the law and most of the societal pressures that have not yet been legislated, but also when it makes an effort to anticipate possible societal problems and responds with timely efforts to prevent them.

Organizational responses to the societal problem of insufficient energy provide a good example to illustrate the three-stage process of social responsibility. During the 1950s, energy organizations felt obligated to supply all the energy needed by society. Then toward the end of the 1960s the first shortages of electricity and gas appeared, which led to a number of brownouts and a large blackout that left the entire East Coast without electricity for about two days. Most organizations began to take steps toward reducing energy consumption. Because the society as a whole seemed to be concerned with the problem, organizations acted in a socially responsible manner. In the 1970s, society has been struggling even more with these energy problems, especially since the oil embargo of 1973. Society has a vague notion that the solution to the energy problem lies with the development of alternative sources of energy and with conservation, and organizations have been at the forefront in developing solar and other nonexhaustible energy sources and simultaneously in promoting conservation. That is an example of social responsiveness.

ILLUSTRATIONS OF BUSINESS-GOVERNMENT RELATIONSHIPS

In most industrialized countries, the role of government is to provide the social and physical infrastructure (formal rules and regulations of social conduct, as well as ports, highways, seaways, and so on) necessary for the smooth and productive functioning of a business enterprise. The government does all this through the expenditure of government revenues derived from taxing individuals and business activities. It traditionally has been expected to perform this role with a minimum of intervention in internal business decision making. After long experience with this so-called laissez-faire philosophy (the best government is the least government), a massive expansion of governmental control of private industry was initiated in the early 1960s and is currently accelerating.[17] This process of governmental intervention is so pervasive today that some people are beginning to talk of the current relationship between business and government as the "Age of Regulation" and others are labelling it "Regulation Overkill."[18]

The question of the desirability, inevitability, or necessity for governmental regulation of business activities must be left to social critics, who, in their pursuit of clarification of present and past events, will pass judgment. At this time there are two predictions that can be made regarding the entire relationship between government and business: the regulatory form of government intervention in the internal decision making of an organization will continue to expand, and this

[17] Weidenbaum, op. cit., p. 4.

[18] James J. Kilpatrick, "A Case of Overkill in Federal Regulation," *Nation's Business,* June 1977, pp. 11–12; also, Paul A. Samuelson, "The State and the Market: The Changing Relationship Between Business and Government," *Management Review* (December 1977) pp. 14–16.

process will adapt to a new form, as already evidenced by the shifts in regulation during the 1970s.

As was pointed out in the previous section, when the government as an environmental sector was discussed, during the entire 10 years of the 1960s, 18 new regulatory commissions were created. In the first four years of the 1970s, 19 new agencies were instituted. In addition, the number of people working for federal regulatory agencies rose by 8% in just two years from 1974 to 1976 (from 64,000 to 72,000), and federal expenditures for business regulation increased by 57% (from $1.9 billion to $3.0 billion) for the same period. Considerably more significant than the quantitative changes in government regulation of business is a change in governmental philosophy, its nature, and the direction it has taken since the beginning of the 1970s.[19]

Table 4-1 provides a summary view of the conventional (pre-1970s) government regulation of business and the new (post-1970s) regulatory activity. Conventional government regulation is industry-related, which means that a specific regulatory commission was created for a specific industry. That commission regulates virtually all operations or functions of that industry and is designed to more or less protect and represent the industry rather than the public or the government. Examples of this type of government regulation are given in the extreme right-hand column of Table 4-1. There are several dozen of these commissions. Because of this strong alliance with the industry being regulated, this form of regulation has been severely criticized as representing lobbying agents rather than regulatory agencies. In addition, critics have accused this type of regulation of practicing the so-called "revolving door" policy in which the heads of these commissions are usually former members of the industry they regulated and also frequently assume key industry positions after leaving the commission.

There are two distinguishing characteristics of the new wave of government regulation of business: it is activity- or function-related, and it is initiated by the public sector of the external environment and is usually headed by a nonindustry person. In short, the overriding objective of this type of regulation is the protection of the public and the physical world. This is indeed a new experience. Most managers of private corporations and some administrators of public works find it difficult to comprehend the rationale and intentions of this regulation. One thing is certain, however, and that is that the new wave of regulation represents the greatest and most thorough penetration of government into the internal decision making of the private sector.

Table 4-1 provides a few examples of this new regulatory activity. It should be noted that these regulation schemes cut across the entire bulk of industrial activity (that is, they are horizontal), as opposed to conventional regulations, which are industry-specific (vertical regulation). These new regulations center around two sectors of the GEBE: the *public* as an employee and a consumer, and the *physical environment* as a resource reservoir and a pollution sink. Figure 4-7

[19] Weidenbaum, op. cit., p. 13.

TABLE 4-1

Evolution of Governmental Regulation of Business.

NATURE	DESCRIPTION	EXAMPLES					
Industry-related Vertical regulation Pre-seventies	As a rule, a Federal Commission is established to regulate a specific industry. Often the public or consumer interest is viewed as subordinated or even ignored, as the commission focuses on the needs and concerns of the industry that it regulates.	Functions \ Industry	Airlines	Autos	Drugs	Utilities	
		Accounting/Finance	↓	↓	↓	↓	
		Marketing	↓	↓	↓	↓	
		Personnel	↓	↓	↓	↓	
		Production	↓	↓	↓	↓	
		Ecology	↓	↓	↓	↓	
		Commissions	CAB	TSA	FDA	FPC	
Specific Function or Operation-related Horizontal Regulation Post-seventies	The focus of the regulatory unit (usually called Agency or Administration) is not limited to a single industry. Rather, its jurisdiction extends to the entire private sector and, to some extent, to the public sector. The concern is with a specific industrial activity, function, or operation and its impact upon a specific sector of the external environment. The main instigator for the creation of such an agency is not the industry being regulated but rather the specific interest group that represents the public at large.	Functions \ Industry	Airlines	Autos	Drugs	Utilities	Agencies
		Accounting/Finance	→	→	→	→	SEC
		Marketing	→	→	→	→	CPSC
		Personnel	→	→	→	→	EEOC ERISA
		Production	→	→	→	→	OSHA
		Ecology	→	→	→	→	EPA DOE

CAB = Civil Aeronautics Board
TSA = Traffic Safety Act
FDA = Food and Drug Administration
FPC = Federal Power Commission

SEC = Securities and Exchange Commission
CPSC = Consumer Product Safety Commission
EEOC = Equal Employment Opportunity Commission
ERISA = Employee Retirement Income Security Act

OSHA = Occupational Safety and Health Act
EPA = Environmental Protection Agency
DOE = Department of Energy

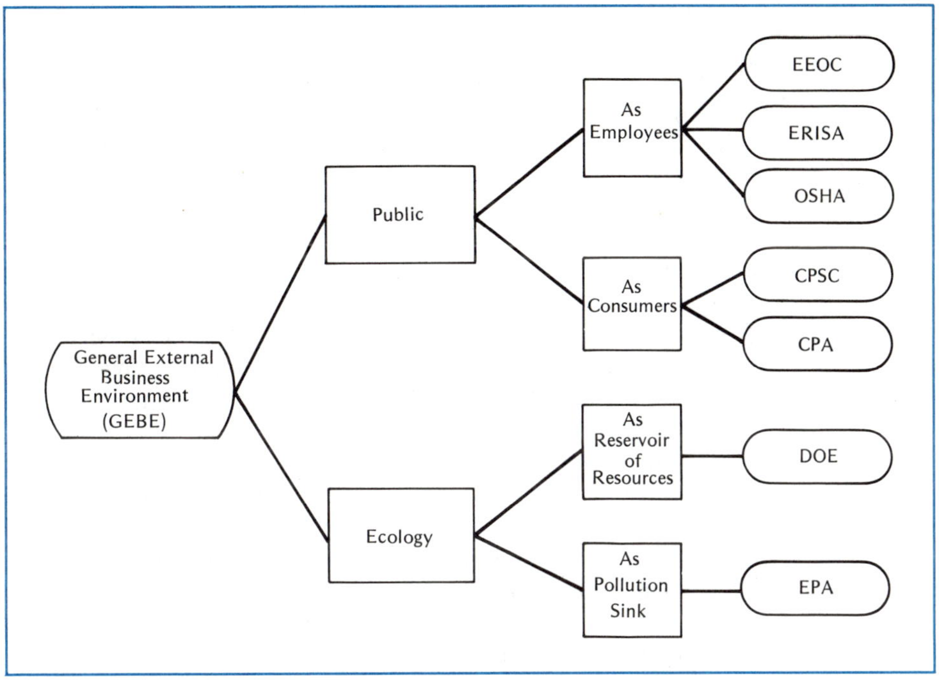

FIGURE 4-7. Horizontal Government Regulation of Business Activities.

provides a summary of the main regulatory agencies and the environmental sectors that serve as their domain.

The Public As Employees

Although local and federal governments have always influenced the employment of individuals by private corporations and to some extent public organizations, the hiring, pay, promotion, and firing of employees were always considered the exclusive job of management. The end of the 1960s and the beginning of the 1970s brought forth the first clouds on the personnel manager's horizon. Apparently society began to suspect that conventional personnel practices used by most businesses were favoring certain classes of individuals at the expense of other groups known as minorities (such as blacks, Hispanics, women, and the elderly). Of the numerous attempts enacted by the government to end these discriminatory personnel practices and to provide fair and equitable hiring, promotion, and termination of employment, the following three acts are of great importance for management:

1. Equal Employment Opportunity Act (EEOA).
2. The Employee Retirement Income Safety Act (ERISA).

3. The Occupational Safety and Health Act (OSHA).[20]

The Equal Employment Opportunity Act of 1972 created the Equal Employment Opportunity Commission (EEOC) to enforce the prohibition of discrimination because of race, color, religion, sex, or national origin in all employment practices, including hiring, firing, layoffs, promotion, wages, training, disciplinary action, and other terms, privileges, conditions, or benefits of employment. EEOC's ultimate objective is to ensure that an organization's work force reflects the population composition of the geographical area within which it operates. For example, if the labor force of a particular city has a 20% black labor force, the person responsible for hiring employees should make allowance for the hiring of 20% blacks. All organizations with 15 or more employees are subject to this regulation, including state and local government agencies, educational institutions, and business corporations.

The Employment Retirement Income Safety Act (ERISA), which was created in 1974, laid down new rules for every employee benefit plan in the nation. ERISA goes far beyond the historical framework of pension plan regulation. In fact, although ERISA is popularly referred to as "pension legislation," it encompasses, in addition, profit-sharing programs and private retirement funds set up by self-employed individuals. The United States Department of Labor provides the following description of the purpose and rationale for ERISA:

> *Private employee benefit plans affect the welfare of millions of workers and their families. The vast assets of such plans have a significant impact on the national economy. New protections and guarantees for employees covered by private employee pension and welfare plans and their beneficiaries are provided in the Employee Retirement Income Security Act of 1974 (ERISA), signed into law on Labor Day, September 2, 1974.*
>
> *Responsibilities for carrying out the law's provisions are assigned to the U.S. Department of Labor, the Internal Revenue Service of the U.S. Treasury Department, and a new government corporation named the Pension Benefit Guaranty Corporation, which was created to administer the plan termination insurance provisions of the law.*
>
> *The law affects two different types of employee benefit plans—pension plans, which provide retirement benefits, and welfare plans, which provide such benefits as health, accident, death, etc. The law applies to plans now in existence and to new ones instituted after enactment. It does not require any employer to establish a plan. However, those that do must meet certain minimum standards. Moreover, the new law provides that each employee not covered by a pension plan other than Social Security may put aside a certain amount of his income tax-free to take care of his retirement years.*[21]

The Occupational Safety and Health Act (OSHA) became law in 1970 and went into effect on April 28, 1971, with the stated purposc to ensure as far as

[20] Weidenbaum, op. cit., Chap. 1; Frances Lean, "EEO Compliance: Behind the Corporate Mask," *Harvard Business Review* (July-August 1975), pp. 138–146.

[21] *ERISA Reporting and Disclosure:* ERISA Act, 1974 (Washington, D.C.: U.S. Department of Labor, 1975), p. 1.

possible every working man and woman in the nation safe and healthy working conditions and to preserve our human resources. As it was pointed out earlier, this act was instigated by the concern over the internal physical environment. The National Safety Council has estimated that the costs of the wage losses, insurance costs, medical expenses, and related costs such as time spent investigating and reporting industrial accidents has exceeded $3.9 billion annually. These costs stem from the fact that some 2.2 million persons are disabled on the job each year, resulting in losses of some 240 million man days' work and that the rate of accident frequency increased from 1958 to 1970 by more than 33%. These were the reasons, both in terms of human suffering and economic losses, which led to the passage of OSHA.[22]

Cost estimates for industry compliance with OSHA are staggering. According to McGraw-Hill Publishing Company, costs increased from 1972 to 1973 by 26% from $2.5 to $3.1 billion for manufacturing and nonmanufacturing companies.[23] In addition to cost considerations, currently of much greater concern is the so-called "no-knock" or "free entry" policy for OSHA inspectors. According to this policy, OSHA inspectors need no search warrant to enter a private industrial establishment for inspection purposes.

The Public As Consumers

The relationship between business and the public as a consumer did not encounter many troubles until the middle of the 1960s when it appeared that the Congress suddenly discovered the existence of the consumer.[24] Public opinion surveys began to show Ralph Nader enjoying high respect in the public's mind. Ralph Nader's publication of a story about GMC's Corvair was a great spur. The Congress, in responding to the public's desires, quickly passed a number of Nader-inspired laws such as the Fair Labeling and Packaging Act, the Truth in Lending Act, the Flammable Fabrics Act, the Poison Prevention Packaging Act, the Refrigerators Safety Act, and the Federal Hazardous Substances Act. To facilitate compliance with these acts, the Consumer Product Safety Commission was created, mandated with the power to ban unsafe products from the market. As a result of these acts, there are now 33 federal agencies and about 400 bureaus carrying out some 1,000 consumer-oriented programs.

The Consumer Product Safety Act of 1972 gave the Consumer Product Safety

[22]Joseph B. Mason, "OSHA: Problems and Prospects," *California Management Review* (Fall, 1976), pp. 21–28; also, William Jensen, Jr., C. L. Mohr, and D. N. Stern, "Administration of OSHA Act in the Face of Criticism from Industry and Labor,"*American Business Law Journal* (Vol. 11), pp. 73–74.

[23]Weidenbaum, op. cit., p. 17.

[24]Margorie Bond, "The Protection Consumers Don't Want," *The Washington Monthly* (September 1977), pp. 29–34; Linda E. Demkorich, "Even a White House Pep Rally May Not Save The Consumer Agency," *National Journal* (June 25, 1977), pp. 456–99; "Consumer Agency Bill Stalled in Congress," *Congressional Quarterly Weekly Report* (June 1977), pp. 1147–50; Burt Schorr, "Why the Consumer Agency Is Stalled," *Wall Street Journal* (July 12, 1977), p. 12; "Consumer Protection: What's the Issue?" *Nation's Business* (June 1977), pp. 18–22.

Commission (CPSC) the mandate to protect the public against unreasonable risks of injury associated with consumer products. In addition to setting standards that regulate product performance, contents, composition, design, construction, finish, packaging, and labeling, the commission can not only order companies to recall and even discontinue the production of an item, but can also charge offending executives with violations that are subject to jail sentences. In 1977, the Carter administration attempted to pass a bill in the Congress that would create a Consumer Protection Agency or, alternatively called, the Agency for Consumer Advocacy, whose main purpose would be to "represent the interest of the consumer before federal agencies and the courts, to receive and transmit consumer complaints, to develop and disseminate information of interest to consumers, and to perform functions to promote and protect the interest of the consumer."[25] The bill passed the House of Representatives' Government Operations Committee with a one-vote margin after some arm twisting by Vice President Walter Mondale.[26] The Senate killed the bill, however, on the grounds of "regulatory overkill" and excessive costs to consumers, among other reasons.

Ecology As a Pollution Sink

The physical environment's ability to provide the resources necessary for human survival (the input to human and industrial systems) and to accept human and industrial wastes (the output of human and industrial systems) did not become questionable until the middle of the 1960s. First, the ecosystem's limitations in absorbing waste became evident. The few isolated instances of pollution that occurred during the 1950s and the beginning of the 1960s accelerated to the point that by the end of the 1960s the United States Congress passed the National Environmental Policy Act, which established a national policy to maintain conditions under which man and nature can exist in productive harmony and fulfill the social, economic, and other requirements of present and future generations of America. The act established the Environmental Protection Agency (EPA) on Dec. 2, 1970, to oversee the execution of this policy. William Ruckelshaus, the first administrator of the EPA, provided the following background for the need for environmental regulation:

> *People all over the country are insisting that we abandon the psychology of the blind bulldozer, that we refrain from paving over the whole world, that we stop polluting the air and the water and the earth. They are taking their cases to the courts. And their voices are being heard in corporate board rooms and by government officials and legislators at every level.*[27]

The United States Environmental Protection Agency brought together for the

[25] *Congressional Quarterly Weekly Report* (May 21, 1977), p. 949.
[26] Burt Schorr, "Consumerism: Down But Not Out," *Wall Street Journal* (March 8, 1978), p. 16.
[27] William D. Ruckelshaus, *Toward a New Environmental Ethic* (EPA, U.S. Government Printing Office, 1971).

first time in a single agency the major environmental control programs of the federal government. EPA is charged with mounting an integrated, coordinated attack on the environmental problems of air and water pollution, solid wastes management, pesticides, radiation, and noise.

To ensure that the agency is truly responsive to environmental needs in every part of the country, it has established a strong field organization, with regional offices located in ten major cities. The regional offices are staffed by specialists in each program area and headed by a regional administrator possessing broad authority to act for EPA in matters within his jurisdiction. EPA's creation marked the end of the piecemeal approach to our nation's environmental problems, which, so often in the past, has inhibited progress, or merely substituted one form of pollution for another.

EPA was created to lead a broad, comprehensive attack on pollution, and its administrative organization has been designed to make this approach a reality. The new organizational structure makes it easier to identify and to take into account all the factors bearing on pollution and its control. It makes it possible to resolve competing or conflicting program aims. It is facilitating the development of better information on the total impact of stresses reaching man from various parts of the environment, and makes possible more sensible choices about what constitutes a healthy, satisying milieu for human life.

The nineteen-seventies absolutely must be the years when America pays its debt to the past by reclaiming the purity of its air, its waters and our living environment. It is literally now or never.—President Richard M. Nixon, January 1, 1970

To ensure full consideration of environmental factors in federal decision making, each federal agency is required to submit to the President's Council on Environmental Quality an environmental impact statement on any proposal for legislation or other major action significantly affecting the quality of the human environment. This statement must include the following:

- The environmental impact of the proposed action.
- Any adverse environmental effects which cannot be avoided should the proposal be implemented.
- Alternatives to the proposed action.
- The relationship between local short-term uses of man's environment and the maintenance and enhancement of long term productivity.
- Any irreversible and irretrievable commitments or resources which would be involved in the proposed action should it be implemented.[28]

Before filing with the Council, the statement must be circulated in draft to EPA and other appropriate federal, state, and local environmental agencies for their

[28] Ruckelshaus, ibid., p. 8.

"The sky is certainly a beautiful blue today, isn't it, Miss Simkins? Check with production and see if something's wrong." (Reprinted with permission of Playboy *magazine. © 1977.)*

comments. These must accompany the final statement. The final environmental impact statement, together with all comments, must be made available to the Congress and the public by the originating agency. Federal agencies must ensure the fullest practicable provision of timely public information and understanding of the environmental impact of federal plans and programs including, whenever appropriate, public hearings.[29]

Of all the criticism leveled against environmental protection[30] actual and projected costs to the public and private sector have been the most well documented. Figure 4-8 summarizes the projected cost of environmental protection for industry for the decade from 1972 to 1981.

As can be seen from Figure 4-8, nearly two thirds of the estimated total environmental expenditures during the decade 1972–1981 will be in the private sector. This compares with a private share of somewhat less than half in 1973. Of an estimated $173 billion in cumulative private spending over the decade, some

[29] Luna B. Leopold, and others, "A Procedure for Evaluating Environmental Impact," Geological Survey Circular No. 645, (Washington, D.C., 1971).

[30] For an empirical investigation into managerial reaction to environmental protection in the United States, see Asterios G. Kefalas and Archie B. Carroll, "Perspectives on Environmental Protection: A Survey of the Executive Viewpoint," *Environmental Systems*, Vol. 6, No. 3, 1976–77, pp. 229–242.

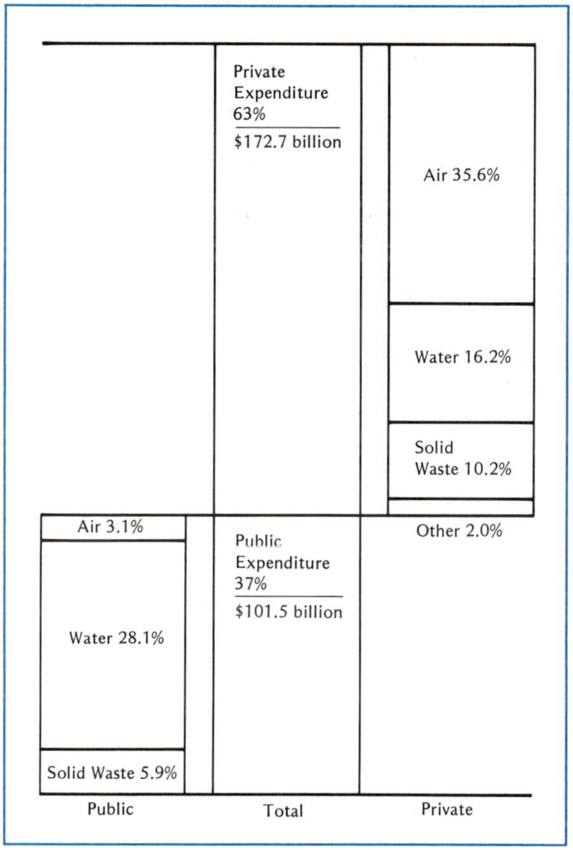

FIGURE 4-8. Distribution of Total Pollution Control Expenditures, 1972–1981. (Source: Committee for Economic Development, p. 35.)

$150 billion will be over and above what would have been spent by business and industry in the absence of recent federal legislation.[31]

Ecology As a Reservoir of Resources

Barely had the governmental regulation on environmental pollution begun to make some progress than a new issue emerged. This new issue involved the environment's capability to supply the necessary resources in general, and energy in particular. When in 1973 the OPEC cartel raised the price of oil and imposed

[31] *More Effective Programs for a Cleaner Environment* (New York Committee for Economic Development, 1974).

some quantitative restrictions in oil production and distribution, the United States Government created the Federal Energy Office (FEO), which was later renamed the Federal Energy Research and Development Administration (ERDA) and finally under the Carter Administration was elevated to cabinet level under the name of the Department of Energy (DOE) in the summer of 1977. Under this legislation, the DOE was given all powers which were formerly held by the Federal Power Commission (FPC), FEA, and ERDA, all of which were abolished.[32]

The rationale and need for governmental regulation of exploitation of resources and energy have been the subject of many studies by academicians, private industry, and governmental institutions. Most of these studies have confirmed that the United States is an energy- and resource-wasteful society. The United States, which represents less than 6% of the world's population, consumes more than 35% of the world's energy and resources. Public opinion polls report that the majority of Americans find that fact to be unreasonable, unethical, and immoral.[33] The American Petroleum Institute summarized the current situation as follows:

> *Many studies now confirm what economists and petroleum officials have been saying for some time. It's a hard pill to swallow, but Americans must come to realize that the era of cheap, abundant domestic supplies of energy is over.*
>
> *The full ramifications of this simple factor of life are enormous. For one thing, energy has a clear relationship with our standard of living and jobs. In short, the economic well-being of this country depends on uninterrupted access to energy supplies.*[34]

SUMMARY

It is becoming abundantly evident that the external environment of an organization is a major determinant of managerial success. Economically and technologically sound decisions may turn into major disasters for an organization if they encounter public disapproval.

This chapter has dealt with the entire organizational environment by breaking it down into two main categories: the internal business environment or organizational climate and the external business environment. The latter was further divided into two interrelated categories: the immediate, operating, or task environment and the general external business environment. Within this framework it was shown that external environmental factors begin as changes in the external

[32] "New Department Given Wide Energy Powers," *Congressional Quarterly Weekly Report* (July 30, 1977), pp. 1581–84; R. Corrigan, "The Federal Energy Administration Is Looking for a Friend," *National Journal* (October 2, 1976) p. 1381; also, "Congress Takes a Chip off Carter's Energy Block," *National Journal* (June 11, 1977), pp. 888–92.

[33] Ervin Laszlo, *Goals for Mankind* (New York: E. P. Dutton, 1977), p. 12.

[34] Charles J. D. Bouse, "Looking for America's Energy Solutions," *Petroleum Today* (Spring, 1977), p. 3.

environment at large—the society or the world—which appear to have no immediate impact upon the organization. In other words, they do not represent part of the business environment. With the passage of time, the build-up of social energy and the corporate response first become part of the GEBE, then of the immediate business environment, and finally end as part of the internal business environment.

The last section of this chapter, entitled *An Illustration: The Business-Government Relationship*, clearly pointed out that there is by now a popular and controversial process of institutionalization, that is, public concerns and public demands for legislating and policing of corporate activity, through a governmental agency. Few corporate executives would dispute the legitimacy of public concerns about the safety and health of a working environment or about the quality of the physical world. By the same token, however, equally few corporate executives agree completely with the direction and intensity of governmental intervention in the internal decision making of an organization.

The subject of the external environment of an organization and its importance for management will appear repeatedly throughout this book. For example, because of the significant role that the external environment plays in the planning process, Chapter 5 deals with it extensively. The same is true for Chapter 12 on organizational development. Because organizational development requires the introduction of changes into an organization's structure and function for the purpose of streamlining it to the changes in the external environment, once again, we discuss the organization's external environment extensively.

Assignments

4-1. Give a definition of the term *environment*.
4-2. What is the internal business environment?
4-3. What is the immediate external business environment?
4-4. What is the general external business environment?
4-5. Describe the process of social energy build-up and the corporate response to it.
4-6. Trace the developments of the six general external environmental sectors over the last three decades.
4-7. What is vertical governmental regulation of business activities? Give some examples.
4-8. What is horizontal governmental regulation of business activities? Give some examples.
4-9. Describe the rationale for the creation of the following regulatory agencies: EEOC, ERISA, OSHA, CPA, DOE, and EPA.
4-10. "Government intervention in the internal decision making of private business corporations is destined to kill the free enterprise system." Refute or support this argument.

Case 4-1

A BITTER AFTERTASTE FOR ANHEUSER-BUSCH

Around Merrimack, New Hampshire, when you say Bud, you've said it all—all that it takes to set a neighbor against a neighbor. Merrimack is the home of Anheuser-Busch, Inc.'s only New England brewery, a sparkling $40 million plant that produces 2 million barrels of Budweiser and Michelob beer annually. The plant was hailed as the town's industrial savior when it located there in 1968, and it pays 40% of the town's taxes today.

But town-brewery relations have seldom been smooth, and this week they veered toward the breaking point in the wake of a Mailogram sent by Merrimack's three top elected officials to August A. Busch III, president of Anheuser-Busch. The message, billed as a "final appeal to reason," charged that the company refuses to pay its fair share of waste-water treatments made necessary by the brewery and thus has created a municipal deficit of $829,173 since 1970. "We can no longer ask the citizens of this town to subsidize the operations of your brewery," the letter says, pleading for Busch's personal attention.

"I'm not sure August Busch knows he has a brewery here," says Edward J. Silva, a truck driver who is chairman of the town's board of selectmen.

Means of Support

In St. Louis, Anheuser-Busch's manager of long-range planning, Robert R. Imsande, wryly comments that he is sure August Busch knows all about Merrimack, a brewery that makes good beer but otherwise has produced trouble because of the sewage plant deficits and another problem with sludge disposal. Imsande says the $829,173 figure Merrimack charges against the firm is far too high. And he laments that Anheuser-Busch and the town had been close to settling on a figure for the 1975 deficit "when this letter came out of the blue sky."

Anheuser-Busch's problems at Merrimack go back to 1968, when it appeared just in time to become the big industrial customer the town needed to support a new waste treatment plant. But the town underestimated operating costs and set rates too low. Ever since, the town has been billing, and Anheuser-Busch paying, deficit payments of up to $120,000 each year in excess of contract obligations.

Now the town is demanding a new contract that would set restrictions on plant usage, which the company says it will not accept. The town is also demanding a new rate of 70 cents per 1,000 gallons of water treated. That is up from about 11 cents in 1968 and 43 cents in 1974. Anheuser-Busch is balking at the higher rate, which other users are paying. "We are willing to pay lump-sum deficits. We are ready to pay about $500,000 in total 1975 sewage costs including deficits. But we won't just sign any contract the town wants us to sign," says Imsande.

Vanished Village

The complex dispute also centers on Merrimack's claim that Anheuser-Busch uses almost all the capacity of the sewage system, a charge the company denies. Company officials agree the brewery provides 90% of the system's waste water but claim there is unused capacity because of failure to connect more than a few homes.

Merrimack is hardly the small Yankee village that either the brewer or some of the newer residents once imagined it to be. Population has grown from 5,000 in 1968 to more than 16,000 now, with onerous school, road, police, fire, and sewage problems escalating taxes and disrupting the countryside. Near Nashua on the Merrimack River, the town has continued to attract new industry with the lure of New Hampshire's low state taxes. Such companies as General Electric and Standard Kollsman Industries have moved in to join the brewery.

Some Merrimackers who have been vocal about the brewery's failure to pay a "fair share" fear this expansion and also fear that the company will double its capacity some day. This would further add to waste treatment costs, they say. Company officials contend that only a minority of citizens are anti-brewery.

"They are making a mountain of a mole hill. We'll pay our share, but we can't let the town tell us how to run the business," says Imsande. Silva counters, "We hope our letter will get decisions makers to come here. I want August Busch to know what's going on."

1. What is the real issue here?
2. Acting as a consultant to the company, develop a five-point plan for Anheuser-Busch's management.
3. Acting as a consultant to the city of Merrimack, what would be your recommendation?*

Case 4-2

EXCITING GAMES, INC.

Exciting Games, Inc. is an organization that has been in business for about seven years. It started by offering game machines to various amusement galleries, bars, restaurants, and other organizations. A recent game the company has put on the market is called "Death Race." For 25 cents the player of the television screen game can drive a small automobile and attempt to run down as many pedestrians as he can in 75 seconds. Each time the player "scores" by striking a pedestrian, the machine emits a loud shriek and a small grave marker appears on the screen at the point of contact. The object, of course, is to tally the most number of "deaths" in 75 seconds.

The National Safety Council has called the game a "sick, sick product that would only be played by someone with sadistic impulses." The management of Exciting Games, Inc. asserts that the pedestrians are meant to be "gremlins" and not people and this therefore takes the game out of the questionable category to which the Safety Council assigns it.

The "Death Race" game was brought to the National Safety Council's attention by a group of concerned parents in South Bend, Indiana, who learned that their children were playing the game at a local amusement gallery in the city.

1. Identify and discuss the social issues involved in this case.
2. What, exactly, is the firm's social responsibility in this case?
3. How would you, as management, respond to the National Safety Council's accusations?

Case 4-3

A NO-WIN SITUATION

George R. Greene, chief executive officer of Southern Super-Powers Company (SSPC), finds himself in a difficult, albeit fairly typical, situation. Since the early 1970s, the EPA has ordered SSPC to reduce its sulfur emissions. After some initial hesitation and legal litigation, SSPC agreed to install "scrubber" devices that are designed to reduce high-sulfur gas into slurry which is in turn dumped. SSPC, in fact, was forced to allocate some $200 million for scrubbers before its subsidiary Southeastern Super-Power could construct and operate a new plant in Georgia. George R. Greene finds the EPA's approach to pollution reduction ineffective. He is fully convinced that "scrubbers" are very costly and

*Reprinted from *Business Week*, Feb. 2, 1976, by special permission, highly ineffective. He thinks that the best and most economical way of reducing pollution is to use low sulfur coal produced in the western part of the United States. Mr. Greene's management strategy will be to import western coal and put money into Research and Development (R&D) to experiment with new processes of pollution abatement. There is one catch: western coal has a larger tax, designed to protect local coal industry and miners.

In view of the potential impact of Mr. Greene's tension on (1) air quality, (2) local coal protection, and (3) utility rate cost, what would be your recommendation acting as:

1. Mr. Greene's immediate subordinate?
2. Mr. Greene's outside consultant?
3. A local citizen?
4. A Congressman?*

References

BAUGHMAN, JAMES P., GEORGE C. LODGE AND HOWARD W. PIFER. *Environmental Analysis for Management.* Homewood, Ill.: Richard D. Irwin, Inc., 1974.

CARROLL, ARCHIE, B., (ed.) *Managing Corporate Social Responsibility.* Boston, Mass.: Little, Brown and Company, 1977.

CHAMBERLAIN, NEIL, W. *Enterprise and Environment: The Firm in Time and Place.* New York: McGraw-Hill Book Company, 1968.

CROSS, FRANK, L., JR., AND ROGER W. ROSS. *Corporate Communicator's Guide for Environmental Control.* Westport, Conn.: Technanic Publishing Co., Inc., 1973.

DAVIS, KEITH, AND RICHARD L. BLOMSTROM. *Business and the Environment.* New York.: McGraw-Hill Book Company, 1966.

EDMUNDS, STAHRL, AND J. LEXEY. *Environmental Administration.* New York.: McGraw-Hill Book Company, 1973.

Environmental Quality. Annual Reports of the Council on Environmental Quality. Washington, D.C.: U.S. Government Printing Office, 1970 henceforth.

FADIMAN, CLIFTON, AND JEAN WHITE. *Ecocide . . . and Thoughts toward Survival.* Santa Barbara, Cal.: Center for the Study of Democratic Institution Interbook, Inc., 1971.

HODGETTS, RICHARD M. *The Business Enterprise: Social Challenge, Social Response.* Philadelphia, Pa.: W. B. Saunders Company, 1977.

KAHN, JAMES W., AND IAN BERG. *Values in a Business Society.* New York.: Harcourt Brace Jovanovich, Inc., 1968.

LAWRENCE, PAUL R., AND JAY W. LORSH. *Organization and Environment.* Homewood, Ill.: Richard D. Irwin, Inc., 1967.

LUTHANS, FRED, AND RICHARD M. HODGETTS. *Social Issues in Business.* New York.: Macmillan Publishing Co., Inc., 1976.

MCGRATH, PHYLLIS S. *Managing Corporate External Relations: Changing Perspectives and Responses.* New York: *The Conference Board* 1976.

MOUSEN, JOSEPH, R. *Business and the Changing Environment.* New York.: McGraw-Hill Book Company, 1973.

STEINER, GEORGE F. *Business and Society,* 2nd Ed. New York.: Random House, Inc., 1975.

*From *Forbes,* February 20, 1978, p. 95.

THOMPSON, JAMES D. *Organizations in Action.* New York.: McGraw-Hill Book Company, 1967.

WEIDENBAUM, MURRAY. *Business, Government, and The Public.* Englewood Cliffs, N.J.: Prentice Hall, Inc. 1977.

ROBERT H. MURPHY
Staff Vice-President, Organization and Executive Development, Rockwell International Corporation

Robert H. Murphy is staff vice-president, Organization and Executive Development, for Rockwell International Corporation, a major, multi-industry company with strengths in aerospace, automotive, consumer, electronic, utility, and industrial businesses.

Murphy joined a predecessor company, North American Aviation, Inc., in 1962, as an employment representative for personnel at the company's Space Division.

Following the merger of North American Aviation and Rockwell Standard Corporation in 1967, he was named manager of Administrative Staffing and Manpower Planning for the Aerospace & Systems group of the newly formed North American Rockwell Corporation.

In 1971, he was transferred to Rockwell's corporate offices and served in several managerial positions for management placement and development, and personnel planning and administration. In 1973, Murphy became director of Personnel Relations for Rockwell Standard group, later to be known as the Automotive Operations.

In 1974, he was promoted to director of Salaried Personnel for Rockwell's automotive operations.

Later that year, Murphy was named corporate director of personnel in Europe, and in 1975, he was appointed vice-president, personnel for automotive operations, a position he held until March 1977 when he was named to his present position.

Executive Commentary

A Corporate Response To Social Responsibility

A century ago when William Vanderbilt was interviewed about his plans, a reporter asked, "What about the public?" Vanderbilt replied, "The public be damned." We have come a long way since then. In fact, we find too narrow the Calvin Coolidge statement that "the chief business of the American people is business."

In today's social environment, social responsibility is another aspect of management's job. Management's basic task remains to make a profit. In the long run, however, profit and social responsibility are compatible because business prospers best in areas where a good social climate prevails.

My particular area of responsibility, Organization and Management Resources for Rockwell International, sounds on the surface to be far removed from the external environment.

Yet, it may be useful to see how the external environment does strongly influence the shaping of our organization and management team. Let's take a look at some of the areas in which we deal:

1. Organization strategies.
2. Recruitment for entry level jobs.
3. Line and functional development.
4. Performance assessment.
5. Identification of people with high potential.
6. Management training.
7. Selection process.
8. Executive review and succession planning.

To look at these in connection with social responsibility, we see many relationships emerging:

1. Organization strategies deal with creating an organization and management climate that homogenizes the external and internal forces that affect our businesses. Today's organization structures must be designed to meet the business needs to communicate with and coordinate its activities with the community, local, state, and federal governments and regulating agencies, as well as special interest groups within society. For example, some of our organization structures include specific functions responsible for coordinating and linking with the business or government legislative activity, environmental control and protection, and other social responsibility items connected with being a "good corporate citizen."

2. It used to be that we seldom had to discuss more than five subjects when we recruited on college campuses—compensation, working conditions, management, opportunity for advancement, and the nature of the work. No longer! A sixth subject—social responsibility—increasingly enters the potential recruit's mind as he or she considers us as an employer. If we had been in the

news lately as an offender, our acceptance ratios undoubtedly would drop. And on our side, we also evaluate the potential recruits. Will he or she be likely to participate in community activities?

3. In line and functional development, the external environment enters in varying ways, depending on the assignment, but it always enters. For example, a person in a factory position must be concerned about employee health and safety, environment, energy, and product quality. In a functional assignment, such as personnel, equal employment considerations prove especially important.

4. We now routinely include in all performance assessments an evaluation of how well the jobholder discharged the responsibilities relating to the external environment. A person who suggests a way to save energy, for instance, would rate well.

5. When we identify people with high potential, one benchmark is their response to the external environment. We are involved extensively in nuclear activities. Many people who have advanced rapidly in this field have done so because of their contributions to nuclear safety.

6. Management training includes instruction in an organized approach to the outside environment. You aren't socially responsible merely because you vaguely wish to save endangered species, prevent pollution, or participate in worthwhile civic activities. How do you do these things effectively? In short, how do you manage your participation?

7. The selection process takes into account the candidate's response to social responsibility, along with other factors. For example, a person who shows exceptional ability in improving a product's quality without increasing its cost would rate well because that is an important response to the external environment.

8. As a person mounts the executive ladder, social responsibilities grow broader and the response necessarily changes. A top manager must lead others in the organization to respond effectively to the external environment. A top manager must speak publicly for the corporation in this area if necessary. Succession planning for key management positions must include an estimate of how well the individual will discharge such duties.

As pointed out in this chapter, public opinion polls show disquieting hostility to business. One reason that has been suggested is that management has not paid sufficient and timely attention to the effects of their activities on the external environment, and vice versa. This can be corrected if social responsibility is made part of the total job from the day a person enters employment after school graduation to the time he or she holds a key management position.

As we and other companies accept this concept and tell that story to Americans, then business as we know it today (the free enterprise system) will continue to provide the opportunities for growth and prosperity that have made this great country what it is today.

CASES FOR PART II

Case II-1

URBAN AFFAIRS AT CHEMICAL BANK

In the spring of 1976, New York City was in the depths of a financial crisis. The city's costs for services of all kinds had for many years outrun its income, and its ability to borrow additional funds was severely constrained. As a result, the mayor was forced to curtail expenditures.

C. Douglas Ades, Vice-President of the Chemical Bank of New York in charge of urban affairs, pondered the implications of the city's plight for Chemical and wondered what actions, if any, he should recommend to the bank's management.

He was moved by the Easter sermon of the Episcopal Bishop of New York, the Rt. Reverend Paul Moore, Jr., delivered in the Cathedral of St. John the Divine on April 18, 1976. In his sermon, Bishop Moore, using the metaphor of death and resurrection, had traced the social and economic ramifications of corporate decisions to leave New York City, asserting that:

> *There are many signs of dying. . . .*
>
> *But perhaps the most sinister sign of all is the announcements that commerce and industry, the very lifeblood of our town, are leaving, sensing like rats, that the ship is sinking.*
>
> *The decisions which lie behind these signs of death are a series of immoral decisions, even though they are clothed in financial considerations, immoral decisions on the part of political and economic leaders on every level of government and business. . . .*
>
> *Industries leave the city. Therefore, fewer jobs and services are needed. Unemployment rises in the Black and Spanish ghettoes. It is now near 50% and perhaps as high as 80% among young people. The tax base is eroded and so educational, social, and health services are cut back because of the diminishing tax income to the city caused by the exodus of business. Inner-city youth are idle; more turn to addiction and violent crime. Crime frightens other New Yorkers, which makes it more difficult to attract employees to the industries. In turn, more industry leaves the city. Such is a simplified description of this tragic cycle.*
>
> *Furthermore, this cycle is exacerbated and distorted by myths. One is the racist, guilt-fear myth surrounding crime. Although crimes of Black against White are small compared to the crimes of Black against Black, the White man sees the crime statistics as a sign of his fear of Black crime against himself. This is basically a racist attitude. The real cause of the high incidence of minority crime is the educational and unemployment deficit of the ghetto, caused ultimately by exploitation and neglect. Another myth is that persons and businesses outside the city limits have no responsibility to the city despite the fact that the vast benefits of the metropolitan area and New York as an international center of commerce drew them here in the first place. The telephones they use, the airports where they land, the clothes they buy, the restaurants where they eat—all float on the back of minority groups who cannot leave the city.*
>
> *Another myth is that the cause of the city's decline is economic. Not so! The symptoms are economic; the cause is moral irresponsibility.*
>
> *The fact that some great corporations stated they they are staying in New York, the fact that the banks and some other businesses must stay in New York, show that it is possible to be here and that exodus is an arbitrary decision made for the purpose of convenience and short-term gain.*
>
> *The religious community, the loyal New Yorkers of goodwill, will not stand by silently in the face of the betrayal of our city, whether the betrayal be by business or government. We will not take this betrayal lying down.*

This case was prepared by Maureen Malin, Research Associate, under the supervision of Professor George C. Lodge, to be used as the basis for classroom discussion.

> *For if the trend continues, we can look ahead to a nightmare town, resorting to physical repression of its frustrated victims, made savage by despair.*
>
> *The gap between rich and poor widens. . . . One tenth of the people of our country are below the poverty level. The major part of these are minority persons.*
>
> *People flee but there is nowhere to flee. These fleeing industries are fooling themselves. People flee, but there is nowhere to flee in a dying land. When industries leave the city, the industrialized suburbs also turn to soulless urban wastelands where social irresponsibility slinks through the night to pull its victims down once more.*
>
> *The struggle for the city's survival is the struggle for the soul of America, for here is being played out what may be the preview of the disintegration of industrialist society, which exploits the poor, the weak, and the old, and then throws them away like refuse. When this occurs, our civilization is doomed. . . .*
>
> *Executives, reverse your decisions and stay in the city. Cut through the fog of statistics and see the moral decision behind them.* Be part of the rising, not the dying. . . .
>
> *There is a role for everyone, not just for politicians and business leaders. . . . Do not let your group spend all its time fighting with others over a smaller and smaller piece of the pie. Unite with other persecuted people and turn the city around.* Be part of the rising, not the dying. . . .[1]

Union Carbide's Decision

Mr. Ades had little doubt that Bishop Moore's remarks would spark considerable debate in the financial and business communities, especially in view of New York City's continued fiscal vulnerability. Impressed by the fervor and clarity of Bishop Moore's views of the city's problems, Mr. Ades in general agreed with the Bishop's conclusions. He wondered, however, what could be done.

It appeared to many that Bishop Moore was speaking directly to Union Carbide. On March 20, 1976, Union Carbide, the nation's second largest chemical manufacturer, had announced its intention to relocate its executive offices in Danbury, Connecticut, a move that would involve the direct loss of 3,500 jobs for the city. The planned move, which was to take three or four years to accomplish, further reduced New York's roster of industrial giants, affected the city's ailing economy, and disappointed the hopes of Mayor Abraham Beame, Governor Hugh Carey, and other public officials who had made personal appeals to the company to remain in the city. The company's plans became known, in fact, just a day after Governor Carey had appealed publicly to Union Carbide and other concerns to suspend considerations of relocation until tax reform and other measures could be considered by the current session of the state legislature. He made the appeal as he announced the appointment of a task force to study the city's tax structure. The governor described the Union Carbide announcement as "unwelcome news" and said it "is precisely this kind of matter that has been the basis for my all-out effort to retain and develop the economy of New York."[2] A spokesperson for Mayor Beame added:

> *We are hopeful that the increasing efforts of the city and the state to generate a vigorous economic development program will more than offset the loss that this move represents.*[3]

In a letter to its employees announcing its decision, Union Carbide stated:

> *While we recognize that New York City does have many advantages, the long-term quality of life needs of our headquarters employees were the overriding factor in arriving at this conclusion.*[4]

In elaborating the reasons behind its decision, the company claimed that the principal problem Union Carbide had in New York was its inability to get middle managers,

[1] Sermon preached by the Rt. Rev. Paul Moore, Jr., on Easter Sunday, April 18, 1976.
[2] *The New York Times*, March 20, 1976.
[3] Ibid.
[4] Ibid.

technicians, engineers, and others to come to the city to work and be trained for senior management posts. The reluctance was attributed to fear of crime, distaste for dirt and congestion, poor public schools, high living costs in the city, and the high cost of commuting expense from suburbs. Connecticut, because of its attractive suburbs and absence of income taxes, had been the principal beneficiary of the corporate exodus from New York that began a decade ago. Company studies had shown that the costs of operating a headquarters in Connecticut would be roughly the same as they were in New York but that there would be considerable tax savings for employees. Thus, for a $20,000-a-year employee, the total of federal, state, and local taxes was $922 less a year in Connecticut than in New York City.

The Union Carbide move was considered to be one of the most severe blows the city's economy had sustained in recent years. Just the week before, Texas Gulf had announced its decision to move its headquarters to Stamford, Connecticut. But unlike Texas Gulf, which has only 135 jobs in New York City, or other large companies which merely maintained pied-à-terre offices in the city, Union Carbide was one of New York City's largest private industrial employers. According to the Economic Development Administration, the goods and services purchased by the company from local concerns accounted for at least 3,500 jobs in addition to its own 3,500.[5] Union Carbide's decision to leave the city cut to 94 the number of large national and multinational corporations that had their headquarters in New York City. In the 1960s, the city was the home of 140 of the top 500. The relocation of these headquarters was one of the prime causes for the loss of 500,000 jobs in New York City since 1969.

Despite the economic impact of its decision, Union Carbide was not without its supporters. In an editorial, entitled "Voting With Your Feet," the *Wall Street Journal* refuted Bishop Moore, claiming that:

> *In themselves, such appeals are irrelevant. Bishop Moore could no more have stayed the exodus of Union Carbide to Connecticut than he could have talked Moses into keeping the Israelities in Egypt. People and corporations will always leave political jurisdictions while costs exceed benefits as long as they believe the spot over the horizon is relatively better.*
>
> *It's called voting with your feet. Immigration. . . .*
>
> *One of the really nice things about the United States is that it contains within it a multitude of political jurisdictions. People and companies can vote with their feet without having to leave the country. If the tax burden or crime rate becomes too unbearable in New York or Newark, people and businessmen will hike to Chicago or Stamford instead. If the authorities in New York or Newark are dismayed by this exodus, they must either reduce costs or increase benefits, or both, until the exodus halts.*
>
> *The financial crisis in New York City has finally caused its authorities to think more in these terms, which is all to the good. But they are also trying to avoid the hard work by making conventional liberal arguments about the need to "federalize." They want to federalize welfare, federalize health, federalize housing, which translates into a system that blocks immigration within the United States as a way of escaping the costs of their programs. If Stamford and Chicago and Salt Lake City were forced to pay for New York City's generosity, there would be no place for the city's businessmen to flee.*
>
> *For the same reason, the liberals have come to despise federal revenue sharing, which permits political jurisdictions to either lower taxes or increase spending. To the degree* [that] *Chicago and Stamford use their shared revenues to lower taxes and New York City and Newark use them to increase spending, businessmen and workers find Chicago and Stamford more attractive, and Bishop Moore must deliver another sermon. And it's true that if all political jurisdictions taxed and spent as foolishly as New York, Union Carbide would have no incentive to leave and would make the moral decision to stay. . . .*[6]

[5] Cited in *The New York Times*, March 22, 1976.

[6] *The Wall Street Journal*, March 29, 1976.

Chemical Bank of New York

Douglas Ades' interest in Bishop Moore's sermon was both personal and professional. As head of the Urban Affairs Department at the Chemical Bank of New York, Mr. Ades was responsible for assessing the impact of recent events in the city on the continued profitable operations of the bank, which, by charter, was required to remain in New York City. With assets of more than $23 billion, Chemical Bank was the fifth largest bank in New York City. It had recognized the need for greater information about the liaison with the community in which it based its operations. To meet these needs, the bank had hired Mr. Ades in 1969 to develop and coordinate its community-oriented activities, particularly those programs initiated in response to pressures from the black and Puerto Rican communities.

Before coming to the bank, Mr. Ades had worked several years for IBM, resigning his position to attend Redlands University. In college, Mr. Ades found that his involvement in the emerging civil rights and anti-war movements had provoked a profound shift in his values and priorities. As a result of considerable soul-searching and his exposure to the suffering of the ghettos, he decided to become a minister. However, after graduation from Union Theological Seminary, Mr. Ades felt that the pulpit would not be the most appropriate or effective means for him to initiate and implement significant social reforms. Mr. Ades described his change of mind:

> *I got tired of being a minister in that community (Harlem) because I had no tools, no resources. I had lots of good wishes but no tools. I got tired of coming down to Wall Street and places like that begging for pennies, so I decided to come down here to work.*[7]

Perceiving the need for a power base and recognizing the importance of money as a source of power, Mr. Ades wrote letters to the presidents of 150 large corporations, telling them he "knew something about the streets," to help them to communicate with and to develop activities for the more disadvantaged persons living in the areas in which they operated. Mr. Ades' first exposure to Chemical Bank had been as a picket opposing its investment policies in South Africa. However, he chose to work there largely because the bank had, until then, done little to respond to the needs of the black and Puerto Rican communities.

In accepting his position, Mr. Ades had explicitly told the bank's senior management the extent of his commitment to the black community:

> *When I came here in August 1969, to organize the (urban affairs) program, I said I had to be honest, and if push came to shove and it had to be the community that took gas or the bank that took gas, I had to let them know right off that I would come down on the side of the community, because that's where my commitment is.*[8]
>
> *Mr. Ades believed, however, that it would be possible: (to skirt) the edge of confrontation and instead (to find) where the nexus is, where it is in the interests of both parties, both the bank and the community, to do something. . . .*
>
> *I'm convinced that if you come up with the program that finds a nexus of interest between the bank and the community both sides will go for it every time. But you have to see yourself in the mainstream of the business, not as an appendage, or as a salver of someone's conscience.*
>
> *Hell, I'm not doing this to show banks are good guys—people will find out if you're doing the job—but to show people there's a way to do it.*[9]

In the seven years that Mr. Ades had been with Chemical Bank, his activities and influence had expanded considerably. From a staff of two in 1969, the urban affairs area

[7] *The New York Times,* December 10, 1972.
[8] *The New York Times,* December 10, 1972.
[9] Ibid.

had grown to a department of nine and an operating budget of $250,000 by 1976. In addition, it was responsible for distributing the bank's contribution budget of $1,070,000 to worthy organizations and programs in the city. Commenting on his department's activities and its growth, Mr. Ades observed:

I came to work (at Chemical Bank) as a skeptic, and I knew that they were going to use me, and I was going to use them, but I didn't know how much it was going to go in either direction. I am not nearly the skeptic I was. I'm amazed at the kind of support that has been given, not just me, but this operation, in terms of staffing and dollars and—even more important—in taking the time to get involved.

Almost everyone in the senior management has walked the streets of Harlem with me, has smelled it, has talked to people, is involved, and cares.[10]

During this same period, the department's formal reporting relationships within the bank had also changed, reflecting, in part, the importance attached to this area by the company, and, in part, the potential impact of external events, such as violence, riots, and the city's fiscal crisis, on the bank's operations. Initially, the Urban Affairs Department had been placed under the Marketing Division, which served as a catch-all for public relations-type activities. In 1971, however, the department was placed under the first vice-president (soon to become the chairman), where it remained until 1973, when Mr. Ades found his department reporting directly to the deputy head of the Metropolitan Bank Divison. This division supervised all 262 of the Chemical Bank branch offices operating in the nine-county New York City metropolitan area and was responsible for coordinating the retail and commercial banking activities of these branch offices. As part of the 1973 reorganization, the Urban Affairs Advisory Committee was reorganized, and met four times a year. Its members included both the president of the bank and the chairman of the board. (Exhibit 1 lists 1976 members of the advisory committee.) The advisory committee provided Mr. Ades and the Urban Affairs Department with direct, albeit informal, reporting lines to the president and the chairman of the board.

Functioning largely as a catalyst and an information processer, the Urban Affairs Department was created to work toward what Norborne Berkeley, Jr., president of Chemical Bank, called "the exciting objective of directly attempting to solve some of the more critical problems of the city, particularly in the low-income areas."[11] To achieve this objective, the department had sponsored or initiated a range of programs and activities to meet the needs of ghetto residents.

The Urban Affairs Department's largest program was its street banker operation. Seven members of the department's staff served as liaison between the community and the bank's branch offices located in Harlem, the Bronx, and the Bedford-Stuyvesant and Williamsburg sections of Brooklyn, areas largely black or Spanish-speaking and generally quite poor. With the streets as their "offices" and affiliated with no single branch office, Mr. Ades' bankers worked with members of the community, helping them to assess their financial and banking needs. In describing their activities, Mr. Ades reported:

Look, all major banks have urban affairs programs of one kind or another. But we're all doing it differently. What we decided was to put street bankers in our branches (in the black and Puerto Rican communities), and their job was not to sit behind desks but to work out in the neighborhoods with people of that community and community organizations, looking for ideas to develop that community, and then translate those ideas into terms a bank can respond to.

That's a key issue. A street banker is a guy or girl who is trained as a banker. I mean, they are not do-gooders in the old sense of the word. They have standard credit training. They know what a bank can perform. They know what it can't do.

But we try to help them get creative with banking. Instead of just seeing banking as helping

[10] Ibid.

[11] Company report, "Banking on New York," preliminary report, 1976.

EXHIBIT 1
Urban Affairs at Chemical Bank.

Membership of the Urban Affairs Advisory Board, Chemical Bank of New York, 1976

Norborne Berkeley, Jr.
Chairman of the Committee
President
Chemical Bank

Richard K. LeBlond II
Vice-Chairman of the Committee
Vice-Chairman
Chemical Bank

Donald C. Platten
Ex Officio Member
Chairman
Chemical Bank

Richard D. S. Bryan
Executive Vice-President
Corporate Bank

Robert I. Lipp
Executive Vice-President
Bank Operations Division

Francis W. Murray III
Executive Vice-President
Metropolitan Bank

William J. Cardew
Senior Vice-President
Metropolitan Bank

Robert J. Collishaw
Senior Vice-President
Public Affairs Department

Alan H. Fishman
Senior Vice-President
Metropolitan Bank

John P. LaWare
Senior Vice-President
Marketing Division

Charles C. Lehing
Senior Vice-President
Metropolitan Bank

Kenneth Porter
Senior Vice-President
Personnel Division

C. Douglas Ades
Secretary of the Committee
Vice-President
Urban Affairs Department

businesses, we try to redefine what a business is, what a customer is. A drug program that has money coming in from the Addiction Services Agency is a business. It has an income and an outgo, and it may need help with its bookkeeping and its disbursements. It may need a loan between the time the contract is signed and the money actually comes out of city government, which we've done a number of times. . . .

But our seven people are dealing not only in a community but in the bank. They're turning on people in the personnel department, they're turning on people in the mortgage and real estate area, they're turning on people in the purchasing department and getting them to be involved. The idea is to be the bridge between the bank and the community.[12]

Although a permanent part of the bank's management structure, the Urban Affairs Department also sought opportunities to undertake projects in which its role was temporary. One such example was Chemical Bank's policy of hiring ex-offenders. According to Mr. Ades, large numbers of ghetto residents had found it difficult, if not impossible, to obtain employment because of their prison records. Under New York law, for instance, ex-offenders were barred from working where liquor was served, thus precluding their seeking employment in restaurants. In 1972, Mr. Ades invited the bank's president, Norborne Berkeley, Jr., to visit a major prison in upstate New York. Appalled by the conditions he encountered in the prison, Mr. Berkeley decided that the bank should

[12] *The New York Times*, December 10, 1972.

do something to ease the re-entry problems of former inmates. Aided by an outside organization with considerable experience in the criminal justice field, the bank selected and hired 12 men and women, most of whom had served time in prison. A training program was developed and, within a year, four of the new employees had won promotions and three more were training as tellers. In the four-year period from the program's inception through 1976, 42 of the 55 ex-offenders who had been hired remained with the bank. Shortly after the program was initiated, however, the task of finding, hiring, and training former prison inmates had become a special recruiting function of the bank's Corporate Personnel Department. The Urban Affairs Department worked as a catalyst; it moved out of operations once a new program's position was assured.

In addition to its direct role, the Urban Affairs Department advised bank management regarding a number of matters. In particular, it provided information about neighborhoods and their residents to the bank's Urban Lending and Urban Housing units and evaluated requests from various community organizations for funds from the company's contribution budget. In assessing the role and importance of the Urban Affairs Department to Chemical Bank's continued profitable operations in New York City, Mr. Ades observed:

> *I think there's a whole new breed of banker that's being created, the urban banker. He's not the guy who deals overwhelmingly with heads of corporations.*
>
> *But any New York City bank has to face what it is to be a bank in this city with 150 or 160 branches. Increasingly, the need is for people who understand the workings of this city, and that means you don't just understand what happens at Rockefeller Center but Jamaica and Harlem and Bedford-Stuyvesant and the South Bronx. . . .*
>
> *In the long range, what we're hoping to do is not just increase the staff of street bankers across New York but increasingly devise methods of incentives to turn on branch managers all through the system to become involved in their communities. . . .*[13]

Commenting further, he added:

> *What's in it for us? Maybe there's not much profit. But you can define profit a couple of ways. One is that corporations exist to increase their long-term equity. That means, in the case of a bank that is limited by law as to where it can operate and that has its headquarters in this city, that this is the market area.*
>
> *If this market area declines or deteriorates, so does the bank. But if we get involved in a housing project and make just a little profit on it, we look 10 years down the line and see that people who have had a chance to move out of some really rotten places, maybe they've gotten off welfare, got a job so they're able to deposit in the bank, borrow from the bank, or work for it—it's a selfish view, but an enlightened one, to see what it means for the short and long term.*[14]

As he reflected on Bishop Moore's sermon and the business community's reactions to it, Mr. Ades realized that this would undoubtedly be a topic of discussion at the upcoming quarterly meeting of the Urban Affairs Advisory Committee. As he prepared for the meeting, to be held in two weeks, Mr. Ades knew that the members would be interested in his assessment of Bishop Moore's claims and the validity of the business community's responses. Just as Mr. Ades had found merit in many of Bishop Moore's comments, so, too, he realized the need for the city to make some hard decisions as it sought to respond to its current fiscal crisis. In Mr. Ades' view, however, the financial problems facing the city had their roots in the political, social, and economic evolution of New York City during the last decade and a half. Similarly, he believed that the exodus of businesses from New York City was an effect as well as a cause of the problems associated with that evolution. Mr. Ades wondered just what Chemical Bank and other businesses

[13] Ibid.
[14] Ibid.

operating, either by choice or necessity, in New York could do to solve the problems confronting the city. He also questioned what the business community could expect in the way of help from government officials and agencies and what the role of business should be in the effort to reestablish the city's financial credibility and to improve the quality of life for its residents. He knew from past experience that many prior attempts at cooperation between the public and the private sectors had failed, largely because there was no forum for regular and frank exchange of views between business and government leaders. At the same time, Mr. Ades recognized the need for a joint effort in the definition of the city's problems and their causes and in the development and implementation of programs designed to alleviate them.

Case II-2

BASF CORPORATION VS. THE HILTON HEAD ISLAND DEVELOPERS

From 1966 to 1969 foreign investment in the United States rose from $9 billion to $12 billion, partially alleviating the balance-of-payments problem. One firm expanding in the United States was a German chemical firm, Badische-Analin and Soda Fabrik Co. (hereafter referred to as BASF). This firm had sales of $2.4 billion in 1969 and property assets of over $550 million. The company produced over 5,000 products for sale in over 130 countries. The firm, which had plants in New Jersey, expanded its operations in the United States in 1969 by acquiring the Wyandotte Chemical Co., located near Detroit, and by acquiring land and announcing plans to build a $100 million petrochemical plant in the Southeast in Beaufort County, South Carolina.

Many European firms have located in recent years in the eastern part of the United States. Some reasons for this are the proximity of the eastern region to the Atlantic Ocean and European markets and the fact that most European firms are more familiar with this area than with other regions of the country. The Southeast appeared particularly attractive to BASF as a location site because of its proximity to many petrochemical and dyestuff customers, and because there were no major petrochemical plants between Philadelphia and Miami.

The company examined sites in 20 states, especially in Georgia, North Carolina, and South Carolina, over a two-year period and talked with state development board officials in many states. BASF had many requirements: 1,800 acres of land, 5 million gallons of fresh water per day, close proximity to a railroad and the seacoast, a free trade area for the tax-free importation of chemical inputs, and an adequate labor force available at competitive prices. An area in the southeastern part of South Carolina in Beaufort County appeared to meet their requirements.

State officials, including then Governor Robert E. McNair and officials of the State Development Board, and many other people in South Carolina badly wanted BASF to locate in Beaufort County because of the poverty and economic imbalances in the area. Although per capita income in Beaufort County is above the national average as a result of military installations (including the Parris Island Marine training base) which account

Much of this material was taken from Chapter 1 of the following monograph: Oliver G. Wood, Jr., John E. Logan, Sandra P. Logan, *et al.*, *The BASF Controversy: Employment vs. Environment* (Columbia, S.C.: University of South Carolina, College of Business Administration, Bureau of Business and Economic Research, 1971), pp. 1–22. The authors' thanks go to Dr. Olin S. Pugh, Director of the Bureau of Business and Economic Research, and Dr. James F. Kane, Dean of the College of Business Administration for allowing us to release this material in case form. This case was first presented at the Southern Case Writer's Association meeting in Miami, Florida, on November 2–4, 1971.

for about 68% of the county's personal income, per capita income in the other three counties in the area was below $2,000 with per capita income in Jasper County standing at $1,192 in 1968.[1] Further, the area was steadily losing agricultural jobs and population at the same time that there was a dearth of manufacturing jobs.[2] A further sign of the severe economic plight of the area is the substantial amount of substandard housing. For example, according to the 1960 census, 55.5% of all housing units in Hampton County were classified as substandard.

BASF was attractive to officials of the State of South Carolina for several other reasons. The Beaufort area had just received unfavorable national publicity during hearings on hunger before a subcommittee of the United States Senate. Also, state officials had been trying to interest industry in state-owned land in this area for about a decade. Further, it was predicted that a business recession might well occur in 1970. The location of such a large facility as the proposed BASF plant would help the South Carolina State Development Board continue its five-year record of having new plant investment in South Carolina exceed $500 million annually.

Initial Plans

By June 1969, BASF representatives were convinced that Victoria Bluffs in Beaufort County best met their requirements. At this time the South Carolina Pollution Control Authority received a copy of the petrochemical company's proposed plans for the site. Although these plans were incomplete. Dr. Hans Lautenschlager, president of BASF in the United States, saw no reason to fear that they would violate South Carolina's pollution laws.[3] In June the Beaufort County Development Board held a confidential advisory meeting with invited representatives of various businesses to discuss BASF's possible location in Beaufort. On June 17, 1969, Charles Fraser, president of Sea Pines Plantation Co., one of the major developers of the Hilton Head Island resort area, wrote a letter to the Beaufort Development Board stating that pollution from the proposed BASF plant could impair the Hilton Head resort industry and affect thousands of jobs[4]

On October 1, 1969, officials of the German company and the South Carolina state government publicly announced plans for the construction by BASF of a dyestuffs plant at Victoria Bluffs. Company officials, at this time, claimed that the investment in this new facility would be approximately $100 million and that this plant would employ about 1,000 people in the production of styrene, polymers, dyestuffs, and pigments. In addition, to help lure BASF to South Carolina, the state had already promised to construct a 13-mile railroad, a four-lane highway, new docking facilities, and to dredge the Colleton River, subject to approval by the Army Corps of Engineers. South Carolina would also grant the company a five-year exemption from state corporate income taxes. The United States Chamber of Commerce forecast the effect of the plant on the Beaufort economy as follows:

> *. . . the influx of 1,000 employees in Beaufort will result in a population increase of 3,590; more than $3,000 more in personal* [*per capita*] *income; 30 more retail establishments; 1,000 more households; 970 more passenger car registrations; $3,310,000 more retail sales per year; 910 more*

[1] Oliver G. Wood, Jr., "Economic Profile of the Beaufort Economic Area," in Oliver G. Wood, Jr., John E. Logan, Sandra P. Logan, *et al.*, *The BASF Controversy: Employment vs. Environment* (Columbia, S.C.: University of South Carolina, 1971).

[2] For example, only 14% of the jobs in the four-county Beaufort Economic Area are in manufacturing industries, as opposed to 34% of all jobs in the State of South Carolina as a whole. Between 1959 and 1967, agricultural employment in the area declined slightly over 33%. In Beaufort County, for example, agricultural employment declined from 11.6% of all civilian employment in 1959 to 5.6% in 1967. At the same time, only 326 people were employed in manufacturing firms employing over 50 and only 2.7% of Beaufort County's work force was employed in the manufacturing industries.

[3] "Why in South Carolina: BASF Needed Area, Water, Labor Force," *The State* (Columbia), Jan. 25, 1970.

[4] From a letter written by Charles Fraser to the Beaufort County Development Board, June 17, 1969.

school children; $2,290,000 more in bank deposits; and 650 more jobs over and above what the plant will employ.[5]

On Ocober 15, 1969, BASF officials announced that their long-range total investment in the site might well be in the neighborhood of $400 million. The dyestuffs plant, to be constructed first, would cost $25 million. The next step would involve the establishment of a $98 million petrochemical plant. In late December, when full details of this second phase were announced, company officials revealed that the petrochemical plant would be constructed only if they could obtain a free foreign trade zone for Port Victoria in Beaufort and permission to import 40,000 barrels a day of naphtha, a chemical used to produce ethylene which in turn is used in the production of plastics.

In November 1969 BASF purchased an 1,800-acre site at Victoria Bluffs from the State Ports Authority for $980,000. The company then announced that they would not lower the quality of the water of the Colleton River into which their wastes would be dumped. All wastes would be treated both at the plant itself and at the water authority treatment facility before being released. At this time neither officials of BASF nor of the South Caroline State Pollution Control Authority publicly expressed any fear that the new plants would violate state pollution laws. Some state officials suggested that the plants would be a boon to the depressed economy of the area.

Charges and Countercharges

The dams of controversy burst on December 2, 1969, when Fred Hack and Charles Fraser, the developers of Hilton Head Island, claimed that the proposed chemical plant would pollute the Colleton River and pose a very serious threat to the existence of the $100 million resort community on Hilton Head Island. Fraser pointed out that the chemical plant could legally pollute the water in the Beaufort area because of the loopholes in the present South Carolina pollution laws.[6] He suggested further that BASF be forced to post a $25 million performance bond which would be forfeited if their plant polluted.

Governor Robert McNair responded to Hack and Fraser the next day:

> *We have assurances from BASF . . . that the company is vitally concerned about the ecology and beauty of the area and that steps are being taken to satisfy all legal, environmental and industrial requirements in safeguarding the air and water from pollutants.*[7]

Hack and Fraser also explained why they had not protested the proposed plant location in October when it had been announced:

> *Hack and Fraser said they withheld judgment for eight weeks after the plant was announced to study the company and the background and experience of other communities that had become the site of chemical plants.*[8]

They also stated they would be willing to buy the Victoria Bluffs land from BASF to develop it as a recreation center, and offered to attempt to find light industry more compatible with the area.[9]

Later that same month various other groups began actively to oppose the construction of the BASF plant in Beaufort County. Among these were the Citizens Association of Beaufort County, Inc., headed by Vice-Admiral Rufus L. Taylor USN (Ret.), and the Environmental Quality Control Council, headed by Franklin Rouse. The Board of Directors of the Hilton Head Chamber of Commerce also announced its belief that the

[5] "Beaufort Getting New Industry," *Columbia Record,* Oct. 1, 1969.
[6] Robert E. Brownlee, "Pollution Prevention Urged for Beaufort," *Columbia Record,* Dec. 9, 1969.
[7] "McNair Assures Pollution Control," *Columbia Record,* Dec. 10, 1969.
[8] "Group Meets to Plan Action Against BASF," *The State,* Dec. 4, 1969.
[9] Ibid.

location of a chemical plant would be a serious threat to the recreation and seafood industry in the area.

Relative peace reigned for the next 10 to 15 days at which time controversy boomed forth again. On December 23, Charles Fraser, in response to the announced plans for the petrochemical plant, claimed that a naphtha import quota of 40,000 barrels a day would allow BASF to escape paying federal import taxes of $20 million a year. On the same day, Dr. Hans Lautenschlager attempted to refute the various accusations against his firm by stating, "BASF intends to be one of the industrial leaders in resolving problems of pollution." He said that his company would continuously measure the quantity and quality of its effluents and that they would make this information public. However, Fraser doubted that these provisions would prevent pollution.

> *We are alarmed that there are indications that BASF is planning to budget only one million dollars for air and water pollution control equipment. We have received private word from executives within the petrochemical industry that a budget of seven or eight million dollars would be a more realistic figure if they genuinely intend to install the most modern and efficient control equipment.*[10]

A few days later company officials announced that construction work at the Victoria Bluffs site would begin in 1970. It was estimated that 800 workers would be employed in construction efforts in 1970 and that the payroll would be $6 million. In 1971 roughly 1,300 construction workers would be needed, with a $9 million payroll, while 1972 would see a $12 million payroll for 1,500 construction workers. (See Table 1.) Skilled, semiskilled, and unskilled laborers, the latter in abundant supply in the Beaufort area, as well as managerial workers would be needed. BASF representatives announced also that by 1975. 1,000 people would be employed in the Port Victoria complex. (However, throughout the dispute, many observers were skeptical as to how many jobs would actually be created and how many of these jobs would actually go to poor residents of the Beaufort Economic Area.)

According to BASF estimates and the analysis of Dr. Robert Rosen and Professor David Pender of what has happened where similar petrochemical plants were built and complexes resulted, operating labor at chemical facilities at Victoria Bluffs would have increased from a little over 600 in 1974 to over 3,000 in 1976 and to over 6,815 in 1978.[11] Even more important, the number of unskilled jobs generated would have amounted to above half of this total. (See Table 2.)

In the last week of December, Hilton Head Island conservationists announced their

TABLE 1
Estimate of Construction Workers to be Used, by Skill and Level, 1970–1972

Construction Workers	1970	1971	1972
Unskilled	200	260	300
Semiskilled	350	650	725
Skilled	150	260	300
Managerial	100	130	175
Total	800	1,300	1,500

Source: BASF ,News Release, December 29, 1969.

[10] "BASF Tells Details of Second Beaufort Plant," *The State*, Dec. 23, 1969.

[11] Robert W. Rosen and David R. Pender, "Economic Impact of the Proposed BASF Project and Satellite Plants," in Oliver G. Wood, Jr., John E. Logan, Sandra P. Logan, *et al.*, op. cit., pp. 44–61.

TABLE 2
Estimated Employment in BASF and Satellite Petrochemical Operations

Types of Worker	1974	1976	1978
Unskilled	315	1,700	4,050
Skilled	240	980	1,870
Management and Salaried	100	445	895
Total	655	3,125	6,815

Source: Robert W. Rosen and David R. Pender, "Economic Impact of the Proposed BASF Project and Satellite Plants," in Oliver G. Wood, Jr., John E. Logan, Sandra P. Logan, op. cit., p. 51.

intentions to meet during the first week of January 1970 to examine the pollution problem; BASF representatives were not invited. While the pollution symposium was taking place, BASF and state government officials agreed to study the problem of pollution in the Victoria Bluffs area, with the state's Water Resources Commission and an independent firm engaged by BASF to conduct separate studies. Meanwhile, conservationists were busy drawing their own conclusions:

Dredging—which the state had promised to do in the Colleton River so ocean-going vessels could dock at Victoria Bluffs—could damage Beaufort County's water supply and severely impair the area's seafood industry.

1. *Oyster beds form on sloping river banks. The dredging would upset this slope and ruin the beds.*
2. *Dredging could alter the pattern of surrounding marshbanks, thereby forcing shrimp to move elsewhere.*[12]

Dr. John O. Withers said, "Changes in the life cycle of one form of sea life could alter the entire ecological balance [of the area]." He argued that as no study of the tidal flows in the area had ever been undertaken, it was possible that the water in the Colleton River at Victoria Bluffs never went into the ocean.[13]

Other conservationists were upset by the company's plans. Conservationist and geographer Alan Ternes pointed out in an April 1970 article in *Natural History:*

If, when it says preserve the ecology, the BASF corporation means to maintain the existing ecosystem, it is proposing to do the impossible. The daily effluent of some 2.5 million gallons from the plant, no matter how it is treated, will change the ecosystem. So will the dredging of a channel to the site.[14]

However, Ternes was equally critical of Hilton Head developers and "conservationists," claiming that they were also guilty of tampering with the environment.

Labor crews and tractors with brush-cutting rigs are constantly assaulting the undergrowth [on Hilton Head Island] so that the landscape will have a parklike appearance. . . . Dredging equipment has cut deep channels through many parts of the island, changing the drainage and destroying wet sites and their distinctive biota. Other areas are filled in with the spill from dredging. . . . Ultimately one tenth of the island will be occupied by golf courses, which may be pretty by some tastes, but which certainly are not examples of natural beauty. . . . Charley Fraser and other developers of Hilton Head Island are concerned about saving an environment, but it is

[12] John David Spade, "Group Warns Against Plan to Dredge Colleton River," *The State*, Jan. 7, 1970.
[13] John David Spade, "Biologist Worries While Local Groups Argue," *The State*, Jan. 10, 1970.
[14] Alan Ternes, "An Introduction to the Setting and Characteristics of the Tragical Farce or Farcical Tragedy of Victoria Bluffs, South Carolina," *Natural History*, LXXIX (April, 1970), p. 12.

an environment they have created, and it is as far removed from the natural environment as the conceptions of BASF.[15]

By January 9, 1970, BASF had announced plans to proceed with construction on schedule and the conservationists had recommended a complete ecological study of the area before construction took place. Orion Hack, the brother of Fred Hack, accused Representative Brantley Harvey of Beaufort of conflict of interests, claiming that Harvey had helped BASF acquire the land under dispute. Harvey denied that his actions created any conflict of interests.

Charles Fraser also pointed out that BASF could hurt employment in the area. He estimated that for every non-high school graduate hired by the new plants, there would be 3 high school dropouts employed in the seafood and recreation industries who would lose their jobs.[16] Although Fraser did not give any reason for his statement concerning loss of jobs, he may have been estimating a decline in employment in these industries because of the threat of pollution. Conservationists also pointed up the possibility of accidental spills from tankers in the Colleton River, a danger which BASF officials admitted they could not prevent.

Dr. Hans Lautenschlager saw little competition between his company and the seafood and recreation industries for labor because, "We won't employ many maids or cooks in the plant." Dr. Lautenschlager also pointed out that 600 people—a somewhat lower estimate than before—would be employed at the plant with half the jobs going to unskilled workers. He thought opposition to the proposed plant was ill-founded.

He said opposition to the plant was confined to a minority of a well organized and economically independent group of people who know how to use the news media and are well acquainted with industry. He said the plant could become a laboratory in which man could learn how to have industry without pollution.[17]

Later in January a State Pollution Control Authority investigation of the Tenneco Corporation plant in the Beaufort area revealed that Tenneco, in spite of promises to the contrary, was indeed polluting the stream into which its effluents poured.[18] In explanation, officials of the State Pollution Control Authority said that due to a lack of funds, they were severely understaffed, and thus, could not effectively monitor all industry. (The South Carolina Legislature subsequently turned down a request by the Pollution Control Authority for 87 new positions and $800,000 more for the 1970–1971 fiscal year.)[19]

In late January opponents of the BASF project began to exclaim that of more importance than the company's promises not to pollute were the facts that the BASF operations in West Germany and Belgium had polluted the Rhine and Schelde Rivers, respectively. In defense of BASF policies and practices. Dr. Lautenschlager claimed that the parent company was only one of many firms dumping waste into the Rhine, but that pollution in this river would be reduced [because of] the strengthening of laws. The company was to invest $45 milion over the next four years to cleanse its operations on the Rhine River. As for the Schelde River, he said it was "dead" before BASF began to dump wastes in it.[20] In defense of BASF operations in New Jersey, the State of New Jersey's pollution controllers asserted that this company was obeying their antipollution laws.[21]

[15] Ibid., pp. 12 ff.

[16] John David Spade, "Legal Action Considered to Halt BASF Construction," *The State*, Jan. 11, 1970.

[17] William D. McDonald, "Advantages of BASF Plant Listed," *The State*, Jan. 21, 1970.

[18] Ternes, op. cit., p. 17.

[19] "Prospects Dim for More Enforcement of Pollution Laws in South Carolina," *The State*, Feb. 18, 1970.

[20] McDonald, loc. cit.

[21] "New Jersey's Tough-Minded Pollution Controllers Give a Clean Bill of Health to BASF's Operations in Their State . . . ," *The State*, Feb. 1, 1970.

In February 1970 South Carolina officials discussed pollution problems. H. J. Webb, associate director of the South Carolina Pollution Control Authority, said the biggest pollution problem in the state might be the hundreds of small sewerage and waste plants built for small real estate developments throughout the state. There were more than 500 of these plants in existence in 1970 and officials estimate that this figure will have doubled by 1980. John C. West, then lieutenant governor of South Carolina, pointed out that over 21 million gallons of waste per day are pumped by the city of Columbia into the Congaree River, or about 10 times the waste it was estimated the new BASF plants would release into the Colleton River, and that air pollution is already a severe problem in North Charleston. The state legislature began to consider various antipollution bills designed to strengthen existing laws. Strom Thurmond, Senator from South Carolina, requested that the Department of the Interior study the BASF plant proposal in order to settle the conflict concerning the plant's ecological effect on the Beaufort County area.

Meanwhile, citizens of Beaufort County presented BASF officials with a petition welcoming them to Beaufort: it contained 7,488 signatures. A Beaufort pharmacist observed "I would say 80% of the people in Beaufort County are in favor of BASF. Those who aren't are rich."[22]

Controls on BASF

The state legislature considered various proposals designed to combat pollution, including a moratorium on construction of the proposed plants, during February. Representative J. Wilson Graves of Beaufort County asked for a concurrent one-year moratorium on inshore fishing and crabbing in Beaufort County in order to help equalize costs between the disputants. This conflict was settled in March with agreement on a one-year moratorium on granting additional waste permits in Beaufort County until a one-year study on pollution in that area could be completed by the South Carolina Water Resources Commission. This study of the effects of industry on the tidelands area was to involve 16 federal and state agencies and would have cost about $156,000.[23] After this compromise had been agreed upon, Representative Graves dropped his proposal for a moratorium on fishing. In February the South Carolina House of Representatives had enacted a bill enabling the South Carolina Pollution Control Authority to appeal to the court for an injunction against any individual or industry polluting the air to the extent that it hampered a person's enjoyment of his own property. The South Carolina Pollution Control Authority also was reorganized to give it more strength.

The controversy entered another arena in February—the federal courts. On February 10 the Hilton Head Fishing Cooperative, Inc.; Blue Channel Corporation; and the Ocean, Lala, and River Fish Companies[24] filed suit in the United States District Court in Aiken, South Carolina, against BASF. The defendant responded that since it had done no business in South Carolina the United States District Court at Aiken had no jurisdiction over it. BASF contended also that the service of the suit was insufficient. About the same time, opponents of the proposed project began to question the cost to taxpayers of the South Carolina State Ports Authority's promises to BASF; i.e., the 13-mile railroad, the new docks and watersheds, the four-lane highway, and the five-year state tax exemption.[25]

[22] William D. McDonald, "Youth Corps Looking for Jobs," *The State*, Feb. 23, 1970.

[23] William D. McDonald, "Study of Effects of Industry on Tiedelands Unveiled," *The State*, March 25, 1970.

[24] Fishing and the packaging of fish is a fairly significant industry in Beaufort County with the manufactured value of fish in the country reaching $2.7 million in 1967, while the value of shellfish harvest, primarily oysters and crabs, was $1.3 million. These totals were about 75% and 46% of South Carolina's total, respectively. The six seafood processing firms employ about 400 people during peak season, while it is estimated that the "fishing cooperatives" in the county employ over 200. Oliver G. Wood, "Economic Profile of the Beaufort Economic Area," Unpublished Manuscript, 1971, p. 28.

[25] Advertisement in *Sea Islander*, Feb. 26, 1970.

In March 1970 the South Carolina Collegiate Press Association sponsored a symposium on pollution problems. Among the speakers was Miss Marion Edey of the Washington, D.C., Office of the Friends of the Earth. Miss Edey said, "South Carolina must choose between making an effort to halt pollution and having an industrialized area as unliveable as New York City, which I fled long ago."[26]

Later in March a survey taken in neighboring North Carolina revealed that chemical workers were the highest paid industrial workers in the state, with average weekly earnings of over $146 as compared with apparel workers in the textile industry in North Carolina who averaged less than $72 a week.[27] (Over 50% of South Carolina's manufacturing workers are employed in the textile industry and receive similar wages. Many people have argued that if South Carolina is to improve its per capita income levels, more high-wage industries must be attracted to the state.)

In spite of the one-year moratorium mentioned previously, the furor continued. The Beaufort Junior Chamber of Commerce joined the forces opposing the location of the plants in Beaufort County. One spokesman for the Beaufort Jaycees said he could see no dearth of employment opportunities in Beaufort County, noting that his "classmates" from school appeared to be employed.[28]

On March 18, 1970, the Hilton Head Company, the Sea Island Development Corporation, and Port Royal Plantation, Inc.—the major developers of Hilton Head Island—filed suit to enjoin BASF permanently from engaging in construction at Victoria Bluffs. One of the principal attorneys for this group later stated that the longer construction could be delayed, the lower the probability that the plants would ever be built on that site since time was extremely important to the company if it were to remain in the vanguard of the chemical industry.

In late March Secretary of the Interior Walter Hickel warned BASF officials not to change the composition of the estuarine waters of the Colleton River. This was interpreted by many observers as a radical change in federal environmental control policy. Others saw it as a dangerous encroachment by the federal government in local and state affairs. Later, most observers felt this was the straw that broke BASF's back. Several days later, company representatives sent a letter to Hickel stating that they would abide by any government regulations. A company spokesman also said that the federal government must set pollution standards and insure that they protect the public interest. Company officials decided to delay all construction at the Victoria Bluffs site until the appropriate federal agencies could formulate these standards. Robert E. McNair, then Governor of South Carolina, expressed concern that the Department of the Interior had become involved in an internal state problem. He wondered whether South Carolina was to become "the guinea pig for a new federal policy on air pollution."[29]

Fraser and the Hack brothers were also busy during late March and April, proposing the possible development of the Victoria Bluffs site into a recreation area to be known as "Seven Flags Over Port Royal," which they envisioned as being similar to the "Six Flags Over Georgia" operation. Although they offered to buy the site from BASF, the three men also said that perhaps they could find another suitable location in the area if the BASF plants did not pollute.[30] Fred Hack said further that the state had sold the Victoria Bluffs site to BASF much too cheaply ($200 per acre). He charged that the company had to pay about $4,000 an acre for the rest of the land at Victoria Bluffs. Hack argued that if BASF had paid $4,000 per acre for the whole package, the state treasury would have been $4.5

[26] Jay A. Gross, "South Carolina Pollution Controversy Called Possible 'Test Case,'" *The State*, March 1, 1970.

[27] "Chemical Workers Top Wage Earners in North Carolina," *Charlotte News*, March 10, 1970.

[28] "Groves: Anti-BASF Forces Ignore Congaree Pollution," *Beaufort Gazette*, March 12, 1970.

[29] "BASF Delays Building of Plant at Beaufort" and "Hickel Statement Blasted," *The State*, April 8, 1970.

[30] "Developers' Plans Depend on BASF," *The State*, April 2, 1970, and "Hilton Head Island Region Could be Model for World," *The State*, April 3, 1970.

million richer.[31] However, his estimate of the total purchase price—approximately $250,000—disagreed with the $980,000 purchase price publicly announced by the state of South Carolina and BASF the previous November.

Proponents of the proposed project were also busy during April. State Senator James M. Waddell. Jr., urged conservationists to be equally concerned about poverty, and the NAACP called for more opportunities for Negroes in nontraditional fields:

> *Isaiah Williams [Field Secretary for the state conference of NAACP branches] said further recreational development of Beaufort County would result in the employment of poor people in traditional jobs as maids, janitors and servants for the wealthy with no hope of upgrading themselves in the future.*[32]

James A. Moore, Chairman of the Committee for the Advancement of Poor People, pointed out that there would be relatively few employment opportunities under present conditions for about 200 youths, black and white, graduating from high school in Hampton County who were not going on to college.[33] Governor McNair, in noting substantial poverty problems on a state-wide level, said that more than 200,000 families in South Carolina had incomes of less than $3,000 per year.[34]

In early May a controversy arose over the legality of funds ($8,500) donated by Beaufort County to the Beaufort Chamber of Commerce, when it became known that the chamber had used part of these funds in its campaign against the proposed BASF plants. The county government was a proponent of the project.

At this time the State Development Board, in conjunction with a consulting firm, issued a new economic profile of Beaufort County. The analysis indicated that the Beaufort area would probably suffer economically if the BASF plant did not locate there. According to these statistics, by 1980 there would be 36,000 jobs in Beaufort without the new plant, while there would be 58,000 jobs with it. Fred Hack argued that these statistics were inaccurate. The Hilton Head Island developers engaged the consulting firm of Skidmore, Owings, and Merrill to draw up a master plan for Beaufort and Jasper Counties. One proposal of the study was a series of agricultural cooperatives in both counties. Skidmore's report also recommended the establishment of more recreation industry and "compatible" light industry, such as a building components plant. The firm estimated that if a mere 130 conventions were held yearly, roughly 20,000 jobs could be created.[35]

However, according to some experts, even "compatible" light industry could be difficult to lure into the area.

> *. . . The image of south Carolina in industrial circles was not enhanced by the long bitter fight by those who felt BASF's pollution potential would ruin one of the few unspoiled marine estuarial areas left in the United States. State officials . . . say that industrial development in the Coastal Plains amounting to many, many millions during the next five years will be lost. A number of firms not wanting to get caught in the crossfire that hit BASF, are said to be shying away from the coastal region [of South Carolina].*[36]

Another aspect in the controversy surfaced in July 1970 when Paul J. Holmes, operator of a Beaufort County landscaping service, filed a class-action suit against State Development Board members in the Courts of Common Pleas in the counties where the board members lived. The suit asked that the State Development Board be prohibited from

[31]"Opponents Say BASF Benefits Gotten at Taxpayers' Expense," *The State*, April 3, 1970.
[32]"NAACP Backs BASF; Reports Jobs Needed," *The State*, April 22, 1970.
[33]"Rally Set to Support BASF Plant," *The State*, May 22, 1970.
[34]"McNair Hits Opposition to BASF," *The State*, April 25, 1970.
[35]John David Spade, "Beaufort-Jasper Co-ops Proposed," *The State*, Aug. 25, 1970.
[36]"Alternative to BASF: Natural Development," *The State*, Sept. 3, 1970.

issuing news releases supporting the proposed BASF plant. Holmes charged that using state funds to support BASF constituted a violation of the state constitution, since the legislature had not appropriated funds for that purpose. Holmes argued further that the board was going beyond "the limit of its authority and violating the very spirit and purpose for which it was created." The board countered by claiming that Holmes' charges were not within any court's jurisdiction. A spokesman for the board stated, "The issues raised by the complainant are of a purely political nature which should be resolved by the legislature and over which the court has no jurisdiction.[37]

In late November 1970 speculation arose, after the removal of Walter Hickel as Secretary of the Interior, that the U.S. Department of the Interior might change its stand against BASF. However, no formal change in policy was announced. Further, no BASF spokesmen made any significant comments concerning possible attempts to begin plant construction.

In January 1971 BASF announced that it would not locate at Victoria Bluffs. The primary reason cited was the decline in the demand for chemicals as a result of the recession. Others felt, however, that BASF's increased financial problems, the expansion room at their recently acquired facilities at Wyandotte, Michigan, and the degree of opposition offered by conservationists and resort developers also affected this decision.

In late January the state of South Carolina was notified that a major oil company had decided to build a half-billion dollar oil refinery at Wilmington, North Carolina, instead of Charleston, South Carolina, and that the Hilton Head developers would not build the major amusement park-resort area they had proposed if BASF did not locate at Victoria Bluffs. The reason for this latter change in plans was that the developers believed the noise from such facilities would disturb guests and residents of Hilton Head Island. This announcement, however, occasioned some strong comments. Charles W. Jones, Jr., of Estill, South Carolina, in a letter to the editor of *The Columbia State* argued:

> *This* [*the decision not to build the amusement park*] *was exactly what I expected. Pollution was only an excuse so they could pay lower wages for their workers in order to survive.*
>
> *May God help our country when a few men of wealth can determine the fate and well-being of people whose only desire is to work and earn an honest living.*
>
> *I hope these men will think of the cold and hungry people who are in that condition because of their selfishness.*[38]

In the meantime, it is not at all certain that the Hilton Head developers have won their battle. J. Bonner Manly, the recently appointed Director of the State Development Board, indicated that the state badly needs an oil refinery and other petrochemical facilities if the state is to break its bonds of poverty. He stated that the primary sites for such developments were at Charleston and Victoria Bluffs. He noted that there was ample technology to prevent pollution, but argued, "Even if it were not we would have to take cognizance of the fact that men remain morally more important than birds, animals, and fishes."[39] Two weeks after this statement was made Orion Hack received an award for being South Carolina Conservationist of the Year.

[37] Ginny Carroll, "Development Board Denies Politics Charge over BASF," *The State*, Aug. 7, 1970.
[38] Letter to the Editor, *The State*, Feb. 1, 1971.
[39] Edward D. Harrill, "Petrochemical Industry Seen as Answer to Poverty," *The State*, Feb. 6, 1971.

III

PROCESS

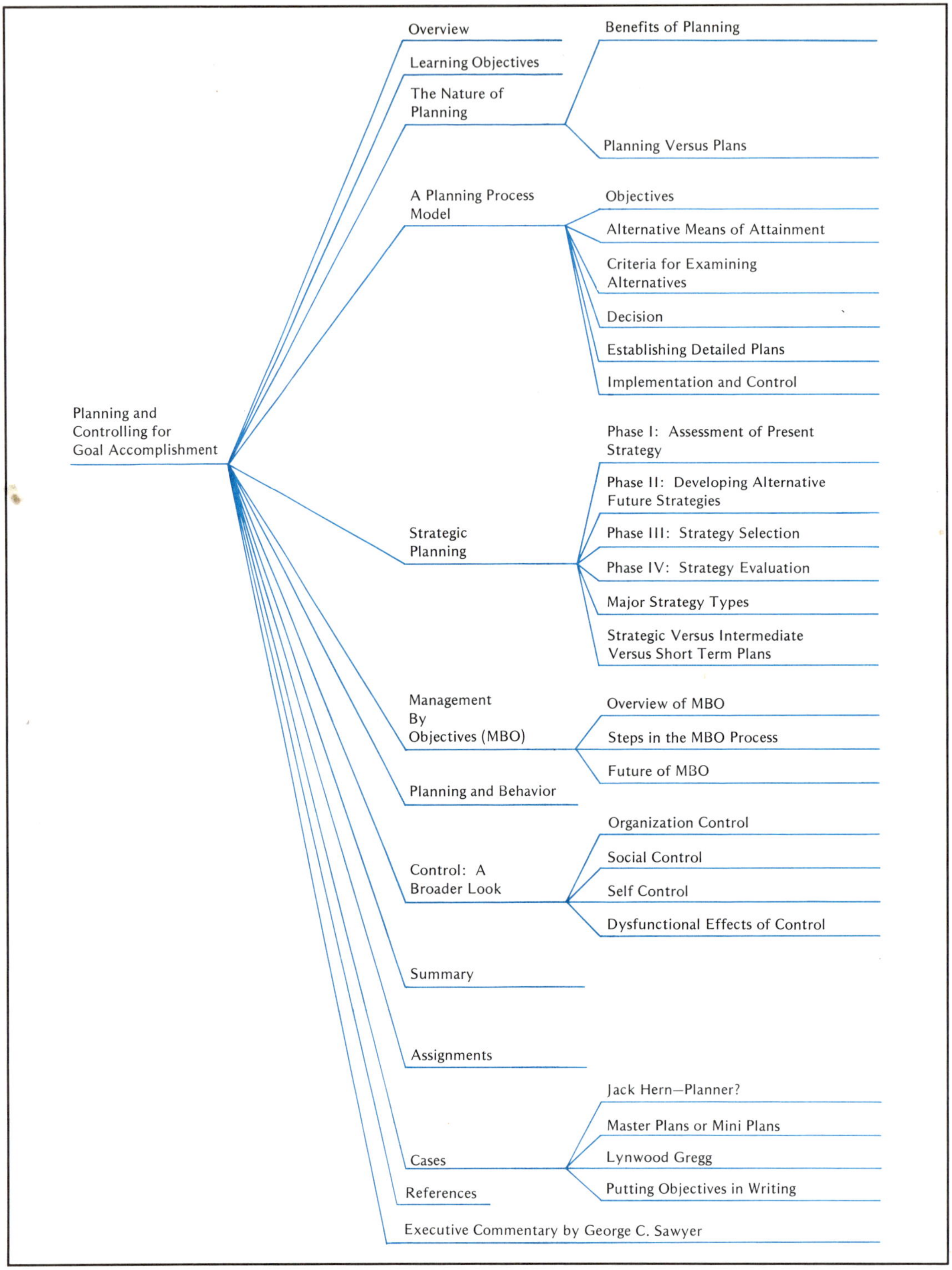
Planning and Controlling for Goal Accomplishment
Overview
Learning Objectives
The Nature of Planning
Benefits of Planning
Planning Versus Plans
A Planning Process Model
Objectives
Alternative Means of Attainment
Criteria for Examining Alternatives
Decision
Establishing Detailed Plans
Implementation and Control
Strategic Planning
Phase I: Assessment of Present Strategy
Phase II: Developing Alternative Future Strategies
Phase III: Strategy Selection
Phase IV: Strategy Evaluation
Major Strategy Types
Strategic Versus Intermediate Versus Short Term Plans
Management By Objectives (MBO)
Overview of MBO
Steps in the MBO Process
Future of MBO
Planning and Behavior
Control: A Broader Look
Organization Control
Social Control
Self Control
Dysfunctional Effects of Control
Summary
Assignments
Cases
Jack Hern—Planner?
Master Plans or Mini Plans
Lynwood Gregg
Putting Objectives in Writing
References
Executive Commentary by George C. Sawyer

5

PLANNING AND CONTROLLING FOR GOAL ACCOMPLISHMENT

OVERVIEW

There is abundant evidence that planning is the most prominent and pervasive of the management functions or processes. Planning is prominent because of the evidence of failure in organizations traceable to poor planning or preparation for the future on management's part. Planning is pervasive in that it cuts through all management functions and is a function that is applicable to all managerial levels. It cuts through the other management functions of organizing, controlling, staffing, directing, and decision making in the sense that it is a vital and necessary component of each of these processes. That is, managers must *plan for* each of the other functions. Planning is applicable to every managerial level because managerial action and decision making, whether at the chief executive's level or at the first-line supervisor's level, should ideally be predicated upon preliminary thought and anticipation of future issues, problems, or details that invariably come into play in the process of making organizations work.

In this chapter we deal with a large number of these and other planning issues. First, we discuss the *nature of planning* and some of the preliminary thoughts that provide the rationality and basis for planning efforts by management. Second, we present a *planning process model* in detail. This is done to conceptualize and discuss the elements or steps that go into the typical planning cycle. In both the first part and second, we make reference to how the *controlling* function is but the other side of planning and, hence, is inextricably linked to it. Third, we provide an overview of *strategic planning*, a special kind of external organizational planning. Strategic planning is external in the sense that it pertains primarily to the future relationship between the organization and its environment. Fourth, we examine *Management By Objectives* (*MBO*), an internally oriented planning approach that has been called by some the most complete management system of the last quarter of a century. Fifth, we consider the relationship between *planning and behavior* in an effort to learn more about the behavioral consequences of planning. And, last, we close out the chapter with a closer examination of the *control function* and its nature and characteristics. Although a coverage of these topics will not make one an expert on planning and control, it will lay a solid foundation for future thought and action in these areas.

LEARNING OBJECTIVES

This chapter is especially intended to help the student:

1. **Gain an appreciation of the planning and controlling functions.**
2. **Understand the nature of planning and the steps involved in the planning process.**
3. **Grasp the essentials of strategic planning and MBO.**
4. **Understand the relationship between planning and its behavioral consequences.**
5. **See how the control function operates within organizations.**
6. **Learn, especially in the context of thinking about management, the meaning of the following concepts:**

planning	**Management By Objectives (MBO)**
planning process	**organizational control**
objectives/goals	**social-control**
control	**self control**
strategic planning	

THE NATURE OF PLANNING

Before planning is anything else, it is a *mental process*. It is a process of thinking through all facets of an issue or a problem before taking action. At the same time, it provides the ingredients for action.

Planning is a process that entails an assessment of the organization, its resources, and its environment, and encompasses the setting of objectives, using that assessment as a backdrop. Planning entails looking at the past, the present, and the future. So often we stress the futurity of planning to such an extent that we fail to make it clear that the past and the present are our points of departure. Using the past and the present as points of reference, in planning we consider both what we *anticipate* the future will be like, and what we *desire* it to be like.

We give consideration to anticipating what the future *will* be like in the *forecasting* process. Forecasting is the part of planning that embodies our estimates, projections, or speculations about what future conditions will be. These future conditions include the *economic,* the *social,* the *political,* and the *technological* environments in which we expect our organizations to reside next month, next year, and many years from now.

We give consideration to what we *desire* the future to be like in our view that by planning we may be able to in some way *shape* the future or to "make a future happen" by our active intervention now. This process is known as *proactive* planning. Proactive planning, in contrast to reactive planning, takes the initiative by attempting to shape a more desirable environment or future than one that might result if left to the vagaries of societal forces.

Perhaps an example of proactive planning would be useful. One of the problems every industry faces today is that of government regulation. Governmental regulation has reached an unprecedented high level in our society and is increasingly placing restrictions on what managers and organizations can and cannot do. In the face of this problem, most business firms in society have done very little outside of the usual lobbying efforts that typify large companies today. One exception is a food processor and canner, the DelMonte Company. DelMonte anticipated that it was just a matter of time before the government intervened to require nutritional labeling of its canned goods. Sensitive to the changing social environment, DelMonte took the initiative—proacted—by coming out years ahead of governmental requirements with nutritional labeling on its products. Thusly, this large company helped "shape" its future by having a significant input into the style, mode, and pattern of nutritional labeling that would have been impossible if it had reacted after the government had acted.

Implicit in the concept of proaction is the belief that *planning is a philosophy,* a way of thinking about managing. Indeed, planning is a philosophy of managing, only then becoming a set of steps to follow or techniques to use. One must fully internalize the spirit of planning before great success can be anticipated from the process of planning.

To fully appreciate the spirit of planning as a philosophy or intellectual activity, it is useful to summarize some of the reasons for planning—some of the reasons that planning is helpful to managers and to organizations. The main reason justifying planning is that research and experience have shown that organizations that do plan, and plan well, are more effective, efficient, and profitable.[1]

Beyond this already sufficient justification for planning, managers plan because of the *uncertainty* of the future. It has been said that uncertainty is the focal point of the "paradox of planning." This paradox holds that uncertainty is both why managers plan, and why they do not plan. Managers plan because the future is uncertain and to deal with uncertainty one must prepare for it in advance.

[1]Robert G. Murdick, "Nature of Planning and Plans," *Advanced Management Journal,* October 1965, pp. 36–46.

Managers do not plan—or are reluctant to plan—also because of uncertainty. That is, they find it *difficult* to plan because of the uncertainty inherent in the future. Hence, the "paradox" of planning.

Benefits of Planning

Although managers find it difficult to plan because of uncertainty and the complexity of the planning process, there are also other justifications for effective planning.

Among the numerous *benefits of planning* are the following:

1. Planning allows managers to identify early problems, threats, or opportunities that may exist in the environment.
2. Planning improves decision making by surfacing all the elements, factors, or forces that may bear on a decision situation.
3. Planning injects rationality, analysis, system, and logic into organizational activities and processes.
4. Planning provides for more optimal acquisition, maintenance, utilization, and replacement of physical and human resources.
5. Planning enhances the behavioral climate in the organization by assuring that job assignments, authority, organization, reward systems, and interpersonal relationships are clearly thought about, designed, and maintained.
6. Planning provides a focus on objectives or clearly specified goals, which should channel behaviors and decisions in directions that are agreed upon and communicated in advance.

Planning, then, is something managers do in advance of taking action. It is a process of deciding what the future will be like, what we would desire the future to be like, what our objectives are in light of those assessments, what our action plans are to achieve those objectives, and what follow-up or control we will exercise to ensure that our objectives are met.

Planning Versus Plans

It is helpful to distinguish between *planning* and *plans* so as to more fully explain the nature of planning. We have defined planning as a process. Elaborating upon this, planning is a *continuous* process, a never-ending process. Thus, we never reach a point at which we can say that planning is over.

Often, managers are tempted to say that their planning is over when a plan has been generated. This is tempting because a plan frequently is written into a document that sketches out the essentials of management's desires. In reality, however, a plan is never final. Plans have to be so developed and articulated that they are adaptable and flexible should future conditions change. As a consequence, a plan is not the final product of the planning process but is, as Ackoff has asserted, an *interim report.*[2]

Viewed in this light, a plan is but one tentative step in the planning process. The end result of a planning effort would be the *results* planning was designed to achieve. Even then, these results are but an interim step in achieving the long-range objectives of the organization, and thus, results achieved after some short time period of, say, one year are but "early returns" on management's progress towards its long-range objectives.

Ways of Conceptualizing Planning

Planning can be conceptualized in many different ways. Some choose to talk about planning in terms of the related functional areas. For example, financial planning, marketing planning, product planning, and manpower planning illustrate this approach. Others view planning in concepts of long-term versus short-term planning, or strategic versus tactical planning. There are numerous ways of conceptualizing planning.

After presenting the planning process in more detail, we will look at two major types of planning that will characterize well the successful areas of management's planning efforts in recent years. First, we will consider *strategic planning,* a long-range type of planning for the overall organization that forms the basis for more short-run oriented planning efforts. Second, we will examine Management By Objectives (MBO), an internal management planning approach that has been used with mixed success by organizations today. We shall examine first, however, a general model of the planning process and discuss its various parts.

A PLANNING PROCESS MODEL

We can better understand all types of planning if we consider first a general planning process model. This model will illustrate the important steps inherent in the planning process and will give us an opportunity to discuss some key concepts that are essential to effective planning. Although the model will highlight some of the common elements of all planning processes, when we examine strategic planning and MBO, we will see both similarities and differences. It is hoped, by taking such an approach, that the various dimensions and characteristics of the managerial planning process can be more fully understood. Within the context of

[2]Russell L. Ackoff, *A Concept of Corporate Planning* (New York: Wiley-Interscience, 1970), p. 5.

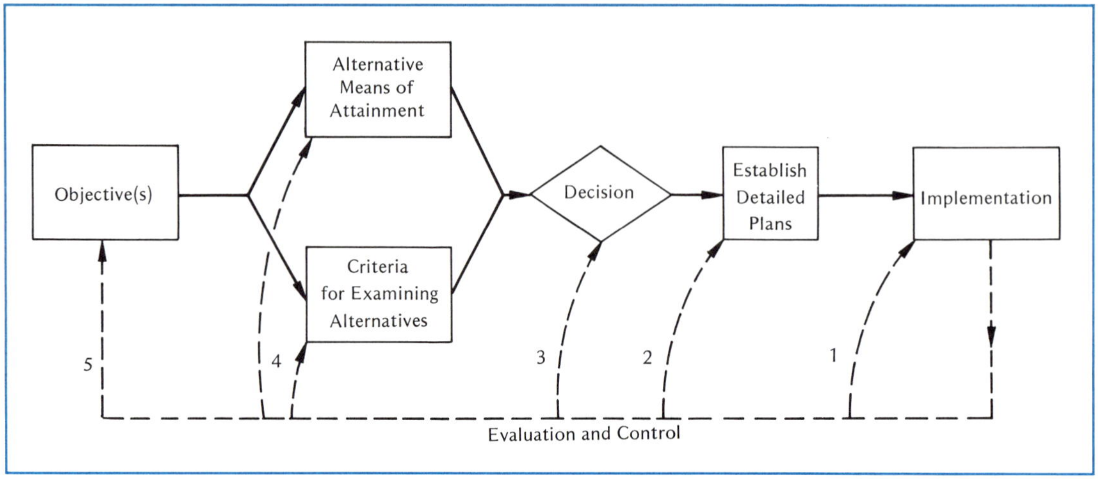

FIGURE 5-1. The Planning Process Model.

the model presented, we will illustrate with an example. The planning process model is shown in Figure 5-1.

Objectives

It is frequently said that objectives are the starting point of all planning. *Objectives* are defined as *ends sought.* Some choose to differentiate between objectives and goals, but the two terms will be used interchangeably here for a specific reason. Sometimes, objectives and goals are used in an opposite manner, by both academicians and management practitioners. Some refer to objectives as those *long-range* ends sought, whereas goals are *shorter-term* ends sought that it is hoped will lead to long-range ends. Others use the terms in just the opposite way. What is important is that one realizes that objectives (or goals) are ends sought (something management is attempting to achieve), and they may be conceptualized according to a number of different levels.

Objectives are said to exist according to a number of different levels to suggest

FIGURE 5-2. Broad Versus Specific Objectives.

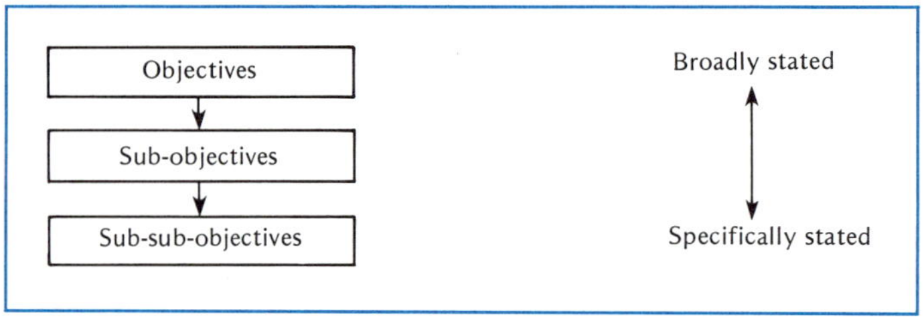

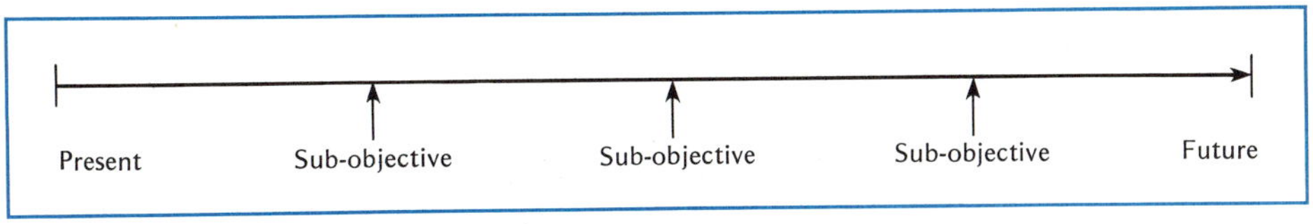

FIGURE 5-3. **Objectives Viewed According to Time.**

that some distinction exists in terms of (1) how *broadly* or *specifically* the objective is stated; (2) the *time frame* over which the objective is being viewed; and (3) how *important* the objective is to the organization.

Figure 5-2 depicts how the objectives can be portrayed, from broad to specific. Figure 5-3 illustrates objectives viewed according to time frame. And, Figure 5-4 depicts objectives viewed according to importance.

Although it is suggested that objectives are the starting point of all planning, in reality, considerable thought should also go into the statement of objectives. This means that planning effort must precede the statement of objectives so that the appropriate objectives are, in fact, set. Viewed in this light, objectives are both the *end result* of significant planning thinking and the *point of departure* toward what the objectives were set to attain. Let us illustrate with an example.

Assume an organization has set an objective to increase sales by 16% for next year. Where did the figure 16% come from? It is to be hoped that it was not just pulled out of the air. If the objective was carefully set, it should have been based upon rational factors. Such factors as past experience, what the competition is doing, the capabilities of those assigned the objective, market conditions, and forecasted prospects are illustrative of the kinds of rational influences that may have helped establish the objective at 16%. Careful research and analysis must go into the setting of objectives; therefore, although we speak of objectives as the beginning of the planning process, we see that, in fact, objectives are in themselves one result of prior planning efforts. This notion that we must plan for objectives, or stated more broadly, plan for planning, is an important consideration in the establishment of an effective planning approach.

There are available a number of guidelines concerning how objectives ought to be set and articulated; however, we will examine these suggestions in our section on MBO.

FIGURE 5-4. **Objectives Viewed According to Importance.**

Plan for Planning

Many attempts at corporate planning have failed because the planners have not planned their own activity. They have attempted to develop a corporate plan on an *ad hoc* basis without thinking through in advance what management wanted to achieve, the work involved, who should participate, and the time required. It is analogous to constructing a building without a blueprint. An essential starting point is a plan for planning that should cover these steps:

1. Assess the present status of planning. How much planning is already being done, and how well? How much reliable information is already available as a basis for sound planning? What are management's attitudes towards planning?
2. Determine how much planning is needed. How serious are the threats facing the company, and how well prepared is it to meet them? What is the magnitude of the opportunities available? How much change appears imminent?
3. Set objectives for the first planning cycle. Because planning is hard work and can require much time, to ensure continuing commitment it is important to balance expectations against the effort required. What is planning expected to achieve by way of tangible or intangible benefits over the next year? What are the key issues to be resolved and decisions that must be made?
4. Develop the organization for planning. It is necessary to establish at the outset the functions of the president, the planning committee, and the planning officer in the planning process. This should include consideration of the responsibility and relationship of line managers and committees in the planning process and in reaching decisions.
5. Design the planning system. This should cover matters such as the scope of strategic and operational planning and their interrelationships with short-term plans and budgets; the flow of information needed to formulate plans; the time span of long-range plans; the annual planning cycle and calendar of events; and the contents of planning documents.
6. Prepare a work program and timetable for the first long-range planning cycle. This should set out the steps of each phase to launch the program, complete business assessment studies, prepare strategic plans, and develop long range operational plans for each major function.

Source: Patrick Irwin, "Romulus and Remus: Two Studies in Corporate Planning," *Management Review*, October 1976, p. 28.

Alternative Means of Attainment

After objectives have been set, two simultaneous steps in the planning process model occur: generating alternative means of attaining the objectives, and establishing criteria for examining these alternatives (see Figure 5-1). Alternative means of attaining objectives refers to possible ways by which the objectives may be accomplished. It is important in effective planning to brainstorm a wide range of possible means of attainment so that the planner can feel secure that all reasonable alternatives have been considered. Possible alternative means in our example of increasing sales 16% over the next time period might include the following:

1. Direct mail promotion.
2. Television promotion.
3. Magazine promotion.
4. Use different packaging of product.
5. Hiring new sales people.
6. Hiring a new sales manager.

Other alternatives may be identified, but let us use these. The question now is how shall we decide which one or several of these alternative means to employ. What is needed to make this decision is a set of criteria that establish the available resources and important parameters of our decision situation.

Criteria for Examining Alternatives

Criteria should be established along with the generation of alternatives. Basically, the criteria help in the decision process by determining what values, resources, and parameters with which there are to work. Usually these criteria are stated in quantitative form, although this is not always either possible or desirable.

In our preceding example, the criteria for choice making may fall into three categories: time, cost, and qualitative considerations. The *time* criterion in this case is established at one year. Because there is such a short time period in which to achieve the 16% increase, we may conclude that alternatives 4, 5, and 6 are not realistic. Each would require lead times that would prohibit achieving our objective in 12 months. The *cost* criterion in this case may be $500,000. Television promotion could use up that amount of money in 10 minutes of advertising, so we may conclude that alternative must be ruled out also. Thus, we have only two alternatives left: direct mail promotion and magazine promotion. Our *qualitative* criterion in this example may be that we not only want a 16% sales increase but also want to make sure that we have a high probability of *repeat* sales from these efforts. Because recent research shows that the continuous exposure to magazine promotion has a more lasting effect than does direct mail advertising, we now narrow our decision down even further by eliminating direct mail as an option. Thus, by comparing our alternative means of attainment with our pertinent criteria, we arrive at a decision to promote the product by means of magazines.

Decision

The foregoing is admittedly a simplistic example. However, it illustrates the mental process that must be undertaken to arrive at a decision—or alternative means—to accomplish an objective. In practice, the comparison of alternatives with pertinent criteria may not be as straightforward as is portrayed here. For example, it is not uncommon today for a manager to have profitability, environmental protection, and energy conservation as relevant criteria in a decision situation. Nevertheless, at this point in the planning process model, we see that planning and decision making are closely related, and also understand how to determine the means for attaining the objective.

Establishing Detailed Plans

A plan is a blueprint for action. Just as a builder needs a detailed blueprint to begin construction, a manager must similarly have a detailed plan of action. This detailed plan will take the course of action chosen—in our example, magazine promotion—and spell out the detailed steps required to carry this option forward. Once a general course of action has been decided upon, there are numerous details—assignments of responsibility, operating budgets, resource plans, timing—that must be stipulated. These detailed plans then form the basis for implementation and control.

Implementation and Control

Some may question whether actual implementation should be included as a part of the planning process, but we want to carry our example through to show how planning affects and is involved with later steps in the process. Significant parts of implementation are *evaluation* and *control.* Evaluation and control are interlinked. These processes refer to the examination of implementation efforts to see that plans are being effectively accomplished.

The *control process* requires three essential elements:

1. The creation of a *standard* against which to measure actual performance (in this case, the standard is the 16% objective).
2. The *comparison* of the standard with actual performance (implicit here, of course, is that performance has been measured).
3. The taking of *appropriate action* (to bring the actual back into line with the standard, if a discrepancy is noted).

To clarify how this control process works, let us assume that one of the specifics worked out in the detailed plans that were established prior to implementation was a more specific time-related statement of the objective. Assume that management concluded from the best knowledge available that the 16% sales increase should occur evenly over the entire year. Thus, the more specific time-related objective appears on page 159.

Obviously, sales would typically not increase according to this constant pattern, but let us assume for purposes of illustration that it is planned to do so. Thus, the objective at the end of three months is a 4% increase in sales. Let us also assume

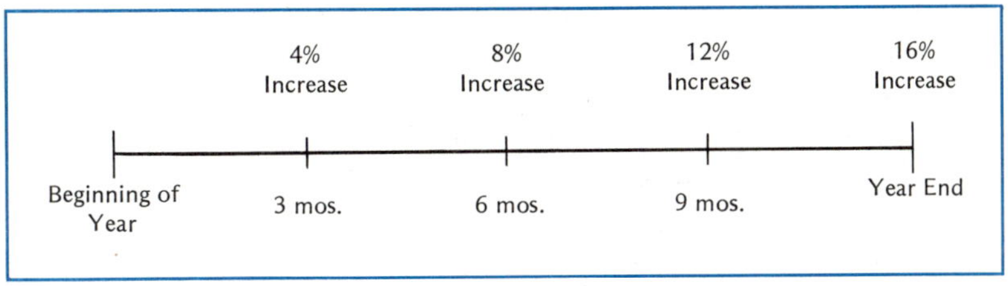

that at the end of this period actual sales have only increased $1\frac{1}{2}\%$. According to the control process outlined, a discrepancy has been noted (the system is out of control), and there is a need for appropriate and, in this case, corrective action.

The question now is what to do in the process of taking corrective action. Do we go back to the original objective and question its validity? Do we go back to the decision criteria and question them? Do we go back to implementation and question whether proper implementation has taken place? The proper procedure is to work back through the model, examining steps in the process in the reverse order in which they occurred. Thus, we would carefully scrutinize first our method of implementation to see if we had made any errors there (see *1* in the model). If so, correct the errors. If not, we must go to the next previous step—the detailed plan (see *2* in the model). In a sequential fashion, then, we would continue working our way back through the model (see numbered feedback loops in the model), attempting to find the error (or perhaps wrong decision) that resulted in our being out of control, or not meeting our objective. The final step we would take in this process is to go back and change (lower) our original objective. We must carefully set that objective initially, and then attempt as best we can to achieve it. By changing the objective, we could immediately bring the entire system back into control; unfortunately, that would be similar to the cartoon situation in which the archer shot his arrows and then had a bulls-eye painted wherever one hit.

We thus see from the planning process model presented how planning entails a sequence of activities including building into the model or process a means of control. If planning is a continuous process, as earlier suggested, it makes sense that this control opportunity is available. We can also see how planning and control must be interrelated and inseparable. Because planning for goal *accomplishment* is our orientation, the control mechanism assumes an essential role. We will discuss control further at a later point; however, presenting it within the context of the planning model vividly illustrates its interrelationship to planning.

STRATEGIC PLANNING

As stated earlier, planning can be viewed according to different dimensions. Although the terms used by experts vary somewhat for different types of planning, two dimensions of planning stand out as primary sources of distinction. These two dimensions are:

1. The *time span* over which planning is done.
2. The *comprehensiveness* of the planning effort.

Time span refers to whether planning is long range, intermediate range, or short range. There is no completely agreed upon view as to how many years are encompassed by each of these types; however, estimates of five years or more for long-range, three to five years for intermediate, and less than three years for short-range planning are reasonable approximations for most companies.

The *comprehensiveness* of the planning effort refers to how encompassing the effort is. Stated differently, it refers to *how much* of the organization is being planned for. Although other dimensions could be considered, these two major characteristics account for the most significant variations in planning efforts.[3]

Both of these dimensions of planning are depicted in the model in Figure 5-5 where strategic planning is displayed in relation to shorter-term planning. It can be seen there that strategic planning is the longest-term planning in which an organization engages and that intermediate and short-term plans are derived from the organization's overall long-term objectives, strategy, or mission.

Strategic planning can best be viewed as that type of planning that results in an organizational *strategy.* The literal meaning of the word *strategy* is "the art of the general," deriving from the ancient Greek word for general, *strategos.*[4] The precise usage of the word dates from at least 400 B.C. but did not appear in writings until the late 1700s. Before Napoleon's time, the word had a military connotation that implied the "art and science of directing military forces to defeat an enemy or to mitigate the results of defeat."[5]

To modern business people, the term *strategy* has come to mean the type of top-level planning decision that stipulates the long-term relationship between the organization and its environment. Strategic planning thus provides answers to the following kinds of questions: (1) In what specific business should a firm be (in terms of the mix of products, services, and customers)? (2) What major market opportunities are most compatible with top management's definition of goals, objectives, or missions? (3) What course of action should the organization pursue (emphasis, timing, priorities)? (4) What is the optimal organizational-environment fit?[6]

The emphasis of strategic planning on such issues illustrates the qualitative

[3]Other dimensions upon which planning could be examined include complex versus simple, major versus minor importance, qualitative versus quantitative, confidential versus public, written versus unwritten, flexible versus inflexible, and so on. For a discussion of these, see George A. Steiner, *Top Management Planning* (London: Collier Macmillan 1969), pp. 19–21.

[4]Steiner, ibid., p. 237.

[5]Ibid., p. 237.

[6]Robert L. Katz, *Cases and Concepts in Corporate Strategy* (Englewood Cliffs, N.J.: Prentice-Hall, 1970), p. 3.

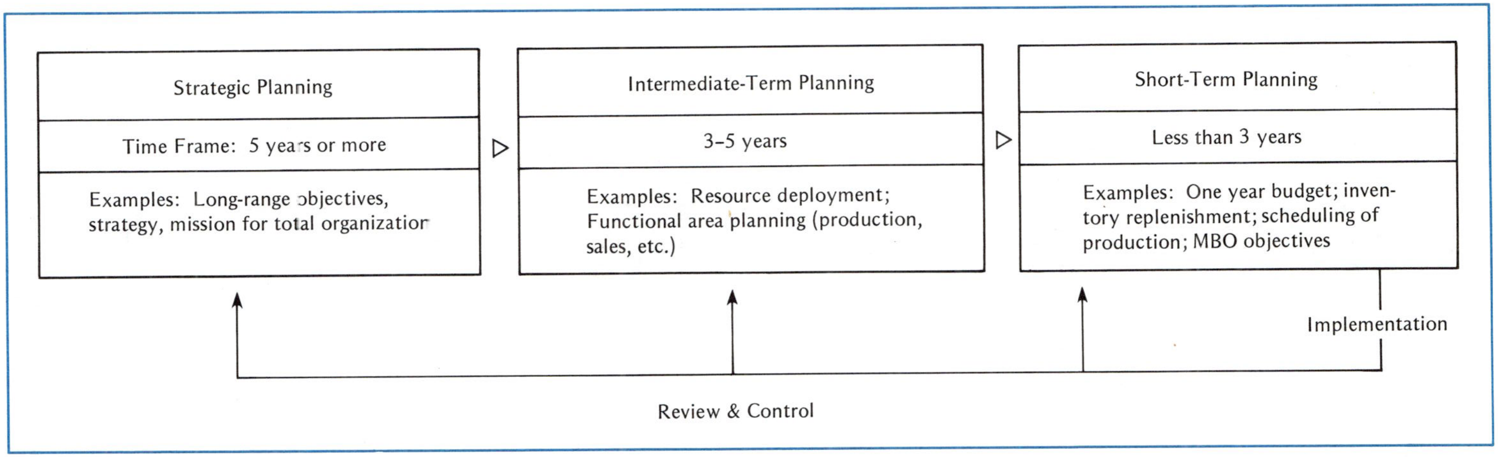

FIGURE 5-5. Strategic, Intermediate, and Short-Term Planning.

difference between strategic planning and long-range planning. Although strategic planning is long-range planning, all long-range planning is not strategic planning. Some long-range planning as done by practicing managers and companies simply projects the future situation to many years into the future without asking the kinds of questions posed here. Real strategic planning entails a continuing assessment of the organization's product/market/service mix, with an eye toward changing the mix should it be necessary.

Because the purpose of strategic planning is to evolve a strategy, it is worthwhile examining a decision process by which an organization's strategy is developed. The major phases in strategy development are (1) assessment of present strategy; (2) development of alternative future strategies; (3) strategy selection; and (4) strategy evaluation. Figure 5-6 presents a schematic representation of these four phases and their interrelationships.[7]

Each major phase in the process deserves a closer examination.

FIGURE 5-6. A Model of Strategy Formulation.

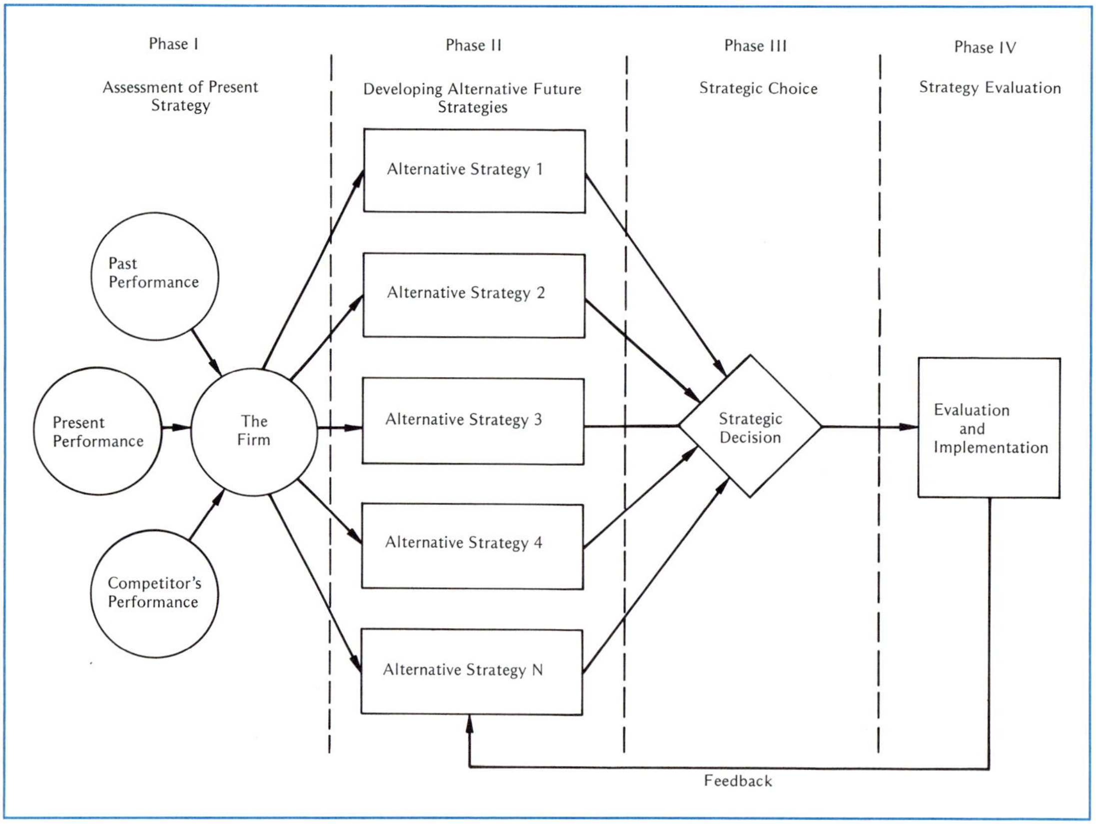

[7]Archie B. Carroll, "Strategic Planning for Boundary Spanning Relations," *Managerial Planning* (January/February 1976), pp. 1–5; 9.

Phase I: Assessment of Present Strategy

The first step in planning or designing an organization's strategy is to rigorously assess past practices and performance. Before a plan for the future can be knowledgeably constructed, it is imperative that the past strategic posture be closely examined. Strategic posture refers to a firm's past decision choices in the strategic decision category. Basically, this entails a process of identifying, describing, rationalizing, and assessing past strategic behavior.

Before an assessment can be made, however, critical strategic success areas must be stipulated. These success areas may vary in relative importance, influence, and sensitivity—depending on the firm and the industry—but will usually encompass such critical areas as product policy, pricing policy, distribution policy, promotion policy, financing policy, and customer policy. With respect to these critical success areas, each must be examined from a number of points of view. These include (1) from the point of view of the organization's behavior vis-a-vis its stated and explicit goals; (2) from the perspective of the organization's past performance or track record; and (3) from a contrast with a competitor's actual behavior and results.

(1) *Past Performance Versus Stated Goals.* The beginning point in a strategy assessment is to examine the organization's strategic posture (what it is and what it has done in the past) relative to what its stated intentions were. Many organizations will have difficulty making this assessment because they have not stated their goals in terms that are tangible and measurable.

The first kind of analysis that should take place is one that evaluates the organization's accomplishments against its own stated targets. If, for example, management chose to keep the organization small so that close control could be maintained, management should not be judged poorly against the criteria of large size and rapid growth. Such an evaluation as this may be quite crude in precision, but it provides some basis against which to say something about the organization's success in the past. In this case, the organization may have made faulty strategic choices in its decision processes, but something favorable must be said for the firm that is able to keep on target—even if the target was not optimally defined or identified initially.

(2) *Present Performance Versus Past Performance.* There is a common managerial tendency to judge the present against the past. This is an additional dimension of an organization's self-evaluation and appraisal and should not be overlooked. Too often, however, organizations judge their present performance against the past and let it go at that. A company's historical record is important but it does not necessarily reflect what it is capable of achieving. Nevertheless, such an examination has merit and should entail a constant questioning of why performance resulted as it did.

(3) Firm's Performance Versus Competitor's Performance. In an effort to complete its self-assessment, the organization must examine closely the parallels between its own performance and competitor's performance in the same industry. It may be faring well against its own stated goals and its own past performance, but still not be performing the way industry averages indicate it should. Therefore, it becomes necessary to examine itself vis-a-vis its competitors and general industry performance standards. This will entail a penetrating analysis of the industry itself, including its past, present, and future trends.

Phase II: Developing Alternative Future Strategies

Against this three-dimensional analysis, the organization must then develop alternative future strategies. The primary purpose of the assessment of the present strategy was to determine its viability as an alternative future strategy. Assuming that the assessment indicates that the organization has achieved a measure of success that it deems appropriate, the continuation of the present strategy then becomes an extremely attractive option.

In developing strategic options or alternatives, the organization must systematically examine the opportunities that exist in the relationship between its resources and capabilities and market opportunities. Quite frequently, an analysis such as this is framed in a matrix similar to the one presented in Figure 5-7.

Utilizing the matrix as a model representing a systematic approach to examining alternatives, the organization can usually encompass most product/service/market strategies within the four basic options presented. In Alternative 1, a business firm chooses the strategy of penetrating present markets further with existing products. Thus, the thrust of the strategy would be to "do better what we are presently doing." In Alternative 2, market development, the firm chooses to seek new markets for present products. This particular strategy has been engaged in by numerous firms producing consumer products and has been a quite satisfactory option.

Alternative 3, product development, entails the modification of existing products for present markets. These modifications or alterations may be necessary for a number of reasons such as adding novelty to the product, responding to technological advances, or modernizing the product line. Alternative 4, diversification, is an option in which the firm chooses to develop or acquire new products/services for previously unexplored markets. Thus, in a systematic fashion, management can explore the possible matches between the organization's capabilities and market opportunities and develop strategic alternatives from which to choose.

Phase III: Strategy Selection

Strategy selection or strategic choice should naturally evolve out of Phase II, the examination of strategic alternatives. Unfortunately, there exists no formula

Markets / Products (Services)	Present	New
Present	(Alternative 1) Market Penetration	(Alternative 2) Market Development
New	(Alternative 3) Product Development	(Alternative 4) Diversification

FIGURE 5-7. Strategy Option Matrix for a Business Firm.

specifying how strategy selection should be made. Ideally, each organization should make an effort to identify the success parameters in its particular industry.

Generally, corporate organizations should possess a strategy that:

1. *Recognizes and understands how the forces of the past have affected the corporation.*
2. *Is responsive to the dynamic forces of change.*
3. *Is capable of implementing programs based upon the first two considerations.*[8]

If management can constructively integrate the wisdom gained from past experiences, a program can be developed for the future that encompasses the critical areas of product, pricing, distribution, promotion, financing, and customer policy. Additionally, the strategic choice should be one that is flexible enough to adapt to changing environmental circumstances with a minimum of organizational disruption.

Finally, strategy selection should be made with *implementation* considerations firmly in mind. Many managers on occasion have been heard to say, "We have a good plan; we just can't seem to implement it." A plan cannot be a good one if it cannot be put into action. Implementation, therefore, is the acid test of strategic planning efforts.

[8]Jack O. Vance, "The Anatomy of a Corporate Strategy," *California Management Review* (Fall, 1970), p. 6.

Phase IV: Strategy Evaluation

Although implementation and its consequences ultimately demonstrate a strategy's success or failure, an evaluative process is a necessary part of designing and assessing strategic planning efforts. By evaluating strategy on a continuing basis, the organization should be able to make adjustments that will continually improve the organization-environment "fit." In determining whether the strategy chosen by management is appropriate for the organization, six criteria are beneficial.[9] These criteria include:

1. Internal consistency of strategy.
2. Consistency of strategy with environment.
3. Strategy's appropriateness in light of available resources.
4. Satisfactory degree of risk.
5. Appropriateness of time horizon.
6. Workability of the strategy.

In a dynamic organization, internal consistency cannot be taken for granted. Internal consistency refers to the extent to which the strategy is congruent with the organization's other policies, modes of operating, goals, and characteristics. The strategy should be consistent with management's philosophy and should be fully integrated into other organizational systems. Consistency also pertains to the external environment. Consistency with the environment pertains to the extent to which the chosen strategy makes sense vis-a-vis what is really going on in the real world—demand conditions, the competitive environment, economic stability, forecasted markets, and so on.

It was earlier suggested that strategy involves a match between available corporate resources and market opportunities. Strategy must therefore be appropriate in light of available resources. This may seem an obvious statement. However, numerous organizations have experienced failure because they believed they could succeed but then could not when it was time. A careful assessment of financial, human, and managerial resources is thus a critical element in the evaluation process.

Each organization must decide in advance how much risk it wants to undertake. This is an especially sensitive decision variable because, to a great extent, it dictates the kinds of ventures that should be pursued. Closely related to the degree of risk is the time span considered in the strategy choice. The history of business is replete with illustrations of strategic choices that either succeeded or failed because of the appropriateness or inappropriateness of the time dimension. The length of time over which an organization is capable of committing itself to a venture, the risk level of the venture, and the inventory of financial resources at the organization's disposal are all intimately related in the strategy choice.

[9]Seymour Tilles, "How to Evaluate Corporate Strategy," *Harvard Business Review* (July–August, 1963), pp. 114–121.

Finally, is the planned strategy workable? Although this has already been stressed, it is important enough to merit additional comment. In the final analysis, some measure of workability of a particular strategy must be developed. Historical figures and industry comparisons are rudimentary approaches to determining a strategy's workability. Profits, growth, returns on investment, and market penetration are all approaches whereby a strategy's viability can be tested. The acid test of implementation and success therefore become the crucial criteria for strategy evaluation.

Major Strategy Types

Within the context of our four-phase model, there are a number of major types of strategies. The first strategy is that of new or changed products or services (as illustrated in Figure 5-7). The second strategy involves present or new markets. Third, there are marketing strategies—ways of getting products or services to the customers and getting them to buy. Fourth, there are growth strategies. These give direction to the organization, such as how much growth, how fast, and where. Fifth, there are financial strategies. How will operations be financed? Sixth, there are organizational strategies. Of interest here is the type of organizational arrangements to use. Issues include structure, centralization of authority, and so on. Seventh, there are personnel strategies. Included here is the complex of issues in the human resources management area. Eighth, there are public relations strategies.[10] Each represents major management decision areas within which we could apply our discussion of strategic planning.

Strategic Versus Intermediate Versus Short-Term Plans

Although we have emphasized the strategic planning part of the model in Figure 5-5, it must be kept in mind that eventually all strategic plans have to be translated into intermediate-term and short-term plans. As stated earlier, these shorter plans are *derived from* strategic plans. That is, they are the more detailed spelling out of the strategic plan. Intermediate-term and short-term plans are typically narrower in scope than strategic plans and, of course, pertain to a shorter-term time span. These shorter-term plans represent the real operational level at which the organization's work gets accomplished.

One of the prevalent ways in which longer-term and intermediate-term planning becomes operational for lower-level managers and workers is in the form of MBO systems of management within organizations. Consequently, it is well worth examining the nature of and characteristics of MBO to gain insights into how this more detailed approach to management relates to planning and controlling for goal accomplishment.

[10] Most of these strategy areas are identified in Harold Koontz, "Making Strategic Planning Work," *Business Horizons* (April 1976), pp. 39–40.

MANAGEMENT BY OBJECTIVES (MBO)

The topic of management by objectives (MBO) is sometimes covered in sections on motivation rather than planning. It fits appropriately in either place. It has only been in recent years that we have explicitly acknowledged the intricate linkage between planning and motivation. Since that linkage has been established, we feel comfortable discussing MBO within a planning and controlling context.[11]

Overview of MBO

Although planning and motivational reference points are most usually tied to MBO, it has long been held to be an *integrative* managerial tool. As early as the 1950s, Peter Drucker proposed the MBO philosophy as an approach to integrating various goals of organizational subunits to achieve overall organizational goals.[12] MBO was developed more fully in the 1950s as an approach to more objective performance appraisal. In the 1960s and early 1970s, MBO has been emphasized as an approach to increasing employee motivation.

Specifically, MBO is a way of achieving integration between an organization's objectives and the individual's objectives by involving individual employees (usually managers) in the setting of their own work objectives. MBO is a way of managing that requires individuals throughout the organizational hierarchy to convert broader organizational objectives into more specific and personalized individual objectives.

The typical MBO process works as follows. Top management establishes the overall corporate-level objectives of the organization, much in line with the strategic planning approach presented earlier. Each successive lower level of managers then develops objectives from the higher-level objectives. Figure 5-8 is helpful in illustrating this process.

Referring to Figure 5-8, once manager A understands the overall corporate-level objectives, he sits down with managers B, C, and D to assist them in the development of their objectives.Then, each of them works with their subordinates in objective-setting sessions. You see in the figure where manager A held a session with his subordinate B to help develop B's objectives, B then held sessions with subordinates E, F, and G, and each of them held sessions with their subordinates to help them derive their (H, I, and J's) objectives.

In succession, then, starting at the top of the organization, the managers at the various lower levels were able to hold mutual goal-setting sessions with their superiors, resulting, eventually, in all managers having personalized objectives. In

[11]For a detailed discussion of this relationship, see David R. Hampton, "The Planning-Motivation Dilemma," *Business Horizons* (June 1973), pp. 79–87.

[12]Peter F. Drucker, *The Practice of Management* (New York: Harper & Row, 1954), Chapters 11 and 12.

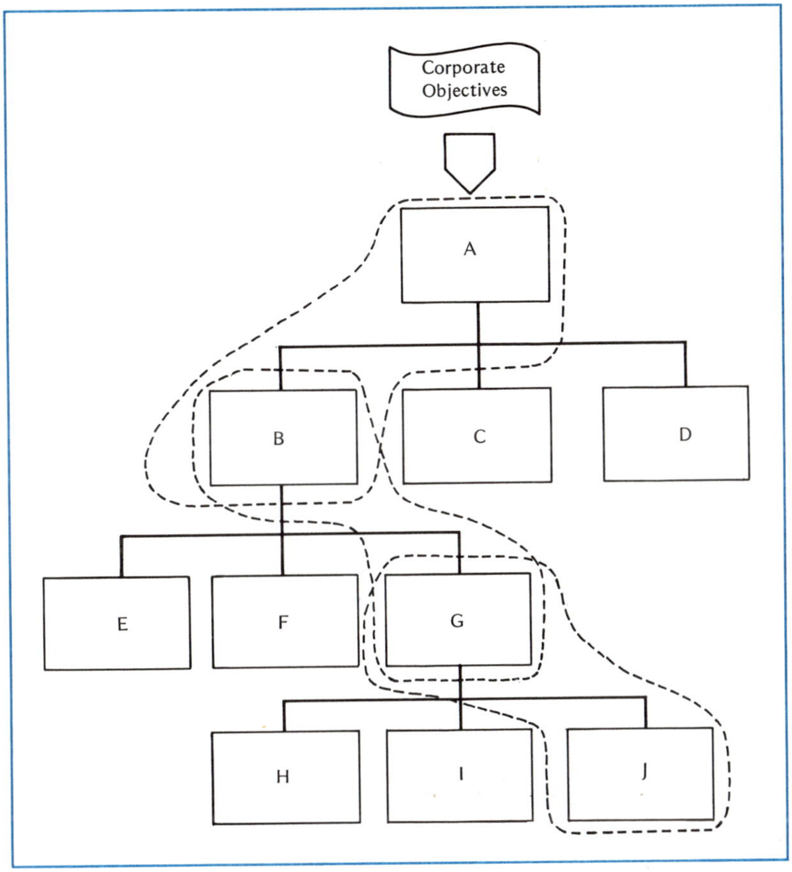

FIGURE 5-8. Applying MBO Throughout the Organization.

a sequential, and increasingly specific, fashion the organization's goals were converted into personal goals for all managers.

Although MBO does not have to start at the top of the organization and work downward, this has been demonstrated to be the most effective approach. Other approaches might be to implement the system at some lower-level segment of the organization only, or to implement the system at all levels at the same time. These latter options are not as desirable, however.

Once objectives have been set for all levels of management, it perhaps becomes obvious that these personalized objectives then become standards or norms against which performance can be specifically measured. As a consequence of this, we begin to see how MBO can be used for planning, motivation, control, and performance appraisal.

Steps in the MBO Process

With no wish to be mechanistic or to detract from the overall philosophy of MBO as a way of managing, we point out that additional facets and benefits of MBO can be seen by considering four main stages or steps in the process. Some experts have conceived of MBO as involving as many as 10 steps,[13] but the four-step approach set forth by William Reif and Gerald Bassford provides an excellent discussional framework. They hold that MBO can be viewed as follows: (1) setting objectives; (2) developing action plans; (3) conducting periodic reviews; and (4) appraising annual performance.[14] Figure 5-9 illustrates the circular relationship of these four components.

Setting Objectives. We described earlier the top-to-bottom process by which objectives are set at each successive lower level. It is appropriate now to provide more detail about the objective-setting process and the objectives that get set. The joint determination of objectives between subordinate and superior is the key part of MBO. This mutual goal-setting session "begins with intensive preparation, focuses on a face-to-face objective-setting interview, and culminates in specific written objectives."[15]

FIGURE 5-9. The MBO Process.

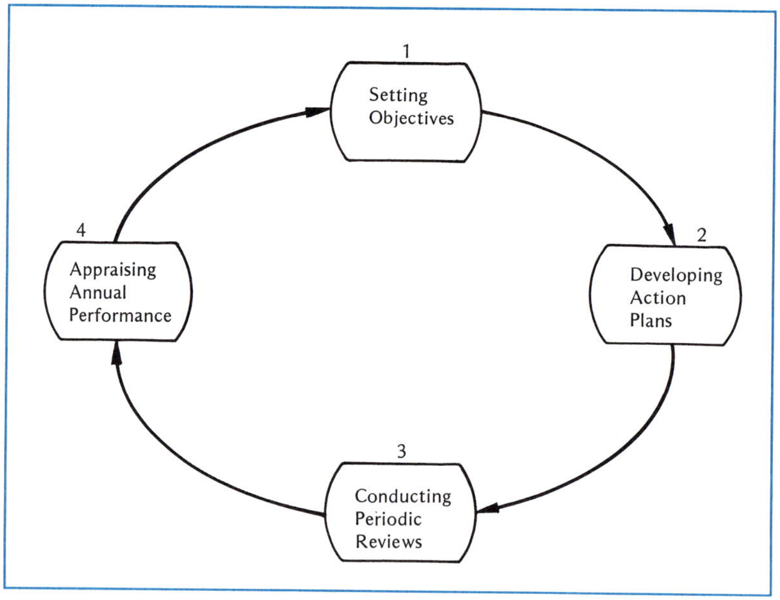

[13]Kae H. Chung, *Motivational Theories and Practices* (Columbus, Ohio: Grid, Inc., 1977), pp. 222–231.

[14]William E. Reif and Gerald Bassford, "What MBO Really Is," *Business Horizons* (June 1973), pp. 23–30.

[15]E. Allen Slusher and Henry P. Sims, Jr., "Commitment Through MBO Interviews," *Business Horizons* (April 1975), p. 6.

In addition to culminating in a sort of psychological contract between the superior and subordinate as to what can be realistically planned for the next time period, the MBO interview often yields other direct benefits for both superior and subordinate. Allen Slusher and Henry Sims suggest these benefits as follows:

For the *superior,* a chance to:

1. *Communicate to the subordinate where help is needed.*
2. *Obtain valuable feedback.*
3. *Enhance the subordinates' motivation and commitment.*

For the *subordinate,* a chance to:

1. *Better understand the superior's priorities.*
2. *Negotiate priorities of the job.*
3. *Influence career development.*[16]

The dynamics of the objective-setting interview are quite important and interesting. However, they are outside our scope here.[17] It is useful, on the other hand, to look more carefully at the nature of the specific objectives that get set during this process. Pertinent here are the categories in which objectives are set and the guidelines for writing effective objectives.

As for the *categories* in which the manager sets personal objectives, four types are typical: regular (or routine), innovative, problem solving, and personal development. *Regular objectives* refers to those usual, routine requirements that are often neccessary for the organization. These would typically be in the key result areas. *Innovative objectives* assume that perfect completion of routine objectives is not enough. These, then, would include any new accomplishments the individual proposes. *Problem solving objectives* are similar to innovative but may simply refer to some special problem that has been plaguing the individual for some time, for which special attention to a solution has not been given. The final category, *personal development,* refers to achievements that the individual sets representing personal (or career) growth and development. Examples might be to attend training seminars, read books, pursue one's education, lose weight, and so on. They are typically objectives that benefit both the individual and the organization.[18]

Numerous guidelines for setting or writing effective objectives have been developed. Stephen Carroll and Henry Tosi suggest that among other characteristics, MBO objectives should be:

1. *Clear, concise, and unambiguous.*
2. *Accurate in terms of the true end state or condition sought.*[19]

16 Slusher and Sims, ibid., pp. 6–8.

17 See the Slusher and Sims article for an elaborate discussion of the MBO interview session dynamics.

18 George Odiorne, *Management By Objectives* (New York: Pitman, 1964), Chapters 7, 8, and 9.

19 Stephen J. Carroll, and Henry L. Tosi, Jr., *Management By Objectives: Application and Research* (New York: Macmillan, 1973), p. 72.

George Morrisey offers even more detailed guidelines for writing objectives. For example, the objective should:

1. Start *with the word* to, *followed by an action word.*
2. *Specify a single* key result *to be accomplished.*
3. *Specify a* target date *for its accomplishment.*
4. *Specify* maximum cost *figures.*
5. *Be as* specific *and* quantitative *(and, hence, measurable and verifiable) as possible.*[20]

Several examples of what might be termed *operational objectives* conforming to these guidelines are:

1. *To reduce the number of electronic component engineering delinquencies for 1982 by 15% over last year's budget.*
2. *To develop and implement a job rotation system that will ensure that each salaried specialist understands and can perform the assignments of any other specialist by January 31, 1982 within the current budget.*
3. *To negotiate all subcontractor cost proposals within 20 days of receipt during the balance of the current year at no increase in the departmental budget.*[21]

The results of such precise statements are goal clarity and specificity, which should enhance goal accomplishment and the pinpointing of accountability. Such precise goals also form the basis for establishing carefully articulated action plans.

Developing Action Plans. Figure 5-9 illustrates the second step in the MBO process, developing action plans. Although the MBO planning process begins with the setting of objectives, the next step is to more carefully spell out action plans to achieve these objectives. The following are useful elements of this overall process. The manager should:

1. *Divide all of the necessary tasks and activities into steps.*
2. *Take note of any relationships between steps, identifying sequences of steps to improve coordination.*
3. *Decide who is responsible for each step.*
4. *Determine resources needed.*
5. *Estimate how long it will take to accomplish each step and assign specific dates for their completion.*[22]

In sum, developing action plans is the stage at which final details are worked out before implementation begins. And, of course, as implementation takes place, the manager is then in a better position to see that goals are accomplished and that activities are smoothly carried out. Consistent with our earlier planning model, if the manager encounters difficulty in achieving a given objective, the

[20]George L. Morrisey, *Management By Objectives and Results* (Reading, Mass.: Addison-Wesley, 1970), pp. 52–54.

[21]Modifications of objectives proposed by Morrisey, ibid., pp. 64–66.

[22]Reif and Bassford, op. cit., pp. 23–30.

first task would be to carefully check out the implementation effort, and then to devise new plans or modify existing ones that take new facts and contingencies into account.

Conducting Periodic Reviews. After objectives have been set and action plans developed, the third step is the conduct of periodic reviews. Whereas the first two steps are more planning-oriented, this step establishes a checking-up or control procedure.

The intent here is to monitor performance to assure that actual results are matching planned results. Reviews are made periodically—perhaps two to four times a year—to assess the degree of goal accomplishment and to provide timely feedback to managers. This feedback then forms the basis for appropriate action being taken by the individuals involved.

Appraising Annual Performance. The main purpose of the annual (or whatever time frame is selected) performance appraisal is to link specific accomplishments with organizational rewards. Prior to the use of MBO and other more recent results-oriented systems, it was not uncommon for employees to be evaluated on the basis of such factors as job qualifications and personality traits. With MBO, the manager evaluates subordinates on the basis of actual performance—results achieved.

Two important performance appraisal purposes are achieved with a well-designed MBO system. First, the quality of performance in the individual's *present assignment* can be assessed. This is done by examining routine, problem solving, and innovative objectives. Second, management potential—or advancement potential—can be assessed by an examination of the individual's achievements on personal development objectives. In this way, the individual's *future prospects* can be assessed.

By linking actual performance to rewards (pay, promotion, recognition), MBO is consistent with most theories of motivation and forms the basis for future expectations the manager may develop about where behavior should be channelled. The annual performance appraisal review then forms the basis for next year's objectives, and the planning cycle is completed.

Future of MBO

MBO is not without weaknesses, and it is not a panacea for management.[23] A well-designed, understood, and implemented approach, however, can yield a number of benefits to management. Among the many benefits are improvements in the following:

[23]See, for example, Bruce D. Jamieson, "Behavioral Problems With Management By Objectives," *Academy of Management Journal* (September 1973), pp. 496–505. See also S. Kerr, "Overcoming the Dysfunctions of MBO," *Management By Objectives,* 1976, **5:** 13–19.

Management performance.
Planning and control.
Coordination.
Superior-subordinate relationships.
Personal development.[24]

Perhaps this last benefit is the key to all the rest. The role of the individual in the building block of relationships that leads to improved management performance is significant. MBO has survived more than 20 years now and its success is attributed to the positive ramifications it has had for the individual. Its future is tied to the future of the individual striving toward personal development, which will at a broader level translate into organizational development. Dale McConkey sums up MBO's future well:

> *Experience has shown that MBO, by itself, will accomplish nothing but chaos. In the hands of a capable management which is ready for it and knows how to use it, it has much to offer. For the right management, it holds promise of a bright future.*[25]

Although we do not wish to conclude on a negative note, it is only fair to point out that MBO has experienced what many new management approaches have experienced—falling victim to "faddism" by managers who adopt some aspect of the approach simply because it is the "in" thing to do. When MBO is taken lightly, the probability rises that it will not be implemented with proper care and, thus, the chances of failure are increased. The future of MBO, therefore, is significantly intertwined with the seriousness with which managers attempt to use it.

PLANNING AND BEHAVIOR

In our overview of MBO, we suggested that it was both a planning and a motivational approach to management. Let us now develop this thought somewhat more by discussing briefly the relationship between planning and behavior. Planning can be viewed in two particular ways, first as "a technical, impersonal, information-developing, and information-using activity."[26] This is basically what strategic planning is, as we discussed it in this chapter. A second way to view planning is "as a motivational tool for shaping the performance and development of people on the job."[27] This latter approach is more closely aligned with MBO and other

[24]Reif and Bassford, op. cit., pp. 29–30.
[25]Dale McConkey, "MBO-Twenty Years Later, Where Do We Stand?" *Business Horizons* (August 1973), p. 36.
[26]Hampton, op. cit., p. 79.
[27]Hampton, ibid.

efforts to get personnel involved on a participative basis in the planning efforts.

Let us expand somewhat on this latter view because it is clear that planning and behavior are linked in that planning has motivational consequences. To see this clearly, let us consider an experience of one of the authors.

The author was called in as a consultant for a small, private telephone company. The company had many different problems, but one problem in particular was relevant to the present discussion. There was a supervisor of a maintenance crew who had been supervisor for only about a year or so. Discussions with the maintenance supervisor's subordinates gave the clear impression that there was a serious morale problem in this man's unit. After interviewing a number of workers, the problem became clear. The supervisor had been with the company for a number of years; in fact, he had worked his way up to supervisor. In this particular company, the supervisors were quite well paid—in fact, they received about $6,000 per year more than the average worker, which represented quite a spread in salary between worker and supervisor.

In addition to making this much money, the supervisor was not married and he could afford to drive a beautiful, large, expensive Lincoln Continental Mark IV automobile. Well, what was the problem? The problem was that the workers in this man's crew were resentful because, instead of really planning and scheduling the work, he would come to work each day (in his Mark IV), roll up his sleeves, and work all day right along side his subordinates. The workers were resentful and had poor morale because he was being paid to be a supervisor and to do the planning and scheduling, but then he would not do it. The supervisor was neglecting the basic planning function and, as a result, work was not getting done in an orderly fashion and the workers had a poor morale level as a result.

Another way to consider the relationship between planning and behavior is to examine how more or less directive or authoritarian approaches to planning impact on behavior. Jeremy Bentham, in the early 1800s, suggested that people behave as they do either to acquire pleasure or to avoid pain. The pain-avoidance motive explains why some people will respond to more painful (strictly authoritarian) forms of planning and/or goal setting. Organizational members may perform, then, to avoid reprimand, poor performance evaluations, or discharge, but the negative consequences evoked are often not desirable. Stress-inducing threats (explicit or implicit) create anxiety that may likely detract from performance. The temptation to cheat in order to meet the often regimented, inflexible goals becomes very strong. We see more about this in our later discussion of the dysfunctional consequences of control.

More participative approaches to goal setting and planning (as in MBO, for example) stand in sharp contrast to goals or planning directives being sent down from above. Douglas McGregor states the basic reasoning for more supportive approaches:

Genuine commitment is seldom achieved when objectives are externally imposed. Passive acceptance is the most that can be expected; indifference or resistance are the more likely consequences. Some degree of mutual involvement in the determination of objectives is a necessary aspect of managerial planning.[28]

In contrast to the directive approaches to planning, involvement methods do not foster anxiety and the human need to reduce it. These approaches create a climate "in which subordinates are provided with arousal cues for achievement, affiliation, power, and esteem."[29] Although the evidence is mixed as to whether the participative method is better than the approach of imposing goals from above, the behavioral consequences in the participative case seem to be clearly more desirable.

Regardless of the method used, the evidence is clear that having specific, as opposed to general or vague, performance goals is more desirable. E. A. Locke, in a series of experiments, showed that subjects were more productive when they set specific goals than when they were simply told to "do their best."[30] The behavioral consequences of specific rather than general goals are likely, therefore, to be more favorable.

One final issue we will discuss here pertains to the behavioral consequences of an excessive emphasis on individual goals and individual pay-offs. Too much emphasis on individual accomplishment can create an environment that stifles cooperation and the achievement of the organization's broader objectives. As an illustration, interviewers in a state employment office were found to be hiding new job openings from one another so that each would have maximum opportunity to get credit for the placement. In another case, the accounting office in a company needed more personnel for a special project, but workers in other departments refused to help out because they saw nothing to gain by leaving their own work and helping accounting.[31]

It is unfortunate that planning efforts are sometimes used without proper care being given to their behavioral consequences. As we have seen, however, there are definite behavioral implications that should be factored into all planning efforts. We have shown that negative behavioral effects can be one possible outcome from not carrying out the planning function as expected of managers by subordinates. We have seen that authoritarian versus participation approaches to goal setting and planning have different behavioral results. The effect of a specific rather than a general goal has also been discussed. Last, we have seen the behavioral consequences of a preoccupation with individual versus cooperative goals. In sum, we have provided some insights into how planning and behavior are interrelated and how managers must be wary that their planning does not become too mechanistic and insulated from the behavioral consequences that follow.

[28]Douglas McGregor, *The Human Side of Enterprise* (New York: McGraw-Hill, 1960), p. 868.

[29]Hampton, op. cit., p. 82.

[30]E. A. Locke, "Toward a Theory of Task Motivation and Incentives," *Organizational Behavior and Human Performance*, III, May 1968.

[31]Examples from Peter M. Blau, *The Dynamics of Bureaucracy* (Chicago: University of Chicago Press, 1963), and Edward Gross, "Some Functional Consequences of Primary Controls in Formal Work Organizations," *American Sociological Review*, XVIII, August 1953, pp. 368–373.

CONTROL: A BROADER LOOK

In our discussion we have alluded to control and its close relationship to planning. In the planning model presented earlier, we saw its role; in the strategic planning model, we saw its place in providing feedback; and in our discussion of MBO, we saw how it manifested itself in the form of periodic reviews. Let us now take a broader look at the control function, its nature and characteristics, and some of the problems it can pose.

It was suggested earlier that there are three essential elements of the control process: (1) *standards* against which performance can be measured; (2) the *comparison* of standard with actual performance; and (3) the taking of *appropriate action.* Quite frequently as we examine control efforts in organizations, these three components do not manifest themselves clearly or explicitly. We would suggest, nevertheless, that they are inherent in organizational processes.

When we view control more broadly—as an effort to channel behavior into desired directions—it is easier to see control at work. In fact, it is important to emphasize that all efforts to channel behavior into appropriate directions are not taken by management. Gene Dalton suggests that there are three major types of control over behavior in organizations and that each of these types has its own standards, monitoring system, and approach to taking appropriate or corrective action. These three types are (1) organizational control, (2) social control, and (3) self-control.[32] Each deserves a closer examination.

Organizational Control

Organizational controls represent those formally designed control efforts originated by management. The general direction of these controls comes from the objectives and plans of the organization. The *standards* come from objectives stated in such areas as profit, market share, growth, and cost reductions. *Monitoring of performance* is handled through devices such as budgets, standard cost reports, and other reports. An MBO interview designed to review periodic performance is also an illustration of the monitoring of performance. The signal for appropriate action is a variance between the planned and the actual. The system for *appropriate action* is the reward system of the organization. Praise, promotion, and salary increases represent positive rewards, whereas negative sanctions include such actions as a request for an explanation, withholding of praise and rewards, and at the extreme end of the spectrum, dismissal.

Social Control

Although social control does not carry with it formal organization sanctions, it is often powerful in channeling behavior in directions desired by various infor-

[32]Gene W. Dalton, "Motivation and Control in Organizations," in *Motivation and Control in Organizations,* Gene Dalton and Paul Lawrence, eds., (Homewood, Ill.: Richard D. Irwin, 1971), pp. 1–35.

mal cliques or social groups. The direction of social control emanates from the mutual commitments that members of informal groups have toward one another. The *standards* here include group norms that have emerged and crystallized in such areas as sharing, helping, levels of work that are acceptable, and dress. Observation and informal communication channels are the *monitoring* mechanism. When deviations are noted, sanctions will likely result. Such negative sanctions may include good-natured kidding, verbal abuse, ostracism, hostility, and rejection from the group. Rewards for conformance also exist, and these include membership, approval, and, perhaps, informal leadership.

Self-Control

Whereas social control comes from an external source, self-control comes from within. Reliance upon this type of control is at the heart of intrinsic motivation systems. An element of self-control exists in most MBO systems. The general direction for self-control comes from individual commitment to personal goals and aspirations. The *standards* are expectations or personally set goals. The *monitoring* system is self-awareness and observation, and the signal for corrective action is any indication that personal expectations will not be met. The system for *appropriate action* includes self-administered sanctions and may range from a mild feeling of disappointment to a deep sense of failure, inadequacy, and, perhaps, withholding of a privilege. Positive reinforcers would include feelings of elation, satisfaction, esteem, and self-mastery. Figure 5-10 summarizes these types of control and their standards, monitoring mechanism, and sanctions.

Taken together, these three types of control create pressures toward goal accomplishment. The three do not work independently of one another; in fact, they combine to support or negate one another. If one system runs counter to one of the others, optimal control is not likely. If all three operate consistently, the total control achieved can be enormous. It is a generally accepted principle that "control is usually highest when it is least felt."[33] If this principle is valid, it points us in the direction of designing control systems that rely more heavily on self- and social control than on organizational controls. The latter are typically necessary, however, so the point is to design them in such a way as to minimize the deviance necessary from the former two types of control, or so as not to evoke negative reactions from those formal controls that are present.

Dysfunctional Effects of Control

The importance of the careful design of control systems becomes clear when one considers the dysfunctional kinds of behavior that experience has shown to be evoked by poorly constructed control systems. Edward Lawler and John Rhode identify four types of dysfunctional effects of control systems that are most frequent. First is *rigid bureaucratic behavior.* This occurs when control systems

[33]Dalton, ibid., p. 16.

(8) Type of Control	(1) Standards	(2) Monitoring Mechanism	(3) Sanctions
Organizational Control	Formally designed by management Objectives; plans	Budgets Standard Cost Reports Other reports	Formal Reward of the Organization (+) Praise, promotion, salary increase (−) Request for explanation Withholding of praise and rewards Dismissal
Social Control	Informally set by cliques or social groups Mutual commitments of group members Group norms (e.g., sharing, helping, levels of work that are acceptable.	Observation and informal communication channels.	By the group (+) Continued membership Approval Informal leadership (−) Good-natured kidding Verbal abuse Ostracism Hostility Rejection
Self-Control	Comes from within the individual (intrinsic) Individual commitment to personal goals/aspirations	Self-awareness and observation	Self-administered sanctions (+) Feelings of elation, satisfaction, esteem, self-mastery (−) Mild feeling of disappointment. Deep sense of failure/inadequacy Personal deprivation of privileges

FIGURE 5-10. Types of Control and Their Characteristics

cause employees "to behave in ways that look good in terms of the control system measures but that are dysfunctional as far as the generally agreed upon goals of the organization are concerned."[34] Second is *strategic behavior.*[35] Strategic behavior represents a short-term behavioral change and "involves actions designed solely to influence information [control] system results so they will look good or acceptable for a certain time period."[36] Third is *invalid data reporting.* This entails employees submitting invalid data about what can be done, and what has been done. The invalid data may be just misleading or may be false.[37] Fourth is *resistance behavior.* When an individual's need satisfaction is threatened by the control system, resistance mechanisms go to work.[38]

It should be noted that dysfunctional behavior is not a necessary outcome of control efforts, but it does occur when control efforts are improperly designed or improperly used. Managers must exercise considerable care as control efforts are formulated, lest rigidities be built into the system. Used properly, control, as stated earlier, is but the other side of planning, and together planning and control can move organizations and human performance and behavior in those directions desired by the organization's leaders.

SUMMARY

Planning is one of the most important of the management functions. It is a mental process, a philosophy, and can include a set of techniques. There are numerous benefits that the organization can derive from planning, and these form the justification for management exerting planning efforts. Whereas planning is a continuing process, a plan is but an interim report or tentative step in the complete cycle.

Planning can be viewed in model form as entailing (1) the setting of objectives, (2) establishing criteria for examining alternatives, (3) generating alternative means of attainment, (4) making a decision, (5) establishing more detailed plans, (6) implementation, and (7) evaluation and control. All of these steps are inherent in both strategic planning and MBO.

Strategic planning is the most comprehensive type of planning that can be done, and all other planning derives from it. Strategic planning results in an organizational strategy, and this strategy defines the organization's relationship with its environment. The major phases in strategy development include (1) an

[34]Edward E. Lawler, III, and John Grant Rhode, *Information and Control in Organizations* (Pacific Palisades, Cal.: Goodyear Publishing Co., 1976), p. 83.

[35]The reader should note that *strategic* is being used in a different sense than its earlier use in the chapter.

[36]Lawler and Rhode, op. cit., p. 86.

[37]Lawler and Rhode, op. cit., pp. 88–91.

[38]Lawler and Rhode, op. cit., pp. 91–94.

assessment of current strategy, (2) the development of alternative future strategies, (3) a strategy decision, and (4) strategy evaluation.

MBO is an operational level type of planning and has been construed to be a motivational and control as well as a planning approach. MBO reveals clearly the interrelationships between planning and control. MBO can be viewed broadly as entailing four steps: (1) setting objectives, (2) developing action plans, (3) conducting periodic reviews, and (4) appraising annual performance. Planning also is related to behavior. Although this relationship is seen more vividly in MBO, the behavioral consequences of planning should be attended to in all planning uses and applications.

The control process is but the other side of planning, and the two are inseparable. Control implies (1) standards against which performance can be measured, (2) a comparison of actual with standard, and (3) the taking of appropriate or corrective action. Three major types of controls are manifest in organizations: (1) organizational (formal) controls, (2) social controls, and (3) self-control. When operating together, they are a powerful force channeling organizational behavior.

Assignments

5-1. Differentiate between planning and controlling but at the same time describe how the two are intimately related.

5-2. How can planning be a mental process, a philosophy, and a set of techniques all at the same time?

5-3. How can objectives be both the end result of and the point of departure for planning efforts? Describe fully.

5-4. Take an example out of your personal life, and show how the planning process model accurately describes the mental activity one really goes through in thinking about the future.

5-5. If planning efforts do not seem to be succeeding, why would you not want to go back and simply change your objective(s), thus bringing the effort back into control? Discuss fully.

5-6. Does the phrase "plan for planning" seem redundant to you? Explain how this could happen. Be sure to present several illustrations.

5-7. Explain the following statement: "All strategic planning is long-range planning, but all long-range planning is not strategic planning." Give several illustrations.

5-8. Taking the strategy option matrix for a business firm presented as Figure 5-4 in this chapter, give some illustrations of consumer products or services of which you are aware that would illustrate each of the four cells in the matrix. Give some nonbusiness illustrations.

5-9. Could MBO be just as fairly referred to as MBG (Management By Goals)? Explain your rationale.

5-10. Taking the guidelines for writing objectives presented in the MBO section, write several operational objectives of your own. Do they meet the criteria laid out for operational objectives?

5-11. It is asserted that the MBO process presented in Figure 5-6 has an element of control in it. Explain, pointing out exactly where it occurs in the model presented.

5-12. Discuss the relationship between planning and behavior in organizations. Give examples of how this relationship manifests itself. Is there a close relationship between control and behavior? Discuss, using examples.

5-13. From your personal experience as a member of any type of organization, illustrate how social control worked; that is, standards set, monitoring, and corrective action.

5-14. Develop a rationale for the statement, "Control is usually highest when it is least felt."

Case 5-1

JACK HERN—PLANNER?

Jack Hern, a supervisor for the National Association of Builders and Contractors, had been inspired by his instructor in a managerial planning session held at a nearby university recently. As a direct result of that inspiration, Jack made a commitment to spend time every morning before the beginning of the workday to plan his work for that day.

Jack typically found, however, that he spent considerable time "fire fighting," that is, coping with spur-of-the-moment problems that arose each day on a fairly regular basis. Consequently, Jack did not see many of his plans carried out during the regular workday. As a result, he became increasingly frustrated each morning as he sat down to plan his activities for the day. Jack cannot put his finger on what is wrong.

1. Is Jack really planning? Why? Why not?
2. Could Jack, in his anxious desire to be an effective planner, have misunderstood some of what his instructor was saying?
3. What steps would you recommend Jack take to get himself out of this predicament?

Case 5-2

MASTER PLANS OR MINI PLANS*

After spending three years and $1 million, the New York City Planning Commission (NYCPC) created a six-volume, 450,000-word master plan that analyzed the character of and suggested the development of the city's 62 planning districts. The debate and controversy over the plan lasted two years, at which time the plan was finally scrapped. It was then outdated. The NYCPC's new chairman, a one-time supporter of the plan, remarked, "Frankly, I don't believe in master plans."

*This case was taken from "The Best Laid Plans," *Wall Street Journal* (June 18, 1973) p. 10.

The fate of the city's master plan suggests what numerous urbanologists have tried for years to emphasize—that there are definite limits to planning, limits that derive from human predictability. In a free society, people will tend to move in, about, and out of cities according to what they see as in their own best self-interests, not according to even the most farsighted blueprint.

There are illustrations of alternatives to government master plans. Continuing to use New York City as an illustration, a privately sponsored group called the Downtown-Lower Manhattan Association proposed plans for the continuing redevelopment and refurbishment of lower Manhattan's trade and financial district. The plan called for providing parks, open spaces, 3,330 housing units, and a community college.

This plan is being viewed as imaginative and realistic. The main reason for this is it is limited in scope, not an effort to transform the city's five diverse boroughs and neighborhoods. In sum, the plan is a mini plan, not a master plan, and is therefore given a good chance of succeeding.

1. Discuss the merits of master versus mini plans. What other issues arise in this case?
2. What is your analysis of the commission chairman's remarks? What does this tell you about the human element in planning?
3. Compare the type of planning illustrated here with planning in businesses and other types of organizations.

Case 5-3

LYNWOOD GREGG

Lynwood Gregg is department head of a branch bank in a city of 100,000 in the Southeast. He has 14 people working for him at the bank. He recently attended a training session held by his bank's home office on Management By Objectives, and he wanted to begin using MBO in his operation immediately.

He called the 14 employees together for a group meeting on Friday afternoon at 3 P.M. After a brief presentation to the group on MBO, he instructed them to discuss the objectives the branch ought to be pursuing. Following their one-hour discussion, he asked each person to prepare a list of specific objectives each hoped to accomplish during the next six months. He then asked that each person prepare the list over the weekend and present the objectives in writing to him no later than the following Tuesday at 5 P.M. The meeting was adjourned, as it typically is, by Costas Alexandras, a supervisor in the teller department, who wanted to get down to K. T. Marty's, a local watering hole.

1. Appraise Gregg's approach to implementing MBO. Do you believe he implemented it in the proper manner? Why? Why not?
2. Describe how your approach to implementation would differ from Gregg's.

Case 5-4

PUTTING OBJECTIVES IN WRITING

The Alexander Company Credit Union (ACCU) publishes its objectives for the forthcoming year in its annual report. The general manager of ACCU argues, "We realize that putting the credit union's objectives for the next year into print can result in considerable embarrassment. However, we feel that the advantages of clearly stating our objectives in advance exceed the possible disadvantages. Our board is convinced that the membership should have as much knowledge as possible of the credit union's advance plans so that it feels more a part of the credit union and has a greater share in the democratic process of determining our goals and direction."

1. List and discuss the advantages and disadvantages of putting objectives in writing and publishing them as ACCU does.
2. To what possible embarrassment was the general manager making reference?
3. Credit unions are organizations that are owned by and run for their members. Would their case differ from a typical business organization on this issue?

References

BRADY, R. H. "MBO Goes to Work in the Public Sector." *Harvard Business Review* (March 1953), pp. 65–74.

CARROLL, ARCHIE B. "Setting Operational Goals for Corporate Social Responsibility." *Long-Range Planning* (April 1978), pp. 35–38.

CARROLL, S. J., JR., AND TOSI, H. L. JR., "A Study of the Goal Setting and Review Process in a Management by Objectives System." *Public Personnel Review,* Vol. 32, No. 3 (July 1971), pp. 177–182.

CYERT, R. M., AND JAMES G. MARCH. "A Behavioral Theory of Organizational Objectives," (ed.) Mason Haire, *Modern Organization Theory.* New York: John Wiley & Sons, Inc., 1959, pp. 76–90.

HOFER, CHARLES W. "Research on Strategic Planning: A Survey of Past Studies and Suggestions for Future Efforts." *Journal of Economics and Business* (Spring-Summer, 1976), pp. 261–286.

LEONTIADES, MILTON. "Planning: A Reexamination of Fundamentals." *Journal of Economics and Business* (Spring-Summer, 1976), pp. 189–194.

MOCKLER, ROBERT J. (editor), *Readings in Business Planning and Policy Formulation.* New York: Appleton-Century-Crafts, 1972.

ODIORNE, G. S. *Management by Objectives: A System of Managerial Leadership.* Belmont, Calif.: Pitman Publishing Corporation, 1965.

SHETTY, Y. K., AND H. M. CARLISLE. "Organizational Correlates of a Management by Objectives Program." *Academy of Management Journal* (March 1974), pp. 155–160.

STEINER, GEORGE A. "Making Long-Range Company Planning Pay Off." *California Management Review,* Volume IV, No. 2, 1962, pp. 28–41.

STEINER, GEORGE A. *Top Management Planning.* New York: Macmillan Publishing Co., Inc., 1969.

VANCIL, R. F. "The Accuracy of Long-Range Planning." *Harvard Business Review* (September/October 1970), pp. 98–101.

GEORGE C. SAWYER
President, Management Technology and Resources

George C. Sawyer is president of his own firm, Management Technology and Resources, which offers consulting services on planning and management. He was formerly director of corporate planning for Hoffmann-La Roche. Dr. Sawyer is a significant contributor to the concepts underlying effective strategic planning in both the corporate and academic worlds.

Executive Commentary
Action Laid Out in Advance

Planning is action laid out in advance. It is a central, essential function of management because a manager must lay out some pattern of action in order effectively to direct the functioning of the organization. While managers plan, by habit and by instinct, the functioning of large modern organizations requires that plans be shared, so that groups of managers are acting in coordinate patterns toward accomplishment of agreed objectives. Thus, planning has become an organizational process in addition to the individual process of each manager.

For planning to be action laid out in advance, as it is, the plans must have the engagement, authority, and support of those who will direct the action. These must be the plans of the line managers, the only true planners in any organization. Although an important staff role exists in aiding line managers to organize, assemble, and coordinate these plans, and to make the necessary supporting information and analyses available to these line managers, the staff cannot plan in the sense that it cannot, by itself, produce a pattern of action laid out in advance that will be executed; for this to happen, the line managers must assimilate the material, take personal responsibility for the strategy defined and issues resolved, and give their authority to the actions.

Although plans are action laid out in advance and the time horizon of plans often extends far into the future, decisions are always made in the present. Line managers live in the present, struggling with the decisions of the day. Good managers are properly concerned that the decisions of the day be timely and that they take proper account of other pending events. Thus, when a decision is needed, the managers will often welcome or even demand information on the future consequences of that decision and will attempt to take proper account of a time horizon as long as the futurity of that decision may require. The planning process model outlined in the chapter tends to function always in the present, with the relevant future related as well as available time and tools permit. The planning staff has the care of the future events not ready for decision and for the gathering of the information that will be necessary when these decisions come to term.

One of the important differences between the plan and the process that produces it is that the process flows on from day to day as a part of the management system, whereas the plan is frozen at a point in time and is written. A good plan should be a useful guide to future action, but it cannot remain totally valid, except briefly, because of the rapid rate at which actual events diverge from the norms on which the plan was based. Actual sales may be less or greater than forecast, competitive efforts more or less effective than expected, the economy stronger or weaker; each such shift changes the starting point upon which future actions should be based. Thus, most organizations revise their plans once a year or more, and consider the plans that result as normative towards a particular decision, rather than mandating its blind execution. And although the series of plans generated over five or ten years will often have strong similarities and a complete consistency in strategy, the details will be quite different as the viewpoint of succeeding moments in time is reflected in each.

In doing its planning, a management will deal strategically with the longest time horizon it attempts to forecast and will at least consider planning for a time span long enough to encompass the full futurity of today's decisions. A decision to build a new electric power generating plant may require 15 years to implement, with payout over the next 25 years, thus apparently requiring a 40-year plan. Yet, the intense uncertainty of the increasingly future years and the limitations of available planning tools may lead the management to plan for 10 years, or even for five, with general projections of trends beyond, and to use this plan as a basis for defining corporate strategy. This strategy may be within the framework of the expected events, or may be made proactive, if it seeks to influence these events.

In doing its planning, a management will use plans and planning staff. The purpose is action laid out in advance. This action should be the wisest and best considered that available information will permit. The formulation for the plan for this action requires diversion of valuable managerial time and resources. This diversion of resources should be kept at the minimum effective level. In organizations, procedures and paper work grow increasingly elaborate spontaneously and unceasingly, unless kept under constructive managerial pressure. Therefore, in a well-managed company the pressure is towards careful use of planning time, allowing only that minimum amount of formality necessary to make the planning an effective part of the management system.

Planning is a part of management, and effective planning is a route to effective managerial action. Plans and planners should be judged on their contribution to this objective.

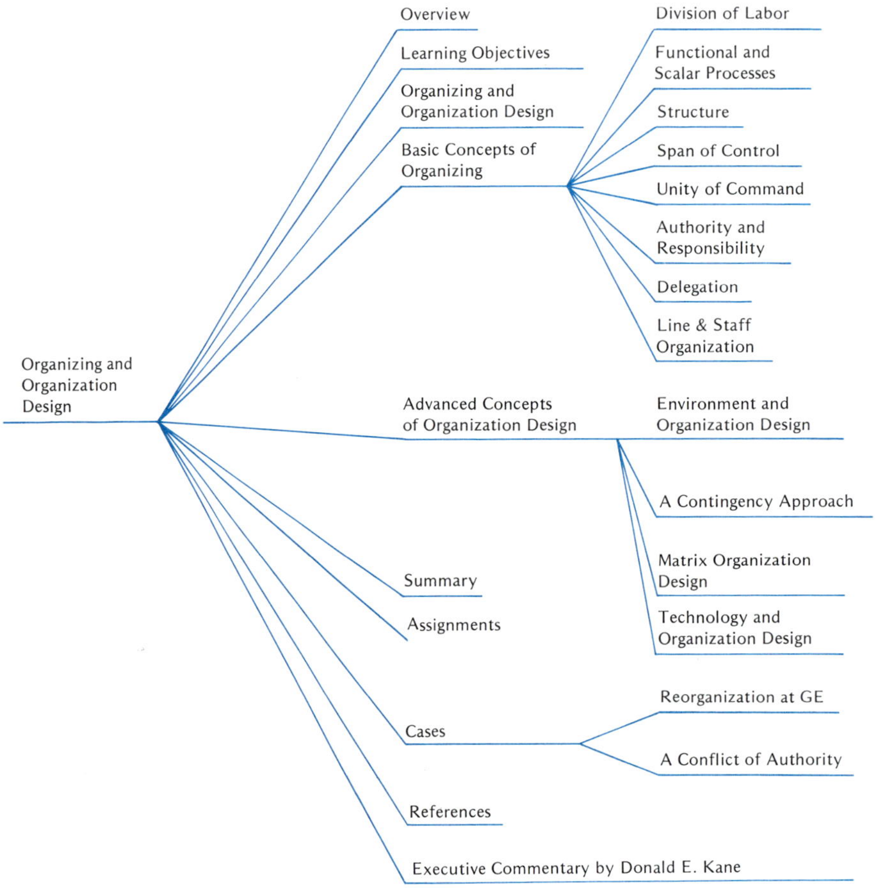
Organizing and Organization Design
Overview
Learning Objectives
Organizing and Organization Design
Basic Concepts of Organizing
Division of Labor
Functional and Scalar Processes
Structure
Span of Control
Unity of Command
Authority and Responsibility
Delegation
Line & Staff Organization
Advanced Concepts of Organization Design
Environment and Organization Design
A Contingency Approach
Matrix Organization Design
Technology and Organization Design
Summary
Assignments
Cases
Reorganization at GE
A Conflict of Authority
References
Executive Commentary by Donald E. Kane

6

ORGANIZING AND ORGANIZATION DESIGN

OVERVIEW

In a sense, the title of this chapter captures the essence of the old and the new insofar as management theory on this topic is concerned. The old is represented by the term *organizing*. Although organizing still takes place and, hence, is not really an outdated concept, in management history it was identified early as one of the basic elements, functions, or processes of management. The new is represented by the term *organization design*. Organization design suggests that the manager, as the architect, assumes an active role in putting together a pattern of relationships that will best achieve the goals desired. Taken together, these two concepts encompass the full breadth of managerial activity having to do with structuring organizations.

LEARNING OBJECTIVES

This chapter is especially intended to help the student:

1. **Understand the subtle distinction between organizing and organization design.**
2. **Gain an appreciation of the basic concepts of organizing.**
3. **Gain insights into the modern notions of organization design.**
4. **See the relationships between environmental factors and organization structure.**
5. **Learn, especially in the context of thinking about management, the meaning of the following concepts:**
   division of labor **responsibility**

functional processes
scalar processes
span of control
unity of command
authority
delegation
line and staff
contingency approach
matrix design
technology

ORGANIZING AND ORGANIZATION DESIGN

Henri Fayol (1841–1925), the French administrative theorist, considered the administrative activities of managing as encompassing planning, organizing, commanding, coordinating, and controlling.[1] Since Fayol's time, many management writers have defined organizing in different ways. We shall define *organizing* for our purposes here as the structuring of the relationships of the elements of the organization in order to provide a cohesive, goal-directed, whole. Although no single definition can fully embody all that goes on in the name of organizing, this definition provides us with a good point of departure for our discussion.

Organization design, in actuality, is just a modern term that implies basically the same notions as our definition of organizing but, perhaps implicitly, somewhat more. Whereas the term *organizing* frequently suggests the *initial* structuring of the pattern by which the organization pursues its objectives, organization design implies that there are choices involved in structuring the organization. These choices are not only a reflection of personal philosophy or predisposition but also of rational thought about the many factors that impinge on the organization, such as the environment and technology, and of the research that has suggested the organization's structure ought to be contingent upon these and other variables such as the organization's strategy. Organization design, therefore, reflects a more sophisticated view of the role of management—that is, as the architect of the system—taking into consideration an analysis of the organization's internal and external environments for design purposes.

Some might suggest that this distinction between organizing and organization design is simply a reflection of a desire to use modern terminology. The latter term does have a more contemporary ring to it, and there is implicit in the expression a belief that not only are we interested in creating *any* structure that will begin moving the organization toward its objectives but, just as an architect building a house, we have a number of variables to work with and we should attempt to construct a more nearly optimal structure—a personalized structure—for the specific variables with which we have to work in any given organization.

With that basic distinction as a backdrop, we will proceed to cover the material in this chapter according to those two understandings. First, we will examine the

[1]Daniel A. Wren, *The Evolution of Management Thought* (New York: Ronald Press, 1972), p. 216.

traditional, or basic, concepts of organizing. Second, we will introduce more advanced concepts of organization design.

BASIC CONCEPTS OF ORGANIZING

It should be clear that an organization (the end result of organizing) should be properly constructed or designed if it is to work effectively; however, many managers often neglect the basic structure or pattern of the organization. Organization structure is neglected in part because it is usually so much simpler to hire a new manager, move managers into different positions, or discharge managers or personnel who are not doing a good job. Another reason for neglecting the basic pattern of organizing is that to alter it would represent much more substantial change—and change is typically perceived as threatening. Still another reason for not working with the basic pattern of organization is that most managers move into a company or organization that is already structured and just assume that it is not a variable they can change. And a final reason why managers are reluctant to alter the basic organization design is that they frequently know so little about basic concepts of organizing.

One reason managers know so little about basic concepts of organizing and organization design is the distorted emphasis given in management education today to behavior theory rather than organization theory. Behavior theory deals with the more tangible problems of managing people—work satisfaction, motivation, leadership, conflict, and communication—and thus is enjoyable to study and discuss. *Organization theory* tends to be more abstract. As a consequence, it in the past has had less appeal to both students and teachers. Also, the field of behavioral theory is more developed and more rigorous than structural theory and thus receives more attention for that reason. Organization theory, however, has gained respect as the field has matured, and it too is now exciting. As the reader works through these basic and then more advanced concepts of organization, it will be seen more vividly how the organization's structure influences its effectiveness and, thus, the very important role that organization theory assumes today.

The classical doctrine of organization dealt almost exclusively with the *anatomy of formal organization,* that is, with its skeleton or structure. It was thus a static analysis. William G. Scott has argued that classical organization theory was built around four key pillars—division of labor, scalar and functional processes, structure, and span of control.[2] We will begin our examination of basic concepts of organizing with these, and then move on to others that are also considered to be fundamental.

[2] William G. Scott, "Organization Theory: An Overview and an Appraisal," *Academy of Management Journal,* April 1961, pp. 7–26.

'For what it's worth, the new organization chart is out and you're not in your box.'

Reprinted by permission of the Chicago Tribune-New York News Syndicate, Inc.

Division of Labor

The *division of labor* concept and the resulting specialization of tasks is at the core of organizing. Although the concept existed prior to Adam Smith's times (1723–1790), Smith was one of the earliest to articulate its importance in a developing economic system. Smith believed that the division of labor and specialization were at the heart of a free market economic system. We might add that it is an important core concept that is at the heart of most effective economic systems. Smith cited the illustration of the pin-makers who, when each performed a limited, specialized operation could produce 48,000 pins per day, whereas one unspecialized worker could make only 20 pins per day.[3] He admitted that this was a trifling example but that this same result could be seen in other industries.

[3] Wren, op. cit., p. 24.

It has been generally established that the productivity of organizations is enhanced when the task to be accomplished is divided into *specialized* elements. Not only did Adam Smith, the economist, stress the importance of this, but so did management writers and thinkers such as Charles Babbage (1792–1871), Henri Fayol, and practically all thinkers since them. Fayol considered the division of work as the first of his famous 14 principles.

In recent years, some criticisms have been raised against the extreme adherence to this key pillar of the classical doctrine. Advocates of job enrichment through combining tasks to form a cohesive work unit hold that specialization has gone too far and that at some point it becomes dysfunctional to further specialize or divide labor. Another kind of criticism has been leveled by Chris Argyris. Argyris holds that there are certain characteristics of modern organizations that inhibit the maturity of the individuals that work in them. He identifies the specialization of labor as one of these factors that limits individual initiative, stifles self-expression, and requires only a few of the individual's abilities.[4] Despite the reservations, however, the division of labor concept and resulting job specialization is a central notion in organizing, and is, in actuality, the notion underlying functional and scalar processes.

Functional and Scalar Processes

The *functional process* of organizing refers to the horizontal specialization that takes place in organizing. It is a special case of the division of labor or specialization into functional work units. It is horizontal in the sense that it shapes the horizontal pattern of the typical organizational pyramid. Figure 6-1 illustrates how the pattern of organization takes on a pyramidal configuration.

Note that Figure 6-1 is only a partial chart in that it does not illustrate all subordinate positions in the organization. Note also that the *scalar,* or vertical, dimension creates the hierarchy of levels, a concept to which we will return.

Departmentation. The name that is given to the horizontal growth of an organization is *departmentation.* These departments, or specialized subunits to handle various tasks can be grouped in a number of different ways. Four main ways by which departmentation occurs are based upon (1) functions, (2) products, (3) territory or place, and (4) customer or clientele. The method chosen is a function of a number of different factors. The main advantages of departmentation accrue from those who have similar tasks, outlooks, and roles being brought together for economies of scale and coordination.

(1) Departmentation by function. Historically, departmentation by function is one of the first used in organizing. The organization is structured according to basic functions that have to be performed to achieve the organization's objectives.

[4]Chris Argyris, *Personality and Organization: The Conflict Between the System and the Individual* (New York: Harper and Row, 1957).

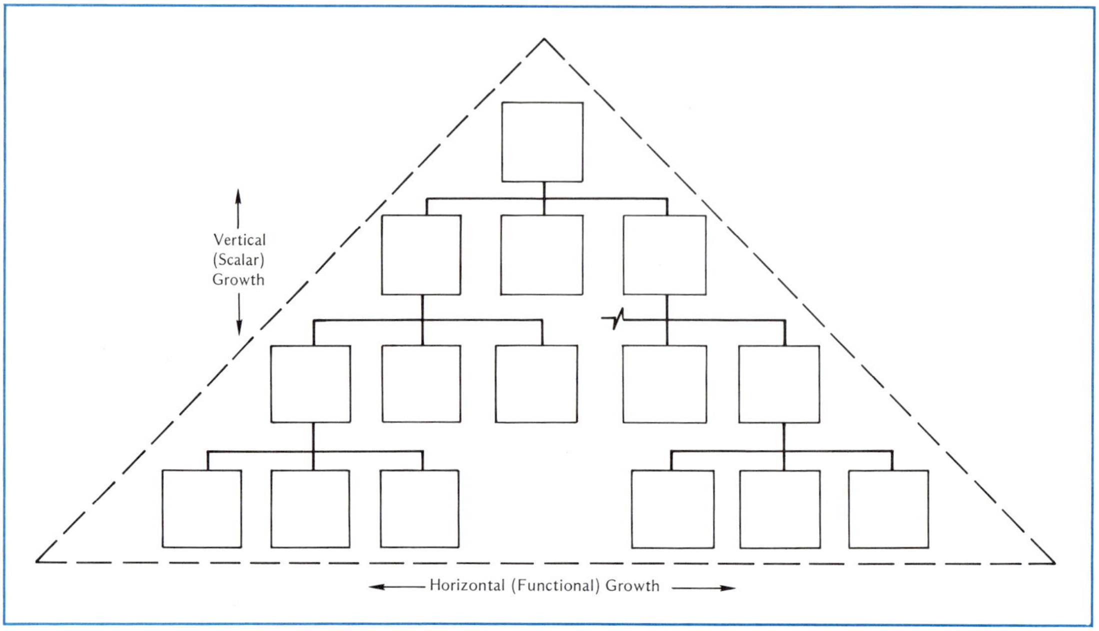

FIGURE 6-1. A Typical Organizational Structure (Pyramid)

Typical functions include production, marketing, finance, personnel, research, and engineering. Depending upon the degree of functional specialization needed, there could be more or fewer than those listed. Figure 6-2 illustrates an electrical equipment company organized at the top level by function.

In this particular company, management has decided that it is best to group those elements together that are doing *similar tasks.* Therefore, grouped together in the research and engineering unit are those working on mechanical design, special components, special devices, and preproduction engineering. In a similar fashion, the other departments are so structured. The chief drawback is the parochial outlook that may result and the difficulty of achieving interunit coordination and integration.

(2) Departmentation by product. Another frequent basis for departmentation is by *product produced.* An organization might structure itself in this manner because of variations in production, marketing, and distribution that necessitate each product unit operating autonomously or semiautonomously. The classical example of this structure is General Motors with its many different auto and product divisions. As another illustration, however, consider the National Metals Corporation, shown in Figure 6-3, which illustrates a structure based upon different metal products.

(3) Departmentation by territory, or place. In some types of organizations it is best to departmentalize according to *place or territory covered.* This is frequently

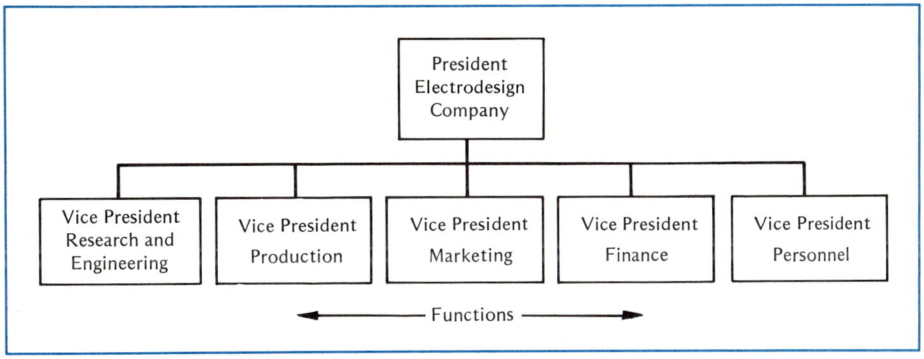

FIGURE 6-2. Departmentation by Function.

the case with marketing or sales-oriented firms that need to be sure of market coverage. In some instances this is because of slight product or promotion differences that may need to vary from region to region, or it may be done simply to assign territory and responsibility to specific departments or units. It is common when this method of organizing is used for a marketing department to be horizontally departmentalized, as we see in Figure 6-4.

Note in this organization chart the company has divided on a territorial basis twice, thus creating a vertical growth as a result of specialized territorial division.

(4) Departmentation by customer or clientele. In some situations it is appropriate for an organization to structure itself by *customer served or clientele.* The reasons would be basically the same as those cited for territory—to better serve the specialized needs of the customers. As an illustration of this method of departmentation, consider the marketing division's structure in a large computer and data processing firm. Figure 6-5 depicts their situation.

The particular needs of each of these types of users or customers are so

FIGURE 6-3. Departmentation by Products.

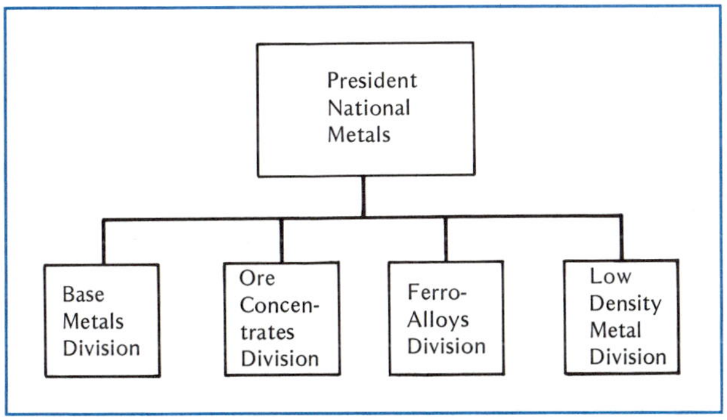

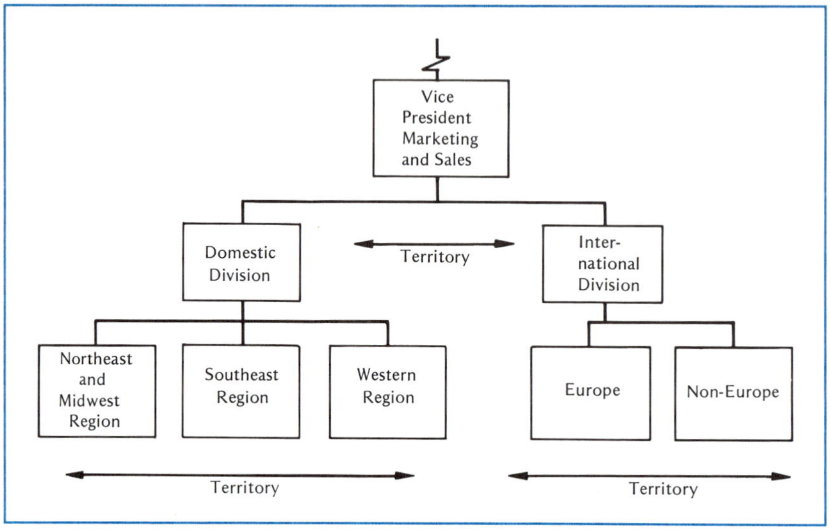

FIGURE 6-4. Departmentation by Territory.

specialized that the company found it useful to departmentalize, as shown in Figure 6-5.

We thus see that departmentation represents the horizontal growth and division of labor of the organization and that the organization can choose from a variety of bases to achieve this horizontal specialization. Presented here, in general, are simple cases illustrating one organization departmentalizing on one basis (function, product, territory, or customer) at a time. In reality, an organization can use a combination of these in structuring itself. In fact, in Figure 6-4 and 6-5, it was implicit in our examples that the organizations had already achieved horizontal departmentation on a functional basis, resulting in the marketing units that were then further subdivided.

FIGURE 6-5. Departmentation by Customer Served.

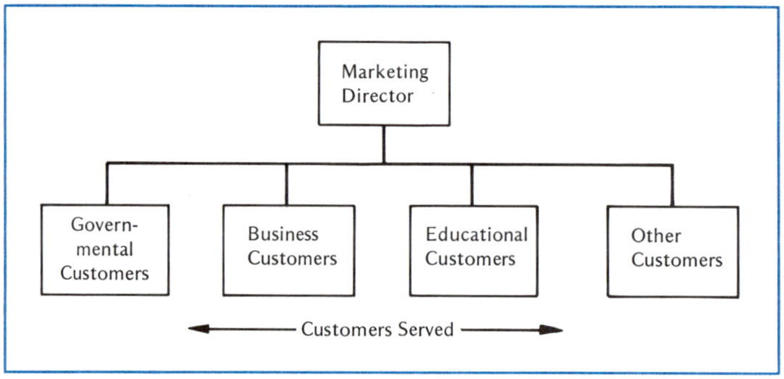

Hierarchy. The companion concept to departmentation is hierarchy. Whereas departmentation represents horizontal growth and specialization, *hierarchy* is vertical or scalar growth and specialization. Hierarchy refers to the creation of a number of different levels in the organization. (Refer back to Figure 6-1.) The hierarchy of an organization creates the superior-subordinate relationships found in the structure and is referred to by some as the *chain of command.* As an illustration of how vertical or hierarchical growth occurs in an organization, let us consider an example that results in an increase in the number of levels of management.

Let us assume a simple organization founded by an individual to whom we shall refer as the manager, who had six subordinates when the organization was formed. See Phase I in Figure 6-6.[5] We use the term *span of control* or span of management to refer to how many subordinates a manager has. In Phase I, the manager's span of control is six. As the organization prospers and grows, the manager hires more employees and the span of control widens to a point at which management cannot be effective because of the large number of subordinates. In Phase II of Figure 6-6, we see that the manager's span of control has grown to 14. At this point, the manager's job needs to be divided into several parts. As this growth occurs and as the manager's physical and mental limits are reached, additional *levels of management* must be created, and scalar growth occurs. In our example, let us assume that management not only decided to divide the manager's job into two, with each submanager in charge of seven subordinates, but that a new level of management was created by the need to coordinate the activities of the two managers. Thus, we see in phase III of Figure 6-6 how the hierarchy continued to evolve. Manager A now has a span of control of two, and managers B and C each have a span of control of seven.

Structure

The third pillar of classical organization doctrine is *structure.* Structure is the "logical relationships of functions in an organization, arranged to accomplish the objectives of the company efficiently."[6] Stated differently, structure—or the pattern of horizontal and vertical authority and responsibility relationships—is the result of the functional and scalar processes we discussed previously. Structure is simply the pattern of relationships emanating out of these concepts.

Span of Control

Span of control was defined earlier as the number of subordinates reporting to a manager. It is an important concept in thinking about an organization's basic structure. If spans of control of managers are wide, that is, many subordinates

[5]This chart was adapted from Hugh J. Watson and Archie B. Carroll, *Computers for Business: A Managerial Emphasis* (Dallas: Business Publications, Inc., 1976), p. 330.

[6]Scott, op. cit., pp. 7–9.

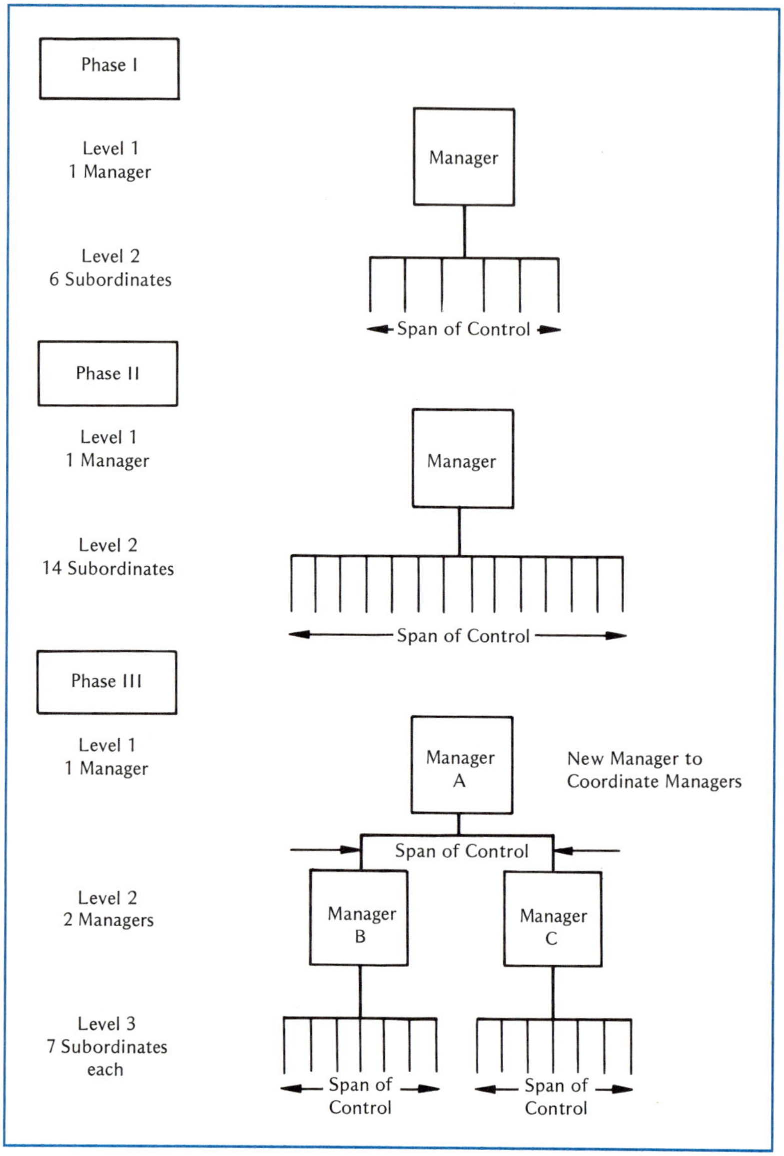

FIGURE 6-6. Organizational Growth and Hierarchy.

reporting to a manager, the organizational structure will be flatter. If spans of control are narrow, the resulting structure will be taller. Figure 6-7 illustrates how spans of control affect the shape of the organization.

The first important question is, Are there limits to the number of persons a manager can effectively supervise? Most managers say yes. Graicunas was one of

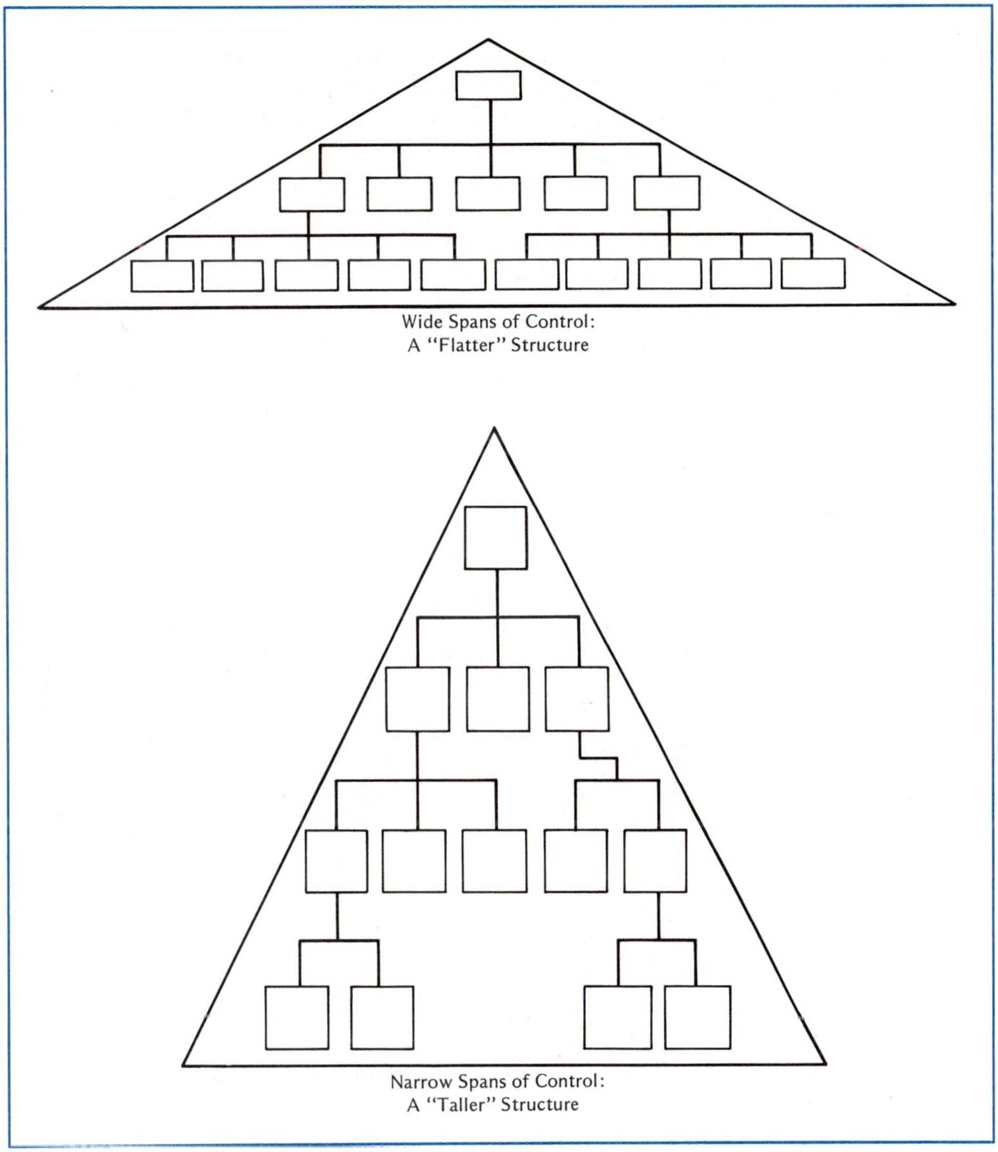

FIGURE 6-7. Spans of Control and Organizational Shape.

the earliest to argue that there are numerical limitations to the number of subordinates one can effectively control.[7] The second important question is, What determines those limits? The research of Joan Woodward into the relation-

[7] V. A. Graicunas, "Relationships in Organizations," *Papers on the Science of Administration* (New York: Columbia University Press, 1937).

ship between technology and organization indicates that spans of control vary with the type of technological system used in organizations. For example, effective organizations with unit technology tended to have narrower spans of control than effective organizations with mass production technology. Technology was also identified by Robert House and John Miner as being related to span of control. Their research revealed that the ideal span of control is likely to fall in the 5–10 range in most situations, with the span increasing at higher, policy-making levels where high echelon executives need more inputs before decisions can be made about the broader system.[8]

In addition to the technology used in an organization, other factors have to be considered when determining what the span of control of any given manager in any given situation ought to be. These other factors include the following:

1. The nature of the work or task being managed.
2. The nature of the people being managed.
3. The leadership ability of the manager.
4. The level of management in the organization.
5. The interdependence of work between employees.

Span of control, combined with departmentation and hierarchy, are the major determinants of an organization's structure and are, therefore, the main variables with which management can work in efforts to shape the organization's configuration.

In addition to the pillars of classical organization doctrine, there are several other concepts that merit inclusion here.

Unity of Command

Henri Fayol suggested *unity of command* as one of his basic principles. The principle holds that in an organization a subordinate should have only one superior. This one-person-one-boss guideline has held up rather well over the years as a fundamental premise upon which organizations should be structured. The basic reason for the principle derives from the belief—which has been documented quite extensively by experience—that an individual cannot effectively serve two masters. Research has also shown that conflict, tension, and anxiety can result when an individual is subjected to multiple directives or authority. Role conflict has resulted in some cases in low job satisfaction, low confidence in the organization, significant decision making difficulty, estranged communications, and other dysfunctional side effects. It is possible that these consequences will result when an individual has more than one person to whom

[8]Robert House and John Miner, "Merging Management and Behavioral Theory: The Interaction Between Span of Control and Group Size," *Administrative Science Quarterly*, 14, 1969, pp. 451–466. For an interesting history of this issue, see David D. Van Fleet and Arthur G. Bedeian, "A History of the Span of Management," *Academy of Management Review*, July 1977, pp. 356–372.

to report. We shall see later, however, that there are some organizational forms in which the principle has been successfully violated, so care must be exercised in being too dogmatic about this concept.

Authority and Responsibility

The twin concepts of authority and responsibility must also be discussed briefly as basic notions of organization. The concept of authority has been implicitly suggested already. Now we shall be more explicit about its role. *Authority* is the *right* of a manager to make decisions and take actions on behalf of the organization. The granting of such rights, of course, flows from the top of the organization down. Thus, the right of managers to take action is *delegated* down the hierarchy so that each manager has the specific right to take actions in those areas so designated by upper management. It can thus be seen that authority is, in a sense, the glue that holds the organization together as the official basis for managerial action.

Authority can be seen pictorially in the organization charts presented earlier. The connecting lines we see between positions refers to a chain of authority. The charts show authority over *people.* There is another kind of authority that has gained widespread usage in organizations, however, and this is known as *functional authority.* Functional authority is the right to make decisions or take actions concerning certain functions or tasks in the organization. For example, an accountant may be given functional authority over all decisions pertaining to forms design and control in the organization. The accountant is given this responsibility because of expertise possessed. Functional authority can collide with hierarchical authority, however, and care must be exercised in its usage.

It is frequently argued that authority and responsibility should go hand-in-hand. By this is meant that just as individuals are given responsibility, so should they be given commensurate authority. These are basic concepts of organization. The question arises, however, whether responsibility can really be delegated. It is axiomatic in classical doctrine that authority can be delegated but responsibility cannot. The basis for this belief is that responsibility *ultimately* resides with the person with whom authority began—the person at the top. But does this preclude those at lower levels from being held responsible?

This debate has been considerably eased by Keith Davis who argues that we need to think of responsibility as having two facets—ultimate and operating.[9] He argues that *operating responsibility* can be delegated whereas *ultimate responsibility* cannot. According to this view, operating responsibility is held by the individual to whom authority has been delegated, whereas ultimate responsibility still resides at the top. This differentiation goes a long way toward clarifying what actually happens with responsibility and accountability in organizations.

[9]Keith Davis, *Human Behavior at Work: Human Relations and Organizational Behavior,* 4th ed. (New York: McGraw-Hill, 1972), p. 200.

The classical thinkers on organization viewed authority as a rather rigid concept creating a definite chain of command and hierarchy. Carried to its extreme, and coupled with the unity of command principle, a rather inflexible organization results. Max Weber combined this classical view of authority, which he called rational-legal authority, with other similarly rigid notions to form what he called bureaucracy, to him the ideal form of organization.

Other views of authority have emerged over the years, however, and although we typically accept the classical view of authority as standard, perspectives have emerged suggesting that authority can be effectively thought of in different ways. For example, Frederick W. Taylor thought that all authority should be based on knowledge and not position. This view is appealing but in practical situations does not seem to make for an ordered approach to decision making. Chester Barnard suggested that an *acceptance theory of authority* should prevail. His position was that the source of authority did not reside in persons of authority but, rather, in the acceptance of that authority by subordinates. Mary Parker Follett's view was that authority should emanate from the situation. Her "law of the situation" held that it was the situation that dictated what ought to be done, not some person with position authority. The views of Taylor, Barnard, and Follett have not considerably altered the basic notion of what authority is in organizations, but these later views have affected somewhat how authority is exercised by position holders.

Delegation

Another concept that helps form the bone and sinew of organizing is that of *delegation.* It is quite appropriate to discuss delegation immediately after looking at authority, because delegation is the process by which authority and responsibility are spread throughout the organization. Effective delegating is one of the truly significant attributes of successful managers. In a sense, delegation *is* management, for it is only by getting work done by others that managers can justify their existence.

Delegation is the passing of authority and responsibility for performance down to lower-level personnel in the organization. Thus, delegation is the process by which managerial positions are created throughout the hierarchy. It may appear that this is a simple process; however, in practice the effectiveness of the delegation process varies widely from manager to manager and from organization to organization.

It has been held that for effective delegation to occur, three vital actions must take place.[10]

1. The assignment of *tasks* to be performed.

[10] William H. Newman, Charles E. Summer, and E. Kirby Warren, *The Process of Management* (Englewood Cliffs, N.J.: Prentice-Hall, 1967), pp. 83–88.

2. The *granting of authority* to carry out these tasks.
3. The creation of *responsibility* to perform.

All three of these must occur to have a successful delegation. Frequently, however, managers fail to make some aspect of this total process clear. If just one of the elements is missing, the delegation may not prove to be successful.

Assignment of Tasks. Clear communication is vital in the assignment of tasks aspect of the delegation process. The person receiving the delegation must understand precisely what is to be done. Some managers prefer to be very general in the assignment of tasks, leaving the individual some leeway or flexibility to display initiative. The major difficulty with this approach is that the manager may not get precisely the results desired. There is a high risk inherent in a general assignment of tasks or jobs to be done. The manager must weigh carefully what room for misunderstanding can be permitted before employing such a general approach.

Typically, more specific assignments of tasks are necessary until managers know well the abilities, capacities for exercising judgment, and the degree of initiative desired by subordinates. The more specific approach requires the manager to provide explicit instruction about what is expected. This approach does not leave as much room for individual initiative, but it does improve upon the probability that the specific task will be accomplished in the desired manner. Whether an assignment of task should be broad or specific will depend, in the final analysis, upon such factors as the task to be accomplished, the time available, the persons involved, and the manager's previous experience.

Granting of Authority. The granting of authority element in the delegation process refers to giving the person to whom a task or job has been assigned the *rights* necessary to accomplish the assignment. This can be another source of difficulty in the delegation process. To begin with, the manager must be in a position (have the authority) to delegate authority to others. On occasion, where managers have not had authority clearly delegated to them from above, they in turn have difficulty communicating to their subordinates what authority is attached to a given delegation. Unclear definitions of authority, therefore, can have a rippling effect down through the organization.

Creation of Responsibility. A third facet of delegation is the creation of an obligation, or sense of duty, to perform. Thus, when a delegation is made, the manager must exercise care to be sure that a sense of accountability is conveyed. Earlier we differentiated between ultimate and operating responsibility. Keith Davis goes on in his discussion to liken the responsibility issue to the "fable of the magic pitcher." This pitcher is one in which the water level remains the same no matter how much is poured out. This is the way it is with responsibility; no matter how much operating responsibility is delegated, the top-level managers' own ultimate responsibility remains the same.[11]

In addition to being fully aware of the three essential elements in the delegation process, management must develop the proper personal attitude if it wants to apply delegation concepts most effectively. Koontz and O'Donnell have found the following attitudes to be most consistent with effective delegators: (1) a willingness to take risks, (2) a willingness to "let go," and (3) a willingness to place trust in subordinates.[12]

The degree of delegation that takes place in an organization plays a role in shaping the structure, for it specifies in part how many subordinate levels will exist in the hierarchy. In addition to affecting the basic structure, however, delegation influences the pattern or mode of decision making that occurs. An organization that delegates decision-making authority down the structure to where specific competence resides is said to be *decentralized.* An organization that retains decision authority at *the top levels* is *centralized.* There are advantages and disadvantages to both approaches, however, and some organizations employ both, depending upon the decision issue involved, the personnel affected, and the nature of the environment.

Line and Staff Organization

The type of organization structure resulting from the typical application of the organizing concepts discussed thus far is the *line and staff organization.* The line and staff organization is one comprised of both line units and staff units. Line units (departments) are those having to do *directly* with the production and distribution of the organization's product or service. In the case of a manufacturing concern, line units would likely be production and marketing. Staff units provide *specialized support* or *services* to the line organization. Although staff units contribute nothing *directly* to production and distribution, their services are nonetheless crucial to the organization. Examples of staff units are the personnel, data processing, legal, and finance departments.

When organizations are first founded, only line units typically exist, and the staff or support activities are handled by the line units. As the organization grows and matures and the line units are no longer able to effectively handle the support functions, separate staff units begin to appear. In the typical modern organization, the structure contains within it both line and staff units, arranged according to the departmentation and hierarchy needs of the organization.

It has not been unusual in organizations to observe conflict between line and the staff units. The basis for this conflict or friction frequently lies in the differences in the characteristics of those who typically hold the two types of jobs and the struggle for influence, authority, or power. Managers in staff positions,

[11] Davis, op. cit., p. 200.

[12] Harold Koontz and Cyril O'Donnell, *Principles of Management,* 4th ed. (New York: McGraw-Hill, 1968), pp. 70–72.

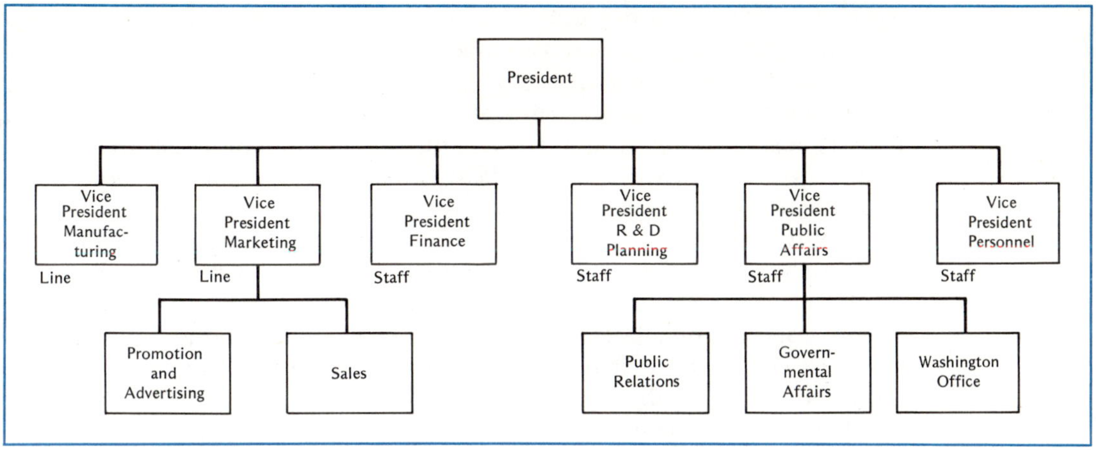

FIGURE 6-8. A Typical Line and Staff Organization.

historically, have tended to be younger, better educated, and in white-collar positions. Managers in line roles have tended to be older and more experienced, but less well educated and at least in the lower echelons in blue-collar roles. The conflict, to a great extent, has therefore been over *status*. As society and the work force has become on the average more educated, some of these historical differences have begun to blur.

The typical line and staff organization has usually been formulated based upon primarily internal needs and factors with little consideration of the external environment of the organization. This trend is changing. As we shall see, external factors have assumed a larger role in providing the basis for how organizations are structured. Figure 6-8 illustrates a partial line and staff organization structure.

ADVANCED CONCEPTS OF ORGANIZATION DESIGN

The 1960s might be said to be the beginning of the modern era insofar as advanced concepts of organization design are concerned. The work of Burns and Stalker (1961); Lawrence and Lorsch (1967); and Woodward (1965) form the core of the advanced notions of organization that emerged.

Environment and Organization Design

Burns and Stalker researched a number of plants in Great Britain to examine the relationships between management processes and systems and their external environments.[13] Specifically, they conducted field research in a rayon factory, a large engineering concern, and a number of firms in the newly emerging electronics field. The rayon manufacturer was the company that operated in the most stable, or most predictable environment. The engineering company operated in a rapidly changing commercial environment, and an embryonic electronics firm operated in the most turbulent, or least stable environment. The researchers found that identifiable patterns of organization tended to correlate with the predictability or certainty of the organizations' environments. In the more certain, stable, or placid environments, the organizational design that seemed most prevalent was "mechanistic." In the more dynamic or turbulent environments, the organizational design that seemed most prevalent was "organic." The researchers concluded that organizations' styles or structures were contingent upon the certainty of the environment in which the organization operated.

Mechanistic organizational systems, which seemed to fare best in stable environments, had characteristics similar to those of the classical doctrine of organization described earlier. Positions in the mechanistic structure tended to be highly specialized and defined. Authority seemed to be concentrated at the top of the structure and in the hands of a few. Communications and interactions seemed to be unidirectional—downward only. In sum, mechanistic systems seemed to be closed, rigid systems with other characteristics similar to those described.

Organic organizational systems possessed characteristics more conducive to conditions of environmentally induced change. Authority was found to be more decentralized and more closely located to where competence resided. Positions in the structure tended to be less specialized. Jobs were not as closely defined and distinguished from one another. Communications and interactions were more multidirectional, with communications tending to resemble lateral consultation rather than vertical command. In sum, organic systems seemed to be more open, less rigid, and adaptive to uncertainty.

Other researchers since Burns and Stalker have more fully articulated the various characteristics of organizations that fit the mechanistic and organic models, but the message that comes through almost consistently is that basic organization design and structure are related to, or contingent upon, the nature of the organization's environment. Figure 6-9 summarizes the most important of these characteristics.

The work of two other researchers on the subject of organization and environment deserves attention here too. Lawrence and Lorsch concluded that because the environments that organizations face are different—varying in certainty-uncertainty and in diversity-homogeneity—organizations need to alter their structures to accommodate these differences.[14] The concepts that describe management efforts at accommodation are differentiation and integration.

[13]Tom Burns and G. M. Stalker, *The Management of Innovation* (London: Tavistock Publications, 1961).

[14]Paul Lawrence and Jay Lorsch, "Differentiation and Integration in Complex Organizations," *Administrative Science Quarterly,* XII, (June 1967).

Mechanistic	Organic
Closed systems	Open systems
Placid environments	Turbulent environments
Certain, homogeneous	Uncertain, heterogeneous
Many hierarchical levels	Few hierarchical levels
Power concentration	Power diffusion
Single goal	Multiple goals
Low knowledge-based authority	High knowledge-based authority
High position-based authority	Low position-based authority

FIGURE 6-9. Characteristics of Mechanistic and Organic Organizations

Differentiation is the process of dividing the organizational system into subsystems so that each subsystem can better adapt to the requirements of its part of the total external environment.[15] This process of developing subunits in the organization is similar to the notions of specialization and departmentation discussed earlier. The differentiation concept, however, takes the process further and specifies the dimensions, or attributes, along which these subunits will vary, once differentiated. Examples of these are (1) the unit's or department's structure, (2) the members' time orientation (such as market versus science), and (3) the interpersonal orientation of the unit's members (concern for task versus relationships).

Lawrence and Lorsch assert that, depending upon the environment the organization faces, it will differentiate itself to deal with that environment. The end result, for example, is a highly differentiated organization structure in the face of a turbulent or dynamic environment. Conversely, a less differentiated organization will function more effectively in a stable or placid environment.

The companion concept to differentiation is *integration.* Although an organization may differentiate itself to more effectively deal with the environment, integration must nevertheless be achieved. *Integration* is defined as the "process of achieving unity of effort among the various subsystems in the accomplishment of the organization's task."[16] Integration, then, refers to achieving coordination among the differentiated units of the organization.

Differentiation and integration might appear to be basically antagonistic forces operating on organization design, but the work of Lawrence and Lorsch shows that both high differentiated firms and low differentiated firms were able to achieve a high level of integration. The difference between the two seems to lie with the *type of integrating devices* used in the respective organizations. Organizations that are more highly differentiated tend to require more sophisticated integrating devices.

The integration devices available to management to assure coordination between organizational units range in complexity. One of the most straightforward integrative devices used is the *management hierarchy* itself. As the organization

[15]Paul Lawrence and Jay Lorsch, *Studies in Organizational Design* (Homewood, Ill.: Richard D. Irwin, 1970), p. 6.

[16]Lawrence and Lorsch, ibid., p. 4.

structure is built by grouping activities into logical units, the management hierarchy of the organization is designed so that integration is built in. For example, if it is decided in an organization that sales units need to be differentiated according to territory or region, these units are then integrated with an overarching superior to whom both units report. Similarly, if the entire marketing unit needs to be tightly integrated with research and development in a high-technology electronics firm, then a common superior, such as a vice-president, may have reporting responsibility for these two units. Thus, integration is designed into the structure by considering at the outset what functions must especially be integrated.

After units have been grouped and the hierarchy established, other integrating devices may also be necessary. These other integrating devices can range from prescriptive rules, operating regulations, and plans for organizations that are basically "mechanistic,"[17] to the use of liaison individuals, integrating departments, or cross-functional teams for more complex organizations.

Liaison individuals, sometimes referred to as "integrators," are individuals who, although they may officially reside in a given functional department of the organization, have the responsibility for integrating the activities of two or more departments. An example of this role is the design engineer who may officially be a part of the engineering department but who works in a special office out in the plant to ensure close coordination between design and manufacturing.

The use of *coordinating departments* and *cross-functional teams* as integrating devices can be seen in Lorsch and Lawrence's investigation of two companies in the plastics industry.[18] The two companies, which they call Rhody and Crown to protect their identities, illustrate what they term the *organizational paradox.* Rhody is the more highly specialized and differentiated of the two firms. The researchers hold that this should mean that Rhody would encounter more problems achieving integration. This does not turn out to be the case, however, and hence the paradox. It turns out that both firms use the same integrating devices—a coordinating department (whose purpose is to coordinate) and cross-functional teams (drawn from several functional areas)—to achieve integration, but their effectiveness differs, with Rhody achieving a more effective integration.

The integration needed in both firms is between the research, sales, and production departments, each of which has varying orientations on the dimensions of *structure,* orientation toward *time,* orientation toward *others,* and orientation toward the *environment.* The researchers conclude that Rhody's coordinating department is more effective because it has a *balanced perspective* of the various orientations in the departments needing integration. The coordinating department at Crown is less effective because it had an imbalanced

[17] Don Hellriegel and John W. Slocum, Jr., "Organization Design: A Contingency Approach," *Business Horizons,* April 1973, p. 67.

[18] Jay W. Lorsch and Paul R. Lawrence, "Organizing for Product Innovation," in Gene Dalton, Paul Lawrence, and Jay Lorsch, (eds.) *Organizational Structure and Design* (Homewood, Ill.: Richard D. Irwin, Inc., 1970,) pp. 280–296.

perspective—one biased toward sales—with respect to the dimensions of time orientation and orientation toward the environment. This imbalanced view resulted in impaired effectiveness of the coordinating department at Crown and hence its weakness as an integrating device.

The companies' other integrating device—the cross-functional committees or teams—revealed also why Rhody more effectively achieved integration. These permanent cross-functional groups brought specialists together for decison-making purposes for the firms. A close examination of how these groups functioned in Rhody and Crown was revealing. They tended to differ in two major respects, in the area of decision authority, and in resolving conflict. At Rhody, knowledge and *decision authority* resided in the supervisors who were made members of the team. These persons had the detailed market and technical knowledge required to make decisions and they were formally delegated authority to make decisions. They were the only ones who attended the cross-functional team meetings. At Crown, members of the teams or committees came from a much higher level than their counterparts at Rhody. Even then, they sometimes were not given the authority to make decisions. Furthermore, they typically did not have the detailed knowledge needed to make decisions. The basic problems, then, were that knowledge and authority often resided in different people at Crown, and their meetings were too large to be effective.

Another difference between Rhody and Crown was how their cross-functional groups *resolved conflict*. At Rhody, members of the team had developed an "ability to confront their differences openly and search persistently for solutions which will provide effective collaboration."[19] At Crown, on the other hand, the norms of behavior sanction withdrawal from conflict. When disagreement occurs, the members avoid discussion in the hope that the conflict will go away. Consequently, the group avoids addressing differences of opinion and forfeits the opportunity to reach a coordinated resolution of conflict. Figure 6-10 summarizes the details of the Rhody and Crown research.

As a result of its more effective use of integrating devices, the Rhody organization achieved a higher level of integration and, hence, innovation, than did Crown. At Rhody new products developed in the five-year period studied accounted for 59% of sales. At Crown the figure was only 20%, or just about one third of Rhody's. The researchers concluded that it is not only the specification of techniques for achieving integration that is important but also how effectively these techniques are employed. That conclusion applies to most of what is discussed in this book.

A Contingency Approach

Lawrence and Lorsch, as well as many others, have argued for a *contingency approach* to organizational design. This approach holds that the differentiation of

[19] Lawrence and Lorsch, ibid.

Company	Rhody	Crown
Industry:	Plastics	Plastics
Degree of specialization and differentiation:	Higher	Lower
Problems *expected* in achieving integration:	More	Less
Actual difficulty in achieving integration experienced:	Less	More
Integration devices employed:	1. Coordinating department 2. Cross-functional team	1. Coordinating department 2. Cross-functional team
Effectiveness of integration:	More effective	Less effective
Level of innovation achieved:	Higher	Lower

FIGURE 6-10. Differentiation and Integration at Rhody and Crown

an organization is a function of the organization's environment and a number of other factors. Likewise, the integration devices needed will vary depending upon the kind and degree of differentiation. It is useful to conceptualize into a simple grid the basic combinations of differentiation and integration needed by organizations in response to environmental uncertainty or turbulence. It is also useful to illustrate the different types of integration devices that can be employed under each set of circumstances. Figure 6-11 presents a differentiation-integration grid that summarizes Hellriegel and Slocum's view of companies and integrating devices, reflecting the conditions in each cell. A brief explanation follows.

In Cell 1—high differentiation/low integration—the example given is the corporate level at General Motors Corporation (GM). Since GM is differentiated along product lines that are profit centers—Chevrolet Division, Pontiac Division, Buick Division—there is little need for integration and this can be achieved by top management committees that provide policy guidelines for the semiautonomous units.

In Cell 2—high differentiation/high integration—the example given is Hughes Aircraft Company, which is organized into seven product lines. The company works on the basis of awarded contracts and a newly awarded contract calls for many people in various divisions to work closely together. The shifting of highly trained personnel between projects and the constant technological change that characterizes the firm's industries, such as electronics, space, and research, demands a special integrative device such as matrix management or a project management structure. These kinds of structures will be discussed separately later.

In Cell 3—low differentiation/low integration—the illustration given is Continental Can Company. The environment and technology are stable in this firm's industry and thus there is a low need for differentiation and integration. High

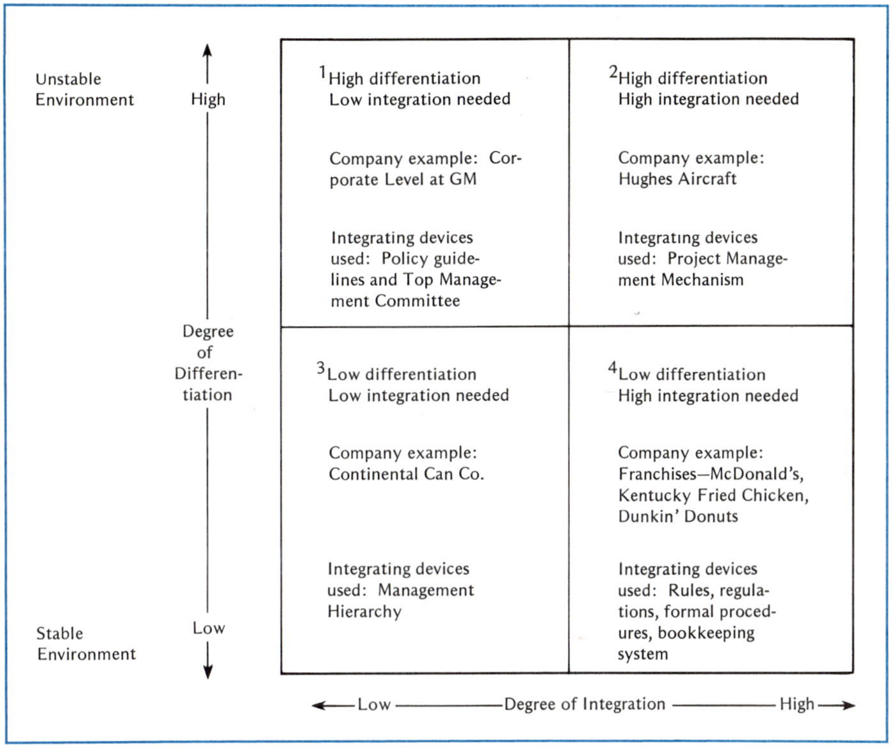

FIGURE 6-11. Companies and Integrating Devices for Differentiation-Integration Grid.[20]

performing firms in the container industry are able to successfully achieve integration by employing the management hierarchy.

In Cell 4—low differentiation/high integration—franchises such as McDonalds, Kentucky Fried Chicken, and Dunkin' Donuts are given as examples. Individual units of these organizations require low differentiation but high integration. Homogeneity and integration of the units are achieved by rules, regulations, formal procedures, and bookkeeping systems to which all units are expected to adhere.

In sum, it can be seen how different companies, facing different combinations of differentiation and integration needs, employ varying kinds of devices to achieve integration. The environments of these organizations assume a prominent role in influencing their organizational design.

[20] Adapted and summarized from Hellreigel and Slocum, pp. 60–68.

Matrix Organization Design

In our discussion of Cell 2, we mentioned project management and matrix organization structures. *Matrix organization designs* (of which project management is one example) sharply contrast with the one-boss command structures that typify many organizations today. These one-boss arrangements adhere to the unity of command principle discussed earlier, although they are moderated somewhat by the power of departments such as personnel. Also, the use of functional authority in conjunction with a line-and-staff organization moves it in the direction of matrix organization, but it is never quite reached.

The origins of the term *matrix* are traceable to the aerospace industry in the United States. This seems quite fitting a term for the quantitatively trained engineers in that industry to apply to the gridlike organizational form that was evolving from its project management beginnings of the 1950s.

Davis and Lawrence define matrix as:

> *any organization that employs a* multiple command system *that includes not only a multiple command structure but also related support mechanisms and an associated organizational culture and behavior pattern.*[21]

Matrix management requires two or more lines of authority in an organization to exercise equal or shared influence over the same resources and to negotiate for the use of those resources. In a typical application, a matrix structure is formed when the functional departments of a company, such as production and marketing, create vertical chains of command, whereas the product or project divisions of the company form the horizontal chains of command, cutting across the functional lines. Figure 6-12 illustrates the effect achieved and, hence, the term *matrix*.

What occurs in a matrix structure, then, is that functional (vertical) lines of authority intersect project or product (horizontal) lines of authority. In the classical aerospace industry illustration, it would not be uncommon for a large firm to have a functional structure of manufacturing, engineering and design, research, and so on, overlayed with another dimension of organization—project lines—which called upon the various resources and persons in the functional divisions at various and sometimes simultaneous points in the completion of a project. For example, TRW Systems at one time had the Titan Missile, Atlas Missile, and Saturn Systems constituting the horizontal dimension of that organization and cutting through several functional lines of authority.

One of the major difficulties inherent in matrix is the potential conflict that results from the violation of the unity of command principle and the multiple flow of authority. What has to emerge out of this is a system based upon negotiation and trust, the open management of conflict, confrontation, and

[21] Stanley M. Davis and Paul R. Lawrence, *Matrix* (Reading, Mass.: Addison-Wesley, 1977), p. 3.

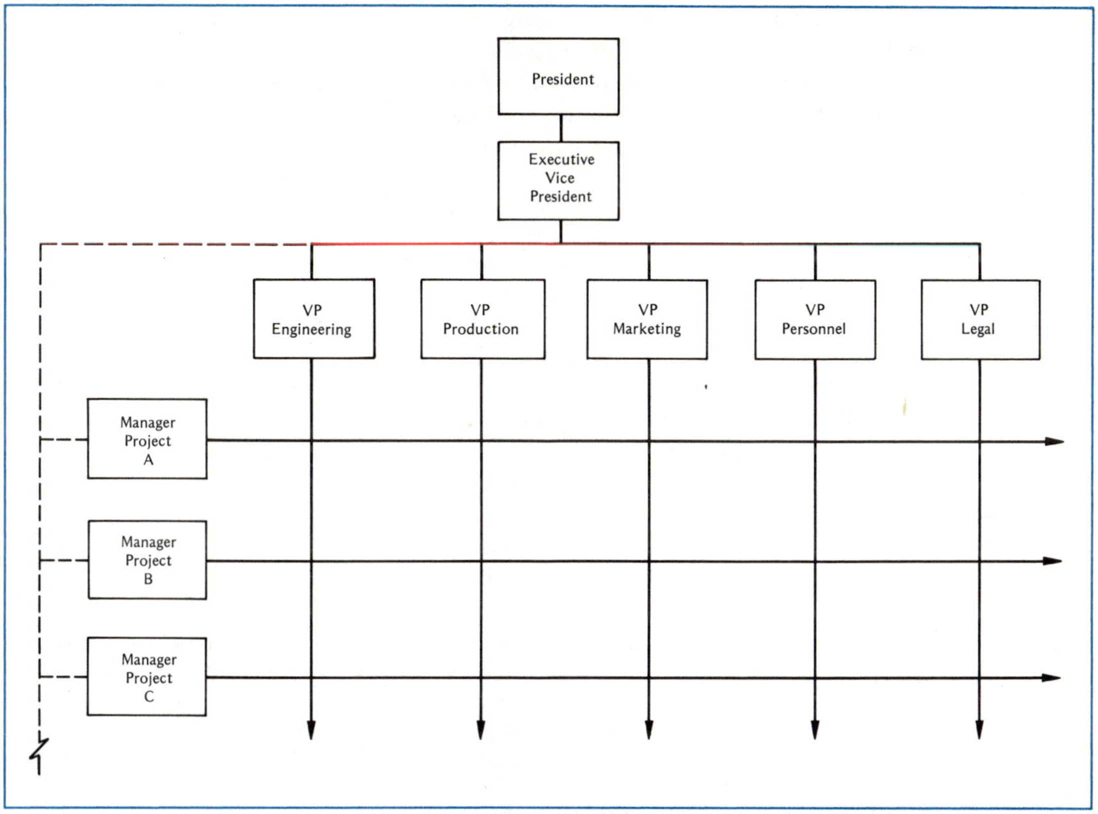

FIGURE 6-12. Matrix Organization Design Showing Vertical and Horizontal Flows of Authority.

problem solving, and a somewhat different style of decision making. The result, however, can be an organization that is readily adaptive to change.

Despite some of the drawbacks inherent in matrix organizational forms, the concept is beginning to break down barriers to action that have become built into traditional hierarchies. The matrix approach pushes decision making down to more people, places a premium on teamwork and collaboration, and restores a measure of flexibility to the large, complex organizations using it. Among the companies that use matrix in one form or another are General Electric, TRW Systems, Equitable Life Insurance, Dow Corning, Shell Oil, and Citicorp.[22]

Davis and Lawrence have commented that three conditions have been identified that suggest the need for a matrix structure.[23] Condition 1 is the *outside*

[22] "How to stop the buck short at the top," *Business Week*, January 16, 1978, pp. 82–83. See also William C. Goggin, "How the multidimensional structure works at Dow Corning," *Harvard Business Review* (January-February 1974), pp. 54–65.

[23] See Davis and Lawrence, op. cit., Chapter 2, pp. 11–18.

pressure for a dual focus. For example, to survive and prosper in the aerospace industry, a firm must give intensive attention to both complex technical issues and the special project orientations of customers. A balance of power must be achieved between project-oriented managers and the managers of engineering and scientific specialists. Neither can be allowed to be relegated to a second-level status. Hence,

> *the needed behavior is epitomized by . . . two middle managers with equal power, but very different orientations and goals, sitting down to debate and argue over each and every point in their search for the answers that would optimize decisions for both technical excellence and unique customer requirements.*[24]

Condition 2 is *pressures for high information-processing capacity.* When the demands placed on the organization are changing, relatively unpredictable, complex, and require a high degree of interdependence, matrix design provides a capacity that exceeds traditional structures.

Condition 3 is *pressures for shared resources.* When the organization is under pressure to "achieve economies of scale in human terms and high performance in terms of both costs and benefits by fully utilizing scarce human resources and by meeting high-quality standards," a matrix design is desirable.[25] Organizations with conventional structures tend to develop rigidities and barriers that inhibit the free movement of specialists across functional lines. When these three conditions are present, Davis and Lawrence hold that a matrix structure is probably indicated.

Technology and Organization Design

The research of Joan Woodward and her colleagues into the relationship between technology and organizational design stimulated considerable thought about this contingency. Although not yet as fully thought out as the work on organizations and environments, the technology research deserves mention here.

Woodward investigated the organizational structure of 100 manufacturing firms located in the south of England. Having found no relationship between organizational characteristics and size of firm or business efficiency, the researchers looked at the relationship between organization and technology. The firms studied were categorized according to *simple technology features* into three major subgroups.

1. Unit or small batch technology.
2. Large batch and mass production technology.
3. Continuous process technology.

[24] Ibid., p. 13.
[25] Ibid., pp. 17–18.

Technology Type	Unit and Small Batch Production	Large Batch and Mass Production	Process Production
Structural Style	Organic	Mechanistic	Organic

FIGURE 6-13. Woodward's View of Technology and Structure

This classification scheme constituted a rather crude scale of technology, but it enabled the researchers to examine organizational characteristics that correlated with technology divisions. Wide differences were found on such measures as number of levels of management authority, span of control, and ratio of managers and supervisors to other personnel.

As a consequence of examining typical characteristics or organizations that fell into the various technology categories and success indicators of these firms, Woodward observed that organizations deviating from the general pattern within a category were often least effective. Organizations that were most effective in the unit or small batch and process production categories tended to be more flexible. Organizations that were most effective in the large batch or mass production technology were those that were more hierarchically organized, specialized, with clearer chains of command, and tighter controls.

These observations led Woodward to conclude as follows:

> *Successful firms inside the large-batch production range tended to have mechanistic management systems. On the other hand, successful firms outside this range tended to have organic systems.*[26]

Figure 6-13 summarizes this relationship.

SUMMARY

Organizing and organization design are crucial responsibilities of management. Organizing entails structuring the relationships of the elements of the organization so as to provide a cohesive, goal-directed whole. Organizing implies the understanding and utilization of basic concepts such as the following: division of labor/specialization, functional and scalar processes (departmentation and hierarchy), structure, span of control, authority and responsibility, delegation, and the line-and-staff organization. Although these are traditional concepts of organizing that have been around for many decades, they remain essential to the operation of contemporary organizations.

[26] Joan Woodward, *Industrial Organization: Theory and Practice* (London: Oxford University Press, 1965).

Organization design is a modern term that implies managers have choices to make in the structuring of organizations and, as the architect, they must examine all of the variables that might bear on design decisions. The objective of organization design is to construct a more nearly optimal structure—a personalized structure—for the specific task of any given organization. Modern organization design builds upon classical or traditional notions of organizing by employing research that addresses the relationship between the environment, technology, and organization. Key concepts of organization design include mechanistic versus organic systems, differentiation, integration, and matrix. These concepts, when taken together with basic concepts of organization, constitute the fundamentals of organization theory.

Assignments

6-1. Differentiate between organizing and organization design.

6-2. Physicians take courses in anatomy and physiology. Which of these provides the best analogy for the study of organization structure? Explain.

6-3. What are meant by functional and scalar processes?

6-4. Describe the various bases for departmentation. Which is most likely to be used by a small business just being formed? What factors influence which basis is used?

6-5. What is meant by span of control? What factors determine what span of control will be used?

6-6. Distinguish clearly between authority and responsibility. How is each related to delegation?

6-7. What are the three essential features of effective delegation? What would happen if one feature was not considered?

6-8. Your superior comes to you and states, "Get started on this right away and let me know next week how you're doing." Is this effective delegation? Discuss.

6-9. Discuss the basis for conflict that may arise between line and staff components in an organization.

6-10. Are universities more nearly mechanistic or organic organizations? Discuss.

6-11. Distinguish between differentiation and integration. Relate these concepts to appropriate basic concepts of organizing.

6-12. Enumerate and describe the various integrating devices management can employ. Is there any way to know which are more desirable?

6-13. Explain why Rhody was more effective than Crown in the case described in the chapter.

6-14. Describe the contingency approach to organization design.

6-15. Using Figure 6-11 as your format, offer your own examples of companies that would fit into each of the four cells.

6-16. What kinds of conflicts are likely to be present in a matrix organizational structure? Discuss.

Case 6-1

REORGANIZATION AT GE*

The General Electric Company (GE) popularized decentralization in the 1950s, strategic planning in the 1970s, and is now pioneering another organizational concept by adding a new layer of senior managers, called sector executives, just below its innovative corporate executive office, which consists of three executives including the chief executive. GE hopes that one major consequence of the move will be to free its three-man executive office from much of the internal work load and permit it to focus on external matters, such as government regulation, which it foresees will be very significant in the 1980s.

Each of the new sector executives will now direct a clearly defined industry multibillion-dollar group of GE units. The group heads who formerly reported to the executive office will report to a sector executive, who will report to one of the two vice-presidents in the executive office. Reports Reginald H. Jones, chief executive since 1972, "Our direct reports would have grown quite substantially if we had not made this change. By 1980 we would have been faced with a really unmanageable situation. We saw the need to inject this new level called sector in order to reduce our span of control and enhance the manageability of the corporation. . ." In each case, the sector executive will now become "Mr. General Electric" in the industry that his sector serves as he begins to absorb many chief executive functions.

Asserts Jones about the changes in organization structure at GE: "We will have to be developing a cadre of managers who are extremely sensitive to externalities, who are able to function in an anticipatory mode, not a reactive one, who will be able to sense that this is what the public wants and should expect of the corporation in terms of what it feels the corporation should be doing."

1. Draw a partial organization chart reflecting the changes described in this case. How do you assess this structure, based upon your understanding of the concepts involved? What are its inherent strengths? Weaknesses?
2. How do you assess Reginald Jones as an organization designer? It may be helpful to examine GE's financial success since 1972.
3. Do you feel Jones is sufficiently concerned about developing a structure that will be responsive to a dynamic environment? Discuss why.
4. Has GE become too large to be manageable? Discuss its probable future.

Case 6-2

A CONFLICT OF AUTHORITY

In February 1980, the Major Jig and Fixtures Department opened a group of jigs to production. Some of these tools had been built by outsiders and shipped in, presumably ready for use in building parts, but this was only the ideal. In practice, many bugs had to be ironed out, and in some instances it was even discovered that subcontracted tools had been built according to obsolete tool design. This meant that major reworking would be required, occasionally even rebuilding the tool involved.

Where this was necessary, production was delayed until the tools could be made ready to build the production assemblies that were needed to turn out parts in quantity. This might require as little as three days or as long as four weeks, depending upon the amount

* This case was developed from the article "GE's new billion-dollar small business," *Business Week*, December 19, 1977, pp. 78–79.

of rework required. It is not surprising that this condition generated a great deal of pressure on the tooling organization from some of the upper echelons of management.

During the peak of this confusion, Fred Larson, a supervisor, found his operation to be one of the hottest spots. Jess Bradley, his division superintendent, inaugurated the practice of walking through the shop a couple of times a day to see how things were moving along. At first, he always came with Phil Hawthorne, Fred's foreman, and discussed the job chiefly with the supervisor in charge. Soon, however, he was coming by himself, and if the supervisor wasn't around, he might talk at length with a lead man or even one or two of the workers. Then as time went on, he went a step beyond talking and asking questions, requesting job builders to tear down a setup in order to incorporate some of his ideas.

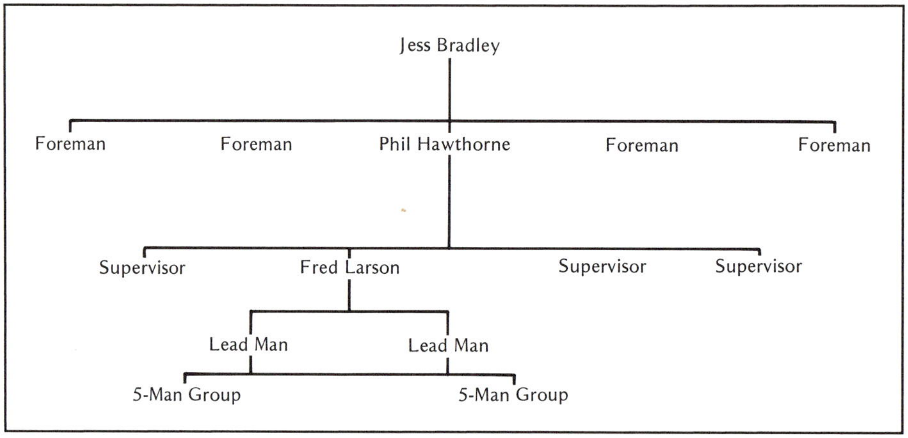

Fred's was not the only work station in the tooling organization to receive this treatment. All of the operations reporting to Phil were also on Jess' itinerary, as were a number of those for which other foremen were responsible, and Phil and his foreman colleagues well knew what was going on. The straw that broke the camel's back, so to speak, was an incident that occurred in Fred's area about 10 days after all of this started. Already, the morale of his men was at low ebb, because they no longer knew whether to go ahead with a given setup as planned, or wait for Jess Bradley to tell them how to proceed. Then, one day, Fred returned to his station after a brief absence to learn that scheduled operations on a large job had just been changed, and that two days' setup time for seven men had thereby gone down the drain.

Profoundly disturbed and thoroughly angry, Fred decided that things could not go on this way any longer.

1. What are the basic organizational issues illustrated in this case?
2. Present your analysis of the problem(s) and recommended solutions. Assume the role of Fred Larson as he feels at the end of the case.

References

CHILD, JOHN. "Organizational Design and Performance: Contingency Theory and Beyond." *Organization and Administrative Sciences.* (Summer/Fall, 1977), pp. 169–183.

DALTON, GENE W., PAUL R. LAWRENCE, AND JAY W. LORSCH. (eds.) *Organizational Structure and Design.* Homewood, Ill.: Richard D. Irwin, Inc., 1970.

GALBRAITH, JAY. "Matrix Organization Designs." *Business Horizons* (February 1971), pp. 29–40.

HREBINIAK, LAWRENCE G. *Complex Organizations.* St. Paul, Minn.: West Publishing Co., 1978.

LORSCH, JAY W. "Organization Design: A Situational Perspective." *Organizational Dynamics* (Autumn, 1977), pp. 2–14.

MCCASKEY, MICHAEL B. "An Introduction to Organizational Design." *California Management Review* (Winter, 1974), pp. 13–20.

PFEFFER, JEFFREY, AND GERALD R. SALANCIK. "Organization Design: The Case for a Coalitional Model of Organizations." *Organizational Dynamics* (Autumn, 1977), pp. 15–29.

PUGH, D. S. (ed.) *Organization Theory.* Baltimore, Md.: Penguin Books, 1971.

THOMPSON, J. D. *Organizations in Action.* New York: McGraw-Hill Book Company, 1967.

DONALD E. KANE
Manager, Corporate Organization Planning Operation, Executive Manpower Staff, General Electric Company

Donald E. Kane joined General Electric in 1956 on their Employee Relations Management Program. After completing several operating assignments in employee compensation, organization planning, and management information systems, he joined the corporate staff in 1968 as an executive manpower consultant. Appointed to his present position at corporate headquarters at Fairfield, Connecticut in 1973, he has overall staff leadership responsibility for organization planning across the company.

Executive Commentary
Growth in Organization Structure Complexity

Rare indeed would be the organization designer who would not agree that simplicity is a highly desirable organization design objective. Yet a comparison of the current organization chart against its counterpart of ten years ago will reveal, for most companies, a dramatic increase in complexity. What's more, I believe that 10 years hence we'll be looking backward longingly at the structures of the late 1970s "when life was a lot more simple than it is here in the 1980s." Whether we like it or not, organization structures are becoming ever more complex, with little chance of respite likely. Thus, the discontinuity between the organization designer's objectives and the results generated can be forecast to continue.

Let's examine several examples of this increasing complexity and some of the reasons behind its growth. All of these examples already exist within General Electric Company. Although few companies today are as large and diversified as GE, increased size and diversification seem to be common characteristics of American industry. Thus, what General Electric and its large diversified peer companies are facing today, many others will probably face tomorrow.

Multiple-role top management structure

General Electric's experience with this difficult, but necessary, top management mode now spans over a decade. Difficult—because shared responsibilities and authorities among several individuals at the top of a company are always somewhat ambiguous and subject to divergent personal interpretation. Necessary—because no single executive, however competent and dedicated, can possibly cover all the bases in our rapidly changing business environment. This is particularly true when one considers the significant amount of time that chief executives need to devote today to government and industry affairs. The days of one-person-leadership would appear to be numbered.

Increasing number of layers in the hierarchy

As large, diversified companies become even more so, the number of management layers between the chief executive officer and first-line supervision increases almost axiomatically. It is a matter of maintaining manageability through realistic spans of control. For selected individual components and managers within a large, diversified company, a broad, flat organization structure may be desirable. Such a structure appears inappropriate for the total company, however, because inadequate control would be the likely result. When General Electric was decentralized in the early 1950s (size then about $2 billion), there were six layers of management between foreman and chief executive officer. Today (size about $18 billion), there are a minimum of seven layers and as many as nine layers. Our recent establishment of sectors as an organizational layer is an example of pertinent organization dynamics.

Increasing diversity of organizational forms

In 1953, upon the completion of the decentralization of General Electric, there was only one type of organization structure allowed—product organization. A quarter century later, we still have product-based structure, but we also have structures based on function, geography, customers, market, process, distribution channel, service provided, body of knowledge or expertise, and a wide variety of matrix organization structures combining two or more of these variables. It has been said, only half in jest, that "You name the type of structure; it exists somewhere within General Electric." Our participation not only in 11 of the 20 basic manufacturing industries but also in eight of the 11 categories under which all industry and commerce is classified makes this broad array of organizational forms both understandable and quite necessary.

Trend toward more complex organizational forms

The trend to not only increased diversity of structures but also more complex and sophisticated structures such as matrix organization tends to mirror the accelerating complexity, uncertainty, and rapid change in the business environment. The requirement for faster response, for incisive changes in strategic direction, and for greater selectivity in resource allocation all have resulted in more sophisticated and differentiated business strategies. Because structure should *follow* strategy, flexible and differentiated organization structures tend to emerge. Today we have matrix organization structure not only in our project-intensive aerospace businesses, but also in our fast-changing consumer businesses. Actually, few of our businesses today have stable environments. For instance, microprocessors are now replacing electromechanical functions in many products that have been design-stable for years. New competitors, based on new technology, are emerging almost overnight. Simple structural forms are increasingly less able to cope with complex and rapidly changing environments.

Affiliates/joint ventures explosion

With most large multinational companies today, an increasing number of affiliates and joint ventures add considerable complexity to the organization structure. General Electric, for instance, has a network of about 130 affiliates (either wholly owned or in which it has an equity investment) and countless internal and external joint venture and consortium arrangements. Soon, barter and countertrade agreements will add further complexity. The causal factors here are many—the impact of nationalism and demand by developing countries for local manufacturing content, worldwide production rationalization aimed at achievement of status of lowest world-cost producer, attempts to preserve identity in an acquisition, necessity for meeting a host of legal requirements, and so on.

Emergence of new functions and issue management organization

Strategic planning, occupational medicine, human resources management—these are examples of emerging functions. Also, many companies are now performing internally certain functions that they used to purchase.

Economic forecasting, trusts investment, and air transport would be typical examples here. Increasingly, we see structure established to deal with issues that transcend functional lines; environmental quality, equal opportunity practices, and wage/price controls are examples. Thus, we are attempting to "issueize the functions" instead of "functionalizing the issues."

Nonstructural integration vehicles

The wholesale elimination of committees was a major concept and highly visible aspect of GE's decentralization in the 1950s. Although committees have not yet crept back into the structure, we do have today a variety of boards and councils as well as appointed area executives, national executives and regional vice-presidents. Thus, continuing necessity for integration across *other* than organizational lines on a formal basis has over the years selectively outweighed the desirable conceptual objective of strict individual responsibility and accountability.

As companies increasingly act in an anticipatory rather than a responsive mode, organization changes are becoming more frequent. Tomorrow's organization chart is destined to be ever more complex; it will also undoubtedly be reissued more frequently.

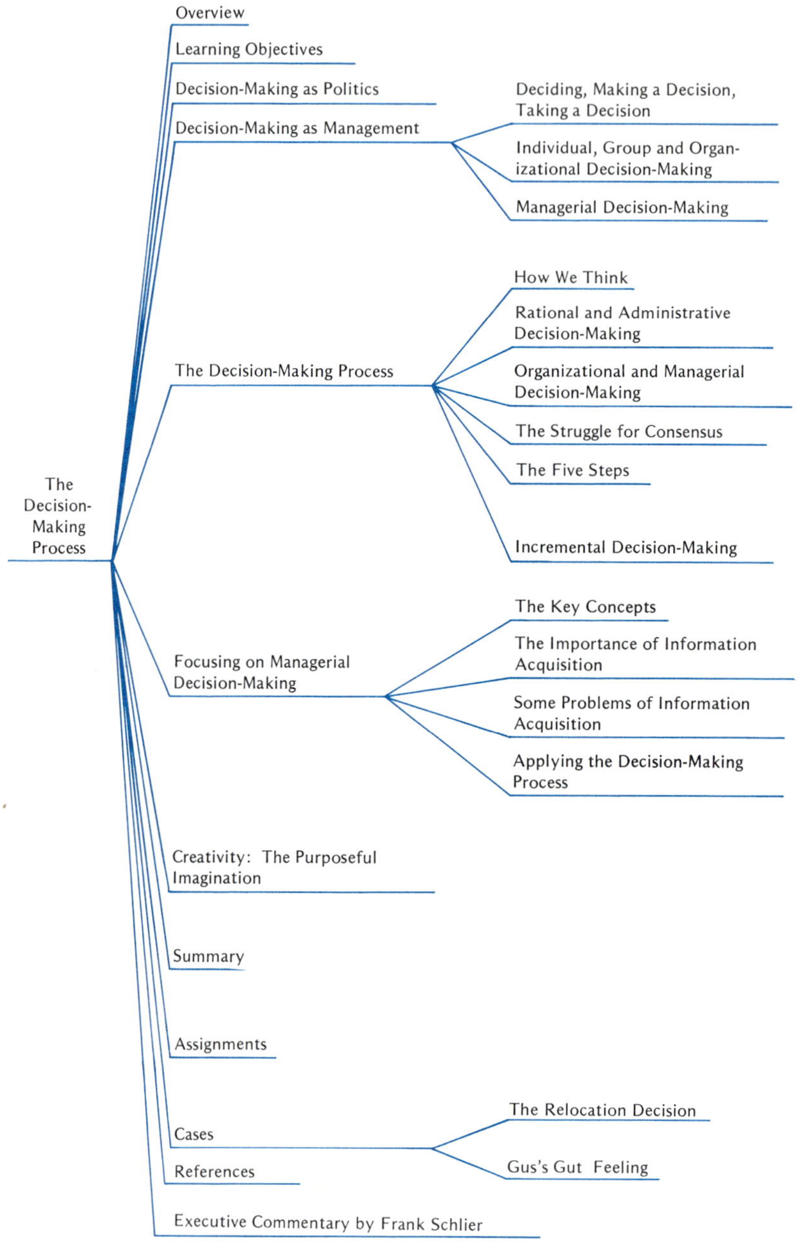
The Decision-Making Process
Overview
Learning Objectives
Decision-Making as Politics
Decision-Making as Management
Deciding, Making a Decision, Taking a Decision
Individual, Group and Organizational Decision-Making
Managerial Decision-Making
The Decision-Making Process
How We Think
Rational and Administrative Decision-Making
Organizational and Managerial Decision-Making
The Struggle for Consensus
The Five Steps
Incremental Decision-Making
Focusing on Managerial Decision-Making
The Key Concepts
The Importance of Information Acquisition
Some Problems of Information Acquisition
Applying the Decision-Making Process
Creativity: The Purposeful Imagination
Summary
Assignments
Cases
The Relocation Decision
Gus's Gut Feeling
References
Executive Commentary by Frank Schlier

7

THE DECISION-MAKING PROCESS

OVERVIEW

This chapter deals with the process of decision making. Decision making, as with all human thought processes, is a complex human activity. A person's life and destiny are determined by the kinds of decisions he or she makes. Some people find it extremely easy to make a decision. The majority of people regard decision making as something that cannot be taken too lightly and should, therefore, be given careful thought. Finally, some people find it impossible to decide. For these people, decision making represents a continuous process of postponements and abandonments of issues that call for a decision. For them the adage "a problem ignored is a problem half-solved" is a golden rule that they follow religiously.

Organizations employ a mixture of all of these three types of individuals. The two extremes, those who find decision making easy and those who find it impossible, represent the minority of organizational decision makers. The majority of managers consider decision making an important function that must be given careful and undivided attention. The first section of this chapter explains what decision making is, beginning with the fact that it is at base a political process. Although some authors would consider decision making as part of one of the functions of management (planning or organizing), in this chapter, we conceive of decision making as a distinct function of management. In addition, decision making is considered a multistep human thought process, rather than a single activity.

The bulk of the chapter deals with the decision-making process. After explaining what the decision-making process is all about, both in terms of analytic and intuitive decision-making, the discussion focuses on the five basic steps of the decision-making process. Finally, the chapter ends with an explanation of the decision-making process within an organizational context. Under the heading, "The Managerial Decision Making Process," the two main styles or modes of decision making (analytic and intuitive) are scrutinized more closely. The last section of this chapter is devoted to a brief examination of creativity conceived of as purposeful imagination.

LEARNING OBJECTIVES

This chapter is especially intended to help the student:

1. **Understand the nature of decision making.**
2. **Learn what the differences are between rational and administrative decision making.**
3. **Ascertain that decision making is not a one-time activity but, rather, represents a well-defined human thought process.**
4. **Become familiar with the five steps of the decision-making process.**
5. **Examine how the decision-making process is applied in managerial situations and how it is supplemented and complemented by some other modes or ways of making decisions, which are known as intuitive and creative decision making.**
6. **Learn, especially in the context of thinking about management, the meaning of the following concepts:**

rationality	**alternative identification and evaluation**
bounded rationality	**payoff matrix**
deciding	**intuition**
problem definition	**creativity**

DECISION MAKING AS POLITICS

At the outset, it will be worthwhile to note that decision making is a very basic kind of human behavior. Let us call this kind of behavior *politics,* or the struggle among human beings associated with one another to get more nearly what they want.

For example, thinking about decision making often begins and ends with the task and the process of making "good" decisions. Of course, we want to get the "best" decisions we can. Unfortunately, however, if care is not taken, the focus on good decisions gives these the status of ends rather than the means they really are.

Specifically, because the organization does not have a will, and because individuals do have wills of their own, organization decisions are made for people, rather than the other way around. In other words, there is no such thing as a good decision apart from the human values that define it as being good. This importance of *values* is very significant for the decision-making process, beginning with the obvious fact that the matter of *what* values quickly becomes *whose* values.

First, two kinds of information must assist that process. One, of course, is understandings about the surrounding situation, the environment. The other, and much of this information is easily overlooked when the focus of attention is on decisions as ends rather than means, is preferences—what the people involved want to get out of the decision being made. Put differently, decisions are close interactions between facts and values.

This approach to decision making was suggested, perhaps partly in jest, by Ambrose Bierce in his classic, *The Devil's Dictionary.*[1] To decide, said Bierce, is "to succumb to the preponderance of one set of influences over another." This way of putting it, however, is precisely what is highlighted by thinking about decision making as politics.

A second key consequence of emphasizing values, *preferences,* as decision information gives *conflict* a central position in decision dynamics. It is of the very nature of individual differences that preferences will do a good bit of colliding with one another. At this point, therefore, politics as the doings of power and the powerful must take the center of this stage. (Note that we will in a later chapter discuss power much more fully.)

In two ways, primarily, power interacts with preferences as a decision factor. One has to do with the preferences of the powerful; of course, leaders seek these positions in substantial part to get more of what they want, and most of what most leaders want is scarce. The other is to inhibit preferences held by the less powerful, whenever there is not enough of whatever is wanted for everyone to have pretty much all they want.

One of the key ways of limiting the preferences of the less powerful is to treat their preferences, in effect, as noninformation. Thus, as power is used to manage diversity so that power holders can have things more nearly their way, values in collision are handled by priority ordering preferences. That is, some preferences, specifically those held by leaders, are taken more seriously than others.

Observe how nicely the priority ordering of preferences as decision information deals with the conflict implications of scarcity. Highest status is thereby given to those preferences that are most certain in any case to force themselves into the decision process; conversely, the preferences of those who have the smallest capacity to create difficulties are placed lowest in this ordering, which is to say that the political dimension of decision making is primarily this weighing or ordering of preferences. More accurately, decisions are for decision makers, and those who are in some way involved in the decisions being made are very different from one another in the scope of their influence on these decisions.

[1] Ambrose Bierce, *The Devil's Dictionary* (New York: Dover, 1958).

DECISION MAKING AS MANAGEMENT

Although few management writers and practitioners would disagree about the importance of decision making for the management of organizations, equally few are able to accurately define and differentiate it from the other managerial tasks and functions of planning, organizing, controlling, and so on. Most writers equate decision making with management in general. Herbert A. Simon, one of the most influential modern writers, stated more than a dozen years ago, "I shall find it convenient to take mild liberties with the English language by using 'decision making' as though it were synonymous with 'management.'"[2] Earlier, in his *Administrative Behavior,* Simon expressed concern about the common neglect of previous attempts to develop a general theory of administration and management on the subject of decision making. He remarked, "Although any practical activity involves both 'deciding' and 'doing,' it has not commonly been recognized that a theory of administration should be concerned with the process of decision as well as with the process of acting."[3] As it will be seen later on, Simon was very influential in the development of a school of thought in management and organization theory known as the Decision Making School, or the Carnegie School.[4]

Some other writers view decision making as the defining characteristic and, perhaps, the distinguishing factor of the executive or top manager. Chester Barnard, for example, in his now classic work, *The Functions of the Executive,* stated that ". . . a characteristic of the service of executives is that they represent a specification of the process of making organization decisions, and this *is the essence* of their functions."[5] Similarly, Peter Drucker echoes Barnard: ". . . only executives make decisions. It is to be expected, by virtue of position or knowledge, to make decisions that have significant impact on the entire organization, its performance and results *defines* the executive."[6] In a similar fashion, David Braybrook has contended that "It is worth investigating the notion that the essential contribution of the man in power . . . is to make decisions, for this is a better description of his activities than many others and, perhaps, is closer to being a *distinctive* description than most."[7]

Finally, some of the recent writers consider decision making as being an integral part of planning. For example, Koontz and O'Donnell, two of the most

[2]Herbert A. Simon, *The Shape of Automation for Man and Management* (New York: Harper Torchbooks, 1965), p. 53.

[3]Herbert A. Simon, *Administrative Behavior: A Study of Decision-Making Processes in Administrative Organizations* (New York: The Free Press, 1976), p. 1.

[4]This school includes the writings of Richard March, James Cyert, William Dill, and other members of the Carnegie Institute of Technology faculty.

[5]Chester Barnard, *The Functions of the Executive* (Cambridge: Harvard University Press, 1968), p. 1.

[6]Peter Drucker, *The Effective Executive* (New York: Harper and Row, Publishers, 1967), p. 113.

[7]David Braybrook, *A Strategy of Decisions: Policy Evaluation on a Social Process* (New York: The Free Press, 1963), p. 31.

Nobel Prize for Economics Is Awarded To Versatile Carnegie-Mellon Professor

Herbert A. Simon of Carnegie-Mellon University in Pittsburgh, who cast doubt on traditional theories of business decision making, won the Nobel Prize for Economics.

Mr. Simon, 62, received a doctorate in policitical science from the University of Chicago in 1943. Since 1965, he has been a professor of computer science and psychology at Carnegie-Mellon.

As the Swedish Academy of Science said in announcing the award, he has worked in science theory, applied mathematics, statistics, operations analysis, and business administration, as well as economics.

In the 1950s when Mr. Simon was teaching psychology and administration at Carnegie-Mellon, he led a challenge to the classical economic theory that business executives always acted to maximize their profits and that, in doing so, they were equipped with perfect information obtained without cost to themselves.

To replace this idea, Mr. Simon developed what he called "profit satisficing." His theory was that executives, possessing incomplete information and facing unknown risks, settled for what they could regard as "satisfactory" profits.

Mr. Simon's research in recent years has led him in new directions. "The more we proved business *decision making,*" he said, "the more it became apparent that we needed to know more about *human thinking* and *problem solving* in general. About that time computers became available as a way to simulate human thinking." He is convinced that his current work with computers will have an important long-term bearing on economics.

Mr. Simon is the seventh American to win or share the Nobel Prize in economics since it was first awarded in 1969. Sune Clarlsson of the Swedish Academy said Mr. Simon is "very sharp, witty, humorous, and it is a great pleasure to attend his seminars. The great advantage with his ideas is that they correspond so closely to the real situation in companies around the world."

The Wall Street Journal, Oct. 17, 1978, p. 8.

influential textbook writers on management, consider decision making as "being at the core of planning."[8] Another textbook views decision making as the end result of the process of planning.[9]

This chapter treats decision making as another task of the manager or the administrator of an organization, not in the sense that there are specific positions within the hierarchy reserved exclusively for decision makers but, rather, that the task is distinct to the extent that it represents an important managerial activity that cuts across most of the other functions of management.

Deciding, Making a Decision, Taking a Decision

The verb *decide* is derived from the Latin word *decidere* and means, literally, "to cut off." In the English language, to decide, to make a decision, or to take a decision, according to Webster's Dictionary, means to "arrive at a solution that ends uncertainty or dispute about; to bring to a definitive end; to induce to come to a choice; to make a choice or judgment."

One can see from this definition that the key concepts in decision making are (1) *uncertainty* or doubt, which comes about as a result of (2) the *existence* of two or more *possible courses of action* or alternatives, from which (3) a *choice* must be made that will lead to (4) the *elimination of uncertainty* or doubt. Thus, it is obvious, that the entire process of decision making begins with a person's feeling of doubt, of not knowing what to do, and ends with a choice of certain courses of action, which removes that doubt, that is, comes to a solution of the problem. Because decision making is triggered by a problem and ends with a solution to that problem, most writers use the terms *decision making* and *problem solving* interchangeably.

Although the distinctions between problem solving and decision making may be difficult and to some extent arbitrary, nevertheless, they do serve a purpose. Problem solving is an activity with which most of us are familiar from early school days. In problem-solving situations, the person is *given* a problem and a set of rudimentary techniques, along with some or all of the information needed to solve the problem. The person or problem solver must select the appropriate technique and find the appropriate information to solve the problem. There are virtually no insolvable problems under these circumstances. A solution must be found and is usually found. Much of the literature on problem solving centers around the kinds and amounts of information, the speed of processing the information, and the quickness of finding a solution.[10]

Decision making, as it is approached in this work, differs from problem solving

[8] Harold Koontz, and Cyril O'Donnell, *Principles of Management* (New York: McGraw-Hill, 1972), p. 123.

[9] William H. Newman, Charles E. Summers, and E. Kirby Warren, *The Process of Management* (Englewood Cliffs, N.J.: Prentice Hall, Inc., 1972), pp. 29–31.

[10] See, for example, Marcus Alexis, and C. Z. Wilson, *Organizational Decision Making* (Englewood Cliffs, N.J.: Prentice-Hall, 1967), pp. 71–78.

to the extent that although it is problem-triggered, the problem is *not given*, but must be defined by the decision maker; and although problems are dealt with in decision making, they are not always solved in the sense that something is done that eliminates the problem. It is possible that the decision maker may choose not to do anything.

As can be seen from this brief discussion, the difference between problem solving and decision making is really negligible. For this reason, many management writers and practitioners use both terms synonymously, with, perhaps, no harm done.

Individual, Group, and Organizational Decision Making

There is a widespread misconception that most managerial and administrative decisions are made by individuals working or deliberating in seclusion in a dark corner of an office, in a resort somewhere up in the mountains, or on a boat on the sea or a lake. The reason for this misconception is, of course, that the news media often report on executive seclusion at a time of big decisions. In addition, most laymen equate decision making with making the final choice and announcing verbally or in a written document the implementation of a specific alternative or plan. Thus, a president of a country, for example, usually takes a trip to his summer or winter retreat before making a decision on a specific issue. So do presidents of large and small private enterprises. Although these situations are actual manifestations of real decision making, they constitute only a very small portion of the entire decision process.

The complexity involved in decision making requires the combined efforts of more than one individual. Thus, most, if not all, important decisions in today's organizations are made by a group of individuals, each contributing his or her own inputs. Whether every member of the group participates equally in the decision-making process is a matter of the leadership style of the organization. Some organizations will allow for greater, more egalitarian participation than others. Some allow for an advisory role by some members whereas other members will be burdened with the final choice and implementation. This group orientation in organizational decision making is prevalent not only because of the belief that "two heads are better than one," but, rather, because the enormous complexity of organizational problems necessitates it.

Managerial Decision Making

Managerial decision making involves both individual and group decisions. The individual not only makes the initial decision to join the organization, what is known in the literature as the "decision to participate," but also each manager makes a host of individual operating decisions as a member of a group and as an individual. By so doing, the manager often contributes partially to another manager's decision making. The reason for this interlocking of individuals and group decision making is that each manager individually and as a member of a group does not make individual or group decisions but, rather, each manager makes *organizational decisions.* It is this kind of organizational decision making by management that is the concern of this book.

In concept, a managerial decision is a present commitment to a particular course of action based upon anticipation of the future course of events. Accordingly, managerial decision making can be defined as an organized human thought process that begins with the necessity to resolve a doubt, conflict, or problem and ends with implementing a chosen course of action.

THE DECISION-MAKING PROCESS

It was pointed out earlier in this chapter that the most fruitful way of understanding decision making is to think of it as a human thought process rather than

Organizational Decisions

Every effort that is a constituent of organization, that is, every coordinated cooperative effort, may involve two acts of decision. The first is the decision of the person affected as to whether or not he will continue this effort as a matter of personal choice. It is a detail of the process of repeated personal decisions that determine whether or not the individual will be or will continue to be a contributor to the organization. . . . This act of decision is *outside* the system of efforts constituting the organization . . . although it is, as we have seen, a subject for organized attention.

The second type of decision has no direct or specific relation to personal results, but views the effort concerning which decision is to be made non-personally from the viewpoint of its organization effect and of its relation to organization purpose. The second act of decision is often made in a direct sense by individuals, but it is impersonal and organizational in its intent and effect. Very often it is also organizational in its process, as for example, in legislatures, or when boards or committees determine action. The act of decision is a part of the organization itself.

This distinction between the two types of decisions is frequently recognized in ordinary affairs. We very often say or hear sentences similar to this: "If this were my business, I think I would decide the question this way—but it is not my personal affair"; or "I think the *situation* requires such and such an answer—but I am not in a position to determine what ought to be done"; or "The decision should be made by someone else.". . . A sort of dual personality is required of individuals contributing to organization action—the private personality, and the organization personality.

Chester Barnard, *The Functions of the Executive*, pp. 187–188.

as a single act. Although this conception of decision making as a process is a very popular view, it is not entirely without its critics who argue that it tends to place heavy, if not exclusive, emphasis on the "rational" aspects of decision making, neglecting other aspects. And two such aspects are especially worth noting.

First, remembering the role of values and preferences in decision making, these are in particular nonrational. That is, we cannot arrive at our values by way of what is commonly called rationality. These must instead emerge from our longer history, including especially the values we were taught beginning when we were very young. As the philosopher Pascal said, "the heart has reasons which reason cannot know." And as Professor Kenneth Schneider put it, what is rational for man must be what has deep meaning for him.[11] In short, it is our values that determine what problems our decision making shall endeavor to solve, not decision making determining what values shall shape our behavior.

Second, even where values have "decreed" that there are problems to be solved, a calculating rationality is not the only possible approach. Intuition is also an important element in human decision making. It will typically take both of these kinds of problem solving for best results. Thus, this chapter views rational and intuitive decision making as a continuum, rather than a dichotomy. Moreover, reason and intuition are, as most effectively used, complementary, rather than mutually exclusive.

How We Think

The decision-making process was referred to as a human thought process. How do people think? John Dewey started his classic work, *How We Think*, as follows:

> *No one can tell another person in any definite way how he should think, any more than how he ought to breathe or to have his blood circulate. But various ways in which men do think can be told and can be described in their general features. Some of those ways are better than others; the reasons [that] they are better can be set forth. The person who understands what the better ways of thinking are and why they are better can, if he will, change his own personal ways until they become more effective.*[12]

The most effective way of thinking that is recommended by Dewey is *reflective thinking:* the kind of thinking that consists of turning a subject over in the mind and giving it serious and consecutive consideration. Dewey further elaborates on reflective thinking by saying:

> *Reflection involves not simply a sequence of ideas, but a* con-sequence *ordering in such a way that each determines the next as its proper outcome, while each outcome in turn leads back on, or refers to, its predecessors. The successive portions of a reflective thought grow out of one another and support one another; they do not come and go in a medley. Each phase is a step from something to something—*

[11] K. R. Schneider, *Destiny of Change* (New York: Holt, Rinehart and Winston, 1968), p. 66.
[12] John Dewey, *How We Think* (Chicago: Henry Regnery Company, 1971), p. 3.

> *technically speaking, it is a* term *of thought. Each term leaves a deposit that is utilized in the next term. The stream or flow becomes a train or chain. There are in any reflective thought definite units that are linked together so that there is a sustained movement to a common end.*[13]

With these words, spoken almost three quarters of a century ago, Dewey established the basic philosophy of the decision-making procss as *successive steps*, each of which determines the next as its proper outcome while, at the same time, it feeds back on its predecessor, thereby forming a train or a sustained movement towards a common end or goal—the ultimate decision. This continued movement of the human mind through the various steps, back and forth, involves both rational deciding, based primarily upon logic and reason, and judgmental deciding, whose main basis is feelings and intuition.

Rational and Administrative Decision Making

It is a popular belief that most managers and administrators base many of their decisions exclusively upon a careful, scientific, and objective thought process. At the minimum, it is asserted that most managers decide in a very rational manner, meaning that (1) they have *complete knowledge* of the *decision situation* or the problem; (2) they have *complete knowledge* of all the *possible alternatives* or *courses of action;* (3) they have a *system of ordering* preferences in a hierarchy of importance; and (4) they always make the final choice so as *to maximize a utility function;* that is, something that is desirable or attractive to the decision maker.[14] Obviously, possession of all of these four characteristics would describe an exceptional human being or a very simplistic decision situation. The organizational world of today is not simple and the citizens of that world are not rare geniuses but, rather, ordinary humans with ordinary capabilities.

Simon was the first management and administrative theory writer to recognize the inability of the rationality theory of managerial decision making to explain the actual decision making in complex organizations performed by ordinary human beings. He delivered a fatal blow to the *economic man* or *objective rationality* theory of decision making, replacing it with the so-called *administrative man* or *bounded rationality* theory. In Simon's words, "actual behavior falls short, in at least three ways, of objective rationality":

1. *Rationality requires a complete knowledge and anticipation of the consequences that will follow on each choice. In fact, knowledge of consequences is always fragmentary.*
2. [*Because*] *these consequences lie in the future, imagination must supply the lack of experienced feeling in attaching value to them, but values can be only imperfectly anticipated.*

[13]Dewey, ibid., pp. 4–5.

[14]James G. March, and Herbert A. Simon, *Organizations* (New York: John Wiley & Sons, 1950), pp. 137–138.

3. *Rationality requires a choice among all possible alternative behaviors. In actual behavior, only a very few of all these possible alternatives ever come to mind.*[15]

Regarding the last criterion, maximization of utility, Simon wrote that "Administrative theory is peculiarly the theory of intended and bounded rationality—of the behavior of human beings who *satisfice* because they have not the wits to maximize,"[16] and 10 years later, "the key to the simplification of the choice process . . . is the replacement of the goal of *maximizing* with the goal of *satisficing*, of finding a course of action that is 'good enough.'"[17] March and Simon explained in more detail this satisficing criteria of decision making: "Most human decision making," they wrote, "whether individual or organizational, is concerned with discovery and selection of satisfactory alternatives; only in exceptional cases is it concerned with the discovery and selection of optimal alternatives.[18]

The management literature, since the original formulation of this theory by Simon and his colleagues at Carnegie, has devoted great efforts in further refining and testing this theory of *bounded rationality/satisficing* managerial decision making.[19] The central focus of theoretical refinements and empirical testings of this theory is "that the capacity of the human mind for formulating and solving complex problems is very small compared with the size of the problem whose solution is required for objective rational behavior in the real world."[20] Research in neurophysiology and psychology has demonstrated that the human brain is subject to two limitations: (1) it has limited information storing capacity, and (2) it has limited retention capacity. In other words, the average human brain not only must leave out some incoming information but also it cannot retain information for a prolonged time span—it forgets.

Regarding the environment within which the human being lives and works and that generates most of the occasions for decisions, research also has shown that it is becoming more and more complex, both in terms of the sheer number of events and happenings and also in terms of the frequency and rate of change. Faced with this doubly difficult situation, the average human not only is incapable of maximizing anything resembling a utility but at best finds himself or herself in a *Future Shock*.[21]

Given the relationship between the human being's cognitive capacities and the ever-increasing complexity of decision situations, and adding to that the fact that

[15]Herbert A. Simon, *Administrative Behavior*, p. 81.
[16]Simon, ibid, p. xxviii.
[17]Herbert A. Simon, *Models of Man* (New York: John Wiley & Sons, 1957), p. 204.
[18]March and Simon, op. cit., p. 140.
[19]For an excellent summary and an extensive bibliography, see Donald W. Taylor, "Decision-Making and Problem-Solving," in *Handbook of Organizations*, J. March, ed., (Chicago: Rand McNally and Co., 1965), pp. 68–86. Also, Richard Cyert, and James March, *The Behavioral Theory of the Firm* (Englewood Cliffs, N.J.: Prentice-Hall, Inc. 1965).
[20]Simon, *Models of Man*, p. 148.
[21]Alvin Toffler, *Future Shock* (New York: Bantam Books, Inc., 1970).

all decision making is future-oriented, one can see why Simon's bounded rationality, satisficing decision making is more realistic and useful in explaining managerial decision making than its predecessor, the economic, rational man theory. It should be emphasized, however, that the bounded rationality/satisficing theory of decision making does not completely replace rationality; after all, it is still a rationality theory. The only difference is that whatever rationality is afforded to the human mind is bounded by its inability to have complete knowledge about the *present* complexity (because of the limited size and retention of the human memory bank) of the task and the invisibility and uncertainty of the *future*. In other words, one's own degree of rationality is determined by one's own capability to comprehend present complexities and the probable future. To that extent, it is a *subjective* rationality. The pre-Simon rationality, on the other hand, is an objective rationality to the extent that it is assumed to be present in a more or less equal quantity and quality in every human being.

Organizational and Managerial Decision Making

As was pointed out in the previous section, Simon's administrative man decision-making theory is more realistic than the previous economic man conception. Simon's bounded rationality/satisficing decision-making theory rests on the following three pillars:

1. Man is unable to anticipate the future because
2. knowledge of the consequences of decision making is always incomplete and fragmentary, and
3. only a very few of all possible alternatives ever come to the decision maker's mind.

These three pillars of Simon's theory define the three constraints within which the average decision maker must operate. Because of this three-way constrained capacity, the administrative man deals with the real world within which a decision must be made through a simplified model. The decision maker then behaves rationally only with respect to this model and not the real world as it is demanded by the economic man theory. In the words of Donald W. Taylor,

> *Economic man is assumed to deal with the 'real world' in all its complexity—with full knowledge of all alternatives, full knowledge of the consequences of each alternative, and even of the probabilities of occurrence of each. In contrast, administrative man is assumed to construct a simplified model of the real situation in order to deal with it. He behaves rationally only with respect to this model—only in terms of his limited knowledge of alternatives and consequences.*[22]

[22] Taylor, op. cit., p. 60.

This model-building process consists, it will be recalled from Chapter 3, of abstracting from the real phenomenon some essential characteristics, called variables or concepts, which enable the model builder to obtain an adequate knowledge. From this initial model, the conceptual model, the manager will then construct a scientific model that eventually will be turned into a system.

The Struggle for Consensus

We shall soon explore at some length the steps, or phases, of analytic decision making, our systematic endeavor to make the best decisions we can despite the constraints Professor Simon describes. It is also important, however, to understand that all of this takes place against the backdrop of what is surely the largest constraint of all. And this points back again to decision making as politics, and keeping these dynamics in mind is another important way to keep our thinking about decision making more realistic.

Of course, the foundation on which organizational decision making must be built is the context of relationships within which decisions are made. That is, those who are working together must continue to be willing to cooperate with one another. Moreover, maintaining such a context is often not easy where the possibility of value collisions are pervasively chronic, and the *consensus* needed for effective decision making is often, at least potentially, interlaced with frustration. The size and strength of this constraint, then, depends upon the effectiveness with which managers keep frustration from damaging cooperativeness.

How is consensus maintained where preferences threaten to seriously overflow the possibilities available for satisfying them? Remember the most basic principle here. Preferences that cannot/will not be satisfied must be kept out of decision making. One way of doing this is to ignore preferences held by the less powerful. A better way is to prevent preferences held by these people, which would then have to be ignored, from coming into being in the first place. That is better because hopes that have become firmly aroused and are then frustrated can become explosively threatening to the spirit of cooperation.

And so it is that competent managers are cautious about the promising they do, including systematically underpromising in many situations in which promising cannot be avoided. However, *expectation shaping,* telling organization members what they can realistically expect from their participation, often cannot do enough balancing of expectations with what may become available. Managers must then also be prepared to engage in expectation finding. Those in charge approach the problem of constraining the preference that gets into the decision process almost precisely the other way around. When they believe they have gone as far as they can in limiting others' expectations, and are unwilling to frustrate some of the hopes that have become aroused, they must, instead, give these others much of what they are expecting. In other words, because scarcity is so likely to be a fundamental fact of life in such situations, this means that the powerful are doing this adjusting by inhibiting their own preferences. Understandably, that will typically be seen by them as something of a last resort.

And let us pass in review some illustrative possibilities associated with another major technique for maintaining the decision-making consensus needed. It might quite accurately be thought of as fashioning agreement out of disagreement. Thus, paradoxical though this does sound, there must in complex organizations be a good bit of using conflict as a key raw material in the creation of consent.[23]

One key dynamic here is the value of conflict in making important information available to the manager; very often, people in power/conflict situations will be much less candid about some of their preferences when everything is going well. Another is the fact that when people find themselves on collision courses with their colleagues, this understanding in and of itself can press them quite hard to work out solutions to their own problems. Because when people discover their own troubles, they are less likely to feel that the powerful are creating difficulties for them, here is yet another large contribution to consensus. A third important possibility for using conflict as a consensus resource is people working together to find strength for the struggle in coalitions with one another. The need for allies is a powerful incentive for agreement, as we voluntarily work out compromises to keep our coalition intact.

The Five Steps

Although the decision-making process is conceived here as consisting of five steps and although each step will be explained separately, it should be kept in mind that what is dealt with here is a sequence of five interrelated and interdependent steps, rather than isolated activities. Just as a person has to walk each step of a stairway to go from the first to the second floor of a building, so also the decision maker has to follow the steps of the decision-making process for the purpose of making a decision. The five steps of the decision-making process are as follows:

Step 1. Definition of the problem.
Step 2. Identification of the possible alternatives.
Step 3. Evaluation of the possible alternatives.
Step 4. Selection of an alternative or choice.
Step 5. Implementation of the chosen alternative.

Step 1: Definition of the Problem. Contrary to popular belief, problems are not always presented to the manager or decision maker for a solution. They must be identified and defined by the manager. Even if a certain problem is presented in a way that appears to be self-explanatory, the decision maker must define the problem anew. It is in this sense that decision making is distinguished

[23]Lewis Coser, *The Functions of Social Conflict* (New York: The Free Press, 1954).

from problem solving as representing a more encompassing concept or activity that includes problem solving but is not confined or restricted to it. Occasions for decision will be presented to the decision maker by (a) superiors; (b) subordinates; (c) peers or colleagues; and (d) the external environment of the organization.

These occasions for decision are manifested as problems. In Chapter 4, "The Organization and Its Environment," a problem was defined as a discrepancy or difference between a desired state (a goal) and the actual state (the actual performance). For example, the general manager of a plant whose actual production falls short of the goal is confronted with a decision occasion of either increasing production (by overtime work or hiring more employees), or lowering the goal. However, the manager may decide to do nothing (decide not to solve the problem) in the hope that somehow things will work out. In any case, the manager must identify and define the problem personally. In the chapter on "Planning and Controlling" it was pointed out that setting goals and monitoring the degree of accomplishment of these goals is a key activity or function of management. Deviations from these goals (discrepancies between a goal and an actual performance) are organizational problems and occasions for decision making.

Obviously, not all occasions for decision making can be as well defined as the example of the manufacturing situation. There are plans in the organization that do not specify the desired goals with a quantitative figure and also cannot measure the actual performance with a comparable quantity. Consequently, the manager will be faced with decision occasions that are known as ill-defined problems.[24] On these occasions, much of the manager's effort will be spent in exactly defining the problem. For example, the case of a discrepancy between desired and actual production may be the result not of insufficient workers (organizational resources), but it may be the result of a new government regulation for environmental pollution, or scarcity of a given material (external environment).

Identification and definition of the occasion for decision or the problem is the most important step in the entire decision-making process. Incorrectly identified and inappropriately defined problems will lead to wrong decisions, no matter how correctly and elegantly the other four steps are carried through. It is not uncommon to hear the statement, "It was one of those things, the right solution to the wrong problem." Ironically, formal education in management emphasizes problem solving (that is, steps 2–5) at the expense of problem defining. The latter is left to experience. Fortunately, as of late, a new field seems to be developing that is exclusively concerned with problem defining. That is the concept of creativity and creative management, and this chapter ends with an exposure to that subject.

[24]Richard Mason, and Ian Mitroff, "A Program for Research on Management Information Systems," *Management Science* (January 1973), pp. 475–487.

Step 2: Identification and Definition of the Possible Alternative. Although the administrative man theory of decision making, which is adapted in this book, rests upon the premise that it is humanly impossible to identify all possible alternatives, the decision maker must make a concerted effort to identify as many alternatives as possible. There is a basic prerequisite implied in decision making that there must be at least two alternatives present; otherwise, there will be no choice, and choice is, of course, a basic characteristic of deciding.

Consider, for example, the person who is planning to hold a product party. An important consideration is whether to hold the party (1) outside, (2) in the carport, or (3) inside the house. These are the decision alternatives that are possible options.

Any thoughts about alternatives must also take into account the possible events that might occur. For example, selecting where to hold the product party is influenced by possible weather events, such as a sunny, cloudy, or rainy day. The decision maker must also consider the likelihood of these varying types of weather occurring on the day of the planned party. For every decision alternative and possible event, there is also an associated payoff. In this illustration, it is the amount of sales realized.

Some decision makers find it useful to systematize their thinking about decision alternatives and the subsequent analysis of a problem. Decision technology provides a variety of techniques that can be used for this purpose. One of these techniques is a subset of statistical decision theory known as *pay-off matrix* analysis. Although it is not formally explored until the chapter on planning models, elements of pay-off matrix analysis can be introduced at this point to help illustrate the steps in the decision-making process and to show how decision technology can be applied to systematize the structuring and analyzing of problems.

A pay-off matrix for the product party is shown in Figure 7-1. The decision alternatives form the rows of the matrix. The columns show the possible events and their probabilities of occurrence. Within the matrix are the outcomes associated with the interaction of the various decision alternatives and events.

Step 3: Evaluation of the Possible Alternatives. Having identified and defined the problem and possible alternatives, the decision maker is now ready to begin evaluating the different alternatives. This evaluation might simply involve a subjective consideration of the important factors, or it might take the form of applying appropriate decision technology. For example, if a pay-off matrix is being used, an expected value (a concept described in Chapter 13) would be calculated for each decision alternative. Continuing with the product party illustration, the alternatives of inside, carport, and outside party have expected values of $175, $220, and $255, respectively.

Step 4: Selection of an Alternative. In this step, the decision maker chooses the *one* alternative that contributes the most toward the accomplishment

		Events		
		Sunny Day (.1)	Cloudy Day (.2)	Rainy Day (.7)
Decision Alternatives	Outside Party	$300	$200	$150
	Carport Party	$200	$300	$200
	Inside Party	$150	$150	$300

FIGURE 7-1. Payoff Matrix for a Tupperware Party.

of the objective. In the previous example, the decision would probably be to hold the party inside, because that offers the highest expected value. A qualifying point does need to be made, however. We are assuming that all of the relevant factors have been included in the pay-off matrix analysis. In many applications of decision technology, important factors do not lend themselves to quantification. In these cases, the output from the analysis must be combined with the decision makers' evaluation of other factors before a final decision is reached.

Step 5: Implementation of the Chosen alternative. Intuitively, one would think that the decision-making process has ended once the choice has been made (Step 4). This would have been true if the primary concern of the decision maker was mental exercise and not a real life situation. Real decision situations call for both making a decision and putting that decision into effect. This is implementation. It is the actual implementation of the decision that ultimately determines the workability, practicality, and effectiveness of the decision. Managers of organizations make effective decisions, that is, decisions that lead to the accomplishment of a purpose. Implementation is the true test of the quality and correctness of the four previous steps of the decision-making process. It is entirely possible that a decision maker performed excellently defining the problem, identifying most of the important possible alternatives, evaluating all the alternatives, and choosing the best one, but finds the implementation virtually impossible. The choice of the best, optimal, or even satisficing alternative provides no guarantee of its implementability. Only implementable decisions are effective decisions.

Whether a final decision will or will not be implementable will depend on a multitude of factors, such as (1) how good a planning job the manager has done; (2) how realistic and well defined the organization's objectives are; (3) how accurate and timely the control and reporting systems and procedures in an organization are; and (4) the frequency and accuracy of the organizational review procedures (see especially Chapter 5). All of these factors will determine the accuracy of the decision maker's problem, alternative identification and definition and, indirectly, his or her realistic conception of the decision occasion. The more realistic (true to the real world) a decision occasion or problem is, the higher the probability of its being implementable.

Provided that the final decision is implementable, the degree of success in actually putting it into effect will depend on the manager's understanding of human and organizational behavior. Part III of this book deals exclusively with the basic requirements for understanding human and organizational behavior. Implementing a decision is primarily a process of communicating both the decision problem and the decision solution to people who will be affected by taking a certain course of action. The purpose of this communication process is to secure acceptance of and identification with the proposed plan for dealing with the decision occasion. Communication, participation, MBO, delegation, and so on are concepts and approaches that are important in the successful implementation of decision (see Chapters 9, 10, 11, and 12).

Incremental Decision Making

Around the edges of the analytical decision-making process in ongoing organizations, an interesting tension often arises. Staff people in organizations, as well as many of those who write about decision making, are likely to recommend decisions involving change that are as large as planners' imaginations can encompass. Line people, by contrast, seem typically to prefer to take on change in substantially smaller pieces.

Superficially, from the standpoint of the threat to consensus which is by definition implicit in significant change, the staff planner's way of doing would seem best. Why not cut off the dog's tail all at once, rather than making the poor animal suffer again and again? But this analogy quickly breaks down. It really does not hurt more to do this kind of change decision-making surgery more often, and it is easy to understand why.

The consensus manager's approach here is called *incrementalism*,[25] defined as mingling the new with what now is in smaller rather than much larger pieces. Its primary value for the consensus foundation on which organizations must do their decision making is that it makes it possible to rebuild consensus before very much has been lost. Because, in other words, all of us do a great deal of moving toward the future with our feelings, these need to be carefully taken into account.

[25] Charles E. Lindblom, *The Intelligence of Democracy* (New York: The Free Press, 1965).

In decision information terms, fears that have not been aroused cannot become troublesome. Thus, near and smaller changes can be assessed more accurately than can distant and larger ventures. Change proposals are therefore much less likely to seem threatening if they do not seem to be as big as the rest of life. Just as miles are traversed one step at a time, so is the difficulty of coming to terms with the new, less formidable when it does not have to be taken on all at once.

Furthermore, giving decision making less of a gap to bridge toward the future almost guarantees less blundering on account of wrong guesses—with all of the implications thereof for loss of confidence by organizational members. When first moves turn out to be minimally harmful, here is a made-to-order morale basis on which next steps can be built. And this is a very important corrective to a common propensity of managers to damage consensus much more severely by pressing for too much too quickly when it seems that their interests would thereby be served.

FOCUSING ON MANAGERIAL DECISION MAKING

Thus far this chapter has provided an explanation of (1) the meaning of decision making as politics and as management; (2) individual, group, and managerial organizational decision making; (3) rational and administrative decision making; and (4) the decision-making process. In explaining the five steps of the decision-making process, emphasis was placed on identifying possible alternatives, calculating, and finally choosing the one alternative that has the highest potential for implementation. A major portion of the remainder of this chapter is devoted to the use of the decision-making process in managerial situations.

It has frequently been emphasized that managerial work is exceedingly complex. This complexity stems from the fact that every manager, whether he or she is engaged in organizing, planning, controlling, leading, or motivating, must develop an adequate knowledge of the past, present, and the future of the organization's interaction with the environment. There are a multitude of factors that constitute the organization (people with their peculiarities, material, equipment, money, processes, and so on), and equally as many, if not more, environmental factors (see Chapter 4). Complex phenomena require equally complex methods for dealing with them. Despite the theoretical excellence and logic of quantitative approaches, they are inadequate in and of themselves as exclusive guides to contemporary managerial decision making. They must be supplemented and enriched by some less structured and more individualized decision-making techniques.[26]

[26]See, for example, Rex W. Brown, "Do Managers Find Decision Theory Useful?" *Harvard Business Review* (May–June 1970), pp. 80–81; E. Sanford, and H. Adelman, *Management Decisions: A Behavioral Approach* (Cambridge, Mass.: Winthrop Publishing, Inc., 1977).

When earlier in this chapter the idea was introduced that decision making is a process rather than a single act, it was mentioned that this viewpoint, although very popular, is not without its critics. The majority of these critics seem to use the term *decision-making process* and *scientific decision making* interchangeably and associate both terms with statistical decision theory. In addition, they label this decision making as rational, analytic, logical, systematic, or secondary-process thinking. This type of decision making is contrasted to nonrational, nonlineal, holistic, primitive, or primary-process thinking.[27] There is no intention here to go into the rich controversy over this dichotomy of analytic versus intuitive decision making. The literature on the subject could fill a personal library. Most respected scholars who have dealt with this controversy have concluded that the two decision-making viewpoints, far from being antithetical, contradictory, or mutually exclusive, are complementary.[28]

The Key Concepts

Managerial decision making is a human thought process involving a *person* who *perceives* a *problem* within an *organizational context* and who must *evaluate* a number of *alternatives* large enough to enable him or her to resolve the uncertainty that is created by the problem. Thus, the basic concepts that must be understood are (1) the person's (manager's) ways of (a) perceiving and (b) evaluating; (2) the organizational context within which managers operate; and (3) the type of problem.

The Manager's Ways of Perceiving and Evaluating Problems. Psychologists who have researched the way people make decisions have determined that people perform two functions: they perceive and they evaluate. People perceive the world around them in one of two ways or modes: sensation, and intuition. People evaluate whatever they perceive in two ways: thinking, and feeling.[29] Figure 7-2 arranges these four modes of perceiving and evaluating into a matrix, representing two psychological types of decision makers, who may be termed Type A, or sensation-thinking, and Type B, or intuition-feeling.

In perceiving the world around themselves, Type A individuals rely exclusively on data received by their senses (sensation). These individuals will define the problem about which they must make a decision as "objective, hard facts," and will give great attention to details. This type of person will start the explanation of a problem with a statement such as, "The facts speak for themselves." Because whatever is factual is real, the decision maker who relies on sensation will take

[27]Sanford and Adelman, Ibid., pp. 16–18.

[28]Sanford and Adelman, Ibid, p. 25. See also, R. Assogiali, *Psychosynthesis* (New York: The Viking Press, 1971), pp. 217–224.

[29]Carl G. Jung, *Psychological Types* (London, England: Rutledge, 1923). See also, Mason and Mitroff, op. cit., p. 476–79.

Perception / Evaluation	Sensation	Intuition
Thinking	Type A	
Feeling		Type B

FIGURE 7-2. Perception and Evaluation.

great care not to attribute to the facts anything more than the facts would justify. For this reason, evaluating tends to run along the lines of abstract, true/false judgments and is based on systems of formal reasoning such as mathematical rules and postulates of formal logic. This type of decision maker who perceives through sensation and evaluates through thinking is called *analytic*.

Type B decision makers perceive the world around them as it might be and as a whole. In defining the problem, the presence or absence of "objective, hard facts" is irrelevant. Whatever facts the intuitive decision maker has, he or she tends to see through them and to extrapolate beyond them. Whereas the sensation-based decision maker may be too data-bound (that is, tends to go on collecting data forever because of a fear of risking a generalization that "goes beyond the available data"), the intuition-based decision maker may be too data-free. In evaluating what has been perceived, this type of a decision maker relies primarily on affective process (feeling). In other words, the evaluation tends to vary along personalistic lines of good/bad, pleasant/unpleasant, and like/dislike.[30] This type of decision maker, who perceives through intuition and evaluates through feeling, is called *intuitive*.

Obviously, decision makers in organizations employ a variety of methods of perception and evaluation, a small portion of which can be classified as belonging to either of these two "pure" categories. And both pure types of perception and evaluation are important for management as well as managers who need to possess a balance between the analytic and intuitive qualities. It will be seen in the following that under certain circumstances and for certain organizational tasks, the one or the other type would be preferable. As a rule, however, the pure type is dangerous. A decision maker who is strictly analytic runs the risk of being too limited, too bound by the current facts, and unable to see future possibilities that might contradict present trends. The purely intuitive decision maker tends to disregard present realities in the fear that they will shatter the future world that is his or her main preoccupation.

[30] Mason and Mitroff, op. cit., p. 477.

Analytic and Intuitive Thinkers

(Analytic) Systematic thinkers tend to:

1. Look for a method and make a plan for solving a problem.
2. Be very conscious of their approach.
3. Defend the quality of a solution largely in terms of the method.
4. Define the specific constraints of the problem early in the process.
5. Discard alternatives quickly.
6 Move through a process of increasing refinement of analysis.
7. Conduct an orderly search for additional information.
8. Complete any discrete step in analysis that they begin.

Intuitive thinkers tend to:

1. Keep the overall problem continuously in mind.
2. Redefine the problem frequently as they proceed.
3. Rely on unverbalized clues, even hunches.
4. Defend a solution in terms of appropriateness.
5. Consider a number of alternatives and options simultaneously.
6. Jump from one step in analysis or search to another and back again.
7. Explore and abandon alternatives very quickly.

Sanford and Adelman, *Managerial Decisions: A Behavioral Approach,* p. 135.

The Organizational Context Within Which the Manager Operates. We show in Chapter 5 that organizations are hierarchical structures. Different persons at various hierarchical levels perform different tasks. Consequently, decision making at each of these levels varies both in nature and complexity. Accordingly, each organizational level requires different decision-making modes. In that chapter, we identified three levels in organizational hierarchies: top, middle, and lower levels. Managers at each of these levels perform interrelated functions whose tasks are nevertheless rather distinct. Robert Anthony, for example, identified three such tasks:

(1) Strategic planning *is the process of deciding* on objectives *of the organization, on* changes in these objectives, *on the* resources *used to attain these objectives, on the* policies *used to attain these objectives, and on the policies that are* to govern the acquistion, *use, and* disposition *of these resources.*
(2) Management control *is the process by which managers* assure that resources *are obtained and used* effectively and efficiently *in the accomplishment of the organization's objectives.*
(3) Operational Control *is the process of assuring that* specific tasks *are carried out efficiently and effectively.*[31]

[31]Robert Anthony, *Planning and Control System: A Framework for Analysis* (Cambridge, Mass.: Harvard University Press, 1965), pp. 16–18.

Types of Decision Problems. Decision problems are usually divided into three categories: (1) decision making under certainty; (2) decision making under risk and uncertainty; and (3) decision making under conflict. This classification is made by using the criterion of knowledge regarding the uncontrollable variables or events. All of these three categories of problems share one common characteristic; that is, they are structured problems. In other words, the decision maker is able to define the problem, the alternatives, the probabilities (either objectively or subjectively), the evaluation techniques, and, finally, he or she can arrive at a decision. This type of decision making is usually referred to as programmed or routine decision making. There is, however, a class of managerial decision problems that can be called unstructured, nonprogrammed, or nonroutine. The more one moves toward the top of the hierarchy (strategic planning), the higher the percentage of unstructured problems, with which one must deal. These kinds of problems are characterized by the absence of one or more of the many parameters of decision making (such as utility function, strategies, events), and for this reason, there is no specific technique to be used.

It is conceptually more useful to think of structured problems as *convergent,* meaning that the more one works on them and the more his or her decision-making techniques improve, the more the possible solutions or decisions converge. Unstructured problems are *divergent;* that is, the more decision makers deal with them, the more the possible solutions or decisions *diverge.*[32] Decision technology and almost all of the modern quantitative methods are very useful in dealing with convergent problems. However, divergent decision problems require a great dose of intuition and feeling. Real life management decision occasions appear overwhelmingly unstructured and divergent. It is for this type of decision occasion that the intuitive decision making, with its emphasis on long-term, futuristic, and holistic orientation, is very appropriate.

The Importance of Information Acquisition

Information is the main ingredient in decision making. From the first step of the decision-making process (identification and definition of the occasion for decision or the problem), to the final and fifth step (the implementation of the chosen alternative), the decision maker is constantly seeking, receiving, evaluating, and disseminating information. Some of this information comes to the manager in an unsolicited manner. Information will be supplied to the manager by superiors, subordinates, or peers. Most of the needed information, however, will have to be actively sought out by the decision maker. Today's organizations spend sizeable amounts of money for a technology that helps the manager organize, process, and disseminate information. It is because of this tremendous importance of information for decision making that this book devotes an entire

[32]E. F. Schumacher, *A Guide for the Perplexed* (New York: Harper and Row, 1977), p. 121.

part to the subject (see Part IV: "Decision Technology," Chapters 13, 14, 15, and 16).

Information is data relevant for a specified decision-making occasion or problem. Data represent numerical expressions of the perceived world of the decision maker. The manager expresses his or her perceptions of a task by using certain numerical languages. For example, a production manager of a manufacturing company would describe his or her job by saying that during the last six months 100,000 units of model XYZ refrigerators were produced, requiring the employment of, let's say, 3,000 people and the use of so much material. In a similar fashion, an insurance officer processes so many insurance applications. Or the bank teller processes so many checks, or the emergency nurse attends to so many patients.

Whether a decision maker will actively engage in seeking out information or will wait to receive information will depend on what step of the decision-making process is being performed. For example, Step 1 (identification and definition of the decision occasion or problem) requires more active information acquisition than the other four remaining steps. Steps 2–4 recognize more processing of information already received and little acquisition of new information. Finally, the last step, implementation, requires mostly information dissemination (communication), rather than either acquisition or processing.

Some Problems of Information Acquisition

Of course, information is vital to the making of acceptable decisions. Not surprisingly, however, because information gets to a decision point by way of human beings, various kinds of human behavior dynamics are likely to complicate that process. We shall here note three important ways in which this often happens.

First, many people will seek as persuasively as they can to make significant decision information out of their preferences. Remember, the thinking animal is only as rational as its values permit it to be. A typical difficulty, however, as people endeavor to make decision information out of their values, is that this is likely to be too easily seen as being precisely what it is. But if preferences, disguised as facts, can be "smuggled" into the decision process, perhaps this danger can be avoided. There are, moreover, more opportunities to do this in complex organizations than might be supposed. Because in that situation everyone will know best what is closest to his/her own responsibilities, what the other person claims to be a fact may often have to be given a substantial amount of face validity.

Second, the masquerade of preferences as facts already overlaps a decision information difficulty that can be extremely troublesome in its own right. Specialization, without which complex organizations could not function, fragments the understanding required to keep such organizations viable. That is, all members in their own setting may be well enough informed to do their jobs quite satisfactorily. But most of this understanding will be out of context with what is often called "the larger picture." Moreover, this is an excellent example of situations in which the pieces do not really add up to the whole. When, then, a number of well-informed people endeavor to make decisions requiring a composite understanding, this can be very difficult upstream against what some of these people do not comprehend but think that they do.

Third, the organization, to do the planning and coordinating it must do, has to treat as "facts" its best guesses about what will happen in the future. This is a sort of "make-believe" reality often called "bureaucratic premises." Thus, if the sales department were to do its planning on the basis of a 5% increase in gross national product, but the production people were doing their planning on the basis of a 5% decrease, that could be chaotically confusing. Of course predicting the future is a highly uncertain business. Also, uncertainty provides a special opportunity to smuggle preferences, disguised as "facts," into the decision process. But there is no avoiding this; organizations must necessarily build much of what they do on premises that may one day be demonstrably in error.

Applying the Decision-Making Process

How do managers make decisions? The answer may be that managers make decisions by using the decision-making process. In other words, managers define problems and alternatives, evaluate alternatives, choose one alternative that satisfies a utility function, and implement that alternative. In going through these basic steps of the decision-making process, the manager may act as an analytic decision maker (that is, as one who perceives problems and alternatives as objective, hard facts and evaluates alternative courses of action by using logical methods such as probability and decision technology). Or he or she may be an intuitive decision maker (problems and alternatives are not defined in terms of objective, hard facts but, rather, are based upon hunches, gut feelings, and other personal sentiments for evaluation). Both of these two pure types are present in organizations. Thus, a subordinate might be dealing with two superiors, one of whom may be insisting, "Give me the figures and don't bother me with feeling," whereas the other might say, "Don't bother me with the facts; I've already made up my mind."

Whether a manager will tend to be an analytic or intuitive decision maker will depend largely on the following four factors:

1. The environment that triggers the decision-making process (both the internal and external environment).
2. The autonomy of the decision maker.
3. The impact of the decision.
4. The personality of the decision maker.

Figure 7-3 provides some suggested relationships between the two main decision-making styles or modes (analytic and intuitive) and the four main factors that influence the decision maker's opportunity to use one or the other as well as a combination of the two. Because the figure is self-explanatory, few examples are provided here as to how these relationships should be interpreted. It was mentioned before that most decision occasions (that is, situations that necessitate the making of a decision) occur as a result of a person perceiving a happening in the environment that can represent a problem, threat, or an opportunity. The frequency of occurrence of these events will depend on how frequently the environment changes. In general, analytic decision making tends to be more appropriate for problems that are created within a stable environment. The reason for this is that in such situations the decision maker has more time and more opportunity to gather and evaluate enough information and to use formal analytic methods. Threats and opportunities also can be dealt with more efficiently through intuitive decision making.

The second class of factors refers to the decider's accountability for decisions that are made. When a manager makes a decision for which he or she is ac-

FIGURE 7-3. Analytic and Intuitive Managerial Decision-Making.

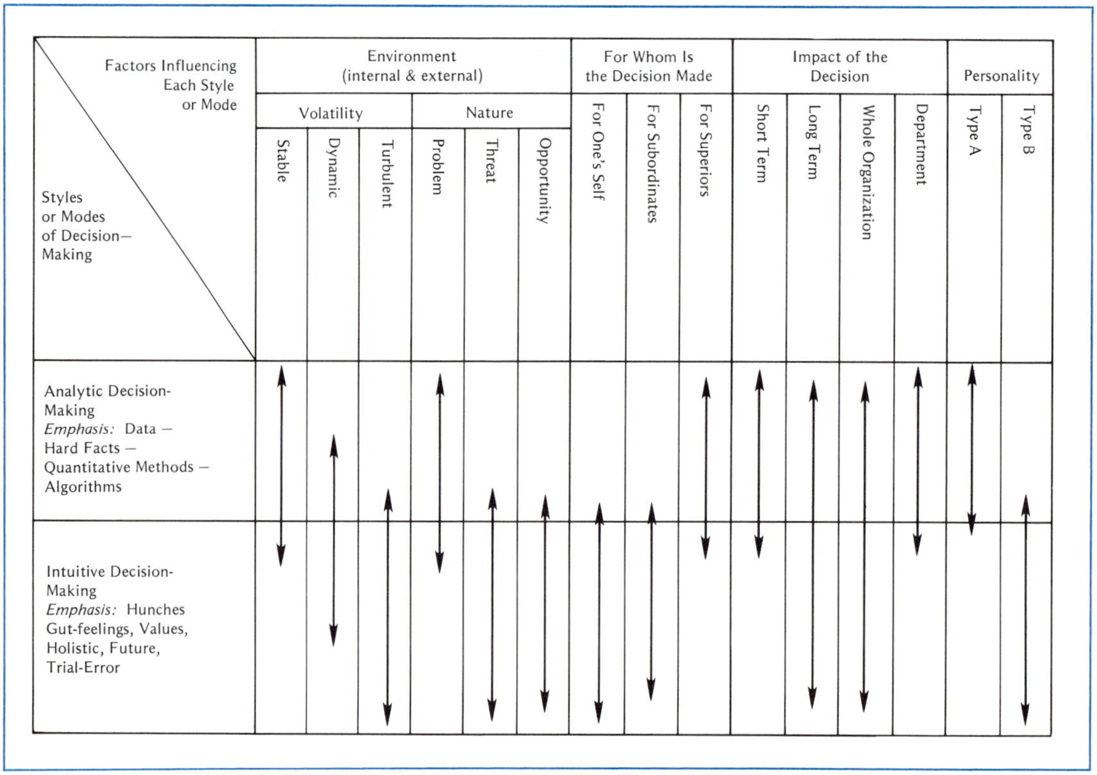

"That's the gist of what I want to say. Now get me some statistics to base it on." (Drawing by Joe Mirachi; © 1977 The New Yorker Magazine, Inc.)

countable, or when the manager makes a decision for subordinates, he or she most likely will use primarily intuitive decision making. Should, however, the manager make a decision for a superior, then, as the cartoon suggests, the superior will insist on analytic decision making.

The impact of a decision also influences the style of decision making. The impact can be conceived both in terms of time (present or short-term, and future or long-term) as well as in terms of the number of people or departments (one's department versus the entire organization). Typically, a decision that has a short-term impact and is destined to affect only the manager's own department is made through analytic decision making. On the other hand, decisions that will have long-term effects and impact on the entire organization require a great mixture of both analytic and intuitive decision making.

All of these suggested relationships between the two styles of decision making and the environment, autonomy, and impact are moderated by the manager's personality. Some psychologists have recently suggested that the human brain is divided into two interrelated parts, known as "hemispheres." This is the concept of the *bifunctional brain* in man.[33] The left hemisphere seems to specialize in the analytic functions of language, rational knowing, sense of time, and other linear functions (Type A). The right hemisphere usually appears to favor nonverbal thinking and knowing such as intuition, spatial orientation, activities, and other nonlinear functions (Type B). Supporters of this concept of the bifunctional brain suggest that in most people one of these two half-brains predominates, so that some people are primarily analytic whereas others are more intuitive and creative.

CREATIVITY: THE PURPOSEFUL IMAGINATION

Management and creativity were traditionally thought of as two antithetical concepts. Managers were supposed to be cold, calculating, rational, money-motivated individuals. Creativity, on the other hand, was a characteristic of the artist, the musician, the writer, and the poet. Children who exhibited any kind of creative tendencies were asked to stay away from professional management.

The Bifunctional Brain

Both the structure and function of these two "half-brains" in some part underlie the two methods of consciousness which simultaneously coexist in each of us. Although each hemisphere shares the potential for many functions, and both sides participate in both activities, in the normal person the two hemispheres tend to specialize. The left hemisphere (connected to the right side of the body) is predominantly involved with analytic, logical thinking, especially in verbal and mathematical functions. Its mode of operation is primarily linear. This hemisphere seems to process information sequentially. This mode of operation of necessity must underlie logical thought, since logic depends upon sequence and order. Language and mathematics, both left hemisphere activities, also depend predominantly on linear time.

If the left hemisphere is specialized for analysis, the right hemisphere (again, remember, connected to the left side of the body) seems specialized for holistic mentation. Its language ability is quite limited. This hemisphere is primarily responsible for our orientation in space, artistic endeavor, crafts, body image, recognition of faces. It processes information more diffusely than does the left hemisphere, and its responsibilities demand a ready integration of many inputs at once. If the left hemisphere can be termed predominantly analytic and sequential in its operation, then the right hemisphere is more holistic and relational, and more simultaneous in its operation.

Robert E. Orstein, *A Psychology of Consciousness*, pp. 51–53.

[33] Robert E. Orstein, *A Psychology of Consciousness* (San Francisco: W. H. Freeman, 1972).

Managers who on occasion tried to be creative found that they were looked upon as persons who somehow never grew up. Recently, however, creativity is a desirable attribute for modern managers. In addition to a brief exposure in formal education in business schools, some organizations further encourage creative management by sending their employees to one of the half a dozen or so "creativity institutes."

Most people conceive of creativity as a very unusual human quality that is an inborn characteristic. In other words, most people believe that nature has endowed some few individuals with the capability to think of and realize things that are unique to the extent that they would not naturally have evolved or come about through ordinary processes. The names of Benjamin Franklin, Graham Bell, Cyrus McCormick, Guglielone Marconi, and other famous inventors are usually thought of as creative individuals credited with great creative powers. Although there is considerable validity in viewing creativity as a unique attribute found only in certain gifted individuals, contemporary researchers perceive creativity as another five-step process that can be learned. James Vargin, founding director of the Psychosynthesis Institute, San Francisco, describes the main logic of the creative problem:

> *Suddenly, in times of frustration or of quiet during the heat of a discussion or while driving on a highway, a flash appears unexpectedly in our mind and forms a new pattern of associations, a new idea, a new vision. Whether it is a simple solution to a trivial problem or a deep intuition that will transform our life, something new has been created. Though it is elusive, we receive it with joy. Though it is imponderable, we may consider it most precious. This moment of insight, this "Aha!" experience, is the central phenomenon of the creative process.*[34]

Although every person's mind functions differently, research involving testimonies of creators and descriptions of their inventions and other creative acts have revealed that the creative process typically goes through the following stages: (1) preparation or saturation—becoming thoroughly familiar with a problem; (2) deliberation or frustration—mulling over ideas, analyzing them, challenging them, thinking of them from several viewpoints; (3) incubation—relaxing, turning off the conscious and purposeful search; (4) illumination—hitting upon a bright idea, new, fresh, different approach, something that gives one the feeling of being the right thing to do; (5) elaboration or accommodation—clarifying the idea, seeing whether it fits the requirements of the problem as it did on first thought, reframing and adapting it, putting it on paper, getting other people's reaction to it.[35]

Contrary to popular belief, creative acts do not fall from the heavens, but, rather, they represent the outcome of hard labor. Benjamin Franklin's remark that

[34] "Creativity," *Synthesis* (Vol. 3-4, Winter 1977), p. 17.

[35] Newman, Summers, and Warren, *The Process of Management* (Englewood Cliffs, New Jersey: Prentice-Hall, Inc., 1967), pp. 335–356; Brewster Ghiselin, *The Creative Process* (Berkeley: University of California Press, 1961); Arthur Koestler, *The Art of Creativity* (New York: Macmillan, 1969); Alex Osborn, *Applied Imagination* (New York: Charles Scribner's Sons, 1961).

On Becoming Creative

Put to other uses? New ways to use as is? Other uses if modified?

Adapt? What else is like this? What other idea does this suggest? Does past offer parallel? What could I copy? Whom could I emulate?

Modify? New twist? Change meaning, color, motion, sound, odor, form, shape? Other changes?

Magnify? What to add? More time? Greater frequency? Stronger? Higher? Longer? Thicker? Extra value? Plus ingredient? Duplicate? Multiply? Exaggerate?

Minify? What to subtract? Smaller? Condensed? Miniature? Lower? Shorter? Lighter? Omit? Streamline? Split up? Understate?

Substitute? Who else instead? What else instead? Other ingredient? Other material? Other process? Other power? Other place? Other approach? Other tone of voice?

Rearrange? Interchange components? Other pattern? Other layout? Other sequence? Transpose cause and effect? Change pace? Change schedule?

Reverse? Transpose positive and negative? How about opposites? Turn it backward? Turn it upside down? Reverse roles? Change shoes? Turn tables? Turn other cheek?

Combine? How about a blend, an alloy, an assortment, an ensemble? Combine units? Combine purposes? Combine appeals? Combine ideas?

Alex Osborn, *Applied Imagination*, p. 18.

"creativity is 95% perspiration and 5% inspiration" is very descriptive. The kind of work involved in building one's conceptual skills for creative work is different from the ordinary activity. Most of the time it involves doing things in exactly the opposite way one has been doing them before. This excessive unorthodoxy is designed to break one's own thinking habits, which tend to constrain and sometimes restrict one's own potential.

SUMMARY

This chapter dealt with the subject of decision making, which was defined as the process of defining a decision occasion or a problem and choosing and implementing a chosen alternative. Traditionally, all decision making was considered to be rational, that is, the decision maker had complete knowledge of the problem and the alternatives and also had a system of ordering performances in such a way as to maximize something desired (such as profits, sales, or goodwill) that was referred to as the utility. Research performed during the last three decades has revealed that humans cannot always act rationally when they are confronted with a decision occasion. The reason is that the human brain is not capable of either comprehending the full complexity of the present situation or of anticipating the future. Consequently, the human's rationality is bounded by those constraints.

This theory of decision making is referred to as the administrative man (or the bounded rationality) theory, as contrasted with the economic man (or objective rationality) theory of the past.

Managerial decisions are present commitments to a particular course of action based upon anticipation of the future. As such, managerial decisions are always made under conditions of incomplete information, or risk and uncertainty. In this chapter, we presented two complementary ways or methods of making decisions: (1) the analytic method, which is extensively used by the decision theory practitioners; and (2) the intuitive method, which depends more on feelings and hunches than on any formal, logical system. Business corporations and organizations in general need and employ both types of decision makers. Although the exact mixture of analytic and intuitive decision making varies from organization to organization and from one manager to another, in general, the more stable the decision environment, and the more the individual manager makes decisions for a superior, the more likely will be an analytic decision-making style. Also the more immediate and the smaller the impact of the decision, the more analytic will be the style with which it will be made. On the other hand, the more long-term and encompassing the impact of a decision, and the more dynamic the environment within which it is being made, the more will this decision making require a judicious mix of analytic and intuitive styles.

Finally, the last part of the chapter dealt briefly with the subject of creativity. Popular belief to the contrary, creativity is not a unique characteristic of a few gifted individuals. Most people are and can learn to be creative, provided that the social stigma that associates engagement in creative work as a waste of time and as unproductive is eliminated. Bright ideas that lead to unusual and unorthodox creations do not fall from heaven like manna. They represent the outcomes of a rather well-defined creative process of saturation, frustration, incubation, illumination, and accommodation. It is for this reason that creativity has been defined in this chapter as purposeful imagination.

Assignments

7-1. Is there any difference between decision making and problem solving?

7-2. What is reflective thinking?

7-3. What does it mean to say that a manager makes a "rational decision" or "behaves rationally?"

7-4. Contrast maximizing to satisficing.

7-5. Explain the "economic man" theory and compare it to Simon's "administrative man" theory of decision making.

7-6. What are the five steps of the decision-making process?

7-7. How do managers perceive and evaluate decision problems?

7-8. What determines or influences the manager's decision-making style? In other words, under what conditions or circumstances could a manager be primarily an intuitive or analytic decision maker?

7-9. In what ways are some people viewed as being primarily right-brain (intuitive) whereas others are left-brain (analytic) decision makers?

7-10. What is creativity? And what is the creative process?

Case 7-1

RELOCATION DECISION

Bill Mihas, a friendly, hard-working Greek immigrant, operated a steakhouse at 1017 Main Street in a small university city in the Midwest. Business was excellent for Bill, although most of the other downtown small businessmen were complaining of a severe recession. One day, a party was thrown by the business community and the local Chamber of Commerce. Bill overheard Ernie, the owner of one of the oldest bars in town located next door to Bill's Steakhouse, telling a group of people about the city council's decision to start an urban renewal project in the city. Both Bill's Steakhouse and Ernie's Bar, as well as numerous other small businesses, would have to be relocated to make room for a new modern mall that the city was contemplating. "That means," Ernie told Bill, "that we're going to have to find a new location within about a year from now."

Bill left the party in a grim mood. He had just completed his sixth year on Main Street. Over the last four years the Steakhouse had been very successful. This was the third time that Bill had opened a steakhouse. The other two times, the first in Chicago and the second in Denver, had been financial disasters. Now that Bill had finally paid for all new equipment, including a new air-conditioning system, he discovered that he'd have to relocate. "This isn't going to be a good year," thought Bill.

Next morning, Bill went to the local banker who confirmed the rumors about relocation. "You see, Bill," he said, "this is the only thing that the city can do. The downtown is dying . . . needs a new face . . . you know . . . new shops . . . new business. You know what I mean?" "Yeah, Dick," said Bill, "I hope you're right." "I know I'm right," said Dick. "Just imagine yourself with a new steakhouse in one of those new shopping malls—doesn't it sound exciting?" "You're forgetting," said Bill, "I don't like shopping centers. I like to be alone. Well, anyway, Dick, how about a loan, let's say $150,000?" "Well," said Dick, "you find a new place first and we'll see."

After the noon rush hour, Bill visited Mr. Johnson, his attorney. "I suppose you heard the news," Bill told Mr. Johnson, "we must move on account of this thing, you know, the urban renewal." "Well," said Mr. Johnson, "it is not all that bad. The way I see it you've got a problem that has several alternative solutions. All of these alternatives are good. Of course, some of them are better than others and, surely, one has got to be the best. It's up to you to determine what that might be. Why, Bill I can give you three alternatives right now. "You see, first. . ." At that moment the phone rang. It was Mr. Johnson's secretary. She reminded him of a trial that was about to start at three P.M.

"Listen, Bill," said Mr. Johnson, "I've got to go to the courthouse. Meanwhile, think about these alternatives I mentioned to you."

You've known Bill for some time now. He sees you entering the steakhouse for your usual dinner. His face brightens immediately. "Hello, Professor," Bill says. (Bill calls all college students professors). He quickly tells you the story about how the city council has decided upon the urban renewal project without asking him. He pays a lot of city taxes . . . has no kids yet, but pays school taxes . . . and so on. Finally, he puts it to you, "Hey, professor, my attorney says I've got at least three alternatives. He says I must make a decision like a rational man. I must consider and weigh all possible alternatives. He says then I'll find the best. Can you help me?"

1. Define Mr. Mihas' problem.
2. Define and evaluate the possible alternatives.
3. Help him make a choice.

Case 7-2

GUS'S GUT FEELING

B. J. Jensen founded Jensen's Construction Company (JCC) in the late 1940's when B. J. was 30 years old. Over the years, JCC grew from a small construction company, operating primarily in upstate New York, to a multimillion dollar organization with offices and branches all over the world. Last year, B. J. celebrated his sixty-second birthday. During dinner, B. J. announced his intention to gradually retire from the day-to-day operations of JCC. He would like to see his two sons, Fredrich and Gustaff ("Gus"), take over complete control of the management of the company. He told the family that he would still like to be the president of the company, with Fredrich, the older son, taking over the technical side of the company, and Gus in charge of administration. Both brothers will be on an equal managerial or hierarchical level within the company.

Fredrich Jensen had gone to college and received his BS in civil engineering. After four years in the Army, Fred started work with JCC. Gus Jensen started college when he was 17 years old. At the beginning of his senior year, Gus dropped out of the engineering school and started taking courses in the business school. After the first few accounting courses, Gus had accumulated enough hours to get a social sciences degree. His family was trying to convince him to go to law school. Instead, Gus joined the Action program and was sent to Latin America. For the last six years, Gus has been working with JCC and enjoying it.

Several months ago, JCC received a request to build a new port for a newly emerged African nation. Fred had already run a computer program that figured out basic cost, time, manpower, and material estimates, and had also given an estimate of the probable profit JCC would be making. "The data look very good," Fred said in a very excited voice. "I mean," he continued "we can hardly go wrong." Fred then asked Gus to draft a letter of intent to participate in the public bidding for the job. When Gus sat at the typewriter, he could not quite start. He had this feeling that something was wrong. He picked up the phone and called Fred. "Fred, this is Gus. Listen, I think we ought to do some more thinking about that job in Africa. I've just got this feeling that something isn't quite right." He paused for a while and then continued. "I think, Fred, we shouldn't even get involved in Africa at all. There is too much turbulence. I know my analysis of the situation isn't as sophisticated as yours, but I just got this feeling, you know. . ."

Fred listened for a while and then replied, "Listen, Gus, we went over that stuff many times. We just can't let your intuition run this business. This is the twentieth century, you know. I mean we've got powerful computers that can do very sophisticated analyses of all possible alternatives, find the best one, and even figure out a best way of implementing a chosen course of action. Now, we just can't disregard all that and follow your gut feeling. You know what I think? I think it's your ulcer acting up again. Yeah, that's it. The feeling you have in your gut . . . it's your good ol' ulcer. Come on, let's have that letter, and then, go out and have a good time. Treat your ulcer to a nice steak."

On his way home, Gus continued thinking about the African job. Things began to crystallize a bit and take a definite shape. What if the government that would sign the contract were to collapse? What if the loan that the country had applied for did not go through? What if there was a war in the area? What if the government imposed an import restriction policy and JCC could not get the necessary material and equipment?

1. How would you go about incorporating Gus's intuition into Fred's analytic decision making?
2. Is there any way that Gus's feeling can be communicated to Fred in a way that he would at least consider rerunning his computer models?
3. Is there anything more to Gus's feeling than what Fred diagnosed as his "good ol' ulcer?"

References

ALEXIS, MARKUS, AND CHARLES Z. WILSON. *Organizational Decision-Making.* Englewood Cliffs, N.J.: Prentice-Hall, Inc., 1967.

BARNARD, CHESTER I. *The Functions of the Executive.* Cambridge, Mass.: Harvard University Press, 1968.

BEER, STAFFORD. *Decision and Control.* New York: John Wiley & Sons, Inc., 1967.

CHURCHMAN, C. WEST. *Challenge to Reason.* New York: McGraw-Hill Book Company, 1968.

CHURCHMAN, C. WEST. *Prediction and Optimal Decision.* Englewood Cliffs, N.J.: Prentice-Hall, Inc., 1961.

EDWARDS, WARD, AND AMOS TVERSKY. *Decision Making.* Middlesex, England: Penguin Books, 1967.

BRINKANS, HENRY S. (ed.) *Decision Making: Creativity, Judgment, and Systems.* Columbus, Ohio: Ohio State University Press, 1972.

LOW, ALBERT. *Zen and Creative Management.* New York: Doubleday & Company, Inc., 1976.

ORSTEIN, R. D. *A Psychology of Consciousness.* San Francisco: W. H. Freeman and Company, Publishers, 1972.

OSBORN, ALEX F. *Applied Imagination: Principles and Procedures of Creative Thinking.* New York: Charles Scribner's Sons, 1957.

SANFORD, EDWARD, AND HARVEY ADELMAN. *Management Decisions: A Behavioral Approach.* Cambridge, Mass.: Winthrop, 1977.

SCHUMACHER, ERNEST F. *A Guide for the Perplexed.* New York: Harper & Row, Publishers, 1977.

SHULL, FREMONT A., ANDRÉ A. DELBECQ, AND LARRY L. CUMMINGS. *Organizational Decision-Making.* New York: McGraw-Hill Book Company, 1970.

SIMON, HERBERT A., *Administrative Behavior.* New York: Macmillan Publishing Co., Inc., 1976.

FRANK SCHLIER
Director of Information Systems
American Bankers Association

Frank Schlier is the Director of Information Systems for the American Bankers Association in Washington, D.C., and is a data processing faculty member of the American Institute of Banking. He serves as a committee member for the U.S. State Department's Committee on International Data Processing and the American National Standards (ANSI) Committee on Data Base Management Systems.

Executive Commentary
Why Wasn't I Consulted?

Business decision making is often viewed as being a solitary function in which the decision maker defines alternatives, evaluates them, and selects the alternative best suited to the situation at hand. In reality, business decisions are seldom made in an environment in which the decision maker has organizational responsibility for all areas affected by the decision, or the organizational power, through hierarchical position, to fully implement the selected alternative.

Implementation of a selected alternative usually requires the cooperation of other managers within the organization and, in many cases, the cooperation of individuals outside of the organization. Often, managers fail in the implementation of a decision result by waiting until after the decision is made to enlist the cooperation of other individuals. The most common battle cry of managers who feel a decision is being forced on them is, "Why wasn't I consulted?" These managers often develop a mental block against the selected alternative, and it becomes extremely difficult to implement the decision.

Often, the alternative selected would be the same with or without consultation, but the implementation of the alternative is viewed from a different perspective by a manager who feels that he was a part of the decision process.

Organizational sensitivity must be considered in the decision process. In the definition of alternatives, the decision maker should define all areas of the organization that might be affected by the alternative and all individuals within the organization whose cooperation is required to fully implement the alternative. Consultation with these individuals will help the decision maker in determining the probability that an alternative will be accepted and will help lay groundwork for the implementation process.

The formation of committees and task forces to address specific decisions is often looked upon as an attempt by the decision maker to "spread the responsibility for the decision," thus protecting him from criticism in the event the decision is wrong. In many cases, this criticism is valid, as weaker managers use the committee process as shield or a crutch. However, the committee process can be used by the strong manager as an effective decision tool. By carefully selecting committee members, the decision maker can ensure that his committee includes individuals with technical expertise in the area of the decision—individuals whose activities will be affected by the decision and individuals who are keys to the implementation of a selected alternative. The decision maker then uses the committee as a source of information in alternative analysis and as a sounding board for various decision scenarios. During this process, he can evaluate each committee member's position on the alternatives. As an alternative becomes apparent to him as the best selection, he can begin the negotiating process with committee members who may favor another alternative. The manager, therefore, can use the committee for decision-making assistance and as a vehicle to aid him in implementing the selected alternative. Often, a manager who disagrees with the selection of a specific alternative will feel better about participating in its implementation if he believes that his recommendations have been considered and evaluated in light of total organization needs.

Organizations are made up of people, each with his/her own set of needs. A common need of most people is to be included. When this need is not fulfilled, it is easy for the individual to find fault in any alternative selected and difficult for him to assist in implementation. When this need is fulfilled, the individual may still find faults in the selected alternative, but, through his participation in the decision process, can understand the basis for the selection and contribute to its implementation.

Decision making, therefore, is not a function that utilizes only the manager's skills in alternative evaluation and selection. The decision maker must be a teacher, a negotiator, and a communicator. He must know the organization in which he is operating and have the interpersonal skills to bring other individuals into the decision process.

CASES FOR PART III

BANK MANAGER'S TIME PROBLEM

At 8 A.M. on a Friday, Paul Spencer, manager of the Stratford branch of the Tri-Cities Bank, swung his car out of the driveway of his suburban home and headed toward his office, located some nine miles away. It was a beautiful day. The sun was shining brightly and a cool, fresh breeze was blowing. The trip to the bank took about 15 minutes and sometimes gave Paul an opportunity to think about bank problems without interruption.

Tri-Cities Bank was centered in Winston-Salem and operated eight branches in the area. Tri-Cities enjoyed a good reputation. Its customers consisted of individual and commercial accounts. It was a closely held bank, with some 70 employees. The Stratford branch employed four tellers and clerks, in addition to Paul. Paul had started with the Tri-Cities bank just after he graduated from business college. After three years, he was promoted to assistant manager of the High Point branch, and, six months later, was promoted to manager when the former manager retired.

Paul was in fine spirits as his car picked up speed and the hum of the tires on the newly paved highway faded into the background. He said to himself, "This is going to be the day to really get things done."

He began to run through the day's work, first one project, then another, trying to establish priorities. After a few minutes, he decided that he needed to get out and open up some new accounts with commercial businesses. Good loans had been lagging lately, and Jim Pitts, the vice-president, branch operations, had been after Paul to develop more and better loan business. Paul frowned for a moment as he recalled that earlier in the week, Jim had called and asked how he was progressing. Actually, he had some ideas that he discussed with other bank officials, but other urgent matters kept getting in the way. "It's time to get going," he said to himself.

Paul's thoughts quickly turned to other projects he was determined to get under way. He needed to do something about employee evaluations. The company had formulated some procedures on this, but they had not been instituted in the Stratford branch. He also needed to get together with the public relations people. Paul felt some of the bank's advertising and promotional pieces were not as effective as they could be and needed overhauling. Then there was that loan delinquency list. . .

Paul's thoughts were interrupted as he pulled into the bank's parking lot. When he entered the building, he knew something was wrong as Jean, one of the tellers, met him at the door. "Great morning, Jean," Paul greeted her cheerfully. "Not so great; Betty called in a minute ago and said she was sick," Jean snapped. "It's Friday and you know how busy we'll be. Think you could get one of the other branches to send someone over?"

"Damn," Paul growled. "She's not very reliable. I'll check with personnel."

He walked to his desk, which was opposite the tellers' cages. One of the other girls brought him a big pile of mail. He asked her to get him a cup of coffee and started to open the mail. The phone rang; it was bookkeeping asking about some of the transactions in yesterday's business. As Paul hung on the phone answering question after question, he thought, "nitpicker." When he finished, he took a swallow of the coffee that was then cold. He started to call personnel about another teller when one of the clerks asked him to check over several of the deposit control sheets. He was trying to find an error when the bank doors were opened and a customer came up to chat with him.

This case was prepared by Jack D. Ferner, lecturer in Management, Babcock Graduate School of Management, Wake Forest University, Winston-Salem, North Carolina. It was adapted from The Case of the Missing Time, copyright 1960, Northwestern University . . . This case is designed to be used as a basis for class discussion rather than to illustrate either effective or ineffective handling of an administrative situation.

The phone rang again and Paul's boss was on the other end. With an obvious edge in his voice, he asked, "the auditors are in and they're asking about your delinquent loans. Did you get the information together yet?" Paul responded that he hadn't had time, but would. There followed a series of questions. The conversation ended with, "Paul, you really need to get after those accounts." Paul sighed. At his desk was a teller asking him to approve a check for payment and a new customer wanting to open an account.

The customers began to pile up as a couple small commercial accounts came in to get their payrolls put together. Paul started to help out when Cecil Hardy, a customer with a couple medium-sized savings accounts, walked up. He came in a couple of times a week to cash checks and liked to have a cup of coffee and chat. He was semi-retired and today wanted to talk about social security benefits. He also was an avid golfer and described in detail a round he had played the day before. Paul had played a lot when he was in school and enjoyed an occasional game.

Paul went to lunch with a young lawyer friend who had recently started his own practice. He had opened a checking account at the bank. He called an hour ahead to say he wanted to discuss a lease on some office furniture as proposed by a finance company. They drove across town to a new restaurant.

When Paul returned at about 2 P.M., the bank was busy again. He suddenly remembered the matter of a replacement teller. "Too late now," he mused. He sat down and began to assemble the files relating to the delinquent accounts. The bookkeeping department called to discuss three checks that had been returned for insufficient funds. A young couple came in to ask about an installment loan. Paul took a break to get a coke from the storage room. He noticed some of the customer files had been pulled out and not returned. As he straightened them out, he thought, "I wonder who the hell did this?"

Paul returned to his desk to find a Boy Scout troop selling advertisements in a program for a rally they were putting on. As the afternoon wore on, Paul became increasingly irritated at not being able to make much progress with the delinquent accounts. The trouble was "what to do about the ones with Reliable Welding and Sally's Supermarket?"

At 5 P.M., the boss called to ask about the business that day. The conversation shifted to a reminder of the branch managers' meeting Monday afternoon. Pitts wanted to discuss the new loan situation that was lagging in most of the branches. He also mentioned that the "computer boys" wanted to schedule a meeting later in the week to see if the computer couldn't be better utilized by the branches. Paul thought, "That's two afternoons shot. Those meetings always drag on so long and we never seem to accomplish anything."

When he finished the call, it was 5:30 P.M. and he was the only one left in the bank. Paul was tired. He put on his coat and headed toward the parking lot. With both eyes on the traffic, Paul reviewed the day he had just completed. "Busy?" he asked himself. "Too much so—but did I accomplish anything?" His mind raced over the day's activities. "Yes and no" seemed to be the answer. There was the usual routine, the same as any other day. The bank kept going and I think it must have been a good day. Any creative or special project work done?" Paul grimaced as he reluctantly answered, "No."

With a feeling of guilt, he probed further. "Am I a manager? I'm paid as one, respected as one, and have a responsible assignment with the necessary authority to carry it out. Yet, one of the greatest values a bank derives from a manager is his creative thinking and accomplishments. What have I done about it? You need some time for thinking. Today was a typical day, just like most other days, and I did little, if any, creative work. The projects that I so enthusiastically planned to work on this morning are exactly as they were yesterday. What's more, I have no guarantee that next week will bring me any closer to their completion. There must be an answer."

Paul continued, "Night work? Yes, occasionally. That's understood. But I've been doing too much of it lately. I owe my wife and family some of my time. When you come down to it, they are the people for whom I'm really working. If I am forced to spend much more time away from them, I'm not meeting my own personal objectives. What about church work? Should I eliminate that? I spend a lot of time on it, but I feel I owe God some time, too. Besides, I believe I'm making a worthwhile contribution. Perhaps I can squeeze a little time from my fraternal activities. But where does recreation fit in?"

Paul groped for the solution. By this time, he had turned off the highway onto the side street leading to his home with the problem still uppermost in his mind. "I guess I really don't know the answer," he told himself as he pulled into his driveway. This morning, everything seemed so simple, but now . . . His son ran toward the car, calling out, "Mommy, Daddy's home."

Questions for discussion

1. What is your analysis of Paul's situation?
2. Is Paul's time problem a planning problem? Discuss.
3. How do you suggest Paul handle his predicament?

RON BLACK IS BACK

Ron Black had just obtained his Master's in hospital administration from a prestigious East Coast university. Ron would readily admit that he owed his degree, in part, to the administrators and trustees of Midvale General Hospital. They had agreed to pay a large part of Ron's college expenses in return for a commitment by Ron to return to Midvale and assume a "high-level management position" for at least four years.

Before going to graduate school, Ron was, in the eyes of practically everyone at Midvale, a superb supervisor of the hospital's purchasing department. His pleasant personality, "can-do" spirit, and uncanny ability to obtain whatever his customers asked for made him the "favorite son" of top management. When it was announced that Midvale Hospital would offer a graduate scholarship to an outstanding member of the staff, Ron was the obvious choice.

Now, having completed graduate school, Ron was anxious to learn what new challenges awaited him at Midvale. He had been asked to meet with the hospital administrator at 10 A.M. to find out. Anxiously, he waited outside the administrator's office, wondering if the sign proclaiming, "John Boone, Administrator" would one day be changed to read "Ron Black."

"Come in, Ron, good to see you again," said Mr. Boone, "you've come back just in time. We've got big plans for you."

"Good," thought Ron, as he and Mr. Boone exchanged pleasantries.

The conversation quickly got down to business.

"Ron, we've been having trouble keeping things under control in some of our administrative support areas—such places as the laundry, security, housekeeping, the internal mail service, and even the food service department. We've had a lot of patient complaints about such things as ward cleanliness, lost linen, cold food, and rising costs. We can't seem to keep a stable security force here, and, these days, if you use the internal mail service you're taking a calculated risk. Just today I got another nasty letter from a patient, complaining about how "surly" our employees are. Something has got to be done, and you're the man to do it."

"Yessir," said Ron.

"I plan to set up a new department, Ron, headed by you. I want to take all these support functions we've been talking about and put them under a strong manager who can get them straightened out."

This case was prepared by Norman G. Oglesby. Used with permission.

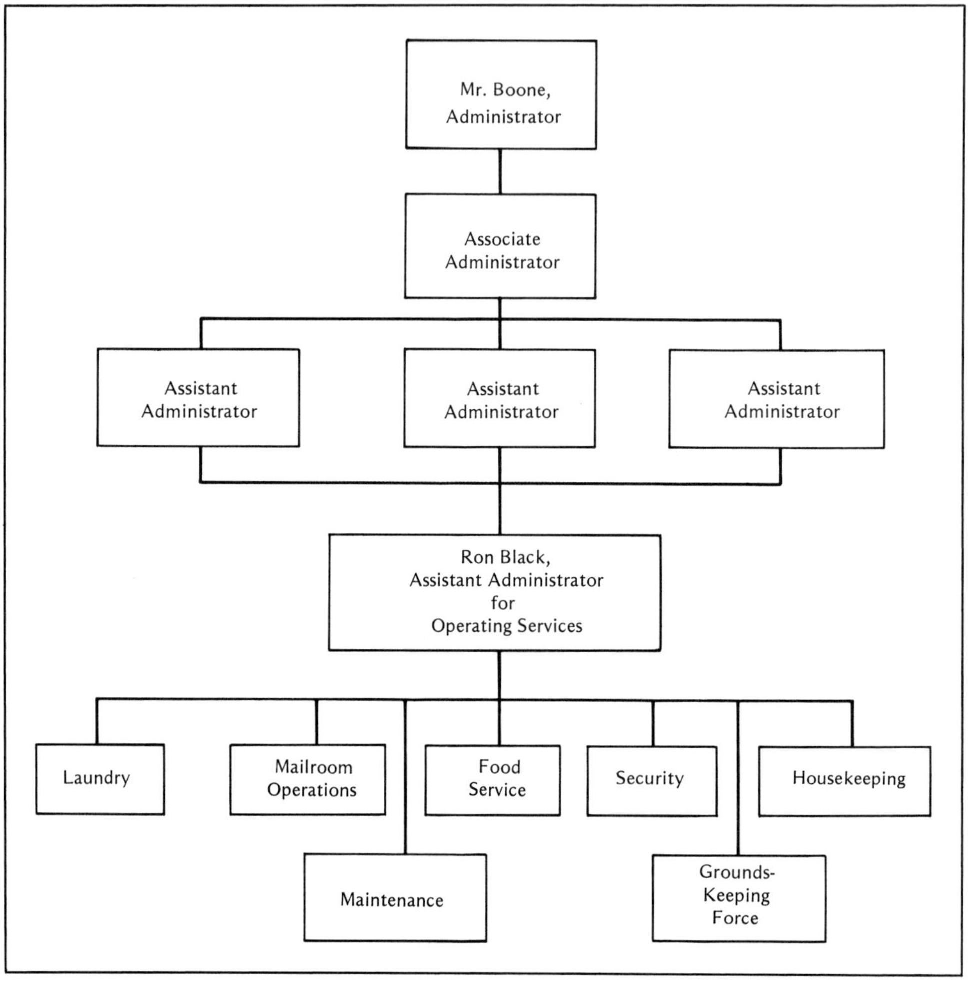

"You've got the right man," Ron thought, as Mr. Boone continued.

"What I want to do is set up a new department called 'Operating Services,' organized like this," showing a chart. "You would be the 'Assistant Administrator for Operating Services.' Of course, I'd want you to work closely with all the other assistant administrators. What do you think?"

"Terrific," said Ron, "when do I start?"

"Right now," said Mr. Boone, "and welcome back!"

Questions for discussion

1. Based on your knowledge of basic organizational concepts, do you see any problems in store for Ron?
2. Using only the organizational units and managers shown on the organizational chart, see if you can propose a better organization structure. Sketch out your plan and be prepared to discuss and defend it.

CREATIVE FASHIONS, INC.*

Following is a letter from a customer of Creative Fashions, Inc., to its president, Mr. Andre Promoter. What are the key management tasks to be performed in this company? What does Andre do well? poorly?

Date: One month into the selling season

Dear Andre:

This is in reference to our order number 1986 for 5,400 dozen women's fashion tops in the amount of $191,700 ($35.50 per dozen). We are very pleased with the designs you developed for our exclusive label. They met with considerable interest among the buyers to whom we showed the samples.

However, a number of problems have arisen:

1. The delivery of the initial shipment of 1,800 dozen arrived three weeks later than your promise. Thus, we came into the market late, which will adversely affect sales.
2. We also have problems with the quality. It appears some of the knitted fabric you purchased has defects (runs). Some of your sewing is sloppy and the sizing is inconsistent.
3. Also, the size distribution we ordered was 1-2-1 (S-M-L). You delivered 4-5-1. Thus, we can sell few proper size distributions.
4. Finally, your request that we consider a price increase of $1.35/dozen would simply put us out of the price bracket at which we aimed the program. I am sorry your costs turned out to be higher than you expected but. . . .

In view of all of this, we are cancelling our order and returning the 1,365 dozen tops that we have not been able to sell or that were defective. Attached are the freight bills. Please adjust our invoice accordingly. Because we were not able to sell the tops as planned, it will take us a bit longer to pay; please let us have 90 days. Also, I have had a lot of trouble finding someone in your organization to answer these questions. I keep getting passed around, which is a bit irritating as it is my long distance call. I tried to call you to discuss this but was told you were on an extended sales trip.

Maybe we can get together next season. I enjoyed meeting with you here in New York—thanks for the fine dinner and evening on the town.

Sincerely,

Mary

TUCSON MINING COMPANY†

The Tucson Mining Company was one of the largest copper producers in the free world. It owned and operated several open-pit copper mines throughout the western United States.

The Soynita open-pit mine operation,[1] which had been in the development stage for nearly six years, had just begun to show a profit. Generally speaking, open-pit mining of

*This case was prepared by Jack D. Ferner, lecturer in Management, Babcock Graduate School of Management, Wake Forest University, Winston-Salem, North Carolina. This case is designed to be used as a basis for class discussion rather than to illustrate either effective or ineffective handling of an administrative situation.

†This case was prepared by Professor Charles E. Watson as a basis for class discussion. It is not designed to present either a correct or incorrect illustration of handling administrative problems.

[1]See Organization Chart, Exhibit 1.

the low-grade ore is only profitable at high levels of volume. Early stages of an open-pit mining operation are not profitable because several years are required just to remove the waste material (overburden), that covers the ore body. The removal of overburden (an operation called stripping) by belly dumps, tractors, and scrapers, and other similar pieces of equipment, continues at the rim of the pit as it deepens and becomes wider at the top.

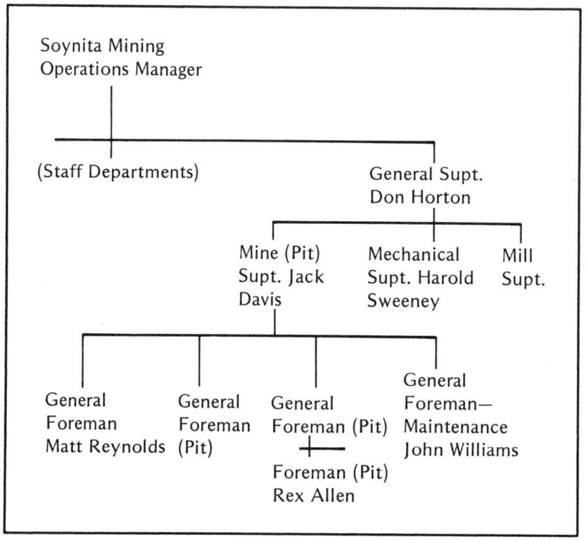

Unlike the overburden, which is essentially soft, the ore body is hard and rock-like. It is freed by means of blasting. It is then scooped up by giant electric shovels and loaded into large electra-haul dump trucks which carry it out of the pit to the concentractor. There the ore is crushed and the copper particles are extracted by a chemical process.

A rift between the pit operators and the mechanical department had been brewing for some time. Pit operators complained that the mechanical department was overly protective of the heavy earth-moving equipment. Interested in getting maximum production, they were known for "pushing" the various pieces of equipment to their limits and those of the mechanical department were unhappy with this practice. One was heard to have made the remark, "No sooner do we get a piece into operation but it's right back in the shop for repairs because of some careless jerk."

In March of 1972, the following events occurred in the maintenance section of the mechanical department.

John Williams, general foreman in the maintenance section, walked down the shop floor just as the whistle blew signifying the beginning of the shift. All the bays[2] were filled with pieces of equipment. "Yes sir," he said to himself, "We're really going to get a lot done today." "Those two scrapers should be nearly finished by the end of this shift," he thought, "and two of the tractors undergoing repairs surely would be ready by noon."

Just as John finished reading the job ticket on one of the tractors, Matt Reynolds, a general foreman in the pit, walked into the shop.

[2]Work areas in the mechanical shop where large pieces of earth-moving equipment are serviced and repaired.

WILLIAMS: "What do you say, Matt?"
REYNOLDS: "How fast can you get me two belly dumps?"
WILLIAMS: "I don't know off-hand."
REYNOLDS: "Well, I have one that needs to come in for repairs pretty soon and I'm already running short."
WILLIAMS: "Yeah?"
REYNOLDS: "No fooling, it's urgent . . . or it will be in a couple of hours! I need 'em bad. You've got to have them ready just as fast as you can."
WILLIAMS: "O.K., Matt. I'll get right on it."
REYNOLDS: "Thanks."

John went to where the scrapers were being repaired and told his men to stop work on them and get working on two belly dumps.

The day was one-eighth over now and it looked like things were coming along fine. As John was in his office looking over some papers, Rex Allen, pit foreman, rushed in.

ALLEN: "What about my scrapers? I don't see your men working on a single one. We just lost another one and I'm really running short. I'll never get any dirt moved if you don't get me that scraper. It's more important to get me that scraper than anything else you have men on now."
WILLIAMS: "O.K., O.K.—I'll get right on it."

John went over to the bay where men were working on a tractor.

VOICE ON PHONE: "John, Harold Sweeney here." (Harold Sweeney was the Mechanical Superintendent and John's immediate superior.)
WILLIAMS: "What's up?"
SWEENEY: "Jack Davis (Mine Supt.) just called and gave me pressure to get out an 80-ton electra-haul truck. How soon can you have one ready?"
WILLIAMS: "I don't know. We're not working on any just now."
SWEENEY: "Well, you better get on it–and quick."
WILLIAMS: "O.K."

John wondered what his men would say when he would tell them to stop what they were doing and start working on the electra-haul.

R. J. GREEN CO.—GENERAL MERCHANDISE

Background

Around 1875, a restless Robert Joshua Green moved with his wife and three children from their hometown of Newberry in South Carolina and settled in a sleepy little town in Georgia called Concord. Concord is situated approximately 90 miles southwest of Atlanta in the heart of Pike County.

For the next 50 years the Green family became involved in a variety of business ventures throughout the area. Cotton farming, mule trading, banking, and wagon manufacturing were but a few of the number of interests pursued by this industrious family.

In 1887, Peter Green, R. J.'s youngest son, decided to enter a business that could best serve the needs of the growing local community. That year, Peter constructed a picturesque two-story, red brick building, measuring 100 × 200 feet, and christened the newest family operation, the R. J. Green Co.—General Merchandise (named after his father

R. J. Green Co.—General Merchandise is a disguised case, written by George S. Vozikis and Timothy S. Mescon.

Robert Joshua). It was a general store that was intended to serve the changing tastes of the local populace.

From the beginning, Peter insisted that the store carry any and all items that may be desired by the townspeople. At one time or another, Peter operated an in-house mortuary, a bank, a post office, a grocery, a general dry goods operation, and a Standard Oil dealership (which still after 90 years of continuous service carries Standard products). As the years rolled by, Peter began to consolidate the family operations into a more formalized structure. The family operations grew and prospered, and based upon Peter's shrewd business acumen, the R. J. Green Co. added three fertilizer plants, six warehouses, a cotton gin, and 10,000 acres of farmland.

The Green family advocated maintaining family control and influence. So it was not surprising that Peter's efforts were continued by his son Joseph, who took over in 1930. Joseph emphasized the financial growth of the R. J. Green Co., and his perseverance helped create the Concord Banking Company, the town's only full-service financial institution. Joseph, an engineering graduate of Georgia Tech, found life in Concord both satisfying and rewarding. A great supporter of small-town living, Joseph states, "Life in those days was great. All the kids went to the same schools and the same parties. On special occasions, we would go to Griffin (20 miles northeast of Concord) and browse around the *huge* department stores. As a graduate of 'Tech,' I could have gone virtually anywhere, but I guess my love for this place was overwhelming because it didn't take me long to come back."

Joseph maintained his father's tradition of carrying a veritable potpourri of merchandise. Freezers, heaters, groceries, pots, pans, stoves, and clothes packed the first floor of the store (the second floor was and still is used for storage).

Joseph's son, Tom, born in 1945, literally grew up in the store. Until he went away to college (the Georgia Tech tradition was sustained), Tom worked at various jobs within the family operation. From stocking groceries to farming cotton, Tom eagerly awaited the day when he could assume the top position in the R. J. Green Co.

Following his 1967 graduation from Tech and a subsequent two-year stint in the Navy, Tom returned to Concord. Joseph, perceiving Tom's intense interest in the family business, allowed him to develop and refine any business talent he felt was lacking.

In 1972, the day Tom had long anticipated at last arrived. Joseph stepped down as president of the R. J. Green Co. and turned over the reigns of directorship to twenty-seven-year-old Tom. Acclimating himself to the role of president was no difficult task; however, Tom quickly discovered that his preconceptions about managing the family businesses, although conceived in good faith, were unfortunately somewhat clouded. Tom soon discovered that the beautiful history of the family store would not pay demanding creditors. With cotton no longer king, Tom decided to sell all but 1,000 acres of the family farmland. He closed two fertilizer plants because of their inability to compete with the agribusiness giants, and leased the warehouses to local farmers.

The wonderful history of the Green family, the store, and the town of Concord were suddenly facing the modern-day realities of business. The store, now grossing in excess of $600,000 yearly, was simply not proving to provide the enjoyment or the monies Tom had once imagined.

Company Structure

The store is owned today by Tom Green and his wife and is run as a partnership, even though Tom's father casts an influential shadow in the manner in which decisions are taking place. Tom once said, "Every time Dad is away, I am trying to initiate as many sweeping changes as I can, but when he comes back, he wants everything to be as it has always been."

In addition to indirect influence, Tom's father still retains the presidency of the local bank, keeping thus a direct financial "trump" card in the management of the family business. "Things are not that bad though," Tom said another time. "Dad and Mom always help with the store when I am flying with the company's plane or when I go shooting the rapids in Chattahoochee. Lots of times, I am the one who makes the wrong decisions, and he is the one to say, 'I told you so.'"

Despite the diversity and the volume of business that the company is generating, it is run as a family business and the organizational chart, even though not formalized, appears as follows:

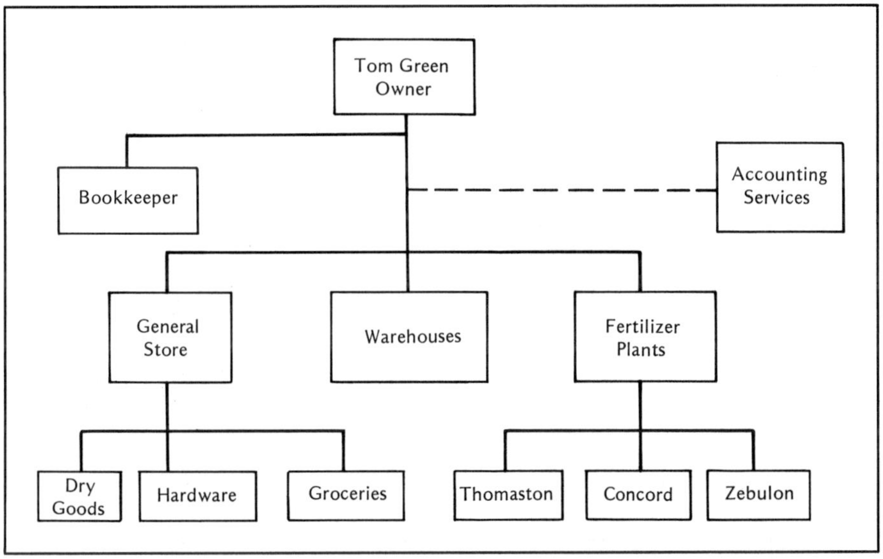

The store in Concord employs two full-time employees and one part-time employee in addition to Tom Green and his wife. The books are kept by a part-time bookkeeper and are later transposed into computer printouts by a computer service bureau in Griffin, 20 miles away.

The operations are broken down into three categories: General Store (the main source of income), warehouse facilities, and three fertilizer plants, where two full-time employees alternate among the three plants to custom-blend fertilizers for the local farmers.

The Store

The general merchandise store appears the same today as it did almost 100 years ago. The main floor of the store (see layout on next page) is literally crammed with thousands of items. Basically, Tom classifies merchandise into three main categories: groceries, hardware, and dry goods.

It would be impractical to list the variety of goods carried, but a sampling of hardware items is given (see next page).

In terms of selection, no resident of Concord is disappointed. A shopper looking for shaving cream, for example, faces the difficult task of selecting from over a dozen brands. Furthermore, fortunately for the shopper, the headache developed from attempting to make the proper selection can be alleviated by any one of ten brands of aspirin.

The second floor of the store has identical floor space to the main level. The upstairs

Oil	Rug cleaner	Axes	Glue
Paint Cans	Screen	Bicycles	Hoses
Spray	Seeds	Blades and drills	Insecticides
Paint equip.	Sporting-hunting goods	Cable	Ladders
Pipe	Storm window equipment	Chains	Locks
Plumbing equip.	Tools	Coolers	Mailboxes
Propane gas	Trash cans	Copper wire	Nails, screws, bolts, nuts
Roof material	Wallpaper	Electric light equipment	Floor covering
Rope	Wash tubs	Electric cultivator	Garden tools
	Wood-burning stoves	Fireplace equipment	

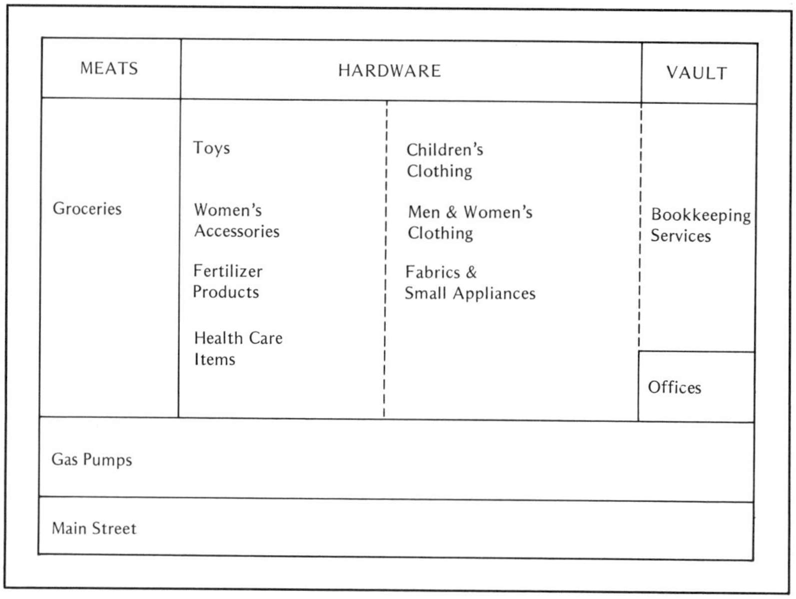

area (there is a hand-operated freight elevator and a stairway leading to the upper level) is covered with a collection of old books and financial records. Interestingly enough, the upstairs has, throughout the years, served as a depository for a number of fascinating objects. Included in the collection are turn-of-the-century costumes from the members of the Knights of Pythias; Ford Model A parts with the original shipping tags still attached; more than 200 old planters; a diverse collection of furniture; snuff tins and bottles from the late 1800s; posters, photographs, and calendars from the early part of this century, just to mention a few.

Each year, in mid-October, Pike County sponsors a crafts festival. Last year, Tom dusted off a few pieces of memorabilia, put what he considered to be an outrageous price on them, and sold everything he had prepared. This year, he is planning to display a greater variety of merchandise during the festival.

Financial Structure

Tom Green receives monthly summarized accounting computer printouts that include in detail monthly payroll, income statements, and balance sheets for each month of the year. When he asked his bookkeeper why inventory breakdown is not included, his bookkeeper told him that it was too much trouble and the costs of an inventory analysis outweighed the benefits. Tom agreed at that particular time and continued to rely on rule-of-thumb measures to reorder or to spot a slow moving item.

The financial statements of the company did not reflect the hard work that Tom was putting into the company. Gross sales for 1977 were almost $600,000, but the business incurred losses, as in the previous five years. (See statements on next page.)

What Now?

Tom Green recognizes that something has to be done; something has to be changed in order to turn the store and the company around. He does not want to transform the general store into a convenience store because of the strong and proud family tradition that he feels on his shoulders. Following the advice of some friends, he tried to project the growth of Pike County in terms of employees, payrolls, and business establishments by

R. J. GREEN CO.
Concord, Georgia
Balance Sheet
December 31, 1977 and 1976

Unaudited **Assets**	*1977*	*1976*
Current Assets		
Cash	$ 4,000	$ 4,226
Accounts receivable—trade	21,952	19,330
Inventories	81,031	76,297
Total current assets	106,983	99,853
Fixed assets		
Land	1	1
Buildings	1	1
Furniture and fixtures	750	750
Equipment	3,807	-0-
	4,559	752
Less, accumulated depreciation	581	50
Net fixed assets	3,978	702
Total assets	$110,961	$100,555

Liabilities and Partners' Equity

Current Liabilities		
Bank overdraft	$ 2,193	$ 5,212
Notes payable—bank	49,422	20,000
Note payable—R. J. Green	25,000	25,000
Accounts payable	23,058	13,797
Accrued and withheld payroll taxes	946	840
Sales tax payable	946	907
Total current liabilities	101,565	65,756
Partners' Equity	9,396	34,799
Total liabilities and partners' equity	$110,961	$100,555

R. J. GREEN CO.
Concord, Georgia
Income Statement
For the Year Ended December 31, 1977

Unaudited		
Sales		$523,000
Cost of Sales		
Beginning Inventory	$ 76,297	
Purchases	452,499	
	528,796	
Less, ending inventory	81,031	477,765
Gross profit		75,235
Expenses		
Salaries	46,725	
Bank charges	20	
Rent	918	
Utilities	4,215	
Telephone	1,716	
Maintenance—repairs	3,076	
Pest control services	1,161	
Vehicle expense	1,017	
Gas and oil	1,744	
Payroll taxes	2,938	
Taxes and licenses	3,451	
Office expense	1,214	
Supplies	308	
Depreciation	531	
Bookkeeping expense	1,970	
Professional fees	876	
Interest	4,730	
Insurance	6,491	
Dues and subscriptions	5	
Advertising	1,268	
Postage and freight	435	
Sundry	940	85,749
Net loss before other income and partner's salary		(10,514)
Other Income		6,018
Net loss before partner's salary		(4,496)
Partner's Salary		6,328
Net loss		($ 10,824)

looking into some statistics of county business patterns for the state of Georgia (see p. 274).

1. In small, rural areas, does the need still exist for a general store?
2. What business is the R. J. Green Co. in?
3. If you were contacted by Tom Green to offer some managerial assistance to the company, what suggestions would you make? Be specific, being sure to offer recommendations in the areas of planning, control, and organization.
4. In what areas do you foresee future growth opportunities for the R. J. Green Co.?
5. What materials could Tom utilize for examining the changing demographics of the area?
6. Fashions, personal preferences, likes and dislikes all fluctuate continuously. What sources of information could Tom turn to in his attempts to "keep up" with the times?

ASTRAL HERB TEA CO.

Astral Herb Tea Co. is located in Colorado. It was originally started by Sheldon and Swope in the summer of 1970, later to be joined by Swope's brother, Swipe, who provided the initial capital of $800. Presently, it is a $5 million operation, employing approximately 180 persons, and with annual growth rates exceeding 100% over the past few years. As a result of an extremely high annual rate of growth (goal of 54% in 1977) and an increasing demand for its products, expansion of present production facilities and acquisition of new equipment are pressing concerns of management.

The organizational structure of Astral Herb Tea Co. is shown in Figure 1. Briefly, there is a board of directors and two co-presidents, Sheldon and Swope. Sheldon's responsibilities include quality control, art, personnel, research (each summer he travels extensively searching for new herbs and solving problems with suppliers) and development, production, and tea tasting. Swope's responsibilities include finance, farming, and administration, and both oversee the purchasing, marketing, and advertising functions. Also, kitchen facilities exist to provide meals for the employees at a minimum cost, but in 1976 this has shown losses of $7,000 on food costs of $32,000.

Because of the relative newness and youthfulness of the organization, Astral Herb Tea Co. is still in the formative stages and has basically operated on a "crisis management" approach; that is, problems are dealt with as they arise. In general, informality is the pervading organizational climate as there are no time clocks; channels of authority and communication are not formally delineated; and no formal performance evaluations exist. Instead, evaluations hinge predominantly on assessments of an individual's loyalty and responsibility to the company. This informality primarily stems from an anti-business attitude by many of its employees and from the spiritual and philosophical bases upon which the company was founded. Consequently, employee motivation is not a problem to management, because the organizational environment in itself provides a positive influence to work. In the future, a profit-sharing scheme, in which employees are given stock in the company, will be implemented.

The marketing department plays an important role in the overall operations of Astral Herb Tea Co. Together with the two co-presidents, marketing sets the goals of the organization. It also initiates the budgetary process. First, the marketing department draws up a temporary budget that it believes accurately reflects demand and sales for the coming year. It is then sent to other departments, such as production, personnel, finance, and so on. Each of these departments makes additions or corrections as to what they

This report was prepared by Bruce R. Neumann with the assistance of J. Nakamura as the basis for class discussion rather than to illustrate either effective or ineffective handling of an administrative situation.

County Business Patterns, Georgia—Employees, Payroll, and Establishments, by Industry: 1974

(Excludes government employees, railroad employees, self-employed persons, etc.—see "General Explanation." Size class 1 to 4 includes establishments having payroll during 1st quarter but no employees during mid-March pay period. "D" denotes figures withheld to avoid disclosure of operations of individual establishments)

SIC Code	Industry	Number of Employees for Week Including March 12	Payroll ($1000)		Number of Establishments, by Employment-Size Class									
			First Quarter	Annual	Total	1 to 4	5 to 9	10 to 19	20 to 49	50 to 99	100 to 249	250 to 499	500 to 999	1000 or more
	PIKE													
	Total	460	490	2466	66	44	8	9	4	1	—	—	—	—
—	Agricultural services, forestry, fisheries	(A)	(D)	(D)	2	2	—	—	—	—	—	—	—	—
—	Contract construction	137	135	574	24	15	3	4	2	—	—	—	—	—
17	Special trade contractors	110	105	448	17	10	3	2	2	—	—	—	—	—
—	Manufacturing	(C)	(D)	(D)	4	—	1	1	1	1	—	—	—	—
23	Apparel and other textile products	(B)	(D)	(D)	1	—	—	—	—	1	—	—	—	—
233	Women's and misses' outerwear	(B)	(D)	(D)	1	—	—	—	—	1	—	—	—	—
2335	Women's and misses' dresses	(B)	(D)	(D)	1	—	—	—	—	1	—	—	—	—
—	Administrative and auxiliary	24	15	261	1	—	—	—	1	—	—	—	—	—
—	Transportation and other public utilities	(A)	(D)	(D)	3	2	—	1	—	—	—	—	—	—
—	Wholesale trade	(A)	(D)	(D)	2	2	—	—	—	—	—	—	—	—
—	Retail trade	56	85	349	19	16	2	1	—	—	—	—	—	—
—	Finance, insurance, and real estate	28	42	213	4	1	2	1	—	—	—	—	—	—
—	Services	85	49	277	5	3	—	1	1	—	—	—	—	—
	PIKE													
	Total, 1975	541	669	2483	62	44	7	6	4	—	1	—	—	—

—	Agricultural services, forestry, fisheries	(A)	(D)	(D)	2	2	—	—	—	—	—	—	—	—
—	Contract construction	90	92	348	20	16	1	1	2	—	—	—	—	—
17	Special trade contractors	72	58	260	14	11	1	—	2	—	—	—	—	—
—	Manufacturing	(E)	(D)	(D)	5	2	—	2	—	—	1	—	—	—
23	Apparel and other textile products	(C)	(D)	(D)	1	—	—	—	—	—	1	—	—	—
233	Women's and misses' outerwear	(C)	(D)	(D)	1	—	—	—	—	—	1	—	—	—
2335	Women's and misses' dresses	(C)	(D)	(D)	1	—	—	—	—	—	1	—	—	—
—	Transportation and other public utilities	(A)	(D)	(D)	1	1	—	—	—	—	—	—	—	—
—	Wholesale trade	(A)	(D)	(D)	2	2	—	—	—	—	—	—	—	—
—	Retail trade	61	67	205	18	14	3	1	—	—	—	—	—	—
—	Finance, insurance, and real estate	23	45	238	4	1	2	1	—	—	—	—	—	—
—	Services	77	80	375	6	3	1	—	2	—	—	—	—	—
—	Nonclassifiable establishments	(A)	(D)	(D)	4	3	—	1	—	—	—	—	—	—
	PIKE													
	Total, 1976	419	606	2538	64	50	9	2	2	—	1	—	—	—
—	Agricultural services, forestry, fisheries	(A)	(D)	(D)	1	1	—	—	—	—	—	—	—	—
	Contract construction	61	86	456	22	18	3	1	—	—	—	—	—	—
—	Manufacturing	(C)	(D)	(D)	2	1	—	—	—	—	1	—	—	—
23	Apparel and other textile products	(C)	(D)	(D)	1	—	—	—	—	—	1	—	—	—
233	Women's and misses' outerwear	(C)	(D)	(D)	1	—	—	—	—	—	1	—	—	—
2335	Women's and misses' dresses	(C)	(D)	(D)	1	—	—	—	—	—	1	—	—	—
—	Transportation and other public utilities	(A)	(D)	(D)	1	1	—	—	—	—	—	—	—	—
—	Wholesale trade	(A)	(D)	(D)	2	2	—	—	—	—	—	—	—	—
—	Retail trade	(B)	(D)	(D)	22	20	2	—	—	—	—	—	—	—
—	Finance, insurance, and real estate	28	51	229	4	1	2	1	—	—	—	—	—	—
—	Services	86	98	372	10	6	2	—	2	—	—	—	—	—

A:0–19; B:20–99; C:100–249; E:250–499; F:500–999; G:1,000–2,499; H:2,500–4,999; I:5,000–9,999; J:10,000–24,999; K:25,000–49,999; L:50,000–99,999; M:100,000 or more

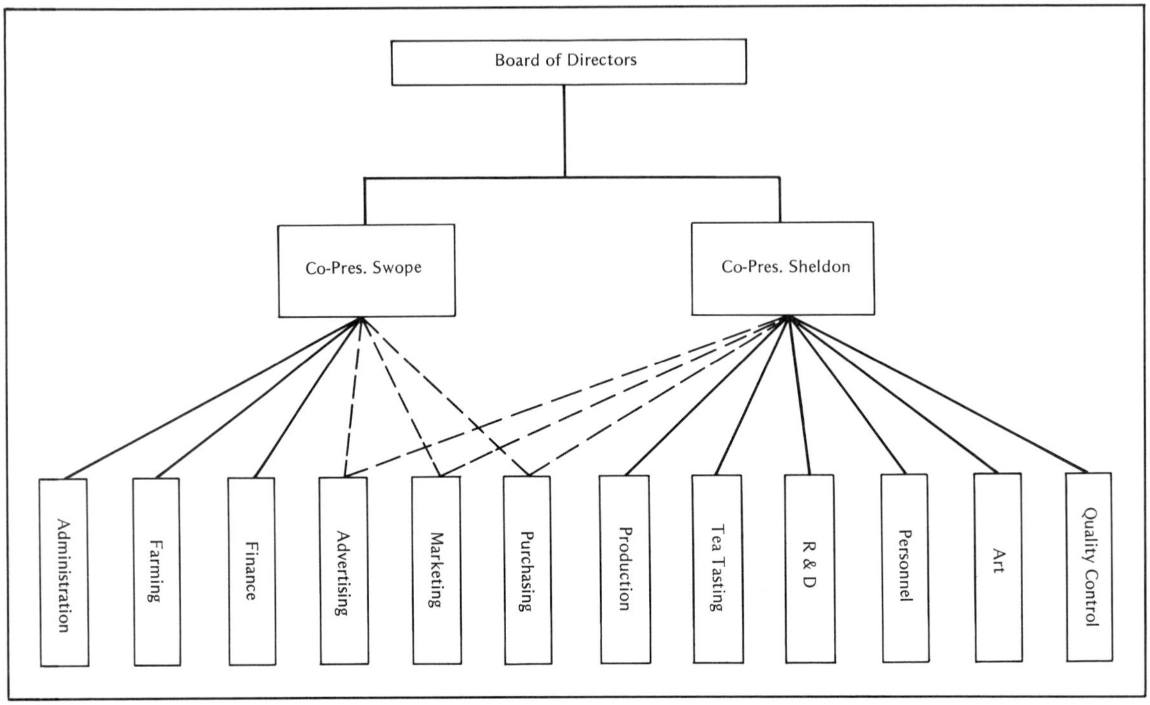

believe they are capable of achieving. After about a six-month process, a fiscal budget is finally agreed upon. To date, the budget has only been used as a short-range planning tool and it is forecast only one year in advance. However, in the coming year, a five-year projection plan will also be instituted.

The budgeting process, in which plans, expressed in monetary terms, are translated into terms of responsibility centers, is carried out by the finance department in Astral Herb Tea Co. and later approved by the co-presidents. Thus, the process of developing a budget is one of negotiation between the manager of a responsibility center and the finance department. The budget is given to each department manager as a statement of projected year's costs. Each department supervisor then allocates the costs over a 12-month period. However, because of the cyclical nature of its business, which is slack during the months of June through September and heavier from October to May, it is difficult to gauge costs each month. Therefore, overruns at the end of the year are not uncommon occurrences.

The operating and accounting as well as the reporting and analysis phases of Astral Herb Tea Co. have generally been limited to the financial area of providing income statements and balance sheets to its stockholders. Some accounting data are used as a basis for measuring and evaluating managerial performance.

The tea products are generally sold to distributors. As an incentive, a rebate is given if a distributor sells its projected sales volume. Recently, Astral Herb Tea Co. has entered grocery chain stores and there are plans for more distribution in international markets (besides Canada and Australia, in which the company is presently distributing).

External environmental factors that could affect the product line are government regulations of the Federal Drug Administration (FDA) and the American Medical

Association. There have recently been articles written about "psycho-active" or mind-altering drugs in certain herbs. Although the vast majority of herbs used as teas (89%) contain no psychoactive drugs and the remaining 11% have such minute amounts that little or no behavioral effects are reported, future FDA regulations may pose some restrictions to production operations.

IV

BEHAVIOR

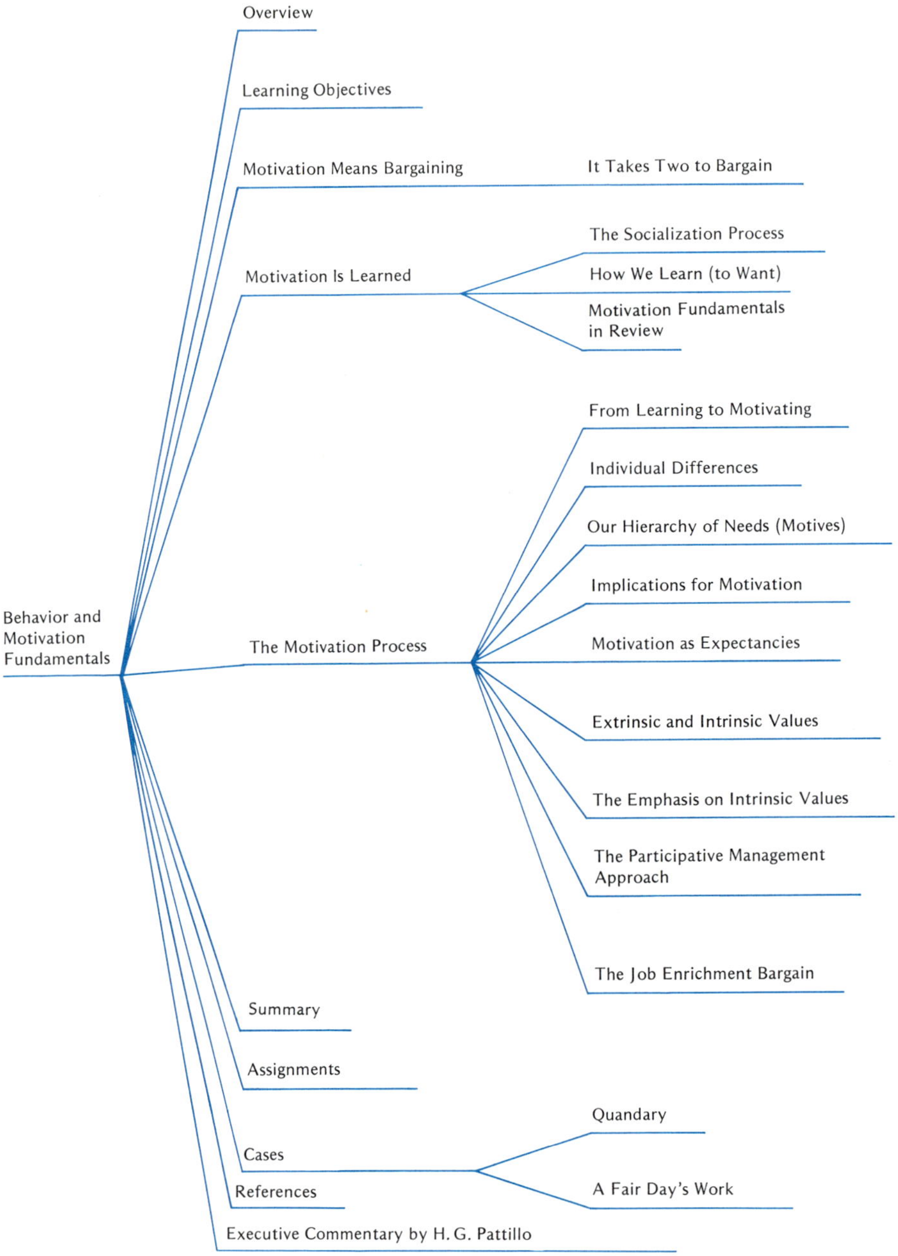
Behavior and Motivation Fundamentals
Overview
Learning Objectives
Motivation Means Bargaining
It Takes Two to Bargain
Motivation Is Learned
The Socialization Process
How We Learn (to Want)
Motivation Fundamentals in Review
The Motivation Process
From Learning to Motivating
Individual Differences
Our Hierarchy of Needs (Motives)
Implications for Motivation
Motivation as Expectancies
Extrinsic and Intrinsic Values
The Emphasis on Intrinsic Values
The Participative Management Approach
The Job Enrichment Bargain
Summary
Assignments
Cases
Quandary
A Fair Day's Work
References
Executive Commentary by H. G. Pattillo

8

BEHAVIOR AND MOTIVATION FUNDAMENTALS

OVERVIEW

The next five chapters will explore several aspects of human *behavior.* This is the most important resource needed for "making organizations perform." Performance, in other words, must be *motivated.* A key way of going at that task is by using *authority* and *power,* which are, in turn, key ingredients in the basic relationship called *leadership.* People working together must interact closely with one another and, therefore, *communication* and *group dynamics* are major dimensions of organization operations. These days, many of our larger, more complex organizations are having so much difficulty keeping pace with their changing environments that *organizational development* has become an important problem.

In this chapter we will look at the motivation of workers from three perspectives. Most fundamentally, we will stress that motivation comes to a principal focus as a *bargaining* process. In this bargaining, employers and employees both endeavor to get as much as they can of what they want out of the work-reward *transaction.* Second, to understand motivation in bargaining terms, it is necessary to explore where *motives* come from. Third, we will most fully examine how managers use worker motives in getting organizations to perform. A particular emphasis here will be the ways in which worker motivation has become different over recent decades, and how these changes have altered the way organizations motivate their members.

LEARNING OBJECTIVES

This chapter is especially intended to help the student:

1. **Understand motivation as a bargaining process.**
2. **Think more concretely about how our motives come to be what they are.**
3. **See clearly the utilization of contingencies, which is the work motivation process.**
4. **Distinguish between content and process ways of thinking about motivation.**
5. **Understand the importance of the fact that there are both intrinisic and extrinsic motives.**
6. **Appreciate how difficult it is in organizations to effectively utilize worker contingencies toward enough productivity.**
7. **Learn, especially in the context of thinking about management, the meaning of the following concepts:**

socialization	**expectancy bargaining**
reinforcement	**extrinsic motivation**
incentives	**intrinsic motivation**
individual differences	**participative management**
psychological contract	**job enrichment**
hierarchy of needs	**bargain trade-offs**

MOTIVATION MEANS BARGAINING

Behavior is what people *do.* Motivation is *why* they do it. Thus "a motive is an inner state that energizes, activates, or moves (hence 'motivation'), and that directs or channels behavior toward goals."[1] In the process of "making organizations perform," what managers need from workers is productive (enough) behavior. Working with them to get production is what is meant by motivating them.

Two aspects of these relationships need particularly to be understood. First, it is not only lower-level workers who must be sufficiently motivated. Higher-level workers, those employees of organizations called supervisors and managers, must also perform adequately. Of course, motivation principles are the same, whatever level of worker is involved. However, the nature of the problem of motivation and the motivation practices followed by organizations are different in the case of higher-level workers. In this book, the motivation specifics discussed will refer primarily to getting enough production from lower-level workers.

Second, it is important to understand what is meant by *productive enough.*

[1]Bernard Berelson and Gary A. Steiner, *Human Behavior* (New York: Harcourt Brace Jovanovich, 1964), p. 240.

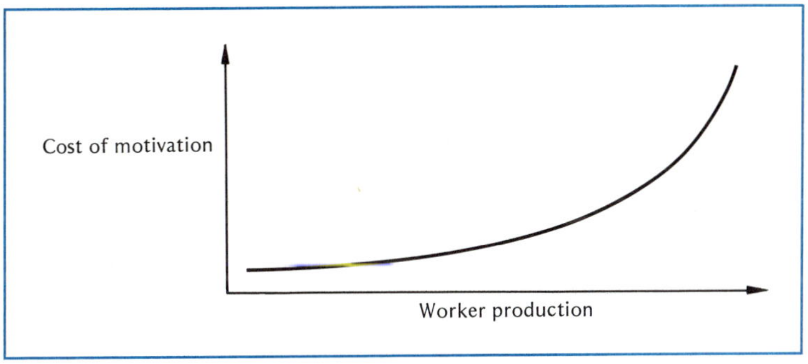

FIGURE 8-1. The Increasing Cost of Output.

When employers respond to employees' motives to induce them to produce, costs will typically be incurred. Note, incidentally, that cost here means all kinds of expense outlays—from paycheck money to making the work environment more pleasant. To a point, the greater this payout, the greater the worker's output. As an organization "buys" more and more work from employees, however, these people will likely come to feel that they are forfeiting other things that are also wanted. As the organization spends additional resources to get what it needs from a worker (see Fig. 8-1), it must always be deciding how much it can afford to pay for how much production. "Enough" means that organizations must develop at least as much cooperation as is required to keep them in business.

Already, this says two things of importance about motivation. First, as an organization decides how best to relate to its workers, these are bargain(ing) calculations. Second, as workers decide how best to interact with their employer, these are also bargain(ing) calculations.

It Takes Two to Bargain

The bargain basis of employer-employee relationships was first discussed in print by a practicing manager, Chester Barnard.[2] He used a fancier language than we are using. His explanation of worker motivation is known as the "inducements-contributions theory." It focuses on workers and organizations endeavoring to find what payouts (*inducements*) to workers in exchange for what degree of cooperation (*contributions*) from workers will be satisfactory to both parties.[3] But whatever the terminology, what is involved in the work-worker transaction is exactly what is involved when a customer makes a purchase in a store. In particular, there is always in bargaining an element of "Nothing is a bargain if it could be bought cheaper."

Because motivating people is bargaining, it will be well to keep in mind the basics of every bargain. What must be achieved is a complicated *double coinci-*

[2]Chester Barnard, *The Functions of the Executive* (Cambridge: Harvard University Press, 1954).
[3]James G. March, and Herbert A. Simon, *Organizations* (New York: John Wiley & Sons, 1958).

The Last Businessman Theorist

Perhaps this title exaggerates; other executive scholars may put in an appearance. But Chester Irving Barnard will even then be one of a kind. A self-made scholar, he studied in his field of major interest, sociology, by reading original texts in both French and German. On becoming president of New Jersey Bell Telephone Company, he was in an excellent position to put theory and practice together. In his classic work, he particularly analyzed the inherent two-sided character of human cooperation arrangements.

dence. A buyer (*B*) and a seller (*S*) must find one another—under circumstances in which *B* wants to buy what *S* wants to sell—and the price *S* wishes to receive is a price *B* is willing to pay. In the work bargain, furthermore, the double coincidence needed is made especially complex by *individual differences.* The fact that every individual is significantly different from everyone else gives organizations a very difficult motivation jigsaw puzzle to put together.[4]

Several other observations will help avoid potential confusions. First, we will begin thinking specifically about the motivation bargain by saying that people are pressed to do what they do by their *wants.* In writings about management, however, and sometimes here as well, the word *needs* is often used instead. Typically, nothing in particular is meant by that usage—as we might say that a family *needs* milk whereas the father *wants* beer. Because no such distinction is usually intended, these words will here be used interchangeably. In bargaining terms, the test of wanting/needing something is willingness to work—which is to say, pay—for it. It then follows that the intensity of needing/wanting is measured roughly by how hard an individual is willing to work, how much people are willing to pay, for whatever is being sought.

Second, it is not to be supposed that big organizations do detailed bargaining with each of their individual employees to precisely tailor-make every bargain for the particular worker covered by it. That would be much too cumbersome a requirement, even if it were seen to be desirable. And it is not thought to be desirable, primarily because workers similarly situated within the organization must be treated very much the same to avoid the tension that can result from perceived "favoritism." To be sure, it is regularly said how valuable/necessary it is to treat people as individuals—and ideally we could induce cooperation more effectively if we did appeal to highly individualized preferences. But there are limits to this, and organizations must therefore do the best motivating they can by dealing with employees in groups.

Conversely and third, it is also not to be supposed that workers are hourly, or even weekly, renegotiating their bargains with their employers. Bargains are by

[4]Professor Homans has elaborately discussed bargains and bargaining in terms of noneconomic values. George C. Homans, *Social Behavior: Its Elementary Forms* (New York: Harcourt Brace Jovanovich, 1961).

definition vulnerable to being worked out differently, but what mostly happens is that people make their determinations about when they are reasonably satisfactorily situated for now, and then avoid the upset of hard bargaining and/or changing their situation except at very substantial intervals. Which is to say that these kinds of relationships are put together so as to give those who are bound by them a substantial element of stability. To illustrate, although, of course, we are not here talking particularly about labor union bargaining, these contracts are very typically intended to hold firm for a year or more.

MOTIVATION IS LEARNED

The foundation fact here, then, is that employees are motivated by being given (some of) what they want in exchange for what they produce. What makes getting work done in an organization difficult, in other words, is knowing what workers want, what they will work to get. We can perhaps best begin thinking about that by asking how people come to have wants in the first place.

The Socialization Process

The sweeping, summary explanation here is that people are taught what to want by their *environment*. There are two important varieties of this teaching.

A few wants were bequeathed to us by the environment that taught our ancestors over the last several millions of years.[5] That is, evolution—the systematic selection of species and individuals that could adapt effectively to their environment—saw to it that everyone comes into the world with, for example, a hunger drive and a sex drive. Of course, that would have to be; these kinds of wantings are essential to the preservation of the species.

With human beings, however, as distinguished from other species, most wants come from the environment in which they grow up.[6] This learning is called *socialization*, because it shapes individuals so that they can live reasonably comfortably in their groups and in their society. In the realm of motivation, socialization means shaping people so that they will work together effectively enough.

Observe in this connection the problem perpetually confronting every society. It (a little later we will emphasize that a society consists of individuals rather than being really an "it") must make certain the next generation will carry on or it cannot survive. It must, therefore, teach each new generation to "pitch in and help," and it does this teaching by the way it relates wants and work deep inside peoples' personalities.

[5] Alexander Alland, *Evolution and Human Behavior* (Garden City: Natural History Press, 1967).
[6] P. B. Bates, and D. Warner Schale, *Life-Span Development Psychology* (New York: Academic Press, 1973).

More specifically, much of a society's business is the production and distribution of goods and services. The "trick" to this production-distribution "balancing act" is to develop the wanting—in the quite explicit meaning of what people are willing to work for—that will produce a high enough level of output. This is a "trick" in the sense that the *balance* that must be achieved really is "tricky." On the one hand, wanting must be intense enough to get the needed work done. On the other hand, it must not generate so much disappointment and, thereby, frustration as to defeat that purpose. In short, a society's citizens must learn to want what their society is prepared to produce, but they must be helped not to want much more than that.

How We Learn (To Want)

Not at all surprisingly, a society achieves the balance it needs between wanting and producing by beginning immediately to relate the wants with which new citizens are born to resources available for satisfying them. Note how useful it is for society that this beginning can be made when the individual to be taught is most dependent and impressionable. What a society quite literally does is use the *helplessness* of new-born infants to transform their simple, desperate needs into the complex, more grown-up wanting that can keep our organizations and therefore our civilization functioning.[7]

A tiny baby, so recently enjoying an effortless existence in its mother's womb, cries because it is hungry and/or because it feels insecure. One or another of its parents (note, now, that it is people, not society as an "it," that really teach us what and how to want) responds to this crying by feeding the child. This response also carries with it an affection, a caring component. Already new citizens are beginning to learn that certain kinds of behaving will bring wanted responses from others. That connection between what is wanted and the significant others who can satisfy that wanting gives them a control over children's lives. This control can then systematically be used to develop adult wanting.

Let us be very explicit about these relationships. What learners want can be made dependent upon their doing what is wanted by those who control these rewards/contingencies. *Contingencies* here means other people managing important "if" relationships toward others' lives; if we do *A*, we can thereby earn, or merit, *B*. As in the "Peanuts" cartoon, "every time you do something right, they pat you on the head." Significant people in our lives, in other words, are by definition those who can give to us, or withhold from us, what we would like to have.

Thus people learn to want what their parents—and/or maybe this or that teacher, an uncle, a dear friend—believe they should want. Included in this wanting is, for example, "success," as society defines success. They do that learning because they must want these things to maintain the goodwill of the

[7] Erik Erickson, *Childhood and Society* (New York: Norton, 1964).

significant people in their lives. Then, having learned what they should want, they find they must do what other significant people in their lives want them to do. In particular, they must do the work these people ask them to do, because getting what they have learned to want binds them to related contingencies, such as responding to the wishes of those who control available resources and, therefore, opportunities. Here are the superiors who motivate subordinates by arranging the rewards by which their work lives will be guided.

There is here another potential confusion. It is very useful to say, as we just did and will frequently do, that supervisors motivate their subordinates. This they cannot really do when what is meant is that motivators are putting motives inside the motivated. To be sure, during the childhood years, the significant people in everyone's life almost literally did that. By the time one's work life begins, however, that creativity has essentially been completed. Organizations are then basically "stuck" with what motivation did get created. In other words, managers do what they do toward their workers—which we often, in shorthand fashion, call motivating them—by controlling the environment around them. That is, supervisors create contingencies affecting workers in such a way as to use for the organization's benefit what was earlier put into them. This is the distinction often made between *motives* and *incentives.* Superiors in control of resources can pay out, or withhold, incentives, and thereby arrange contingencies that will trigger workers' motives in the interest of organization productivity.

Motivation Fundamentals in Review

In thinking about motivation, there are only a few fundamentals, but these then quickly become a multitude of complexities. Let us next, therefore, review the fundamentals as a preface to pursuing some complications that are particularly of concern to managers.

First, one of the emphases of this book is the systems character of making organizations perform. Especially to be noted about motivation is that it is a *person-environment system.* Thus a person is what it, interacting with its environment, has made it, and what the person then does is respond to the environment within and around it.

Second, a major emphasis in thinking about management these days is the contingency nature of what managers do.[8] Not only is motivation a person-environment system; it is a system of *contingency relationships.* People focus their learning to receive contingent rewards. That is, they assume that they will more certainly get what they want if they do their learning well. Having learned what to want and what is wanted, people then work to earn other contingent outcomes, other possibilities they expect will be more certainly achieved or avoided if they do their work well.

[8]Fremont Kast, and James E. Rosenzweig, *Contingency Views of Organization and Management* (Chicago: Science Research Associates, 1973).

Third, although the socialization and motivation processes are in one sense exactly the same kind of transaction, the latter is really a *mirror image* of the former. The socialization process shapes new arrivals into a society by rewarding them, and in this process a great deal of what each individual will be is very deeply rooted. After this basic personality has been put in place, people thus shaped are motivated by rewards that satisfy the wanting developed in them earlier. By analogy, human beings are made to be a bank of push buttons attached to behaviors that will one day be useful. This mirror image, moreover, must be a fairly faithful reflection. Because the employer-employee relationship is a bargaining one, workers must be induced to cooperate, primarily by being given what they have been taught to want.

THE MOTIVATION PROCESS

Asking where wants come from, of course, was only to help us look more closely at the bargaining process that is motivation. Here, furthermore, is where complexity takes over from the simplicity of the fundamentals. Let us next, therefore, focus on these complications.

From Learning to Motivating

Again, it will be helpful to begin with the learning-motivating mirror image. The key relationship here is called *reinforcement.*[9] When a baby behaves in a certain way and feels rewarded by receiving a valued outcome, it is said that its behavior has been reinforced. Reinforced behavior will likely be repeated, and behavior that is again and again reinforced will likely become deeply rooted. The behaviors of adults, in short, are a product of their behaving-reinforcement history.

That product, in turn, is the raw material with which managers must work. Contingencies must be arranged, incentives used, to reinforce the behavior wanted by the organization. In simple work-worker terms, workers must be helped by pay-offs to want to do better, rather than worse, for their employers. Of course, that objective requires a careful use of available resources that are certain to be limited.

Although incentives are quite commonly thought of as money payouts, actually a very broad spectrum of *contingent outcomes* can function in this way. Specifically, whatever an individual values can be used to reinforce wanted behavior, as, for example, a smile, a compliment, a key to the executive restroom. It is important to organizations, furthermore, that there is a large number of possibilities. This gives them more freedom to choose contingencies, or pay-offs, that are less expensive. The key requirement, if motivation is to be achieved by a

[9] F. S. Keller, *Learning: Reinforcement Theory* (New York: Random House, 1954).

particular reward, is that it be used systematically enough to reinforce the behavior wanted.

Nor is this a small caution; managing reward contingencies for a sizable organization is very complicated. For example, using *punishment,* often called *negative reinforcement,* is quite difficult.[10] The principal problem is that punishing a behavior tells behavers what not to do. They must still determine which of many other behaviors should be selected. If a succession of wrong behaviors has to be punished, both punisher and punished can become seriously frustrated, as they feel they are getting nowhere. A special perplexity here for supervisors is the employee who seems rarely to do anything right enough to be worth positively reinforcing.

In fact, it is not easy to know how best to reinforce behavior that supervisors want repeated. To be sure, if such behavior is never or rarely rewarded, that would not be motivating. Similarly, to reinforce wanted behavior so occasionally that the worker cannot tell what is being rewarded would also not be motivating. Unfortunately, however, these easy understandings do not mean it would be best always to reinforce "good" behavior. Evidence seems rather to suggest that *intermittent reinforcement* may achieve the most productive results.[11] That is, behavers will most intensely work for incentives that are forthcoming often enough to make them real reinforcers of wanted behavior, but with enough gaps in this pay-off program to keep behavers feeling that perhaps working even harder would be better.

There is one other complexity in the reinforcement realm worth an emphatic repetition; it is critically important that there not be too much wanting. Thus, as managers struggle to keep a proper balance between what is wanted and what is available, a society must do a good bit of guarding against too much disappointment. In consequence, there are a number of people in the labor force who are not at all optimistic about what their work lives will bring them.[12] From the standpoint of motivation, the implications of this outlook are obvious. When a low level of wanting is all that is available to organizations in some of their employees, the arranging of contingencies toward that wanting can produce only a low level of cooperation.

Individual Differences

We have already emphasized that people differ greatly from one another. In motivation terms, this means that everyone has different needs, and that even when people want the same things, the *intensity* of that wanting will vary from one person to another. Because it is possible to motivate people only with

[10]Fred Luthans, and Robert Kreitner, "The Role of Punishment in Organizational Behavior Modification," *Public Personnel Management,* May–June 1973, pp. 156–61.

[11]Walter R. Nord, "Beyond the Teaching Machine," *Organizational Behavior and Human Performance,* Volume 4, 1969, pp. 375–401.

[12]G. Lorenz, "Aspirations of Low-Income Blacks and Whites," *American Journal of Sociology,* Volume 78, 1973, pp. 371–98.

incentives that are important to them, individual differences can produce an extremely wide variety of bargaining possibilities. Whereas most people are likely to be warmly motivated by judicious pattings on the back, there are those who are annoyed by that. It is well known that an expression of disapproval from a superior may be positively reinforcing to some subordinates.

More specifically, we are all different from one another in the way we see and evaluate what is going on. This difference is called *perception,* and everyone is guided and limited by the way he or she perceives what is happening to and around him or her. That is why "the eye of the beholder" is so important in *motivation bargaining.* Although workers are not always motivated by what would motivate their superiors, this assumption is a mistake often made in organizations. Also, employees are often not motivated by what managers wish would motivate them, or what superiors believe would motivate them if they "knew what was good for them." People are, in short, motivated by only those incentives they perceive to be satisfying enough to make it worth their while to do what is being asked of them. The contingencies people are arranging around us to shape what we do are only as significant as we perceive them to be.

This, too, is why the employment bargain is often called a *psychological contract.*[13] It is inside, within their psyches, that workers determine the value to them of what they are getting from their employer and what they are being asked to give for it. This caution then explains a relationship important to everyone who must deal with other peoples' behavior. We are often exasperated by how "illogical" others' responses seem to us to be. We forget, in other words, that so much human behaving conforms to a *psycho-logic* that is unique to whoever has it. This uniqueness, of course, arises from the fact that everyone was developed by a different behavior-reinforcement history.

Finally, it is quite necessary from the standpoint of getting the work of the world done that people do perceive things differently from one another. In a bargaining situation, people seeing things differently is the only way the double coincidence problem can be solved. In a grocery store, for example, if both buyer and seller put the same value on the dollars and goods to be exchanged, there could be no transaction. In motivation bargaining, this is also the case. Organizations must feel that what they will be getting from workers is more valuable to them than the incentive payouts to workers. Workers, in turn, must see these values the other way around, valuing what the organization will be getting from them less highly than what they will be getting from the organization.

The Hierarchy of Needs (Motives)

There are, of course, some useful approaches that supervisors in motivating their workers can take on the basis of individual differences. In some respects,

[13] J. P. Kotter, "The Psychological Contract: Managing the Joining-Up Process," *California Management Review,* Volume 15, 1973, pp. 91–9.

workers can be treated as the unique individuals they are—with valuable consequences for the organization. In substantial part, however, as we have already noted, motivation actions taken by organizations must be on a more wholesale basis. That is, they must more particularly take into account the motivation characteristics of workers in general. Let us, therefore, do some thinking about what workers in the plural want that can be used in organizations for motivation purposes. What bargain outcomes will move them to do more of what is wanted by their superiors?

One of the most widely quoted descriptions of human wants in general was developed by Abraham Maslow.[14] Thus, as shown in Figure 8-2, human beings have five kinds of needs. The most fundamental, called by Maslow *physiological* needs, are what millions of years of evolution history commanded people to want—such things as food, water, and protection from the elements. Next in importance is *security;* people want not only to eat today, but also to "know where the next meal is coming from." More generally, workers needed to feel that they live in a reasonably stable, predictable, and, therefore, manageable environment.

Physiological and security needs together are called *primary needs.* Beyond them, and a little later it will be noted more specifically what that means, are our *higher-order needs.*

The first of these is the need almost everyone has for social acceptance, approval, typically called our *social,* or *belongingness,* needs. A second higher-order need is for prestige, respect, or status in the eyes of those whose good will we value. Above these *ego* needs is the need in some people to achieve the greatest richness of experience, the highest level of personal creativity, they can. This need for *self-actualization* is seen as the highest-order need one can have.

FIGURE 8-2. Maslow's Hierarchy of Needs.

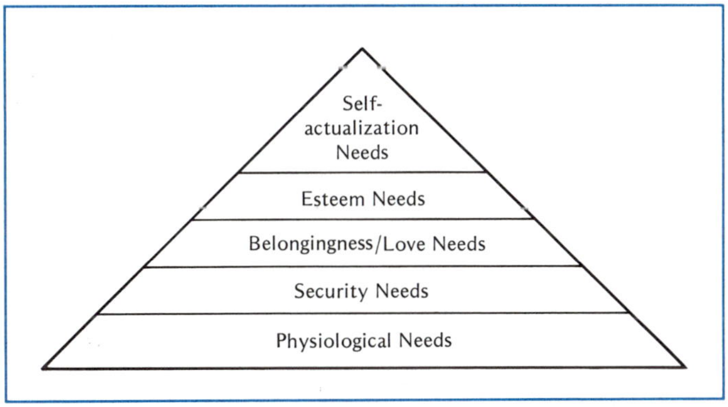

[14] A. H. Maslow, "A Theory of Human Motivation," *Psychological Review,* Volume 50, 1943, pp. 370–96.

Abraham Maslow

Implications for Motivation

Given such an array of human needs, what are the implications from the standpoint of getting organizations to perform? What does this say about the motivation bargain—how managers might most effectively use "if" possibilities in workers' lives?

A first implication reflects the fact that Maslow is describing a *need hierarchy*, needs that are higher and lower relative to the *unsatisfied needs* we are most wanting to satisfy. In other words, it is only unsatisfied needs that trigger behavior. If, therefore, one is fairly well off from the standpoint of primary needs, only higher-order need satisfactions will be motivating.

Maslow's need hierarchy also suggests some important things about changes in wanting and, therefore, the changing character of the motivation task over time. In a poor, developing economy, it may be that primary needs will be managers' principal grip on worker motivation. As is often said, when one is hungry, one is not likely to be preoccupied with poetry or philosophy. Note that to whatever extent this is true, in the last 100 years in the United States, many workers' most important unsatisfied needs would have done a great deal of shifting toward higher-order needs.

Yet another implication of needs as a hierarchy is a down-to-earth way of looking at how workers make *bargain trade-offs* in their own motivation decision making. Suppose, for example, an individual whose want satisfaction situation is as shown by line *X* in Figure 8-3. Observe that many, probably most, workers will endeavor to satisfy some of their higher-order needs long before they have satisfied all of their primary needs. Put differently, it is unlikely these days that many individuals would be so desperate in their physiological and security need

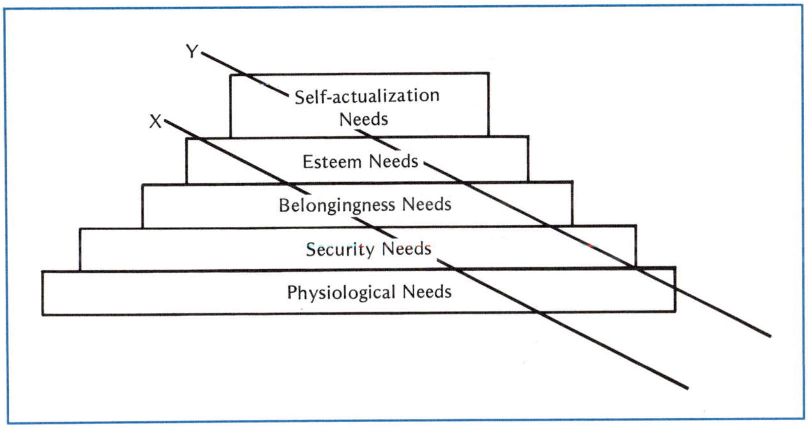

FIGURE 8-3. A Further Look at Need Hierarchies (A)

realms that they would not work to achieve also some higher-order need satisfactions.

Look now at line *Y* in Figure 8-3; it represents an improvement in a worker's reward situation. Note that this improvement includes becoming better off in all five want categories. No doubt many workers choosing the improvement they would prefer in their pay-off situation would elect this kind of change from *X* to *Y* as the "price" they would "charge" for being more productive for the organization. This begins to explain why workers often do not rate money compensation as the most important unsatisfied want in their lives.

A final implication of needs ordered hierarchically says something else that is important about money side by side with other wanting in the motivation trade-off thinking of many workers. Suppose a worker were given the opportunity to choose between lines *K* and *L* in Figure 8-4 in deciding what kind of a work bargain would be most acceptable. That might be the situation in which a worker would elect to be a cab driver (the situation described by line *L*), rather than an automobile plant assembly-line foreman (the option pictured by line *K*). It is well known that many workers will, in fact, happily choose less primary need satisfaction in order to achieve more of a feeling of both belongingness and self-esteem.[15] Elliot Liebow has given us a book-length case study of the circumstances under which a group of men did with some regularity make that trade-off.[16]

Motivation As Expectancies

Maslow's hierarchy of needs is one important way of thinking about the *content* of motives, the more specific characteristics of the needs managers may

[15] Charles R. Walker, and Robert H. Guest, *The Man on the Assembly Line* (Cambridge: Harvard University Press, 1952).

[16] Elliot Liebow, *Tally's Corner* (Boston: Little, Brown and Company, 1967).

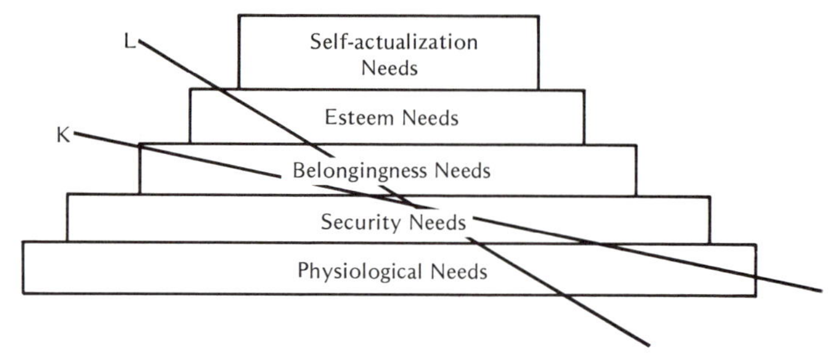

FIGURE 8-4. A Further Look at Need Hierarchies (B)

be able to convert into work for the organization. We will look at other useful ways of thinking about motivation content a little later. First, however, let us see how learning reinforcement, individual differences, perception, and motivation content of whatever kind come together in the ongoing process of workers making their work-reward decisions.

These calculations have come to be called the *expectancy approach* to motivation.[17] The focus of attention here is on what is expected by workers in supervisor-worker situations—and why worker *expectations* often trigger less performance from workers than their organizations want.

First, it is not enough that there be within a worker an unsatisfied want that might be used by an organization to induce performance. This performing must also be perceived by the worker as a way of satisfying that want (or wants) at a cost, an expenditure of effort, deemed to be acceptable. That is, expectations on all sides of this transaction are important; there must be a likelihood that performing for the organization will bring with it rewards making the cost/effort to be expended worthwhile.

Second, it follows that these effort-reward expectations are not the product of simple decisions. Whether, and how much, work will get done depends especially on the intensity of worker feelings about what is in fact expected. How great will be the value of the pay-off and how great the discomfort of the effort required to earn it? Only, thus, if some *net gain* is seen by the worker, will the superior's will get done. Note, of course, that it is not the superior who weighs positive and negative values within the employee. As already emphasized, everyone manages his own psycho-logic.

Third, most decisions of this kind are complicated in another way as well; they are not one-value-one-cost affairs. Perhaps typically we want a number of outcomes as we determine what course of action we shall take—and must often also weigh a number of costs. This complexity does not alter the character of the

[17] Victor Vroom, *Work and Motivation* (New York: John Wiley & Sons, 1964).

motivation transaction; it is first, last, and always a *cost-benefit* determination. The fact that there are multiple considerations in significant decision making, however, does say a great deal about why people so often do not understand what those around them are really doing, why managers regularly have so much difficulty comprehending their employees' calculations.

Everything we have said about the motivation process comes to a focus on perceptions/expectations—the understanding of probabilities and the weighing of outcomes. What an individual expects the future to bring must necessarily be a product of his or her learning, the reinforcement of behaviors history that has been experienced. Here, too, is where individual differences can be plainly seen; one worker will respond in one way in a situation, and another will act quite differently, because these *life histories* somehow were built into different expectation patterns. Necessarily, then, the probabilities one sees and their importance are most of what motivation content is all about.

Figure 8-5 depicts an expectancy model of motivation. As individuals see values (1) there is some likelihood they can achieve (2), they will decide that expending effort to get them is worthwhile (3). Applying their capacities (4) in the best way they can as they understand available possibilities (5), they will perform for the organization (6). In some cases, it may begin soon to seem that

FIGURE 8-5. The Porter-Lawler Model of Motivation.[18]

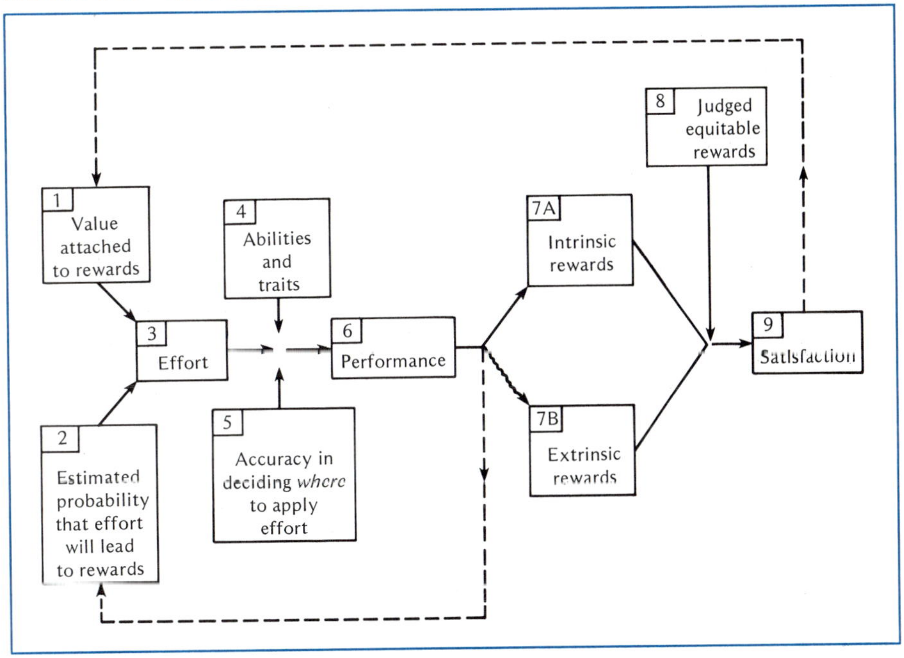

[18]As adapted in Raymond E. Miles, *Theories of Management* (New York: McGraw-Hill, 1975), p. 141.

this situation was not very accurately assessed and will require rethinking whether or not to expend this (much) effort. Otherwise, workers will continue along this decision path. Thus, they will receive the rewards expected (7), some of which will be valuable in and of themselves (7A), and some of which will be valuable only as they make it possible to secure other values (7B). If, finally, this work-reward situation seems fair (8), the transaction will produce enough satisfaction (9) to be continued.

Extrinsic and Intrinsic Values

Against the backdrop of expectancy theory, let us look more closely at what people want. An important way of doing that, still thinking in terms of people in general, is to emphasize a contrast between worker motives that are more and those that are less easily used as contingencies in motivation. This involves the distinction between *intrinsic* and *extrinsic* motives. As already noted, this distinction refers to whether a reward is valued for itself (intrinsic), or as a means of acquiring some other value (extrinsic).

For example, let us look at the use by managers of incentives that are of use to workers only after they leave work. In particular, that is the way the extrinsic reward called money mostly works. It is not the money in and of itself that workers seek. It is what they are able to do with it as they live their away-from-work lives. Nor is this in any way to belittle money as an incentive; it can be a very significant element in worker expectations.[19] But there are complications in its use, stemming from the fact that it is a long step removed from what those receiving it really want.

Given a fixed amount of money a worker is to receive for a day's work, over a substantial range of circumstances, the less effort he or she must expend to earn it and therefore, very likely, the less output produced for the organization, the better. Note the *bargain basics* here. By working less hard, the worker gives up nothing of value. Indeed, "goofing off" may even mean opportunities to do enjoyable things at work that would not be possible if one tackled the work to be done much more rigorously. It follows that dealing with workers who are not interested in what they are doing may require a more expensive supervision program. Even then, if a number of workers as a group decide to do less than they easily could for what they are getting, an intensive supervision effort often cannot prevent that.

We shall be saying more about workers subtly sabotaging output in our next chapter. Suffice it here to add one other observation about workers seeing work as someone else's concern rather than theirs. Remember, precisely this was the problem Frederick Taylor set out to solve by way of scientific management. Understandably, too, men grappling scientifically with that problem would emphasize relating money payouts to worker contributions, thereby making a

[19] William F. Whyte, *Money and Motivation* (New York: Harper, 1955).

contingency out of wage payments. In principle, this would prevent workers from endeavoring to get their pay-offs without performing reasonably well for the organization. But, it will also be recalled, there were difficulties with this way out.[20] In particular, employers were quite consistently unwilling to hold to anything closely resembling the letter of the *incentive compensation* promise. When workers then adjusted their expectations accordingly, employers were all the more forced back to the expensive supervision solution—insofar as that could be a solution.

Contrast this history, now, with the situation in which the work itself, as an intrinsic reward, is valued by those doing it. Moreover, it does not matter whether work is valued because workers enjoy their work, or are absorbed in its challenge, or secure pleasure—perhaps in the form of status—out of getting a great deal of work done. The key fact is that the value to the worker of working cannot, in this situation, be separated from the work that is to be done. Because the worker cannot, therefore, gain by being indifferent to the requirements of the organization, there is needed no elaborate supervision to make sure he or she does not trade off on-the-job and after-work values against what the organization believes it must get from its workers.

Understandably, given the very different dynamics of extrinsic and intrinsic motivation, much thinking triggered by Maslow's hierarchy of needs would focus on intrinsic values as by far the better way to motivate work. Immediately, however, there are complications surrounding the endeavor to make use of intrinsic values competently.

First, there is the temptation to do this with tongue in cheek. That is, it might be supposed that workers can simply be given a few words that make it seem as if they are, or will be, doing intrinsically rewarding work. However, it will likely soon be clear that such words are a hoax rather than really a reward.

Second, there was a time when it was widely thought that *high morale,* defined as workers enjoying the fellowship of one another in the work situation, was a fairly sure road to high-level motivation. High morale—which does, indeed, signify important intrinsic values—can contribute to high productivity. However, as was gradually learned the hard way, there is no sure connection between the intrinsic value of fellowship and the amount and quality of work that gets done. Intrinsic values *at* work are not necessarily the same thing as intrinsic values *in* work; workers doing this kind of expectation planning may not arrive at more and/or better work as a likely route to greater well-being.

Putting it differently, a fellowship can be intrinsically enjoyed whether it is pressing for output or preoccupying itself with such things as the upcoming employees bowling tournament. There is no dependably systematic way supervisors can use this intrinsic value as a contingency to motivate workers toward employer concerns. On the fellowship front, superiors can readily make a con-

[20] Arch Patton, "Why Incentive Plans Fail," *Harvard Business Review,* May–June 1972, pp. 58–66.

tingency only out of their interaction with subordinates, not interactions among subordinates. This hard truth is that fellowship between superiors and those they supervise often seems not to be promising as a usable intrinsic value.

Third, it is worth noting that there is an inherent difficulty in the use of intrinsic motivation to get an organization's work done. We have emphasized that workers may be tempted to neglect the organization's needs if they can get extrinsic rewards more "cheaply" that way. Interestingly enough, they may also be tempted to neglect the organization's needs if they can thereby concentrate more satisfyingly on their intrinsic wants. For example, an organization may need its salesmen to focus a good bit more of their attention on larger accounts, whereas it is more intrinsically rewarding to these people to spend more time in the less formal atmosphere of smaller-scale operations. And is it not paradoxical that organizations find themselves on occasion using extrinsic rewards to "buy" employees "away from" some of their preoccupation with intrinsic satisfactions?

The Emphasis on Intrinsic Values

Because not all intrinsic values are easily used as motivation contingencies, there has developed an intense interest in finding intrinsic needs that are usable in that way. There are three primary reasons. One is that so many workers have become much less dependent on a particular employer and, with the help of unions, can often more effectively bargain with the one they have. Another is that much of the work we must ask many workers to do is of a kind that cannot easily be closely supervised, needing therefore to be done with a higher degree of worker willingness than was once thought to be needed. The third is that, although we call ourselves an affluent society, we do not have nearly enough material reward resources to induce the output we have come to believe we need. Perhaps these three factors could almost be summarized by suggesting that contingencies triggered by threat—which is to say, fear—have become much less useful for getting the work of organizations done.

An early, important intrinsic motivation emphasis was provided by Douglas McGregor. Writing shortly after World War II, McGregor observed that managers were still making contemptuous, degrading assumptions about workers. They thought of workers as being lazy, uncreative, and indifferent to work. Unfortunately, he continued, people are likely to behave much as important people in their lives assume that they will. Why should we be "good" if these important others will in any case believe that we are "bad"? What McGregor called for was replacing these *Theory X* assumptions with *Theory Y* beliefs about workers. If, in other words, managers can bring themselves to expect workers to be diligent, responsible, and helpful, and then treat them accordingly, they will almost certainly be pleasantly surprised at how much more productive their work force will become.

More specifically, McGregor well understood that workers would have to be met at least halfway if something resembling a revolution in their outlook were to

The Assumptions of

Theory X

1. The average human being has an inherent dislike of work and will avoid it if he can.
2. Because of this human characteristic of dislike of work most people must be coerced, controlled, directed, threatened with punishment to get them to put forth adequate effort toward the achievement of organizational objectives.
3. The average human being prefers to be directed, wishes to avoid responsibility, has relatively little ambition, wants security above all.

Theory Y

1. The expenditure of physical effort is as natural as play or rest.
2. Men will exercise self-direction and self-control in the service of objectives to which they are committed.
3. Commitment to objectives is a function of the rewards associated with their achievement.
4. The average human being learns, under proper conditions, not only to accept, but to seek responsibility.
5. The capacity to exercise a relatively high degree of imagination, ingenuity, and creativity in the solution of organizational problems is widely, not narrowly, distributed in the population.
6. Under the conditions of modern industrial life, the intellectual potentialities of the average human being are only partially utilized.

Douglas McGregor, *The Human Side of Enterprise* (New York: McGraw-Hill, 1960), pp. 33–4, 47–8.

be achieved. Thus, he recognized that work would have to be made *desirable* before it would be *desired.* He did, however, think that it would not be difficult to make much of the work to be done much more attractive than it is.[21]

Clearly, that would mean doing a good bit of reversing of the economic history that had made work more and more routine and specific tasks more and more remote from the worker's comprehension of the larger picture of what is being done. What was called for, in short, was nothing less than the opportunity for employees to join with managers in much more of a program of *participative management.*[22] On the one hand, it was supposed that people would much more enthusiastically endeavor to achieve outcomes toward which they had some say in making decisions. On the other hand, it was believed that better decisions for

[21] McGregor, ibid., Chapter 4.

[22] George Strauss, "Some Notes on Power-Equalization," in Harold Leavitt (Ed.), *The Social Science of Organizations* (Englewood Cliffs, N.J.: Prentice–Hall, 1963).

the organization might often be made if those who will be carrying them out help make them. If, thus, the organization could be made to seem to workers more like "one big, happy family," they would more enthusiastically enter into its endeavors.

The Participative Management Approach

Since McGregor gave us *Theory X* and *Theory Y*, a great deal of thinking has been devoted to a search for better ways of utilizing intrinsic motivation to make organizations perform more effectively. And the term *search* is so important to an understanding of this endeavor that we can appropriately note two key things about it. First, quite a number of approaches have been suggested, of which we will be able to describe only a few, and these very briefly. We have as yet much less definitive understanding about how to motivate work in our organizations than we would like to have. Also, we are not sure how much of what we think we understand is "for real" and how much is the wishful thinking of management writers who are more sure about what would be desirable than about what would be both possible and helpful. This, by the way, is one of the principal reasons that in this chapter we are looking a little more closely at the Maslow–McGregor beginnings than we are at later variations on these themes.

As a summary overview, these approaches tend strongly to point toward what is now called *participative management.* One of these emphases is *achievement motivation* as an important way of inducing more effort from employees at higher levels in the organization. Associated particularly with David McClelland, that emphasis points to a variety of esteem and self-actualization values called the *need to achieve.*[23] Not everyone is equally "turned on" by the opportunity to solve problems and overcome obstacles on the way to accomplishments in which one can take pride. However, it is widely supposed that the work ethic of Western civilization created a sizable reservoir of achievement motivation, much of which is still available. It would seem to follow that if achievement opportunities can be created for some of an organization's workers, a great deal of organization accomplishment can be obtained from them in exchange.

An approach applying to a much larger group of employees was suggested by Rensis Likert. He has called this approach *System IV,* to distinguish it from several other managerial styles that are, in varying degrees, less participative.[24] Thus, he lists a number of organizational characteristics that will likely provide useful motivation contingencies for many members of a work force. Thus, workers will probably respond by being more cooperative if there are the following:

1. A network of supportive relationships.
2. A high task involvement.

[23] David McClelland and Associates, *The Achievement Motive* (New York: Appleton, 1953).
[24] Rensis Likert, *The Human Organization* (New York: McGraw-Hill, 1967).

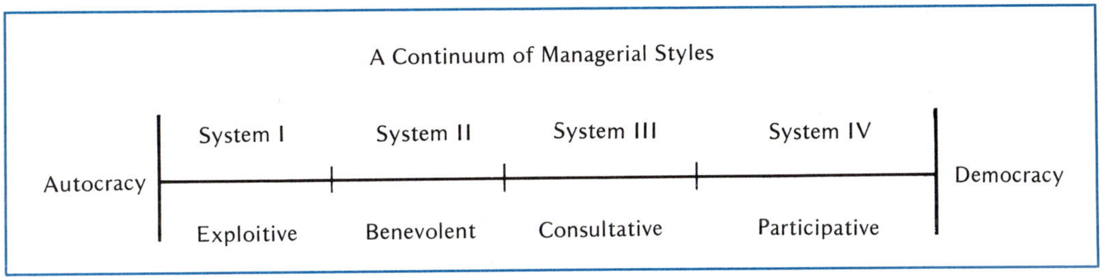

3. A compensation program developed through participation.
4. A generous flow of mutual confidence and trust.
5. A widely dispersed decision process.
6. A wide responsibility for review and control.

It is interesting, too, to note the relationship between the intrinsic values approach to motivation and management by objectives (MBO), which was discussed in Chapter 5. This is an *ego-involvement* way of relating workers to their work, which, if effectively done, may well induce them to work more productively. Especially is MBO intended to give participating workers a goal to achieve that they have helped to establish and to set them an achievement task they have agreed to accept. These dimensions of MBO are designed to give workers a self-concept they will feel compelled to live up to so as to maintain their view of themselves, as well as the view important others have of them.[25]

Yet another intrinsic-type approach to motivation bargaining is *teambuilding*. Managers endeavor to develop cohesive groups that will transform their cohesiveness into greater productivity. More concretely, often an individual's peers can exert pressures far greater than can be exerted by supervisors. Without question, this technique can have valuable motivation consequences. It is well to keep in mind, however, as has already been noted, that group cohesion and high morale do not necessarily mean high productivity. Here is a particular case of intrinsic values *at* work that may not be intrinsic values *in* work. Note, furthermore, that even when the team-building strategy is successful, a turn of events a little later may transform a group's cohesiveness into one enforcing lower rather than higher output norms.

The Job Enrichment Bargain

A final participative management way of motivating workers will be looked at more fully. In part, this is because *job enrichment* is so much talked about these days, and many job enrichment programs are actually being implemented. In part, however, we shall focus a special attention on job enrichment to illustrate that in bargaining terms some of our ideas about how to get more out of workers

[25] E. R. Hilgard and Associates, *Introduction to Psychology* (New York: Harcourt Brace Jovanovich, 1971), Chapter 3.

may not be as promising as they can be made to seem[26]—and there is the possibility that wishful thinking may get intermingled with our understandings about motivation.

First, a look at job enrichment basics. The unquestioned "father" of *job enrichment* is Frederick Herzberg, whose research makes a distinction between a *hygiene* and a *motivation* dimension of worker situations.[27] Hygiene factors are such things as supervision, pay, working conditions, rules and regulations, job security, and interpersonal relationships. They are important in the motivation realm because, although they can create dissatisfaction in workers, they cannot motivate work. By contrast, work, according to this understanding, can be motivated only by satisfiers/motivators. These are such things as responsibility, achievement, advancement, recognition, and possibilities for personal growth. In other words, workers must be motivated by *the work itself*—hence the name *job enrichment.*

The idea behind job enrichment, then, is to make work challenging/inviting enough so that the task itself is intrinsicially worth doing. Over the years, especially since the Industrial Revolution, much of the work we have been asking many people to do has been systematically de-enriched; the planning of tasks has been more and more separated from doing them. The job enrichment approach to motivation suggests that a good bit of the planning opportunity be given back to those who are doing the work. Workers will then get enough satisfaction and sense of accomplishment that their work will become intrinsically desirable. In Theory *Y* terms, when workers are given more than the dull, routine parts of the job to be done, they will not shun work and avoid responsibility for it. Note, incidentally, that this rejoining of planning and doing clearly distinguishes *job enlargement* from *job enrichment,* for the former only gives the worker a greater variety of unenriched tasks.

Nothing we will say here is intended in any way to belittle what can be accomplished by job enrichment. Furthermore, even the most staunch advocates of job enrichment well understand that some kinds of work as, for example, assembly-line operations, are much more difficult to enrich than others. In between two ends of a spectrum of possibilities, however, there is a large realm of relationships within which workers will decide quite carefully whether or not job enrichment will buy from them more of what their organizations want. Looking at these relationships from that perspective, what kind of a bargain is job enrichment?

A quotation from Thomas Carlyle is often cited by job enrichment enthusiasts: "Blessed is he who has found his work; let him ask no other blessedness." Already, workers have reason to wonder what is being done to them in this realm. At higher levels in the organization, where job enrichment is called delegation, greater responsibility is almost invariably accompanied by a higher level of compensation.

[26] Howard R. Smith, "The Half Loaf of Job Enrichment," *Personnel,* March–April 1976, pp. 24–29.
[27] F. Herzberg, B. Mausner, and B. Snyderman, *The Motivation to Work* (New York: Wiley, 1959).

Why is it, workers are so likely to ask, that those above us are entitled to "multiple blessedness" whereas our lot is supposed to be the "single blessedness" of more work to do? If they conclude that their "single blessedness," in a world of scarcity, is some of what makes it possible for those above them to enjoy "multiple blessedness," how can one convince them they are wrong? As one worker put it, after seeing first-hand some work-enriched situations in Scandinavia, "If I've got to bust my ass to be meaningful, forget it; I'd rather be monotonous."

It is small wonder that at this point many workers begin looking beyond job enrichment at various possibilities for *life enrichment*, which, of course, is what job enrichment is all about in any case. And why, indeed, should they limit their thinking about enrichment to "repackaging" their lives at work?

This is where it becomes important, whether it is work that many workers dislike, or only boring work. And if, in thinking about job enrichment, it is appropriate to quote Thomas Carlyle, surely it is as useful to misquote Elizabeth Barrett Browning: "Work," many workers might say, "how do I hate thee, let me count the ways." Making work less disagreeable does not necessarily make it inviting; making work richer is not at all the same thing as making it rich. And

Job Enrichment/Work Humanization: Labor Leaders Versus the Professors

Trade union spokesmen and those with like-minded views perceive the humanization of work as . . . hostile to trade unionism. . . . The content of the humanization ideology is . . . viewed by unions as a put-down of the union's high valuation of economic benefits and job security.

The humanization movement overrates the importance of the work satisfaction problem in workers' values. . . . The first condition of work humanization is the humanization of compensation.

. . . the humanization of work movement is seen as a disguised method for increasing productivity and reducing costs at the expense of wages and workers' rights. . . . For unionists, productivity is a code word for speed-up.

[At this point] . . . the humanization advocates . . . [remind us of] Taylorism. Both Taylorism and the modern humanization movement are really aimed at increased productivity without appropriate payouts.

. . . the humanization movement . . . is mainly based on the needs of middle-class managers for participation and self-actualization. The advocates seem incapable of understanding that the economic calculation is the prism through which other values are filtered.

More time-off, not phony schemes of 'humanizing,' is the only way that the monotony and strain of these jobs can be eased: longer vacations, more paid holidays, and the shorter work week with no reduction in pay.

Excerpted from Jack Barbash, "Humanizing Work—A New Ideology," *CIO-AFL American Federationist*, July 1977, pp. 8–15.

workers must therefore still determine whether newly enriched work will now be attractive enough to deserve a more dedicated interest.[28]

When, in short, the struggle of job enrichment against other varieties of life enrichment takes the center of the stage, some other possibilities may come to seem promising. For example, why not "soldier" on the job in order to have a greater opportunity for fun throughout the work day? One important kind of "fun" might even be "gaming" with superiors who are attempting to find out if there is "soldiering"—and to put a stop to it if there is. Observe, once more, that the "soldiering" problem has been chronically with us ever since scientific management set out with such missionary zeal to solve it.

Moreover, why not go at the life enrichment challenge in some part by staying away from work? Here, of course, are workers trading off some of their primary values for a greater share of the higher-order values that are available. That trade-off can be accomplished not merely by way of *absenteeism;* it is quite likely that much of this kind of trading off takes the form also of *turnover.*

SUMMARY

Work motivation is a bargain in which bargaining partners must decide how they will deal with one another. Workers will evaluate what they are getting from employers, employers will evaluate what they are getting from workers, and both will evaluate the cost of what they are getting. The problem of motivating workers then becomes one of arriving at compensations to workers that will "coax" from them the output that is needed.

The motives that must be used in organizations to induce workers to produce adequately are already mostly learned behavior. This learning is a product of a socialization process in which the significant people in children's lives use the latters' simple wants and their own control over need-satisfaction resources to develop adult wanting patterns. Motivating work is then a mirror image of socialization, as adult wanting is used to get work done by the control over want-satisfying resources by the significant people in workers' lives.

The motivation process uses the wants that workers bring into organizations by making their satisfaction contingent upon doing the work assigned. As employers thus become managers of the contingency relationships governing worker output, a critical problem becomes knowing what workers want and will therefore work to get. Most of the vigorous discussion about motivation in recent years principally addresses that problem.

Of course, much of this focus of attention must look beyond individual differences, although these do greatly complicate the motivation-to-work task. So

[28]Not surprisingly, there is a good bit of evidence suggesting that there is much difference among workers in the appeal of enriched work. C. Hulin and M. Blood, "Job Enlargement, Individual Differences, and Worker Responses," *Psychological Bulletin,* Volume 69, 1968, p. 41–55.

much of what complex organizations must do with workers requires that they be handled as classes of people rather than as individuals. A great deal of thinking about the wants of people in general now emanates from Maslow's hierarchy of needs theory. This approach stresses that over recent decades American wanting has done a great deal of shifting from lower-order to higher-order needs—from extrinsic to intrinsic values.

A variety of ways of emphasizing intrinsic values have been suggested. All of them, however, highlight two approaches. The first of these is participative management, the idea that workers who help decide what will happen to them will cooperate more actively with their organizations. The second is job enrichment, and note that these are in substantial part two sides of the same coin. Here the thinking is that workers often have trouble dedicating themselves to what they are supposed to do because it is so dully monotonous. There seems to be a significant gap between workers' emphases on these approaches to the motivation problem as contrasted with those who primarily write about management.

Assignments

8-1. Referring to Figure 8-1, how does an organization decide how much output to buy from its workers?

8-2. What really is meant when evolution is called a "teacher"?

8-3. Why must people be taught what to want before they can be motivated to work?

8-4. How are the wants we are born with used to develop the wants that will be needed to trigger our motivation to work?

8-5. Explain the learning-motivation mirror image in terms of the way significant people become significant in our lives.

8-6. Discuss the proposition that individual differences are more of a liability than an asset in the motivation of work.

8-7. Explain the expectancy approach to motivation, as summarized in Figure 8-5, in terms of double-coincidence bargaining.

8-8. Relate intrinsic and extrinsic values to primary and higher-order needs. What implications do you see here for today's motivation problem?

8-9. Why, do you suppose, do the various participative management approaches to motivation seem to have no place in them for labor union participation?

8-10. Similarly, explain why union efforts seem to be so much less preoccupied with intrinsic values than are professors writing about management.

Case 8-1

QUANDARY

All of us in the section were pleased when Rowena came to work with us. And I guess I was about as happy as anyone because she was everything that a supervisor could want in the work that we are doing. She was pleasant, enthusiastic, efficient in everything that she did. And, perhaps as important as anything, the way she dressed and cared for herself were particularly important in view of the public relations character of the work in our department at the bank.

But that was six months ago, and things have not continued to go as they then promised. Oh, Rowena is still cooperative and efficient, but she has certainly let some other things slide rather badly. Specifically, beginning about two months ago, she has seemed not to care about how she looks, and even, sometimes, how she acts with customers and other people who are important to our operation.

I have talked with Rowena about this several times. Each time, I noticed some improvement for a few days, but then she slips right back into her more slovenly ways. It is a little embarrassing to us all.

What I want you to tell me is how I can get this girl straightened out. And don't tell me that I ought to let her go and get someone else. Perhaps, in a way, I should. But I have another problem, too. For the last three months the people above me have been suggesting that maybe I have one too many girls in my section. That means that if I were to let Rowena go, I probably wouldn't get a replacement.

1. What might be motivating Rowena to behave so differently these days?
2. What is probably motivating her supervisor to keep her on, rather than to let her go?
3. How might Rowena's supervisor turn her behavior around sufficiently so that she will no longer be a problem?
4. Should the bank let Rowena go and not replace her?

Case 8-2

A FAIR DAY'S WORK

Elrood Skraggs is the plant manager of a medium-sized needle-trades plant in a small southern town. His plant employs about 200 people, of whom 190 are women. It is the main source of employment for three counties. Employees are paid on a straight piecework basis, with the exception that a base rate complying with the Fair Labor Standards Act is also paid.

Average production in the plant is running about 110% of standard. Plant policy, as set by Elrood, called for adherence to the standard on the part of the company. On the other hand, there had been no retiming of loose standards installed by the company since he had taken over eight years ago. Because the runs on any specific standard were relatively short, this didn't hurt dollar-wise to any serious degree.

Elrood's own policy was that everyone should work at her own maximum and strive to turn out a little more each day than the day before. He briefed each new employee on this, and firmly believed in it.

Two of his women workers, Ann Crane and Sue Billups, had been turning out approximately 125% of standard for more than a year. They were both adept and efficient, and their work was of high quality. The girls were close friends both on the job and off. They sat side by side at their work stations.

After being employed for about two years, the girls decided to limit their production to about 115% of standard and to "live a little." They thought that they were getting too tired at work to really enjoy life. The girls' approach to the problem was anything but subtle or devious. Their production figures started to match each other's, piece by piece, dozen by dozen. Of course, as a result, their paychecks matched dollar for dollar and penny for penny. The figures were always enough to keep up the 115% pace—no more, and no less.

When Elrood noticed the coincidence and inquired into the matter, there was no attempt to hide the scheme. The girls, in fact, expressed surprise at his displeasure and concern. They pointed out that they were producing 15% over standard and five points over the plant average.

Elrood pointed out that his policy called for all employees to produce according to their ability—to give his or her best. If they continued to restrict their production, he added, he would be forced to let them go.

As he walked back to his office, a nagging thought crossed his mind. How many other employees were restricting production, but not so openly? And in any case, what should be done about Ann's and Sue's defiance of management standards?

1. Explain the life-enrichment trade-off Ann and Sue are making here.
2. How many other workers do you suppose are making a similar trade-off?
3. Why might Sue and Ann have told Elrood what they are doing rather than keep it to themselves?
4. What should this organization do about Ann and Sue? About the larger situation here?
5. How is "a fair day's work" determined?

References

Argyris, Chris. *Personality and Organization.* New York: Harper & Row, Publishers, 1957.

Bass, Bernard M., and James A. Vaughn. *Training in Industry: The Management of Learning.* New York: Wadsworth Publishing Co., Inc., 1966.

Cummings, L. L., and Donald P. Schwab. *Performance in Organizations.* Glenview, Ill.; Scott, Foresman and Company, 1973.

Dollard, John, and Neal E. Miller. *Personality and Psychotherapy: An Analysis in Terms of Learning, Thinking, and Culture.* New York: McGraw-Hill Book Company, 1950.

Fuller, John L. *Motivation: A Biological Perspective.* New York: Random House, Inc., 1962.

Gellerman, Saul W. *Motivation and Productivity.* New York: American Management Associations, Inc., 1963.

Haire, Mason. *Psychology in Management.* New York: McGraw-Hill Book Company, 1956.

Herzberg, Frederic, *The Motivation to Work.* New York: John Wiley & Sons, Inc., 1959.

Lawler, E. E. *Pay and Organizational Effectiveness.* New York: McGraw-Hill Book Company, 1971.

Leavitt, Harold J. *Managerial Psychology.* Chicago: University of Chicago Press, 1964.

Schein, Edgar H. *Organizational Psychology,* 2nd ed. (Englewood Cliffs, N.J.: Prentice-Hall, Inc., 1970.

Sheppard, Harold L., and Neil O. Herrick. *Where Have All the Robots Gone?* New York: The Free Press, 1972.

Sutermeister, Robert A. *People and Productivity.* 3rd ed. New York: McGraw-Hill Book Company, 1976.

H. G. PATTILLO
Chairman of the Board,
Pattillo Construction Company, Inc.,
Decatur, Georgia.

In addition to a distinguished career in his own business, Pattillo has been actively involved in community service—especially as Chairman of the Federal Reserve Bank of Atlanta, and as Chairman of the Board of Regents of the University System of Georgia. He is also a member of the Board of Directors of a number of other business concerns.

Executive Commentary
Short Term Versus Long Term

Motivation for a short stretch of work is important to the construction industry. No general contractor is able to maintain an even volume of contracts to sustain a level work force. Consequently, craftsmen perform their trades on one project for one contractor and then move on to another project with another company.

For a bricklayer, the quantity of bricks to be laid on a particular job is finite. The brick work must be completed before the roof deck is laid. The roof deck must be in place before the floor slab is poured. The job superintendent has the responsibility of coordinating these trades. He has the additional responsibility of completing the job on a predetermined schedule within an estimated cost.

How does the job superintendent encourage the bricklayer to lay a reasonable number of bricks each day?

First, the job superintendent must understand brick work. He needs to know an average rate of production, acceptable workmanship, the equipment required to support the workman, the special features of this particular project, and the general attitude of a bricklayer crew.

Second, the superintendent uses the wage rates to obtain acceptable production. The rate varies from area to area. Construction rates are higher than manufacturing rates. The hourly rate is still the best motivation in the construction industry and is probably the best motivation for short-term work in any industry. Unfortunately, union agreements fix the same hourly rate for all bricklayers on a job. The inefficient worker is paid the same as the efficient worker. Extra pay for extra production is forbidden. Compensation motivates. Union agreements dilute its effectiveness.

Third, the superintendent usually has a bricklayer whom he has used through the years. This favored person is a member of the crew when the work begins and the crew is assembled. He works "steady" through the bulge and is the last man laid off when the brick work is being finished. His loyalty to the superintendent sets the tone of the job. For short-term performance, every leader needs a dependable example.

Fourth, the superintendent keeps up with the performance of his crews. Climbing onto the scaffold once a day can be as helpful as a computer printout. A problem is easy to spot for an experienced leader. The successful one knows the solution. He is quick to haul off faulty brick, repair equipment, or encourage a mason who is not carrying his share of the load.

Fifth, the amount of work performed by bricklayers has a bearing on the amount of brick to be laid. When masonry production slipped badly in the 1960s, tilt-up concrete panels were used for exterior walls. When concrete panels became expensive, insulated metal wall sections were used for the same purpose. These materials do not use bricklayers. Indeed, these materials require less hours of any kind of labor. Wages and rates of production design buildings. The labor union can use the constraint of the building codes to sustain a trade for a time. The power of the marketplace eventually wins. Short-term performance affects long-term opportunity.

Motivation for the short term is needed in every work force. The construction industry makes an extreme example.

Motivation for the long term is more complex. Most workers seeking a long-term reward work indoors. Many factories are air-conditioned. The number of toilet fixtures is dictated by OSHA. Parking spaces are free.

Farmers moved from the harshness of the outdoors to the relative comfort of a manufacturing plant. The uncertainty of a crop was exchanged for 40 hours of consistent pay. Wages have been enhanced with Social Security, unemployment compensation, hospital benefits, and the suggestion box.

For the next generation, and the one following, the regularity of work was no longer a blessing, but a bore. However, the factory worker is the backbone of the economic system of our country. His working conditions are set by Japan and West Germany. His strength provides for his family. His persistence establishes the standard of living in this country. His attitude shapes the culture of our population.

The factory worker is paid with money, security, fringe benefits, influence in politics, and association with other workers.

The search for additional compensation continues. Probably, it will not be found in gimmicks. Perhaps, a new generation will find the fundamental worth of the individual to the society of our country and appreciate the price he pays for belonging to it. It will not be measured in wages or working conditions.

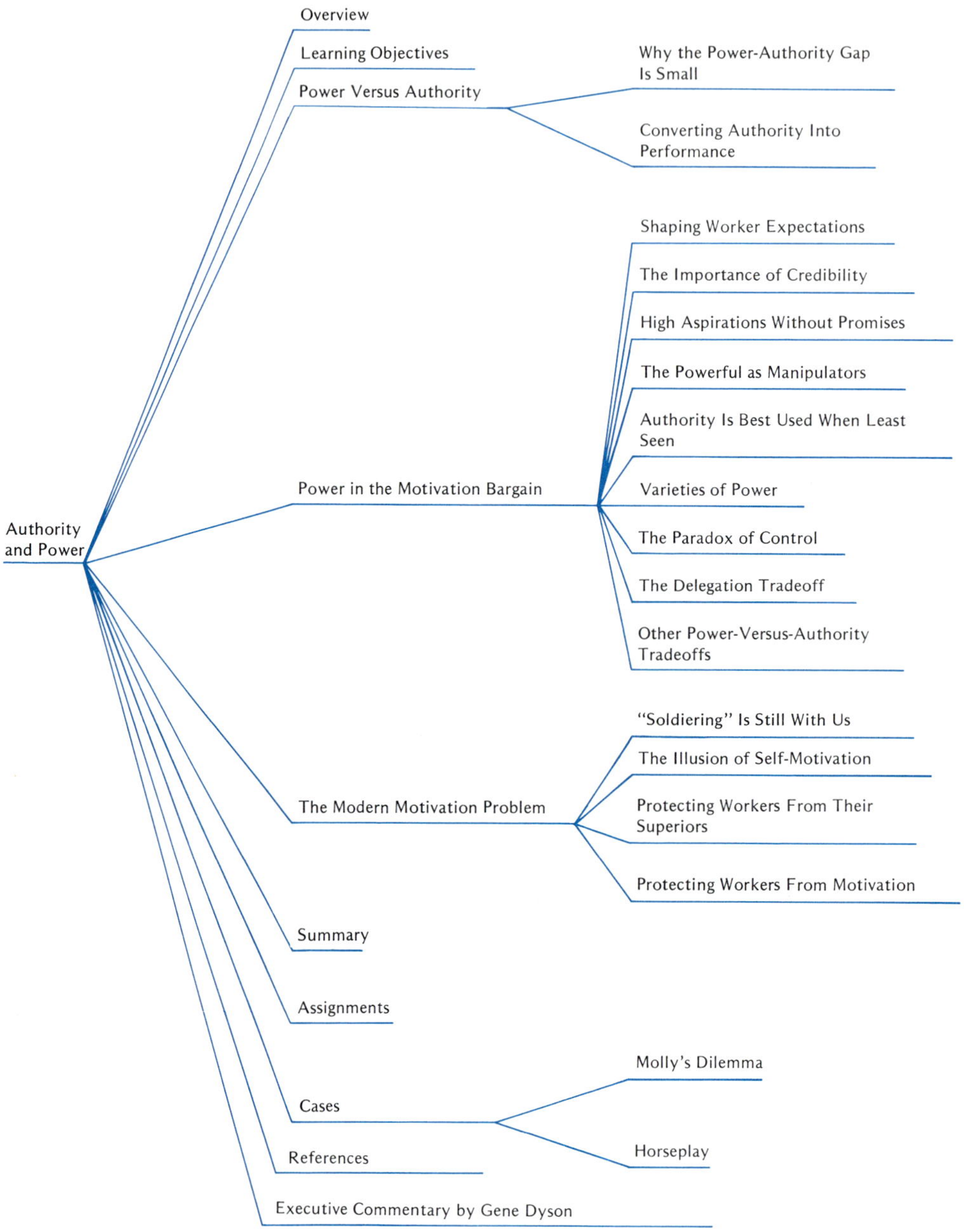
Authority and Power
Overview
Learning Objectives
Power Versus Authority
Why the Power-Authority Gap Is Small
Converting Authority Into Performance
Power in the Motivation Bargain
Shaping Worker Expectations
The Importance of Credibility
High Aspirations Without Promises
The Powerful as Manipulators
Authority Is Best Used When Least Seen
Varieties of Power
The Paradox of Control
The Delegation Tradeoff
Other Power-Versus-Authority Tradeoffs
The Modern Motivation Problem
"Soldiering" Is Still With Us
The Illusion of Self-Motivation
Protecting Workers From Their Superiors
Protecting Workers From Motivation
Summary
Assignments
Cases
Molly's Dilemma
Horseplay
References
Executive Commentary by Gene Dyson

9

AUTHORITY AND POWER

OVERVIEW

In this chapter we will discuss *authority* and *power* as they, along with motivation, interact to "make organizations perform." First, we will distinguish between authority and power. In particular, we will discuss the problem of converting authority into power, stressing that the willingess of workers to contribute to their organizations' objectives is critically important. When workers are reluctant to do their best, authority is in proportion diluted. In other words, to whatever extent authority is not successfully converted into power, organizational effectiveness will be limited. Our focus on these relationships will therefore be on the problem of converting authority into enough power to keep the organization functioning effectively. The chapter concludes with a discussion of some particularly important aspects of authority-power relationships in today's world.

LEARNING OBJECTIVES

This chapter is especially intended to help the student:

1. **Understand the problem of converting authority into performance.**
2. **See the relationship between authority and the motivation bargain.**
3. **Appreciate the significance of manipulation as an important managerial activity.**
4. **Become familiar with the operation of the process that makes authority best used when least seen.**

5. **Understand the most important trade-offs between power and authority.**
6. **Note some special problems of authority in the motivation bargain in today's environment.**
7. **Learn, especially in the context of thinking about management, the meaning of the following concepts:**

authority	**lottery motivation**
power	**paradox of control**
reluctance	**functional foremanship**
expectation shaping	**frozen group**
self-fulfilling prophecies	**worker volition**
credibility	**entitlements**

POWER VERSUS AUTHORITY

Authority is, of course, a familiar concept. In a general sense, it means that one person can *compel* another person to do what the first one wants. But the term *compel* does not accurately explain authority, because in organizational situations subordinates can, and frequently do, say "no" to their supervisors. However, this does not mean that authority is not present.

Why the Power-Authority Gap Is Small

Let us then define authority somewhat differently, recognizing that those with authority cannot always have their way. *Authority* is the right, given to managers by an organization, to *command,* to give orders to employees so as to get work done. Authority also includes the right to *manipulate rewards* in such a way that subordinates will be happier when they follow orders than when they do not.

The right to command, however, does not ensure that employees will always follow orders. Still needed is a term explicitly recognizing that there is a gap between authority and the response of workers to authority.[1] We will use the term *power* for this and define it as the extent to which authority is accepted by workers. Early in the history of organization theory, a classic work particularly emphasized the need for managers to focus much of their attention on this gap between how much a manager has a right to expect from workers and how much they are willing to give.[2]

Much of this chapter will center on why authority does not convert into as much power as is desired. First, however, it is worth noting why the gap is sufficiently small that organizations are still able to function. A major reason for

[1]Robert V. Presthus, "Authority in Organizations," in Mailick, Sidney, and Van Ness, Edward H., *Concepts and Issues in Administrative Behavior* (Englewood Cliffs, N.J.: Prentice-Hall, 1962).

[2]See, especially, Chester Barnard, *The Functions of the Executive* (Cambridge, Mass.: Harvard University Press, 1954).

A Definition

manipulate. 1: to treat or operate with the hands or by mechanical means esp. in a skillful manner; 2: to manage or utilize skillfully; b: to control or play upon by artful, unfair, or insidious means esp. to one's own advantage; 3: to change by artful or unfair means so as to serve one's purpose.

Webster's New Collegiate Dictionary (Springfield, Mass.: Merriam, 1973), p. 699.

the smallness of this gap is the socialization process. We all learn as infants and children to depend on authority figures—for example, our parents—to satisfy our wants and needs. This dependence then remains with us and is later transferred to employers whom we, as employees, work for later in life. This early learning is therefore a very important resource available to those in power.

Converting Authority into Performance

Although socialization makes available to managers a very basic resource, it does not follow that performance is obtained without managerial effort and skill. On the contrary, a great deal of both are needed to achieve production by bridging the gap between authority and power. The key fact here is that even successful organizations are a reluctant merger of purposes. Workers want what they want; managers want what they want; and the mission of the organization can be accomplished only if everyone gets enough of what he or she wants. A primary task of power, therefore, is to minimize the friction between supervisor and worker—to keep the cost of worker cooperation as low as possible.

Figure 9-1 shows these relationships. Each individual in the organization has a will of his own and managers must thus face multiple wills. This, of course, is where reluctance resides; many people would rather do more of what they would like to do, even if that would mean doing less of what the organization would like them to do. The organization, however, must combat this *diversity.* It must convert reluctance into the *conformity* that will accomplish the mission the organization has set for itself.

In other words, managers obtain adequate performance by manufacturing or creating power out of the authority given them by their organizations. In motivation terms, however, they must do this by giving subordinates an "offer" they "won't refuse."[3] It then follows that power, as it contributes to performance, becomes a part of the motivation bargain.

The use of power to induce conformity, and especially thinking about this in manipulation terms, must bring to mind the idea of some people exploiting other people. Moreover, this can, of course, happen. But there are a number of other

[3] George C. Homans, *Social Behavior: Its Elementary Forms* (New York: Harcourt Brace Jovanovich, 1961).

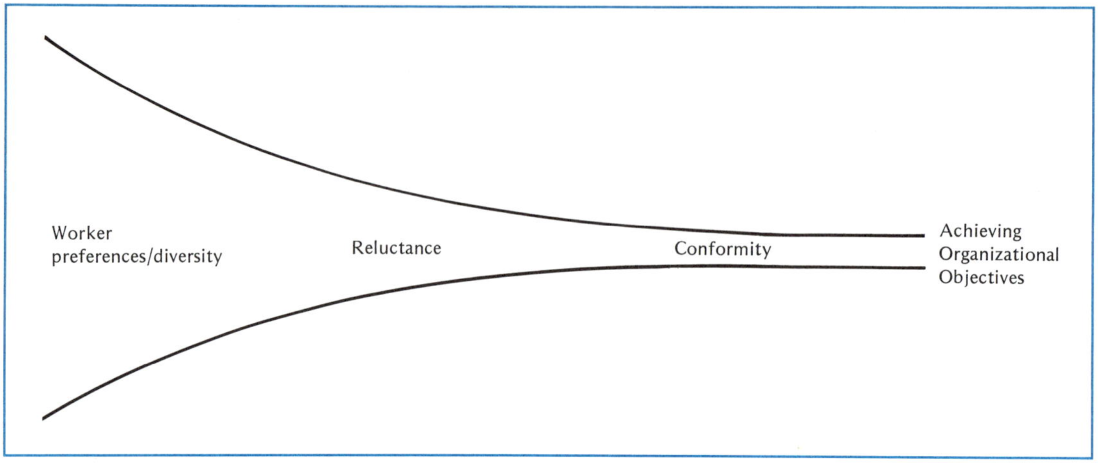

FIGURE 9-1. Converting Diversity Into Conformity.

aspects of these relationships, and those will primarily be the context of our discussion.

First, pressing people to conform is often thought of as negative. It is therefore quite basic here that the very fact of a gap between authority and power means that those who have authority are limited in how much conformity they can command. Second, and even more important, managers are dependent upon, as well as being in a position to command, their subordinates. Worker reluctance then becomes a *reciprocal manipulation* upward in the organization. Third, and this is the most fundamental fact here, throughout this discussion of authority and power, the few pushing the many for performance is one of the core elements of the dynamics that gives us civilization.

POWER IN THE MOTIVATION BARGAIN

Those who have authority possess a bargaining advantage over those who do not.[4] That is, those in authority are able to work things out more nearly as they need them to be for the organization. Let us look at some ways of using authority to secure worker conformity and therefore satisfy organizational objectives.

It might seem that those with authority would simply command conformity by ordering workers to do what needs to be done. However, it must be kept in mind that people do have wills of their own. Overcoming reluctance means bending those wills, channelling worker *volition,* toward the organization's objectives. We all, to some extent, take a dim view of this when we are on the receiving end. We

[4]Peter M. Blau, *The Dynamics of Bureaucracy* (Chicago: University of Chicago Press, 1963).

prefer to do more nearly what we want rather than what the organization wants. As Johnny Paycheck said in a popular song, "Take this job and shove it."

Thus we see why there is always a gap between authority and power.[5] The deference to authority that everyone acquires from the socialization process has a certain fragility and must therefore be handled carefully. As managers and workers seek to fulfill their wills and objectives, the power-performance bargain necessarily becomes quite critical.[6]

Shaping Worker Expectations

A fundamental technique of those who have authority is convincing individuals lower in the organization that they should want less rather than more. However, we noted at some length in the chapter on motivation that we are motivated only when we have unsatisfied wants. Consequently, wanting must be

"Know why I go for Jerry Brown? He lowered my expectations. Now, I don't have any!" (Reprinted by permission of NEA.)

[5] A fascinating study of this in a highly authoritarian society is Joseph S. Berliner, *Factory and Manager in the USSR* (Cambridge, Mass.: Harvard University Press, 1957).

[6] James G. March, and Herbert A. Simon, *Organizations* (New York: Wiley, 1958), is a full-length study of the complexities of bargaining between employers and employees.

kept active for the sake of motivation. This is not too difficult, fortunately, for human beings have a way of taking on more and more hopes and aspirations.

That is especially the case in a so-called affluent society. The problem of managers is to maintain a balance between the wanting necessary for the motivation needs of the organization and the available rewards. Great care is required so that employees with active imaginations do not demand higher pay-offs than management can or cares to supply.

A few observations will make clear why this balance is so fundamental and delicate. First, motivating workers involves a cost that cannot be allowed to become too high. There will always be a scarcity of material goods, power, and status—the kinds of rewards most people are willing to work hard to get. Second, the few who possess authority are nearly always given a disproportionate share of the available rewards. On the one hand, those in power will use their power to get more of what they want. On the other hand, managers must be compensated well enough to be willing to take on the difficulties and discomforts of management responsibilities. Third, when expectations have been strongly aroused and are then frustrated, productivity is likely to be adversely affected. Employee attitudes may then even become explosively dangerous. Because unmade promises cannot be broken, it is worth a great deal of trouble to see to it that employees do not feel they have been promised more than managers can or will deliver.[7]

A key activity of an alert leadership interested in bridging the gap between authority and power, therefore, is *expectation shaping*. This means helping employees understand that they must be content with less than they might like to have. New supervisors quickly learn about this aspect of their new jobs as they come to realize that making promises they cannot keep can be very treacherous.

This does not mean that managers should never make promises. Rather, the lesson is that optimistic expectations must not be encouraged to develop, only to be later frustrated. A technique learned early by supervisors for coping with this danger is to *underpromise* when promises must be made.

The Importance of Credibility

Managers, of course, cannot fully shape the expectations of employees. As we noted in our discussion of motivation, the largest element in human wanting is learned during childhood. The learning-motivation mirror, the fact that later in life people can be motivated only by what they have learned to want, dictates that people must be given a large proportion of what they were earlier taught to want. However, people can learn to be less optimistic about what will happen to them. Because expectations can become so dangerously domineering, here is a situation in which an ounce of prevention really is worth a pound of cure. This is one of

[7] A brief but pointed discussion of reactions to frustration will be found in Henry L. Tosi, and Stephen J. Carroll, *Management: Contingencies, Structure and Process* (Chicago: St. Clair, 1976), pp. 77 ff.

the problems faced when subordinates participate in decision making. This style of management is likely to enlarge expectations, rather than making them realistic.[8]

Why is it, though, that people listen to those who have power when these people tell them what and how much to want? There are three principal reasons for this, and all of these further emphasize the importance and the difficulty of expectation shaping by managers.

First, and once again, subordinates believe those above them because the socialization process left them with a deference to authority (figures) that does not easily disappear. Therefore, a benefit of the doubt is given to what these people say; it is assumed that those in power say what is true rather than what is not true. (Note, by the way, that *truth* here may mean in large part the capacity of managers, because they have power, to make true what they say is or will become true.) Thus, managers have *credibility.*[9]

Although deference to authority does not easily erode, it is not set in concrete. It will not withstand any and all shocks, such as the careless handling of employees, not being wholly honest, or not seeming to be capable. Maintaining credibility, in other words, demands attention, effort, and competence.

Second, subordinates tend to believe superiors who effectively use available resources to reward subordinates. This is called *distributing patronage*—to couch this in a terminology often used by political scientists to describe how political leaders "buy" support. As we have said, managers have ways of making their people glad they did, or sorry they did not, do as was wanted. In short, leaders pay out available rewards to those who are most supportive of them and the organization. When that is competently done, patronage reinforces belief, making what those with authority say and do more readily believable.

Third, this patronage dimension of the way power is used enters also into expectation shaping. Remember that authority holders do this shaping in the context of the learning-motivation mirror through which the future unfolds mostly as *self-fulfilling prophecies.* Those in power, however, with their control over resources, have a basic grip on what the future will bring to those they supervise. Managers, thus, can shape subordinates' expectations and tell them much about their future, secure in their own power to make the future turn out as they said it would. This correlation between expectation shaping and what managers can make happen reinforces their power by making them even more believable.

High Aspirations Without Promises

Attention, effort, and competence, then, are what managers must bring to the task of converting authority into power for the organization. One dimension of

[8]This is, of course, why participative management is often in name only. See for example, Toby Moffett, *The Participation Put-On* (New York: Delacorte, 1971).

[9]Howard R. Smith, *The Capitalistic Imperative* (New York: Exposition, 1975), Chapters 8 and 20.

competence, the careful handling of promises, has already been mentioned. Let us now think about the competence needed for handling authority well. We will begin by exploring further problems and possibilities connected with promises.

It is sometimes possible for motivation to be so strong that no promises have to be made. That is the epitome of getting the most out of people for the benefit of the organization. Those in control can thus secure the advantage of high aspirations without risking the fury likely to be caused by the breaking of real promises.

The kind of contributions-inducement program capable of accomplishing this can appropriately be called *lottery motivation.*[10] Note that lottery here does not mean luck and chance gains; it means, rather, few winners and many losers. Observe how this works in the case of the Irish Sweepstakes. The success of the sweepstakes depends upon all participants believing they have a chance to win, with no one feeling assured of winning. This is how many of the higher-level rewards are allocated in a *merit society* such as ours. We widely advertise that handsome pay-offs—power, status, and money—will be available to those who are capable enough to merit them. Having spread that word, we leave it to the "rat-race" to determine which few will win. Of course, some will be disappointed. We need only remind the losers, however, that no promises were made and that if they had been "good enough" they would have received one of the most desirable prizes. As a result, society has received the benefit of the valuable efforts of people who do not have to be paid off in proportion to their contribution.

Observe the promotion process in organizations from this perspective. Available opportunities will be sought by several candidates, even though only one can be successful. One of the candidates who does not win this promotion may get the next one. Furthermore, most of these people will live quite comfortably with the lesser rewards they receive. But what this process shows is that an effective lottery motivation program can keep many contributors vigorously active even after they have suffered defeats.

The Powerful As Manipulators

It would seem that the lottery way of motivating almost runs itself, requiring no special handling by those in power. But that is not the case. Managers must keep some potentially high-level performers from getting discouraged, despite the odds they are up against, without having them feel that they have been promised success. They must also discourage some people whose failure might be quite disruptive. They will have situations to smooth over in which disappointed candidates believed that solid commitments had been made. All of this is often awkwardly complicated by the fact that decisions based on merit are highly subjective.

The lottery way of motivating is a type of manipulating that is widely used.

[10] Without using that term, Professor Joseph A. Schumpeter described this phenomenon in his *Capitalism, Socialism, and Democracy* (New York: Harper, 1942), Chapter VI.

Raises are going increasingly to the swift, leaving little or nothing for the also-rans. (Joseph Farris for Business Week. *© 1975.)*

Interestingly enough, however, that use of authority as a bargaining advantage is a specific variety of a more general use of the expectation shaping process.

It has already been emphasized that those who have authority can more confidently make predictions about what can appropriately be wanted, because they can more nearly shape the future. Often, they can maneuver a situation in such a way that what is wanted just seems to happen naturally. Observe what has now been accomplished. Instead of a situation appearing to be the will of a superior, it appears that a neutral environment has brought adverse developments. The phrase "that's the way the cookie crumbles" serves as a reminder that sometimes events just come together "wrong" for us. Note the close parallel here with the results of lottery motivation. Much of what happens can be blamed on the neutral fact of merit, even though there is much that managers can do to determine the "obvious" outcome of merit determinations.

A major event in the history of management thinking focused on these dynamics. Mary Parker Follett in the 1920s undertook to show how conflict in organizations can often be worked out much more harmoniously. Her primary argument was that leaders do not exercise power nearly as much as they simply follow the *law of the situation.* That is, she argued, it is not really an organiza-

Mary Parker Follett

In these days of warfare against sexism, it is well worth taking note of this outstanding woman. Along with Lillian Gilbreth, although from a very different perspective, Mary Parker Follett made a large contribution to management by helping us think our way beyond scientific management.

Henry C. Metcalf, and Tyndall F. Urwick, (eds.) *Dynamic Administration: Mary Parker Follett* (New York: Harper, 1941).

tion's managers who give commands. Rather what needs to be done "speaks for itself," and a technique used too little by leaders is helping those who are unhappy about a decision understand that things could not have been done or come out any other way.

Follett was right in emphasizing that when workers see what is happening as obvious and necessary, rather than a leader deciding who shall and shall not be advantaged, the gap between authority and power remains smaller. Most of us are much more likely to see in events "an offer we won't refuse" if these developments do not seem to be deliberately maneuvered. But she was less discerning when she suggested that the "law of the situation" is typically not itself a manipulation. After all, it is the principal business of managers to make things come out as they wish. What so often happens, therefore, is that managers create "the situation"—shape expectations by shaping the circumstances under which they are or are not fulfilled.

Authority Is Best Used When Least Seen

There are other ramifications, too, of authority as a key ingredient in the motivation bargain. Let us now look beyond the importance of expectation shaping and lottery motivation as one way of letting what happens seem more spontaneous than it is. All of this is, in turn, only a special use of a more general technique that might meaningfully be called *perception shaping*. Workers, just as other human beings, regularly respond to the way they "see" things rather than the way things are. Because they do, superiors can bridge some of the gap between authority and power by helping subordinates "see" what is happening to and around them in ways that are more useful to the organization.

There are three realms in which it is important that workers "see" themselves in their organization in a certain way. First, they need to feel that their leaders are doing their jobs well. After all, superiors and subordinates are joined together in what they are doing and, to some extent, have the same interest in how things go.

Second, workers need to feel as nearly as possible that the organization is being run with their interests in mind. This feeling is often diluted by guesses about the "real" motivations of those who run the organization. But there are many opportunities to help workers feel that they are being well cared for, and it is important that leaders take advantage of these. Most people will often quite willingly accept "facts of life" as being more congenial than they really are, especially when that will allow them to live more comfortably with the authority they know they cannot escape.

Third, it is useful for workers to "see" the authority in their work lives as less constraining than it is. Accordingly, a great deal of perception shaping effort will often go into this project[11]—a challenge to leaders often thought of in terms of "authority is best used when least seen."

Perception shaping as a key element in using authority in motivation bargaining can itself be seen in several dimensions. First, everyone has a limited threshold of tolerance for visible authority, often called *naked power.* To a point, we can accept the fact that we are dependent upon other people who may or may not be concerned about our interests. Beyond that, we want this dependence to be subtle rather than obvious. One meaning of the saying "more flies are caught with honey than with vinegar" is that an offer that will not be refused is more likely to be seen in a pleasant than in a naked power situation.[12]

Second, it is important to emphasize that authority, over a wide range of circumstances, must be used as a last resort. As individuals with their vast differences live together, a number of techniques for dealing with interpersonal friction have been developed. One of these is to command conformity. But this tool really must be used primarily as a last resort, because the overuse of commands can stifle cooperation. In other words, all other ways of bridging the gap between authority and power should be used before resorting to naked commands.[13]

Varieties of Power

Central to keeping the gap between authority and power as small as possible by perception shaping is the fact that there are several bases for the exercise of power. They are "reward power, coercive power, legitimate power, referent power, and expert power."[14]

Reward power means that superiors are perceived as being able to reward behavior that is useful to the organization. A person who has *legitimate power* is seen by subordinates as possessing a legitimate right to tell others what and how to do. *Referent power* can be enjoyed by those who are accepted as models, ideals, by other people. Whoever is recognized as having an expertise, a special skill or knowledge, has *expert power* over associates who need this expertise in what they are doing.

[11]Howard R. Smith, "How Much 'Con' in Consensus?", unpublished manuscript.

[12]Fred Luthans, and Robert Kreitner, "The Role of Punishment in Organizational Behavior Modification," *Public Personnel Management,* May-June, 1973, pp. 156–61.

[13]Smith, *The Capitalistic Imperative,* op. cit., pp. 82–3, 202–3.

[14]J.R.P. French, and B. Raven, "The Basis of Social Power," in Dorwin Cartwright, Ed. *Studies in Social Power* (Ann Arbor, Mich.: Institute of Social Research, 1959).

The Importance of Power

The care, constraint, with which power must be used, be it explicitly noted, is a consequence of its very great importance. As Bertrand Russell says in his book on power: "the fundamental concept in social science is Power in the same sense that Energy is the fundamental concept in physics.

Bertrand Russell, *Power* (New York: Norton, 1927).

Clearly, in one way or another, these four varieties of power will help power be less uncomfortable to those who respond to them. The fifth, *coercive power,* is likely to describe a sharply contrasting relationship. Thus, when power is seen to be starkly, nakedly coercive, power itself can easily increase reluctance. In other words, when power is used basically to punish, those it threatens are most apt to develop nonconformist attitudes.

It follows that managers will want to make as much use they can of varieties of power that are more, rather than less, acceptable. Note that this is a more general statement of what Mary Parker Follett saw as the value of "commands" that seem to be the "law of the situation." Ideally, in short, those who command would wholly avoid the use of coercive power. Unfortunately, from the standpoint of keeping the gap between authority and power smaller, it sometimes does not seem to practicing managers that the other varieties of power will accomplish enough.

The Paradox of Control

Another way of thinking about coercive power brings into focus a special dimension of the problem of converting authority into enough power. It is quite appropriately called the *paradox of control.*[15] This paradox notes the possibility that people in organizations, in a wide variety of circumstances, may feel so burdened by authority that they will go to a great deal of trouble to frustrate its use. When this point in the relationship between superiors and subordinates is reached, attempts to correct performance difficulties by using power even a little more strongly will likely "backfire." That is, workers who feel abused will find some other way of avoiding doing what the organization wants whenever the organization succeeds in closing any given "loophole."

Summarized differently, the paradox of control can result from these basic characteristics of the superior-subordinate interaction: (1) obtaining organizational performance is a two-sided bargain; (2) one of the principal uses of authority in organizations is to generate conformity despite reluctance; and (3) we all have a limited threshold of tolerance for authority. As these dimensions of the motivation-authority bargain come together, workers can come to feel too badgered by a very visible exercise of authority. Insofar, then, as they can work

[15] This is discussed in several variations in March and Simon, op. cit., pp. 36 ff.

out a sufficiently subtle and effective response, the exercise of more authority by management may create a situation that is as damaging to the organization as the one its leaders were endeavoring to correct.

It follows, thus, that it is important for managers to use their authority, for example, to do their perception and expectation shaping, so that a paradox of control impasse does not develop. Let us next, therefore, note a few illustrations of using authority more effectively by making it less visible, so that it is not caught in a paradox of control trap. It is important to keep in mind in this connection, by the way, that the perception shaping used in keeping authority more nearly out of sight is valuable to all partners to the motivation bargain. It should be observed, too, that the supervisors who are able to do this best have to be actors to some extent.

In the realm of authority and its use, there are a number of ways in which managers can make it seem to be less ever-present than it is. A few of these are the following:

1. *Clear job assignments* so that supervisors need not hover nearby to clarify uncertainties.
2. *Standard rules and procedures* so that the voice of authority need not be raised so often.
3. *Established norms concerning fairness and legitimacy* to keep superiors from appearing to be looking for ways to further constrain employees.
4. *Delegation* to keep employees from being constantly reminded that they are in fact closely constrained.

Other examples further illustrate this principle. Military officers wear evidence of their rank on their uniforms. This helps subordinates separate authority from the person who holds it. Instead, they associate authority with the system the power-holder represents. Ceremony is often used to emphasize that respect is given to an office rather than to the man who holds it. This also helps subordinates see themselves in relation to a system rather than to a person. Superiors often go to some pains to make subordinates feel they care about them; the actor dimension of being an effective supervisor is especially useful here. Because superiors will in any case have difficult interactions with workers, these should be adequately balanced whenever possible by pleasantness.

Handling authority in such a way that it is less visible is much like puppeteers in relation to their puppets and their audiences. It is fascinating that grown men and women, knowing all the time they are being "conned," get emotionally involved with stuffed rag figures cavorting on a stage. What is even more fascinating, however, is that these remarkable results can be achieved only so long as the puppeteers, the performers, are skillful enough so that the audience does not clearly see the strings by which the puppets are being manipulated. So it is between those who have power and those they are supervising. As long as the strings of authority are not too plainly in sight, those being maneuvered by them may be quite willing to join in a "game" of pretending they are not there.

The Delegation Trade-off

In an earlier chapter we discussed at some length a number of aspects of organizing—how organizations are best put together, and why organizational structure decisions are made the way they are. The necessity of keeping the gap between authority and power as small as possible is another context in which the rationale for structure decisions is quite important.[16] Specifically, a number of organizational structure trade-offs must be made as it is decided that sacrifices of some possibilities must be made to achieve other possibilities.

For example, every organization of some size and complexity must work through the *delegation trade-off*. One or even a few managers cannot supervise the functioning of the entire organization. Top management must, therefore, place substantial authority and resources with key subordinates so that they can and will make their best capacities fully available to the organization. Having done that, top management then risks what these people may do with that authority and those resources, because these can often be used in such a way that they are more useful to these middle managers than to the organization. How can this risk be minimized? It will, of course, be a smaller risk if there are not too many delegatees and if these few are carefully selected in terms of their competence and their full acceptance of the organization's mission.

As Figure 9-2 illustrates, the delegation trade-off dictates much of the basic shape of organizations. The smaller number of people who top managers believe have both high competence and a high level of loyalty to the organization's interests will be in Quadrant I, whereas the largest number of employees will be in Quandrant III. When this situation is related to the scarcity of reward resources, the familiar hierarchical organization shape is especially demanded.

The problem and process of organizing for economic development in Communist China dramatically illustrates the workings of the delegation trade-off. The difficulty there, and on a smaller scale this is precisely the delegation problem top managers confront in organizations, was finding enough high-talent people who were also loyal to the new regime. Perhaps, moreover, the way China's leaders pressed for conformity in the face of this difficulty is also illustrative of what happens in smaller-scale situations.

What China, in fact, did was to set in motion pendulum swings from "Redness" to "expertness" and back again.[17] First, top leaders tolerated a drift toward less competence in management to be certain that the ideological stance remained acceptably intact. Then the focus shifted to management competence at the risk of some dilution of ideological purity. The result is pendulum swings that alternate in guarding against the two most basic difficulties those who hold power must stuggle against as they endeavor to interact with worker reluctance effectively enough.

[16] Bertram M. Gross, "The Power-Authority-Responsibility Triangle," *Organizations and Their Managing* (New York: Free Press, 1964), Chapter 4.

[17] Franz Schurmann, *Ideology and Organization in Communist China* (Berkeley: University of California Press, 1966).

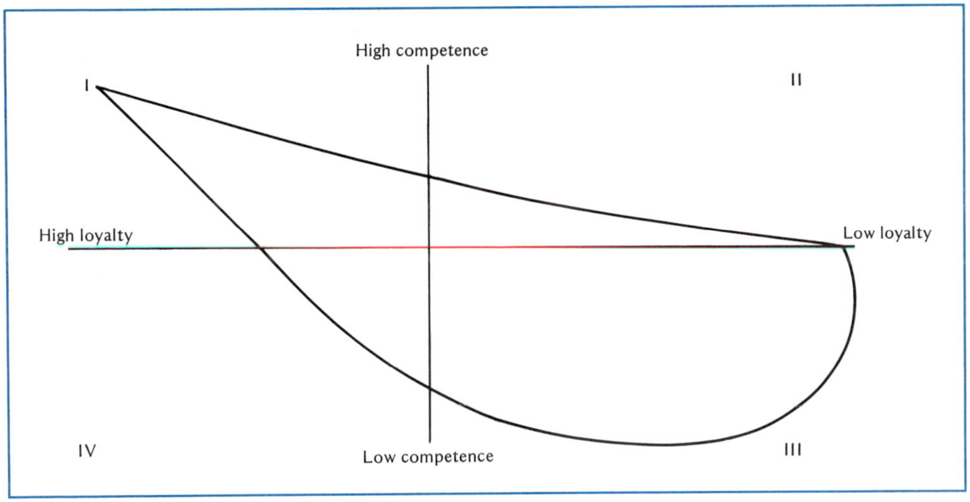

FIGURE 9-2. The Competence-Loyalty Mix.

Other Power Versus Authority Trade-offs

Lower in organizations another significant trade-off is important. We will call this the *span-of-control trade-off,* because it deals with how many subordinates a supervisor can efficiently manage. A number of factors determine the number of subordinates a supervisor should have.[18] Factors suggesting a smaller number of subordinates, a smaller span of control, are primarily as follows:

1. The sameness of the work of subordinates.
2. The simplicity of the work subordinates are doing.
3. A minimum need for subordinate training and supervision.
4. A minimum need for task interaction among subordinates.
5. A minimum need for planning the work of subordinates.

It is easy to understand the principal elements in the span-of-control trade-off. Too small a span of control is expensive and may make authority too visible to workers. Too few supervisors may allow the gap between authority and power to become too wide, doing too little to overcome worker reluctance.

As managers in complex organizations endeavor to achieve the best motivation/conformity bargain they can, they must also make other power versus authority decisions. One of these is the *line-staff trade-off.* Because line managers cannot master all of the specialized understandings that go into running their operations, they must be given staff people to provide them with technical help.

[18] Gerald D. Bell, "Determinants of Span of Control," *The American Journal of Sociology,* June 1967, pp. 100–109.

But how, as these helpers are made as valuable as possible to the managers to whom they report, shall staff people relate to the line subordinates of their own superiors?

In principle, it was long ago agreed that staff should be advisory so as to keep authority lines "clean." This helps ensure control toward organizational objectives. In practice, however, staff personnel are often most helpful to their superiors when they interact directly with the latter's line subordinates, even though the latter view this as giving them another superior.[19] This is confusing and annoying to them; coordination can in this way be made much more difficult, and authority, at times, thereby becomes too visible. In consequence, line people endeavor to escape some of this authority by finding "dodging room" in their interaction with two authority channels. This trade-off, therefore, tries to find a golden mean between using staff people as fully as possible without eroding the full value of a single source of supervision.

Closely related to the line-staff trade-off is another golden mean quest we might call the *functional foremanship trade-off.* At one point, Frederick Taylor—and, of course, this thinking is quite congenial with a scientific management emphasis—seriously proposed that knowledge rather than authority should be the basic principle behind supervision. Accordingly, he suggested organizing so that workers would be supervised primarily by functional specialists (Figure 9-3). Understandably, managers in that day and time believed that so extreme a violation of the traditional way of managing was not acceptable.

Over the years, however, we have structured many organizations along the lines of this Taylor "ideal." We have done so because of the great complexity in so many modern organizations. Nevertheless, a decision must be made here closely paralleling the line-staff trade-off. A number of supervisors focusing on the same work station will almost certainly create supervision and coordination difficulties. It follows that the "trick" is to use functional competence as fully as can be managed and at the same time to erode as little as possible the conversion of authority into power.[20]

There is one other key power versus authority trade-off involving organizational structure that must be made. It will be described later in our discussion of recent developments involving the gap between authority and power. We will conclude our thinking about trade-offs here, therefore, by noting one that is not a consequence of organizational structure. It is just as exasperating to top management, however, as any of the others. Often called the *competence-credibility trade-off,* it focuses on the relationship between authority handling by superiors and the acceptance of authority by subordinates.

Using authority effectively requires a good bit of finesse, but some of those who have been given authority handle it clumsily. Sometimes authority is handled so

[19]Douglas McGregor, *The Human Side of Enterprise* (New York: McGraw-Hill, 1960), Chapter 11.

[20]Robert J. House, "Role Conflict and Multiple Authority in Complex Organizations," *California Management Review,* Spring 1970, pp. 53–60.

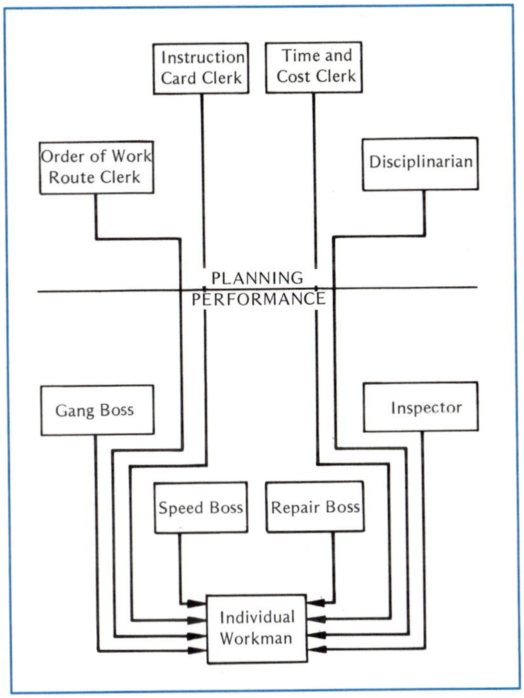

FIGURE 9-3. Taylor's Functional Foremanship. [Source: Frederick W. Taylor, Shop Management (New York: Harper, 1911), p. 99.]

clumsily as to be quite obvious. How shall higher-level managers respond to this mishandling of a crucial organizational resource? As they carry on their search for credibility with rank-and-file people, mangers know that authority incompetently handled erodes acceptance, thereby widening the gap between authority and power. Unfortunately, however, to recognize management incompetence, even by endeavoring to correct it, also risks an erosion of credibility. Therefore, leaders manage this trade-off by sometimes reluctantly protecting authority-handling bunglers and sometimes by rejecting them. In this way, it is hoped that subordinates can maintain a useful distinction between belief in authority and belief in particular power holders.

THE MODERN MOTIVATION PROBLEM

It may seem beside the point to embark on a discussion of the *modern motivation problem* in a chapter on authority and power. But that is a superficial view; as we have repeatedly emphasized in this chapter, the principal task of authority in organizations is to interact with worker reluctance, worker motivation, in the interest of increasing organizational output. Quite literally, organizations can usefully be thought of as, among other things, *motivation-authority systems.*

Much of what is being said and written about management these days makes it seem as if motivation is one thing and power another. Really, however, authority is the basic, down-to-earth dimension of motivation. When what is being said and written about management is looked at more closely, it becomes apparent that virtually everything managers do or are urged to do in the realm of motivation consists of manipulating something (or some things) in the interest of more and better work.[21] Stated differently, the whole area of more effectively motivating workers really is "giving them an offer they won't refuse"—endeavoring to make them happier when they do, regretful when they do not, do more satisfactorily what management asks them to do.

"Soldiering" Is Still with Us

A backward look at some of the historical developments described in Chapter 2 will give us the more specific point of departure we now need. It will be recalled that the problem Frederick Taylor endeavored to resolve was "soldiering," workers systematically doing much less than they easily could have done. The scientific management approach to that problem was to intensify—make more scientific—traditional management techniques for utilizing human resources. It will also be recalled that after half a century of struggling to solve the motivation problem in this way, a fundamental piece of research demonstrated quite conclusively that no real headway had been made toward a solution.[22]

If we were not on the road to a solution at the end of the 1920s, however, perhaps in the 1930s we took a very large step toward more fully defining the problem. Let us, therefore, look at the most tangible finding of the Hawthorne Studies. For one of these studies had an excellent opportunity to examine closely the phenomenon Mathewson had studied much more extensively.

What the Hawthorne researchers, purely by chance, found their microscope focused on at one point was the so-called *frozen group.*[23] Here was a group of workers so cohesively knit together that it could closely shape the behavior of its members. Much of this cohesion, moreover, was built out of a deeply shared feeling that members needed the help of a strong group to protect them from management. The concept of frozenness therefore meant primarily two things. The group's members were frozen together, and the resultant cohesion was frozen out of control by management, much as the water supply in a home is put out of control when the pipes freeze.

In terms of the Mathewson research, one can only wonder how many frozen

[21] Smith, *The Capitalistic Imperative,* op. cit., Chapters 12 and 13.

[22] S. B. Mathewson, *Restriction of Output Among Unorganized Workers* (New York: Viking, 1931).

[23] F. J. Roethlisberger, and Dickson, W. J., *Management and the Worker* (Cambridge, Mass.: Harvard University Press, 1946).

groups were involved in the results he reported. The answer is probably many, because work restriction must almost always be a total group effort if one or two *ratebusters* are not to "give the game away." Note in particular here that one relationship that was expressly seen in the Hawthorne studies was the importance of peer pressure in the shaping of individual behavior. It is then interesting to look at all of this in the context of experience with incentive pay programs. It was suggested earlier that workers may have decided a game that could not be won should not be vigorously played. But perhaps many workers decided a game that could be lost should be intensely pursued, if only in self-defense.

In short, what was becoming unmistakably clear was that we could not take worker motivation nearly as much for granted as we had through most of the nineteenth century. In bargaining terms, Western civilization was discovering worker volition—the willingness and capacity of workers to "talk back" to their employers—and this represented a marked increase in the amount of reluctance to be overcome by management. Employer-employee relations, in other words, really had been a comfortably one-sided affair from the standpoint of managers during the first century after the Industrial Revolution.

It is worth noting several reasons why this marked change in relationships took place. We had been teaching Americans for many decades that power must be used for the benefit of those who are controlled by it. The task of developing viable labor organizations in a capitalistic society was well underway. A large and growing middle class had begun to take a sympathetic interest in the well-being of workers. There was emerging a new public policy that even before the beginning of World War I had put laissez faire painfully on the defensive. Vastly improved transportation, coupled with a dramatic advance of urbanization, had made workers much less dependent upon a single employer. A greatly enlarged capital investment per worker was making the exercise of any given level of volition by workers much more consequential for the organization.

What is more important, however, is that the "talking back" dimension of what was happening became both more frequent and more sophisticated after the Taylorites made "soldiering" a major issue. For example, workers' experiences with incentive pay program speed-up practices heightened their "soldiering" inclinations. Also, during the 1920s, a prime management endeavor was to

The Divine Right of Property

As late as 1904 it could seriously be said by a prominent industrialist: "The rights and interests of the laboring man will be protected and cared for not by the labor agitators but by the Christian men to whom God in his infinite wisdom has given the control of the public interests of the country."

Howard R. Smith, *Government and Business* (New York: Ronald, 1958), p. 212.

weaken labor unions.[24] It is not surprising that workers responded to that assault by "talking back" in other ways. An obvious possibility was the work restriction so thoroughly documented by Professor Mathewson and the Hawthorne Studies.

It follows that this phenomenon would almost certainly be with us from then on. A cartoon from the days of student unrest in the late 1960s shows a mother and her high school daughter. The latter is saying, "Mother, you didn't demonstrate when you were in school, did you?" To which her mother responds, "No, dear, we didn't know we could." Once workers learned that they could exercise much more volition, the employer-employee bargaining process, of course, became much more intense.

The Illusion of Self-Motivation

Given the decisive appearance of more worker volition, how should workers' bargaining partners—managers—respond? How could they best reshape authority in its relationship to power in the interest of getting the organization's work done?

That question of what might be the best response is, of course, difficult to answer at this time. With issues of this magnitude at stake, most of the next half century may be required to be sure how things do work out. Meanwhile, however, let us suggest as explicitly as we can what may be taking place.

As a beginning, let us offer a hypothesis. We may well be in the process of over-responding to work volition. Put differently, we may be reacting too drastically to the need to interact with worker reluctance more carefully. We can perhaps most definitively get at that possibility by discussing what might, without too much exaggeration, be called the *illusion of self-motivation.*

It is not difficult to demonstrate, of course, that there is such a thing as self-motivation; a persuasive case can be made for the proposition that all motivation is self-motivation. As we said in the preceding chapter, "Behavior is what people do. Motivation is why they do it." By definition, the reasons people do what they do are key dimensions of the decision-making apparatus inside them. But that fact can be greatly overstated. This is done by concluding that because motivation is always inside the person, what is inside a worker is all there is to motivation. It is all too easy to suppose that because motivation is an internal process, it is unnecessary to supplement these internal dynamics.

Professor Herzberg refers to the negative and positive dimensions of motivation by superiors, sanctions and rewards, as, respectively, "rape" and "seduction." Professor Levinson similarly decries both "carrot" and "stick" management, calling them "The Great Jackass Fallacy."[25] Daniel Bell observes the powerful tendency of "modernism" to think in terms of the "untrammelled" self.[26] A

[24] Smith, ibid., pp. 325 ff.

[25] Harry Levinson, *The Great Jackass Fallacy* (Cambridge, Mass.: Harvard Graduate School of Business Administration, 1973).

[26] Daniel Bell, *The Cultural Contradictions of Capitalism* (New York: Basic Books, 1976).

booklet entitled *Incentives For Executives* begins by asserting the importance of emphasizing "the other kind of motivation":

> . . . the kind that comes from within—the motivation that, *stripped of outside influences,* constitutes an inner drive. (Italics added.)

And a brochure advertising a job-enrichment program put it this way:

> The key principle to be grasped is that there is no way in which he can motivate his workers. You cannot motivate anybody. Nobody can motivate you. Only you can motivate yourself. In other words, *motivation is a completely individual and internal process.* (Italics added.)

What can be seriously misunderstood about this is the man-environment-system character of human beings—or as discussed earlier, the learning-motivation mirror, which demands that motivation rewards correspond closely to the wants people learned in their younger years. On the one hand, the entire range of our learned behavior potentialities is put into every child by outside influences. On the other hand, it is then outside opportunities and probabilities that draw particular behaviors out of us. At neither end of this operation is motivation "completely individual and internal, stripped of outside influences." Organizational motivation involves leaders using sufficiently attractive rewards that workers will perform more effectively in exchange for these pay-offs. Beyond expectation shaping, in other words, expectation finding must be much of the way those in power go about their motivation task.

As we have emphasized throughout this chapter, power is maneuvering by superiors that makes use of worker motivation, whereas motivation is the behavior that maneuvering generates. A great deal of maneuvering can and must be done by managers to bring out, to focus toward the organization's work, the motivation that is inside people. It is, therefore, as accurate to say that no motivation is self-motivation as to say that all motivation is self-motivation. Employees decide what and how much they will do, but the available options have been maneuvered by authority in the hands of managers. Thus, the bargaining concept of "giving them an offer they won't refuse" does not necessarily mean a coercive situation. If in a work-worker situation there is a motivation to "soldier," such "soldiering" can be prevented if those involved are helped by management to have enough reason(s) not to "soldier."

Protecting Workers from Their Superiors

It is easy to understand that the discovery of volition would make motivating workers more difficult. However, we do not refer to that as the "modern motivation problem." No one argues against a worker's right to participate in bargaining that is of great importance to him. Only when a greatly enhanced volition is vigorously intermingled with "the illusion of self-motivation" do we arrive at a problem of sizable proportions.

Drawing by H. Martin; © 1974 The New Yorker Magazine, Inc.

What we seem more often to be doing is acting as if worker reluctance can be effectively managed, over a wide range of circumstances, by abandoning the task of maneuvering contingencies.[27] More specifically, we have again and again placed decisions concerning workers out of the reach of supervisors, those who have the responsibility for motivating them.

One large realm in which this has been done is labor union negotiating, where public policy has powerfully supported *collective* (as distinguished from individual) *bargaining*. Whatever is settled between employers and employees in union contract terms is then not available for use as rewards by superiors. A closely related phenomenon in government work, where collective bargaining is severely diluted by making strikes illegal, is civil service regulations that similarly protect millions of American workers.

There is no mystery about why we have done and are continuing to do these

[27] Dow Votaw, "What Do We Believe About Power?", *California Management Review*, Summer, 1966, pp. 71–88.

kinds of things. Managers, being very human, are likely at times to deal arbitrarily with subordinates. Moreover, organizations, because they are managed by human beings, are likely to make some of their decisions in terms of narrower interests, rather than larger public policy concerns. Put more bluntly, we are endeavoring to make certain that *human rights* are adequately guaranteed—that the push for productivity does not override fairness—that power does not prejudice decency or crowd out justice. In short, what we are doing is protecting workers from their supervisors.

It will be useful to illustrate this further by noting yet another power versus authority trade-off. Let us call it the *personnel specialization trade-off.* What is involved here is internal—as distinguished from labor unions and civil service regulations as external—constraints also designed to protect workers from supervisor decisions. Thus, personnel/industrial relations departments have been created so that specialists in them can do much of the thinking and planning about how employees shall be handled. In this process, what is in almost every respect an internal civil service organization is created.

One of the primary reasons for doing this, of course, is to prevent certain kinds of discrimination that are legally prohibited. Whatever the reasons, it is clear that what is involved in this trade-off enables workers to play one authority figure against another, just as in the case of line-staff and functional-foremanship trade-offs. Care must be taken to see to it that the gains achieved by centralizing certain personnel functions do not too seriously erode the authority exercised by lower-level supervisors. But note the implications from the standpoint of motivation. However effectively this trade-off is managed, the centralization of personnel/industrial relations decisions must place many decisions concerning workers beyond the reach of those who are expected to motivate them.[28]

Protecting Workers from Motivation

And now, considering the current emphasis on preventing certain kinds of discrimination, we will explore some further implications. The most crucial relationship is the necessity in the realm of motivation to be discriminating, in truth, to *practice discrimination,* if the motivation endeavor is to go well. Discrimination here means that those who perform better for the organization will be treated better, and those who perform less well for the organization will be treated less well. Otherwise, those who are more productive will have no reason to continue to be good workers, and those who are less productive will have no reason to perform better.

Let us then note a number of the major areas within which superiors are prevented from discriminating or distinguishing among their workers. Recent figures suggest that more than one fifth of the total wage bill in the United States

[28] Morris Janowitz, "Changing Patterns of Organizational Authority," *Administrative Science Quarterly,* March 1959, pp. 473–93.

goes to workers in the form of fringe benefits, and this percentage is steadily increasing. Because these are systematically paid out to classes of workers (for example, a one-week vacation with pay for all who have been on the payroll two years), they are not available as *discretionary payouts* to workers on the basis of performance. Moreover, it is also remarkable the extent to which wages are determined in a context of collective bargaining (even in many organizations that have no union), civil service regulations, and centralized personnel/industrial relations decisions, rather than by superiors, who must to that extent supervise without motivating their subordinates.

None of this says anything about those areas in which discrimination as we ordinarly use that term is expressly prohibited. It will certainly not be argued that we must discriminate against females and minority workers in order to further production, or that fairness and equality are beside the point. Rather, what is involved is that these are highly qualitative contexts in which it is often not easy to be sure where one kind of discriminating leaves off and another begins. The issue here, therefore, is one of priorities. To whatever extent we support what is coming to be called the *divine right of fairness, of equality,* to whatever extent we lean over backwards to avoid discrimination of certain kinds, to that extent do we make it more difficult for lower-level supervisors to maneuver contingencies in favor of greater productivity.

One final way of looking at this is also useful. Professor Daniel Bell is perhaps the originator in this context of the term *entitlements.* Whatever an individual receives because he or she is entitled to receive it, rather than because it was earned by effective performance, cannot be used for motivation purposes.

A powerful trend these days is to distribute more and more of the national product in the form of *entitlements* instead of, using this term in its quite literal sense, *earnings.* One of the key emphases in motivation theory these days is how little motivating can be accomplished by naked authority through the use of fear. That, of course, is true. But it is interesting to wonder how much of that is because, in one way or another, we have gone so far toward supplying people's lower-order needs as entitlements in guaranteeing their human rights. The fundamental question then is, how much can we protect workers from their supervisors without protecting them from motivation and from work?

SUMMARY

A major problem of those in charge of organizations is productivity. Their most basic productivity resource is the willingness of rank-and-file organization members to do what they are asked to do. In principle, of course, giving orders is all managers need to do to get the organization's work done. But in the management of organizations an unavoidable gap separates what managers want and what they can translate into performance. Recognizing that gap, we use the term *power* to stand for the extent to which authority can get workers to do what is wanted.

It follows that a basic challenge to authority is to convert its potential into as much power, and therefore performance, as possible. One fundamental here is expectation shaping—helping workers not arrive at expectations that will later have to be, painfully for workers and expensively for the organization, frustrated. Indeed, it turns out that superiors, as they interact with subordinates, must first, last, and always, be manipulators of the way workers see things. Most basically, what must be accomplished is helping workers see authority as less constraining than it really is. But there are a number of trade-offs that must be made; these are situations in which some ways that power might be used to induce performance must be sacrificed in favor of other ways of getting enough work done in the organization.

These trade-offs then merge into what we have called the *modern motivation problem.* This is an appropriate topic in a chapter on authority and power, because what power primarily does is maneuver the contingencies that trigger motivation. In modern times, the bargaining that motivation represents has become much less one-sided than it was in the nineteenth century. However, we have evidently let ourselves, to a considerable extent, be taken in by the illusion of self-motivation. These two elements have then merged into a powerful force that drastically erodes what can be done by using power effectively. The overall consequence of this evolution seems to be a large and still growing phenomenon that might, with considerable accuracy, be called "protecting workers from work."

Assignments

9-1. Explain why there is a gap between authority and power and why that gap is as large as it is.

9-2. Explain what is meant by the idea that power is a key element in a motivation bargain.

9-3. Why is *expectation shaping,* in the sense of limiting aspirations, so much more important than *expectation finding,* which means learning what workers want and giving it to them in exchange for their output?

9-4. Which portion, or elements, in a work force would be most readily controlled through *lottery motivation?* Which would be least readily controlled that way? In both cases, why?

9-5. Explain the *law of the situation* in terms of using power more effectively by keeping it less visible.

9-6. Explain *the paradox of control* in terms of two-way bargaining. Why is this kind of bargaining worked out implicitly rather than explicitly?

9-7. Why in power-motivation dynamics are trade-offs made?

9-8. Explain the *illusion of self-motivation.*

9-9. What are the principal ways in which motivation and authority-power are related to one another?

9-10. What are the major differences between the motivation problem Frederick Taylor confronted and what is here called the *modern motivation problem?* How did we get from there to here?

Case 9-1

MOLLY'S DILEMMA

A strictly enforced company rule states that any employee leaving his or her area of work without first obtaining permission from the responsible supervisor shall be considered to have quit his job.

Molly Cummings reported for work as usual on the second shift one Wednesday afternoon. Shortly after she arrived, she asked her supervisor if she might be absent during the second half of the shift to attend a PTA meeting.

The supervisor denied her request in a friendly, courteous manner, explaining that if she excused Molly to go to PTA, she would in all fairness have to assent to any other similar request from anyone else.

Molly replied that in that case she should not have reported for work at all. The fact is that because she had a perfect attendance record for the year to date, she could have been absent the entire shift without fear of disciplinary action. (In this organization, four such AWOL's within a year means automatic discharge.)

Because only a half hour is allowed for lunch, employees eat in the company canteen. However, at lunch time this day, Molly left the plant and did not return for the remainder of the shift.

When she reported for work the following afternoon, her supervisor informed her that because she had walked off the job, she was presumed to have quit—that, in other words, she was no longer working there.

Within minutes, Molly, accompanied by her shop steward, was in the office of the personnel director filing a grievance.

1. How well, or otherwise, do you believe this supervisor handled Molly's initial request? Explain.
2. To what extent should an employer endeavor to accommodate employees' personal business? Why?
3. Explain what has happened in this situation from the standpoint of converting authority into power.
4. How should the situation regarding Molly be resolved?

Case 9-2

HOSRSEPLAY

John Jones was operator-lead man on a machine requiring a three-man crew. He, along with his crew, reported for work on the third shift on a Friday night. They were given three orders that were to be run. These orders required a little extra effort over average runs, but standards were attainable.

In the incentive system used in this organization, 80% efficiency or less is rewarded with minimum pay. The maximum that can be earned is 120%, this spread amounting to 70 or 75 cents an hour pay difference. Average efficiency is 110%.

John and his crew made the setup on the first order and ran the order with an efficiency of 86%. The second order was set up and run with an efficiency of 72%.

By that time, the supervisor had put up with this dragging of feet as long as he thought he could. He approached John and asked if there was some difficulty that was holding down efficiency. The answer John gave was that he was having a hard time getting his crew to work together.

The supervisor thought this over for a couple of minutes and then told John that if they didn't pick up their speed, he and his crew would be sent home for the remainder of the shift.

John's reply was, "I'll see what I can do."

The supervisor went on with his rounds, making a mental note to check back in 30 to 45 minutes to see what improvement had been made. A little less than an hour later, he returned to John's operation. As he approached, Tom Brown, first helper on the crew, came around the machine holding a piece of board fashioned into a banjo.

"Horseplay!" The supervisor now felt that he had had it—and then some. He checked the crew's efficiency and found it only 56%. The men were sent home two and a half hours before the end of the shift.

They filed a grievance asking for pay for the two and a half hours. Their reason was that the union contract stated they would not be sent home as long as work was available for their machine.

1. What does this situation tell us about what power cannot do?
2. What does it tell us about the work-reward bargain in which these workers are interested?
3. What thoughts do you have about the grievance that has been filed? What thoughts about the contract the supervisor's action is said to violate?
4. In some organizations, horseplay is all but prohibited. What do you think of that way of getting at this problem?

References

ARDREY, ROBERT. *The Social Contract.* New York: Atheneum Publishers, 1970.

BERLE, A. A. *Power.* New York: Harcourt Brace Jovanovich, Inc., 1969.

BLAU, PETER M. *Exchange and Power in Social Life.* New York: John Wiley & Sons, Inc., 1967.

DALTON, MELVILLE. *Men Who Manage.* New York: John Wiley & Sons, Inc., 1959.

ETZIONI, AMITAI. *A Comparative Analysis of Complex Organizations.* New York: The Free Press, 1961.

GOLEMBIEWSKI, ROBERT T. *Organizing Men and Power.* Chicago: Rand McNally & Company, 1967.

GROSS, BERTRAM M. *Organizations and Their Managing.* New York: The Free Press, 1964.

LASSWELL, HAROLD P., AND ABRAHAM KAPLAN. *Power and Society.* New Haven, Conn.: Yale University Press, 1950.

MCCLELLAND, DAVID C. *Power.* New York: Irvington, 1975.

MACIVER, ROBERT M. *The Web of Government.* New York: Macmillan Publishing Co., Inc., 1947.

MACHIAVELLI, NICCOLO. *The Prince.* (written in the early sixteenth century.)

ORWELL, GEORGE. *Animal Farm.* New York: New American Library, 1946.

PRESTHUS, R. V. *The Organizational Society.* New York: Alfred A. Knopf, Inc., 1962.

SELZNICK, PHILIP. *TVA and the Grass Roots.* Berkeley, Calif.: University of California Press, 1949.

SKINNER, B. F. *Beyond Freedom and Dignity.* New York: Alfred A. Knopf, Inc., 1972.

GENE DYSON
President, Georgia Business & Industry Association

Prior to joining GBIA 14 years ago, Mr. Dyson worked for the General Motors Corporation. As a result of appointments by Governors Carter and Busbee, he is the only chairman the Georgia World Congress Center Authority has ever had, serving in this capacity for more than five years. He is also the vice-chairman of the Georgia Economic Development Council.

Named twice as one of the Outstanding Young Men in America, Dyson is listed in *Who's Who* and is a Certified Association Executive. He has recently been chosen as the Outstanding Association Executive in Georgia and as the Outstanding State Association Executive in America.

Executive Commentary
A Perspective on Power

What is power?

Power is almost as elusive to define as sex appeal or charisma. You either have it or you don't—at least so it seems. But power can be acquired. Bookstores and newsstands are filled with self-help books by authors who profess various ways and means to get and keep power. Some say a corner office connotes power and that such symbols as tape dispensers and staplers on your desk top do not. Conservative clothes intimidate. And the hype goes on. Another new book, another new theory.

But power does not come from a corner office, or a clean desk top, or a pin-stripe suit. Power comes from within—from knowing who you are. It is your sense of self that equips you to deal with the myriad of roles you encounter on a daily basis. External trappings cannot give you power; internal confidence can.

Power, in essence, is the ability to make things happen, to get things done. It is your ability to work with others and, at the same time, command their respect. Power is motivating subordinates to accomplishment. Power is acquired by knowing who you are, being aware of your shortcomings as well as your strengths. Power is not using every opportunity to prove your own importance. Power is having others work for you because their importance somehow depends on your importance. Individuals with inflated egos rarely achieve power as it equates with motivating others to perform. They are sometimes found in positions of authority, but authority and power are not necessarily synonymous.

Authority is simply a designated role inherent in any management position. Authority equals "person in charge," but the "person in charge" does not always cause things to happen. The boss is always in charge, but unless his "people skills," his ability to command respect, and his credibility are strong, he has only authority, not power. And to have the necessary people skills, one must know himself and be comfortable with who he is, and recognize the strengths and weaknesses of others. Let me illustrate the importance of people skills in differentiating between authority and power.

> *The small office had a casual, friendly atmosphere, and employees and supervisors were on a first name basis. This was one of the factors that appealed to Susan when she considered accepting the secretarial position there. Margaret Malone, the chief executive officer, was about 45 years old and made a positive first impression as a dynamic, aggressive, and busy person. During Susan's job interview, Margaret was often paged on the office intercom for phone calls. "Margaret, you have a call on line one." One of Susan's new duties was to answer the telephone. A call came in for the "Boss," and Susan activated the intercom. "Margaret," she said. "you have a call on line one." It was at that point that Susan's fascination with her new job ended. "Margaret" flew out of her office in a rage. "You," she said, shaking her finger at Susan, "are NOT to call me Margaret." To you and the other secretaries, I am Mrs. Malone!*

Gone was respect, and power. Authority had definitely been asserted. Mrs. Malone had certainly reinforced that she was "the boss." But using this everyday occurrence to prove her own importance was self-defeating. Mrs. Malone's role as boss was already recognized by the staff. But evidently her personal sense of self was lacking. Mrs. Malone needed to prove that she was more important than those who worked under her. However, the price she paid for the assertion was the loss of power. Her ability to work with others, to command their respect, and to motivate them to accomplishment was sacrificed for a moment of glory in playing the role, "I am the boss."

Respect is not something you can demand from subordinates. Persuasiveness, your ability to cause something to happen, your power is largely a matter of having people agree with you because they *want to*. Not because you have demanded it.

Knowing what power is—and isn't—is a keystone to successful management.

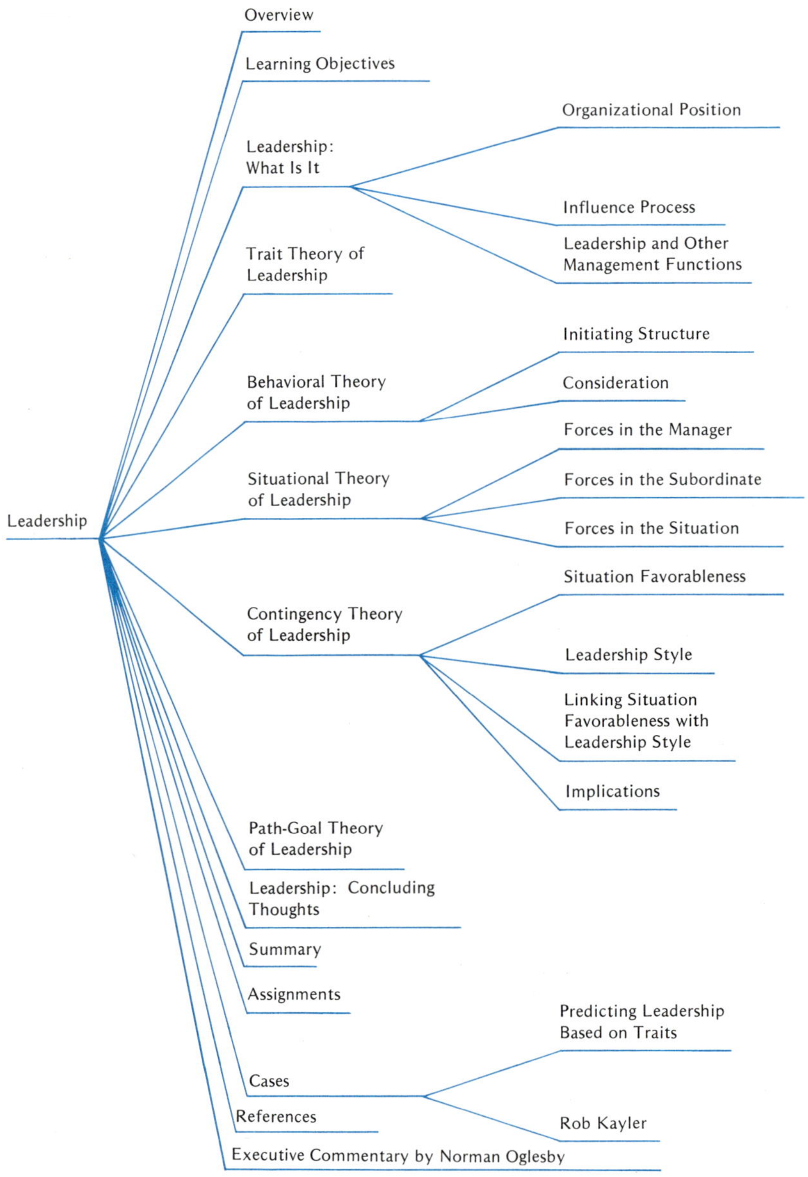

Leadership
Overview
Learning Objectives
Leadership: What Is It
Organizational Position
Influence Process
Leadership and Other Management Functions
Trait Theory of Leadership
Behavioral Theory of Leadership
Initiating Structure
Consideration
Situational Theory of Leadership
Forces in the Manager
Forces in the Subordinate
Forces in the Situation
Contingency Theory of Leadership
Situation Favorableness
Leadership Style
Linking Situation Favorableness with Leadership Style
Implications
Path-Goal Theory of Leadership
Leadership: Concluding Thoughts
Summary
Assignments
Cases
Predicting Leadership Based on Traits
Rob Kayler
References
Executive Commentary by Norman Oglesby

10

LEADERSHIP

OVERVIEW

Leadership is one of the most important behavioral roles assumed by managers in their efforts to make organizations perform. Leadership is much more than simply a behavioral role or position, however. Although leadership is viewed by some as an organizational position, it is most typically viewed in the management and behavioral literature as a process of influencing others towards the achievement of the organization's objectives.

It is sometimes difficult to engage in a separate discussion of leadership because it permeates so many of the management functions discussed and is intertwined with the other behavioral topics. In addition, it is a function that transcends the kind of formal organizations we have been addressing. Thus, empirical studies of leadership demonstrate that it is a global term that is indiscriminately used to describe such varied roles as politician, soldier, playground leader, committee chairman, business executive, or club president. Regardless of these various usages, we will look at the theories of leadership that have evolved for the most part in the realm of business organizations.

In this chapter, we intend to examine carefully what is meant by leadership, discuss its relationship to other management processes and functions, and explore the particulars of the various theories or views of leadership that have evolved in the management body of knowledge.

Learning Objectives

This chapter is especially intended to help the student:

1. Differentiate between leadership as a position and as an active process.

2. **Relate leadership to the other management functions.**
3. **Appreciate the evolution of leadership theory from its beginnings as a trait theory to the modern path-goal theory.**
4. **Learn, especially in the context of thinking about management, the meaning of the following concepts:**

trait theory	**consideration**
behavioral theory	**situation favorableness**
situational theory	**least-preferred co-worker**
contingency theory	**leadership style**
initiating structure	**path-goal theory**

LEADERSHIP: WHAT IS IT?

Leadership can be conceived of in two basic ways: as an *organizational position*, or as an *influence process*. As an organizational position, leadership refers to the individual who has been placed in a leadership role by management. According to this view, all managers are leaders by definition. The deficiency in this view is that it does not emphasize the *dynamic* aspect of the manager's role but, rather, stresses the static occupation of a post of authority within the organization.[1] Furthermore, we all know of individuals who are managers or who have held formally designated roles that make them the leader by definition, but they are not really leaders in other senses of the word.

The other meaning of leadership suggests that to be a leader one must *inspire* others to follow. This view suggests the dynamics of leadership; that is, that leadership is a *process of influencing* others towards the achievement of the organization's objectives.

The distinction between leadership as an organizational position and leadership as an influence process is brought into clearer focus when we pose the questions, Is a manager also a leader? and Is a leader also a manager? Ideally, the answers to both of these questions would be "yes." In reality, however, we find that neither of these statements is necessarily true. As to the first question, organizations commonly have individuals who are managers by virtue of their official positions but who simply do not have the capacity or ability to energize others. Similarly, there are those in organizations who truly inspire or influence others but are not managers in the position sense. An example of the latter would be an *informal leader* in a work group or department. Informal leaders do not have organizational sanction for their positions, but their charisma, unique personalities, interpersonal skills, or expertise provide them with a capacity or ability to influence others.

[1]For an interesting discussion of this distinction, see Charles R. Holloman, "Leadership and Headship: There Is a Difference," *Personnel Administration*, July-August 1968, pp. 38–44.

What Is Leadership?

In a recent management development seminar, one of the authors posed the question, "What is leadership?" The answers given by these practicing managers suggest a rather broad view of leadership. The prevailing view was, however, that the ability to inspire or influence others is what it is all about.

A sampling of the answers received follows:

1. "Is the ability to inspire in others the desire to perform."
2. "Certain traits an individual has that influences others."
3. "The ability to inspire others to perform or work."
4. "The ability to direct and control the actions of others toward a set goal."
5. "Processes by which you direct others."
6. "Provide atmosphere to result in motivation."

The focus in the chapter on motivation was on developing reward systems to energize the behavior of others. In the chapter on authority and power, we stressed the importance of those two attributes in channeling behavior. Now, in this chapter on leadership, we discuss the importance of the manager using himself—his own interpersonal style—to shape employees' behavior. Thus we see the essential role of three different but interrelated emphases that managers use to get employees to comply with their wishes.

Leadership and Other Management Functions

How does leadership relate to other management functions such as motivating, planning, organizing, and controlling? Leadership is certainly *implicit* in the effective accomplishment of these other functions. Consequently, these functions are interrelated. Leadership and motivation are closely interrelated, for example. They resemble two sides of the same coin in that knowing something about each is essential to effective management. For a manager to effectively influence others toward organizational objectives, the manager must be able to diagnose the motivational state of the individuals and groups with whom he is working. Similarly, even though the manager may have a firm grasp of the motivational characteristics of his subordinates, that does not necessarily mean he has the ability to effectively use such information for influence purposes. Leadership and motivation, therefore, must operate in tandem.

Leadership is also related to the management processes of planning, organizing, and controlling. These functions become intertwined and inseparable. The total manager would be one who possessed technical, administrative, and behavioral proficiency with respect to each of these crucial functions. It would be desirable, then, to develop managers in all facets of effectiveness, as defined by these essential processes, if the most competent leaders are wanted. Leadership as a capacity and ability to influence, ideally cuts through and permeates the traditional management functions.

The history of management is replete with efforts to identify what it is that makes for effective leadership. In an effort to trace the progress that has been made on this important topic, it is useful to discuss in some detail the various theories of leadership that have evolved over time. The major leadership theories can be categorized as follows: (1) trait theory, (2) behavioral theory, (3) situational theory, (4) contingency theory, and (5) path-goal theory.

TRAIT THEORY OF LEADERSHIP

Very early in the study of leadership it was believed that one should be able to identify those traits, attributes, or qualities possessed by effective leaders. This is the essence of the *trait theory of leadership.* This theory was appealing because it seemed so straightforward—identify those leaders who have been successful, isolate their traits, and assume that all persons who possessed these traits would be effective also.

Trait theory ran into difficulty rather quickly, however, in attempting to pinpoint the specific kinds and number of traits held in common by successful leaders. Traits that seemed intuitively connected with effective leaders—intelligence, independence, friendliness, ambition, integrity, enthusiasm—were found to be present in both leaders and nonleaders and never uniformly present in effective leaders.

Years of research have failed to identify a cluster of attributes or traits that consistently correlate with effective leadership. Some of the difficulties inherent in his search should be noted. First, it is difficult to define traits that are mutually exclusive in operational terms. From factor analysis research, we know that numerous traits are merely variations of a common dimension. One research effort disclosed approximately 17,000 one-word descriptions of leadership qualities found by combing the literature. Another study disclosed that in 106 leadership studies only 5% of the traits identified appeared in four or more studies.[2] A second, but related, problem is that it is difficult to define leadership qualities in a manner that will be generally accepted, much less amenable to accurate measurement.

Trait theory research has not been entirely fruitless, however. R. M. Stogdill, in a classic 1948 article, reports his review of a large number of empirical studies of personal factors associated with leadership.[3] His conclusions suggested that there are a few dimensions of leaders by which they stand out from others. Two key dimensions were height and intelligence; leaders tended to be taller and more

[2]James J. Cribbin, *Effective Managerial Leadership* (New York: American Management Associations, Inc., 1972), pp. 29–30.

[3]R. M. Stogdill, "Personal factors associated with leadership: A survey of the literature," *Journal of Psychology,* 1948, **25:** pp. 35–71.

intelligent. Other identifiable traits that seemed to stand out with some reliability were knowledge, insight, verbal fluency, originality, and initiative. Another reason Stogdill's review of 30 years or so ago stands out was his identification of a number of studies that suggested leadership traits as varying with the situation, a factor that will take on more importance in our discussion later.

Most serious trait theory research ended in the 1950s because of the frustration of being unable to pin down a reliable set of traits associated with effective leadership. Trait theory was the point of departure, however, for more intensive thought about the nature of leadership. What would have been the implications for management had the trait approach proved successful? For one thing, it might have suggested that one could not learn to become an effective leader because individuals were either born with leadership qualities or were not. Those born with the proper traits would then be promoted to managerial positions, and those that did not have them would have been left out. Many current managers today, we are sure, are thankful that trait theory bore no more fruit than it did.

The World's Most Successful Leaders

Tredgold justly remarks in his *Human Relations in Modern Industry* that "certain of these qualities did not exist in some of the most successful, or temporarily successful leaders in history," and that "the longer and more comprehensive the list of qualities, the more obvious it must be that their possessor would be of no use as a junior leader in industry, for he would inevitably be in demand elsewhere as a prime minister, or maybe as an archangel." When we consider such men as Hitler, Napoleon, the Wesleys, John Knox, and Oliver Cromwell, or such women as Mary Baker Eddy, Queen Elizabeth, and Mrs. Pankhurst, it becomes absurd to say that a leader should be well-balanced, possess a sense of humour, or a sense of justice. Some of the most successful leaders in history have been neurotic, insane, epileptic, humourless, narrow-minded, unjust and authoritarian; there have been religious leaders with a pathological sense of guilt, political leaders with delusions of omnipotence, and military leaders with delusions of persecution. If the objection is made that we are concerned with industry . . . it is easy to show that the great "captains of industry" have been equally lacking in the qualities recommended by psychologists: such men as Hearst, Ford, Carnegie, and Morgan were by no means paragons of either virtue or normality. Looking at the problem historically, we have good reason for supposing that mental abnormality is no drawback in a leader and, indeed, may be an advantage, so long as he is insane in the appropriate direction. Hitler with his paranoia and Hearst and Ford with their obsessional neuroses were successful precisely because they had these defects and the defects happened to be in some sense appropriate to the existing situation.

J.A.C. Brown, *The Social Psychology of Industry* (Baltimore, Md.: Penguin Books, 1954), pp. 219–220.

BEHAVIORAL THEORY OF LEADERSHIP

Because of the many inherent problems and ambiguities with the trait approach, attention shifted to other notions of leadership. Prominent in the thinking of the 1950s was what has come to be known as the *behavioral theory of leadership.*

The view of behavioral theory was that what makes a leader effective is simply what the leader does, quite independent of personal traits. The focus in this theory, then, was more on leader effectiveness than on personal attributes or characteristics. Behavioral theory had intuitive appeal because it centered around efforts to discover the behaviors in which good leaders engaged. The early efforts in behavioral theory identified such behaviors as communication, delegation, motivation, planning, handling meetings, and so on, as desirable leader behaviors. One real value of the theory was its implication that leaders need not be born as such but could be trained to do the right things.[4]

As a result of research undertaken at Ohio State University and the University of Michigan, behavioral theory became more refined. The overall mission of the *Ohio State Leadership Studies* was to discover the determinants of leader behavior and to investigate the impact of leadership styles on worker satisfaction and performance. The major result of these research efforts was that two relatively independent dimensions of leadership were identified. The dimensions were termed *initiating structure* and *consideration.*

Initiating structure was a dimension that pertained to the degree or extent to which the leader defined and organized the task, work relationships, established communications, and specified goals. Initiating structure was essentially a *task-oriented style.*

Consideration was a dimension that pertained to the degree or extent to which the leader displayed trust, mutual respect, friendship, rapport, support, and a concern for employees as individuals. Consideration was essentially an *employee-oriented style.*

What was particularly notable about the research and identification of these two leader behaviors was that it was concluded that they were not opposites of one another but, rather, that they were relatively independent of one another. Thus, the early view was that they occupied opposite ends of a continuum:

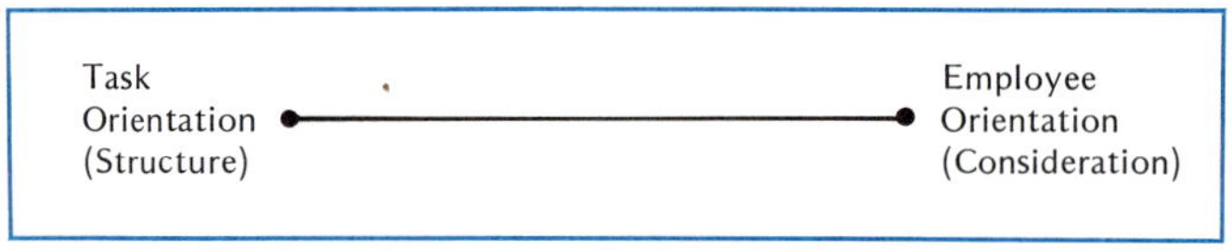

The later view, on the other hand, was that they were relatively independent measures on which a leader could either be high or low:

[4]James Owens, "The Uses of Leadership Theory," *Michigan Business Review,* January 1973.

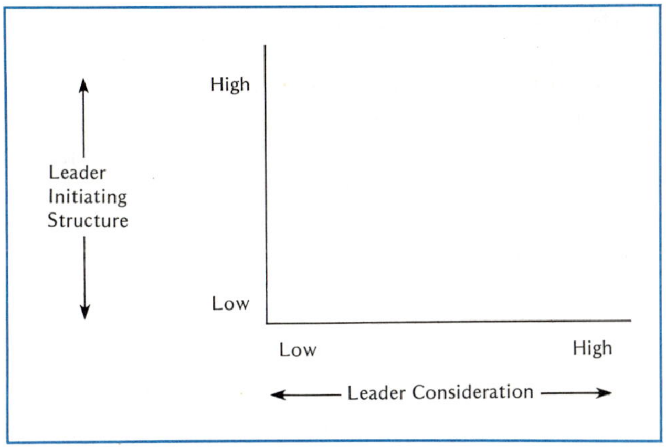

During the same period that the Ohio State studies were underway, research was progressing in a parallel vein at the University of Michigan. The *Michigan Leadership Studies* identified two dimensions of leadership behavior that they called job-centered and employee-centered. *Job-centered* leader behavior correlated closely with initiating structure, and *employee-centered* leader behavior correlated closely with consideration.

Both the Ohio State and Michigan studies were interested in the relationships between leader behavior displayed and various measures of leadership effectiveness or success. The measures of leadership effectiveness most often examined were the *satisfaction* of subordinates with the leader and the *performance* or productivity of the subordinates.

In connection with these relationships, Ivancevich, Szilagyi, and Wallace summarize with respect to these two streams of research:

> Ohio State Studies: *The findings indicate that a mix of initiating structure and consideration leader behavior which achieved the highest effectiveness depends largely on situational factors.*
>
> Michigan Studies: *Employee-centered and job-centered styles result in productivity increases. However, job-centered behavior created tension and pressure that resulted in lower satisfaction and increased turnover and absenteeism. Employee-centered is the best leadership style.*[5]

Although the contrasting orientations toward the task and toward employees were identified several decades ago, research into these two dimensions continues. The finding that there were situational variables that seemed to dictate the needed mix of task-employee orientations paved the way for further thinking about leadership theory.

[5]John M. Ivancevich, Andrew D. Szilagyi, Jr., and Marc J. Wallace, Jr., *Organizational Behavior and Human Performance* (Pacific Palisades, Calif.: Goodyear Publishing Co., 1977), p. 281.

SITUATIONAL THEORY OF LEADERSHIP

Bridging the gap between behavioral theory and situational theory stands the classic article by Robert Tannenbaum and Warren H. Schmidt.[6] Although these authors cannot be credited with inventing or discovering situational theory—for its roots appeared many years before—they did perhaps more than anyone else to popularize the view that the leader behavior displayed was a function of a number of situational variables. Their article was so popular, in fact, that it was published again in an update in 1973.[7]

Although Tannenbaum and Schmidt were not the first to conceptualize leader behaviors or styles along a continuum ranging from autocratic to free rein, they were among the first to spell out what factors needed to be considered in choosing a leadership pattern. Their basic view was that managers had a choice of leadership style, as portrayed in Figure 10-1.

The continuum shows seven basic positions, or choices, of leader behavior. Note that unlike the behavioral theory discussed earlier, particularly the identification of initiating structure and consideration as relatively independent emphases, this model assumes a continuum ranging from boss-centered to subordinate-centered leadership. Close attention should be given to the verbal descriptions of the leader behaviors at each of the seven points. One can see that the main theme at each point is the degree of participation or involvement in decision making allowed by the subordinate. It is for this reason that participation or participative management is frequently discussed as a leadership topic. That topic was discussed in Chapter 8 on Behavior and Motivation Fundamentals; therefore, we will not discuss it further as a leadership style.

By outlining basic behaviors that a manager could display, the Tannenbaum and Schmidt work earns its position as an offshoot of the behavioral school. The key to their role in situational theory, however, is anchored to their identifying the basic factors or forces that a manager should examine before choosing one of the leadership patterns. They identify three major sets of forces, each of which will be briefly elaborated upon.

1. Forces in the manager.
2. Forces in the subordinate.
3. Forces in the situation.

Forces in the Manager

Forces in the manager are those operating within the leader's own personality or style. Included here are such considerations as the following:

1. *The leader's* value system. *How strongly does the leader feel that subordinates ought to share in decision making? How convinced is the leader that the person who is being paid to make decisions should carry this burden mostly alone?*

[6]Robert Tannenbaum, and Warren H. Schmidt, "How to Chose a Leadership Pattern," *Harvard Business Review*, March-April 1958, pp. 95–101.

[7]*Harvard Business Review*, May-June 1973, pp. 162ff.

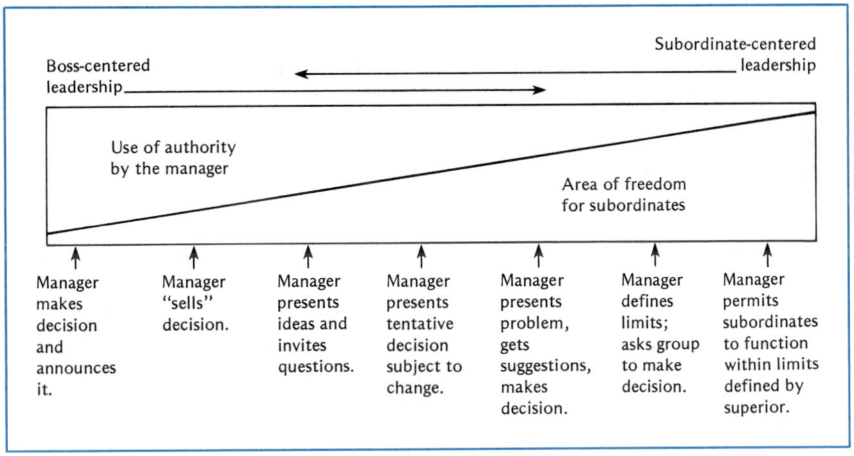

FIGURE 10-1. The Continuum of Leader Behavior.

2. *The leader's* confidence in subordinates. *How much trust does the leader have in the subordinates? What knowledge and/or competence can they bring to bear on the problem?*
3. *The leader's own leadership* inclinations. *Does the leader function more naturally and comfortably as a highly directive leader or in a team role?*
4. *The leader's* feelings of security *in an uncertain situation. Can the manager operate effectively with loss of control over the predictability of outcomes? Can the leader tolerate ambiguity?*[8]

Forces in the Subordinate

Just as the leader considers internal forces before choosing a style forces residing in subordinates should also be considered. Like the leader, each subordinate possesses a personality and a set of expectations that will impinge on the leadership situation, and it is desirable that they be factored into the leadership style choice.

The manager can allow greater subordinate freedom if subordinates have the following characteristics:

1. *High needs for independence.*
2. *A readiness to assume responsibility.*
3. *A high tolerance for ambiguity.*
4. *An interest in the problem at hand.*
5. *An understanding and identification with organization goals.*
6. *The necessary knowledge and experience to deal with the problem.*
7. *An expectation to share in decision making.*[9]

Of course, if these conditions are not present, the leader may be more inclined to choose a boss-centered style.

[8]Tannenbaum and Schmidt, op. cit., 1958.
[9]Tannenbaum and Schmidt, op. cit., 1958.

Forces in the Situation

In addition to forces in the manager and the subordinates, there may exist certain characteristics of the situation that will affect the manager's leadership style choice. The following are pertinent:

1. *Type of organization.* Organizations, as individuals, possess certain values and traditions that influence the behavior of those who work in them. A newcomer to an organization quickly discovers that some behaviors are appropriate and others are not. The leader's style, therefore, may be greatly shaped by the history or culture of the organization. In addition, such variables as the size of working units and the units' geographical location affect what leadership styles are feasible and desirable. Even more dramatic is the comparison of a military organization with a history of autocratic leadership and a high technology research and development firm with a historical climate of democracy or laissez-faire leadership style. The type of organization, thus, constrains which leadership styles are possible.

2. *Group effectiveness.* Before involving a group in decision making, the leader should carefully analyze how effectively the group can work together. Questions that may be asked to obtain this information might include the following: Has the group had experience working together before? Has the group established habits of cooperation? Does the group have confidence in itself? Is the group cohesive and does it have a common purpose? Answers to these questions are essential to the manager in deciding upon a leadership style.

3. *The problem itself.* The nature of the problem faced may assume a significant role in determining the degree of involvement that a manager may choose to use. Pertinent here are whether it is the type of problem in which the group *expects* to contribute and whether the group has the needed *expertise* to be involved with the problem's solution. If the manager possesses the needed information and knowledge to make the decision, it may be better to do so than attempt to inform others as to the facts of the case.

4. *The pressure of time.* Frequently, the immediacy of a time constraint clearly precludes involving subordinates in a decision. Many organizations operate in a continual state of crisis and thus managers are required to maintain complete autonomy over decisions. With less intense time pressures, however, the manager can more fully involve others in the decisions that need to be made.

Each of these—and perhaps other factors—may influence the leadership style choice of the manager.

Taken together, these sets of situational factors play a large role in the manager's choice of leadership style. The basic view of situational theory is that there is no one ideal leadership style but that the choice of style is a function of a number of variables in the situation. Furthermore, alternate styles could be successful if the particular combination or mix of factors is appropriate to the style being used. Tannenbaum and Schmidt summarize situational theory as follows:

> *Thus, the successful manager . . . can be primarily characterized neither as a strong leader nor as a permissive one. Rather, he is one who maintains a high batting average in accurately assessing the forces* that determine what his most appropriate behavior at any given time should be and in *actually being able* to behave accordingly.[10] (Emphasis added)

CONTINGENCY THEORY OF LEADERSHIP

There is some ambiguity in the leadership literature as to whether situational theory and contingency theory are one and the same. The two terms are often used interchangeably, and this adds to the problem. For our purposes, however, we have chosen to treat situational and contingency theory separately but to acknowledge similarities between the two. Whereas some researchers have tended to place Tannenbaum and Schmidt's work into behavioral theory, we noted in the last section how their efforts formed a bridge with situational theory, and, therefore, could be considered a situational theory. Another way of looking at the similarities between situational theory and contingency theory is to suggest that whereas situational theory states that leadership style depends on the situation (without suggesting which style is appropriate for which situation), contingency theory goes one step further and attempts to suggest the type of leadership style that will be effective in specific kinds of situations. Thus, contingency theory, in a sense, represents an evolution in sophistication of situational leadership theory.

Contingency theory research has revolved, for the most part, around the work of Fred Fiedler and his contingency model of leadership.[11] Fiedler and his associates studied numerous industrial, educational, and military leaders to evolve this theory. The attractiveness of the contingency theory is that it is based upon the actual collection of data from managers and thus is undergirded with an empirical base.

In developing the view that particular leadership styles work best under certain conditions, several key concepts must be presented. The two major concepts are *situational favorableness* and *leadership style.* Fiedler suggests that the performance of groups is contingent upon the interaction of situational favorableness and leadership style. More simply stated, the contingency theory addresses the question, "What kind of leadership for what kind of situation?"[12] A brief review of the major concepts will be helpful in understanding Fiedler's theory. Figure 10-2 conceptualizes contingency theory.

Situational Favorableness

The favorableness of a situation for a leader consists of three main elements: (1) leader-member relations, (2) task structure, and (3) position power of the leader.

[10]Tannenbaum and Schmidt, ibid.

[11]Fred E. Fiedler, *A Theory of Leadership Effectiveness* (New York: McGraw-Hill, 1967).

[12]Fred E. Fiedler, "Validation and Extension of the Contingency Model of Leadership Effectiveness: A Review of Empirical Findings," *Psychological Bulletin,* Vol. 76, No. 2, 1971, pp. 128–148.

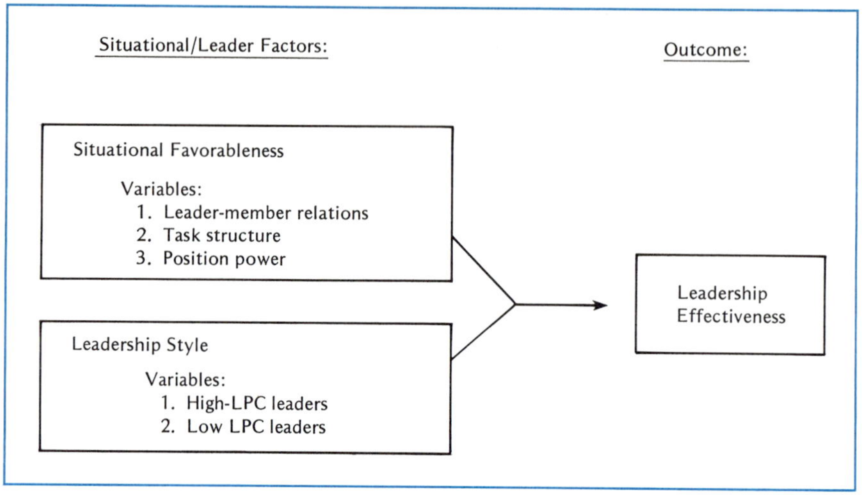

FIGURE 10-2. Contingency Theory Conceptualized.

Leader-Member Relations. Fiedler's basic view is that leaders have more power and influence if they have a good working relationship with their members (employees, subordinates, co-workers) than if they do not. Thus, the more friendly the leader-member relations, the easier it is for the leader to obtain good group cooperation and effort. Leader-member relations can range from good to poor.

Task Structure. If a task is more highly structured, specified, or programmed, the situation is more favorable for the leader. In these situations the leader has more influence. As Fiedler states:

> *It is easier, for example, to be a leader whose task it is to set up a sales display according to clearly delineated steps than it is to be a chairman of a committee preparing a new sales campaign.*[13]

Task structure, then, can range from high to low.

Position Power. The position power facet of situational favorableness refers to the leader's ability to influence the behavior of others by the use of coercive, legitimate, or reward power that is inherent in the job. Thus, for example, if the leader's position has been vested with such prerogatives as hiring and firing, being able to discipline, to reprimand, and so on, the leader's position in relation to members is strong. If a foreman has been given this type of authority, his position power would be stronger, for example, than that of a chairperson of a local charity in the community. Position power can range from strong to weak.

These three elements define the favorableness of the situation for the leader. If

[13]Fred E. Fiedler, "How Do You Make Leaders More Effective? New Answers to an Old Puzzle," *Organizational Dynamics*, Autumn, 1972, pp. 3–18.

the leader has good leader-member relations, a highly structured task, and strong position power, the overall situation is said to be favorable for the leader.

Leadership Style

The second major concept necessary to understand the contingency theory is that of leadership style. Fiedler measured leadership style by how high a leader scored on a *least preferred co-worker* (LPC) measure. To ascertain leadership style, Fielder used a questionnaire that required the leader to describe the person with whom he or she has been *least* able to work well—the person he or she least prefers as a co-worker. The description was made on a number of 8-point, bipolar adjective scales, such as the following:

Friendly: ____:____:____:____:____:____:____:____: Unfriendly
8 7 6 5 4 3 2 1

Cooperative: ____:____:____:____:____:____:____:____: Uncooperative
8 7 6 5 4 3 2 1

A high LPC score means that the leader has described his least preferred co-worker in favorable terms and that the leader is, therefore, an employee-oriented or relations-oriented leader. This high-LPC leader is concerned with maintaining good relationships in the work situation. A low LPC score means that the leader has described his least preferred co-worker in unfavorable terms and that the leader, therefore, is task-oriented, tending to reject those with whom he cannot work. The low-LPC leader is concerned not so much with maintaining a friendly, working environment as with getting the work of the group accomplished. Research by Mitchell has produced evidence that high-LPC leaders tend to be more cognitively complex in their thinking about groups, whereas low-LPC leaders are inclined to give more stereotyped, cognitively simple responses.[14]

Linking Situation Favorableness with Leadership Style

Having defined the key concepts in Fiedler's work, the question still remains, "What kind of leadership style for what kind of situation?" Figure 10-3 summarizes the results of 63 analyses based on a total of 454 separate groups. Included in this research were numerous types of leaders—managers of consumer cooperatives, open hearth shop leaders, antiaircraft artillery leaders, members of boards of directors, and so on.

The horizontal axis in Figure 10-3 displays "situational favorableness," classified into eight groups, with variations on the three elements of that measure. The vertical axis displays the relationship (correlations) between the leader's style (as

[14] T. R. Mitchell, "Leader complexity and leadership style," *Journal of Personality and Social Psychology*, 16, 1970, pp. 166–174.

defined by LPC measures) and the leader's group performance. A median correlation above the middle line demonstrates that the relationship-oriented leaders tends to perform better than did task-oriented leaders. A median correlation below the middle line demonstrates that the task-oriented leader performed better than the relationships-oriented leader.

The data suggest the following:

1. Task-oriented leaders tend to be more effective in situations at each extreme—when the situation is highly favorable for the leader (cells 1,2,3) and when the situation is unfavorable for the leader (cell 8).
2. Relationship-oriented leaders tend to be more effective in situations that are intermediate or moderate in favorableness.

Implications

Fiedler's empirical research has shown those situations in which relationships-oriented versus task-oriented leadership styles tended to be more effective. Although researchers have found a number of limitations to the contingency

FIGURE 10-3. Fiedler's Contingency Theory Data. (From Organizational Dynamics, *Autumn 1972, pp. 3–18.)*

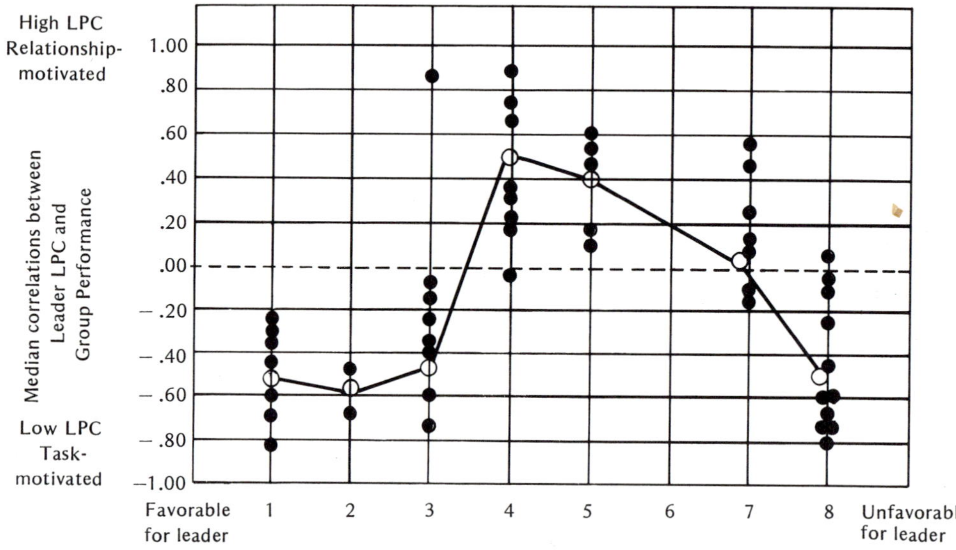

Leader-member Relations	good	good	good	good	mod. poor	mod. poor	mod. poor	mod. poor
Task Structure	str.	str.	unstr.	unstr.	str.	str.	unstr.	unstr.
Leader Position Power	strong	weak	strong	weak	strong	weak	strong	weak

theory research, the general approach used suggests possible directions for further research into the connection between leader style and situations. The Fiedler model continues to be an important source of new propositions and hypotheses to be tested and strongly suggests to us that our search for the one best leadership style is likely to be a disappointment. Fiedler suggests further that leadership effectiveness can be shaped in several basic ways: (1) the situational factors can be modified or changed in the organizations so that the leader's situation more closely corresponds to his leadership style, or (2) the leader can be trained, thus resulting in a more flexible leadership style. Both of these approaches offer fruitful avenues for further thought.[15]

PATH-GOAL THEORY OF LEADERSHIP

The newest theory of leadership is the path-goal theory as postulated by Robert House.[16] The path-goal theory builds upon the concepts of expectancy motivation, as discussed in Chapter 8. Earlier, we stressed the importance in expectancy motivation of the individual deciding whether to behave (e.g., "work hard,") based upon his calculations or assumptions as to the probabilities that his *efforts* would lead to *performance* and performance would lead to *rewards* that were valued. Thus, in effect, expectancy theory is a path-to-a-goal theory in that it addresses those elements comprising the decision process that lead to an individual acting or behaving in a certain way to achieve certain outcomes.

The leader in the path-goal theory assumes the role of (1) influencing the value of rewards to the individual and (2) influencing or improving upon the effort-to-performance and performance-to-reward probabilities. The leader's responsibility in the path-goal approach is summarized by House, who argues that the function of the leader

> *consists of increasing personal pay-offs to subordinates for work-goal attainment, and making the path to these pay-offs easier to travel by clarifying it, reducing roadblocks and pitfalls, and increasing the opportunities for personal satisfaction in route.*[17]

The leader assumes a role in influencing the value of rewards in that he determines what extrinsic rewards are to be associated with work-goal accomplishment. For example, the leader determines to a great extent in some organizations the degree to which accomplishments will be rewarded with salary increases, bonuses, promotions, assignments to more enriching jobs, and so on.

[15] Fred E. Fiedler, "Engineering the Job to Fit the Manager," *Harvard Business Review*, Vol. 43, 1965, pp. 115–122.

[16] Robert J. House, "A Path Goal Theory of Leader Effectiveness," *Administrative Science Quarterly*, Vol. 16, No. 3, September 1971, pp. 321–338.

[17] House, ibid., p. 323.

The leader's behavior can also increase the subordinate's belief that high-quality work will lead to desirable rewards or, possibly to the administering of negative sanctions. Thus, the leader has a number of ways of affecting the worker's "paths" toward his and the organization's goals.

The primary techniques available to the leader to clarify goals or to facilitate subordinate goal achievement are initiating structure and consideration. By initiating structure, the leader has a technique or approach to more clearly define paths for followers. Consideration, on the other hand, does not clarify paths so much as it provides for a warmer and supportive climate in which to operate.

By utilizing the concepts of initiating structure (IS) and consideration (C) along with situations in which they seem more or less appropriate, a number of hypotheses or propositions could then be stated and empirically tested. Some of the more important of these propositions were that the leader's effect on subordinate satisfaction and performance by showing IS and C depended upon whether the subordinate's task itself was satisfying and whether the task was a clearly defined or an ambiguous one. If the task the subordinate was working on was already a satisfying one, showing C will not have much effect—it is redundant. If the task is a boring or dissatisfying one, C will offset the unpleasantness. If the task the employee is working on is an ambiguous one, IS will serve a useful function by lending definition or structure to the situation. If the task is clearly defined already, IS is not necessary and may be found dissatisfying.

Although the research is somewhat mixed as to whether these propositions are supported, the research in general is supportive of the path-goal hypotheses. The hypotheses certainly have a high intuitive appeal, and it is encouraging to find empirical support when it is forthcoming. Perhaps one of the forms in which path-goal theory research might be reported in the future would be in a matrix such as that shown here. All that is needed now is that researchers be able to fill in the cells with decisive research findings. In the meantime, it may serve as a useful frame of reference for thinking about the differential impact of IS and C on subordinate satisfaction and performance.

		Impact on:	
		Subordinate Satisfaction	Subordinate Performance
Factors:	Initiating Structure (IS)		
	Consideration (C)		

LEADERSHIP: CONCLUDING THOUGHTS

One is left with a rather uneasy feeling after studying the evolution of leadership theories. It seems that research methodology for investigating leadership has become more sophisticated, but definite conclusions as to what leadership is, how it relates to motivation, and which theory best captures the truly important facets of individual efforts to make organizations perform are not as readily forthcoming.

This chapter could easily have gone in a number of other directions. Some writers choose to discuss at length the advantages and disadvantages of various leadership behavioral models—the autocratic leader, the bureaucratic leader, the diplomatic leader, the democratic leader, and the free-rein leader.[18] Others choose to speak of leadership as evolving along a continuum of emotional tone ranging from anger or resentment (a hardly desirable style) to excitement (a charismatic style).[19] And, recently, others have discussed it from the standpoint of "what it is that you really want to know about leadership" as a basis for the approach you use.[20]

Our approach has been to survey the emergence of leadership theory through an examination of a variety of means and the progress that has been made. No unifying concept seems to be emerging as the answer to what leadership is all about, and such a development is not likely to happen in the near future. As with other subjects of investigation in management and the social sciences, progress will be evolutionary, with each stage in that evolution making its own contribution to our understanding of what leadership as a process *is* and *will be* in the future.

What can best be said, depending upon how one elects to look at the leadership issue, is that different kinds of conclusions are suggested. We can see, briefly, where these different approaches point. First, we can reiterate that the trait theory is not especially helpful to us. Even if we could find traits that correlated with effectiveness, these findings would hardly negate the relationships we have found in the other approaches. Furthermore, traits are inherent and cannot be taught and, therefore, would not be useful from a leadership development perspective.

The behavioral theory suggested that what leaders do is important. A focus on the task is not the opposite of a focus on employees. The two are dimensions that are relatively independent. A mix of initiating structure and consideration lead to the highest effectiveness, with the mix depending on situational factors. The Michigan Studies suggested, however, that the employee-centered style has the most potential.

The situational theory looks at leadership from the perspective of three sets of forces or factors that moderate the degree of the use of authority by the manager

[18] Owens, op. cit., pp. 68–71.

[19] David E. Berlow, "Leadership and Organizational Excitement," *California Management Review*, Winter, 1974, pp. 21–30.

[20] Jeffrey Pfeffer, "The Ambiguity of Leadership," *Academy of Management Review*, Vol. 2, No. 1, January 1977, p. 104–112.

versus involvement by subordinates. Thus, how much the leader lets subordinates be involved in decision making is a function of forces in the manager, in the subordinate, and in the situation. Some of these forces dictate clearly to the leader what style should be employed. The attractiveness of the situational theory is that it encourages the manager to think about leadership as a range or continuum of styles that may vary depending upon the circumstances.

The contingency theory is an empirically based approach, demonstrating that leader effectiveness depends on situation favorableness and leadership style. Data gathered suggest that task-oriented leaders tend to be more effective in the extreme conditions when the situation is highly favorable for the leader and when the situation is highly unfavorable. Relationship-oriented leaders tend to be more effective when situations are intermediate or moderate in favorableness. Although these findings are somewhat useful to the practicing manager who is able to make these kinds of assessments, the theory has most potential as a research tool.

The path-goal theory is most appealing to those who want to draw a close conceptual linkage between leadership and motivation. This approach builds upon the expectancy model of behavior and views leadership as a process of enhancing goal attainment of subordinates. The manager assumes a facilitating role by selectively employing initiating structure and consideration as the need arises. If the employee is already working on a satisfying task, for example, using consideration may be redundant. If the task is boring or unpleasant, on the other hand, consideration may help offset the unpleasantness. If the employee's task is ambiguous, the leader can use initiating structure to lend clarity to the task. If the task is already clear, lending additional structure may be dissatisfying. The leader's objective, thus, is to enhance the subordinate's effort-performance-reward probabilities.

All this knowledge about leadership has not and likely will not surface as a unified theory, but valuable threads can be found in each of the approaches. Each of the approaches conceptualizes leadership slightly differently, but each tends to complement one another, rather than to be contradictory. Taken together, they tell us a good deal about the nature of the relationship that must exist between and among the key variables in the leadership process. Most importantly, the various approaches convince us that there are a multitude of ways of learning more about the leadership issue and that this diversity can be educationally profitable.

SUMMARY

Although leadership can be viewed as both an organizational position and as an influence process, we have developed the latter, more dynamic view, because it more fully embraces what leadership means to managers, researchers, and others.

After a brief discussion of the linkage between leadership and other management functions, we provided an overview of the major leadership theories in existence today.

The trait theory sought to identify those characteristics of individuals that tended to be associated with effectiveness as a leader. We discarded the trait theory as being a fruitless avenue of research, but we all still cling to the intuitive belief that there are a group of traits that seem to be common to successful leaders. The behavioral theory was a useful evolutionary step, because it shifted our focus from inherent characteristics of successful leaders to what behaviors these successful leaders displayed. Identified with this body of thought were the dimensions of initiating structure (task orientation) and consideration (employee orientation), which carried through the later theories and still remain useful research conceptualizations.

The work of Tannenbaum and Schmidt crystallized the notion that leader behaviors must be associated with situational factors to be useful. Fiedler carried this view forward by empirical research that linked specific leader styles to specific situations. This situation/contingency thrust continues and is woven into the fabric of House's path-goal theory of leadership. In the path-goal theory, the leader assumes the responsibility for clarifying employees' paths to goals or enhancing the work climate, which is done in a significant way by the use of initiating structure and consideration. Taken together, the evolutionary development of leadership theory provides us with an undergirding that will be valuable as new leadership understandings emerge in the future.

Assignments

10-1. Does leadership differ when one examines *formal* leaders versus *informal* leaders? Discuss the differences.

10-2. In this chapter, we argued that leadership differed from other management functions such as motivation, planning, organizing, and controlling. Can you see the differences? Discuss what they are.

10-3. Is there necessarily a difference between a manager and a leader? Discuss what the differences might be.

10-4. Discuss the linkage between the behavioral theory of leadership and the situational theory of leadership.

10-5. It could be argued that situational theory and contingency theory could be called, respectively, situational theory I and II, or contingency theory I and II. Does this make sense to you, based upon the chapter?

10-6. Using Tannenbaum's and Schmidt's leader styles and situational factors, identify the type of leadership style that would most likely be used in the following situations:

a. A fireman instructing his work crew at the scene of a fire.

b. A volunteer leader of a charity drive in the community who is working with other volunteers.
c. A member of a sorority who has been given the responsibility to plan and coordinate rush.
d. A foreman of a drill-press operating group of highly skilled workers.
e. A military officer in peacetime.

What are some of the difficulties you have in responding?

10-7. What characteristics (personality, attitude, and so on) would you tend to ascribe to a person who had received a low-LPC score? A high-LPC score?

10-8. Do you tend to view your least preferred co-worker (in class, for example) in positive or negative terms? What does this say to you about the leadership style you should use on a group project?

10-9. Is there any question in your mind as to whether leadership style influences others' performances? What if we were unable to identify any significant relationships between the two? Should we cease research on leadership?

10-10. Identify clearly how leadership differs from motivation. Be prepared to articulate your answers to others.

10-11. Do research and reading in the literature on leadership. Are there any conclusions we can put into the cells of the matrix shown in our discussion of the path-goal theory?

Case 10-1

PREDICTING LEADERSHIP BASED ON TRAITS

From the following descriptions of two 25-year-old young men, select the one you believe was the most successful in life. Why?

He was pudgy in appearance, genial, open, and sometimes, rude. He was not brilliant or incisive but was energetic, methodical, conscientious, and dependable, and had sound common sense. His personality was not captivating. He was stubborn, cautious, and conservative, and had little interest in ideas. When opportunities presented themselves to him, he accepted them, but he did not go out of his way to create them for himself.

He was of medium height and thin. He wore glasses, had an unpleasant, toothy grin, and affected flashy clothes. He spoke indistinctly, stumbled, and hesitated, appearing almost to have a speech impediment. His companions thought he was eccentric, and his seniors were irritated by him. He was a particular nuisance in class, bumptious, cocky, boyishly positive, know-it-all. He was earnest, enthusiastic, outspoken, and tactless. His hot temper, nervousness, and boyish manner made an unfavorable impression. He was a good student, making Phi Beta Kappa in his senior year. He had an array of interests, and for some time after college graduation, he was unable to decide what he wanted to do in life.

1. What characteristics do each of these persons have that would lead you to think they would be successful leaders?
2. Do you believe they could be successful leaders, given the traits they possess?

Case 10-2

ROB KAYLER

Rob Kayler was the new supervisor of Midvale Hospital's Central Surgical Supply Service (CSSS). This was Rob's first managerial position, although he had worked for several years in central service at nearby Valleydale Hospital. At Valleydale, according to Rob's former supervisor, Rob had been "the best surgical nurse Valleydale ever had."

Today is Rob's first day as CSSS supervisor. Having received no special instructions on how to proceed, Rob decided that he would spend this first day getting to know his staff. He further decided that the best way to do this was to tour the department and visit with each employee on the job. This, Rob believed, would afford an opportunity to see the staff in action and to discuss any problems of interest to them, without disrupting normal routine.

Rob first encountered Ms. Lisa Lux, R.N. After an exchange of introductory pleasantries, the following conversation ensued:

MR. KAYLER: Say, Lisa, isn't that a surgical pack you're working on?

MS. LUX: Yes. It's for cardiac cases. We make them up in advance each week.

MR. KAYLER: Right. I believe most hospitals do the same thing. Are we still using those old sterilization indicators in surgical packs? There's a new type out now, you know.

MS. LUX: I didn't know that, sir.

MR. KAYLER: Let me show you a better way to pack those instruments—and throw this one away, Lisa, it has seen better days. (Mr. Kayler proceeds to rearrange Ms. Lux's work). There! That's what a good cardiac pack should look like!

MS. LUX: Thank you.

MR. KAYLER: You're welcome. See if you can come up with some more better ideas on your own, ok?

MS. LUX: Yes, sir.

As Rob Kayler's tour of the department continued, Rob repeatedly showed why he was called the "best surgical nurse" at Valleydale Hospital. He was able to speak knowledgeably about the job of every employee. He gave almost everyone new instructions on how to do his or her job, and some of his ideas were obviously more efficient than existing methods. Later, at the end of the day, Rob felt quite satisfied that, at least in his first day of leadership, he had accomplished a great deal.

After a relaxing weekend, Rob was asked to meet with Mr. Peter Brucker, the assistant administrator. The following conversation ensued:

MR. BRUCKER: Well, Rob, how are things in Central Service?

MR. KAYLER: Fine so far, sir. I went around and met everyone on Friday, and I discussed the work with them.

MR. BRUCKER: Oh? How did it go?

MR. KAYLER: Fine, Pete. I think they were delighted to find better ways to do things. I tried to show them all I could, and I think they all appreciated it.

MR. BRUCKER: At least two of them didn't, Rob. Ms. Lux, the most experienced nurse in CSSS, and another employee have filed a grievance alleging that they were treated unfairly by you. They called it "unfair supervision," I believe.

MR. KAYLER: What? I don't understand.

MR. BRUCKER: I don't either, Rob. They've never complained before. I think you'd better

This case was written by Norman G. Oglesby. Used with permission.

read these complaints and let me know what you recommend. The sooner, the better.

MR. KAYLER: Yes, sir.

1. Can you explain why Rob Kayler's approach to leadership may have resulted in a grievance being filed?
2. If you were Rob Kayler, what would you do now?
3. How would you respond to the popular saying, "Leaders are born, not made"?

References

BAVELAS, ALEX. "Leadership: Man and Function." *Administrative Science Quarterly,* Vol. 4, 1960, pp. 491–498.

DOWNEY, H. K., J. E. SHERIDAN, AND J. W. SLOCUM. "The Path-Goal Theory of Leadership: A Longitudinal Analysis." *Organizational Behavior and Human Performance,* Vol. 16, 1976, pp. 156–176.

FLEISHMAN, EDWIN A. "Twenty Years of Consideration and Structure," in E. A. Fleishman and J. G. Hunt (Eds.) *Current Development in the Study of Leadership.* Carbondale, Ill.: Southern Illinois University Press, 1973, pp. 1–37.

HOLLANDER, EDWIN P., AND JAMES JULIAN. "Contemporary Trends in the Analysis of Leadership Process. *Psychological Bulletin,* Vol. 71, 1969, pp. 387–397.

JENNINGS, EUGENE E. *An Anatomy of Leadership.* New York: McGraw-Hill Book Company, 1960.

KERR, STEVEN, AND CHESTER SCHRIESHEIM. "Consideration, Initiating Structure and Organizational Criteria— An Update of Korman's 1966 Review." *Personnel Psychology,* Vol. 27, 1974, pp. 555–568.

KORMAN, A. K. "Consideration, Initiating Structure, and Organizational Criteria—A Review." *Personnel Psychology,* Vol. 19, 1966, pp. 349–362.

SCHRIESHEIM, CHESTER, AND MARY ANN VON GLINOW. "The Path-Goal Theory of Leadership: A Theoretical and Empirical Analysis." *Academy of Management Journal,* Vol. 20, No. 3 (September 1977), pp. 398–405.

STOGDILL, RALPH M. *Handbook of Leadership.* New York: The Free Press, 1974.

STOGDILL, RALPH M. "Personal Factors Associated With Leadership." *Journal of Applied Psychology* (January 1948), pp. 35–71.

SZILAGYI, A. D., AND H. P. SIMS. "An Exploration of the Path-Goal Theory of Leadership in a Health Care Environment." *Academy of Management Journal,* Vol. 17, 1974, pp. 622–634.

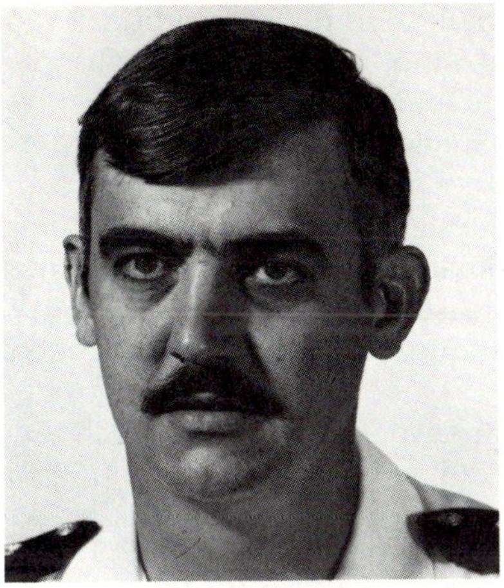

NORMAN OGLESBY
Naval Hospital Corps School
Great Lakes, Illinois

Norman Oglesby is a naval officer who has served more than 21 years in the U.S. Navy. A health care administration specialist, he has held management positions in Navy hospitals throughout the United States and abroad. He previously taught management theory and case studies at The Naval School of Health Sciences, Bethesda, Maryland. He is currently Commander of the Naval Hospital Corps School, Great Lakes, Illinois.

Executive Commentary

The Realities of Un-leadership (for Those who Dislike Surprises)

I still remember that day in 1957 when I decided to join the Navy. A young man ready for adventure, romance, and travel, I saw a large poster displayed in front of the post office in Atlanta, Georgia. On it, there was a full-color picture of a brawny, tanned sailor standing on the deck of a destroyer. Binoculars in hand, with wind and surf in his face, this virile leader of men was obviously in command of all he surveyed. Peering intently over the horizon, he was clearly in charge of several awed underlings whose pictures had been blended softly into the background. A bold caption across the top of the poster proclaimed, "IN COMMAND-IN THE NAVY." I soon learned that getting in the Navy was the easy part. Being a leader, in command, proved to be quite another matter, surprisingly unlike I had imagined.

My first surprise was finding out that leaders rarely get to play the classic command role ("Here are the orders, men; now go carry them out, because I said so.") There are two good reasons for this:

1. Most matters of any consequence are complex, and the leader's freedom to act on them is usually limited by legal, administrative, and resource con-

straints. Some of these are so complicated that it is simply not possible to act intelligently without the advice (and, possibly, consent) of staff experts. Important decisions come slowly and painfully, and they are almost never made in the off-the-cuff, macho manner popularized by generations of John Wayne movies.

2. The "divine rights" of managers are dead—at least, on this side of heaven. Leaders are fallible, and subordinates know it. Given a directive from the leader, subordinates are not the least bit timid about asking *"Why?"* You had better be prepared to answer that question, if you expect good people to stay around very long.

My next surprise was that a leader spends about as much time *being led* as he does in leading. The *crew* leading the ship's captain? Heresy, say you. Reality, say I.

The fact is that a leader must be as adept in reacting to human events as in causing them. As often as not, the demand for a leader to act is not generated by the leader, but by the subordinates. The captain, of course, has final say on the course the ship will sail. But, having set that course, he or she spends a great deal of time *reacting* to human contingencies posed by the crew. Taking charge or taking notes; being tough or being quiet; counseling or commanding—these and many other leadership options are available. Please note, however, that their use is *not* preordained by the captain but dictated by the peculiarities of the *crew* with whom he or she sails—and every voyage is different. In such cases, who is leading whom?

Another surprise was that a leader cannot motivate anyone. All subordinates come with motivation as standard equipment. The best one can hope for is to influence favorably the motivation that is present. This, I have learned, cannot be done with any overnight, instant motivation scheme. On the contrary, *time* and *doing things as a team* are required to build the mutually respectful, productive relationships that every leader wants. If, over time, the leader pays scrupulous attention to matching abilities with jobs, performance with rewards for performance, then *subordinates will motivate themselves.* In the final analysis, they are the *only* ones who can. Given motivated subordinates, the leader's most important task may be staying out of the way—"un-leading"—and letting subordinates do what they are capable of doing (and *want to do*) to get the job done.

As I see it, then, there are a lot of important, nondirective aspects to a leader's job. That poster I saw in front of the Atlanta Post Office (and a lot of management training since) did not prepare me for those passive-reactive parts of leading that I have called "un-leadership." Depending on subordinates, helping instead of bossing, leading through consulting—these under-discussed facets of leadership I learned the hard way, in a 21-year course called Naval Service.

I trust that you, dear reader, will not take as long.

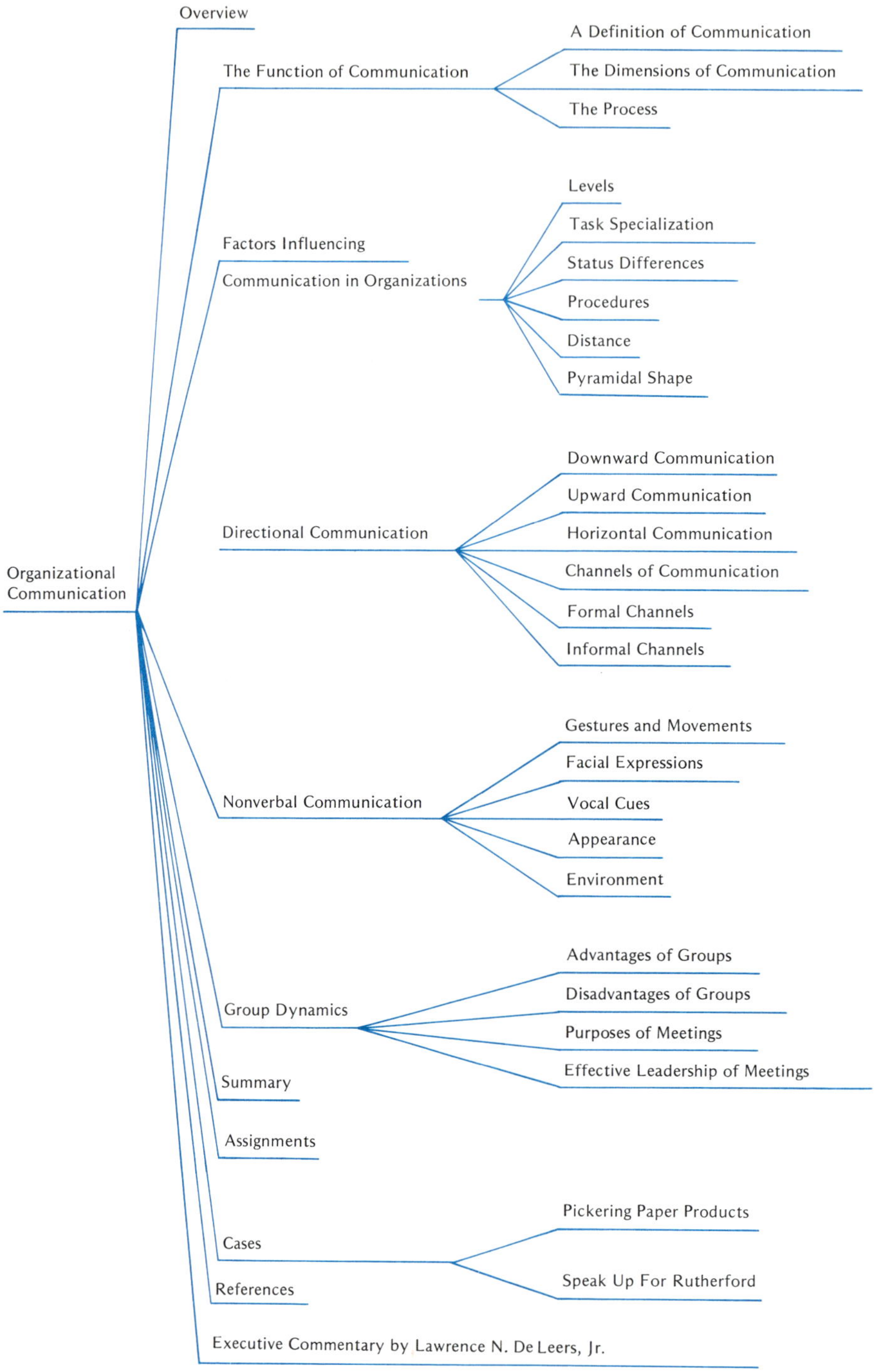
Organizational Communication
Overview
The Function of Communication
A Definition of Communication
The Dimensions of Communication
The Process
Factors Influencing Communication in Organizations
Levels
Task Specialization
Status Differences
Procedures
Distance
Pyramidal Shape
Directional Communication
Downward Communication
Upward Communication
Horizontal Communication
Channels of Communication
Formal Channels
Informal Channels
Nonverbal Communication
Gestures and Movements
Facial Expressions
Vocal Cues
Appearance
Environment
Group Dynamics
Advantages of Groups
Disadvantages of Groups
Purposes of Meetings
Effective Leadership of Meetings
Summary
Assignments
Cases
Pickering Paper Products
Speak Up For Rutherford
References
Executive Commentary by Lawrence N. De Leers, Jr.

11

ORGANIZATIONAL COMMUNICATION AND GROUP DYNAMICS*

OVERVIEW

Some authorities compare the structure of an organization to the circulatory system of the human body, with communication being the "life blood" of the organization. Although this analogy may strike some as overly dramatic, few managers deny the extreme importance of communication to the effective functioning of their organizations. There are very few also who claim to be completely satisfied with communication between themselves and their colleagues.

The purpose of this chapter is to investigate communication within the business organization. Whether the communication is verbal (oral or written) or nonverbal, the communication process is the same. In this chapter, the role of each of the components will be analyzed. Downward communication is traditionally emphasized in business organizations and the horizontal and upward flow of information is often neglected. Because each type of directional communication must confront special barriers, each is examined individually, and ways to minimize the barriers are indicated. Those characteristics of the organization that have the greatest impact on internal communication as well as their probable influence will also be examined.

*This chapter was written by James M. Lahiff, Associate Professor of Management, College of Business Administration, University of Georgia.

Our society and its organizations have a pervasive group orientation. To be an effective manager requires that a person recognize the strengths and limitations of groups and be able to employ groups when appropriate. Overall, therefore, this chapter is devoted to the attainment of organizational goals through communication.

LEARNING OBJECTIVES

This chapter is especially intended to help the student:

1. **Understand the importance of communication to the business organization.**
2. **Recognize the main purposes of communication in the organization.**
3. **Learn the organizational characteristics that most affect communication and their impact on the communication process.**
4. **Describe the significant barriers to the various types of directional communication.**
5. **Explain the possible sources of nonverbal information about others.**
6. **Learn what a manager can do to maximize a group's effectiveness.**
7. **Learn, especially in the context of thinking about management, the meaning of the following concepts:**

communication	**directional communication**
feedback	**nonverbal communication**
formal channels	**group climate**
informal channels	**cohesiveness**
environment	

THE FUNCTION OF COMMUNICATION

Although the functions of planning, organizing, controlling, and decision making can be more or less isolated, the function of communication cannot. It pervades all of the core functions as well as most other activities in which managers participate. The relationship between communication and the core functions is one in which the success of the various functions depends largely on effective communication. Without effective communication effective management is impossible.

Definition

As with any word or concept that is widely referred to, there are numerous different definitions of communication.[1] Figure 11-1 shows some of the defini-

[1] F. E. X. Dance, "The Concept of Communication," *Journal of Communication*, Vol. 20 (1970), 201–210.

communication. 1. the act or process of communicating. **2.** the imparting or interchange of thoughts, opinions, or information by speech, writing, etc. **3.** something imparted, interchanged, or transmitted. **4.** a document or message imparting information, opinion, etc. **5.** a passage or means of passage between places. **6. communications, a.** the means of sending messages, orders, etc., including telephone, telegraph, radio, and couriers. **b.** routes and transportation for moving troops and supplies from a base to an area of operations.

Source: The Random House College Dictionary (New York: Random House, 1975) p. 272.

communication. 1: the act or action of imparting or transmitting (the—of the common cold. . the—of power to the machine) **2a:** facts or information communicated **b:** a letter, note, or other instance of written information (he had not yet read the spy's—) **3a** *obs:* conversation, talk **b** *archaic:* personal dealings **c** *archaic:* sexual intercourse **4** *archaic:* common participation **5a:** access between persons or places; opportunity of communicating (maintaining—between regulars and guerrillas) **b communications** *pl:* means of communicating **1:** a system (as of telephones or telegraphs for communicating information and orders (as in a naval service) **2:** a system of routes for moving troops, supplies, and vehicles in military operations **3:** the function in an industrial organization that transmits ideas, policies, and orders **4:** *sometimes cap:* personnel engaged in communicating **5:** a medium through which information is carried (channels of—in industry) **6a:** interchange of thoughts or opinions: a process by which meanings are exchanged between individuals through a common system of symbols as language, signs, or gestures **b:** close or intimate rapport that is sometimes intellectual and often affective **7:** a Masonic lodge meeting **8** *or* **communications** *pl but sing or pl in const:* an art that deals with expressing and ex- changing ideas effectively in speech or writing or through the graphic or dramatic arts and that is taught as an integrated program at various levels.

Source: Webster's Third International Dictionary (Springfield, Mass., Merriam Co., 1971) p. 460.

FIGURE 11-1. Some Definitions of Communication

tions included in standard reference sources. The different definitions, however, do not indicate major disagreements as to what communication is as much as they do reflect its recognized importance. Harry Bridges, a former president of Shell Oil, attested to its importance thusly, "This business of communicating has become as important as finding more oil."[2]

By communication we mean the exchange of information, whether planned or unintentional, between two or more individuals. The kinds of communicating that managers do are either interpersonal, organizational, or public. *Interpersonal* communication occurs in a face-to-face setting and involves a small enough group

[2]Robin D. Willits, "Company Performance and Interpersonal Relations," *Industrial Management Review,* Vol. 7 (1967), 91–107.

of individuals so that they are able to readily talk together. *Organizational* communication is characterized by the formal relationship between the interactants and by a predetermined system through which information is disseminated. *Public* communication occurs outside of the confines of the organization and is sometimes referred to as external communication. When the vice-president of public relations explains a company's selection of a site for a new plant, it is public communication. The same can be said for the manager speaking before the local Rotary Club. All three types of communication may be described by the same general definition, the sending and receiving of messages. They differ primarily in the milieu in which the interaction occurs.

Dimensions of Communication

Although communication cannot be isolated as a separate managerial function, there are several main dimensions of the communication process that are evident in any organizational setting. These dimensions that help describe the manager's roles as a communicator are as follows:

1. Coordination dimension: Ideas and contributions of others must be elicited and integrated by the manager so as to accomplish the organizational goals.
2. Maintenance dimension: The manager communicates that information regarding organizational policies and procedures necessary to keep the organization operating effectively.
3. Orientation dimension: The manager transmits work-related information to the employees in order to keep them aware of their responsibilities and of the changing aspects of their work.
4. Developmental dimension: Growth opportunities are provided for employees formally through training programs, job enrichment, and job enlargement and informally through a supportive atmosphere developed by management.
5. Decision-making dimension: The manager must solicit varying points of view regarding alternative approaches in order to reach decisions compatible with organizational goals.

THE PROCESS

The model of the communication process presented in Figure 11-2 is typical of many such models, and the same components of the process are present regardless of the nature of the communication. Because communication is an ongoing process and never stops, it should be noted that these components are constantly changing. The humans involved, as well as the nonhuman elements, are in a constant state of flux, and, even in the most mundane conversations, changes

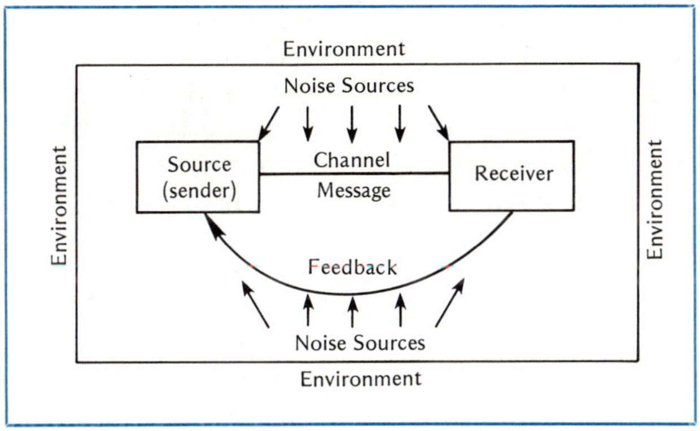

FIGURE 11-2. The Communication Process.

continue. In order for there to be communication certain components are necessary. There must be the following:

1. A source (sender).
2. A message.
3. A channel.
4. A receiver.
5. Feedback.
6. The environment.

Regardless of the type of organization in which communication occurs, the *source* of the information greatly influences the manner in which it is received. When the members of the route sales crew are reminded by the accounting clerk to turn their expense statements in on time, they respond indifferently, having grown immune to such appeals over the years. However, when the same persons are contacted by the company comptroller about the same matter, their response is immediate and they then find a way to get their next expense statements in on time. Not only do different sources elicit different kinds of responses, but they vary also in the credibility attached to them. According to researchers, credibility of a source is comprised of two major dimensions: authoritativeness and character.[3] Research suggests that a person who is perceived as being an expert in a certain subject and who is perceived as trustworthy will have higher credibility than will a source lacking in either of those qualities.

Another research study involving sources of information found that creative scientists rely on more diverse sources of information than do less creative scientists. In the same study, it was shown that superiors, as an information source, were found to be less useful to the creative scientist than to others. The

[3] James C. McCroskey, "Scales for the Measurement of Ethos," *Speech Monographs*, Vol. 33 (1966), 65–72.

researcher speculates that this is because of the role played by the superior, that of administrator or manager. Such a role is unlikely to make the superior a relevant source of research information.[4] Whether the initiator of communication is called the source or sender, that individual cannot be disassociated from the message as it traverses the channels of communication. It will influence the eventual acceptance and interpretation of the message.

The *message* is another necessary component in the communication process. There are numerous factors in a message that influence the manner in which a message is received. Such factors as message length, complexity of the information, and the way in which the information is organized will influence its reception. Whether the message is spoken or written, many of the same factors exert influence on its reception. It sometimes happens that in a manager's attempt to prepare a report or memo for subordinates the manager also seeks to impress a superior, who is also sent a copy of the message. The message that results from such a scheme is usually written at too high a level for the subordinates to understand. Although such attempts are often made, it is difficult for a person to communicate with equal effectiveness with several diverse groups or individuals. There are formulas that can measure the readability of written messages and can indicate the likelihood that the message will be understood. The Flesch readability formula,[5] and the Gunning Fog Index[6] are two such formulas.

Being able to construct an understandable message is a necessary skill in a manager, but that in itself is not enough. Managers should know what to communicate about. Many organizations suffer from communication overload, that is, too much information, and this in part is often caused by management's inability to recognize what should be communicated. As quoted by Aronson, J. D. Salinger had a character in a short story critique another's writing ability in this way.

> *You really are a terrific craftsman. You really know how to write. You really know how to put a sentence together. You've mastered the technique. You know how to take these sentences and string them together into paragraphs. Your stories are constructed beautifully. The one thing you haven't learned yet is what to write about, and that's a really important problem.*[7]

Management could minimize many of the communication problems by which organizations are traditionally buffeted by learning what should be communicated as well as how to communicate.

Managers often falsely assume that all of the messages that they transmit are planned and clearly purposeful. Whereas this is more true of written messages

[4] Conrad J. Kasperson, "An Analysis of the Relationship Between Information Sources in Creativity in Scientists and Engineers," *Human Communication Research*, Vol. 4 (1978), 113–119.

[5] Rudolph Flesch, *The Art of Plain Talk* (New York: Collier Books, 1962).

[6] Robert Gunning, *How to Take the Fog Out of Writing* (Chicago: Dartnell Press, 1964).

[7] E. Aronson, "Research in Social Psychology as a Leap in Faith," *Personality and Social Psychology Bulletin*, Vol. 3 (1977), 190–195.

than of spoken ones, it is far from completely true of either. Many of the messages we send each day are neither planned nor purposeful. In fact, many messages do not employ words; they are nonverbal and largely unconscious. Researchers believe that only 30 to 35% of the meaning obtained from others is verbal.[8]

In any organizational setting a person has the choice of a wide variety of *channels* to use for communicating. When analyzing the communication process, the channels are frequently divided into visual, linguistic, and auditory. Although touch and smell are sometimes included in this list, they are not frequently relied upon. Several channels are sometimes used simultaneously. When a manager conducts a meeting with some subordinates, for example, the visual, linguistic, and auditory channels are all used. If the communication between those parties is restricted to writing, however, only the visual and linguistic channels are employed. In a comparison of the effectiveness of various channels, Dahle found that the combination of oral and written was more effective than was any single channel.[9]

In order to complete the communication process, there must be someone to *receive* the message. When considering organizational communication, however, the sender and the receiver are different individuals, and frequently there are multiple receivers. It should be noted that the receivers possess certain filters, either physical or psychological, which color the messages they receive as well as their eventual interpretation.

A problem with most communication models is that they fail to convey the ongoing nature of communication and, instead, imply that the process ends when the message is received. What actually does happen at this point is that the roles of the participants are reversed. The receiver now becomes the sender and vice versa.

Two other factors that are significant in the communication process are feedback and the environment. *Feedback* refers to the messages sent back from the receiver to the sender. It is a response to a previous message and provides the sender with knowledge of what is being accomplished. The *environment* refers to the setting in which communication occurs and to the various forces which comprise that environment. Feedback and the environment influence the success of the communication as reflected by the response elicited.

Also, the pervasive influence of noise upon all components of the communication process must be considered. Although noise is usually thought of as something audible, from a communication standpoint it should be regarded as anything that disrupts communication. The audible types of noise are the ones most easily overcome. The crew of the paper machine, for example, must work amidst a deafening roar. Because it is futile to try to talk under such circumstances, a system of gestural signals usually evolves. It is difficult to overcome

[8]Raymond L. Birdwhistell, *Kinesics and Context* (Philadelphia: University of Pennsylvania, 1970), 158.

[9]Thomas L. Dahle, "An Objective and Comparative Study of Five Methods of Transmitting Information to Business and Industrial Employees," *Speech Monographs*, Vol. 21 (1954), 21–28.

inaudible noise, however, for the involved parties are frequently unaware of its presence. In any work setting there are many examples of inaudible noise; some actually disrupt communication and others have the potential to do so. When a supervisor gives instructions to a worker, the movements of others in the vicinity may distract the worker and result in misunderstood instructions. The attitudes of workers towards their supervisors and toward their jobs in general also have the potential to disrupt communication. The possible sources of noise are numerous, and the influence of these sources varies greatly.

FACTORS INFLUENCING COMMUNICATION IN ORGANIZATIONS

The more formal the environment in which communication occurs, the greater are the constraints placed upon it. When the communication is interpersonal, that is, face-to-face within a small group or with a single individual, there are fewer constraints regarding the topics to be covered and the manner in which the topics are considered. Organizational communication, however, is more dependent upon the special characteristics of the organization. These characteristics include the following:

1. Levels of the organization.
2. Task specialization.
3. Status differences based on organizational-level constraints.
4. Procedures imposed by the organization.
5. Physical distance between people.
6. Pyramidal shape.

Levels. The levels present in an organizational structure greatly influence the flow of information within that organization. A "tall" organization features more levels and, therefore, more links in the channel of communication. With increased links comes a greater likelihood of distortions occurring. A "flat" organization, on the other hand, has fewer levels and a reduced likelihood of distortions. The tall organization tends to allow for more face-to-face contacts, however, because the span of control will ordinarily be narrower.

Task Specialization. With the advent of task specialization came increased organizational efficiency. Individual duties became more limited and specific and, as areas of specialization were more clearly defined, verbal shortcuts intended to facilitate goal accomplishment were developed. The aspect of task specialization that has the greatest effect on organizational communication is the growth of special jargons. Webster defines *jargon* as "technical terminology or characteristic idiom of specialists or workers in a particular activity or area of knowledge."[10] Jargons are sublanguages that simplify communication within a given area of specialization. Thus, accountants use certain terms likely to be understood by other accountants in communicating with them. Because certain assumptions can usually be made about the level of knowledge of others, it is possible to introduce greater brevity and specificity through the appropriate jargon. Jargon becomes dysfunctional, however, when used by a specialist to communicate with outsiders. Computer specialists and government administrators are especially notorious in this respect. Haney illustrated the problem nicely in describing the efforts of some government scientists to inform a foreign-born plumber to stop using hydrochloric acid for clearing clogged water pipes.

> *When the plumber first discovered that hydrochloric acid was effective, he wrote to the National Bureau of Standards to find out if it was a good thing to use. In his reply, a scientist wrote that "the efficacy of hydrochloric acid is indisputable, but the corrosive residue is incompatible with metallic permanence."*
>
> *The plumber wrote back thanking the Bureau for telling him that hydrochloric acid was all right. The scientist was disturbed about the misunderstanding and showed the correspondence to his boss—another scientist—who wrote the plumber: "We cannot assume responsibility for the production of toxic and noxious residue with hydrochloric acid and suggest you use an alternative procedure."*
>
> *The plumber wrote back thanking the Bureau for telling him that hydrochloric acid works fine. Greatly disturbed, the scientists took their problem to the top boss. He broke with scientific jargon and wrote the plumber: "Don't use hydrochloric acid. It eats the hell out of pipes."*[11]

Status Differences. Intrinsic to the notion of different levels that characterize organizational structure is the notion of status differences between jobholders at the various levels. When a superior and a subordinate interact, there is also an interaction between their roles and this has definite implications regarding organizational communication. When the plant manager communicates with the head of the shipping department, there are some significant differences between them in terms of formal authority and of status. This status difference may result in the department head accepting without question what the plant manager says. Research on superior-subordinate relationships has shown that such a status difference will inhibit the subordinate from transmitting information to a superior if that information will reflect adversely on that superior. Tesser termed this phenomenon the *MUM effect.*[12]

Procedures. Of the many constraints imposed on employees by the typical business organization, the need to *go through channels* has special significance

[10] *Webster's Third New International Dictionary* (Springfield, Mass: Merriam Co., 1971), 1211.

[11] William V. Haney, *Communication and Organizational Behavior* (Homewood, Ill.: R. D. Irwin, 1973), 275.

[12] Abraham Tesser, Sidney Rosen, and Thomas Batchelor, "Some Message Variables and the MUM Effect," *The Journal of Communication,* Vol. 22 (1972), 239–256.

from a communication standpoint. By stressing the use of channels, management attempts to ensure a systematic approach to the transmission of work-related information. It is easier for management to control and monitor the formal channels and to ensure that the attainment of organizational goals is being realized. The formal channels consist of all those recognized by management and illustrated on the organizational chart.

The required use of formal channels is not the only procedure with communication implications for the manager. Organizations differ in their policies regarding such activities as production reporting and personnel appraisals, and most such activities have special meaning for the communicator.

Distance. The greater the distance between the sender and the receiver, the greater the likelihood of breakdowns in communication. This has already been shown regarding the number of links in the channel, but it is not limited to that. Geographical distance is another significant factor that is often reflected in language differences among the widely separated branches of a multinational organization. When the branches are located in different time zones, it increases the complexities of effective communication. Such factors present problems, but they are not insurmountable.

An even more significant problem relating to distance concerns the differing environments of the various business locations. A frequent complaint in the branches is that "the home office doesn't understand us," and that complaint often has merit. It has been shown that perceptual differences can be traced to differences based on hierarchical position or based on different functional areas.[13] Differences between production and sales are a common example of this. From the home office in New York City, it is difficult to envision the environment within which the sales staff in Milan must function. It is equally difficult for upper management to accurately sense the mood of employees based at distant locations.

Pyramidal Shape. The pyramidal shape of the traditional business organization exerts certain constraints on the flow of information. Downward communication is facilitated because there are fewer senders than receivers. Because there are so many more people at the bottom of the organization than at the top, however, upward communication is often hindered. A line worker must frequently wait for a response from above, whereas the opposite is much less of a problem.

DIRECTIONAL COMMUNICATION

A frequent basis for analyzing or evaluating communication is the direction in which messages travel. Message direction may be classified as *upward, downward,*

[13] J. G. March, and H. A. Simon, *Organizations* (New York: John Wiley and Sons, Inc., 1955).

or *horizontal*. Regardless of the type of organization, communication flows in certain directions. Several researchers have concluded that approximately two thirds of a manager's communication time is spent with superiors and subordinates, in vertical communication. About one third is spent in horizontal communication.

Downward Communication. Downward communication has traditionally been emphasized in business organizations. It has been a fundamental concern of management ever since organizations were first viewed as a desirable and effective approach to maximizing the efforts of people.

Most of the task activities of any organization are directed through downward communication. Order-giving and instructions are usually facilitated in this way. However, downward communication is certainly not limited to such kinds of messages. Whenever management attempts to make itself understood to its employees, the communication is downward.

Figure 11-3 is based on a survey of business organizations and illustrates the effectiveness of the organizations' downward communication. It shows how much of what upper management says is correctly understood at lower levels. According to the findings of the survey, the production line workers correctly understand only 20% of what top management communicates downward.

As a message travels through an organization some filtering of the message occurs. Either consciously or unconsciously, both the sender and the receiver of a message emphasize certain aspects of the message and deemphasize other aspects. The greater the number of levels that a message traverses, the more filtering occurs.

FIGURE 11-3. Downward Communication. [Source: Edward E. Scannell, Communications for Leadership (New York: McGraw-Hill/Gregg Management Series in Marketing, 1970)].

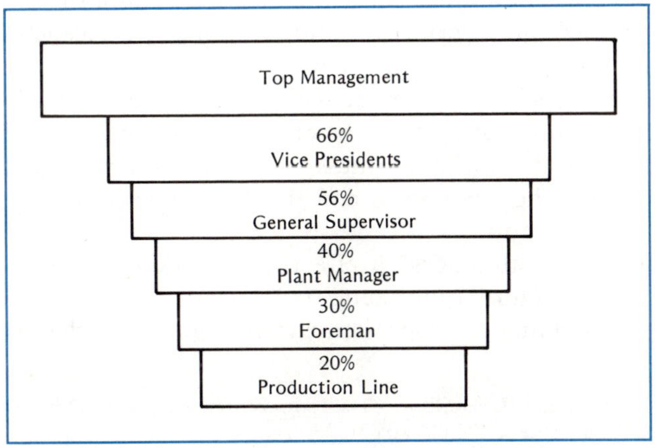

There are a multitude of possible purposes for downward communication. In addition to varying greatly in terms of generality or specificity, it also varies as regards its audience. Whereas reports about production quotas or quality-control information may be directed toward a small number of individuals, much of the downward communication is directed toward a large number of employees, a mass audience, and therein is one of the most significant problems inherent in downward communication. In order to reach these large numbers, management often resorts to the written word and sends the same message out to all of its employees. An alternative approach, sometimes used to reach large numbers of employees, is to assemble them in sizeable groups to listen to the message from their superiors. In either case, there may be a problem with the message, in terms of its appeal to large numbers of workers. Within the work force of most large organzations, for example, there is a wide range of intelligence levels. A message that will be easily understood by one worker may be incomprehensible to another. In addition, some workers will be more interested in the subject than will others. Hence, the former will work harder to understand the message than will the latter whose ignorance will probably not be detected because of the large size of the audience.

Through carefully controlled downward communication, it is possible for management to ensure that all of its employees will get the message at exactly the same time. It is also possible to ensure that exactly the same message will be transmitted to all. Because of individual differences among the workers, however, this mass approach cannot ensure that all the employees will interpret the message in the same way.

The crux of the downward communication problem lies in the long-held view of it as being one-way in nature from sender to receiver without any consideration of feedback. Because the downward flow of information has for so long been associated with "orders from headquarters," there remains a certain resistance within many organizations to the idea that downward communication should be anything other than one-way.

Much downward communication is intended to accomplish two goals: to make employees aware of the information and to gain their acceptance of it. Katz, Levin, and Hamilton have shown that a mass media approach often is appropriate for creating awareness but acceptance will not be gained through it. To accomplish that, the communication must be of a more personal nature.[14] A personal approach is the opposite of what business organizations have long subscribed to in attempting to reach the employees, and therein lies an underlying problem in downward communication.

Another factor that influences the effectiveness of downward communication is the nature of the information being transmitted. Davis (1968) found higher accuracy in the sending of job-related information than that which was not

[14] E. Katz, M. L. Levin, and H. Hamilton, "Traditions of Research as the Diffusion of Innovation," *American Sociological Review*, Vol. 28 (1963), 237–252.

job-related.[15] It appears that information contributing to the accomplishment of the job is more likely to be communicated accurately than that which does not.

Upward Communication. Although the value and necessity of downward communication has been recognized since humans first began to organize in hierarchies, such has not been the case with upward communication. Because upward messages must travel against the normal flow of information, management should overtly encourage the free flow of upward information for there are many benefits to be derived from doing so.

It is through upward communication that management is best able to learn the extent to which its downward messages are being understood and accepted. There are also other ways in which management will benefit from committing the necessary time and resources to the improvement of upward communication. By encouraging upward communication, management is making it easier for employees to offer their ideas and thereby provide a wider range of inputs into the organization than is normally the case. This greater diversity of inputs may result in better decisions simply because more viewpoints have been introduced into the decision-making process. An additional benefit of facilitating upward communication in an organization is that there will often be an increase in the commitment and loyalty of employees to the organization. Although upward communication is usually viewed in terms of its value to subordinates, there are also substantial benefits to be derived by upper management.

Subordinates benefit from upward communication both directly and indirectly. Foremost among the direct benefits is the increased sense of worth that accompanies the opportunity to communicate regularly with one's superior. When workers are asked for their ideas on work-related matters and are otherwise encouraged to communicate with their superiors, they are almost certain to consider themselves more of a part of the organization than if their only role in the communication process is as targets of orders, instructions, and other directives. Managers have more favorable attitudes towards contacts with their superiors than those with their subordinates, probably because the superior's reward power over the subordinate makes such interactions very significant for the subordinate.

A less direct but equally important benefit to subordinates is the opportunity to "let off steam" by giving management their feelings on such things as organizational policies, procedures, and managerial practices. When subordinates are given the opportunity to express their feelings and are encouraged to do so, what results is a catharsis in a more positive direction than might otherwise be the case. When such opportunities are not available within an organization, the employees will often find other outlets. For example, workers are likely to be both more critical and more vocal about their employer when in the outside community

[15] K. Davis, "Success of Chain-of-Command Oral Communication in a Manufacturing Management Group," *Academy of Management Journal,* Vol. 11 (1968), 379–387.

because they are not afforded the opportunity within the organization. Such frustration is also sometimes reflected in a loss of efficiency or general decline in performance on the part of those who are chafing uder such restricted upward communication. Because of their extreme interest in facilitating upward communication with their superiors, many managers, either consciously or unconsciously, underplay the value of eliciting communication from their subordinates, thereby creating conditions that inhibit effective upward communication.

There are barriers to upward communication that inhibit the flow of information from subordinates to superiors. As indicated earlier in this chapter, the number of levels through which a message travels results in a proportionate dilution of that message. Also, as indicated earlier, when the message might reflect adversely on the subordinate who is sending it or on the superior who would receive it, the subordinate will probably choose not to send it. That phenomenon, again, is called "the MUM Effect."[16] Unless management instills a climate of trust and openness, information of this sort will go unreported and what originated as a minor problem can become a full-blown crisis by the time it is detected. Defensiveness on the part of managers often keeps subordinates from pointing out errors made by superiors.

Managers sometimes encourage upward communication but then proceed to ignore it. Their thinking is that providing workers with an opportunity to express themselves to their superiors in itself will make them feel better about their jobs and about their employers. It usually does not take workers long to recognize this for the ploy it is. Sometimes it is the superior's failure to act on previous suggestions or complaints that helps the workers identify these attempts to maneuver them, and what follows then is greater resistance to the idea of upward communication.

At this stage, unfortunately, management sometimes identifies the silence of the workers as proof that there are no problems in the organization. Hence, it makes no attempts to encourage upward communication and the problem festers.

The concept of upward communication has grown more socially acceptable over the years and there is a general managerial recognition of its worth. Many managers continue to feel, however, that they just do not have time for it. It is true that listening to employees is time-consuming. However, many managers who were once beset by problems of motivation or loyalty among personnel can attest to the fact that not listening can be even more time-consuming.

Horizontal Communication. Although managers spend more time in vertical communication than in horizontal, horizontal or lateral communication still represents a significant managerial activity. In fact, several researchers have found that managers devote about one third of their communication time to communication of this type, which includes all exchanges of messages among people on the same level of the organization.

[16] Tesser, Abraham, Sidney Rosen, and Thomas Batchelor, op. cit.

Horizontal communication encompasses several different types of interactions. The most prevalent type of horizontal communication is that among *peers* within a work group. In most organizations, much of the satisfaction that individuals derive from their employment comes from this type of interaction. In addition to providing satisfaction of workers' social needs, it is also through horizontal communication that many job-related problems are solved and decisions are made.

Interactions *between individuals* who are on the same level but are members of *different units* is another type of horizontal communication. Communication between members of different departments typifies this sort of interaction. Because horizontal communication so often involves individuals with a departmental orientation other than an organizational one, therein lies high potential for conflict. When two such individuals interact, there are vested interests to protect, and the sharing of information is often viewed with extreme apprehension.

The third type of horizontal communication is that between line and staff. As with interdepartmental communication, there is a potential for conflict here also. Even though the staff may be viewed by line managers as being of lower status than line, the fact that staff has greater knowledge of organization-wide events and a correspondingly heightened awareness gives staff an informal power that the line comes to recognize. Zajonc and Wolfe concluded that staff employees in fact do have more extensive communication contacts than do line employees.[17] Any differences in formal power can be offset by such contacts and can help explain the dynamics of line-staff interaction.

CHANNELS OF COMMUNICATION

One need only look at an organizational chart to identify many of the communication channels that management relies upon. These are the formal channels of communication, and they are based on such factors as formal systems of authority and delegation of such authority. Many of the messages that travel through the formal channels are routine in nature. That is, they are transmitted on a periodic basis and the receivers of them are accustomed to their regular arrival. In any organization there are regularly recurring reports and directives that are intended to contribute to the smooth functioning of the organization. Because they are intended to guide specific operations, a certain amount of importance is attached to them and more consideration is accorded them than might otherwise be the case.

[17]R. Zajonc, and D. Wolfe, "Cognitive Consequence of a Person's Position in a Formal Organization," *Human Relations*, Vol. 19 (1966), 139–150.

Formal Channels

The formal channels of communication in any organization are the "official" channels. It is through them that most task-related information is conveyed and, because these channels are sanctioned by management, information should flow through them unhampered by distortion and subject to few questions by the recipients. As indicated on most organizational charts, the formal channels can accommodate upward, downward, and horizontal communication.

Prior to going through channels with a message, the sender must select the most appropriate technique to use. The fact that there are usually several different techniques from which to choose greatly complicates this decision. Research of the Bureau of National Affairs (BNA) casts light on some of the techniques and media currently being used in the formal communication systems of business organizations.[18] In this survey of personnel executives, it was found that they considered the following techniques to be the most effective in management's efforts to communicate with its employees. They are presented in the order of their effectiveness:

1. Small group meetings of employees.
2. Regularly appearing company publications.
3. Meetings of supervisors.
4. Mass meetings of employees.
5. Letters to employees' homes.
6. Pay inserts.
7. Bulletin boards.

Although no single reason explains the effectiveness of each of these techniques, each features certain characteristics that suggest the reason for its effectiveness in reaching employees.

Small group meetings of employees provide a forum for true two-way communication. They offer management an opportunity to give a full explanation of its position and to encourage questions that are then answered immediately. Because there is face-to-face interaction, there is an ongoing exchange. Through the give-and-take that characterizes such meetings, management anticipates these two end results: 1) a more complete understanding by the employees of the subjects discussed, and 2) an increased commitment of the employees.

Regularly appearing company publications are viewed as being regularly read by most employees. Some employers mail them to the employees' homes so that their families will have access to them. The content of such publications is often confined to important subjects, and the publications explain the company's position on these subjects.

Meetings of supervisors are intended to provide information to supervisors that will enable them to explain company policies to subordinates and thereby keep

[18] Bureau of National Affairs, *Personnel Policies Forum* (1974–75) (July 1975), 1–46.

them updated on other organizational matters of which they should be aware. Because such meetings ordinarily involve small numbers of supervisors, there is an opportunity for two-way communication.

Mass meetings of employees are usually reserved for important announcements that affect all employees. The source of the announcement is usually an authority who is high in organizational position and in credibility. By disseminating a message in this way, a company is able to ensure that all employees receive it simultaneously and from an authoritative source.

Letters to employees' homes are an attempt by the company to interest the family of each worker in company matters. It is also thought that employees who are contacted in this way will have more opportunity at home to read and think about the message.

Pay inserts are messages attached to the employees' paychecks or enclosed in envelopes with the checks. It is thought that this indicates to the employee that the message is very important so that the employee will attend to it. By relying on pay inserts, management can be sure that the employee will at least see it.

Bulletin boards are relatively easy to prepare. They are considered effective in reaching employees quickly and are easily controlled by management.

Although these seven techniques are believed to be the most effective means to reach the workers, there are many others also available to management. The following are some of the other techniques mentioned in the BNA survey:

posters	closed circuit television
plant tours	videotape programs
public address systems	cassette recordings
advertisements in local news media	memos

Although it is true that more organizational effort is devoted to establishing and maintaining channels for effective communication from management to the employees, various attempts are also made to improve the sending of information upward from the workers to management. The BNA found that the following techniques were thought to be the most effective:

1. Informal inquiries or discussions with employees.
2. First-level supervisors.
3. Formal attitude surveys.
4. Grievance or complaint procedures.
5. Counseling.
6. Exit interviews.

Informal inquiries or discussions with employees are believed to be effective because of the spontaneity engendered by the format. It is thought that real problems can be easily recognized and resolved in this type of setting.

Because *first-line supervisors* are the main link between management and the workers, they are seen in many organizations as a vital key to the success of any communication effort. It is believed that without first-line supervisors who are knowledgeable and aware, communication either to or from the line workers will be neither thorough nor effective.

Formal attitude surveys can provide management with the thoughts and feelings of workers but protect their anonymity. This approach will usually elicit candid responses from the workers, and it requires a minimal expenditure of the workers' time.

Grievance or complaint procedures vary from one organization to the next; however, most organizations do have some sort of system for administering them. Such procedures usually aid management in recognizing areas of potential trouble that may otherwise be considered insignificant by management.

Counseling is considered appropriate and necessary in some organizations for the resolution of employee complaints or personal problems. Skilled counselors are often able to bring out the true feelings of the aggrieved workers.

Exit interviews are conducted with employees who are leaving voluntarily. Because they are about to leave the organization, they usually feel freer to discuss its strengths and shortcomings than they did while employed.

Some of the other techniques employed by the organizations polled by the BNA and intended to provide formal channels for the workers to communicate with management include the following:

Union representatives.
Formal meetings.
Suggestion systems.
Question-and-answer column in employee publication.
Open door policy.
Employee committees.

Thus, there are many different techniques that might be and are applied to formal communication efforts. One last issue to be examined from the BNA survey concerns the *kind of information* companies seek to communicate to employees. According to the survey, companies make an effort to emphasize these types of information in employee communications:

1. Company news and future prospects.
2. Employee compensations and benefits.
3. Personal news.
4. Company rules, policies, and programs.

This survey is not exhaustive in its coverage of formal communication techniques nor in the kinds of information communicated. It does, however, accurately depict communication practices common to many organizations.

Informal Channels

If all of the messages flowing through an organization followed the channels dictated by the organizational chart, management could readily control communication. That is not the case, however, nor is it ever likely to become the case.

Many of the messages in any organization travel through informal channels. This is inevitable as people normally talk to others with whom they come in contact. Invariably, and regardless of the nature of the organization, many of these contacts are with people outside of one's formal channels.

Grapevine is the name commonly given to the informal channels that traverse organizations. In management circles, it is sometimes referred to as the "gripevine." In the minds of some managers it has negative connotations because it is beyond management's control. These managers are the ones who view the grapevine as a cause of many of their problems, so they are not above looking for ways to eliminate it. More realistic managers recognize that the grapevine will not be eliminated, but they understand that they must live with it and that, at some times, it can be a helpful tool for management to use. The grapevine has earned its dubious reputation by being regularly associated with rumors. For that reason, many managers perceive it as the distribution system for the local rumor mill.

To this day many also misperceive the manner in which the grapevine operates. Although it is often viewed as a chain along which messages travel, Davis found that it operated in clusters with one person telling several, not each of whom would relay the information to others. Those who did pass it along would usually tell more than one, and the process would be repeated.[19] Figure 11-4 illustrates how the cluster grapevine operates.

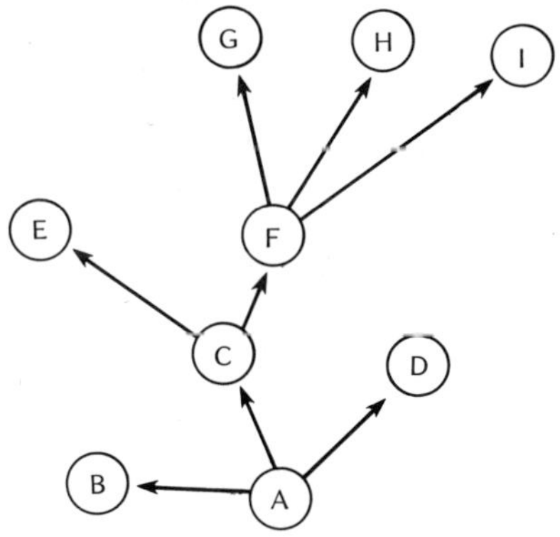

[19] Keith Davis, "Management Communication and the Grapevine," *Harvard Business Review*, Vol. 31 (May 1953), 43–49.

Some of the most significant characteristics of the grapevine are its speed, its influence among workers, and its accuracy. In his research on the grapevine, Davis found it to be accurate in anywhere from 75 to 95% of its information.[20]

Contrary to much of what is written on the subject, the grapevine is not inherently evil. When the bank examiners descend unexpectedly upon a large bank, for example, the news circulates quickly throughout the organization. Those employees who may be approached by them can plan accordingly, and little time is wasted in speculation about who the strangers are.

When management makes an effort to keep its formal channels viable and emphasizes upward as well as downward communication, the function of the grapevine will be to support and reinforce the formal channels. It is in the absence of effective formal communication that the grapevine fills the void, and what results is often contrary to the best interests of management.

NONVERBAL COMMUNICATION

When most people think about communication they think only of verbal communication, and it is true that approximately 75% of an adult's waking time is given to verbal communication activities.[21] There is another dimension of communicating that is usually neither planned nor purposeful, but it exerts great influence on the way in which people and their messages are received. Although a considerable portion of any manager's workday is devoted to speaking and writing, much more time is spent communicating nonverbally. In fact, Mehrabian found that only 7% of the total meaning transmitted is expressed by words only. Tone and inflection accounted for 38%, and 55% of the meaning is transmitted through body language.[22]

Until recent years it was thought that one's ability as a communicator was a function of and limited to one's aptitude for speaking and writing. There has been a great deal of research on nonverbal communication, however, and it has resulted in a general acceptance of the idea that body language is a significant component of one's makeup as a communicator. Research in nonverbal communication has encompassed an incredibly wide variety of different areas. Some of those that are most pertinent for the manager are the following:

Gestures and movements.
Facial expressions.
Vocal cues.

[20] Keith Davis, "Care and Cultivation of the Corporate Grapevine," *Dun's Review*, Vol. 120 (July 1973), 46.

[21] Larry A. Samovar, Robert D. Brooks, and Richard E. Porter, "A Survey of Adult Communication Activities," *The Journal of Communication*, Vol. 19, (Dec. 1969), 301–307.

[22] Albert Mehrabian, "Communication Without Words," *Psychology Today*, Vol. 2 (Sept. 1968), 53–55.

Appearance.
Environment.

Gestures and Movements. *Kinesics* refers to the study of body movements, and it has been the subject of extensive research. Although it is not possible to summarize that research briefly, an overall finding is that people communicate much information through gestures and body movements. These are learned behaviors and they vary from one culture to another. Research suggests that through the study of such behaviors an observer can gain insights into a person's attitudes, status, warmth, and tendency to deceive. Warren Lamb, British management consultant, has developed a system for recognizing a person's likely managerial style by observing that person's posture and gestures.[23]

Facial Expressions. Facial cues are more revealing of a person's attitudes and emotions than are any other means of nonverbal communication. The eyebrows and the mouth have been the subject of research, but the eyes are recognized as an especially good source of information. One of many researchers in this area, Hess found that a person's pupils expand when interested and contract when disinterested.[24]

"Barton, do you have something you want to share with the rest of us?" (Reprinted with permission of Henry R. Martin. First published in **The Wall Street Journal.)**

[23]Jean Ross-Skinner, "Those Telltale Executive Gestures," *Dun's Review*, Vol. 95, (March 1970), 66–67.
[24]E. H. Hess, "Attitude and Pupil Size," *Scientific American*, Vol. 212, (April 1965), 46–54.

Vocal Cues. Often termed *paralanguage,* vocal cues refer to such qualities as pitch, volume, and rate of speech. Research has shown that an alert observer will learn much about a speaker through such vocal cues. Mehrabian has shown that message will be evaluated negatively when vocal cues are not consistent with it.[25]

Appearance. Whether a person is meeting another for the first time or is simply arriving at the office to begin another workday, physical appearance usually precedes any verbal interaction. The primary means of communication by appearance for most people is through the clothing they wear. Gibbins found that people judge others in part on the basis of their clothes and that people generally agree as to what meanings certain types of clothes convey.[26]

Environment. Individuals communicate through numerous different aspects of the environment they occupy. The way in which one uses space tells others much about a person. *Proxemics* is the study of the use of space. An observer can tell much about a person's status by looking at the person's office. Goldhaber presented these principles regarding the use of space or territory in organizations:

1. The higher a person is within an organization, the more space a person will have and the better it will be.
2. The higher a person is, the more protected that person's space will be.
3. The higher a person is, the easier it is for that person to invade the territory of those who are at lower levels within the organization.[27]

This treatment of nonverbal communication included gestures and movement, facial expression, vocal cues, appearance, and environment, but the body of research on the subject is much broader than that. People also communicate through such avenues as touch, color, silence, and time. Managers who are most effective in their interactions with others are usually those who are perceptive to the various "silent messages" being transmitted by their co-workers. Although they may not be cognizant of the voluminous research done on the subject, they are aware of the fact that there is more to communication than the words being spoken.

[25] Albert Mehrabian, and M. Winer, "Decoding of Inconsistent Communication," *Journal of Personality and Social Psychology,* Vol. 6 (1967), 109F.

[26] K. Gibbins, "Communication Aspects of Women's Clothes and Their Relation to Fashionability," *British Journal of Social and Clinical Psychology,* Vol. 8 (1969) 306–307.

[27] Gerald M. Goldhaber, *Organizational Communication* (Dubuque, Iowa: William C. Brown, 1974).

GROUP DYNAMICS

Managers have long complained about the amount of time they must spend in meetings. Research in time management has confirmed that this is a significant problem. Managers cite the frustration of enduring three-hour meetings in which nothing pertaining to their own duties is even discussed. Equally disturbing is the tendency to hold a meeting when there is no need for one, simply because it is Wednesday and that is the day the group meets.

Over the years, the use of groups has grown in significance in most business organizations. The participation of employees in decision making was considered controversial when first implemented in the 1930s but became increasingly accepted with the passing decades until it is now recognized as a fact of organizational life. Participative management went from being perceived as a radical concept to an accepted term in the management lexicon. Much of what is presented as participative management, however, is what is termed *pseudo-participation.*[28] This occurs when managers attempt to get their subordinates involved in the task but not actually in decision making. Regardless of whether management is seeking actual participation or pseudo-participation, the fact remains that a great deal of organizational time and energy is devoted to group efforts.

Advantages of Groups

It stands to reason that business would not be that supportive of the group approach if it did not offer some distinct advantages to the organization. It also follows that the group approach would not be viewed so negatively by so many managers if there were not some dysfunctional aspects of it. These factors are usually included among the advantages in using groups:

1. Better decisions.
2. Individual recognition.
3. Concurrence.
4. Commitment.

Better Decisions. Among the advantages associated with the use of groups, the quality of the decision is usually considered foremost. The idea of two heads being better than one, although a cliche, has been confirmed through research into small groups. If the group is to be effective, however, it is a prerequisite that the group members be knowledgeable on the subject in question. Becoming a member of a group will not confer instant intelligence upon the individual lacking expertise in the area. In other words, groupness is no substitute for understanding.

[28] Fred Luthans, *Organizational Behavior* (New York: McGraw-Hill, 1973), 227.

Individual Recognition. An advantage accruing directly to the group members is the feeling of recognition engendered by the group experience. Being a part of a group helps an individual satisfy some of the recognition needs that everyone has. Despite the fact that managers bemoan the time they waste in meetings, some researchers have found that this sense of recognition does accompany participation in groups.[29] Ideally, this feeling of recognition has a positive effect on all aspects of the participants' work.

Concurrence. When a decision is made by a group, the members of the group are more likely to concur in the decision than if the decision had been handed down to them. The fact that the group members were given the opportunity to offer their ideas will usually ensure a higher rate of concurrence. This concurrence should be reflected in the larger organization, where the fact that the workers' colleagues participated in the decision will increase overall support.

Commitment. Just as concurrence may result from group participation, so also may commitment. Having played a role in solving a problem, the group members will have more of a stake in the solution's success. Thus, their commitment to the effective implementation of the solution should be high, and the same holds true for the commitment of their colleagues who have been aware of the use of the group approach.

Disadvantages of Groups

Thus, in looking at such factors as decision quality, individual recognition, concurrence, and commitment, it is obvious why the group approach is attractive to management. There is, however, another side to this issue. There are reasons that the group approach is viewed with skepticism in some circles.

Because meetings are the source of so many complaints, it would seem to follow that there are some inherent disadvantages in the use of groups. The main disadvantages are that they are:

1. Time-consuming.
2. Often unnecessary.
3. Conformity-inducing.
4. Unbalanced in participation.

Time-consuming. It is no secret that managers spend a great deal of time in meetings and that they also must devote time preparing for those meetings. Parkinson's thesis that work expands to fill the time available is as applicable to meetings as to work in general. Meetings that start late and continue longer than

[29] Howard H. Martin, "Communication Settings," *Speech Communication: Analysis and Readings*, Howard H. Martin & Kenneth E. Anderson, eds. (Boston: Allyn & Bacon, 1968), 70–74.

expected seem to be the rule rather than the exception. When one calculates the worker hours spent in meetings and the pay involved, the result is staggering. The realization that time is indeed money is never more meaningful than as one observes the 10 participants in their weekly two-hour production meeting. While the production manager drones on, the other nine participants feign interest while the time clock whirs along.

Often unnecessary. Man is a creature of habit, and this is never more obvious than in the use and abuse of meetings. In many organizations, meetings are not scheduled on the basis of need but on the basis of precedent. All too often, the safety committee meets simply because it is Monday afternoon and that is when that group regularly meets. It is immaterial if there is nothing important to discuss. Members of such groups grow increasingly resentful of these abuses of their time, and these feelings color their involvement in other work groups also. At times there is a task to be accomplished, but it requires the expertise of only a few of the group members. Too often the entire group is assembled regardless, supposedly because the leader wants to keep everyone informed.

Conformity-inducing. Although one advantage of groups is the diversity of viewpoints elicited, it often occurs that this diversity disappears as the group recognizes how the leader feels about the subject under consideration. It is not, however, always the leader who causes this. Sometimes participants who are somewhat overbearing are able to convince the other participants, either correctly or incorrectly, of their expertise and its relevancy. When exposed to such a show of force, many participants are happy to fall in behind the supposed expert. Thus, a format intended to enhance creativity, instead, may reinforce conformity. Janis terms this condition "groupthink."[30] He describes it as the condition that prevails when critical thinking is overshadowed by the wish for concurrence.

Unbalanced in Participation. A group may be structured so as to provide a certain mix in terms of areas of responsibility or areas of expertise. Although this is an appropriate step, its effect will be minimal if each participant does not provide inputs. When there is considerable variation in the willingness and ability of group members to actively participate, the group leader must strive to ensure more balanced participation. Too many leaders expect this to take care of itself but, just as the meek are not currently on the verge of inheriting the earth, the reticent group members usually will allow the more talkative and aggressive members to dominate meetings. If an individual has the necessary credentials to attend a meeting, that person should actively participate, and it is the leader's responsibility to overcome the problem of unbalanced participation.

[30] Irving L. Janis, *Victims of Groupthink: A Psychological Study of Foreign Policy Decisions and Fiascoes* (Boston: Houghton-Mifflin, 1972).

Purposes of Meetings

Meetings are a predictable occurrence in the work week of most managers. Some managers contend that meetings are an overused device in business, but others feel differently. If one were to categorize meetings on the basis of specific purpose, numerous categories would result. Categorization on the basis of general purpose, however, yields the following list of mutually exclusive purposes of meetings:

1. Information receiving.
2. Information giving.
3. Information exchanging.
4. Problem solving.

Information Receiving. When the purpose of the meeting is information receiving, the leader will attempt to elicit balanced participation from the group members, each of whom will be an authority in a certain area. When a decision must be made on whether or not to introduce a new product, for example, there would probably be representatives from production, marketing, finance, and research and development at the meeting. The leader will draw upon the expertise of these individuals in order to garner the necessary information that will enable the leader to eventually make an intelligent decision.

Information Giving. In the information giving type of meeting, the primary flow of information is from the group leader to the members. When the sales manager, for example, meets with the sales force to explain changes in company policy regarding the documentation of travel expenses, the meeting is an information giving one. The group leader is the main source of information and the other participants are there to be informed. Although the participants may exert some degree of control by their questions and in their nonverbal responses, the group leader will not relinquish the role of information source.

Information Exchanging. A meeting held for purposes of exchanging information is analogous to a refueling stop on the road to a decision. Perhaps the ultimate goal is a revised fringe benefits package, but there may be several meetings for purposes of exchanging and pooling information that will precede the ultimate goal. The manager of compensation administration may assign several subordinates the task of investigating various components of the compensation package. For example, while one person is researching various insurance plans, another is investigating the sick leave policies of similar companies. When the group meets there is an exchange of information and this enables the leaders and the other participants together to work toward a revised compensation package. After several such sessions the group will attain closure. That is, they will have put all of the components together into a well-balanced benefit program.

Problem Solving. Many automatically associate meetings with problem solving, and that is probably the most frequent purpose of meetings. By using groups for this purpose, not only is the solution generally superior to that proposed by an individual, but the commitment of the group members to the solution will be greater.

Having recognized four main purposes for group meetings, it should be pointed out that in most meetings there is a combining of purposes. Rare is the meeting that is devoted solely to information giving or to any other single purpose. Because there is a blending of purposes, it follows that a single style of leadership may be less than ideal. Whereas a more autocratic style would be desirable for the information-giving session, this would not be true for the other types in which a more democratic style would be effective to accomplish the group's purpose. These four types of meetings and the usual communication flow therein are illustrated in Figure 11-5.

Effective Leadership of Meetings

The two preceding sections have emphasized group climate and various means of developing group cohesiveness. Those sections have been general in nature.

FIGURE 11-5.

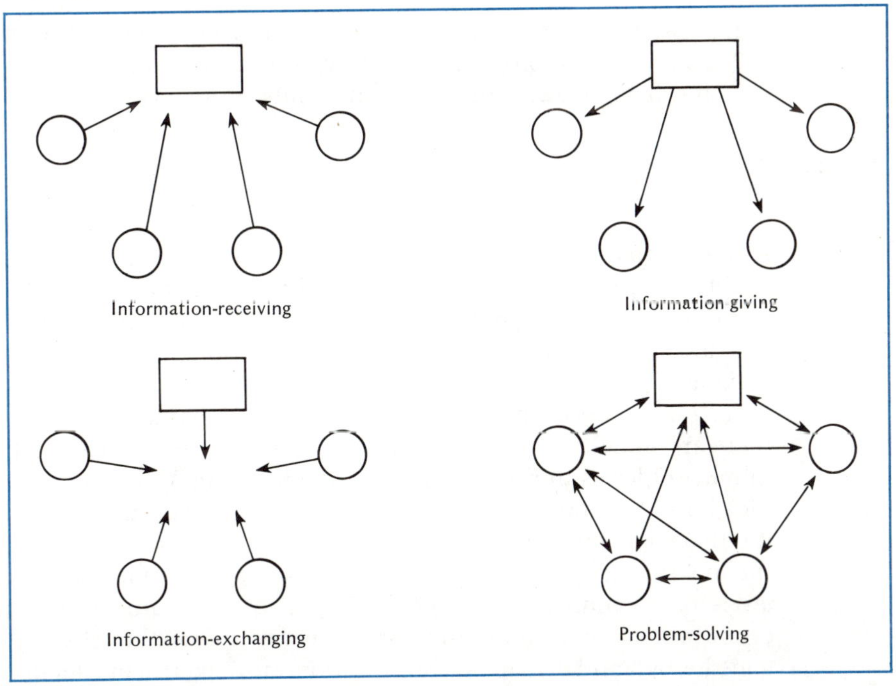

There are, however, some specific things that a group leader can do to increase the likelihood of an effective meeting. Before the meeting, the leader should:

1. Contact participants to get input as to what, if anything, they believe should be discussed at the meeting.
2. Determine if a meeting is actually necessary and, if so, determine the exact purpose of it.
3. Select an appropriate site for the meeting.
4. Prepare an agenda, stating topics to be discussed, starting and finishing times, and location of the meeting. Distribute the agendas to those who should participate in the meeting.

During the meeting, the leader should:

1. Begin on time.
2. Follow the agenda and do not allow a digression from it unless there is a genuine need for one.
3. If participants are being assigned tasks, make sure that the tasks are described clearly and completely.
4. End the meeting on time.

Following the meeting, the leader should:

1. Disseminate the minutes of the meeting, if they are kept, as soon as possible.
2. Follow up the progress being made on the assignments given. If progress is not being made, prod the delinquents into activity.

SUMMARY

Although there has been extensive research in organizational communication during the past three decades, there is little agreement as to the definition of communication. The most common dimensions of communication for a manager are coordination, maintenance, orientation, development, and decision making.

Each organization has certain characteristics that affect communication, but there are some characteristics that pertain to all organizations. The greater the number of levels in the organization, the more likely are distortions in communication. The more specialized the tasks within the organization, the more likely it is that jargons will develop within the various areas of specialization. Because of the hierarchical nature of organizations, status differences between the various levels often constitute barriers to effective communication. Such factors as organizational procedures, the distance between branches of some organizations, and the pyramidal shape of organizations also exert considerable influence on communication.

Downward communication has traditionally been emphasized in business organizations because of the importance of giving orders and instructions. The value of upward communication is now recognized, and it is used to determine how downward communication is being accepted as well as to provide all employees with easy access to upper management. Horizontal communication is that which occurs between individuals on the same level of the organization.

The formal communication channels are identified on organizational charts and are those routinely used by management. Whereas the number of formal channels is limited, a message sender has various options in terms of techniques and media to use. Many messages travel through informal channels and the *grapevine* is a name applied to such channels.

Much of the communication in any organization is nonverbal; it does not involve language. People communicate through gestures and body movements, and the study of such communication is called kinesics. Facial cues reveal more about attitude and emotion than any other means of nonverbal communication. Paralanguage refers to vocal qualities such as pitch and volume, which are nonverbal and which communicate information to others. Effective managers are perceptive of the many nonverbal messages to which they are exposed.

Management has become more group-oriented as it seeks to involve more workers in the operation of the organization. Foremost among the advantages of using groups is the fact that knowledgeable groups usually make better decisions than do individuals. Also, individuals have an opportunity for recognition as group members, and there is an increase in both concurrence and commitment. Among the disadvantages of groups is the fact that they are time-consuming and are often employed unnecessarily. Conformity is sometimes induced inappropriately among group members, and sometimes more talkative members are accorded more power than they actually merit.

An effective manager is aware of the importance of group climate and strives to establish one that is supportive and likely to develop group cohesiveness. Managers' knowledge of group dynamics becomes apparent in their manner of conducting and participating in meetings.

Assignments

11-1. Rank the different dimensions of organizational communication in terms of their importance to the organization, as you see it. Be prepared to justify your answer.

11-2. What are the main components in the process of communication?

11-3. Status differences between individuals are reflected in the hierarchical arrangement of jobs in an organizational chart. Explain how status differences may hinder effective communication. What can be done to minimize their effect?

11-4. What is there about the structure of most organizations that facilitates downward communication?

11-5. For what reasons does management stress the need for using the formal channels for communication?

11-6. Some managers maintain that there would be fewer communication problems if the grapevine could be eliminated. Do you agree or disagree? Why?

11-7. What factors should be taken into consideration when determining what medium of communication to use?

11-8. How does a jargon develop? What are the advantages and disadvantages of a jargon?

11-9. When a decision must be made, what should a manager consider in determining whether or not to appoint a group to reach it?

11-10. What are some steps that a first-line supervisor on an assembly line could take to improve the climate for his subordinates?

Case 11-1

PICKERING PAPER PRODUCTS

Pickering Paper Products, although a small, family-owned and nonunion corporation, has been able to carve out a niche in the coated paper industry. In the past year, however, its competitors have cut into Pickering's share of the market because of their ability to hold the line on price increases, whereas Pickering had to twice increase its prices. Having become alarmed at the precariousness of the company's position, Phillip Pickering, III, the president, announced that new efforts must be made to cut costs.

Phillip took this problem so seriously that he had posters designed reading, "By Cutting Costs We're Staying Alive; By Producing More We're All Gonna Thrive." These green and white posters carried the Pickering logo and were posted throughout the plant.

He instructed his staff and all the members of management to get "a little extra" out of their workers. The first-line supervisors were told to "bear down" on their workers. Management was able to make inroads into the problem through such tactics as speeding up certain machines, reducing waste, and reducing the length of the workers' coffee breaks.

This was not accomplished, however, without some human costs. The rate of employee turnover increased, as did absenteeism. Supervisors complained increasingly about the attitude of the workers, and President Pickering was by now extremely apprehensive.

1. In what ways is this a communication problem?
2. Looking at this as a communication problem, what do you advise President Pickering to do? Indicate what specific steps he should take and why he should take them.

Case 11-2

SPEAK UP FOR RUTHERFORD

When Blake Rutherford received his undergraduate degree in business, he immediately went to work for his father, Rustin Rutherford the owner of Rutherford Tube and Pipe Company. Blake's job title was Director of Special Projects, and, although he was not given much responsibility for his first year, he later began receiving more challenging assignments. Although the company had never experienced an unusually high rate of turnover, Blake initiated an exit interview program to learn the reasons for which employees left the company. Blake conducted the exit interviews, and he soon learned that the first-line supervisors were frequently given as the main reason for workers quitting their jobs. Blake made it a point to discuss these reasons with the supervisors as well as with upper management.

Six months after the start of the exit interview program, a new factory opened in the community, and several outstanding first-line supervisors quit Rutherford abruptly. They claimed that upper management was interested only in seeing that its orders were followed. These supervisors felt that they were not given the authority needed to do their jobs and that management was always second-guessing them. They viewed themselves as "trapped in the middle" between the line workers who did not trust them and management that did not support them.

Both Blake and his father recognized the seriousness of the situation and together they developed a program to encourage upward communication that they called "Speak Up." Three of the more popular aspects of the "Speak Up" program were the suggestion system, Rustin Rutherford's new open-door policy, and weekly awareness sessions.

The suggestion system appeared to be a success from the start, as many employees competed for the cash awards given for the best suggestions. So many suggestions were offered, in fact, that it was taking management much longer to respond to them than anticipated. To alleviate this problem, it was decided that only those contributors of suggestions deemed acceptable would be notified. Those whose suggestions were not acceptable would receive their suggestions back with "Unacceptable, but thanks" stamped on them. This reduced the turnover time considerably, and it gave the contributor almost immediate feedback.

When Rustin Rutherford announced that his door would be open to any employee, his colleagues were surprised because he already had more obligations than he could handle. He worked 10 to 12 hours a day, but he now managed to talk with those workers who had questions or complaints. He assured those with problems that he would personally investigate them, and he made a list of them, fully intending to look into them when time allowed. Rustin felt that the workers would become more committed to the company through such easy access to him.

Each week, 10 workers were selected at random to participate in an awareness session. This was a 90-minute meeting at which either Rustin or Blake gave a 60-minute informative presentation entitled, "The Rutherford Way—Yesterday, Today and Tomorrow." This was followed by a question- and- answer session during which coffee and donuts were served.

Initially, both Rustin and Blake were pleased with the results of their efforts. After one year, however, worker interest in the Speak Up program seemed to diminish for no explainable reason.

1. What do you consider the strong points of the Speak Up program to be? What are the weak points?
2. Looking at this as a communication problem, what do you think should be done by management?
3. What could have been done to prevent this problem from occurring?

References

BIRDWHISTELL, RAYMOND L. *Kinesics and Context.* Philadelphia: University of Pennsylvania, 1970.

BORMANN, ERNEST G., WILLIAM S. HOWELL, RALPH G. NICHOLS, AND GEORGE L. SHAPIRO. *Interpersonal Communication in the Modern Organization.* Englewood Cliffs, N.J.: Prentice-Hall, Inc., 1969.

GOLDHABER, GERALD M. *Organization Communication.* Dubuque, Iowa: William C. Brown Company, Publishers, 1974.

HANEY, WILLIAM V. *Communication and Organizational Behavior.* Homewood, Ill.: Richard D. Irwin, Inc., 1973.

HUSEMAN, RICHARD C., JAMES M. LAHIFF, AND JOHN D. HATFIELD. *Interpersonal Communication in the Organization.* Boston: Holbrook, 1976.

KATZ, E., M. L. LEVIN, AND H. HAMILTON. "Traditions of Research as the Diffusion of Innovation." *American Sociological Review.* Vol. 28 (1963).

LEATHERS, DALE G. *Nonverbal Communication Systems.* Boston: Allyn & Bacon, Inc., 1976.

LEWIS, PHILLIP V. *Organizational Communications.* Columbus: Grid, Inc., 1975.

MARCH, J. G., AND H. A. SIMON. *Organizations.* New York: John Wiley & Sons, Inc., 1955.

MEHRABIAN, ALBERT. *Silent Messages.* Belmont, Calif.: Wadsworth Publishing Co., Inc., 1971.

REDDING, W. CHARLES. *Communication Within the Organization.* New York: Industrial Communication Council, Inc., 1972.

SCANNELL, EDWARD E. *Communications for Leadership.* New York: McGraw-Hill/Gregg Management Series in Marketing, 1970.

SIGBAND, NORMAN B. *Communication for Management.* Glenview, Ill.: Scott, Foresman and Company, 1969.

TORTORIELLO, THOMAS R., STEPHEN J. BLATT, AND SUE DEWINE. *Communication in the Organization.* New York: McGraw-Hill Book Company, 1978.

TUBBS, STEWART L., AND SYLVIA MOSS. *Human Communication—An Interpersonal Perspective.* New York: Random House, Inc., 1974.

LAWRENCE N. DeLEERS, JR.
First Vice-President
International Banking Division,
First Wisconsin National Bank
of Milwaukee

Lawrence N. DeLeers joined the First Wisconsin National Bank in 1959 after previous experience with Bank of America, N.T. & S.A. in California. His experience with the First Wisconsin National Bank has involved assignments in the following divisions: credit, personnel, corporate planning, economics and research, and international banking.

He has contributed written works on technical banking matters and made numerous presentations on related subjects for the American Management Association and other interested groups.

He is a member of the Bankers Association for Foreign Trade.

Executive Commentary

Communicating Efficiently

Business communications skills at the senior management level have become crucial to the timely and intelligent conduct of nearly any enterprise. Issues are more complex and information is more plentiful in today's world. Good communication in the decision-making process is therefore crucial.

I would like to share with you in this commentary some feelings developed through experience on the elements of effective business communications. At the outset, let me define the type of communications I am speaking about. Specifically, I would like to cover bottom-line, decision-making communications with and/or between senior managers and executives. I am not speaking about either sales pitches or imparting new, complex conceptual information. Rather, I am talking about imparting factual information and/or recommendations designed to produce everyday business decisions and the actions resulting therefrom.

There are, I believe, certain key rules to be followed if communication (written or verbal) of this type is to be efficient and successful. To my mind, the most important of these rules are:

1. Be direct.
2. Be honest.
3. Address yourself to the competence of the recipient.
4. Be prepared to back what you say.

Be direct. Get to the point. Do not engage in hedging or beating around the bush. Every executive is deluged with information. As a result of the vast amount of data he deals with each day, he must be selective in what he reads and what he listens to. Communications that lack directness activate an involuntary defense mechanism and all too often lose the attention that may be deserved.

Today's environment emphasizes the need for honesty in communications. Probably the most common violation of the rule of honesty is to fail to relate all truly relevant facts—emphasizing the positive and avoiding that which is perceived to be negative. With the vast interrelationship of factors often involved in business situations, it is difficult enough to make good decisions.

Dealing with less than a complete story decreases the odds. Blatant dishonesty, even inadvertant omission, in communications may appear to produce favorable short-term results but generally backfires in the long run.

The third rule (addressing the competence of the recipient) relates to the first (be direct). In communicating facts and/or recommendations, lay only such background or framework as the recipient can be presumed to require. Knowing what the recipient already knows will go a long way toward being direct. Of course, the presumption as to the knowledge of the recipient must be an informed presumption, not a guess. If there is doubt, the road to directness in verbal communications is by such a question as, "Are you familiar with . . . ?" In written communications, a simple statement such as, "Given the nature of . . . ." Too often, junior managers, in their zeal to display their own newly acquired knowledge, go into great background detail with which their superiors are fully familiar. If the effort is taken to draw an informed presumption of the competence (familiarity with the subject) of the recipient, directness will be assured.

A particular decision-making communication may be honestly structured, delivered directly, and addressed to the competence of the recipient, but still fail. The failure results when a request for expansion or support of one or more of the key factors involved cannot be backed up by either a citation of facts or a tightly structured rationale. "Being prepared to back what you say," then, is as critical a factor to effective decision-making communications as are the first three rules cited. Being unable to back key points detracts from the credibility of both the individual and his presentation.

It is my observation that successful executives are successful communicators. Different situations, such as sales, motivation, and conceptual communications require different techniques and emphases. In communicating facts and/or recommendations designed to produce day-to-day business decisions, the four rules cited appear to me to be among the most important.

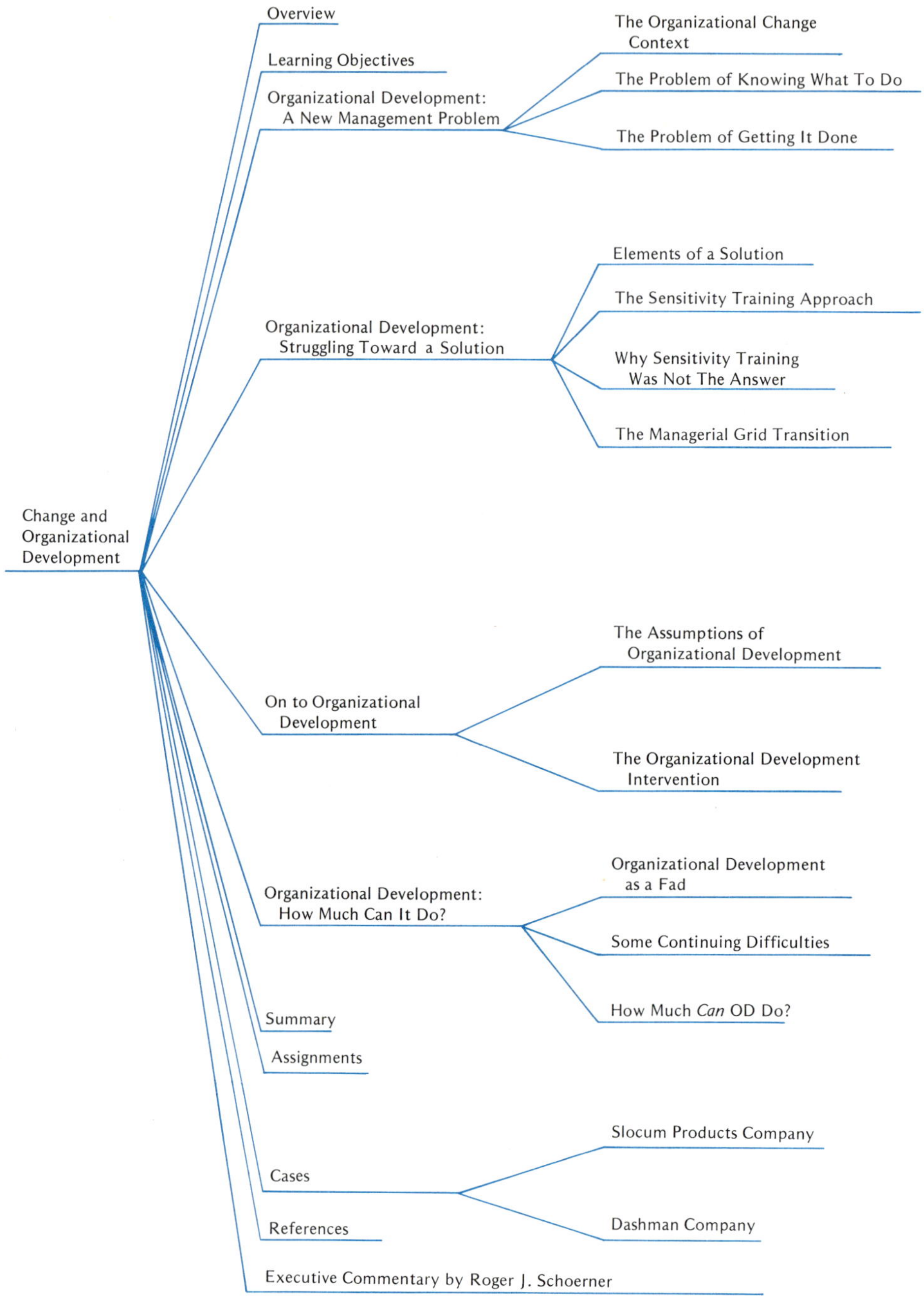
Change and Organizational Development
Overview
Learning Objectives
Organizational Development: A New Management Problem
The Organizational Change Context
The Problem of Knowing What To Do
The Problem of Getting It Done
Organizational Development: Struggling Toward a Solution
Elements of a Solution
The Sensitivity Training Approach
Why Sensitivity Training Was Not The Answer
The Managerial Grid Transition
On to Organizational Development
The Assumptions of Organizational Development
The Organizational Development Intervention
Organizational Development: How Much Can It Do?
Organizational Development as a Fad
Some Continuing Difficulties
How Much *Can* OD Do?
Summary
Assignments
Cases
Slocum Products Company
Dashman Company
References
Executive Commentary by Roger J. Schoerner

12

CHANGE AND ORGANIZATIONAL DEVELOPMENT

OVERVIEW

Organizational development as it will be discussed here is two things. First, it is a way of stating a difficulty, the need for a comprehensive and long-term effort to improve an organization's problem-solving processes. This need primarily arises from the organization's failure to perform satisfactorily in an *environment* that is changing so rapidly that the organization's decision making cannot keep pace. Second, it is a way of describing how organizations endeavor to solve this problem. As a solution, organizational development is a comprehensive and long-term effort to improve an organization's decision making in relation to its environment—especially by using applied behavioral science to develop collaborative problem solving. In this chapter we will look at organizational development from several points of view. First, we will discuss why comprehensively changing organizations has recently become a major matter. Second, we will overview the history of efforts to deal with this new problem in the interest of more effective organization functioning. A third focus will be on organizational development as a process, how *organization developers* go about this task. These people include those who will manage the organization while it is being, and after it has been, effectively changed. Also included are the *behavioral scientists* who often assist organizational development efforts as *consultants*. Finally, attention will be given to the limitations of organizational development, emphasizing especially the danger of expecting this approach to managing change to do more than it can do.

LEARNING OBJECTIVES

This chapter is especially intended to help the student:

1. **Understand what the organizational development problem is.**
2. **Think about why the problem of organizational development has become much more important in recent years.**
3. **See the principal endeavors that have gone into the struggle toward a solution to the organizational development problem.**
4. **Appreciate why first attempts to solve the organizational development problem did not succeed.**
5. **Become familiar with the major elements of organizational development as an approach to a solution.**
6. **Understand why organizational development provides a special opportunity for "faddism."**
7. **Learn, especially in the context of thinking about management, the meaning of the following concepts:**

resistance to change	**team building**
hidden agendas	**change agents**
sensitivity training	**intervention**
family T-groups	**action research**
the managerial grid	**survey feedback**

ORGANIZATIONAL DEVELOPMENT: A NEW MANAGEMENT PROBLEM

Organizational development has become a very important approach to organizational change. Of course, organizational decision making typically involves adapting to the organization's outside environment. An organization's decision making, however, must also adapt, and adapt to its own internal situation. In fact, internal adjustments are one of the most essential elements in adaptations toward the organization's external environment. Making internal adjustments as needed for organizational effectiveness is what is commonly called *change management.*

The Organizational Change Context

One of the most widely used clichés in the field of change management is that it is human nature to resist change. Certainly that must be the way many eager, but frustrated, managers see it. Actually it is, of course, not human nature to resist change any more than it is human nature to promote change; wherever one sees people endeavoring to reject the new, one sees other people endeavoring to promote innovation. It is sometimes said, only half in jest, that if it were human nature to resist change, we would all be naked, hungry, and, above all, single.

The human nature proposition therefore becomes that it is human nature to resist whatever is perceived to be injurious to one's physical or psychological well-being. There are few places in the status quo in which at least some people have not put down deep personality roots, and there are therefore few changes that can be made that will not be seen as damaging by some of those affected by them. A primary reason that the management of change is so challenging is that individual differences make it difficult to guess where perceived damage from change will strike.

Injury as a dimension of change is what makes power, and especially the gap between authority and power, important in the change management process. On the one hand, upper-level managers, by contrast with rank-and-file workers, can most nearly get the organizational changes they want and avoid those they do not want. On the other hand, leaders cannot have everything their way in the change management realm. Because motivation is a bargain, managers must trade off the amount and rate of change they insist on against the motivation consequences of the resulting injury to workers.

The central characteristic of organizational development as one variety of change management is its *comprehensiveness.* Other kinds of change efforts in organizations are piecemeal. That is, a need may be felt to alter some aspect of an organization's operations so that it will perform more effectively. With organizational development, however, the problem to be solved is rather seen to be a failure of the entire organization to be sufficiently adaptive to the world outside to continue to be effective.

Because organizational development is a total organization approach to change management, it makes use of a wide variety of approaches. Of course, a comprehensive assault on inadequate, *total organization adaptiveness* would seize upon anything and everything that holds out some promise of being helpful. Literally everything that has been found useful in piecemeal organizational change has been put to work in organizational development efforts. For example, as illustrated in Figure 12-1, such things as team building, MBO programs, job enrichment, sensitivity training, and managerial grid seminars are sometimes used as

FIGURE 12-1. The Organizational Change Spectrum.

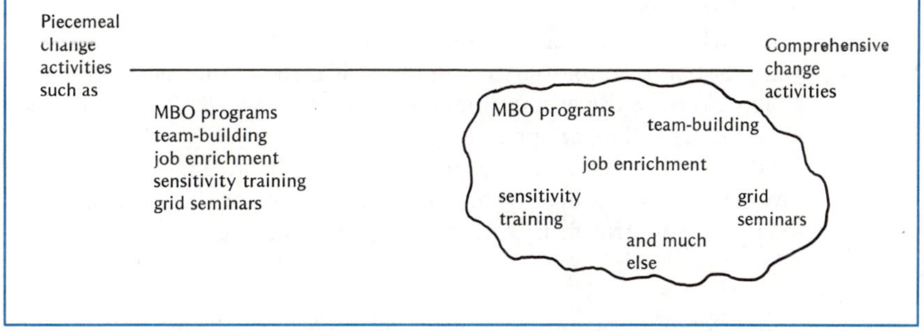

piecemeal approaches to helping organizations improve their effectiveness—and sometimes as a part of more comprehensive organizational development endeavors. Because, then, different organizational development efforts are quite likely to use a somewhat different mix of approaches and emphases, organizational development can seem to the observer to be a hodge-podge of techniques.

In fact, one of the confusions surrounding organizational development activities is a tendency to give the name organizational development to one or another of the techniques used in these endeavors. Business leaders, for example, sometimes in this way identify the part with the whole. However, organizational development is best thought about in terms of its *core element.* Among those who study and put into practice the science and the art of organizational development this core is quite distinctive. Our discussion will build primarily around that common denominator, although we shall first note why a comprehensive organizational change approach has recently become prominent, and then trace the efforts over a period of time to find an effective way to go about changing an entire organization.

The Problem of Knowing What to Do

Because organizational development has only recently become a large concern in the world of management, it is worthwhile asking at the outset why this concern has come to be so chronically with us.[1] A summary explanation would say simply that managers can no longer *command change* as effectively as was once possible. Although that is true, it is too simple an explanation. We must also understand why command is now less useful in bringing about the changes organizations need. Note, by the way, that it already begins to say a good bit about this that the core element in organizational development includes a great deal of participative decision making.

William Faulkner on the Challenge of Change

What's wrong with the world is, it's not finished yet. It is not completed to the point where man can put his signature to the job and say, "It is finished. We made it, and it works."

Because only man can complete it. Not God, but man. It is man's high destiny and proof of his immortality, too, that his is the choice between ending the world, effacing it from the wrong annals of time and space, and completing it. This is not only his right, but his privilege, too.

Like the Phoenix, it arises from the ashes of its own failure with each generation, until it is our turn now in our flash and flicker of time and space which we call today . . . to perform this duty, accept this privilege, bear this right . . . .

[1] Warren Bennis, *Organization Development: Its Nature, Origins, and Prospects* (Reading, Mass.: Addison-Wesley, 1969), Chapter 2.

One hundred years ago we were living in a laissez-faire, leave businessmen alone era. Bureauracies were simpler then; especially was there more *centralization of authority* toward the top of organizations. With few constraints, either inside or outside the organization, it was relatively easy for competent managers both to know what to do and to get it done. In the simplest case, one man would make these decisions, and then tell everyone else where they fit into the new program.

The organization's situation in relation to needed changes is now quite different. For one thing, so much is happening in and around today's organizations—and so rapidly—that it is difficult to know what organizational changes will be useful. We may indeed be living with a *law of acceleration,* changes coming at us at an ever-increasing rate.[2]

This can perhaps most easily be seen in what is happening to the environment organizations must make their way within. In the realm of the technology used by organizations, one breakthrough seems often these days to trigger a variety of other advances.[3] The organization's legal environment seems to be subject to much the same change explosiveness. Every year, in our federal and state legislatures, tens of thousands of new business-related laws are proposed. Unfortunately, too, as most businessmen would say, many of these proposals become law.

Vigorous change outside the organization is one reason managers have difficulty knowing what should be done to keep in step with the times. Another is the size and complexity of many of today's organizations. With some regularity, America's 50 largest corporations have revenues greater than the combined revenues of all of our 50 states. Increases in organization size, furthermore, typically mean greater organization complexity. When, then, organization complexity is accentuated by technology complexity, the result is the need for more and more *elaborate coordination arrangements.* Where the work of many people is closely interlocked, a few top-level managers can all the more not be sure what organizational changes will be useful.

Perhaps it exaggerates a little to summarize this challenge of knowing what to do as Peter Drucker did in 1954.

> *At some unmarked point during the last twenty years we imperceptibly moved out of the modern age and into a new, as yet nameless, era. . . . The old view of the world, the old tasks and the old center, calling themselves 'modern' and 'up-to-date' only a few years ago, just make no sense anymore. They still provide our rhetoric whether of politics or science, at home or in foreign affairs. But the slogans and battle cries of all parties, be they political, philosophical, aesthetic, or scientific, no longer serve to unify for action—though they still can divide in heat and emotion. Our actions are still measured against the stern demands of the 'today,' the 'post-modern' world: and yet we have no theories, no concepts, no slogans—no real knowledge—about the new reality.*[4]

[2] Townsend Hoopes, "The Corporate Planner (New Edition)," *Business Horizons,* Winter, 1962, p. 59; and Alvin Toffler, *Future Shock* (New York: Random House, 1971).

[3] G. D. Brewer, "On Innovation, Social Change, and Reality," *Technological Forecasting and Social Change,* Volume 5, Number 1, 1973, pp. 19–24.

[4] Peter F. Drucker, *The Practice of Management* (New York: Harper, 1954), p. 375.

But Warren Bennis, one of today's authorities on organizational development, did not think so.

> *Writing in August 1968, I find it impossible to dispute Peter Drucker's gloomy statement. The two recent national political conventions with the "new politics" have revealed the trouble we are in, and we are in trouble because we have no "real knowledge" about the new reality, this post-industrial world.*[5]

Warren Bennis.
(Courtesy of Wide World Photos.)

The Problem of Getting It Done

The problem of making the right change decisions is only the beginning of the organizational development difficulty. That problem merges with another one. How can we get organization members, including managers and supervisors, to accept the changing that might be needed? Here, especially, is where command, and what it can and cannot do, becomes intimately involved. For why would top managers not simply order what they believe should be done?

The problem of getting cooperation for the implementation of needed changes must be understood first from the standpoint of what people are like. As we have already emphasized, all behavior is motivated. That means, to repeat, that whatever anyone does in organizations is to get something he or she wants. It follows that people will do whatever they can to get what they are after.[6] Of course, there are times when people will oppose changes their organizations want; that is why this behavior is called *resistance to change.* Resistance to change, then, is why organizational development is often defined as finding and removing barriers to effective organizational performance. Resistance to change is also why

[5]Bennis, op. cit., p. 1.
[6]R. M. Cyert, and J. G. March, *A Behavioral Theory of the Firm* (Englewood Cliffs, N.J.: Prentice-Hall, 1963), especially Chapters 3 and 6.

the core element in organizational development emphasizes getting people to work together more comfortably from the standpoint of their own needs, and thereby more productively from the standpoint of the organization's needs.

It is primarily because organizational change is often resisted that it has many times been said that it is human nature to resist change. One of the reasons this is not true is that quite often there is resistance to changes wanted by the organization because those who are resisting want other changes instead. Or resisters of organizational changes may be in that way resisting the manager-changers, "getting back at" the organization for "wronging" its people in their eyes. To be sure, we human beings do feel we must be cautious about the changing we accept, because guessing how proposed changes will affect us is very difficult. As Shakespeare had Hamlet say:

We'd rather bear those ills we have
than fly to others that we know not of.

Again, it is perceived injury, not change, that our human nature presses us to resist. Most sweepingly, organization members are likely to feel threatened when change is pushed at them by superiors, because subordinates are not sure that leaders either understand their followers' situations or that they really have subordinates' interests at heart. More specifically, people are likely to see in proposed changes:

1. Threats to traditional norms and values, and therefore the comfort people have found in these traditions.
2. Threats to group relationships, the warmth people find in their associations with others.
3. Threats to economic well-being—as especially, for instance, loss of income.
4. Threats to skills that have been useful—vis a vis the cost or the impossibility of developing new skills.[7]

The problem of getting cooperation for the implementation of needed changes must also be understood from the standpoint of what today's organizations are like. Here in particular, the organizational development problem takes reference from the size and complexity of so many of our organizations and the difficulty managers have commanding the changes they want.[8]

A primary consequence of organizations becoming larger and more complex has been a decrease in the control exercised by a tiny handful of top managers. That is, as the challenge to managers overran their capacity, they were compelled to delegate authority and responsibility to subordinate managers. By definition,

[7]Richard A. Johnson, R. Joseph Monsen, Henry P. Knowles, and Borje O. Saxberg, *Management, Systems, and Society* (Pacific Palisades, Calif.: Goodyear, 1976), pp. 210–11.

[8]Victor A. Thompson, "Bureaucracy and Innovation," *Administrative Science Quarterly*, June 1965, p. 2.

(Reprinted by permission of NEA.)

however, delegation means a degree of *autonomy* for middle managers. That is, these managers come to have "command rights" over their "domains." To be sure, that kind of autonomy is limited; a manager cannot do whatever he would like with the organization resources entrusted to him. But in the resistance to change realm, the autonomous manager does have a partial veto over what is proposed for his unit.

Of course, veto does not mean that a manager says to those around him—as, for example, his own superior—"I will not do that." Rather, a specialist department head will subtly twist his understanding of what is expected of his unit. He can then get more nearly what he wants, even at the expense of some change wanted by those above him in the organization. When this manager is confronted with this "misunderstanding," he can say, "Oh, I had no idea that was what you meant," or, "If I had supposed that was what was involved, I would never have agreed to go along." Or a key figure in some proposed change can simply "sit on his hands," giving later the excuse that his resource or his priority situation took such a turn for the worse that he just couldn't take on a new requirement.

It would not matter much in an organization if a few subordinate managers occasionally resisted change. When, however, many managers are regularly avoiding wanted changes, that can indeed become a paralyzing organizational development problem. This may particularly be the case, given the close interlinking of relationships within complex organizations. One veto can then hamper activities all around it. In short, the top management group, although quite confident it knows what should be done to keep pace with a dramatically changing environment, often cannot do what needs to be done. The dilution of authority makes it impossible to command the changes that seem needed.[9] There is, in truth, reason enough to define organizational development as finding and removing barriers to effective organization performance.

In summary, getting it done—even after deciding what should be done—can

[9] Alexander Winn, "Social Change in Industry: From Insight to Implementation," *Journal of Applied Behavioral Science*, April 1966, pp. 170–84.

indeed be exceedingly difficult. Perhaps this difficulty has never been better said than by Machiavelli, as he warned his "Prince" to take the problem of change making very seriously.

> *There is nothing more difficult to carry out, nor more doubtful of success, nor more dangerous to handle, than to initiate a new order of things. For the reformer has enemies in all those who profit by the old order, and only lukewarm defenders in all those who would profit by the new order, this lukewarmness arising partly from fear of their adversaries, who have the laws in their favour, and partly from the incredulity of mankind, who do not truly believe in anything new until they have actual experience of it.*

Observe, incidentally, how exactly the organizational development problem reflects the meaning of organizational development. Introducing change into organizations must be a systematic effort in large part because resistance to change is both chronic and pervasive. Organizational development efforts must then especially make use of what we know about human behavior because that is where the roots of resistance to change are.

It is also worth emphasizing, to keep our discussion of organizational development in perspective, that resistance to change is not the only barrier to effective organizational adaptations. Such things as the neglect and/or misdirection of programs of searching for both problems and solutions—the inadequacy of resources allocated to or priorities directed toward needed changing—and learning processes within organizations that do not work well—also contribute to poor performances by organizations vis a vis their environments. In other words, resistance to change is given top billing here because in thinking about organizational development it is the principal concern.

ORGANIZATIONAL DEVELOPMENT: STRUGGLING TOWARD A SOLUTION

Let us now look at how management practitioners have sought to solve the very sticky problem of keeping large, complex organizations in tune with their environments. As a preface, it may be worthwhile to emphasize how important finding a solution to the organizational development problem is thought to be. Thus:

> *The essential task of modern management is to deal with change. Management is the agency through which changes enter our society, and it is the agency that then must cope with the environment it has set in turbulent motion.*[10]

[10] Max Ways, "Tomorrow's Management: A More Adventurous Life in a Free-Form Corporation," *Fortune*, July 1, 1966, p. 84.

And as Alfred Sloan once said:

> *The circumstances of an ever-changing market and an ever-changing product are capable of breaking any business organization if that organization is unprepared for change—indeed, in my opinion, if it has not provided procedures for anticipating change.*

Efforts directed toward solving the problem of organizational development date from World War II. Quite understandably, the difficulty of achieving needed changes in organizations might especially surface during a massive war challenge.

Elements of a Solution

The first approaches toward solutions to the organizational development challenge were almost implicit in the difficulty that had to be surmounted. What particularly had to be assaulted was resistance to change. To achieve change, the first step must be to *unfreeze* the bonds that powerfully hold organization members to the way things now are. Only after that has been done can new opportunities be exploited and *new behaviors* put in place that can then, though perhaps again only temporarily, be *refrozen*.[11]

How shall we unfreeze, or open to needed changes organization members who see the status quo as more attractive than their perception of how proposed changes will affect them? A key strategy settled upon was to develop a feeling of mutual trust and confidence among those who would need to cooperate toward needed changes. Of course, it was asserted, people cannot work together effectively if they are fearful of one another. Where there is fear or insecurity, people will do much of their planning on the basis of *hidden agendas,* ideas about what is wanted that are not shared openly with associates. Fear and insecurity will also result in a less than candid sharing of information as data are gathered for making change decisions. Of course, planning built quite literally out of deceptions would often be very poorly done.

What was seen to be most needed was a different kind of *manager training.* Heretofore the principal emphases in developing managers had been to improve knowledge and to develop skills. Against the backdrop of trust and confidence deficiencies, however, it was concluded that something else must now be given high priority. Much needed, too, was the willingness and the ability to be personally open with organization associates. That is, those who must plan together would have to learn to share understandings and feelings that are important to thinking about needed organizational changes.[12]

[11] Edgar H. Schein, "Management Development as a Process of Influence," *Industrial Management Review,* May 1961, pp. 59–77.

[12] Sheldon A. Davis, and Robert Tannenbaum, "Values, Man, and Organization," *Industrial Management Review,* Volume 10, Number 2, 1969, pp. 67–86.

The Sensitivity Training Approach

A first major endeavor to help managers achieve more personal openness was appropriately called *sensitivity training.* That meant the sensitivity of people to one another, their awareness of others' understandings, but more especially of their own needs and feelings. Sensitivity training was to help people become more aware of their fellows, which, of course, would require them to be more willing to reveal themselves.

The principal technique used was the so-called *T(raining)* Group, the nature of which gives training participants an excellent opportunity to (learn to) reveal themselves.[13] More specifically, the T-group is a basically *unstructured group situation,* in which the *trainer* is primarily an observer, rather than a leader. Leader behavior then compels participants to find their own identity in relation to this group and to struggle with the group leadership problems that necessarily arise. In this process of searching for personal identity and struggling with group structure issues, information is developed that enables group members to learn a great deal about themselves and one another.

Perhaps predictably, the lack of guidance by a designated leader would result in many painful *confrontations* of participants by one another. That is, there is likely to be in such a context a great deal of bluntly telling one another how he or she is behaving poorly and how to become more interpersonally competent. In time, moreover, confrontations came to be seen as a very essential element in the achievement of openness.[14] How else, it was argued, could people be unfrozen from the resistances to change that were hampering organizational development other than by being compelled to look closely at themselves and their impact on others.

Understandably, the unguided group situation with its confrontation discomforts was threatening to men and women who had never experienced it before. Not surprisingly, therefore, a small proportion of those put into T-groups suffered at least some of the elements of a nervous breakdown. Yet, in many kinds of circumstances, sensitivity training accomplished its purpose. Granted that a price did have to be paid, the sensitivity toward others often achieved was nevertheless

An Existentialist Overview

Sensitivity training addresses itself to ways of being with other people. "Hell," as Sartre wrote, may be "other people," but on this earth there is virtually no escape from them. If a psychological hell is embedded in relationships between people, "happiness" is no less dependent on human society.

[13]Martin Lakin, *Interpersonal Encounter: Theory and Practice in Sensitivity Training* (New York: McGraw-Hill, 1972).

[14]Robert T. Golembiewski, *Renewing Organizations* (Itasca, Ill.: Peacock, 1972), pp. 28–44.

thought by many to be well worth the initial discomfort. The "joy of openness," being open with others and receiving their openness in return, seemed to many T-group participants to be a treasure of great value. Over a dozen or so years after 1950, thousands of managers were sent by their companies to be developed in T-group programs.

Why Sensitivity Training Was Not the Answer

As it turned out, however, T-groups as such were not what the organizational development problem called for. As time went along, it became increasingly evident that the sensitivity training approach to manager training often fell far short.

Not everyone believed that the keen discomfort experienced by many T-group participants, to say nothing of the risk of breakdown, was a price worth paying for what was gained. Moreover, a comparison of costs with benefits only in part reflected how high the costs actually were. In addition, negative conclusions stemmed from the feeling that a high degree of openness is not necessarily a valuable outcome.

Many people began to have reservations about what some T-group-trained people were taking back to their organizations. Being open with people one has struggled to achieve openness with is one thing. Being open with people one has not gone through the struggle for openness with—for example, subordinates and peers—is quite another. Specifically, a strangeness of fit began to be seen between many managers who had learned to be much more open and the organizations that had paid for their T-group training.[15]

Imagine, for example, a manager who has developed the joy and skills of openness. Of course, too, he would be encouraged to make use of his newly achieved personal growth because the company, after all, did send him to the T-group experience. Immediately on his return, therefore, he launches himself on a new career of being open with his organization associates. Suppose, moreover, that this new career includes the confrontations that have become an important part of his human relationships. A very early discovery will be that frankness with colleagues who have not yet learned the "joy of openness" will often be painfully unwelcome. In particular, where the sensitivity-trained manager assumes that his not sensitivity-trained superior wants frankness, the "joy of openness" may suddenly turn into a search for another job.

The Managerial Grid Transition

As the shortcomings of the T-group approach to organizational development became increasingly evident, the number of managers sent to such programs declined sharply. Sensitivity training proponents endeavored to adjust what they

[15]Ross A. Webber, *Management: Basic Elements* (Homewood, Ill.: Irwin, 1975), p. 678.

"This new, more positive self-image of yours, Clarkson—get rid of it." (Drawing by Stevenson; © 1977 The New Yorker Magazine, Inc.)

were doing to make it more useful. There was a great deal of experimentation with what came to be called *family T-groups,* in which those who would later be working together would achieve openness together. But the discomfort was still present, as well as some risk of more serious emotional difficulties.

Understandably, therefore, efforts were directed toward replacing sensitivity training as the manager development approach to organizational development. A different approach was soon being devised—one that became in a few years perhaps even more popular than sensitivity training had been.

This next step toward organizational development was called *managerial grid* training.[16] In this type of training, managers gather for, perhaps typically, a

[16]Robert Blake, and Jane Mouton, *The Managerial Grid* (Houston: Gulf Publishing Company, 1964).

one-week program. On the basis of their knowledge of one another, whether that knowledge was gained in their organization back home or in the training situation, participants are asked to describe one another's managerial style. That view of oneself from others provides a mirror image that each manager can then compare with his view of himself for the purpose of achieving a better understanding of his effectiveness as a manager. It will, of course, be noted that mirror images of participants provided by others are here also confrontations intended to unfreeze behavior and make it less resistant to change.

Armed with a better understanding of themselves, these managers-in-training are then given for study a "picture" of a variety of managerial styles so that they can see their own style in fuller perspective. This "picture" is the managerial grid (Figure 12-2). It highlights manager outlooks and behaviors from the standpoint of two key variables: *concern for production* and *concern for people.* Note, by the way, how closely these ways of thinking about managers *vis a vis* their tasks and their subordinates parallel the Ohio State and Michigan leadership research discussed in Chapter 10.

The manager being trained has now looked at himself closely as a manager and has compared his personal style with a wide variety of manager-style possibilities. It is hoped he is now ready to move toward becoming more nearly the manager

FIGURE 12-2. The Managerial Grid.

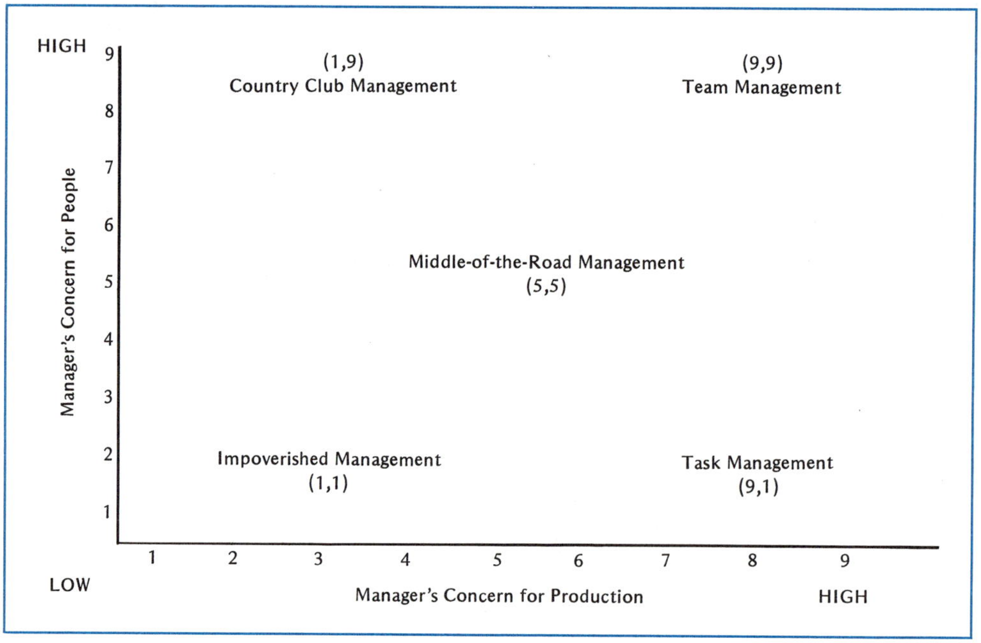

he should be. The basic assumption underlying the managerial grid model is that concern for production and concern for people are both important. More specifically, it is assumed that a 1,9 managerial style, where good relationships are much more important than production, will lead to a sort of "Country Club Management," which will likely not get very much work done. The opposite of "Country Club Management," a 9,1 managerial style, making high production much more important than good relationships, may backfire and therefore also get too little work done. Of course, a 1,1 managerial style, a concern for neither production nor good relationships, is not promising. Only, therefore, as one achieves a balance between these two concerns—at the 5,5 or, better yet, the 9,9 level—will he develop into a truly effective manager.

ON TO ORGANIZATIONAL DEVELOPMENT

Managerial grid training had helped offset some of the difficulties that were rapidly eroding the manager training value of T-groups. A training leader provided a structure for the group experience that lessened the need for deep confrontations. This in turn by-passed much of the danger of emotional upset. The extreme emphasis on trust and confidence also disappeared from the managerial grid approach. Those were the largest changes from sensitivity training. The "joy of openness," which had on occasion been so tragically destructive to participants' careers, was no longer the end in view. Rather, what was wanted was organizational development.

However, the managerial grid was only a *transition* in the evolution toward organizational development. Whatever assumptions proponents of this approach had that grid training for managers would be a sufficient lever to achieve organizational development proved to be exaggerated. It is no longer taken for granted that a 9,9 managerial style is ideal; good relationships seem not to be quite as important to organizational performance as was once thought. More specifically, it was by now evident to many people that no amount of or approach to manager training, in and of itself, would really achieve organizational development. It came to be seen, in other words, as not enough to work around the hazards of sensitivity training. Also essential would be keeping the larger organizational development need in sharp focus.

It is important to be very clear about this. It was not that manager development was not helpful. But there is something of a controversy between organizational development enthusiasts and other management people who feel that much more emphasis should be placed instead on manager development.

Organizational development enthusiasts were beginning to insist that manager development, however valuable, is not necessarily organizational development. Thus, sensitivity training has lived vigorously on in the form of what has come to be called encounter groups. However, many fewer managers as such are participants in these programs. In fact, a close cousin of family T-groups is often a key element in more comprehensive organizational development programs.[17] Similarly, managerial grid training has continued to be an important way in which organizations endeavor to develop their managers. In many cases, these endeavors are also part of a larger organizational development program.

Numerous other varieties of manager training continue to be popular as well. For example, manager training in the implementation of *management by objectives* is widely used, often making in the process a contribution to whatever organizational development work is going on.[18] The same is true, to mention only one other example, of *transactional analysis training,* in which managers are helped to understand the difference between "parent," "child," and "adult" communicating.[19] Again, however, what is important here is not that manager development became less useful; rather, we were learning to make the hard, but perhaps critically needed, distinction between manager training and organizational development and to do whatever of these two things seems indicated.

Several threads of continuity moved from sensitivity training beginnings, through the managerial grid transition, into organizational development. One was the importance of sensitivity, awareness. Resistance to change is, after all, the key obstacle to the effective adaptation of organizations to their environments, and interpersonal sensitivity is one of the key ways of meeting resistance to change. A second is the confrontation technique of unfreezing managers to change. Although a less threatening kind of confrontation is used in grid training, it also recognizes that people may have to be confronted by themselves and by others so as to become more aware of where they are in relation to where they ought to be. It had become evident that confrontation must be cautiously and expertly employed if it is to build trust and confidence without doing damage.[20] Finally, the family T-group method of organizational development training continued to be seen as valuable, to help those who would later be developing their organization together to achieve openness and information sharing with one another.

This concept of *team building* had appeared in the later stages of the sensitivity training period. In managerial grid training, it began to be much more thoroughly accepted that putting organization associates together in training situations could be highly beneficial. Then, putting all of these carry-overs together, it was only a short step to another key understanding. Confrontation, the struggle toward interpersonal sensitivity, can contribute much more to organizational development if that struggling takes place in the context of the organizational development problem.

[17] Golembiewski, op. cit., pp. 156 ff.

[18] George Odiorne, *Management By Objectives* (New York: Pitman, 1965).

[19] Thomas A. Harris, *I'm OK, You're OK* (New York: Harper, 1967).

[20] William Gomberg, "Problems in Management Development Programs," *The Personnel Administrator,* September-October 1964, pp. 1–6.

The Assumptions of Organizational Development

The core element in modern organizational development builds most fundamentally from what we know about human behavior. The point of departure of practitioners serving as *change agents* is, therefore, assumptions. And note in these assumptions how closely they reflect both the organizational development problem and the history of efforts to solve it.[21]

Organizational change agents first make some assumptions about people. They assume that many people have unfilled needs for personal growth. Given these needs, such people can make a much larger contribution to their organizations than they now are making. The organization, however, must help them become more nearly what they are capable of becoming. There is available, then, a *mutual interest* in change, an interest that often comes to a focus on resistance to change obstacles. Where these obstacles can be surmounted, manager development and organizational development can usefully become two sides of the same process.

Also, organizational development work is based on assumptions about people in relation to groups. Here what is important is everyone's need for cooperative interaction within at least one group. Work groups can, of course, become vital in the lives of people. These groups, therefore, can become an especially available handle for moving people from a frozen status quo toward needed organizational change. When people have reasons rooted in their own needs to take on developmental opportunities, they will probably work much more effectively in groups that are important to them than they have done previously. Work situations, moreover, are particularly likely to be developmental if it is not taken for granted that a group's leader will make virtually all of its decisions.

These two sets of assumptions then interlink with a third set, organizational development assumptions about people vis a vis the larger organization.[22] First, assumptions are made about the nature of the organizational development problem. It is assumed that work groups and other organization subdivisions overlap. This, in turn, suggests that what happens at one point in an organization may create a wide circle of consequences. It would seem then to follow that

The "Father" of Organizational Development

Most would agree that if anyone merits this title, that person is Kurt Lewin. His special interests in this emerging area of study were his field theory of social psychology and a passion for applied behavioral science. Although Lewin died before organizational development became a full-fledged discipline, he was a central figure in the origin of both sensitivity training and survey research.

[21]Wendell French, "Organization Development: Objectives, Assumptions, and Strategies," *California Management Review*, Winter, 1969, pp. 23–24.

[22]Paul R. Lawrence, "How To Deal With Resistance to Change," *Harvard Business Review*, January-February 1969, pp. 4–13.

change planning must carefully take into account these *interdependent relationships.*

Some further assumptions even more pointedly anticipate the need for behavioral science in guiding organizational development. It is assumed that *organization climates* tend to suppress the expression of the feelings people have about one another and about their own difficulties. It is then assumed that suppressed feelings must adversely affect both personal growth and group problem solving. Limited personal growth opportunities and problem solving, then, will likely go hand in hand with a low level of interpersonal trust and support. These several relationships together will probably result in behavior strategies that serve personal and smaller-group interests rather than the larger organization.

In the realm of solving the organizational development problem, it is primarily assumed that *mutually acceptable strategies* for serving organization-wide interests can more frequently be devised than is now the case. A first principle in developing such strategies is to make much more use of feelings as data. As was emphasized in the discussion of decision making, how people feel about what is happening to them is the most crucial information there is for an organization's decision process. Again, observe the behavioral science emphasis; surely, it is assumed, better understanding of the outlooks of the organization's members can open up new avenues toward goal setting, leadership, communication, and intergroup cooperation. What is thereby made possible, it is then finally assumed, must be implemented by making appropriate changes in how the organization deals with its people. For, of course, such activities as staffing, training, task subdivisions, work appraisal, and compensation can either reinforce or fight against whatever management is endeavoring to do.

The Organizational Development Intervention

Reaching into a large, complex organization to make it more adaptive is clearly a large order. Perhaps the term *intervention* does not exaggerate as a description of what must typically happen. That terminology does not overtstate in view of the fact that a full-scale organizational development effort really must be comprehensive, involving all organizational levels and all aspects (technology, structure, people) of the organization.

Let us next, therefore, look at the organizational development intervention—the way(s) change agents do reach comprehensively into an organization to make it perform more satisfactorily.[23] In looking more specifically at what organizational development is, we can quite plainly see the importance of the sensitivity training and managerial grid predecessors in setting the stage for today's organizational development endeavors.

The organizational development intervention is often called *action research*

[23]Richard Beckhard, *Organization Development: Strategies and Models* (Reading, Mass.: Addison-Wesley, 1969).

(Figure 12-3), because systematic data collection—*diagnosis*—becomes the basis for ensuing actions. It is appropriate that this kind of learning about a particular organization's dynamics is called *process learning.* The push for needed change must, of course, begin with the organization's internal processes; the key factors are how the organization functions and why it does not function better. Mastering and then effectively using this kind of learning in effecting organizational change are thought of as developing *process skills.*

Because action is what is wanted from diagnosis, a first premise of organizational development work is that it must begin at the top. That is not because organizational development decisions will primarily be implemented by force. Often, the organizational development problem may in substantial part be a product of endeavoring to do too much by naked coercion. Rather, the understanding is that top management can too easily veto change programs if those people are not a basic element in what is being proposed.

There is, of course, a special problem of confrontation where top managers are involved. An insightful saying goes, "The boss may not always be right, but he is

FIGURE 12-3. ***An Action Research Model for Organizational Development. [Source: Newton Margulies and Anthony P. Raia,* Organizational Development: Values, Process, and Technology *(New York: McGraw-Hill, 1972), p. 36.]***

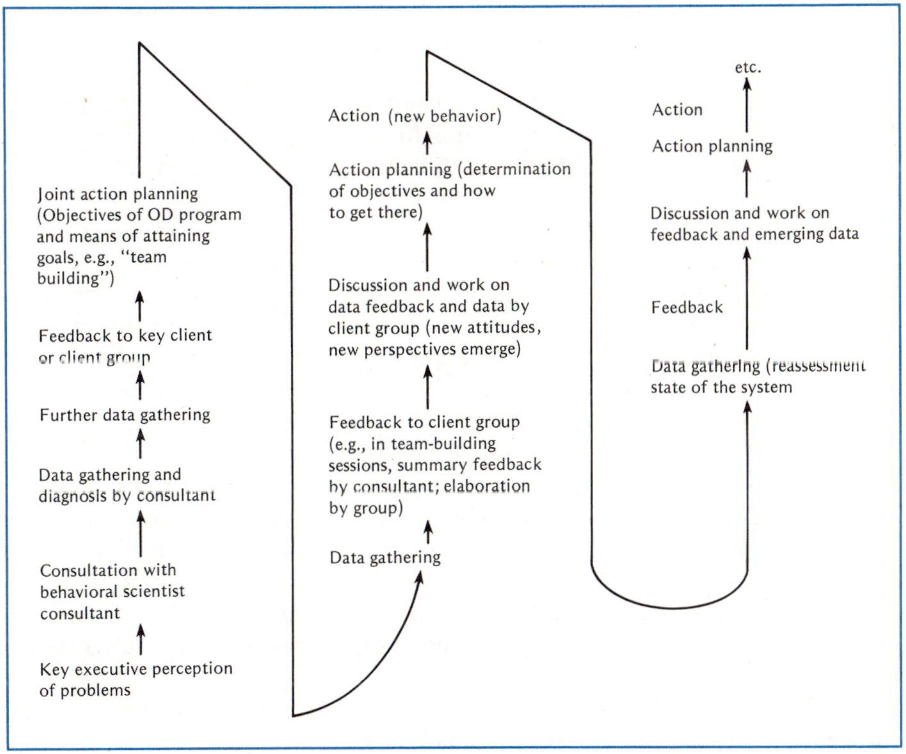

still the boss." But top managers cannot be exempt. They must be helped to see themselves as others in the organization see them, as a first step toward jarring them out of their frozenness. Again, if the powerful are not convinced about doing their part toward organizational development, the needed changing cannot be achieved beneath them in the organizational hierarchy. As with mental illness and alcoholism, the prognosis for an organization in difficulty is poor unless the patient acknowledges the problem and seeks help.

To assist with this confronting of the powerful is one of the principal reasons change agents are so often *outside consultants.*[24] Outsiders can probe with top managers into relationships and possibilities that are personally sensitive to these people without fear for their own futures. Equally important, however, outsiders can, by their interacting with top managers help make certain that there will be *top management support* for an organization climate that is supportive of organizational development. Without that, of course, securing openness lower in the organization would be impossible.

Change agent interaction with upper managers is a first data-gathering operation, a research program designed to find a conceptual and organizational framework within which to begin an action program. With this framework in mind, change agents can then begin gathering data one step farther down in the organization. Personal feelings must be an important part of the diagnosis data collected. At all levels in an organization, how people feel about their situations will be important to how effectively they perform for their organization. Again, too, confrontation must be an element in this data collection. Always, much of what is needed is an understanding of some of the deeper feelings of those involved. Always, it is vital for the organizational development endeavor to achieve much sharing of real feelings and to have available a substantial degree of mutual trust and confidence.

As each next organization level is brought into the development effort, it is essential that there be a two-way information flow between levels. A common way of achieving this is by using *survey feedback*. The term *survey* may mean anything from a not very systematic interviewing of those from whom information is wanted to elaborate questionnaires filled out by these people. But more important than the kind of survey is the fact of feedback; what is learned will thereby be made available to those supplying the information and to organization members closely associated with these informants.

The function, and therefore the necessity, of information feedback is readily apparent. How else can people be confronted in real-world terms except by those who as close associates are particularly knowledgeable about one another? Obviously, this process can be very treacherous. Feedback between levels means subordinates candidly telling their superiors, if only indirectly, what problems they see and how they feel about superior-subordinate relationships. Once more,

[24]Johnson, and others, op. cit., pp. 219 ff.

a full-scale organizational development program requires that people feel safe with one another.

By now, if the action research effort is going well, managers and their subordinates at upper organization levels have begun a process of team building. They are beginning to be much more sensitive to one another's needs and potential contributions and the need to take one another more fully into account. By now, therefore, it is hoped they are finding the mutual interests, the personal growth, and satisfaction possibilities, without which the resistance to change problem cannot be surmounted. By now, too, organizational interdependence can begin to be built into a broadly based assault on frozenness. Focusing on the most fundamental dimension of the organizational development process, these are the *behavioral science data* that must now be translated into change actions.[25]

The organizational development process must move down the organization hierarchy one step at a time (Figure 12-4), always then feeding back diagnosis data

FIGURE 12-4. Organization Development Phases. (Source: Margulies and Raia, p. 38.)

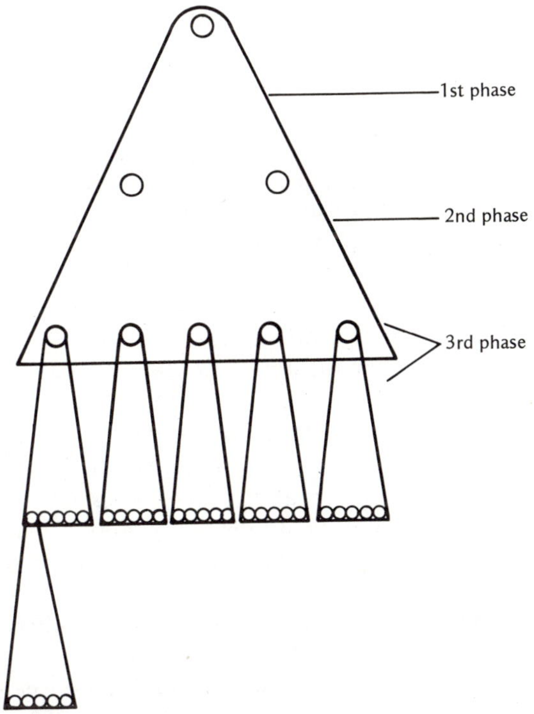

1st phase. Data gathering, feedback, and diagnosis—consultant and top executive only

2nd phase. Data gathering, feedback, and revised diagnosis—consultant and two or more key staff or line people.

3rd phase. Data gathering and feedback to total top executive team in "team building" laboratory with or without key subordinates from level below

4th and additional phases. Data gathering and team building sessions with 2nd or 3rd level teams.
Subsequent phases. Data gathering, feedback and interface problem solving sessions across groups.
Simultaneous phases. Several managers may attend "stranger" T-Groups; courses in the management development program may supplement this learning.

[25] Bernard Berelson, and Gary A. Steiner, *Human Behavior* (New York: Harcourt Brace Jovanovich, 1964).

from each lower level to the level immediately above, and vice versa. Furthermore, every organizational development program differs from every other one because organizations are different, because change agents are different, and because organizational development is not an exact science. When the end of data gathering and its use in analysis are in sight, the problem of reshaping the organization's *system of behavior reinforcements,* its overall personnel system, takes on greatest significance. As you can see, modern organizational development has become complex and therefore difficult.

ORGANIZATIONAL DEVELOPMENT: HOW MUCH CAN IT DO?

There is a long history in management of expecting too much of new approaches. This overoptimism began in recent times with scientific management, and has moved to such things as "the caring supervisor," Theory Y, management by objectives, and job enrichment. It will be useful, therefore, to look closely at organizational development from the standpoint of what can and cannot be expected from it.

"Missionaries" and "Opportunists"

It has long been a cliché in American politics that local option prohibition is supported primarily by bootleggers and ministers. That kind of union between strange bedfellows may have something of a counterpart in the organizational development field. For example, just as scientific management came to be thought of by many as a gospel, organizational development has been promoted by some people who would have to be thought of as missionaries. There are two dangers in a missionary approach that presents organizational development as a panacea for organization ills. On the one hand, "true believers"[26] are likely to advertise organizational development in misleading and glowing terms. Exaggeration can invite organizational development endeavors in situations that are not appropriate to such an effort, or by consultant change agents who are not equal to the tasks they are assuming. The result is likely to be disappointed hopes that will reflect against the very real contributions to organizational health that organizational development can unquestionably make.

On the other hand, overoptimism on the part of missionaries assists those who do organizational development work primarily to earn consultant fees. The more missionaries do to make organizational development endeavors seem valuable ("let us release the imprisoned potential in your people") and certain to succeed

[26]This is Eric Hoffer's term, describing people whose lives come to be literally taken over by some reform cause. Eric Hoffer, *The True Believer* (New York: Harper, 1951).

("how could a fuller use of your human resources fail to make your organization more healthy?"), the easier it will be for opportunists to expand their role. Adding to this possibility is the fact that typically change agents in organizational development efforts are outsiders.

There are, let us strongly emphasize, many competent organizational development professionals, who can point to impressive successes. However, these very successes can greatly assist opportunists to increase their business. At that point, both missionaries and successful practitioners are unintentionally, but substantially, helping to expand the activities of opportunists, some of whom may be of the hard-sell variety. Whatever inappropriate and unsuccessful organizational development work is done must cast a shadow on the fine work that can be done.

Organizational Development As Fad

If only one thing is then added to this combination of missionaries, opportunists, and successful organizational development practitioners, we have all of the ingredients of a *fad.* That added element is potential clients who are not carefully discriminating, a possibility well described by Professor George Strauss:

> *American companies are suckers for gimmicks. Managers are too anxious to find short-cut solutions to complicated problems, particularly in the area of human relations. Companies try one attractive package after another, just as long as each promises a painless solution to their problems. Human relations, suggestions systems, the open door policy, brainstorming, zero-defect programs—all have had their day. Each is tried in turn and then allowed to lapse gradually into oblivion. When instant success is not achieved, there is a tendency to switch one's attention to other areas. And false expectations may lead to cynical disillusionment.*
>
> *Staff training men often contribute to fadism, even when they should know better. Staff effectiveness is not easily measurable, and staff men must prove their worth by making contributions that are easily dramatized. The training director who is in his seventh successful year with the same program may not have the visibility of the man who introduces a completely new program with great fanfare each year.*[27]

Given so open an invitation to fadists, it is not surprising that organizational development endeavors are sometimes launched under unlikely circumstances. Ideally, such endeavors should reflect fully mutual goal setting, a collaboration based on as nearly equal power among associates as can be managed, a genuine spirit of inquiry using publicly shared data, and equal freedom to terminate the program. Because, however, ideal conditions so rarely exist, in practice organizational development consultants are often brought in for other reasons. Again, Strauss has succinctly sorted these out.[28]

First, there is the *conversion motive.* An influential manager is exposed to an

[27] George Strauss, "Organization and Development," in Robert Dubin, (Ed.), *Handbook of Work, Organization, and Society* (Chicago: Rand McNally, 1976), p. 669.

[28] Strauss, ibid., pp. 646–7.

organizational development missionary—who may also be a competent organizational development professional. Captivated by this exposure, the manager develops a keen desire to introduce this into his own organization. But conversions are rarely contagious, except in the revival meeting setting. By definition, the organizational development prognosis is poor if the impetus behind it is not the concrete difficulties of the organization launching it.

Second, there is the *morale motive.* Those responsible for getting an organizational development program underway may well understand that they are embarking on much less than a full-scale effort. No great difficulty is in sight; no large consequences are expected. The collaborative sharing principle behind organizational development, however, provides an opportunity to "get people together" to show them that top management is interested in working closely with them. The morale motive is often triggered by personnel people and accepted by managers as something that "might be helpful."

Third, there is the *handyman motive.* An organization may have a specific problem, as distinguished from an organizational development need. There is, in other words, no thought that the organization will be significantly changed. Furthermore, it will often be that top management—for example, the chief executive—will know exactly what it/he wants done about this problem before the outside consultants are called in. Here, by the way, is an especially attractive situation for opportunists. With top management already committed to a workable solution to a small problem, the handyman motive can frequently produce tangible successes that facilitate organizational development advertising.

Finally, there is the *Mafia motive.* Outside consultants are brought in by one manager (or group of managers) to "take care of" another manager (or group of managers). Quite possibly, in this "hired gunman" setting, some organization changes will be made. That changing will probably, too, be done in a context of going through the motions of democratic decision making. Those who are to be "taken care of," however, will, of course, have little to say about what is being done. It is obvious, incidentally, how useful it is to get outsiders to do an organization's dirty work for it. An uncomfortable unpleasantness can thereby be put off on someone else, and the full onus of what was done can then later be put on people who are no longer around.

Some Continuing Difficulties

In addition to the missionary/opportunist possibility, perhaps accentuated by fadism, organizational development can easily promise too much for other reasons. So much that is written about organizational development sounds as if there is a full-blown behavioral science ready to be used in organization change contexts by competent specialists. Unhappily, that is not so—and unhappily in part because the limits of the science dimension of organizational development can assist both missionaries and opportunists.

We have already emphasized the relatively large proportion of art mixed with the science that can be used by managers. Not only is that true in the organizational development realm, but the proportion of art in managing is significantly higher in the behavior areas than where more technical decisions are involved. The extreme of the pretensions of organizational development on the science front are quite comparable to the pretensions that brought scientific management to gospel status. Every genuine organizational development task requires more trial, error, and hoping than is required in all but a small proportion of medical or engineering problem situations.

Furthermore, it is possible that many organizational development people, because there is a sizable missionary element in these efforts, are sometimes more preoccupied with sensitivity and confrontation than with organizational development. Such a preoccupation with interpersonal relationships can get in the way of careful thinking about very real problems. In additon, organizational development programs are not the only way to upgrade an organization's health. It may be that improvement endeavors that are more modest, less costly, and inviting fewer confrontation risks should more frequently be tried before the more wholesale organizational development approach is undertaken.[29]

There are other ways, too, of emphasizing the dysfunctions of a preoccupation with the personal interactions side of life in organizations. The limits of that approach to organization therapy—and recall here our earlier discussion of T-group training—were largely responsible for its becoming much more of a program for individual than for organizational health. There are no doubt, too, many situations in which less complicated changes in organization structure might accomplish more for an organization than exploring some of the emotional depths of organization members.[30] It is still much easier to devise effective confrontation experiences—with all of their discomforts and risks—than it is to be reasonably certain that such experiences will be usefully put to work in the organization.

There is one other way in which much of the continuing problem of organizational development can be stated. There is a strange gap in organizational development thinking, perhaps because of its missionary point of departure. One of its most important emphases is enough mutual trust to promote information sharing. Yet, the organizational development literature is oddly silent about why the lack of trust among human beings is so pervasive. What many individuals do, of course, is to keep from others information they feel it would be unsafe to share. A fully successful organizational development program may create a situation in which mutual sharing of understandings is safe. Who will guarantee, however, that it will continue to be safe to share understandings with one another. And

[29]John H. Miner, "The O D–Management Development Conflict," *Business Horizons*, December 1973, pp. 31–6.

[30]W. Wohlking, "Attitude Change, Behavior Change," *California Management Review*, Volume 13, Number 2, 1970, pp. 45–50.

A Grim Reminder

I have yet to see an organization development program that uses an interventional strategy other than an interpersonal one; and this is serious when one considers that the most pivotal strategies of change in our society are political, legal and technological. We call ourselves "change agents," but the real changes in our society have been wrought by the pill, the bomb, the automobile, industrialization, communication media, and other forces of modernization.

Bennis, *Changing Organizations*, pp. 78–9.

long before it is known that the organization will not always be safe for sharing, one may have done serious damage to oneself by previous sharing.[31]

Given the possibilities for organizational development as a fad—note here especially the "handyman" and "Mafia" orientations—a particular organizational development program may not be all that it is advertised as being. Top managers may want an organizational development program to change people so that they will be more congenial within the organization as it now is, rather than really changing the organization. When there are upper-manager agendas that are likely to remain hidden, the sharing that may be induced may not be mutually useful. Of course, experienced members of organizations well understand these possibilities. Wherever, as a result, organization members become quite reluctant to be candid with one another, organizational development is already unlikely. It is small wonder voices are being raised suggesting that more often than is now the case we might be better off endeavoring to make our organizations manageable by members as they are, rather than endeavoring to make these people quite different.[32]

How Much *Can* OD Do?

But if around the edges of what is being done in the name of organizational development there are activities that fall short of the ideal, organizational development is nevertheless a vigorous dimension of the current management scene. On both the practitioner and literature fronts, organizational development is a booming business.

On the practitioner-outside consultant front, the number of professionals holding memberships in OD organizations now number in the low thousands. An OD emphasis sponsored by the National Training Laboratories, the organization

[31]Howard R. Smith, "Communication By Ambiguity," in Richard Huseman, Calvin Logue, and Dwight Freshley, *Readings in Interpersonal and Organizational Communication* (Boston: Holbrook, 1973), pp. 173–87.

[32]Amitai Etzioni, "Human Beings Are Not So Easy to Change After All," *Saturday Review,* June 3, 1972, pp. 45–47.

that pioneered sensitivity training possibilities, has several hundred members. The American Society for Training and Development, an organization for personnel development and training people, created an OD division in the late 1960s that now has approximately 1,000 members. The Academy of Management established its OD division in 1971, and it has since become one of the most active groups in the Academy. A number of universities are offering curricula to prepare students in OD work.

From the standpoint of practitioner work, there is a great diversity in the OD programs being implemented. Much that OD specialists are doing within organizations is not OD work in the comprehensive sense in which that term has been used here. In more strictly OD operations, the top priority is changing the organization climate by building mutual trust and in other ways removing barriers to communication. The techniques OD people find particularly useful include team building, MBO, outside consultants, job enrichment, survey feedback, and participative methods of problem identification and problem solving.

Organizational development is set to and is doing quite a lot. Moreover, it augurs well for the longer-term future of OD endeavors that managers are broadly satisfied with what OD people are helping them do.[33] And it is worth emphasizing that many types of organizations, including service and not-for-profit kinds of operations, are seeking help by way of OD.

A large majority of the leaders of what might be called experienced OD organizations believes that this experience has been successful enough that they will continue these efforts. And that is the acid test of success in the OD field, precisely because it is a comprehensive program that can only be successful over a period of many months. Few of these leaders are completely happy about their OD results. For example, many wish the effectiveness of OD programs was not as difficult to evaluate as it is and that the programs did not require so long a period of time to implement. But both of these conditions are inherent in OD, and OD people have been quite effective in helping OD consumers understand that.

Finally, it might be useful to say a few things about the conditions that evidently must be present if a successful OD program is to be developed. Although it is difficult to define these terms closely, there is no doubt a mixture of "warm-hearted idealism" and "hard-headed realism" which would promise best results. Such endeavors can carry only a limited load of wishful thinking, but important and difficult tasks must always be supported by some optimism. This caution about avoiding misleading expectations is as applicable to managers, who are "suckers for gimmicks" in Professor Strauss' phrase, as to missionaries who make OD seem a panacea.

Organizational development is perhaps an excellent example of the value of doing the right thing for the right reasons. This means making sure that organizational development rather than manager development is what is needed. There

[33] See, for example, W. J. Heisler, "Patterns of OD in Practice," *Business Horizons*, February 1975, pp. 77–84.

also must be a wide acceptance within the organization of the need for a really basic therapy, an equally wide willingness to participate in an effort that must necessarily be quite demanding, and a leadership that is prepared to make decisions on the basis of the data developed by OD research. Specifically, these requirements mean avoiding the "conversion," "morale," "handyman," and "Mafia" motives for launching a so-called OD endeavor.

SUMMARY

Organizational development needs have become one of the large, new problems of our time. The heart of these needs is resistance within organizations to changes needed for better performance within their environments. The organizational development problem has become much larger recently for two reasons. First, organization environments are changing so much. Second, in modern organizations, with their widely delegated authority and tightly interlocking parts, resistance to change has become a much greater obstacle.

Perhaps not surprisingly, first attempts at solving the new organizational development problem centered around manager development. The thinking was that better (trained) managers make organizations more effectively adaptive to their surroundings.

As the manager development approach was pressed, however, difficulties developed with that way of thinking. People, it turned out, are what they are in large part because of their environments. Therefore, taking a manager from his work environment and helping him become significantly different in a training environment did not necessarily make him a better performer.

In fact, in the first major attempt to achieve organizational development by way of manager development, the reverse often happened. Managers exposed to sensitivity training, T-group experiences, sometimes emerged from those situations so different that they were less useful back at work.

The reason for these adverse results was the unstructured group situation that compelled trainees to find their own way to personality openness. Within that very unusual environment, with strangers, managers achieved an interpersonal candidness that could not be used in the very different, unchanged work environment.

Thinking toward organizational development would have to move beyond so fundamental a difficulty. An intermediate step was managerial grid training. That training situation was less dramatic, pressing toward a less basic changing of trainees. More and more, too, the grid approach, as it sought to achieve organizational development status, moved from "stranger" to "family" training sessions. Family training for managers, of course, begins to simulate the living together these same people will be doing back in their organizations.

The next step in this evolution was organizational development, a broad-based approach to organization change by way of total organization action research. This more comprehensive approach includes the sharing of important, sometimes sensitive, information among organization members who have been helped to be open with one another. In that way, much of the earlier struggle did make a contribution to what might be thought of as the organizational development finished product.

Modern organizational development is the most fundamental effort ever undertaken to apply science to the "people problem" of complex organizations. Much fine work is being done in that realm. This work is somewhat hampered by the fact that organizational development endeavors find both missionaries and opportunists pushing their interests. Even so, however, a great deal of effective organizational development work will no doubt continue to be done. And that will particularly be so if we do not expect too much from these efforts, especially by neglecting other ways of building toward better organizations.

Assignments

12-1. What is the organizational change problem? Why has it become a much larger problem since, say, World War II?

12-2. What does the organizational development problem tell us about the usefulness of authority in today's organizations?

12-3. Why is manager autonomy, as it contributes to the organizational development problem, sometimes called "the autonomy dilemma"?

12-4. What is the value for our human living together of the frozen behavior that sometimes gets in the way of organizations trying to keep pace with change?

12-5. Why is the unstructured nature of T-groups so helpful in creating openness?

12-6. What does 1,9 ("Country Club") management tell us about the relation ship between satisfaction and productivity?

12-7. How was the managerial grid a transition to organizational development, and why was it no more than a transition?

12-8. Explain team building in terms of the assumptions made by organizational development people.

12-9. In what ways does the term *intervention* accurately describe what happens in successful organizational development programs?

12-10. How might the opportunism in organizational development be lessened, or would you argue that it is not really a problem? Explain.

12-11. Is the missionary aspect in organizational development more of an asset or more of a liability? Explain.

Case 12-1

SLOCUM PRODUCTS COMPANY*

Thomas Slocum, president of Slocum Products Company, a small manufacturer of household plastic tableware, returned from a one-week sensitivity training workshop sponsored by a local university. He was enthusiastic about his experience and told one of his associates that in his opinion, "Every manager should attend a T-group."

His associate, Jim Cassady, plant superintendent, was puzzled about what Slocum said. He wondered why Mr. Slocum believed that Slocum Products managers needed to learn something about their own behavior. He also wondered whether other company executives would benefit from such an experience. If so, should they all go to the same training group, or would it be better to go to separate sessions? What would be the objective of such training and what would it cost?

Jim remembered a recent conversation he had with his general foreman, who had attended a church-sponsored T-group. Mike had remarked that he believed, "It was pretty much a waste of time for most people," and "Only the real talkative ones got anything out of it." Cassady had recently read several articles about the organizational development approach to organization problems. He wondered if this approach might not be better.

The following day, Cassady received a telephone call from Slocum, inviting him to a meeting in the latter's office for the purpose of discussing informally the question of management training and T-groups. All of the company executives were to be there. Cassady wondered how to approach this meeting and what to say.

1. Would you expect this meeting to be the beginning of an organizational development effort? Why, or why not?
2. Should Cassady recommend sensitivity training for his company's managers, whether or not organizational development is to be involved? Why, or why not?
3. How should Cassady prepare for this meeting?
4. How should he conduct himself at the meeting?

Case 12-2

A NEW PLANT MANAGER†

Several years ago a new plant manager arrived at a continuous process facility (a plant where there is a continuous shaping of raw materials into finished products, [such as] a steel-making plant or an oil refinery). He surveyed the scene and found the following characteristics: the plant had over two thousand employees; there were several layers of managers arranged in functional departments (production, maintenance, technical research, purchasing and stores, engineering, etc.); the plant performed fairly well in terms of productivity and profitability. The new manager's predecessor had been an energetic and autocratic man who had made all the operational and administrative decisions at the plant. The rest of the upper and middle management were called "superintendents"—they superintended their bailiwicks, supplied information to the plant manager, and received orders from the manager about what should be done in their departments and divisions, as the plant was run on a day-to-day basis.

The new manager had a different managerial philosophy and a different leadership style: he believed in delegating as much responsibility to his subordinates as possible; he

*This case was taken, with permission, from Johnson, Monsen, Knowles, and Kasberg (Pacific Palisades, Calif.: Goodyear, 1976), p. 230.

†W. L. French, C. H. Bell, Jr., *Organization Development*, 2nd ed., © 1978, pp. 11–12. Reprinted by permission of Prentice-Hall, Inc., Englewood Cliffs, N.J.

believed in allowing wide participation in the important decisions affecting the work and the work forces; he believed that better information and decisions would come from involved, committed "managers"; he wanted to develop subordinates so that they would move to higher positions of responsibility; and, as he told the managers at one of his first meetings with them, he wanted them to "share in the work and share in the fun." The new manager knew that he needed to build strong individual managers, an effective "management team," and that he needed to change the managerial culture and climate in the plant. He knew that this change in the way things were done would require new skills and a new management climate in the plant. And that would require training; the habits of ten years could not be changed just by his issuing an order. He called in several consultants, told them his desires, and solicited their aid.

As things evolved, there turned out to be six goals of the change project: (1) to increase the abilities and skills of the individual managers; (2) to build an effective top management team; (3) to build stronger division and department teams; (4) to improve the relations between work groups, such as between production and maintenance, and thus reduce the level of energy spent in competition; (5) to change the managerial culture from one in which one person made all the decisions to one in which all managers made or participated in decisions that affected them; and (6) to improve the long-range planning and decision-making abilities of managers at all levels. These change goals and the ideas of the new plant manager were public knowledge, just as was the information about the consultants and the OD program.

1. Does this sound as if it is to be a real OD program? Explain.
2. How much manager development is needed in this situation, and will an OD program accomplish this?
3. What must the new plant manager do to help this effort become an effective OD program?

References

ARGYRIS, CHRIS. *The Applicability of Organizational Sociology.* London: Cambridge University Press, 1972.

BENNIS, WARREN G. *Changing Organizations.* New York: McGraw-Hill Book Company, 1966.

BENNIS, WARREN, KENNETH BENNE, AND ROBERT CHIN (Eds.) *The Planning of Change.* 2nd ed. New York: Holt, Rinehart and Winston, 1969.

BLAKE, ROBERT, AND JANE MOUTON. *Consultation.* Reading, Mass.: Addison-Wesley Publishing Co., Inc., 1976.

BOWEN, DONALD D., AND RAGHU NATH. "Transactional Analysis in OD." *Academy of Management Review* (Jan. 1978), 79–89.

BRIGHT, JAMES R. *Research, Development, and Technological Innovation.* Homewood, Ill.: Richard D. Irwin, Inc., 1964.

BURKE, W. WARNER (Ed.). *Current Issues and Strategies in Organization Development.* New York: Human Sciences Press, 1977.

CONNOR, PATRICK E. "A Critical Inquiry into Some Assumptions and Values Characterizing OD." *Academy of Management Review* (Oct. 1977), 635–644.

COSER, LEWIS A. *The Functions of Social Conflict.* New York: The Free Press, 1956.

CRAIG, ROBERT, AND LESTER BITTEL (Eds.). *Training and Development Handbook.* New York: McGraw-Hill Book Company, 1967.

DRISCOLL, JAMES W. "Trust and Participation in Organizational Decision Making as Predictors of Satisfaction." *Academy of Management Journal* (March 1978), 44–56.

FRENCH, WENDELL, AND CECIL BELL. *Organization Development.* Englewood Cliffs, N.J.: Prentice-Hall, Inc., 1973.

LEWIN, KURT. *Field Theory in Social Science.* New York: Harper & Row, Publishers, 1951.

LOWI, T. J. *The Politics of Disorder.* New York: Basic Books, Inc., Publishers, 1971.

MARGULIES, NEWTON, AND ANTHONY RAIA. *Conceptual Formulations of Organizational Development.* New York: McGraw-Hill Book Company, 1978.

MARGULIES, NEWTON, AND ANTHONY RAIA (Eds.). *Organizational Development: Values, Process, and Technology.* New York: McGraw-Hill Book Company, 1972.

National Industrial Conference Board. *Behavioral Science: Concepts and Management Applications.* Washington, D.C.: National Industrial Conference Board, 1969.

ROGER J. SCHOERNER
Senior Vice President,
Southwire Company

Roger J. Schoerner, a Massachusetts native, is senior vice-president of Southwire Company in Carrollton, Georgia.

He worked for 10 years with a major wire and cable company before moving to Carrollton in 1949, when he co-founded Southwire.

Mr. Schoerner is a board member or participates in activities of numerous state, trade, and civic organizations and holds 34 U.S. and 115 foreign patents.

Executive Commentary
Is It in the Stars?

In 28 years, Southwire Company has grown from a new firm with two principal organizers, 15 employees, and first year's sales of $566,000, to a worldwide organization today, with sales of $600,000,000 and direct or indirect employment of more than 5,000 persons in 14 domestic and overseas plants. During these 28 years, Southwire has experienced at least five organizational changes, and many executives on the management team are now discussing a possible sixth major structural change. Southwire's experience in organizational development is probably quite typical.

In general, no organization can be perfect in the eyes of more than one person. Although it has been stated that it is human nature to resist change, my experience would indicate that very few in an organization are entirely in favor of status quo. As a matter of fact, any time an employee at any level of management has his authority increased, the inevitable change process begins. Therefore, the only way a company could possibly maintain status quo is to cease making any changes at all within the organization in personnel or job functions. This, of course, is virtually impossible.

Changes can vary from the simple routing of a purchase requisition to the major reorganization by product line or profit center or central versus divisional control. When external forces of change are exerted on the organization, a change as subtle as wood warping or as obvious as glass shattering can occur within that organization. It has been our experience that the major sudden changes can be, and usually are,the highest risk and could even be disastrous in the loss of personnel and the disruption of an organization. If profitability and overall objectives of a company are to be maintained, obviously, the slight warping is far more desirable than the complete shattering with the costly rebuilding it would entail. If a major change is believed advisable by the executives in control at any given time, a gradual move to the new structure will probably result in the loss of fewer desirable personnel and a minimum of confusion. I don't recall ever seeing a major change that did not continue to have modifications until it again functioned reasonably well.

Through the years, Southwire has explored every organizational and management fad or whim that has come along, and each of them had some appeal and some success to at least a small group of employees. However, in no case has there been universal acceptance of any idea or plan, and I suspect no matter how enthusiastic a proponent of organizational development may be, universal acceptance will not prevail. Every organization is an association of people, whether within a social group, a private enterprise company, or an Israeli commune. Each organization has internal stresses that are not apparent to most others within the group, let alone to outsiders.

One of the basic problems in changing or restructuring any organization is that each person within the group is different. It is, therefore, impossible to have them all react in a predetermined, hoped-for pattern. Another basic problem is that no person from the lowest echelon to the chairman of the board is likely to score 100% in accomplishing his job. Therefore, it is highly desirable to have an organization with enough flexibility so that the weaknesses of the person assigned to any slot at any time can be covered by others around him. It is also evident to me, from watching the many changes of the personnel in the same organizational format as well as major organizational changes, that no person will fill the same slot in exactly the same manner, regardless of how explicit the job description and definition might be.

Consequently, within any healthy organization there is continual change at every level of management. The size and direction of the change are in proportion to the amount of authority and responsibility each person has within the organization. In general, I believe that people within an organization generally expend more energy and show greater productivity during a period of change. This, in itself, would indicate that perhaps change is beneficial to maximize productivity.

As we grow, it is hoped we learn. New organizational methods are tried; some work and some don't. Not all of the predominent concepts of management in years past were entirely wrong. The most ideal management is perhaps a blend of some part of every management concept that has ever been taught or practiced.

There is no rule of thumb, no easy magic words to say that will make an unprofitable organization turn profitable. What works for one company may be disastrous for another. One of the challenges managers and teachers of managerial philosophy probably will always face is the mystery of what determines whether reorganization and change will result in a company continuing to grow and prosper or to fall by the wayside.

The secret of successful management may well lie in other than the organizational format. Some of these ideas can be found in Confucius' sayings or the many maxims from *Poor Richard's Almanac* of early America. Of the more recent ones, I prefer a saying attributed to McGraw: "There is a way to do it—better find it," or the one attributed to Edison: "There is a way to do it better—find it." Any system that develops leadership that can in turn promote enthusiasm and perseverance will probably be successful. The following quotes fit this philosophy quite well:

> *"Enthusiasm is the greatest business asset in the world. It beats money and power and influence. Single-handed, the enthusiast convinces and dominates where a small army of workers would scarcely raise a tremor of interest. Enthusiasm tramples over prejudice and opposition, spurns inaction, storms the citadel of its object, and like an avalanche overwhelms and engulfs all obstacles. Enthusiasm is faith in action; and faith and initiative rightly combined remove mountainous barriers and achieve the unheard of and miraculous. Set the germ of enthusiasm afloat in your business; carry it in your attitude and manner; it spreads like a contagion and influences every fiber of your industry; it begets and inspires effects you did not dream of; it means increase in production and decrease in costs; it means joy and pleasure and satisfaction to your workers; it means life real and virile; it means spontaneous bedrock results—the vital things that pay dividends."*

> *"Press On—Nothing in the world can take the place of Persistence. Talent will not; . . . Nothing is more common than unsuccessful men with talent. Genius will not; . . . Unrewarded genius is almost a proverb. Education alone will not; . . . The world is full of educated derelicts. Persistence and Determination alone are omnipotent."*

Much of an organization's success or failure probably hinges more on the overall environment created by the interpersonal relationships developed both within the organization and between the organization and external groups.

After all the analyses of companies employing various forms of management, whether termed good or bad, one could almost reach the conclusion that "it really might be in the stars."

CASES FOR PART IV

Case IV-1

CHOOSING A PROPER LEADERSHIP STYLE

Young Harry Carbonotti spent a restless night mulling over his latest challenge. Because of economic pressures, the firm in which he was shipping foreman was coming under increasing strain to reduce costs in shipping operations. His father and older brother, both officers of the firm, had instructed him to accomplish what he thought was near impossible—to decrease employee overtime work by increasing productivity during normal working hours. Harry thought of the problems he had previously experienced with his subordinates. "I just can't seem to get it all together. And I've tried everything—good guy, bad guy, even no guy. Nothing seems to work the way it should. How can I be expected to get more work from the crew without more hassles?"

The Firm

G. Carbonotti, Inc. is a specialty foods wholesale distributor in an eastern city of 250,000. It was established shortly after the Great Depression by George Carbonotti, an aggressive and talented entrepreneur. The firm has enjoyed continuous growth since its inception, with gross sales in 1975 in excess of $2.2 million. The firm is entirely family-held, with George as the principal stockholder, president, and chairman of the board. George attributes the success of the firm to hard work, wise money management, and to what he refers to as a "no-nonsense attitude toward employees."

The operations of the firm consist primarily of the purchase from producers and distribution to grocers of high-quality, relatively expensive specialty foods. A substantial portion of the goods are imported from throughout the world. Operations require a traveling sales staff, office personnel, warehousemen (technically dockworkers), and truck drivers.

Although George Carbonotti is still actively in control of the company, his first son, George, Jr., sits as vice-president. Since entering the firm after graduating from a prominent eastern business school in 1970, George, Jr. has generally held the reins on day-to-day operations.

Shipping Operations
(prior to Nov. 1975)

The shipping operations group, headed by foreman Charlie Dowd, performed the laborious tasks typically associated with wholesale distributors. Goods were received from producers by railroad car or trailer truck and then were stocked by product line in specific locations within the warehouse. Each product was coded with a number that was also associated with its stock location within the warehouse. In order to fill specific orders for goods, computerized pickup sheets were produced that indicated the stock numbers, names of goods, and quantity of each required by a wholesale purchaser. Dockworkers would each take one pickup sheet and walk around the warehouse, pushing a hand-truck and picking off each item indicated on the sheet. Although the automated inventory system was to provide for a minimum of walking distance on each pickup, for various

This case was prepared by Professor Dennis Callaghan of the University of Rhode Island as a basis for class discussion rather than to illustrate either effective or ineffective handling of an administrative situation. Presented at a Case Workshop and distributed by the International Case Clearing House, Soldiers Field, Boston, Mass.

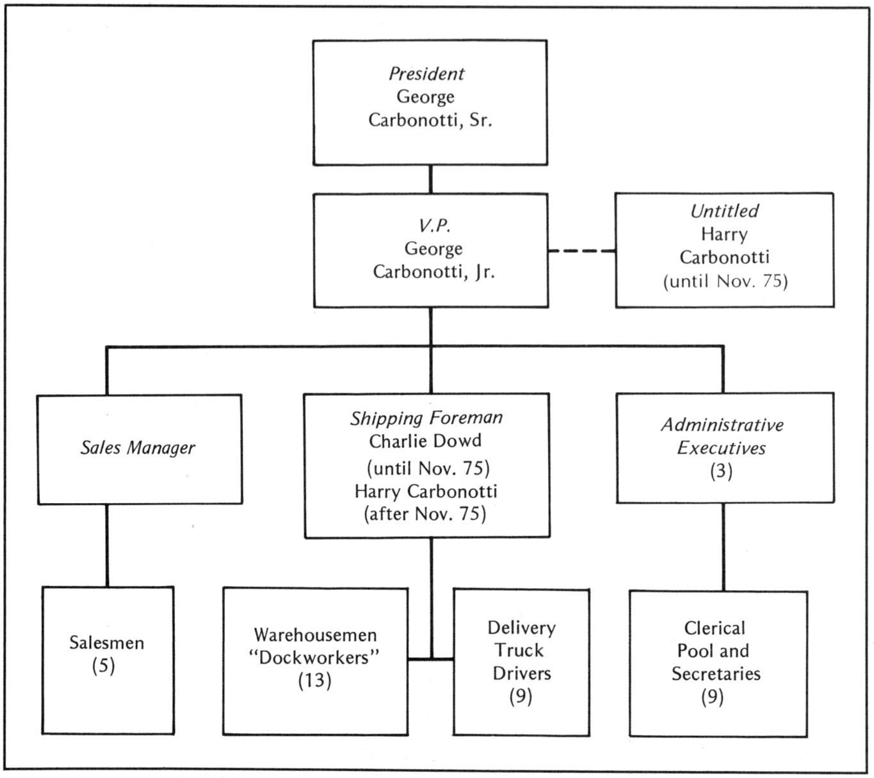

FIGURE 1. Organization: G. Carbonotti, Inc.

reasons certain products would often not be in their proper stock location. This meant that efficient pickup required knowledge by workers of the unusual product locations. New dockworkers usually took about two weeks to become proficient in keeping up with what they called the maverick product locations.

As each order was filled or when a warehouseman had a full hand-truck, the picked goods would be taken to the loading dock where they would be stacked for loading onto a specified delivery truck. The warehousemen would then choose another from the stack of pickup sheets and continue the process. The normal routine involved receiving and picking for the 6 A.M. to 3 P.M. shift of eight workers. At 11 A.M. the second shift of five men would arrive and pick until all orders were completed. At that time all efforts would be shifted to the loading of delivery trucks. Usually five or six trucks would be loaded per day because some of the nine delivery routes required two or more days to complete.

Charlie at the Helm

Because the orders seemed to fluctuate widely from day to day, overtime work would often be required on particularly busy days. Charlie Dowd had been with the firm since its inception and, as foreman for 12 years, had become very adept at forecasting overload days. He was also able to estimate with relative accuracy the overtime required to complete operations on a busy day. This enabled him to spread the overtime work evenly between both shifts. Although the dockworkers generally were indifferent to overtime work, they did become annoyed when one shift received a greater proportion of the overtime during any pay period.

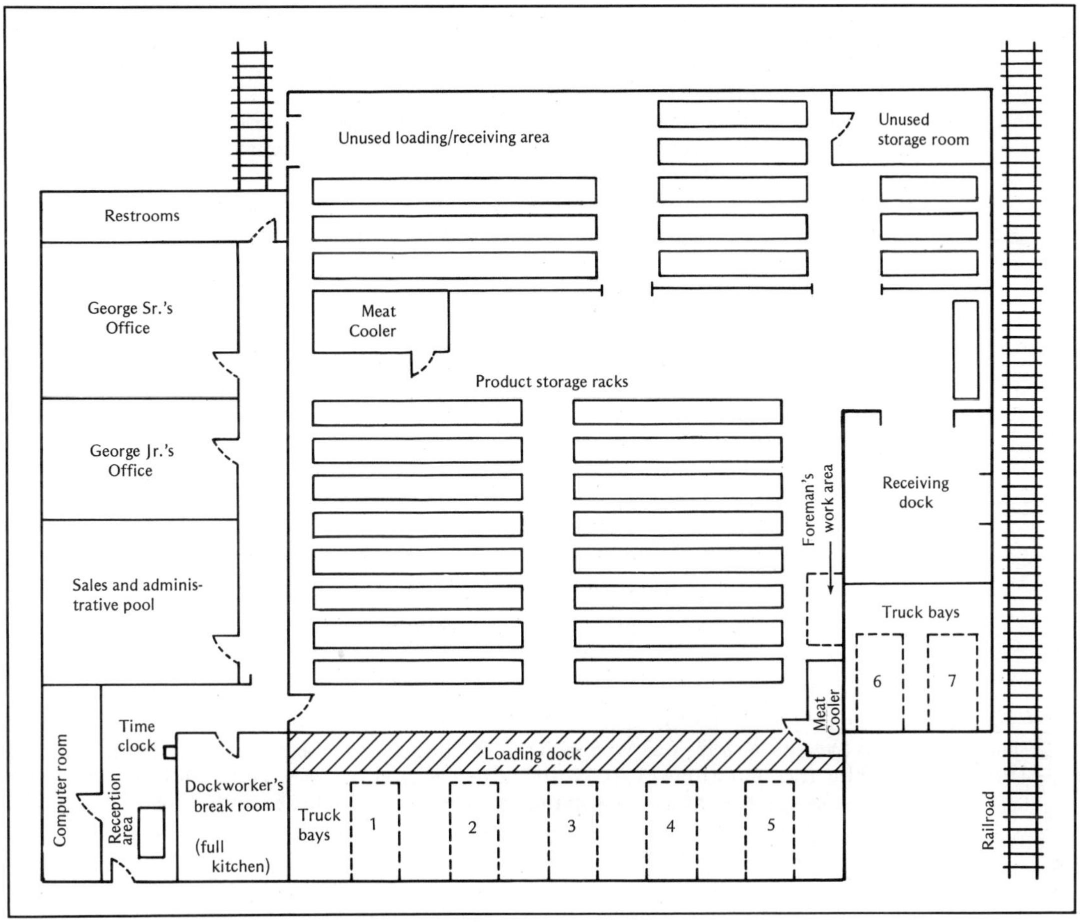

FIGURE 2. Warehouse layout.

Balance in overtime work was only one of many means through which Charlie Dowd maintained his positive relations with both dockworkers and truck drivers. His relaxed, almost lethargic presence, coupled with an astonishing memory for detail, led most of his subordinates to respect him and respond without question to his infrequent instructions. In particular, Charlie rarely interacted with the delivery truck drivers as they were usually senior employees, proficient in their jobs, who operated relatively independently. Generally, all his subordinates felt very comfortable working for him. In his 12 years as foreman, the firm had only been struck twice. This was indeed a remarkable record. Both strikes were of the general type by the Teamsters Union of which his men were members.

Sandbagging and More

Although Charlie maintained good relations with his subordinates, he certainly did not inspire them to work at anywhere near capacity. The relatively relaxed atmosphere seemed to permeate all facets of the operations, resulting in what appeared to be utter boredom among employees. This was particularly obvious when new men came to work in the warehouse. For the first week or so, the rookies would perform their tasks briskly and with interest, stopping only to ask questions as they learned their jobs. Typically, these new men picked more orders in their first few days than did their veteran comrades, even though the rookies were learning their jobs. It didn't take long, however, for new men to fall into the groove followed by the veterans. Only two men, Larry Hinkle and Bob Carmoli, appeared to be conscientiously and diligently performing their jobs. Both had been with the firm for nine years and both appeared content with their jobs. The average tenure for dockworkers was about 13 months.

Along with the high rate of turnover, pilferage and frequent absenteeism were also problems encountered; Charlie Dowd generally ignored these unless they became blatantly obvious. In extreme cases, Charlie would report their occurrences to George Jr. and, after clearance with the union, individuals involved would be fired. These cases were rare, however.

Even though problems existed among warehouse personnel, both George, Sr. and George, Jr. were generally not aware of them. Their occasional presence in the warehouse was always well known by the dockworkers. The pace of work would always pick up for the duration of their visit, usually for less than five minutes per day. New employees were always indoctrinated by the veterans to look sharp when either of the front office Carbonottis was around. There were plenty of stories circulating about the fierce tempers of the Carbonottis, most of them unfounded. It could not be disputed, however, that the Carbonotti approach to employee management was considerably more strict than that practiced by Charlie Dowd.

Harry Carbonotti (prior to Nov. 1975)

Harry, the second son of George Carbonotti, Sr., formally joined the firm on a full-time basis in July, 1973. Unlike George, Jr., Harry had spent a number of summers during his teen years doing odd jobs around the warehouse. After Harry dropped out of college following four semesters of study, his father offered the 21-year-old an untitled position with the firm. Reluctantly, he accepted and began varied duties under the direction of his older brother, George, Jr. Nearly all the duties involved manual labor. Typical jobs included filling in for absent dockworkers, assisting salesmen in setting merchandise displays in stores, and on occasion sorting spoiled merchandise in the warehouse (one of the most objectionable tasks in the company).

There were a number of problems in fitting Harry into the organization. First of all, no openings were immediately available in administration or sales. Even if there were, it was doubtful that Harry was qualified for them. Ironically, family pride prevented his being permanently assigned as a dockworker even though some of the tasks he did perform were of the lowest status. Further, Harry suffered from a chronic lack of self-confidence, possibly in part because of his slight stature (5'2", 115 lbs). He had never had any real responsibility in the firm. George, Sr. constantly cited Harry's persistence in wearing shoulder-length hair and modish clothes as the reason for not delegating responsibility and authority to him.

Harry was in an unusual position in working with the warehouse personnel. He knew the shipping operations as well as anyone but Charlie Dowd. Unfortunately, however, he was neither accepted nor respected by the dockworkers. They continuously felt that he was a family spy within their midst. This forced uncomfortable working situations for both Harry and the dockworkers. On a few occasions, Harry had mentioned specific pilferage and "sandbagging" to George, Jr. Each time, George, Jr. reacted swiftly and robustly in personally reprimanding those involved in the presence of their fellow workers. These occasions continually worsened the relationship between Harry and the dockworkers.

Shipping Operations (Nov. 1975–May, 1976)

Late in November, 1975, Charlie Dowd was stricken with a heart attack and died. After a great deal of deliberation, George, Sr. and George, Jr. decided to move Harry into the foreman position. Surprisingly, Harry was not the least bit reluctant to accept the responsibility. Within four days of Charlie's death, Harry had full responsibility for shipping operations.

Harry's First Month

Harry took on the job with new-found vigor. He recognized the potential problems he would have in dealing with the dockworkers, so he began to carefully think through the approach he would use in leading them. He decided that he would try to befriend his subordinates by showing genuine interest in each of them. By doing so, he hoped he could generate the respect that Charlie had enjoyed.

For the first two weeks, Harry took coffee breaks and ate lunch every day with the men, something that Charlie had never done. On a number of occasions, Harry bought coffee and donuts for the entire crew. In the morning when the men arrived, he allowed them to choose the order in which each of the loads would be picked. He offered the crew the option of changing coffee break and lunch times as long as they were kept to the previous durations of two 10-minute and one half hour break per day. The first shift of men chose to have their coffee breaks 15 minutes earlier and their lunch break the same as in the past. The second shift decided not to change their break times.

For the first few days under Harry's leadership there was much talk among the dockworkers. Many boasted among themselves that they would quit if Harry didn't "pan out." They clearly understood why Harry had got the job—he was family—but they didn't like it. Initially, they toyed with the possibility of sabotaging operations so that Harry would appear to be performing poorly. This talk was short-lived, however. Harry's approach seemed to be working. At first, the men's reactions were characterized by utter disbelief that a Carbonotti could treat them as well as Harry did. Soon they began to believe that Harry was going to "pan out." On one occasion, Harry found one of the men leaving work with a $14 box of imported cheese. He called the individual aside and clearly laid out the repercussions of pilferage. Here the matter ended. No report was made to the front office. The individual reported for work as usual the following day. In a short period of time, all the dockworkers were aware of the incident.

The first month of Harry's new job went well for him. Although overtime work seemed to be increasing, Harry rationalized this as being a result of holiday season demands. Most important to him, he felt that he had successfully managed to generate an effective working relationship with his men. Unfortunately, his success did not continue for long.

Harry Shifts Gears

After the holiday season, the men began to take extended coffee breaks, some up to half an hour. The amount of merchandise broken in the warehouse started to increase drastically, On a number of occasions, workers totally ignored the directions given to them by Harry. Aisles in the warehouse became overly cluttered with scrap boxes and papers, so that it was increasingly difficult to effectively pick the stacks. In Harry's eyes, the most distressing problem was the fact that pilferage appeared to be on the upswing. Although he had discovered no one in the act of stealing, the inventory reports showed an increasing amount of merchandise missing from stock.

Early in February 1976, an incident occurred that significantly changed Harry's attitude toward the dockworkers. Upon inspecting a small, unused storeroom for the purpose of making possible use of it, he discovered more than $1000 worth of selected goods stacked neatly beneath a window. The window had been unlocked and the burglar alarm bypassed so that it would be inoperative. It was obvious to him that some one had plans to return after closing and retrieve the goods. His first reaction was to report what he had found to his older brother. George, Jr. was outraged and came storming into the warehouse. He called all of the dockworkers together. In no uncertain terms, he expressed his disgust with the "crooked and conniving bastards" he had working for him. His explicit and graphic language came straight across to all of the men. None of them made any comments. George, Jr. then told Harry to report to the front office for a "discussion."

The "discussion" was no less than a chewing out. George, Jr. was obviously dissatisfied completely with Harry's leadership style. Said the young V.P., "There is no place in this organization for pussyfooting. You've got to clamp down and get your men in line. This isn't a country club."

Harry clearly understood what his brother said. Actually, Harry had begun to think this way recently but was reluctant to make any changes in his style. Now he had the impetus. He returned to the warehouse and laid out specific instructions for the completion of the day's tasks. He also told the men to report to him any knowledge they had of the attempted theft. He knew, however, that he'd get no response. Discovering the guilty individual was a lost cause.

The following few weeks were traumatic for Harry and his crew. Harry continually bellowed out instructions to his men. He pressed them to work faster and chastized those he found erring in their jobs. He forced the men to return to the original coffee break schedule. In doing all of this, Harry felt totally out of character and very uncomfortable. He tried to rationalize his behavior in the name of profits, but that didn't seem to help. Compounding his discomfort was the fact that George, Jr. was making more frequent and longer visits to the warehouse each day.

The results of Harry's new approach were varied. The amount of overtime work required had not changed substantially, even though absenteeism had risen drastically. This could only have been the result of increased productivity by the men present. All indications were that pilferage had ceased altogether. Unfortunately, four men had quit over one three-day period. There was talk among most of the men about quitting. In fact, Harry had overheard Bob Carmoli and Larry Hinkle, the two "company men," discussing leaving the firm. Further, there was much griping among the men about Harry's inability to evenly schedule the overtime work. Harry had not been as adept at scheduling as Charlie Dowd, but the men had only begun to express concern since the pilferage incident.

More Pressure

In the second week of March, the firm was dealt a crushing blow. The dockworkers' shop steward reported to George, Jr. with a formalized list of demands, accompanied by a threat of specific strike against G. Carbonotti, Inc. The demands and the potential strike had been certified by the local office of the Teamsters Union. The demands included specific changes in working conditions, the assurance of equalized overtime, and the clear delineation of tasks to be performed by the dockworkers.

Fortunately, George, Jr. was able to skillfully avoid the strike. He met most of the working condition demands by installing new equipment in the warehouse, including better heating units, safety devices, and the like. The overtime problem was satisfied by a compensation plan. When the discrepancy between the two shifts was greater than two hours per week, workers offered less than the average overtime for the two shifts (as a percentage of regular hours) would be paid the average anyway. Finally, George, Jr. drew up a list of tasks expected of the dockworkers. All of these efforts proved to be very expensive for the firm, but the potentially devastating strike was averted.

During the three-week period when George, Jr. was developing the means to meet the union demands, he persistently pressed his father to remove Harry from the foreman position. Although the elder Carbonotti reluctantly considered it, he decided to give

Harry a few more months on a probational basis. Harry was well aware of the tenuous position he would be in if he stayed on. His determination to succeed overcame his thoughts of leaving voluntarily. After all, he knew he had let his father down when he left college, and he did not want to do that again.

Since the threatened strike, Harry had lost nearly all his confidence in effectively dealing with his men. He no longer felt that he could consciously develop a proper leadership style. His behavior in the warehouse came to be characterized by partial withdrawal. He no longer intentionally sought a specific manner in dealing with the men. It was as though he stood on the sidelines, occasionally giving necessary instructions. At first, the men would only reluctantly come to him with questions. Eventually, they became more willing to ask his advice and direction in operational matters. Slowly the men realized that Harry, like Charlie Dowd, had developed a keen memory for detail.

Back to "Normal"

Althought it took a number of months for things to settle down in the warehouse, it appeared that activity was getting back "in the groove." Overtime work returned to its normal level and scheduling was improving. Inventory reports showed that the amount of missing and broken items was comparable to the previous year's average. In fact, nearly all facets of the shipping operation seemed to be settling back to where they were under Charlie Dowd's direction.

Even with conditions improving, Harry was not satisfied with the job he was doing. He did not feel as though he was leading his men. He strongly felt that much of the overtime work was unnecessary and that his performance, or lack of it, was accountable for the below-capacity output. Harry was, however, beginning to feel more comfortable in his job because primary tasks were being accomplished with few personnel problems.

"Normal" is Not Enough

Late in June 1976, Harry had dinner with his father and brother in order to discuss the progress of the firm. Both of the older Carbonottis expressed their pleasure with Harry's rapid recovery from the unpleasant conditions experienced earlier in the year. In fact, George, Jr. apologized for ever suggesting that Harry should be removed as foreman. The conversation then moved to future operations. Of primary focus was the economic strain the firm was beginning to be subject to as a result of continual escalations in import product prices. Only portions of the rising costs could be passed on to food purchasers in the form of higher prices, so the firm was experiencing a squeeze on profits. Further, the elder Carbonotti speculated that the problem was going to get much worse in the future.

The course was then set for Harry—he would have to cut costs in the shipping group. It was clear that one of the few ways this could be done was to decrease overtime work but to maintain the volume shipped. George, Sr.'s only suggestion about how to do so was, "You've got to put a little more pressure on the union scum—they'll get in gear." Harry thought, "If only that's all there was to it."

Case IV-2

DILEMMA OF A YOUNG MANAGER*

"Where will it all end?" ponders Johnny Woods as he sits at his desk recalling the events of the past six weeks.

* This case was prepared by Professors Bill D. Fortune of Northeast Louisiana University and Brian Belt of Texas A & M University at Corpus Christi as a basis for classroom discussion and not to illustrate either effective or ineffective handling of an administrative situation. Presented at a Case Workshop and distributed by the Intercollegiate Case Clearing House, Soldiers Field, Boston, Mass.

He thinks of what he studied about human relations in college. He wishes he had a workable and equitable solution to his problem.

Johnny thinks to himself, "I know I've been fair enough with those two guys—maybe, too fair at times. More than once I've jeopardized my job to protect them."

He momentarily remembers a question raised by one of his college buddies one day during the discussion of a case assigned in his personnel/human relations management course, "What if your subordinates don't like you?" Johnny wonders if being liked is really worth it and if being liked is the answer to his problem.

"Maybe," Johnny thinks, "Professor Bates can give me some advice as to how I might solve this problem."

Johnny decided to give Professor Bates a call and see if he could discuss his problem with the professor. Johnny called Professor Bates and he agreed to discuss Johnny's problem with him the next day.[2] The following is an account of Johnny's discussion of his problem with the professor.

Events of the Past Six Weeks

Johnny Woods, age 24, started to work for the Futuristic Automotive Electrical Corporation six weeks ago immediately upon completing all the requirements for "A Certificate of Completion" in electrical theory and practice at The Community Technical Institute.[3] Johnny is the supervisor of the lathe-machines shop where he supervises the work of seven lathe operators. (Exhibit 1 presents a description of Johnny's job.) He has had problems with Billy Adams and Charles Pierce almost from his first day on the job. For instance, at the end of the first week on the job, Johnny overheard the following parts of a conversation among Mr. Adams, Mr. Pierce, and another of the lathe operators as he walked into the shower room this Friday morning:

ADAMS: Those kids think they're just it! Why, I bet he isn't 20 years old. What do they teach these kids today—how to comb their sideburns? All that schoolboy ever thinks about is work.

PIERCE: I remember when old man Jones had his [Johnny's] job.[4] He let us do our own thing. What's happening to the company when they'll let a kid come in here and boss around seven experienced machinists? Billy, you and me are at the top of our labor grade.

LAROQUE: Hey, you guys better shut up! Mr. Woods is standing over there. Let's go to work; it's time to punch in.

The following conversation ensued when Johnny conferred with his professor:

PROFFESSOR BATES: How would you describe your relationship with the other lathe operators and with your boss, the general supervisor?

JOHNNY: I get along well with all the men except Adams and Pierce. With the exception of these two guys, everyone goes about doing his job without causing problems for me or anyone else. Adams and Pierce, no doubt, are good at their work.

[2] Professor Bates was the instructor of the personnel/human relations management course mentioned. Johnny took the course under Professor Bates at Lack University (LU), a four-year academic university. Johnny dropped out of LU during his junior year after making the decision to attend The Community Technical Institute located in his hometown.

[3] The Futuristic Automotive Electrical Corporation rebuilds automobile, truck, and farm tractor starters, generators, alternators, distributors, and voltage regulators that are marketed all across the United States. Its products are distributed primarily through automobile and truck parts and accessories shops. However, approximately 25% of its sales is to a national mail-order company. The corporation also provides machine-shop service, such as turning armatures, to local automobile and truck garages.

[4] Mr. Jones held Johnny's job for eight years. Johnny was selected to replace Jones when he retired from the corporation.

My boss seems to be satisfied with my work and the work of my shop. In fact, he complimented me several times for "getting the work out." But, I don't know how long this will last, if those two guys keep fouling things up for me.

PROFESSOR BATES: How would you characterize your boss?

JOHNNY: As I pointed out, he seems to be satisfied with my work. However, when he interviewed me for this job, he emphasized several times that he takes "a hands-off approach" to the people who work under him. He said that he thinks a supervisor should be capable of handling his [the supervisor's] problems without intervention from him [the General Supervisor]. This is why I've tried to work out my own problems.

PROFESSOR BATES: Are there other events of the past six weeks you would like to discuss?

JOHNNY: Five times within the past six weeks, twice during my first week on the job, Billy Adams has been from 10–35 minutes late for work. Each time, I reminded him that it was important for all the men to be at work on time because of the high volume of work that had to be turned out by our shop in order to meet delivery dates set by Production Control. On each occasion, I told Adams that I saw no need to report his being late to the Personnel Office, as long as he was not late to work again.

Twice I have seen Adams leaving work early. Both times I checked his time card to see if he had punched out. He had not. On both occasions, I checked his time card again after 5 P.M., the shop's regular quitting time, to see if it had then been punched. As I suspected, someone had punched the time cards at 5 o'clock so that Adams' leaving early was not reflected on the cards. Although I realized that it was a Class A offense,[5] according to the existing labor contract, for a person to punch another employee's time card, I made no attempt to find out who punched the card. I have no evidence of it, but, I suspect Pierce of punching Adams' card. Again, although I have no evidence of it, I suspect the other lathe operators are aware of Adams' leaving early and having someone else punch his time card. I just have a feeling the others are aware; it's the way they act.

PROFESSOR BATES: Johnny, are there other incidents similar to the ones you have just described?

JOHNNY: Yeah, I'll tell you about a few of them.

Both Adams and Pierce have missed the last three biweekly safety meetings. In other words, they haven't attended a single safety meeting since I started to work here at Futuristic. I did not report their absence to either the General Supervisor, even though he is a stickler for safety, or to the Personnel Office. Each time I didn't think it would be necessary. After each of their first two absences, I reminded them of the company rule that requires their attendance at the safety meetings. They sounded so sincere each time when they told me they wouldn't miss another meeting and when they asked me please not to report them. I noticed at the last safety meeting that they were both absent again. Also, Mr. LaRoque was absent. He had never been absent before during my time here. The next morning I was able to catch Adams and Pierce in the shower room before work and after everyone else had left to go to the shop. I started out by asking them why they were absent from the safety meeting. Boy! Did they blow up! Pierce told me quite frankly that he had been working at Futuristic for three years and he already knew everything that was ever said at the meetings.

There are two more incidents I can tell you about.

One day, the manager of Stores, who fills requisitions for materials, parts, and

[5] A Class A offense is an infraction of company rules considered so serious as to warrant summary dismissal on the first offense, regardless of mitigating factors. Each of the seven lathe operators in Johnny's shop is a member of the United Automobile, Aircraft and Agricultural Implement Workers.

hand tools called me and pointed out that Adams and Pierce had come to him several times requesting various hand tools without first having me sign the requisition forms, which I'm supposed to do. He very carefully explained to me, as if I didn't already know, that company policy required me to sign the requisition for all hand tools. This incident really made me look like a fool. I called this incident to the attention of Adams and Pierce. In no uncertain terms, Pierce was quick to tell me what I could do with the requisition forms.

But, wait until you hear about what happened yesterday a few hours before I called you, Professor Bates. After this incident, I just knew I had to ask someone for advice.

The bananas really hit the fan yesterday! It is company policy that working overtime be assigned to the men in the shop on a revolving basis. That is, each lathe operator in the shop works overtime in an emergency as his turn comes up. Well, yesterday I needed three men to work a few hours' overtime in order to get out a rush order for one of the local garages. I checked the overtime schedule and found that Adams' name was among those persons whose turn it was to work overtime. I went to each of the three men just before quitting time and pointed out to them that we had to get out a rush order and that their names had come up to work overtime. [According to Johnny, he was informed of the rush order just a few minutes before he talked to the three lathe operators.] After a few seconds of the normal grumbling that always comes from the men who are asked to work overtime, the first two guys said they would work late. Adams' reaction was something else, though. He said he was tired and didn't want to work late. He turned and walked out of the shop. I had to get another guy to work in his place. Adams showed up for work this morning and acted as if nothing had happened.

PROFESSOR BATES: Johnny, tell me something about the characteristics of Adams and Pierce.

JOHNNY: Adams is 32 and Pierce is 29 years old. Adams has been with the company five years and Pierce, three years. Both of them are at the top of their labor grade. Both are high school graduates. Neither one of them is married, although I think Pierce used to be. I, quite naturally, would characterize them both as being smart alecks, to say the least. That's about all I can tell you about them.

PROFESSOR BATES: Was either of them a candidate for your job?

JOHNNY: No. From what I've been able to pick up, neither one was interested in the job. Besides, my boss wanted a graduate of The Community Technical Institute for the job. So, I don't think there's any hard feelings because I got the job.

PROFESSOR BATES: Johnny, tell me something about yourself.

JOHNNY: As you know, my father has owned a machine shop and garage for more than 20 years. I started helping my father in the shop when I was about 10 years old. I learned to operate every machine in the shop—lathe, boring and honing machines, milling machines, valve grinding machines, and so on. I learned to completely rebuild any part of a car, truck, and tractor such as the motor, starter, generator, carburetor. You name it, and my father taught me how to rebuild it. However, I've always been most interested in automotive electronics. That's the reason I went to The Institute for formal training in electrical theory and practice. I learned things there in two years that I could never have learned in my father's shop. My interest in and desire to learn more about automotive electronics is what prompted me to take this job with Futuristic. Too, if I work up to General Supervisor, then I will have an opportunity to learn about the entire field of automotive electrical systems. I would like someday to be the owner-manager of my own shop. The experience I get here at Futuristic will help me realize this long-run goal.

PROFESSOR BATES: I gather you know a great deal about the technical side of your job. What would you say are your qualifications as a manager of people? That is, what are your qualifications as they pertain to the human side of your job?

JOHNNY: As far as formal training goes, I had a course in working with people and a course in shop management at The Community Technical Institute. Also, I had your personnel/human relations course at LU. As a matter of fact, recalling some of the things we discussed in the course is what prompted me to call you.

PROFESSOR BATES: Such as?

JOHNNY: Well, things like Theory *X* and Theory *Y*; role behavior and conflict; Chester Barnard's acceptance theory of authority; making unpopular decisions; and, taking disciplinary action.

PROFESSOR BATES: What about practical experience in directing people?

JOHNNY: This job with Futuristic is what I would consider to be the first job I've had where I am formally responsible for directing people. When I worked for my father, I helped him oversee the machinists and mechanics who worked in his shop. But, that's not quite the same as here at Futuristic. I guess I've got a lot to learn.

How do I solve this dilemma? I've only been here six weeks. What do I do? Do I take the problem to my hands-off boss who thinks I'm doing such a good job? Do I do nothing and jeopardize losing my job because I fail to meet production schedules or fail to carry out some other job responsibility? Maybe I should quit my job?

PROFESSOR BATES: You've told me something about Billy Adams and Charles Pierce. What about the other lathe operators in your department? Is there anything you can tell me about them that might have a bearing on the resolution of your problem?

JOHNNY: Not much. I've not had time in only six weeks to learn much about them. My job is not the kind that requires that I directly supervise and interact with the people in my department or shop. It's not really necessary; everyone knows his job and more or less takes his orders from the situation at hand. Also, because of the tight production schedules in my department, my men do not have a great deal of time away from their jobs so that I could get to know them better.

I do know that all the other lathe operators are married and have families and are older than I am. They all are experienced lathe machine operators. They seem to accept me. Other than this, there's not anything more I can tell you about them.

Resolution of the Problem

PROFESSOR BATES: You alluded to your concern as to whether being liked was the answer to your problem. Do you think this is your problem? Why don't you reflect on all you've told me and then do the following, which should help to guide your thinking in determining a solution to your problem.

1. Define the problem(s).
2. Analyze the cause(s) of the problem.
3. Develop alternative ways of removing the causes and thus solving the problem. Remember that these alternatives should deal with causes, not symptoms of the problem.
4. Evaluate the alternatives, according to criteria such as these:
   a. How well does the alternative meet the corporation's objectives?
   b. How much time and organizational resources are required?
   c. Does the alternative conform to personal and organizational values for equitable and responsible behavior?
   d. What are the ramifications of each alternative?
   e. What is the probability of success?
5. Select an alternative.
6. Develop a detailed plan of implementing the solution to the problem. Who should do what? How? When?

EXHIBIT 1
The Futuristic Automotive Electrical Corporation

Position Description

Position: Supervisor
Department: Lathe-machines shop

Primary function: Under the supervision of the General Supervisor, supervises 7–12 (varies) lathe operators and through them provides the highest quality machine services that he is capable of to the entire plant.

Position content:

1. Seventy-five%: Performs supervisory duties as follows:
   a. Observes all work of subordinates to ascertain that the work conforms to work orders, as generated by Production Control.
   b. Supervises the machining of work pieces and directs the general work assignments made to his department.
   c. Schedules assignments as determined by work orders received from other activities and sees that tools, materials, equipment, and personnel are available as needed for best performance.
   d. Inspects equipment and tools to insure proper conditions and use; requests repairs as needed.
2. Ten%: Performs managerial duties as follows:
   a. Conducts safety meetings; revises work practices and equipment to alleviate hazards; sees that safety regulations are observed; procures, issues, or inspects individual safety equipment.
   b. Interprets standard practices and procedures for unusual conditions and checks for compliance with standard practices and procedures applying to machining activities.
   c. Initiates notices of employees' performance; reprimands for violations of regulations or for deficient work; participates in settlement of step-1 grievances; rates probationary employees.
   d. Transfers or promotes personnel to fill temporary vacancies in hourly positions; grants employees time off; prepares employee working schedules.
   e. Signs time cards; originates labor distribution; originates and signs Supervisor's accident reports, requests for medical attention, reports on unsafe practice or condition, safety charts, and safety meeting report.
3. Fifteen%: Performs technical and administrative duties as follows:
   a. Originates and signs work orders as needed for repair of equipment.
   b. Originates and signs material requisitions for supplies, tools, etc.
   c. Collaborates with various operating and maintenance personnel regarding work orders pertaining to jobs requiring services of Lathe-Machines Shop.
   d. Analyzes work orders and determines labor and equipment requirements for efficient operation. Assigns overtime according to company policy.

Working conditions:

1. Works day shift.
2. Works overtime during emergencies.
3. Subject to normal plant and Lathe-Machines Shop conditions.

Case IV-3

REGIMENTED CAFETERIA*

Whalen College is a private liberal arts institution located in a rural town in mid-Ohio. Because of its low enrollment and small campus, the school is able to provide meal service

*This case was prepared by Dr. John A. Pearce II of West Virginia University as an exercise for classroom use and not to illustrate either effective or ineffective handling of an administrative situation.

for its students by maintaining one central cafeteria that employs 30 food service workers, janitors, and part-time helpers in addition to a food service manager and a kitchen supervisor.

For 10 years, the food service manager was Mrs. Helen Larson, a quiet, easygoing woman who devoted much of her time to planning menus and work schedules and attending to the administrative details of the kitchen and cafeteria. She seemed to be well liked by the staff and had created an amicable work atmosphere, which was noted by Mr. David Tarkley, the school's director of personnel services and Helen's immediate supervisor.

Her assistant, Mrs. Emily Harris, supervised the actual operation of the kitchen. Emily had worked in the kitchen for 12 years before becoming the kitchen supervisor in 1968. She had a pleasant relationship with the staff and often helped them with their work if help or time were short.

The apparent harmony of the kitchen was threatened in 1975 when Helen was fatally injured in an automobile accident. Two weeks later, Emily surprised both the staff and Mr. Tarkley by announcing her own resignation. Because she was already 63 years old and because she deeply missed Helen's companionship, Emily decided to retire early in order to spend more time with her family.

Mr. Tarkley faced an immediate and serious problem. After Helen's death, he had intended to ask Emily to become the new food service manager. She was the only one on the staff who he felt could effectively handle the position, and there was little hope of finding another qualified candidate in the small town where Whalen was located. However, Mr. Tarkley's problem seemed to be solved when he was visited by Lou Jackson.

Mr. Jackson had recently moved to the town after finishing a successful 20-year career in the military. His initial assignment in the Army had been as a cook's helper, and he had found both the work and the atmosphere of the mess hall quite enjoyable. He had received favorable efficiency reports regularly, and after a few years and several promotions, he had been placed in charge of his company's mess hall. Then, in 1970, shortly after the army began consolidating company mess halls into larger battalion-sized dining facilities, Lou was promoted to sergeant first class and spent his last five years of service as mess sergeant for his battalion. Lou was just 40 years old when he retired from the army, and after moving to Ohio, he began looking for a civilian job to supplement his retirement income.

Lou hoped to utilize and broaden his experience, planning eventually to own and manage a restaurant business. As a starting point, he had inquired at two of the town's larger restaurants concerning management positions, and although the meetings did not produce the job he desired, he did learn of the recent events at Whalen College. He immediately called Whalen's personnel services director and was given an appointment with Mr. Tarkley the following afternoon. A few days later, Lou became the school's new food service manager.

During his first week at Whalen, Lou was dismayed by what he perceived as the lack of organization in the kitchen. Although Mr. Tarkley had warned him that the work atmosphere would probably be much different than what he was used to, Lou was quite sure that the situation had worsened as a result of the events of the past month. Although the employees seemed concerned about their work, their friendships and coffee breaks appeared to be of much greater importance. Lou decided that a more efficient work situation was needed rather than this "family atmosphere" he had inherited.

Under Helen, the employees had been allowed to take their breaks and eat lunch at a large table in the corner of the work area. However, Lou felt that efficiency could be improved if a sharper distinction were drawn between those times when the employees were supposed to be working and those times when they were not. His first changes, therefore, were the installation of a time clock and the removal of the corner dining table. Then, in order to ensure that the women would use the ladies' lounge upstairs for their breaks, Lou instituted a rule that nothing, other than water, could be eaten or drunk within the work area.

Lou also decided that it would be a good idea to plan the menus monthly, as it had been done in the Army. The military's system had proven to be highly effective for organizing work schedules and ensuring that the dietetic storeroom had the items on hand for each day's meals.

Finding that the administrative details of the cafeteria did not give him ample time to thoroughly supervise the kitchen and janitorial staffs, Lou recruited and hired a replacement for Emily Harris as kitchen supervisor. Giving her complete control over the kitchen staff, Lou began spending most of his working hours alone in his office, but he often ate lunch and talked with the janitors. Some of these discussions led Lou to believe that there were serious inequalities between the work requirements for the kitchen employees and those for the janitors. Accordingly, he rewrote some of the formal job descriptions and shifted a few of the janitors' responsibilities to the women.

The new kitchen supervisor was Mrs. Betty Corbin, a recent home economics graduate, who was anxious to try out her college-level training. She was cautious, though, when it came to exercising her "academic expertise." She often asked for suggestions and consulted with the employees in order to learn about the details of their jobs.

Betty noticed that one of the older workers, Mrs. Marie Arnold, had become the informal leader. Most of the other cafeteria employees, and even Lou, went to Marie for advice or background information on various kitchen matters. Seeing this, Betty sensed that her position of authority was threatened and began making efforts to be more assertive. One such effort compelled Betty to give a letter of reprimand to Marie, charging that she had failed to follow prescribed communication channels and had been otherwise insubordinate in assigning salad makers to cooking duties twice in as many weeks. Further, Betty threatened to write a formal letter to the director of personnel services the next time her authority was not respected.

Marie was confused, hurt, and angered. The following day, she requested an interview with Lou and asked Mrs. Cambi, her union steward, to accompany her to the meeting. Mrs. Cambi, who also worked in the kitchen, was almost as emotionally upset as Marie. During the meeting, Lou felt that it was best to support Betty's actions. He tried to soothe Marie each time she asked a question, without actually saying that either woman had been wrong in the situation. Marie was still sure that she was falsely accused by Betty, but after her side of the story was so poorly received in the interview, she decided not to appeal the possible grievance further.

In the days following the meeting, Lou began noticing a change in the kitchen. The formality with which the staff was conducting its work and the obvious dissatisfaction of some of the women employees became so apparent that Lou started questioning his own supervisory methods. For this reason, he visited Mr. Tarkley and asked him to informally review his handling of the Arnold complaint. He also told Mr. Tarkley about the seemingly haphazard operation of the kitchen as he had initially encountered it and about the changes he had instituted.

Before making any recommendations to Lou, Mr. Tarkley decided to talk with Mrs. Cambi, the union steward.

Mrs. Cambi's View[1]

Helen had been able to create a family atmosphere in which everyone willingly worked hard and long hours. The employees received personal satisfaction from their jobs and were able to form close social ties with their fellow employees. Lou Jackson failed to appreciate that atmosphere and started immediately to force more regimentation upon the women. Most of this control was unnecessary and unfair. A good example is the time clock, which is a double-edged insult. On the one hand, being forced to punch the clock

[1]The "views" were developed by the author, based upon written and oral interviews he conducted with Mrs. Cambi and Mr. Tarkley six months after Mrs. Arnold's complaint was filed.

tells these very reliable women that they are no longer trusted. At the same time, Lou's failure to pay the earned overtime registered by the clock suggests that their extra efforts are not really appreciated.

Another example of Lou's senseless regimentation was his removal of the corner dining table. This took away the only decent place for the women to eat lunch and take their breaks. The ladies' lounge consists of two straight-back wooden chairs in the restroom. The women now have to go upstairs from the cafeteria to take a break or stop for a cup of coffee. Because preparing certain foods requires constant attention, some employees have to stay in the kitchen area during their breaks because they cannot take the time to leave their cooking or baking to go upstairs. Standing on their feet hour after hour leaves these women totally exhausted at the end of the day.

Lou also makes no attempt to understand the occasional need to change the planned menus when employees are absent. When someone is ill or on vacation, there is often just one worker to prepare a portion of a meal. If the women complain about the situation, Lou just laughs and talks about his days in the Army and how easily his workers adjusted then. He tells the women that they will get done, even without any other help.

The favoritism he shows toward the janitors in the assignment of duties really constitutes mistreatment of the women. Since arriving, he has shifted the janitorial jobs of mopping floors and emptying trashcans to the kitchen help. Considering all of the time that Lou spends with them, it is surprising that the janitors have not talked him into having us do all of their work.

Lou's selection of Betty Corbin as the new kitchen supervisor was well intended and her credentials were adequate, but he neglected to realize that there would be many new problems she would have to face. Giving her complete control of the staff from the start forced Betty to seek so much information from others that some of the women felt she was incompetent. Perhaps their feelings show, because Betty has become increasingly authoritarian. In fact, it was probably her fear or jealousy of Marie that led to her totally unjustified attack. Now that Lou has failed to resolve the problem, the majority of the employees fear that any independent action will result in a similar reprimand or even dismissal.

Mr. Tarkley's View

The fact that Lou has begun to realize the change in the employees' attitude is a big step forward. Undoubtedly, part of his problem is that his previous experience in the military was quite different from the cafeteria environment. Under Army regulations, everyone knows his place in the hierarchy and his specific duties. But in our cafeteria the lines of formal authority have traditionally been overshadowed by a cooperative effort to get the meals ready on time.

Lou should seek help from my office in order to get more in-depth information on the personnel policies and procedures. Upon review, he will learn that policy requires payment of overtime and rest periods for his employees. Because the time clock is already installed, Lou should use the information it provides to help him regulate behavior in a positive way. For example, he should make every effort to recognize any extra work, both monetarily and through personal expressions of appreciation to the employees.

Because there is never a time that food preparation is not in process, some form of a rotation system could be devised so that the work area is always covered while employees are taking their breaks. Perhaps the women's lounge facilities could be improved by the addition of a couch and another chair or two to provide for any employees who feel ill on the job, wish to smoke, and so on.

Lou's idea of planning his menus ahead is fine, but he might want to consider providing for enough flexibility to allow for the substitution of some less time-consuming items in order to help compensate for employee absence problems.

Even if Lou does not realize his seemingly preferential treatment of the male staff in evaluating employee workloads on a day-to-day basis, it should soon become apparent that the women employees are carrying more responsibilities than they should. It might be wise for Lou to discuss the idea of evaluating his unit with me and representatives of the union like Mrs. Cambi. If the idea is workable, he should consider holding a general employee meeting to explain the reasons for his request and the expectations he has for the review. This would show his employees that he is acting in good faith in attempting to provide an equal workload distribution for the employees.

Lou's realization of the change in employee attitudes must lead him to reconsider his handling of the Arnold situation. It is obvious that he needs to review the formal grievance policies here at Whalen College and to gain some insight into the proper way this type of interview session should be handled. Lou must also leave himself some time both to allow his employees the opportunity to discuss their work problems directly with him and to spend with Betty in acquainting her with the day-to-day procedures to be used in the cafeteria.

Case IV-4

HUDSON TEXTILES, INC.*

Hudson Textiles, Inc., a large manufacturing company, with 12 plants throughout the nation and with head office in New York, will pay full tuition refund to those New York office employees who have completed one year's service and who are matriculated in a degree-granting institution. Originally designed to combine business experience with formal education for the benefit of the company, which pays the bills, the plan is generally regarded as a fringe benefit and as an incentive to ambitious employees to go to college. At the present time, 44 of the 200 eligible employees in the New York office take advantage of this benefit.

A recent survey showed that over the past four years an average of 75% of those obtaining a college degree at company expense quit Hudson within one year and 12% quit before attaining a degree. The company is expanding each year and needs college-trained personnel for middle-management positions, not only in the New York office but also in the various plants throughout the country. Thus, Hudson pays college tuition for lost employees and is forced to hire college-trained personnel from the outside at substantial wages for middle-management positions, and then train these employees who have had no company experience. More than three-quarters of the existing middle-management positions are filled with employees having fewer than four years with Hudson.

You have been asked by Mr. Thomas J. Robertson, president of Hudson Textiles, to make some recommendations to ease this situation.

As a beginning, assume you review written exit interviews of lost employees for the past four years and find that 92% of 125 ex-employees who received their college degrees at Hudson expense gave as their reason for leaving Hudson the fact that they had received no recognition in the form of promotion after their graduation. Further, 84% added that they believed "mere payment" of tuition had not been sufficient reward for their six to eight years of attending evening classes for a degree. More than half of these ex-employees (67) expressed a feeling of bitterness toward Hudson because "outsiders" with college degrees held management positions.

Assume also that you collect data by conducting a series of individual interviews with a sample of 100 employees (44 student-employees, 50 nonstudent employees eligible for college entrance,and six recent college graduates at Hudson expense) in the New York office.

*This case was prepared by Ruth G. Batchelor of New York University. Reprinted with permission from *Business Communication Case Book*, copyright 1974 by the American Business Communication Association.

Of the 44 student-employees, five frankly state they intend to clear out of Hudson for better jobs as soon as they complete their degrees; ten hint at the same by saying they will "probably" look around after graduating; and the remaining 29 say they have no plans. None indicate any definite plans to stay with Hudson.

Of the six graduates, two were promoted to middle-management positions after receiving their degrees, but only one of these seems happy with his promotion, which included a raise as well as a title. The remaining four are frankly looking around for jobs with other companies. One of these four summed up the feelings of the others when he said: "No one in Management or in Personnel ever asked me how I was getting along (in college) nor congratulated me when my name was on the Dean's List for five successive semesters. I thought surely when I graduated, Mr. Robertson would write me a letter. If Dean Crosby had not sent me carbons of the letters he sent on six separate occasions to Mr. Robertson regarding the honor I had received, I would have believed no one at Hudson knew I was attending college. . . . Of course, I'm grateful to Hudson for paying my tuition, but I represented Hudson at the university and I can honestly say I was a good representative . . . frankly, I expected a promotion and a raise."

You select the 50 non-student employees out of the total of 156 of those eligible on the basis of their indicated interest in obtaining a college education, although they are not currently participating in Hudson's tuition refund plan. Forty-eight of these 50 expressed their belief that it is company policy to fill middle-management positions from the outside; 27 of these 48 feel the extra work involved in getting a degree would not pay because the degree apparently would not lead to a promotion. Two of these 50 employees are not in the plan because they are momentarily expecting transfer to a western branch. Both express the hope that Hudson will extend the benefit to employees in other cities where colleges offer evening degree programs.

All of the student-employees and the six graduates indicate that there is no periodic review made of their academic progress or achievements, that no recognition is given in the form of raises or promotions based on academic achievement, and that some supervisors are seemingly not aware of the fact than an employee in their charge is attending school. Ten of the 44 student-employees and only one of the college graduates indicate they think it Hudson's policy to recruit outsiders for middle-management positions.

Write a report to Mr. Robertson, clearly defining the problem and its implications to the company, using the information given to you but presenting it logically and in your own words. Before you present your data, tell how you secured it and why you chose this particular way of collecting data. Why was it necessary to interview the non-student employees? State specifically the questions you asked each group of employees. Present the data clearly, draw your conclusions from the data, and state your recommendations to Mr. Robertson.

Case IV-5

FOREIGN AUTOS, INCORPORATED*

Ralph Johnson, owner of Foreign Autos, Inc., was sitting alone in his office late one Friday night pondering what he should do about Wil Michaels who had been with Foreign since its inception 30 years ago.

*This case was prepared by Professor Mary Ann Lederhaus of Virginia Polytechnic Institute and State University as a basis for class discussion to illustrate leadership problems in resolving informal small group issues.

History

Foreign Autos, Inc., a medium-sized sales and service dealership for several makes of foreign prestigious automobiles, was founded in Virginia soon after World War II. From the sale of his very first automobile, Ralph Johnson realized a potential market existed among consumers who found themselves ready to purchase durables, especially automobiles, after the hardships of the war ended. Ralph knew that in order to develop a successful auto business, he must not only sell autos but also must be prepared to offer service commensurate with the prestigiousness of these autos. To do this, Ralph very carefully hired auto mechanics who were familiar with his product. This was not an easy task for Ralph, a salesman with a degree in Business Administration from a midwestern university, but with the help of a former army buddy, he was able to locate two mechanics who were familiar with foreign autos. Hendrick, a former mechanic from Munich, Germany, was a middle-aged widower who lost his wife just prior to the war and was able to emigrate to the United States. Hendrick was happy to have the opportunity to work on engines with which he was so familiar. Although his ability to communicate was restricted by his heavy German accent, he welcomed the opportunity to teach his trade to a young mechanic from Wisconsin, Wilson Michaels.

Hendrick and Wil carried the service end of Foreign Autos for almost five years. One day, however, in a conference with Mr. Johnson, both men requested an oil change and grease mechanic to relieve them of these more mundane duties. Foreign Autos had grown to the point where Hendrick and Wil were working 10 to 12 hours a day and barely meeting customer time demands. A grease mechanic, they felt, would allow them to handle the mechanical work in a more efficient manner. Ralph, who was somewhat surprised at the request, said he certainly would look into the matter and apologized to Hendrick and Wil for not spending more time with his service responsibilities.

Ralph realized then that he could not be a salesman and a service manager at the same time. Therefore, he was willing to relinquish his sales duties to his son and his service duties to a newly hired service manager. So, by 1966, the family business had burgeoned into a corporation with six salesman, headed by Ralph, Jr. as sales manager, and Don Evans as service manager with five mechanics. Although Hendrick retired just prior to Don's coming, Wil, now a twenty-year veteran, remained as a valuable product of Hendrick's careful teaching.

Although attrition had been minimal prior to 1966, Foreign experienced considerable turnover in its service department during the following 10 years. It lost three service managers during that time and none of the mechanics other than Wil had more than three years with Foreign.

Ned Thomas, Foreign's current service manager, was a young mechanic with a two-year associate degree in auto repair. In addition, Ned minored in business management at college. Although Ralph felt Ned was well qualified to handle the service manager's job, problems continued in the service department.

The Issue

Ned stormed into Ralph's office late last week and told Ralph that he had to get rid of Wil. Although Wil was an outstanding mechanic, the other mechanics would not work with Wil. "Wil is trying to show us up," said one young mechanic. "I've been here only two months, but I can see it already. He comes in at 7 A.M. and works 'til 6 at night, or later. That stuff can be done the next day."

"He won't even eat lunch with the rest of us guys," said the air-conditioning mechanic, "He eats while he works. Granted, a lot of people ask for Wil because he's been here so long, but if he would not tinker on a job, he would get through. The other day he was fixing a door lock and he said it just didn't sound right when he got it back together, so he took the whole thing apart again. Hell, it worked and that's what matters."

"This is creating a problem, Ralph," said Ned. "Let me cite a few other instances."

"One day about two weeks ago, a lady came in to get new wiper blades. She walked into the service area and was greeted by a big hello from Wil. You've got to admit, Wil's mighty friendly. To make a long story short, Wil left his job and put the wiper blades on for her. We've got people to do those small tasks. It was okay for him to retorque her engine after the head replacement, but why this nonsense? We've got a minimum charge for labor and he put those blades on for just the cost of the parts. We'll go bankrupt this way."

"You'll probably remember last Friday night when we all were going to leave exactly on time to go to the ball game—well, Wil was still working on this car he promised to have done. He had all the major work done by 4:45. Instead of quitting, he started tinkering with the seat belt adjustment. The customer told Wil that he would be very happy to bring the car in some other more convenient time—but, no, Wil had to fool around with that, too. You know, I don't leave until all the mechanics are gone, but I just couldn't stay and I decided to leave about ten after five. I don't know how long he kept the cashier there, on top of which he had me blocked in the parking lot with his car. Boy, I burned rubber when I got out of there!"

"What concerns me most right now, Ralph, is that I overheard some of the guys planning to place one of Wil's wrenches in the cowl behind the fan. You know what that will do."

"I guess this problem is just getting too big for me to handle. I'd fire him immediately, but I learned in business school not to overstep my authority, so I'm coming to you to ask you to do it."

Ralph's train of thought suddenly was interrupted by the pile of mail on his desk. He had been so involved in his thoughts about his service department he failed to look through the day's mail. Only bills, he thought, until he came to a post card—a glossy color print of Vancouver—addressed to Wil! Curiosity forced him to read the card. "We're having a lovely trip—no car trouble, thanks to your wonderful service, time, and effort on our car. We'll always be your loyal customers."

Ralph turned back to his thoughts. He really didn't know what to do. Should he say something to Wil tomorrow during their fishing trip?

V

DECISION TECHNOLOGY

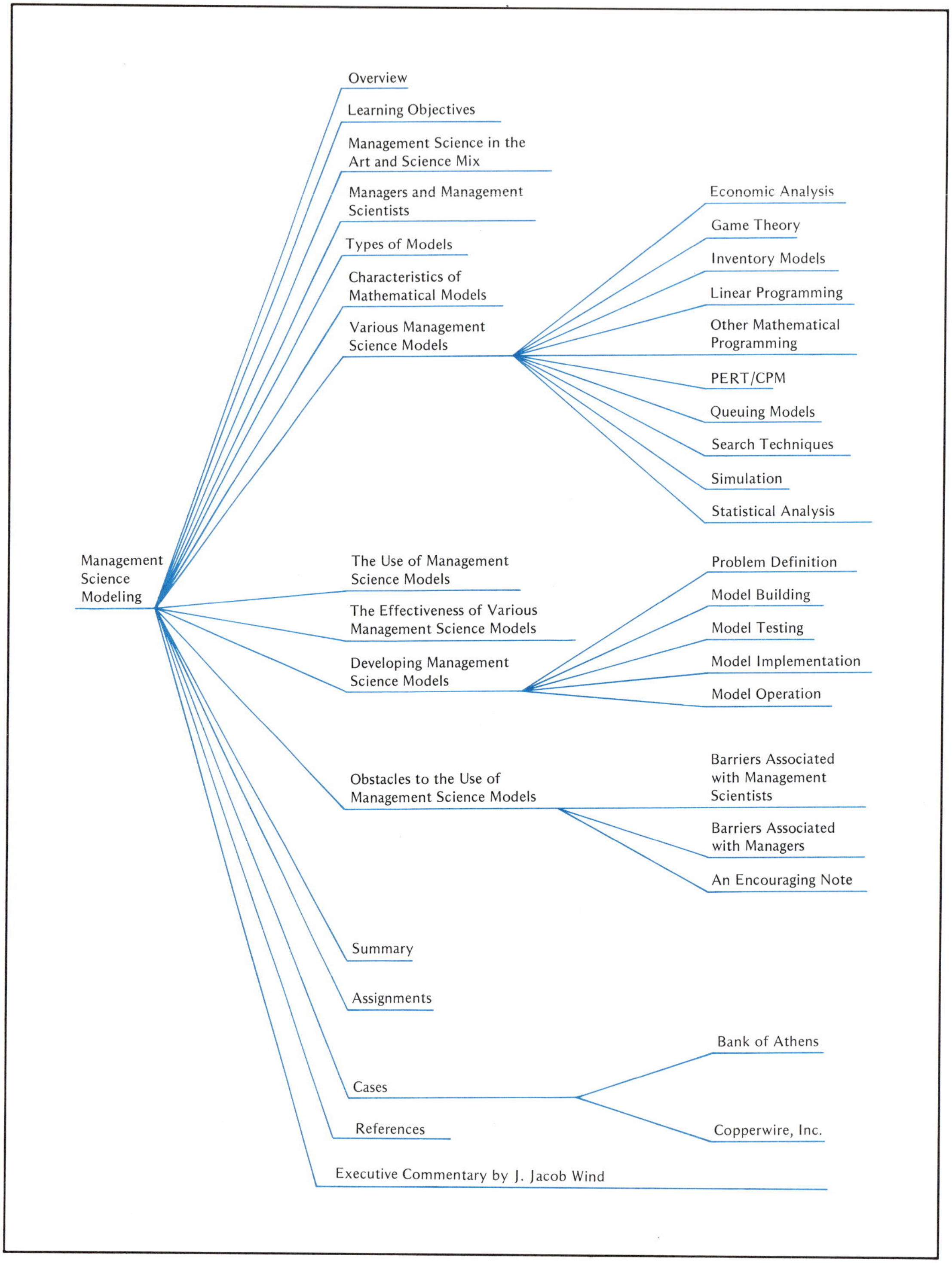
Management Science Modeling
Overview
Learning Objectives
Management Science in the Art and Science Mix
Managers and Management Scientists
Types of Models
Characteristics of Mathematical Models
Various Management Science Models
Economic Analysis
Game Theory
Inventory Models
Linear Programming
Other Mathematical Programming
PERT/CPM
Queuing Models
Search Techniques
Simulation
Statistical Analysis
The Use of Management Science Models
The Effectiveness of Various Management Science Models
Developing Management Science Models
Problem Definition
Model Building
Model Testing
Model Implementation
Model Operation
Obstacles to the Use of Management Science Models
Barriers Associated with Management Scientists
Barriers Associated with Managers
An Encouraging Note
Summary
Assignments
Cases
Bank of Athens
Copperwire, Inc.
References
Executive Commentary by J. Jacob Wind

13

MANAGEMENT SCIENCE MODELING

OVERVIEW

The book's next four chapters direct your attention to some of the *decision technology* that is making an impact on contemporary management practice. Decision technology refers to scientific advancements that are influencing the ways managers make decisions. These advancements include the widespread development of *computer-based information systems* and the use of *management science models.* Both of these developments are having a significant effect on the management of organizations.

This chapter provides a broad overview of *management science modeling.* It discusses what models are, possible model characteristics, the different types of models, organizational use and reaction to various models, the model development process, management's role in this process, and obstacles to the use of management science models. The next chapter will examine in detail several important *planning models,* followed by a chapter on *controlling models.* The decision technology chapters conclude with a look at *computer-based information systems.*

It is important to keep decision technology in the proper perspective. By itself, the use of decision technology does not guarantee managerial and organizational success. It is only one component of many (experience, judgment, interpersonal skills) that make organizations perform effectively and efficiently.

LEARNING OBJECTIVES

This chapter is especially intended to help the student:

1. **Distinguish between the roles of managers and management scientists.**
2. **Identify various types of models.**
3. **Spot situations where management science models might be used.**
4. **Direct the development of management science models.**
5. **Minimize the problems sometimes associated with using management science models.**
6. **Learn, especially in the context of thinking about management, the meaning of the following concepts:**

management scientists	**verbal model**
physical model	**mathematical model**
iconic model	**deterministic model**
analog model	**probabilistic model**
symbolic model	**optimization**

MANAGEMENT SCIENCE IN THE ART AND SCIENCE MIX

The practice of management has always been a mix of *art and science,* and in Chapter 1 we saw how this mix has been changing over time. A major factor in the movement to more science has been the coming of age of the management sciences. Its real take-off point occurred during World War II when complex, large-scale logistical problems had to be solved. A second major factor was the commercial introduction of the digital computer in the mid-1950s, which made it computationally feasible to investigate and solve many complex business problems. Today, there are many groups, such as The Institute of Management Sciences (TIMS), the American Institute for Decision Sciences (AIDS), and the Operations Research Society of America (ORSA), which are organized to encourage, promote and develop methods, models, and procedures for adding more science to the practice of management.

MANAGERS AND MANAGEMENT SCIENTISTS

In general, managers and management scientists are not the same people. *Management scientists* (operations researchers) are usually specialists who are employed to help analyze quantifiable organizational problems. They have undertaken specialized studies in disciplines such as mathematics, statistics, computer science, industrial and systems engineering, and operations research in order to master the available technology. In most instances, management scientists are not the final decision makers; rather, they supply data, analyses, and recommendations that are used by managers in support of their decision-making responsibilities.

Most management scientists are best classified as staff specialists. They are often part of a separate organizational unit that serves the remainder of the organization. In some instances, the management science group works on problems of their own choosing but, in many instances, their efforts are in response to a specific request for assistance from other parts of the organization.

Given the availability of management scientists in an organization, the question is, "How much do managers need to know about the management sciences?" To be sure, managers do not need to be able to actually perform most of the methods of analysis that are available, but they should to be able to identify when a technique might be profitably used. Amplifying upon this point, managers can benefit from (1) knowing what methods of analysis are available; (2) possessing a sufficient understanding of the methods so that possible applications can be identified as situations arise; and (3) maintaining an awareness of what is required in using the methods. All of this suggests that managers should have a broad-based understanding of the nature, role, and use of management science models as well as basic computational skills for some of the simpler, more important models.

TYPES OF MODELS

What exactly is a model? In the most general sense, a *model* is a representation of reality. It represents but is not actually reality. As was pointed out in Chapter 3, it is a simplified representation of reality. However, the model often allows one to better understand the behavior of a real world system.

Our definition of a model includes many types. Model airplanes, mannequins, job descriptions, and econometric models are all examples of widely differing types of models. In this chapter, we will describe many different models.

Although many different classification systems for models are possible, a useful one is to categorize models as being either physical or symbolic, and then to subcategorize them as being either iconic, analog, verbal, or mathematical.[1] Figure 13-1 presents the relationships among the various model categories.

Physical models employ a physical representation to depict reality. Iconic and analog are two types of physical models. An *iconic model* looks like the repre-

[1]This classification system is suggested by Clifford H. Springer, Robert E. Herlihy, and Robert I. Beggs, *Advanced Methods and Models* (Homewood, Ill.: Irwin, 1965), pp. 7–10.

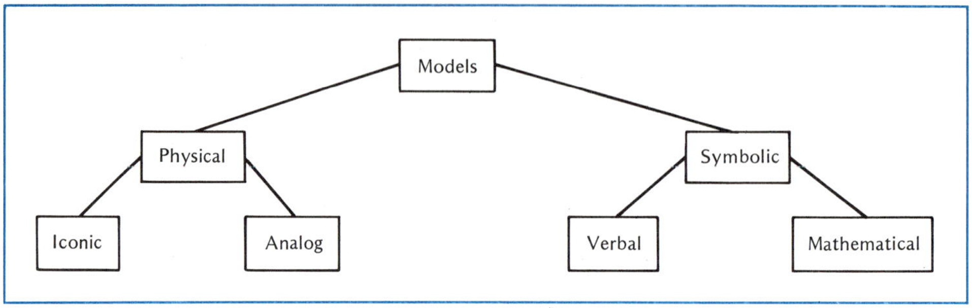

FIGURE 13-1. A Classification System for Models.

sented reality. It is a physical representation that is visually similar to a real-world system. A diagram showing the layout of a plant is an example of an iconic model. A model airplane is an iconic model when it is patterned after a real-world plane. In each of these cases, the model looks like the represented reality.

An *analog model* acts like the represented reality. It has the same behavior characteristics as the real-world system it models. Frequently before a chemical processing plant is constructed, a small-scale working replica is built in order to test the proposed design. Because the replica acts like the proposed full-scale plant, it is an analog model. The model airplane that was mentioned previously as an example of an iconic model might also be categorized as an analog model if it also flies. Our categories are not mutually exclusive; a model can possess the characteristics of several different types of models.

Symbolic models employ symbols to represent reality and include both verbal and mathematical models. *Verbal models* employ verbal statements such as we use in everyday speaking and writing. A course description is an example of a verbal model because it uses verbal symbols to describe the course for which the description was written. A job description is a verbal model because it describes the education, experience, and task requirements of the job. We probably employ more verbal models than any other type.

The last type of model is a *mathematical model.* It employs mathematical symbols to depict reality. In accounting, it is common to describe total cost as being a function of fixed costs, per unit variable costs, and volume of output.

$$\text{Total Cost} = f(\text{Fixed Costs, Per Unit Variable Costs, Volume of Output})$$

Total costs can be estimated by adding fixed costs to the multiplication of per unit variable costs times the volume of output.

$$\text{Total Cost} = \text{Fixed Costs} + \text{Per Unit Variable Costs} \times \text{Output}$$

Or being even more symbolic in our representation,

$$TC = FC + VC \times O$$

This basic accounting model is commonly used to describe cost behavior in organizations and is a good example of a mathematical model.

As you have seen, there are a number of different types of models. Each serves useful roles in organizations, but it is mathematical models that receive most of the attention of management scientists. The power of mathematical representation is used by management scientists when investigating the complex systems that typify the contemporary business world.

CHARACTERISTICS OF MATHEMATICAL MODELS

There are several types of mathematical models possessing varying characteristics. Figure 13-2 illustrates two important dimensions in which mathematical models differ.[2]

Mathematical models vary in the *purpose* for which they are used by managers. Some models only *describe* the system they model. However, such models are often useful for answering "what if" questions. For example, we might ask, "What will be the effect on our cash position if operating expenses increase by 10% and we increase our dividends to $1.50 per share?" By using a descriptive mathematical model, we can often gain insights into what might happen to the real-world system if certain conditions occur or certain policies are followed—all without exposing the organization to real-world dangers.

Mathematical models are sometimes used in *optimization* studies. In an optimization study, we are searching for a best solution to a problem. For business organizations, the problem typically is to find a revenue or profit maximization or a cost minimization. For example, a common problem for manufacturing firms is

FIGURE 13-2. Characteristics of Mathematical Models.

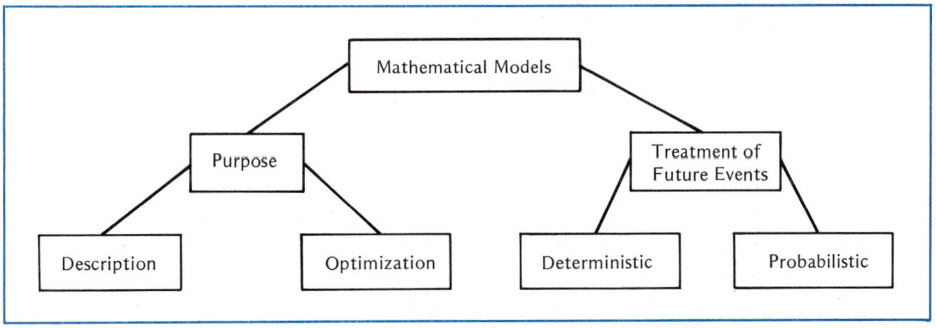

[2]In addition to purpose and treatment of future events, mathematical models can also be categorized on the basis of mode of analysis and generality of application; see Hugh J. Watson, and Archie B. Carroll, *Computers for Business: A Managerial Emphasis* (Dallas, Texas: Business Publications, Inc., 1976), pp. 227–229.

to determine the quantities of different products to produce in order to maximize profits. In the next chapter, we will see how this *production mix problem* can be solved by an optimization technique known as *linear programming.*

Mathematical models also vary in *how future events are treated.* A *deterministic model* assumes for analysis purposes that all of the future events are known with certainty. For each variable in the model, a single-valued input is provided for the input variables and a single-valued output is generated from the analysis for the output variables. Most real-world systems are not deterministic but, frequently, we can gain the information we seek from a deterministic model.

Probabilistic models reflect the uncertainty that often exists in the real world about future events. Probabilistic, multi-valued inputs are entered to the model and probabilistic outputs are generated. These multi-valued inputs and outputs may be appropriately used when the future is not known with certainty. For example, rather than saying that our profit forecast for next year is $200,000, with a probabilistic model we might use probabilistic data inputs and later be able to say that we are 95% confident that profit will be between $180,000 and $220,000. This additional information frequently allows management to better plan and control future activities. With a probabilistic model we are able to estimate and quantify the uncertainty that exists. Unfortunately, probabilistic models are more costly and difficult to build, operate, and understand than are deterministic models, and consequently are not as widely used. However, their use is increasing in the business world. For example, probabilistic models are increasingly being used in the area of financial planning.

VARIOUS MANAGEMENT SCIENCE MODELS

Over the years, a wide variety of management science models and methods have been developed and put into practice. Although it is not feasible to describe all of the models or provide an in-depth treatment of their characteristics and applications, it does seem useful to provide an overview of the most important ones. Our coverage will be in alphabetical order, and let us begin by considering a rather general category referred to as *economic analysis.*

Economic Analysis

Almost all organizational undertakings involve costs and benefits, that is to say, economic considerations. A number of methods have been developed to assist in the systematic analysis of economic factors. The methods vary from simplistic approaches such as breakeven analysis to more sophisticated techniques such as net discounted present value analysis.[3] With *breakeven analysis,* the objective is

[3]See J. Fred Weston, and Eugene F. Brigham, *Managerial Finance,* 6th ed. (Hinsdale, Ill.: Dryden Press, 1978).

to determine how many units must be sold in order that the cash inflows equal the cash outflows. It is one of the planning models that we will consider in the next chapter. With *net discounted present value analysis,* all of the cash inflows and outflows are placed on an equal time basis through a process known as *discounting.* This method accommodates the important consideration that a dollar today is worth more than a dollar received at a later date, because today's dollar can be invested and earn more money. An examination of the wide variety of economic analysis models finds some of them having description as their purpose, whereas others are employed for optimization. In most cases, the models treat future events in a deterministic manner, but some models are probabilistic.

Game Theory

In the competitive business world, there are many situations in which decisions must be made in light of possible decisions made by competitors. For example, service stations must price their gasoline not knowing what pricing decisions are determined by their competitors. Banks must locate their branches taking into consideration the branch-banking decisions being made by competitors.

The management science area known as *game theory* is concerned with the analysis of decision making under conflict caused by opposing interests. Game theory employs a matrix format in the analysis of situations. The alternatives from which the manager can choose form the rows of the matrix. The alternatives that are open to the opponent constitute the columns of the matrix. Within the cells of the matrix are the outcomes resulting from the interaction of the manager's decision alternatives with those of the competitor. Through the use of sophisticated mathematics and statistics, game theory identifies for the manager the optimal alternative to choose.

As we will see when data on the use of various management science models is presented, game theory is less frequently used than other methods. Despite earlier optimism about the potential for game theory, it now appears to be most important as a conceptual framework for considering important factors in competitive decision-making situations.[4] Most real-world decision-making situations are either too complex or deviate too widely from the theoretical constructs of game theory to permit useful analysis. When game theory is employed as a conceptual framework, its purpose is system description, but game theory as a management science technique is an optimization method. It is deterministic, but sometimes probability concepts are employed in its analysis procedures.

Inventory Models

A common denominator to almost all organizations is that inventories must be maintained. Inventories are quantities of items that are being held by the organi-

[4] Shiv K. Gupta, and John M. Cozzolino, *Fundamentals of Operations Research for Management* (San Francisco: Holden-Day, 1974), pp. 265–291.

zation for future use. Because of the importance of inventory in the operation of organizations, it is not surprising that management scientists have devoted considerable attention to developing inventory models.

Because inventory by itself does not create revenues or profits, inventory models attempt to minimize the costs associated with maintaining an item in inventory. Inventory costs can be divided into four general categories—purchase costs, carrying costs, ordering costs, and out-of-stock costs. Most inventory models strive to identify how many units of an item should be ordered at a time and the timing of the orders so that the sum of all the inventory costs is minimized.[5] We will examine a simple, yet useful, inventory model in the chapter on controlling models. Most inventory models have optimization as their purpose. Some inventory models are probabilistic but most of them are deterministic.

Linear Programming

There are many real-world situations in which the objective is to allocate scarce resources in an optimal manner. For example, the production mix problem mentioned previously deals with the question of what quantity of products (the mix) should be produced so as to maximize the contribution to profits when there are limits on product demand, skilled labor time, raw materials, machine time, and so on. A similar situation occurs in marketing when the problem is to decide what mix of advertising media to select in order to optimize advertising effectiveness. Constraints exist in such areas as the total advertising budget and the maximum amount of exposure thought wise in various types of media. As mentioned previously, we will explore linear programming in the chapter on planning models. *Linear programming* is used for optimization and is a deterministic method of analysis.[6]

Other Mathematical Programming

Linear programming is only one type of mathematical programming. There are, however, many other tvpes that are designed to analyze particular kinds of problems. The common bond that ties them together is the optimization of an objective while satisfying real-world constraints. Let us consider some of the methods that might be collectively referred to as *other mathematical programming.*[7]

With *integer programming* the solution to the problem can contain only integer values. For example, integer programming is sometimes used to select projects for investment. Because there is no fraction of an investment, the

[5]See Elwood S. Buffa, *Modern Production Management,* 5th ed. (Santa Barbara, Calif., Wiley / Hamilton, 1977), pp. 371–404.

[6]Gupta and Cozzolino, op.cit., pp. 95–143.

[7]An in-depth treatment of mathematical programming is provided in Harvey M. Wagner, *Principles of Operations Research* (Englewood Cliffs, N.J.: Prentice-Hall, 1969).

problem solution must be integer valued. *Dynamic programming* is used when there is a sequence of decisions rather than a single decision to optimize. For example, in manufacturing plants, decisions have to be made on scheduling routine and major overhauls of machinery. Dynamic programming has been applied to this problem. *Nonlinear programming* is employed when the real-world situation demands the use of nonlinear mathematical relationships. For example, production costs and revenues commonly vary nonlinearly with the scale of operations. Optimization models dealing with these variables often require nonlinear relationships. There are other types of mathematical programming not described here. In general, however, all of these methods are used for optimization and are deterministic in their treatment of randomness.

PERT/CPM

In the late 1950s, PERT (Program Evaluation and Review Technique) and CPM (Critical Path Method) were independently developed. The U.S. Navy, working in conjunction with several prime contractors, developed PERT for use in planning and controlling the Polaris missile project. CPM was developed by DuPont for use in managing projects in the chemical processing industry. Although PERT and CPM originally had several major differences, over time the advantages of one were incorporated in the other, which has resulted in the many PERT/CPM hybrids being used today.[8]

PERT/CPM is used to assist in planning and controlling projects made up of many component activities. For example, it is used in developing the military's weapons systems. National parks are developed using PERT/CPM. Major construction projects, such as the space gantrys at Cape Canaveral and Atlanta Stadium in Atlanta, Georgia, employed PERT/CPM. You will have the opportunity to explore the PERT model in the chapter on controlling models, although it is also useful in planning. PERT/CPM can be used in both deterministic and probabilistic forms. The purpose of the technique is to describe the project that is being undertaken.

Queuing Models

Many systems are characterized by elements waiting in line to receive service. Shoppers wait in checkout lines at grocery stores. Cars line up to pass through a toll booth. Work-in-process inventory waits for work stations to become free. These *waiting line*, or *queuing*, situations are very common in the business world. Because of their frequency of occurrence and importance, queuing situations have received considerable attention from management scientists.[9]

In designing queuing systems, the objective is typically to minimize the sum of

[8]Buffa, op.cit., pp. 450–480.
[9]Gupta and Cozzolino, op.cit., pp. 313–344.

the costs of elements waiting in line and the costs of servicing the elements. Consider, for example, the decision as to how many checkout lines to provide in a grocery store. From the store manager's perspective, the costs of customers waiting in line include the lost profits resulting from customers laying down their intended purchases and walking out of the store, plus the foregone profits resulting from customers remembering how bad the lines were last time and taking their business elsewhere. The costs on the service side include the costs of creating and operating the service facilities. Well-designed systems attempt to minimize the sum of the waiting and service costs. Most queuing models are developed to describe real-world systems, but the models are often manipulated to try to discover better system designs. Because most queuing systems are probabilistic, their random characteristics are included in nearly all modeling efforts.

Search Techniques

Search techniques provide another approach to optimizing system performance.[10] A search technique typically employs a computerized analysis that contains a combination of mathematical techniques and sophisticated trial-and-error procedures to identify an optimal solution. The techniques are used in analyzing systems in which there are multiple variables that affect the system's behavior, and the objective is to identify optimizing values for the variables. For example, the engineering department of a chemical processing plant might be interested in what combination of temperature and pressure maximizes a particular product's yield. This and other multifactor problems are sometimes amenable to investigation through search techniques. Although most search techniques are deterministic, some allow probabilistic factors.

Simulation

When complex systems are investigated, *simulation* is often the method of analysis selected.[11] Many real-world systems are so complex that to simulate their behavior is often the only practical analysis alternative. In fact, simulation has been referred to as a "method of last resort," because it is often used when there are no other analysis options.

Simulation models are found in all of the functional areas of business. In marketing, simulation models are used to investigate the effectiveness of proposed promotion plans. Accountants use simulation in forecasting the future financial condition of the firm. Inventory control managers simulate the cost-effectiveness of alternative inventory control policies. In the chapter on controlling models, we will discuss a model that simulates human decision making. In general, simulation is a descriptive method of analysis. A mathematical model is built that

[10] See Douglas J. Wilde, *Optimum Seeking Methods* (Englewood Cliffs, N.J.: Prentice-Hall, 1964).
[11] See Robert E. Shannon, *Systems Simulation* (Englewood Cliffs, N.J.: Prentice-Hall, 1975).

describes the behavior of a system over time. Given a simulation model, different policies, conditions, courses of action, and system configurations can be investigated. In this sense, simulation models can be used for optimization purposes. They can be either probabilistic or deterministic depending upon the uncertainty associated with future events and the intended use of the model.

Statistical Analysis

There are many methods and models that fall within the general category of *statistical analysis.*[12] This category includes, for example, probability theory, statistical inference, multivariate methods, and statistical decision theory. Because so many methods of analysis are included in the category, it is not surprising that one or more methods are employed by many organizations.

Almost all statistical methods of analysis are based upon probability concepts. *Probability theory* provides information about the characteristics of probabilistic relationships and systems; for example, probability theory can tell us the probability of an arrival at a ticket counter in the next minute, if the arrival times can be described by some known probability distribution. With *statistical inference* we make probability statements about a population of interest, based upon sample data; for example, we might estimate the proportion of the consuming public that prefers our new product over our competitor's. *Multivariate methods* allow us to make probabilistic statements about the relationship between or among variables of interest; for example, they can indicate to what extent increases in absenteeism are explained by bad weather. *Statistical decision theory* employs probability concepts in analyzing which decision alternative(s) are optimal; for example, it can help management decide whether a large or small plant should be built when future demand is uncertain. You will see an example of the use of statistical decision theory in the chapter on planning models. Being that statistical methods of analysis are based upon probability concepts, it is not surprising that they treat randomness in a probabilitistic rather than a deterministic manner. Statistical analysis is used for both description and optimization purposes.

THE USE OF MANAGEMENT SCIENCE MODELS

Having reviewed various types of management science models, a logical question is, "Which ones are most often used?" This question is answered in Table 13-1, which presents the findings of a recent survey of more than 100 nonacademic members of the Operations Research Society of America and The Institute of

[12] See William A. Spurr, and Charles P. Bonini, *Statistical Analysis for Business Decisions,* 2nd ed., (Homewood, Ill.: Irwin 1973).

TABLE 13-1
Frequency of Use of Various Management Science Methods

Rank	Method
1	Economic analysis (payback, breakeven, net discounted present value)
2	Statistical analysis (probability, statistical inference, statistical decision theory)
3	Simulation
4	Linear programming
5	Inventory models
6	PERT/CPM
7	Other mathematical programming (integer, goal, dynamic)
8	Search techniques
9	Queuing models
10	Game theory

Management Sciences. The data report the frequency of use of various management science models and methods.[13] Respondents were asked to rank in order the models described in this chapter.

Not surprisingly, the most frequently used methods were economic analysis and statistical analysis. There are few organizations that do not employ some type of economic or statistical analysis. Simulation is also widely used, undoubtably because of its wide applicability. Linear programming is one of the most fundamental management science methods with a large and well-known set of possible applications that contribute to its use. Organizations are not continually engaged in large projects, but when they are, PERT/CPM is commonly used. Other mathematical programming methods are still evolving, possible applications are still being developed, and over time their use should increase. Search techniques are used by some organizations, and their employment should also increase. It is interesting that queuing models are not more frequently used, because queuing systems are so prevalent. As was mentioned previously, game theory is formally employed by relatively few organizations.

THE EFFECTIVENESS OF VARIOUS MANAGEMENT SCIENCE MODELS

The survey cited previously also investigated the effectiveness of various management science models.[14] Table 13-2 presents the findings. The results of using

[13]Hugh J. Watson, and Joan M. Baecher, "A Survey of Industrial Usage of Operations Research Techniques," *Proceedings of the Fifteenth Annual Meeting, Southeastern Chapter, The Institute of Management Sciences*, Myrtle Beach, South Carolina (October 1979).

[14]Watson and Baecher, ibid.

TABLE 13-2
The Results from Employing Various Management Science Methods

	Results			
Method	**Poor**	**Fair**	**Good**	**Uncertain**
Economic analysis (payback, breakeven, net discounted present value)	1%	20%	78%	1%
Statistical analysis (probability, statistical inference, statistical decision theory)	1%	17%	80%	2%
Simulation	3%	20%	73%	4%
Linear programming	14%	28%	49%	9%
Inventory models	9%	36%	51%	4%
PERT/CPM	10%	40%	47%	3%
Other mathematical programming (integer, goal, dynamic)	7%	33%	51%	9%
Search techniques	6%	33%	56%	5%
Queuing models	7%	24%	60%	9%
Game theory	21%	31%	26%	22%

each type of model were indicated as being either poor, fair, good, or uncertain.

The data show that the results of using the various management science methods are fair or good in the majority of the cases for all of the methods. In general, there is a direct relationship between the methods' frequency of use (Table 13-1) and their effectiveness (Table 13-2). For example, economic analysis and statistical analysis are the highest ranked in both frequency of use and favorable results. This relationship is to be expected because people tend to use those methods that work well.

DEVELOPING MANAGEMENT SCIENCE MODELS

Models do not mysteriously appear in organizations for managers and others to use. Rather, they are the end product of a substantial commitment of organizational resources, including not only the efforts of management scientists but also of managers and other end users. If there is any one key ingredient in the successful use of models, it has to be *user involvement.* This involvement must begin with the definition of the problem and continue through to the operation of the model. Consequently, it is important for management to understand the model development process and management's role and responsibilities at each stage.

Although many classification systems are possible for describing the model development process, the following is useful for our present purposes. It is consistent with the conceptualization, measurement/quantification, and computerization steps of the systems approach that was described in Chapter 3.

1. Problem definition.
2. Model building.
3. Model testing.
4. Model implementation.
5. Model operation.

Let us now briefly consider each of these five stages.

Problem Definition

As elementary as it might at first seem, problem definition is far from being a straightforward procedure. For example, a manager might know that orders are being delivered late to customers. But is this the problem? Actually, it is probably only a symptom of the true problem. With further investigation, it might be discovered that orders are being delivered late because there have been production scheduling problems caused by certain key inventory items being out of stock. The real problem might originate with poor forecasts of the demand for the inventory items. This is a problem that can be attacked by management science methods, but only after it has been correctly identified as the true problem.

Charles J. Hitch of the Department of Defense has said:

> *It is my experience that the hardest problems for the systems analyst are not those of analytical techniques. In fact, the techniques we use in the Office of the Secretary of Defense are usually rather simple and old-fashioned. What distinguishes the useful and productive analyst is his ability to formulate* (or design) *the problem. . . .*[15]

Although Hitch's message is to the analyst, managers must remember that most analysts or management scientists do not have as broad an organizational viewpoint and perspective as they do and, consequently, can benefit from managerial guidance in identifying the true problem.

Model Building

With proper problem identification, the next step is to build an appropriate model. From the problem definition should emerge an understanding of the type of information that should be generated from the model and what type of model might be most applicable.

Management must be sure that its information requirements are clearly understood by the management scientists. The Charlie Brown cartoon illustrates

[15] Charles J. Hitch, *Decision Making for Defense* (Berkeley, Calif.: University of California Press, 1967), p. 54.

***A Tool Not Fitting the User's Needs.* (© 1976 United Features Syndicate, Inc. Reprinted by permission.)**

what happens when a tool, no matter how powerful or elegant, does not fit the needs of the user.[16]

The determination of the model's output specifications is the beginning of the model-building process and sets the stage for the specification of the input requirements and the actual development of the model. The organization's information system can usually supply at least some of the required data inputs. Other data will often have to be carefully gathered for use with the model. In general, models that support higher-level organizational decision making (strategic planning as compared with day-to-day decision making) pose the greatest data problems, because upper management's decision making often involves subjective factors and recognition of factors in the firm's external environment. In this type of decision-making situation, the manager will probably have to work closely with the analyst to make sure that subjective and environmental factors are being appropriately included in the model.

[16] Stafford Beer first used this cartoon to illustrate this point in *Management Science* (New York: Doubleday, 1967).

The type of model that is built depends upon the problem and management's information requirements. In general, management scientists should be encouraged to build simple models first, and expand upon them only when more complexity is needed. This approach ensures that substantial sums are not spent on inappropriate models and also helps control the urge of some management scientists to build "aesthetically pure" models when "rough" models are all that are needed.

Model Testing

After the model has been developed, it must be tested in two major ways. First, it must be validated to make sure that it provides a sufficiently accurate representation of the real-world system. Second, its operation must be tested to ensure that it meets management's needs.

Model validation is a complex subject. Appropriate validation procedures depend upon a variety of factors, including the model's intended use, benefit/cost considerations, the type of model that has been built, and, to some extent, one's beliefs on appropriate methods of scientific inquiry. However, validation most commonly requires: (1) checking the assumptions and internal logic of the model to make certain that it is consistent with what is known about the real world; (2) testing the equations in the model against real-world data; and (3) comparing output from the model with output from the real-world system.

As early as possible, management should be given sample output from the model. In this way, the appropriateness and usefulness of the model can be judged when there is still the opportunity for making relatively inexpensive changes.

It is rare for the initial version of a model to become the final version. Model building and model testing are interactive processes that typically are repeated many times until the model is judged satisfactory for its intended purposes. The model must accurately describe the real-world system and meet management's needs.

Model Implementation

After the model has passed the formal testing stage, it must be implemented in its organizational setting. By this we mean that it must be made ready for management's use. For many management science models, this requires that computer programs be written and that a data base be established to maintain required data. These are technical considerations that usually need not concern the manager, except for giving needed authorizations, especially for the collection and maintenance of data.

Model implementation should also include training programs for users of the model. Unless the manager understands basically how the model functions, how to operate the model, and the uses and limitations of the model's output, it is unlikely that the model will be fully utilized. Although training programs are helpful in serving this purpose, they do not substitute for managerial involvement in the entire model development process.

Model Operation

After the model has been implemented, it is ready for use. It is now at the point at which it can be turned over to the end user. However, even when the preceding steps have been carefully followed, modifications are sometimes required. Perhaps the computerized output is not in the best format, or additional information in selected areas is required. This points out once again the looping nature of the development process.

One of the potentially serious problems is that in time models become out of date. Most systems are subject to constant change and, unless models are modified to reflect change, they become obsolete. Two things can then happen. Either the user recognizes that the model is no longer relevant and stops using it, or the model continues to be used and supplies misleading information. Both situations are bad. Consequently, management must take special care to ensure that models are updated over time.

The development of a management science model has many stages, each with its own peculiar characteristics. A common bond, however, is a need for managerial involvement in each stage. Decision technology can be of great assistance to management, but it must be kept in mind that managerial responsibilities go along with using and benefiting from the technology.

OBSTACLES TO THE USE OF MANAGEMENT SCIENCE MODELS[17]

Despite the potential value of management science models, their impact and use have not been as great and widespread as one might first expect. Many managers, even successful ones, still rely upon elementary analysis procedures when more powerful methods of analysis are available. This condition does not mean that the newer methods are impractical; rather, it reflects some of the real-world obstacles or barriers to the use of management science models. Some of these obstacles are not easily eliminated, but an understanding of their nature and origin provides a starting point for their removal.

Barriers Associated with Management Scientists

Barriers to the use of management science models originate with both management scientists and managers. These barriers reflect natural differences in

[17] The material in this section is adapted from Archie B. Carroll, "Obstacles to Progress in the Managerial Adoption of Analytical Methods," *Marquette Business Review* (Spring 1976), p. 18–23.

education, organizational perspective, professional values, and so on. First, let us consider a few of the obstacles that tend to be associated with management scientists and their methods (See Table 13-3).

It has been suggested that management scientists do not fully understand the process by which managers accept new knowledge.[18] In fact, insufficient research has been conducted on managerial acceptance of innovative knowledge. As a result, management scientists are often stifled and frustrated in their attempts to implement their approaches with the speed and ease they would like.

Some management scientists do not appreciate management as a total process that involves a multitude of interfaces, relationships, constraints, and problems with which the staff specialist is often only vaguely familiar and is perhaps even less interested.[19] A high-level executive of one of the nation's largest corporations suggests that some management scientists are much like ". . . evangelical bearers of the Solution trying to make contact with the Problem."[20] Management scientists must recognize that management is much more than making a series of optimizing decisions. Many nonquantitative factors often have to be taken into consideration in the decision-making process. There is an analogy here with Taylor's "gospel of efficiency," which was discussed in earlier chapters.

Management scientists often do not fully understand how ideas must be conveyed. Because the typical practicing manager is not mathematically oriented, he has difficulty understanding logic expressed in mathematical symbols. Unfortunately, the management scientist too often has difficulty communicating his reasoning without the use of mathematical representation. The communications problem also exists in the jargon used by management scientists. Words such as *heuristic, stochastic,* and *algorithm* are not in the vocabulary of the typical manager. This dilemma was dramatized by the president of a $50 million division of a large pharmaceutical firm who had the following to say about the communication problem: "We're continually being talked at by our operations researchers, but they don't explain and, damn it, I would like to know."[21]

TABLE 13-3
Management Scientists' Barriers to the Use of Management Science Models

1. Not understanding the knowledge transfer process.
2. Not appreciating management as a total process.
3. Communication problems.
4. Management science oversell.
5. Modeling limitations.

[18] William H. Gruber, and John S. Niles, "Problems in the Utilization of Management Science/Operations Research: A State of the Art Survey," *Interfaces* (November 1971), p. 14.
[19] Gruber and Niles, ibid., p. 13.
[20] Louis T. Rader, "Roadblocks to Progress in the Management Sciences and Operations Research," *Management Science* (February 1965), p. C-1.
[21] Harvey N. Shycon, "Perspectives on MS Applications," *Interfaces* (November 1971), p. 31.

There has been a tendency for management specialists to oversell themselves and their techniques.[22] Management scientists, as other specialists, want a piece of the action. They want to get their ideas, theories, and techniques used by managers. As a result, there are some who believe that ". . . from the massive oversell in the early days of the decision (management) sciences, there still remains the lingering bad taste of a product that didn't live up to the user's expectations."[23]

There are often important and significant limitations to modeling real-world systems. It is difficult, for example, to include human and nonquantitative variables in the modeling effort.[24] This exclusion is why many managers are often reluctant to place too much reliance on a solution derived through quantitative analysis.

Barriers Associated with Managers

Not all of the barriers related to the use of management science models are attributable to management scientists. Some of them originate with the manager. Let us now consider some of these obstacles (See Table 13-4).

Traditionally, managers have a strong unwillingness to forsake old customs and practices. This resistance to change is a phenomenon common among people. Green and Schilagi provide an insightful perspective on the resistance to change problem. They assert that the concept of "territorial imperative" assists in explaining managerial resistance to change.[25] The *territorial imperative* concept relates to managers' tendencies, similar to territorial animals, to be defensive of their own territory. A manager's territory is the decision-making realm over which he or she has authority. It may be the person's department, functional speciality, or a given class of decisions. As the manager's territory gets larger, he is self-protective of territorial "rights." Management scientists, in this context, are potential invaders of the manager's drive to gain, maintain, and defend decision-making powers over an organizational domain.

TABLE 13-4
Managements' Barriers to the Use of Management Science Models

1. Resistance to change.
2. Overrelying on experience and intuition.
3. Incomplete or out-of-date education.
4. Misunderstanding the investment required.

[22] Rader, op.cit., p. C-2.

[23] Thad B. Green, and Frank Shilagi, "Organizational Reluctance to Employ Decision Science Methods," paper presented to the March 30, 1972, Southwestern AIDS Meeting, San Antonio, Texas, p. 8.

[24] Gruber and Niles, op.cit., p. 13.

[25] Green and Schilagi, op.cit., p. 8.

Managers rise and fall on the basis of their experience, judgment, intuition, and insight, and are therefore reluctant to substitute something they do not understand for something they do.[26] Francis F. Bradshaw, former president of the Society for the Advancement of Management, characterized this problem when he stated, "Most managers would rather live with a problem they can't solve than use a solution they don't understand."[27]

A precondition to effective management participation in the use of management science techniques is basic training in the management sciences. Unfortunately, many of today's managers in the middle and upper levels of business organizations were educated prior to the mid-1960s when significant quantitative training in business schools first began.[28] Consequently, an educational barrier exists, which inhibits widespread use of quantitative approaches. The implication, of course, is that management science models would be more extensively employed if managers possessed greater quantitative training. This problem should decrease in time as more quantitatively trained managers climb the organizational ladder.

Managers are characteristically action-oriented. Daily they face decision-making situations that demand quick and effective action. These job and behavior characteristics can create problems, however, when the manager does not understand the time, dollars, and commitment that are often required in the development of management science models. One effective management science department head known by the authors takes an interesting approach to this potential problem. He permits his staff to work on only problems in which the expected benefits exceed the costs by a factor of 5 to 1, and a member of the end user group is assigned to his staff for the duration of the study.

An Encouraging Note

The obstacles to the use of management science methods are not insurmountable. Developments are taking place that promise to increase the use of models. Educational changes are helping both managers and management scientists. Managers are receiving better quantitative training, and management scientists are learning that there is much more to managing organizations than finding optimal solutions. Managers are learning what to expect and what is required in developing, implementing, and using management science models, and also the competitive disadvantage they face if they cannot use the new decision technology. Management scientists are increasingly making their methods easier to use, if not more understandable to the layman. They are beginning to realize that managers are not management scientists, and if management scientists are to continue their organizational role, the needs of managers must be met. All of these are encouraging developments.

[26] Russell L. Ackoff, "Frontiers of Management Science," *The Bulletin* (*TIMS*) (February 1971), p. 20.
[27] Rader, op.cit., p. C–2.
[28] Harvey N. Shycon, "Perspectives on MS Applications," *Interfaces* (May 1972), p. 28.

SUMMARY

Contemporary management practice is being substantially affected by emerging decision technology. This technology can be seen in the use of management science models and the development of computer-based information systems. Consequently, the art and science mix of management is changing with increased emphasis on the science component.

Much of the new decision technology is being brought to organizations by staff specialists who are commonly referred to as management scientists. These individuals employ models to depict real-world systems. There are iconic, analog, and verbal models, but mathematical models are the principal tools of management scientists. These models can differ in terms of purpose (optimization or description) and their treatment of randomness (deterministic or probabilistic).

There are many different types of management science models or methods—economic analysis, game theory, inventory models, linear programming, other mathematical programming, PERT/CPM, queuing models, search techniques, simulation, and statistical analysis. Each is useful in analyzing particular types of situations, but economic analysis, statistical analysis, and simulation are most frequently used and appear to produce the most favorable results.

A key to the successful use of management science models is managerial involvement. This involvement is required in differing ways throughout all stages of the model development process. These stages can be identified as problem definition, model building, model testing, model implementation, and model operation.

Despite the potential value of management science models to management, there are obstacles to their use. These barriers are found to exist with both management scientists and managers. Management scientists often fail to understand the knowledge transfer process, to appreciate management as a total process, to communicate in nontechnical terms, and to honestly state model usefulness and limitations. Managers, on the other hand, sometimes tend to resist changing to new methods, rely too much on experience and judgment, have out-of-date training, and fail to appreciate the time and financial commitments that management science models require. It does appear, however, that some of these obstacles are decreasing.

Assignments

13-1. Discuss the factors that have led to the use of management science models in organizations.

13-2. What courses in the business school curriculum contribute to your knowledge of the management sciences?

13-3. Categorize the following models as iconic, analog, verbal, or mathematical.
a. A wind tunnel.
b. $E = mC^2$.
c. A friend's description of a blind date.
d. A Barbie doll.
e. A Donald Duck cartoon.
f. The game of Monopoly.

13-4. The total cost model, $TC = FC + VC^*O$, is common in the business world. Categorize it by purpose and treatment of randomness.

13-5. Identify the three most frequently used management science models and give a real-world application of each that was not mentioned here.

13-6. Identify an application of linear programming and PERT/CPM that was not mentioned in the chapter.

13-7. A highly sophisticated, probabilistic financial planning system was developed by the management science group, but is not being used. What might have gone wrong in the development process? What can be done to improve the situation?

13-8. There are other barriers to the use of management science models that were not discussed in the chapter. What might some of these be?

Case 13-1

BANK OF ATHENS

A manager of the Bank of Athens has been reading about some banks turning to a single *quick line* approach to providing banking services. Traditionally, banks employ several tellers, and customers choose one of the several lines to join; see Figure 1.

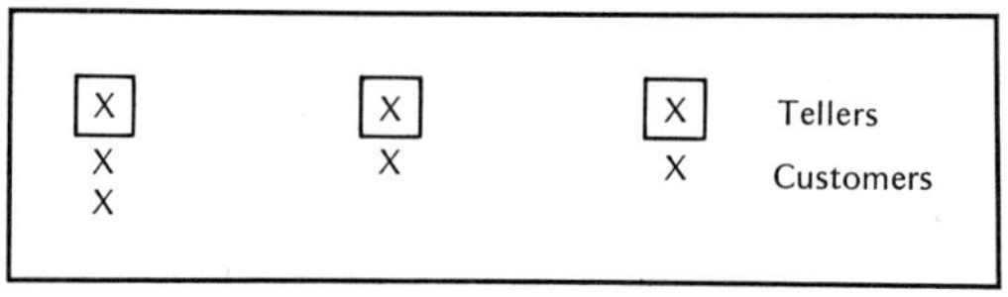

FIGURE 1. Traditional Service Concept.

With the quick line concept, there are still several servers, but all customers join a single line to await service; see Figure 2. Each teller has control over a light that flashes and a bell that rings in order to signal the customer at the head of the line that the teller is free and ready to provide service.

FIGURE 2. Quick Line Concept.

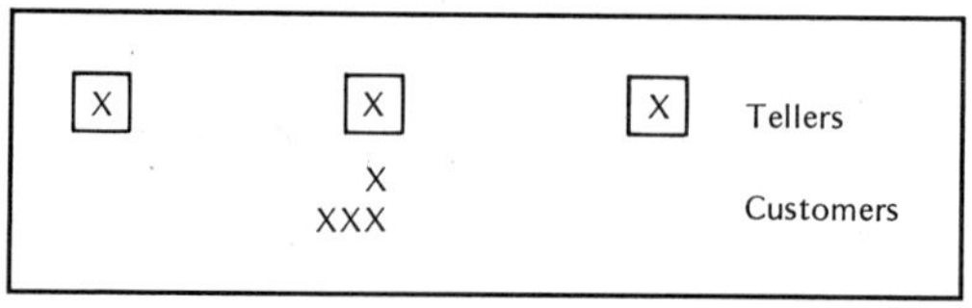

Answer the following questions for the bank manager.

1. What management science technique(s) might be used to compare the merits of the traditional and quick line approaches?
2. What performance criteria should be used in comparing the two approaches?
3. What data would be necessary in modeling the two alternatives?
4. What subjective considerations are important in comparing the two approaches?

Case 13-2

COPPERWIRE, INC.

Copperwire, Inc., produces copper wire and has just ordered an expensive smelter to produce the copper that goes into its copper wire. Interestingly, there is no set formula for producing copper. There are many combinations of ingredients that can be put into a smelter and still have copper flow out. It is not quite as easy as it sounds, however. Some combinations will not produce copper, whereas others produce a copper product that is not viscous enough to flow out of the smelter. When this latter condition occurs, the copper has to be chipped out of the smelter before the smelter can be used again. Obviously, this is an expensive condition.

In the past, an old-timer has been employed to decide which of the available ingredients should be thrown into the smelter to produce copper that day. The salaries paid these old-timers is quite high, however, and there is no way of knowing whether the cost of producing the copper is being minimized.

Some of the company's chemical engineers have suggested that there must be some management science technique that might be used to make the copper smelter production more scientific. They indicate that they can write the chemical reaction formulas that will ensure the ingredients will produce copper and it will flow out of the smelter. The engineers believe this more scientific approach will eliminate the need for the old-timer's services and should also result in cost-reducing efficiencies in producing copper.

Since management has ordered a new smelter, it agrees that perhaps now is a good time to look at new approaches to copper production. Answer the following questions for management about the situation just described.

1. What costs are important in deciding whether or not to adopt a new approach?
2. What management science technique might be applied to the copper production problem?
3. What data inputs would the management science technique require?
4. What kinds of people would be required to develop and implement the new approach?

References

BEER, STAFFORD. *Management Science.* New York: Doubleday, 1967.

CHURCHMAN, C. WEST, RUSSELL L. ACKOFF, and E. LEONARD ARNOFF. *Introduction to Operations Research.* New York: John Wiley & Sons, Inc., 1957.

GRAYSON, C. JACKSON. "Management Science and Business Practice." *Harvard Business Review* (July-August 1973), pp. 41–48.

HAMMOND, JOHN S. "Do's and Don't's of Computer Models for Planning." *Harvard Business Review* (March-April 1974), pp. 110–123.

HAMMOND, JOHN S. "The Roles of the Manager and Management Scientist in Successful Implementation," *Sloan Management Review* (Winter 1974), pp. 1–24.

MCCOUBREY, CHARLES A., AND MADIS SULG. "OR/MS Implementation at Converse Rubber." *Sloan Management Review* (Winter 1976), pp. 63–76.

MILLER, DAVID, AND MARTIN STARR. *The Structure of Human Decisions.* Englewood Cliffs, N.J.: Prentice-Hall, Inc., 1967.

WATSON, HUGH J., AND PATRICIA GILL MARETT, "A Survey of Management Science Implementation Problems." *Interfaces* (August 1979), pp. 124–128.

J. JACOB WIND
Consultant/Analyst
American Management Systems
Arlington, Virginia

J. Jacob Wind is a member of a team that is exploring the U.S. Navy's ship maintenance systems and creating new, cost-effective systems. At American Management Systems (AMS), he has also worked on data base management for the Bureau of Public Debt and on a unified system to automate financial management for the District of Columbia. Mr. Wind's work brings him into daily contact with management science models—and with resistance to their adoption.

Mr. Wind coordinated testing of AMS's Assignment Management and Planning System for the U.S. General Accounting Office (GAO). The system enables GAO to track progress on GAO's 4,000 ongoing audits, as well as preparing payroll data for GAO's 5,000 employees.

Executive Commentary

On Implementing Management Science Models

As this chapter on management science modeling suggests, organizational inertia is a powerful deterrent to the successful implementation of management science models. Effecting any form of change is difficult. Franklin Roosevelt wrote of his efforts as Secretary of the Navy, "To change anything in the Navy is like punching a feather bed. You punch it with your right and you punch it with your left until you are finally exhausted, and then you find the damn bed just as it was before you started punching."

Corporate resistance to change comes in many forms: adherence to corporate traditions; hesitance to invest in implementation despite demonstrable benefits; and continuing insistence on further study. Overcoming inertia and selling the model are large parts of the management scientist's job.

Readers of this chapter who become managers will find themselves confronted increasingly with problems requiring the mathematical application of common sense, that is, management science. Readers who become management scientists will frequently face the need to justify models to management. In either case, readers should prepare themselves by understanding the model development process described in this chapter.

At American Management Systems, a consulting firm, we have succeeded in building many substantial models for small users, as well as users as large as New York City, the District of Columbia, and the U.S. Navy.

Although our terminology differs slightly from that in the chapter, our steps are much the same:

System Concept: we define the problem, analyze the user's major requirements, and outline the scope of the project.

General Design: we lay out on paper for client review the main issues and features of the system. Only after the major issues are resolved and the goals defined can the model-building process proceed.

Detail Design: we define the system inputs and outputs, the exact format of reports, and how the data will be processed. The client must review the specifications to ensure they meet the needs. This step is analogous to model building.

Programming: we explicitly code the processing formulas and format the inputs and outputs in computer language. We then test the system with sample data first, ideal data, then, flawed data to catch errors. It is far cheaper to correct errors early than to risk system failure after model installation.

Implementation: we define this as actual installation of the model at the user's facilities. Old and new systems should run parallel for at least one accounting cycle to eliminate "bugs," compare results, and verify efficiency.

Feedback: we provide continuing feedback once the user fully shifts to the new system. Users often require model updates to meet changing needs. Often, continuing contact leads to follow-on contracts.

These additional thoughts about management science modeling come to mind:

The chapter suggests that game theory is not widely used. However, it is used increasingly in the military to simulate high-conflict situations. Teams take opposing sides in mock battles to examine their responses and to gauge the actions of a real enemy.

Queuing, despite its potential power, has not grown in popularity because of the difficulty in mathematically describing and analyzing the complex systems that abound in the real world. Alert management scientists, however, frequently see single-server systems where long queues can be cut to size just by adding more serving lines.

In the business world, probabilistic models are rare. More often, managers use deterministic or simplified best/worst/most likely terms. Too often, people ignore low probabilities, assuming that with only a 10% chance the river will flood, their home on the banks is doubtless safe. Explaining basic probability concepts to the lay person is a challenge to the management scientist.

Models are useful in two broad classes of situations: high use and high cost. Repetitive calculations, such as cattle-feed optimization or production-line scheduling, are well suited for modeling, and here linear programming is particularly useful. For expensive endeavors, careful planning, using such tools as PERT/CPM, enables firms to deliver on time and within budget. Model development costs can be small compared to the dollars the model will save.

Resist the urge to create an all-encompassing model at the start. Instead, formulate a simple model. Once it runs successfully, add error detection routines, multiple report capabilities, and the like.

Always stick with the model-building process from beginning to end. Many managers focus on the system analysis and programming, supervising their staff marvelously. But then they leave implementation to someone else, or to no one. Models do not implement themselves. The excitement of finding a successful solution must be followed by the real work of selling it to clients and corporate decision makers. Following models through from design to implementation and allowing frequent feedback are how management scientists provide guarantees to their customers.

Management scientists must be politicians, developing constituencies, often fighting to convince others. One must find allies at various organizational levels and build a track record of profitable implementations. As the problems get bigger, organizational inertia will grow, and one needs more momentum to surmount it.

- Planning Models
  - Overview
  - Learning Objectives
  - Breakeven Analysis
    - Cost-Profit-Volume Relationships
    - The Breakeven Model
    - An Illustration
    - Limitations of Breakeven Analysis
  - Linear Programming
    - A Production Mix Illustration
    - Stating the Problem Mathematically
    - The Graphical Method
    - Post Optimality Analysis
    - The Simplex Method
  - The Payoff Matrix
    - Basic Probability Concepts
    - The Concept of Expected Value
    - The Payoff Matrix Structure
    - An Illustration
  - Summary
  - Assignments
  - Cases
    - Summer Sail, Inc.
    - Taylor Industries
    - Hightower Manufacturing Company
    - Gerloff Equipment Company
    - King Manufacturing Company
    - Tuttle Manufacturing Company
    - Income Property, Inc.
    - Current Publications, Inc.
    - James B. Megabucks
  - References
  - Executive Commentary by R. Miles Waugh

14

PLANNING MODELS

OVERVIEW

As you saw in the previous chapter, there are many types of mathematical models that have been developed for a variety of applications. We are limited, however, in the number and depth in which these models can be examined in this book. Consequently, only some of the most useful models are presented.

This and the following chapter are the only ones dedicated to actually showing how to use various management science models. This chapter covers models that are primarily used for planning purposes, and the next chapter explores controlling models. However, this separation is somewhat artificial, for as you saw in the planning and controlling chapter, these two functions are highly interrelated. Not surprisingly, most models are used for both planning and controlling purposes.

Three planning models are presented in this chapter. The first is the *breakeven model,* which is quite likely the most popular financial planning model in use today. We not only discuss how and when to apply the breakeven model, but also its limitations as a method of analysis. The second model presented is the *linear programming model.* It is illustrated through its application to the production mix problem. The third model comes from statistical decision theory and is the *payoff matrix.* Its use is illustrated through an application to an equipment selection decision.

LEARNING OBJECTIVES

This chapter is especially intended to help the student:

1. Better understand the role and use of planning models.

2. **Know how and when to apply breakeven analysis.**
3. **Know how and when to apply linear programming.**
4. **Know how and when to apply the payoff matrix.**
5. **Learn, especially in the context of thinking about management, the meaning of the following concepts:**

breakeven analysis
contribution margin
linear programming
objective function
constraints
feasible solution space
post-optimality or sensitivity analysis
expected value
payoff matrix

BREAKEVEN ANALYSIS

As you learned in the preceding chapter, economic analysis is the most frequently used management science technique. Of the methods employed for this purpose, none is more popular than breakeven analysis.[1] For many managers in a variety of settings, breakeven analysis provides useful information to support decision making.

The breakeven model is conceptually quite simple to understand. It identifies the number of units that must be sold so the revenues received equal the costs incurred.[2] As the name *breakeven* implies, no profits or losses are realized at the breakeven point; the organization is simply breaking even.

One of the most popular applications of breakeven analysis is in planning whether or not to introduce a new product. In this role, it is best used as an initial screening device. If it seems unlikely that sufficient units of the new product will be sold to at least break even, the proposed product should probably be discarded without further consideration. If, on the other hand, it seems likely that the product will be at least break even, it should be subjected to more complex and sophisticated methods of financial analysis such as net discounted present value analysis.[3] Later in the chapter we will talk about the limitations of breakeven analysis and why more advanced methods of analysis are also used.

Cost-Profit-Volume Relationships

Before introducing the breakeven model, it is necessary to talk about what accountants refer to as *cost-profit-volume relationships.* These relationships describe how costs and profits vary with the volume of output. Let us begin our discussion with a consideration of cost behavior.

[1] J. Fred Weston, and Eugene F. Brigham, *Managerial Finance,* 6th ed. (Hinsdale, Ill.: Dryden Press, 1978), pp. 71–82.
[2] The breakeven point can also be expressed in terms of dollar sales or percentage of utilization of plant capacity.
[3] Weston and Brigham, op. cit., Chapters 9 and 10.

Costs. *Total costs* are made up of fixed and variable cost components. *Fixed costs* are costs that do not vary with the level of output; for example, the insurance on a building is independent of the number of units produced by a manufacturing firm or the amount of service provided by a service organization. Figure 14-1 graphically shows the relationship between fixed costs and output.

Total variable costs exhibit a direct relationship with the volume of output. The more units produced or services provided, the greater become the total variable costs. For example, raw materials and direct labor tend to vary proportionately with the level of output. Total variable costs are found by multiplying the per unit variable costs times the volume of output. Figure 14-2 depicts the relationship between total variable costs and output.

When describing total cost behavior, the fixed and variable cost components are summed. This process results in the total cost behavior, as shown in Figure 14-3.

In actuality, few costs are completely fixed or variable, as a few examples will illustrate. Consider, for example, that costs may be fixed, but only over a limited range of output. One machine might satisfy a manufacturing firm's needs up to a certain volume of output, but beyond that point a second machine is required. Consequently, the fixed cost behavior in this example is best described by a *staircase* function (See Figure 14-4).

Variable costs do not always vary proportionately with output. For example, at high levels of output, some of the raw materials purchased may qualify for a quantity discount on the purchase price. Quantity discounts result in total variable cost behavior, such as described in Figure 14-5.

Some costs are *semivariable* and have both fixed and variable components. For example, selling expense is usually a semivariable cost, because it includes a fixed component such as manager's salaries and a variable component such as salesmen's commissions. Semivariable cost behavior is shown in Figure 14-6.

These latter examples are not intended to show that categorizing costs as fixed and variable is not useful. Rather, they show that the real world is sometimes more complex than the fixed and variable cost accounting model implies. How-

FIGURE 14-1. Fixed Cost Behavior Relative to Output.

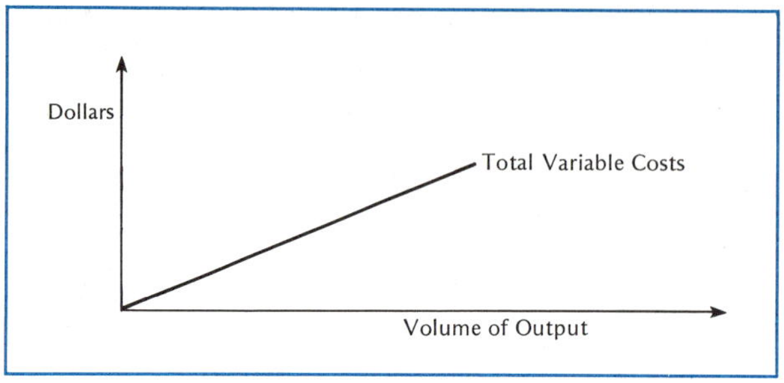

FIGURE 14-2. Total Variable Cost Behavior Relative to Output.

ever, this poses no real problem as long as the model provides a useful approximation of reality. Given that we usually talk about breaking even over a limited range of output, that quantity discounts are usually relatively small and occur at known points, and that semivariable costs can be broken down into fixed and variable components, the fixed and variable cost descriptions are still useful.

Revenues. In most organizations there are revenues resulting from the sale of goods or services. The greater the number of goods or services sold, the greater the revenues. *Total revenue* is found by multiplying the selling price by the number of units sold. This revenue behavior is shown in Figure 14-7.

As was the case with cost behavior, the real world can deviate from the revenue model depicted in Figure 14-7. For example, in order to achieve extremely high levels of sales, the organization may have to offer price discounts. Consequently, the total revenue curve may not be a straight line. Once again, however, the simple revenue model is often useful for analysis purposes in many situations.

Profits. Profits are determined by putting the total cost and revenue components together. By subtracting total costs from the total revenues, the organization's *profit* is determined. Figure 14-8 graphically shows the relationship between

FIGURE 14-3. Total Cost Behavior Relative to Output.

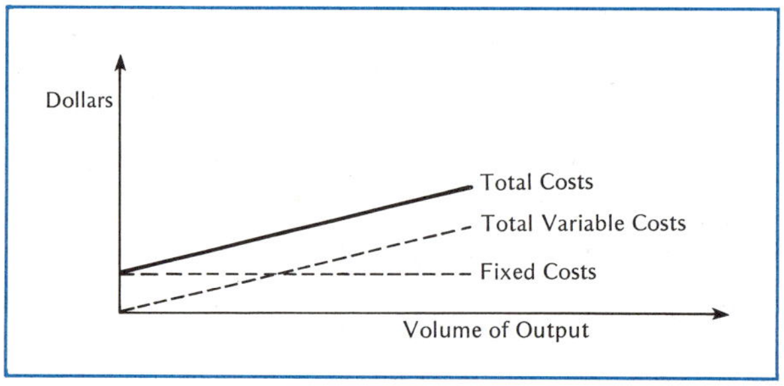

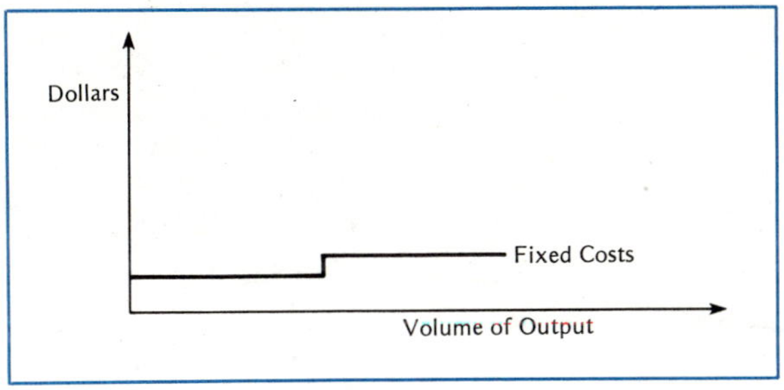

FIGURE 14-4. A Staircase Function of Fixed Cost Behavior.

costs, revenues, and profits at various volumes of output. It can be seen that losses are being incurred up to the *breakeven point,* but beyond the breakeven point there are profits.

The Breakeven Model

The breakeven model can be developed after adding mathematical notation to the concepts developed so far. The starting point is the recognition that at the breakeven point total revenues are equal to total costs.

$$\text{Total Revenues} = \text{Total Costs} \qquad [14\text{-}1]$$

Next, the revenue and cost terms are broken down into their component parts.

$$\text{Selling Price} \times \text{Output} = \text{Fixed Cost} + \text{Per Unit Variable Cost} \times \text{Output} \qquad [14\text{-}2]$$

Adding more mathematical notation, we have,

$$P \times O = FC + VC \times O \qquad [14\text{-}3]$$

FIGURE 14-5. Total Variable Cost Behavior with Quantity Discounts.

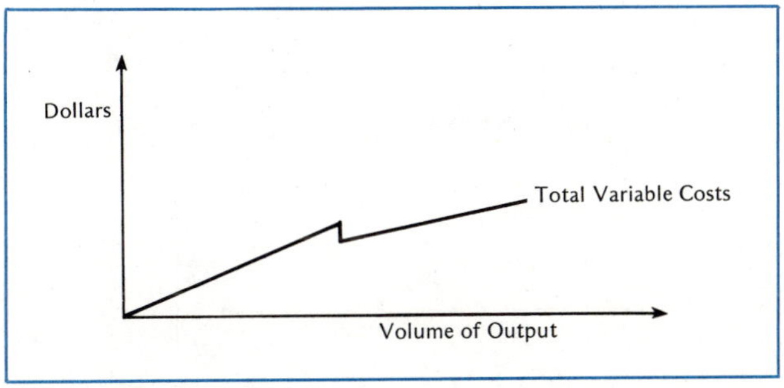

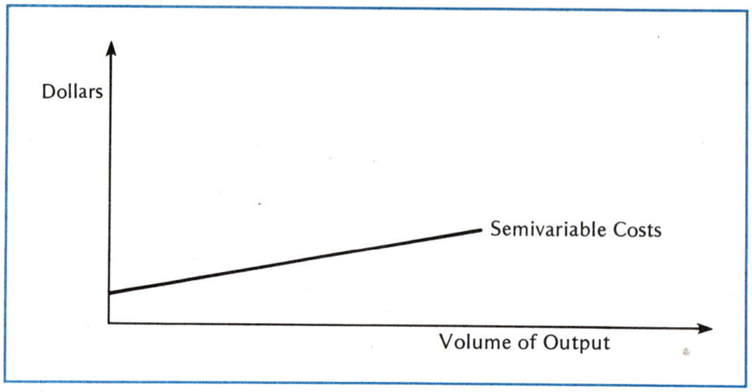

FIGURE 14-6. Semivariable Cost Behavior Relative to Output.

Now we need only to manipulate expression [14-3] so that O is a function of P, FC, and VC.

$$P \times O - VC \times O = FC$$
$$O \times (P\text{-}VC) = FC$$
$$O = \frac{FC}{(P\text{-}VC)}$$

This volume of output where the costs and revenues are equal is the breakeven point (BEP).

$$BEP_{\text{units}} = \frac{FC}{(P\text{-}VC)} \qquad [14\text{-}4]$$

The breakeven model tells us that we can find the breakeven point by dividing the fixed costs by the difference between the selling price and the per unit variable costs.

FIGURE 14-7. Total Revenue Behavior Relative to Output.

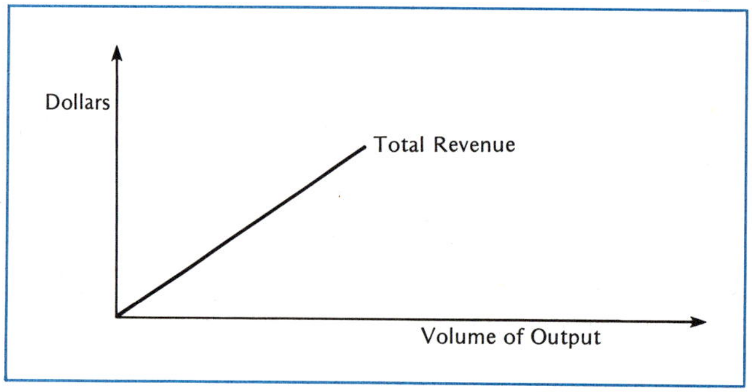

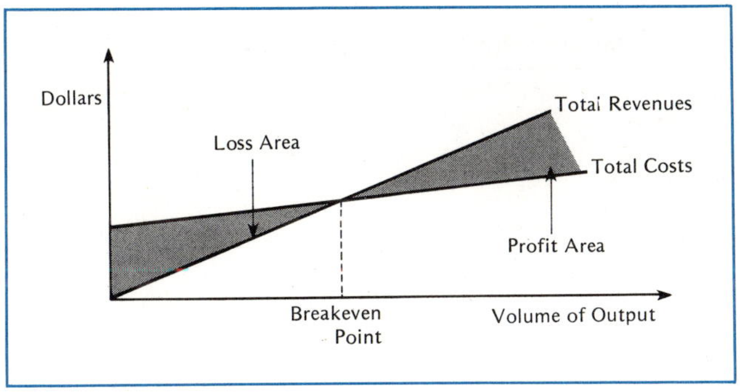

FIGURE 14-8. Profit Behavior Relative to Output.

It seems appropriate to make several additional comments about the breakeven model. Marketing people frequently refer to the denominator of the breakeven model, $(P\text{-}VC)$, as the *contribution margin.* It shows the contribution that each unit produced and sold makes toward covering the fixed costs. The contribution margin is a useful figure to watch, because it greatly affects the number of units that must be sold in order to break even. It is a bad sign for most business operations when per unit variable costs begin to approach the selling price.

It is also interesting to note that a characteristic of successful small businessmen is that they watch their fixed costs very carefully and try to make as many costs variable as possible.[4] Small businessmen commonly do not have a large financial base from which to operate and can be affected disastrously by business slowdowns. By keeping their fixed costs down, they keep their breakeven point low and, consequently, improve their chances of surviving occasional declines in sales.

An Illustration

Let us now employ the breakeven model in an illustration. The focus of our attention is the number of units of a new product the Creative Toy Company must sell in order to break even. The data in Table 14-1 is needed for our analysis. It can be seen that the fixed costs total \$170,000, the per unit variable costs run \$5.65, and the proposed selling price is \$9.95. Using the breakeven model [14 4], the breakeven point is shown as follows to be 39,535 units.

$$\text{Breakeven Point} = \frac{170{,}000}{(9.95\text{-}5.65)} = 39{,}535 \text{ units}$$

[4] A further discussion of the variability of fixed costs can be found in W. M. Harper, "Business Mathematics-Fixing the Fixed," *Management Accounting,* (February 1971), p. 66.

TABLE 14-1
Breakeven Analysis Data for the Creative Toy Company

Anticipated Selling Price			$9.95
Manufacturing Expenses:			
Raw Materials (per unit)		$2.50	
Direct Labor (per unit)		1.75	
Factory Overhead			
Variable (per unit)		.80	
Fixed	$10,000		
Equipment Expenses:			
Fixed	100,000		
Operating Expenses:			
Selling Expenses:			
Variable (per unit)		.50	
Fixed	30,000		
General & Administration Expenses:			
Variable (per unit)		.10	
Fixed	30,000		
	$170,000	$5.65	$9.95

The breakeven point can also be expressed in terms of dollar sales. This expression of the breakeven point can be found by multiplying the selling price times the breakeven point in units (See expression [14-5] shown as follows).

$$BEP_{\text{dollar sales}} = P \times BEP_{\text{units}} \quad [14\text{-}5]$$

For our Creative Toy Company illustration, the breakeven point in dollar sales is shown as follows to be $393,373.25.

$$BEP_{\text{dollar sales}} = \$9.95 \times 39{,}535 = \$393{,}373.25$$

Limitations of Breakeven Analysis

Despite the popularity of breakeven analysis, financial experts have reservations about its use. It has several inherent limitations that suggest it is best used only as an initial screening device. Let us now consider the most important limitations of breakeven analysis.

Most financial planning models have a meaningful time horizon. For example, internal rate of return analysis, which is a more sophisticated technique, calculates the average return over the *lifetime* of the investment.[5] However, breakeven analysis considers the returns only *up to* breakeven point. The returns after the breakeven point are completely neglected.

Breakeven analysis does not include the *time value of money* concept. Future dollars are treated as being worth as much as today's dollars. The timing of cash inflows and outflows can substantially affect the attractiveness of an investment, and breakeven analysis does not take this important fact into consideration.

[5] Weston and Brigham, op. cit., Chapters 9 and 10.

Breakeven analysis is simple to use and understand; however, it must be properly used.[6] As long as it is employed as an initial screening device, its limitations are minor. However, in a thorough financial analysis, more sophisticated decision technology should also be used (for example, internal rate of return analysis, net discounted present value analysis).

LINEAR PROGRAMMING

As stated in the preceding chapter, *linear programming* is one of the most frequently used management science techniques. It has been applied in areas ranging from selecting advertising media to the racial balancing of schools. Linear programming is employed in situations in which there is an objective to be met within a set of constraints. It is a type of mathematical programming in which all of the important relationships in the real-world system can be expressed in linear terms.

Perhaps the best way to understand the basics of linear programming is through an example. An important and useful application of linear programming is to the production mix problem.

George B. Dantzig was the primary developer of linear programming. He is shown here receiving the National Medal of Science from President Ford.

[6]An excellent application of breakeven analysis is found in C. J. Gibson, "Selecting Pricing Strategies with Breakeven Analysis," *Cost and Management,* (November-December 1972), pp. 8–11.

A Production Mix Illustration

The *production mix problem* involves the determination of the combination of quantities of different products to produce so as to maximize profits. Problems of a similar nature are also found, however, outside of the production realm. Apartment complex developers must determine the mix of different size apartments to build. Financial managers are involved in determining the mix of projects for investment. In all of these cases, the objective is to determine the best single combination out of many possible combinations.

In a world of unlimited resources, there would be no production mix problem. An infinite quantity of all products would be produced and sold, resulting in an infinite profit for the organization. Obviously, however, such a situation does not exist, and in this world of ever-decreasing resources, it becomes increasingly farther from reality.

In the short run, there is often only a limited supply of certain key resources. A manufacturing firm may have access to only a limited quantity of raw materials. There may be only a limited amount of skilled labor and machine time available. Most products do not have an infinite demand and, consequently, production schedules must be established in light of product demand forecasts. All of this suggests, therefore, that the production mix must be selected within many constraints.

Linear programming can be used to identify the optimal quantity of items to produce and yet satisfy existing constraints. In the typical industrial setting there is a large number of possible product combinations and constraints. Although the constraints limit the possible, or feasible, solutions to the problem, there usually still remains a large number of possibilities. Linear programming locates the best of the feasible alternatives.

Stating the Problem Mathematically

In order to introduce some of the concepts associated with linear programming, let us consider the Video Products Company's decision as to how many black-and-white and color television sets to produce during the coming time period. Obviously, the products are related and require many of the same organizational resources. However, there are also important differences in such areas as component parts, skilled labor time, production costs, and selling price. The question is, "How many of each should be produced in order to maximize the contribution to profits?"

Linear programming requires that the problem be set up in a particular format. Specifically, a mathematical statement known as the *objective function* must be specified to express the objective of the analysis. For the Video Products illustration, the objective function is a profit equation that indicates the profit associated with producing color and black-and-white television sets. This expression is important in identifying the optimum combination of color and black-and-white sets to produce. The *constraints* that bound the possible solutions to the problem must also be expressed mathematically. For Video Products, constraints sometimes exist in areas such as raw materials availability, skilled labor time, machine time, accepted sales orders, product demand, and so on. Once the problem is stated in terms of an objective function and constraints, it can be analyzed using linear programming.

Video Products has a good understanding of the revenues, costs, and profits associated with the production of its television sets. Table 14-2 presents data on these factors for the black-and-white and color sets. From Table 14-2 it can be seen that every black-and-white set produced and sold generates $60 in profit, whereas every color set produces $100. Let us now express this fact mathematically in an objective function.

The symbolic notation of mathematical modeling requires that variable names and mathematical operators be used. In our example, X_C will represent the number of color sets produced and $X_{B\&W}$ the number of black-and-white sets produced. If $60 is realized from every black-and-white set produced and sold, $\$60X_{B\&W}$ must be the total contribution from this type of set. Likewise, $\$100X_C$ is the total profit from color sets. The contribution from both sets is the objective function that we want to maximize and is expressed as follows:

$$\text{Profit}_{\text{maximize}} = \$100X_C + \$60X_{B\&W}$$

For Video Products, it would be ideal if there was an unlimited demand for its television sets. Unfortunately, however, the marketing staff indicates that only a limited number of black-and-white and color television sets should be produced during the coming time period. This is just one of several important constraints that affects Video Products' production mix. The marketing people state that no more than 300 black-and-white and 500 color sets should be made. Expressed mathematically, the demand constraints would appear as follows:

$$X_{B\&W} \leq 300$$
$$X_C \leq 500$$

The marketing staff has already committed Video Products to manufacture 100 black-and-white sets, because a sales order for that amount has already been

TABLE 14-2
Revenue, Cost, and Profit Data for Video Products' Television Sets

	Black and White	Color
Revenue (per unit)	$120	$400
Cost	− 60	−300
Profit	$ 60	$100

accepted. Consequently, the number of black-and-white sets produced must be equal to or greater than 100.

$$X_{B\&W} \geq 100$$

Skilled labor also affects the production mix decision. Each black-and-white set requires 8 hours of skilled labor time, and each color set demands 10 hours. During the planning period, only a total of 4,000 hours are going to be available. This skilled labor constraint is expressed mathematically as follows:

$$8X_{B\&W} + 10X_C \leqq 4{,}000$$

Other factors also potentially affect Video Products' production decision, but those that have already been expressed are believed by management to be the most important and binding. The objective function and constraint equations summarized in Table 14-3 capture the essential characteristics of Video Products' situation.

Even though this example is quite simple, the optimal production mix is not immediately obvious. Just imagine the difficulty of trying to solve a problem in which there are five or ten different products and several hundred constraints, which is not at all an uncommon situation. In such a case, managerial intuition and simple computational analysis must be replaced by the systematic analysis procedures of linear programming. Let us now examine some of the analysis procedures by continuing with our Video Products' example.

The Graphical Method

Our production mix problem contains only two *choice* or *decision variables*—$X_{B\&W}$ and X_C. It is our choice or decision as to what value each will ultimately have, assuming, of course, that all of the constraints are satisfied. When there are only two choice variables, a *graphical method* of analysis can be employed.

TABLE 14-3
Video Products' Objective Function and Constraints

Objective Function

$$\text{Profit}_{max} = 100X_C + 60X_{B\&W}$$

Constraints

(1) $X_{B\&W} \leqq 300$
(2) $X_C \leqq 500$
(3) $X_{B\&W} \geqq 100$
(4) $8X_{B\&W} + 10X_C \leqq 4{,}000$

The graphical method requires that a graph such as in Figure 14-9 be prepared with the choice variables on each axis. We have chosen to place X_C on the horizontal axis and $X_{B\&W}$ on the vertical axis, although the selections could have been reversed. The constraints equations are then drawn. The demand constraints are identified as (1) and (2), the previous commitment for black-and-white sets as (3), and the skilled labor constraint as (4).

When the $X_{B\&W} \leqq 300$ demand constraint equation was drawn, it eliminated some of the possible solutions to the problem. Any points above the horizontal line drawn at $X_{B\&W} \leqq 300$ are not possible solutions because they violate the constraint on the demand for black-and-white sets. Figure 14-9 has been shaded with the lighter area representing the *area of feasible solutions* to the problem. Notice that all of the area above $X_{B\&W} = 300$ is darkened.

The constraint on the demand for color sets, $X_C \leqq 500$, results in a vertical line. Because the demand for color sets is equal to or less than 500, all points to the

FIGURE 14-9. A Graphical Analysis of Video Products' Production Mix Decision.

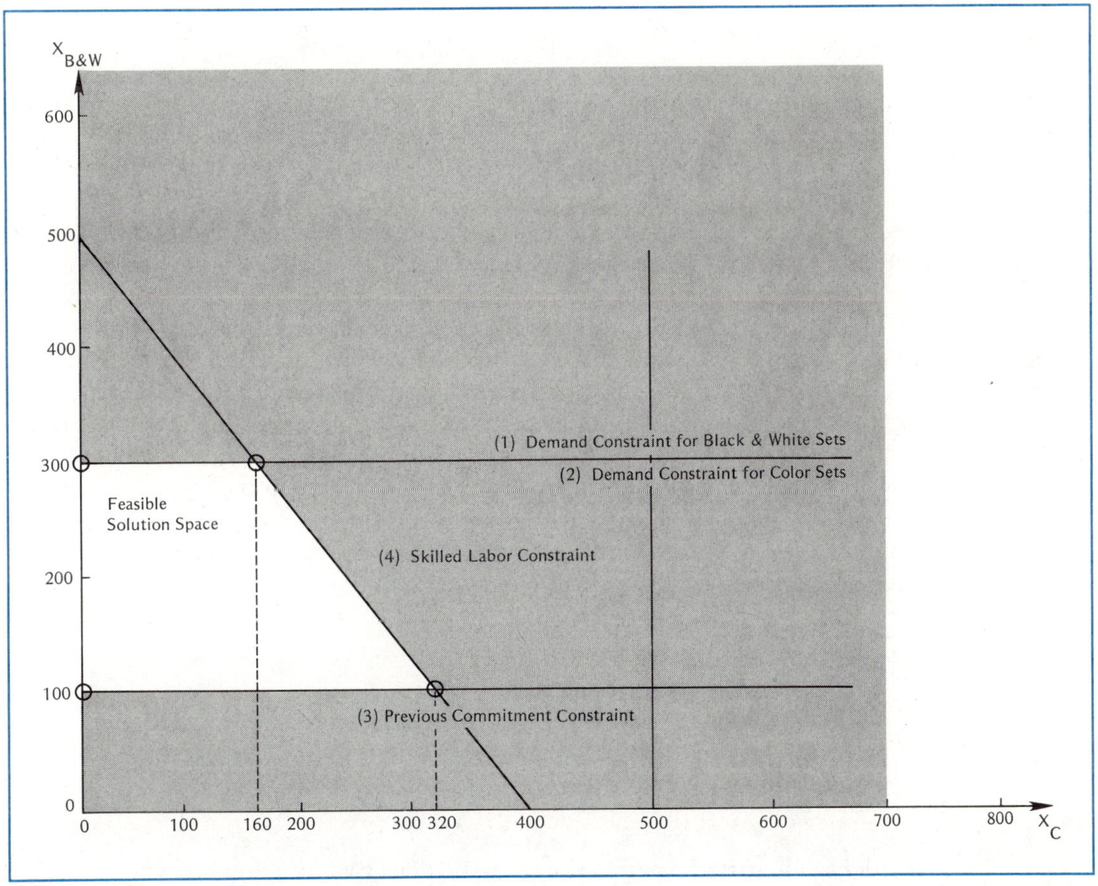

right of constraint (2) are shown as being shaded, that is, not feasible solutions.

Because of our commitment to produce 100 black-and-white sets, the horizontal line at $X_{B\&W} \geqq 100$ is drawn. Because we cannot produce fewer than 100 black-and-white sets, the area below constraint (3) is shaded.

The fourth and final constraint involves the availability of skilled labor. It is most easily drawn by plotting two points, first where it is assumed that no black-and-white sets are produced (each constraint is drawn independently of other constraints), and second where it is assumed that no color sets are produced. First consider constraint (4) when $X_{B\&W} = 0$,

$$8(0) + 10X_C = 4{,}000$$
$$X_C = 400$$

Next, when $X_C = 0$,

$$8X_{B\&W} + 10(0) = 4{,}000$$
$$X_{B\&W} = 500$$

A line drawn through the two points (400,0) and (0,500) reflects the various ways that the skilled labor can be used to produce the two types of television sets. Because no more than 4,000 labor hours can be used, the area to the top and right of constraint (4) is shaded.

After all of the constraints have been drawn and the nonfeasible areas shaded, there is a "window" of feasible solutions left. This window is referred to as the *feasible solution space,* and any problem solution must be within this space. We still do not know, though, which of the feasible solutions is optimal. With a little thought, however, we can discover that the optimal solution has to be on the perimeter of the feasible solution space. Any point within the perimeter can be improved upon by producing an additional color or black-and-white set. It is less intuitive that an optimal solution has to occur at a vertex of the feasible solution space. This fact can be proven but is of little interest to us.

Figure 14-9 has four vertices, which we have circled for identification purposes, and one of them is the optimal production mix for Video Products. The coordinates of the four points are read from the graph as,

$(X_C, X_{B\&W})$

1. (0,100).
2. (0,300).
3. (160,300).
4. (320,100).

In order to identify the best of the four, the objective function must be used. The combination that produces the highest profit is obviously the optimal solution to the problem.

1. Profit = 100(0) + 60(100) = \$6,000
2. Profit = 100(0) + 60(300) = \$18,000
3. Profit = 100(160) + 60(300) = \$34,000
4. Profit + 100(320) + 60(100) = \$38,000 (the optimal solution)

After comparing the possible solutions in the objective function, the combination of 320 color and 100 black-and-white television sets is found to be optimal, because it generates a profit of \$38,000, the highest possible profit. No other feasible production mix produces as great a profit.

Post-Optimality Analysis

The value of the linear programming model is not exhausted when the optimal solution is found. There still is additional information, which can and should be gained. This information results from performing *post-optimality* or *sensitivity analysis.*

Let us consider a case in point. Suppose the marketing manager of Video Products suggests that by offering a \$30 rebate on the sale of all color sets, the demand could be increased from 500 to 600 sets. Management's reaction to this suggestion should be negative. By reexamining Figure 14-9, you can see that the optimal production mix is relatively insensitive to the demand for color sets. In fact, the color set demand constraint is a *superseded* constraint, because it does not contribute to forming the final feasible solution space. Its impact is *superseded* by other constraint equations. In fact, the demand for color sets could drop as low as 320 before the optimal production mix is affected.

Let us now consider another possibility. It is obvious that the availability of skilled labor is having a large impact upon our profit picture. What would be the effect of increasing skilled labor hours from 4,000 to 5,000 hours by authorizing overtime, even if it decreases the per set profit on color and black-and-white sets from \$100 and \$60 to \$95 and \$55, respectively? Figure 14-10 provides the answer to this question. With the new skilled labor constraint, the optimal production mix becomes 100 black-and-white and 420 color sets, resulting in a profit of \$45,400. Obviously, the authorization of overtime is advisable, because it increases profits from \$38,000 to \$45,400.

Most decisions are made within the framework of an initial conceptualization of how the real world is or should be. Any model we develop reflects this conceptualization. However, as we saw with the possibility of authorizing overtime, our initial conceptualization of a system need not be the final one. Through considering the possibility of using overtime, we saw that the profits of Video Products could be increased. And that is what post-optimality analysis is all about. The initial optimal solution is for the first conceptualization of the problem.

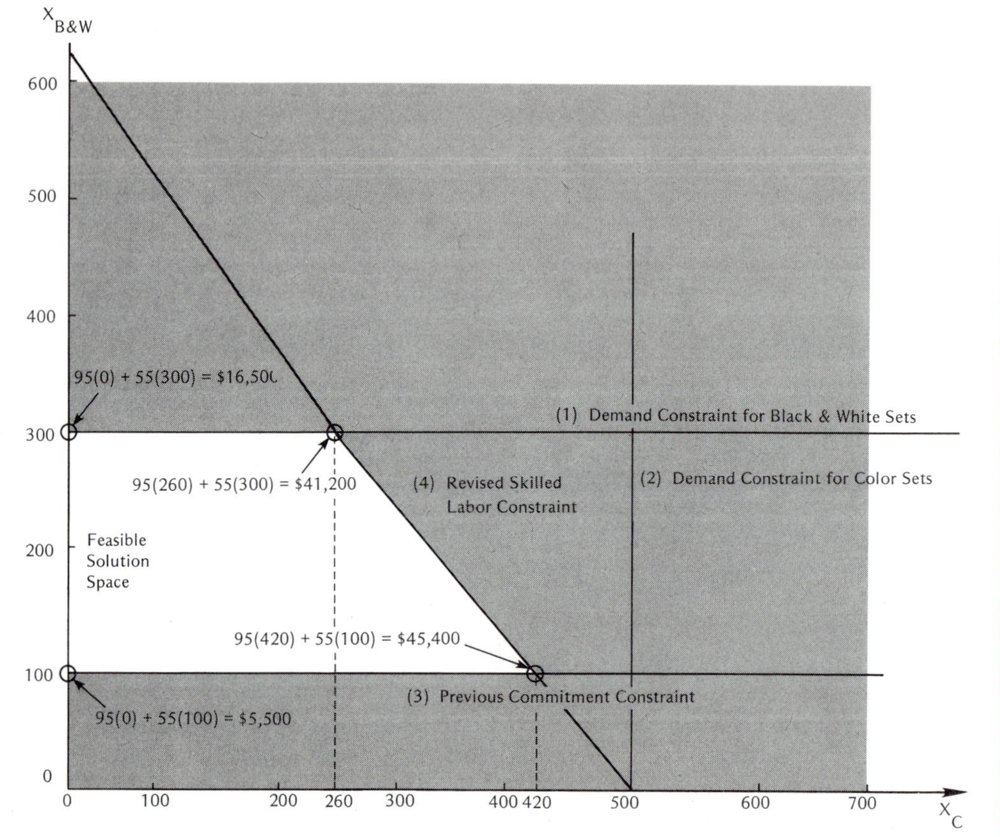

FIGURE 14-10. Post Optimality Analysis for Video Products' Production Mix Decision.

Post-optimality analysis investigates the behavior of the system when conditions are altered. When post-optimality analysis is not performed, much of the usefulness of a model is wasted, because valuable information is being neglected.[7]

The Simplex Method

Our linear programming problem was solved using a graphical method of analysis. You might have wondered, however, what would have happened if Video Products produced three rather than two different types of television sets. Obviously, we would have had difficulty in graphically investigating a three-

[7]Further discussion of sensitivity analysis is provided in Marvin W. Tucker, "Sensitivity Analysis for Linear Programming," *Management Accounting* (October 1975), pp. 324–326.

dimensional problem, and if there were four products, a graphical solution would have been completely impossible.

There is a general mathematical solution for linear programming problems known as the *simplex method.* Any problem that can be set up in a linear programming format of an objective function and constraints can be solved by the simplex method. Our introduction to linear programming will not include the simplex method, because it is a rather detailed analysis procedure that is better covered in management science courses. Basically, however, the simplex method identifies the vertices of the feasible solution space and moves from vertex to vertex, always moving to a better solution until the optimal one is found. Because of the importance of linear programming as a management science technique, a large number of packaged (prewritten) computer programs have been developed to perform the computations required by the simplex method. Consequently, the problem need only be set up in the correct format and entered as data inputs to the packaged program, and the computer performs the simplex analysis.[8]

THE PAYOFF MATRIX

Decision theory is one of the methods of analysis included in the category of statistical analysis. Its objective is to provide systematic analysis procedures for probabilistic decision-making situations.

The *payoff matrix* is one of the simpler and most useful of the decision theory models. It is employed when there are multiple decision alternatives, multiple probabilistic events that might occur, and consequences that depend upon which alternative is selected and which event occurs. It provides a structure for evaluating which alternative is best among management's possible courses of action.

The payoff matrix requires the use of probabilities. It therefore seems important to introduce several basic probability concepts. We will limit the discussion to those that are required when using the payoff matrix.

Basic Probability Concepts

A *probability* is the likelihood, or chance, that some future event will occur. For example, we might say that there is a 0.20 probability that it will rain tomorrow, or that there is a 0.75 chance that our company will be awarded a desired contract. Probabilities are quantitative assessments of the relative likelihood of possible future events.

Probabilities are based upon either *historical data* or *subjective judgment.* First consider using historical data as a source of probabilities. Here we assume that

[8] An excellent reference on this subject is Harold Bierman, Charles P. Bonini, and Warren H. Hausman, *Introduction To Linear Programming,* 4th ed., (Homewood, Ill.: Irwin, 1973), pp. 199–313.

what has taken place in the past is appropriate for assessing what will take place in the future. To illustrate, assume that an insurance salesman keeps records of how frequently he is able to set up a meeting with prospective clients based upon unsolicited telephone calls. The salesman's records show that he is able to set up an appointment 10% of the time. This being the case, if a number is called at random, what is the probability that a meeting will be arranged? Based upon the historical data, the probability is 0.10. There is also a 0.90 probability that there will be no meeting, because the events in this case are mutually exclusive and collectively exhaustive. *Mutually exclusive events* are those in which the occurrence of one event excludes the possibility of the occurrence of any other event. For example, either a meeting is arranged or it is not. *Collectively exhaustive events* are those that include every possible outcome. For example, there is no third alternative to success or failure in arranging a meeting. When events are mutually exclusive and collectively exhaustive, their probabilities sum to 1.00. Consequently, if the probability of arranging a meeting is 0.10, the probability of not meeting must be 1.00 − 0.10, or 0.90. Use of the payoff matrix requires that the events be mutually exclusive and collectively exhaustive.

Probabilities can also be based upon subjective judgment. In this case, data may be available, but are not directly applicable for assigning probabilities. For example, assessing the probability that our company will receive a contract requires subjective judgment. We may have experience in the bidding behavior of our competitors, but none of these data are directly convertible into a probability. Instead, we must combine this with our "gut feelings" in order to generate a probability.

Some people initially believe that probabilities based upon subjective judgment are unscientific and should not be used. To a limited extent, subjective probabilities might be considered unscientific, but most important business decision-making situations require subjective judgment. It is not a question of whether subjective probabilities will or will not be used; it is a question of whether they will be quantitatively expressed and systematically processed in a model, or whether the human mind will process them without the aid of a model. Given the limited data processing capabilities of the mind, using a model is often advisable.

The Concept of Expected Value

At the heart of decision theory and the payoff matrix is the concept of *expected value.* Mathematically, it is defined as follows:

$$E(x) = \Sigma\, x \times p(x) \qquad [14\text{-}5]$$

The expected value of a random variable is equal to the sum of the possible values for the variable multiplied by their probability of occurrence.

Most of us have an intuitive understanding of the expected value concept. Let us consider a simple example. What if someone offers to play a gambling game with you. A coin will be flipped, and if you correctly call whether it comes up heads or tails, you win \$1.00. However, if you guess incorrectly, you win nothing. Obviously, the person offering to play this game with you will want an entrance fee before each flip of the coin so as to give him or her a chance of winning as well as losing money. The question is, "How much should you be willing to pay in a fair contest?" Without a whole lot of thought, you would probably answer \$0.50, which is, indeed, the correct response. But do you realize that your answer implies the occurrence of an expected value calculation? The probability of guessing correctly (0.50) multiplied by its consequence (\$1.00 won) plus the probability of guessing incorrectly (0.50) times its consequence (\$0.00 won) equals \$0.50.

$$\begin{aligned} E(x) &= 0.50\ (\$1.00) + 0.50\ (\$0.00) \\ &= \$0.50 \end{aligned}$$

Expected value is a long-run concept. It is analogous to a mean projected into the future. It reveals what would be the mean outcome if the same experiment was repeated over and over again. In our gambling game, on any one coin flip, we would be paid either \$1.00 or \$0.00 (neglecting the entrance fee), but in the long run, we would expect to average \$0.50. This is why we might be willing to pay up to a \$0.50 entrance fee to play the game.

In business decision making, we seldom face the same situation over and over again. However, we face many similar decisions in terms of the costs and revenues involved. Consequently, and this is a bit of an inductive leap, if we consistently base our decisions on the basis of optimizing expected value, over the course of our managerial careers we should hope to optimize the decisions we make.

The Payoff Matrix Structure

Having introduced the necessary probability concepts, we should now examine the structure of *payoff matrix analysis.* A payoff matrix has four basic components.

1. The alternative courses of action.
2. The possible events.
3. The probabilities of the events occurring.
4. The consequences of the interactions of the courses of action and the events.

Figure 14-11 shows how these components are included in a payoff matrix structure. The courses of action open to the decision maker form the rows of the matrix. The possible future events and their probabilities are the columns. The

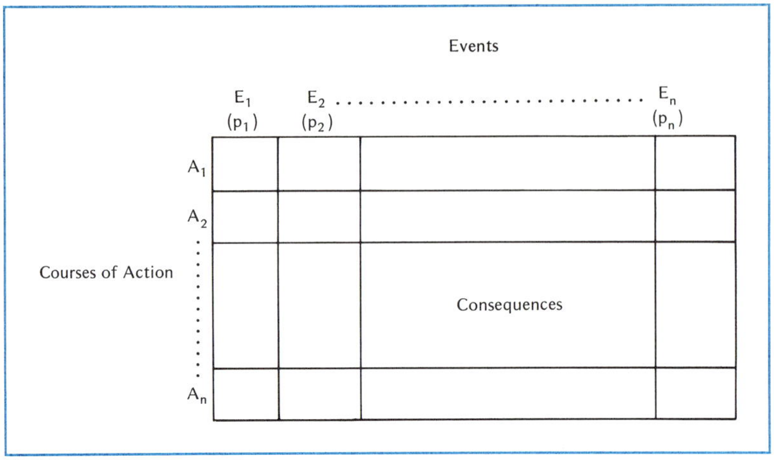

FIGURE 14-11. Structure of a Payoff Matrix.

cells within the matrix show the consequences of the interactions of the courses of action and the events.

The optimal course of action is determined by making expected value calculations across the rows for each decision alternative. The probability associated with each event is multiplied by the consequence, and the products are summed to find the expected value for each course of action. In a maximization situation, the alternative that offers the highest expected value is chosen; in a minimization situation, just the reverse occurs. Let us now consider an example.

An Illustration

The management of Sprague Electronics is considering which of two machines to buy. The first machine has a lower purchase price but its operating expenses are higher because of additional scrappage and labor requirements. The second machine initially costs more but has lower operating costs. Relevant data for the two machines are presented in Table 14-4.

If Sprague Electronics could predict with certainty the demand for its product made on the new machine, the decision as to which machine to buy could be

TABLE 14-4
Cost Data for the Two Machines Being Considered by Sprague Electronics

	Machine 1	Machine 2
Purchase Cost	$100,000	$140,000
Operating Costs (per unit)	$0.14	$0.06
Lifetime	10 years	10 years

TABLE 14-5
Demand Data for the Product Made by Sprague Electronics

Demand Level	Units Demanded	Probability
High	800,000	0.2
Moderate	600,000	0.5
Low	400,000	0.3
		1.0

made in a straightforward manner. Assuming that the selling price of the product made by each machine is the same, the total costs of satisfying the demand could be calculated and compared for the two machines. The machine that had the least total cost would be purchased. Unfortunately, however, Sprague Electronics is not able to predict with certainty what the future demand will be.

It is thought that the demand might be high, moderate, or low, but with different probabilities. Table 14-5 shows the possible demand levels, units demanded, and their probabilities for the lifetime of the product made on the two machines.

Sprague's equipment selection problem is amenable to analysis through a payoff matrix approach. The decision alternatives involve which of the two machines to buy. The events are the possible demand levels, and we have probabilistic estimates for their likelihood of occurrence. From the cost data and the possible number of units demanded, the economic consequences can be calculated. We use the total cost model presented earlier in the chapter ($TC = FC + VC \times O$). All of these data are summarized in the payoff matrix shown in Figure 14-12.

The analysis proceeds by making expected value calculations across the rows of the matrix for two decision alternatives.

$$E(\text{Machine 1}) = (0.2)\,(212{,}000) + (0.5)\,(184{,}000) + (0.3)\,(156{,}000)$$
$$= \$181{,}200$$
$$E(\text{Machine 2}) = (0.2)\,(188{,}000) + (0.5)\,(176{,}000) + (0.3)\,(164{,}000)$$
$$= \$174{,}800$$

FIGURE 14-12. A Payoff Matrix for Sprague Electronic's Equipment Selection Decision

		Events		
		High (0.2)	**Moderate (0.5)**	**Low (0.3)**
Courses of Action	Machine 1	100,000 + (.14) × (800,000) = \$212,000	100,000 + (.14) × (600,000) = \$184,000	100,000 + (.14) × (400,000) = \$156,000
	Machine 2	140,000 + (.06) × (800,000) = \$188,000	14,000 + (.06) × (600,000) = \$176,000	140,000 + (.06) × (400,000) = \$164,000

Based upon this analysis, we would recommend that Sprague Electronics purchase Machine 2, because it has the least expected cost. It might also be noted that Machine 2 involves the least risk, because its range of possible costs is only from $188,000 to $164,000 whereas the range for Machine 1 varies from $212,000 to $156,000.

SUMMARY

It is useful for managers to possess computational skills for some of the more important management science models. This chapter presented three models that are particularly useful in support of management's planning responsibilities. The three models considered were breakeven analysis, linear programming, and the payoff matrix.

Breakeven analysis is concerned with how many units of an item must be sold in order that the revenues received equal the costs incurred. It is a highly popular method of analysis that is particularly appropriate for evaluating new product proposals. If it appears likely that the new product has the potential to at least break even, it should be subjected to more sophisticated methods of financial analysis.

Linear programming is often applicable to situations in which scarce resources are to be allocated in an optimal manner. In order to use linear programming, the problem must be structured in the format of an objective function and constraints. If there are only two choice variables, a graphical method of analysis can be employed. Otherwise, the more general simplex method must be used.

The payoff matrix can be used to structure decision making in situations when there are multiple courses of action, probabilistic events, and consequences that depend upon the action selected and the event which occurs. In order to select the optimal decision alternative, expected value calculations are made across the rows of the matrix for the various courses of action. Decision making is based upon optimizing expected value.

Assignments

14-1. What information is provided from breakeven analysis?

14-2. What data are required in performing breakeven analysis?

14-3. What is the general effect on the breakeven point for the following changes?

a. An increase in the selling price with no change in units sold.

b. A reduction in variable costs.

c. A change from leasing a piece of equipment for $5,000 per year to the purchase of an equivalent machine for $100,000. The useful life of the purchased machine will be 20 years, with no salvage value.

14-4. What type of problem can be analyzed by linear programming?
14-5. What format must be used with all linear programming problems?
14-6. Is it possible to graphically solve any linear programming problem? Why, or why not?
14-7. Give several examples of probabilities that are based on (1) historical data and (2) subjective judgment.
14-8. Explain what is meant by the concept of expected value. Give an example.
14-9. What are the elements and concepts used in any payoff matrix analysis?
14-10. Management planning models are abstractions from, or simplifications of, reality. Explain how this is true with respect to breakeven analysis, linear programming, and the payoff matrix.

Case 14-1

SUMMER SAIL, INC.

A businessman is considering starting Summer Sail, Inc., a small summer sailboat rental business in a resort beach area. A local motel has agreed to rent a strip of land on the beach for the summer for $1,500 plus $.50 of every hourly rental fee received. It is estimated that 30 scorpion sailboats would fit conveniently on the strip, and that with a quantity discount, they could be purchased for $500 each. Rather than worrying about storing the boats from one summer to the next, the businessman plans to sell them at the end of the summer, and hopes to realize $7,000 from the 30 used boats. A student at a local university has agreed to manage the rentals from June 1 to August 31 (90 days) for $20 per day. It is estimated that life jackets and cushions would cost approximately $100, and the cost of materials for a shed to store the equipment would be about $500. The businessman and the student have agreed to erect the shed together before the season starts. The businessman has decided that a reasonable rental would be $3.50 per hour.

1. How many hours of sailboat rental time would be required in order to break even on this investment?
2. How many hours of rental time would be required in order to realize a $5,000 profit?
3. What would happen to the breakeven point if the student demanded $.50 of every rental hour fee?

Case 14-2

TAYLOR INDUSTRIES

Taylor Industries has found that because of the characteristics of its production facilities and methods of manufacturing, one of its products has fixed costs that vary at three different levels of output. Specifically, for output of up to 10,000 units, fixed costs are $250,000. For output between 10,000 and 15,000 units, fixed costs are found to be $350,000. For output of more than 15,000 units, fixed costs are found to be $370,000. Variable costs per unit, though, remain constant at all three levels of output, and consist of $23 per unit for materials and $37 per unit for direct labor.

1. If the current selling price per unit is $80, what is the breakeven point for Taylor Industries' product?

Case 14-3

HIGHTOWER MANUFACTURING COMPANY

Hightower Manufacturing Company produces building materials and related products. Management is considering whether or not to change the method it currently uses to make and package one of its products. The present technique employs a relatively equal mix of equipment and labor. However, the company could purchase and install a newly developed machine that would reduce the number of operators needed, thus reducing labor costs but increasing fixed costs. Comparative data on the two alternatives for one month of operations are as follows:

Alternative	Fixed Costs per Month	Variable Costs per 100-lb bag
Current method	$2,500	$40
Buy new machine	5,000	20

1. Assuming the selling price of each 100-lb bag to be $100, what are the breakeven volumes per month for the two alternatives?
2. If the company expects to sell about 50 of the 100-lb bags per month, which alternative should be chosen?

Case 14-4

GERLOFF EQUIPMENT COMPANY

Gerloff Equipment Company manufactures and sells heavy construction equipment. Management wishes to find the optimum combination of its two most profitable products, bulldozers and steam shovels, in order to maximize total profit. Bulldozers contribute $2,500 to profit, and steam shovels contribute $3,000. Each piece of machinery must go through two departments—production and engineering. In the production department, the machinery is assembled, and then it is sent to engineering where it passes through a rigorous inspection test. One bulldozer require 15 hours in the production department and 5 hours in engineering. Steam shovels, on the other hand, require 25 hours in production and 8 hours in engineering. There is a total of 500 hours available in production and 250 hours in engineering.

1. Find the optimum combination of the two pieces of machinery in order to maximize total profit.

Case 14-5

KING MANUFACTURING COMPANY

The King Manufacturing Company has a contract to produce 10,000 pounds of a cement coating mixture for a customer. The mix consists of two ingredients *A* and *B*, each costing $8 and $11 per pound, respectively. No more than 3,000 pounds of *A* can be used, and least 1,500 pounds of *B* must be used.

1. Calculate the number of pounds of each ingredient to use in order to minimize total costs for producing the 10,000 pounds of cement coating mixture.

2. Calculate the lowest possible cost.
3. Because of a shortage of ingredient *A*, its cost per pound increases $4. How is the optimal blend affected?
4. Suppose the customer prefers to have at least 2,000 pounds of ingredient *B* in the mixture because it makes the cement coating more water resistant. How does this affect the optimal blend?

Case 14-6

TUTTLE MANUFACTURING COMPANY

The president of the Tuttle Manufacturing Company is considering hiring another salesman. She has limited her choice to three candidates, each of whom she believes would successfully fill the position, but in different degrees. Because of their varying educational degrees and working experience, they each demand a different starting salary. Candidates *A*, *B*, and *C* want salaries of $20,000, $15,000, and $17,000, respectively. The president believes that each applicant deserves the requested salary. However, she also believes that the company may not be able to afford the added salesman at the present time, no matter who the choice may be. It all depends upon projected sales, and the president is very uncertain about what future sales will be. When questioned, she stated that she believed there is a 30% chance the company will experience heavy sales and a 50% chance for moderate sales. Earnings, projected for each of the three possible salesmen for the coming year, are as follows:

Discounted Future Contribution of the Salesmen for the Coming Year (Excluding Yearly Salary)

		Sales		
		Heavy	Moderate	Light
Applicants	Salesman *A*	$50,000	30,000	15,000
	Salesman *B*	30,000	10,000	5,000
	Salesman *C*	30,000	20,000	10,000

1. Which salesman should the president hire? Why?

Case 14-7

INCOME PROPERTY, INC.

Income Property, Inc., is considering the purchase of a piece of land for investment purposes. The land's purchase price is $825,000. It is believed that a major highway will be built in the area, thus making the land highly desirable. The company believes it could sell the land for as much as $1,500,000 if the site is chosen for the highway. After talking with several legislators, management feels that the chance of that location being chosen for the highway is about 15%. If the site is not chosen, Income Property, Inc. would quickly sell the land at a price of $700,000 in order to obtain funds for other investments.

1. Would you recommend that Income Property, Inc. purchase the land? Why, or why not? At what probability of the site being chosen would you be indifferent between the two courses of action?

Case 14-8

CURRENT PUBLICATIONS, INC.

Current Publications, Inc. is considering the purchase of a new high-speed printer to make its operations more efficient. It has narrowed its choice to one of two models, one with a lower purchase price but higher operating costs per page, and the other with a higher purchase price but lower operating costs per page. Comparative data for the two models are as follows:

	Model A	Model B
Purchase cost	$350,000	$200,000
Operating costs	$0.0061 per page	$0.0251 per page
Lifetime	10 years	10 years

The number of pages the company will print during the next 10 years depends upon the number of its printing contracts. Management assesses the probability of a large number of contracts to be 0.2, a moderate number to be 0.5, and a small number to be 0.3. The number of pages associated with the contracts in each condition is 1,000,000, 600,000, and 300,000, respectively.

1. What model of the printer should the company purchase? Why?

Case 14-9

JAMES B. MEGABUCKS

James B. Megabucks, world-renowned oil tycoon, high roller and sportsman, was on his annual South American safari. Accompanying him was Homer Jones, his close but financially impoverished friend. While tracking along a stream infested with vicious piranha, James B. Megabucks tripped over a tree root and fell into the stream. Jones, seeing his friend being attacked by the horrible piranha, jumped into the stream and rescued Megabucks. Needless to say, Megabucks was extremely grateful to his friend for risking his life, and said, "Jones, I'm going to give you $1,000,000 for saving my life." The life of poverty has come to an end for Jones. However, after taking several more steps, Jones hears Megabucks say, "Jones, I've always loved a gamble. I'll tell you what I'll do. I'll flip a coin, and if you call it right, I'll give you $2,100,00. But if you call it wrong, that $1,000,000 I was going to give you, well, we will just forget about it."

1. If you were Jones, what would you say to Megabucks?
2. Is your answer consistent with the concept of optimizing expected value?
3. What are the characteristics of this decision-making situation that make it unusual?
4. How is the economic concept of diminishing marginal utility applicable here?

References

ANDERSON, DAVID R., DENNIS J. SWEENEY, AND THOMAS A. WILLIAMS. *Management Science*. St. Paul, Minn.: West, 1976.

ANTHONY, ROBERT N. *Management Accounting Principles.* Homewood, Ill.: Richard D. Irwin, Inc., 1970.

BROSTER, E. J. "Breakeven Analysis." *Certified Accountant.* (January-February 1974), pp. 3–4, 9–11, 56.

BROWN, REX V., ANDREW S. KAHR, AND CAMERON R. PETERSON. *Decision Analysis for the Manager.* New York: Holt, Rinehart and Winston, 1974.

BROWN, REX. "Do Managers Find Decision Theory Useful." *Harvard Business Review,* (May-June 1970), pp. 78–89.

GEORGE, PHILIP M. "The New Breakeven Chart." *Accountancy.* (November 1973), pp. 41–45.

GIBSON, J. "Introduction to the Graphical Approach to Linear Programming." *Certified Accountant.* (October 1973), pp. 550, 553, 567.

GUPTA, SHIV K., AND JOHN M. COZZOLINO. *Fundamentals of Operations Research for Management.* San Francisco: Holden-Day, Inc., 1974.

MUKIRJI, D. "Breakeven Analysis: An Appraisal." *Management Accountant.* (October 1972), pp. 603–608.

SHORE, BARRY. *Quantitative Methods for Business Decisions.* New York: McGraw-Hill, Book Company, 1978.

SPURR, WILLIAM A., AND CHARLES P. BONINI. *Statistical Analysis for Business Decisions.* 2nd ed. Homewood, Ill.: Robert D. Irwin, Inc., 1973.

ULIVILA, JACOB, REX V. BROWN, AND KARLE S. PACKARD. "A Case in On-Line Decision Analysis for Product Planning." *Decision Sciences.* (July 1977), pp. 598–615.

R. MILES WAUGH
Manager of Management Sciences Department, Philip Morris, USA

R. Miles Waugh is the Manager of the Management Sciences Department at Philip Morris, USA. The department was created by Waugh in 1975 to serve the management science needs of Manufacturing Management at the new plant of Philip Morris in Richmond, Virginia. The department provides both simulation and optimization analysis. Both types are used heavily in the areas of contingency planning, policy assessment, and so on.

Executive Commentary
Title: Planning Models at Philip Morris, USA

One of the first questions I asked myself when I came to Philip Morris, USA in 1974 to form the Management Sciences Department was, What kinds of planning models do you develop for a company that previously achieved a 13% and a 20% annual growth rate in operating revenues and income, respectively, over the period 1970–1974? (These exceptional growth rates were just as rapid for the period 1974–1977.) And better yet, how do you sell them? My thoughts and observations regarding these and other questions will be expressed in this commentary.

The company's top management was not lulled into complacency by all this success. They realized that new skills and talents, new analytical techniques, and more systematic and comprehensive planning would be required to maintain this growth into an increasingly complex and uncertain future. Philip Morris, USA is turning increasingly to the use of computer-based models to more quickly and fully evaluate the consequences, risks, and uncertainties of alternative planning scenarios.

Management has become aware that the old ways of "feeling your way along" are in many cases not adequate to handle the increasingly complex nature of our cigarette business. In the manufacturing area, for example, the number of cigarette brands produced at the new Richmond Manufacturing Center is 50% greater than originally anticipated, and our export production in 1978 is running 50% ahead of what was forecast as recently as 1975. Planning for both production and material requirements has been complicated by an increase in the number of finished goods product items, by the addition of new manufacturing facilities, and by the new technologies necessary to meet the ever-growing demand for our products.

Hence, in many areas, traditional methods have been replaced or at least complemented by modeling methods. A manual and time-consuming analysis once performed by the director of production planning and control has been replaced by a computer-based planning tool that helps him determine the optimal (least cost) monthly schedule of hiring and overtime to meet specified inventory goals over a multi-year planning horizon. This model is not only much quicker than the old manual procedure, but is also more comprehensive, because it is able to take into account factors and relationships that the director previously did not have time to consider.

Other planning models, which the management sciences department has or is developing, run the gamut from financial applications to production and even some marketing activity. A cash flow analysis and profitability model performs "what-iffing" and sensitivity analysis on capital investment projects. A production allocation model, which currently is formulated as a linear programming problem, determines what brands should be produced where in order to minimize total production and distribution costs, subject to capacity and demand constraints. A production forecasting system forecasts monthly production by product code and by plant for material requirements planning. A distribution model determines optimal distribution modes (including interplant transhipments) from manufacturing plants to field warehouses, subject to plant production forecasts and warehouse demand constraints.

Models must be described and sold in operational terms that managers can appreciate, understand, and identify with on a personal basis. To assist the analysts who work in my department in this selling task, I advise them to

- Think big, but start small.
- Be inquiring.
- Be responsive.
- Avoid interdepartmental entanglements.

In developing planning models, it pays to think big but start small. Initial costs should be minimized until the benefits of a model can be demonstrated through some concrete results. The natural initial tendency to incorporate everything one can think of into the model should be avoided. The model for the director of production planning, for example, started out as a simple computer-based tool that merely duplicated the results he had been obtaining by hand. Later on, additional features were incorporated into the model, but only after the model's usefulness and credibility and the user's interest had been established.

Planning models must be developed and implemented within a given organizational environment. Frequently, such an environment involves conflicting interdepartmental objectives and a preoccupation with short-term considerations. Such facts may be deplored from an intellectual viewpoint, but they cannot be ignored if one is interested in developing planning models that will actually be used by management to aid in their decision making. The model builder must attempt to get to know his user population, its objectives, and the underlying motivations of the key decision makers. For this reason, I encourage my analysts to inquire into how other departments and key managers are operating, what motivates them, what their problems are, and where we may play a role.

Responsiveness, in terms of the ability to respond to today's "hot issue" or problem, can go a long way toward gaining the type of managerial support required to maintain a sound modeling effort.

Model builders should avoid becoming actually entangled in the interdepartmental rivalries of a company. This, in effect, imposes a prudent limit on the level of visibility and inquisitiveness. Recognize the forces at work, but try to maintain an independent and detached posture. Ultimately, planning models must be accepted for their relatively objective nature as a decision input, or not at all.

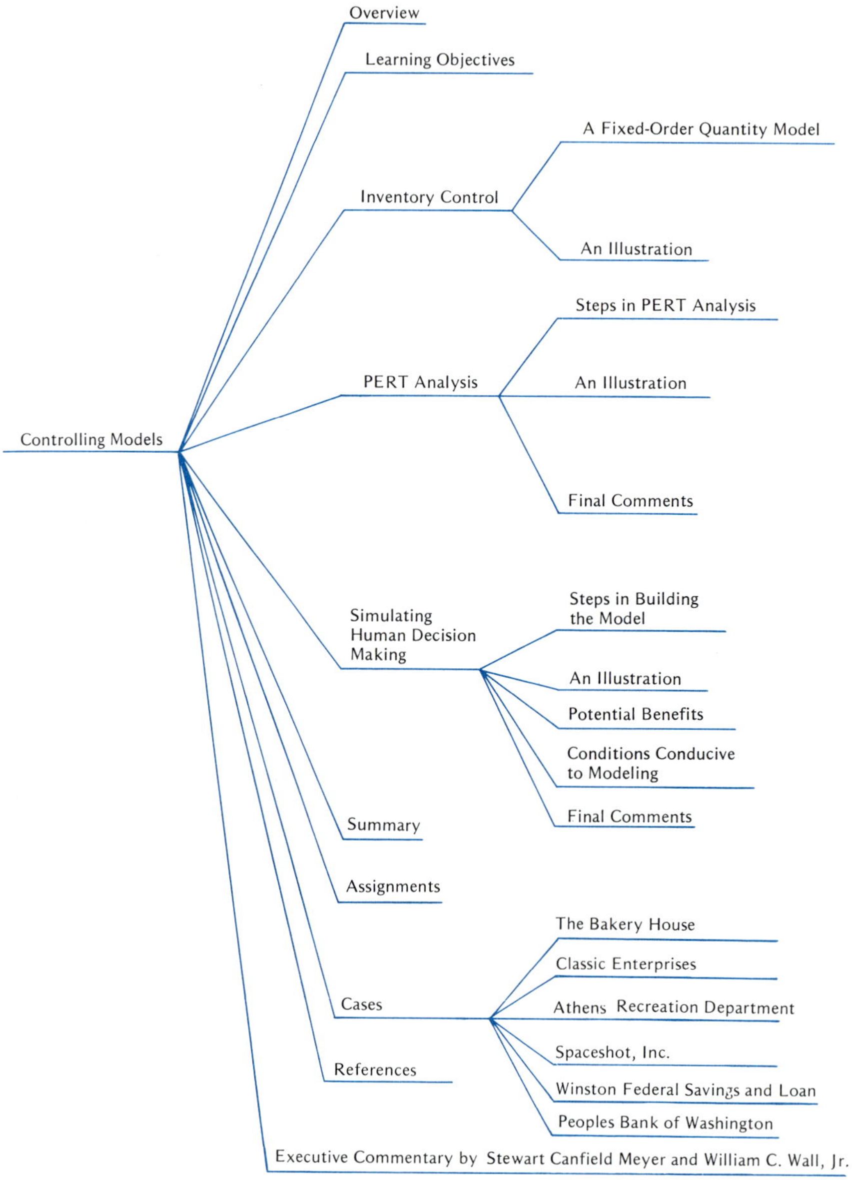
Controlling Models
Overview
Learning Objectives
Inventory Control
A Fixed-Order Quantity Model
An Illustration
PERT Analysis
Steps in PERT Analysis
An Illustration
Final Comments
Simulating Human Decision Making
Steps in Building the Model
An Illustration
Potential Benefits
Conditions Conducive to Modeling
Final Comments
Summary
Assignments
Cases
The Bakery House
Classic Enterprises
Athens Recreation Department
Spaceshot, Inc.
Winston Federal Savings and Loan
Peoples Bank of Washington
References
Executive Commentary by Stewart Canfield Meyer and William C. Wall, Jr.

15

CONTROLLING MODELS

OVERVIEW

In the preceding chapter, three widely used planning models were presented—breakeven analysis, linear programming, and the payoff matrix. This chapter introduces three additional models that are valuable when used in support of management's controlling responsibilities. These models come from the areas of inventory control, project management, and simulating human decision making. They provide an exposure to the wide variety of models that are employed for controlling purposes.

The controlling of inventories is a concern for almost all organizations. Because of its importance and relatively structured nature, it is not surprising that inventory control problems were among the first to attract the attention of management scientists. We will look at the inventory problem in general, develop a simple but often-used model, and present an illustration.

Complex projects made up of many interrelated activities often pose difficult management problems. However, PERT analysis provides decision technology that assists in planning and controlling such projects. We will examine the PERT analysis model and its application to a project that involves the development of an industrial park.

The final model we will consider takes us into the fascinating realm of simulating human decision making. Through a controlling model for processing a bank's overdrafts (bad checks), we will see how models can be profitably used to simulate routine, judgmental decision making.

LEARNING OBJECTIVES

This chapter is especially intended to help the student:

1. **Understand the role, nature, and use of controlling models.**
2. **Learn to apply a basic fixed-order quantity inventory model to items with independent demand.**
3. **Learn to apply PERT analysis to project management.**
4. **Understand the steps, benefits, and conditions that go with simulating human decision making.**
5. **Learn, especially in the context of thinking about management, the meaning of the following concepts:**

independent demand	**events**
dependent demand	**activities**
MRP systems	**critical path**
fixed-order period models	**heuristics**
fixed-order quantity models	**tree diagram**
PERT	

INVENTORY CONTROL

Inventories are required by all systems that transform inputs into goods or services. *Inventory* can best be described as quantities of items held for future use by an organization. Raw materials inventory is kept so that the product can be produced or a service provided. Work-in-process inventory of partially completed items is found in most production systems. Completed items in a production system are placed into finished goods inventory. Retailers and wholesalers maintain inventories of items sold to customers.

There are many types of decisions that need to be made about inventory. They include what kinds of and how much inventory to maintain, when items should be ordered, and how many items should be ordered at a time. These are important decisions, because for most organizations it is common to find a large proportion of their capital assets tied up in inventory.

In this section we will look at only a portion of the problems of managing inventory. The primary focus of attention will be on controlling raw materials inventory. Furthermore, it will be assumed that we already know what items are needed and we must only decide how many items to order and the timing of the orders. Depending upon the nature of the demand for the inventory item, an appropriate inventory control method is selected.

In controlling inventories, it is useful to make a distinction between items that experience independent, as opposed to dependent, demand. *Independent demand* refers to demand situations in which the need for an item is independent or distinct from the demand for any other item. For example, the demand for refrigerators depends only on the need for them. With *dependent demand,* the need for the item depends upon the demand for other items. For example, if 5,000 new cars are going to be produced during a time period, there will be a need for 25,000 new tires (assuming a spare tire for each car). In this example, the demand for tires is linked to the production of new cars.

Control procedures for independent and dependent demand items tend to be handled differently by industry. Material Requirements Planning (MRP) systems are finding wide acceptance for use with dependent demand items.[1] These are computerized systems that "create schedules identifying the specific parts and materials required to produce an end item, the exact numbers needed, and the dates when orders for these materials should be released and be received or completed within the production cycle."[2] A schematic of the input and output from a typical MRP system is shown in Figure 15-1. The Bill of Material file

FIGURE 15-1. The Functioning of an MRP System. (Source: Chase and Aquilano, p. 425.)

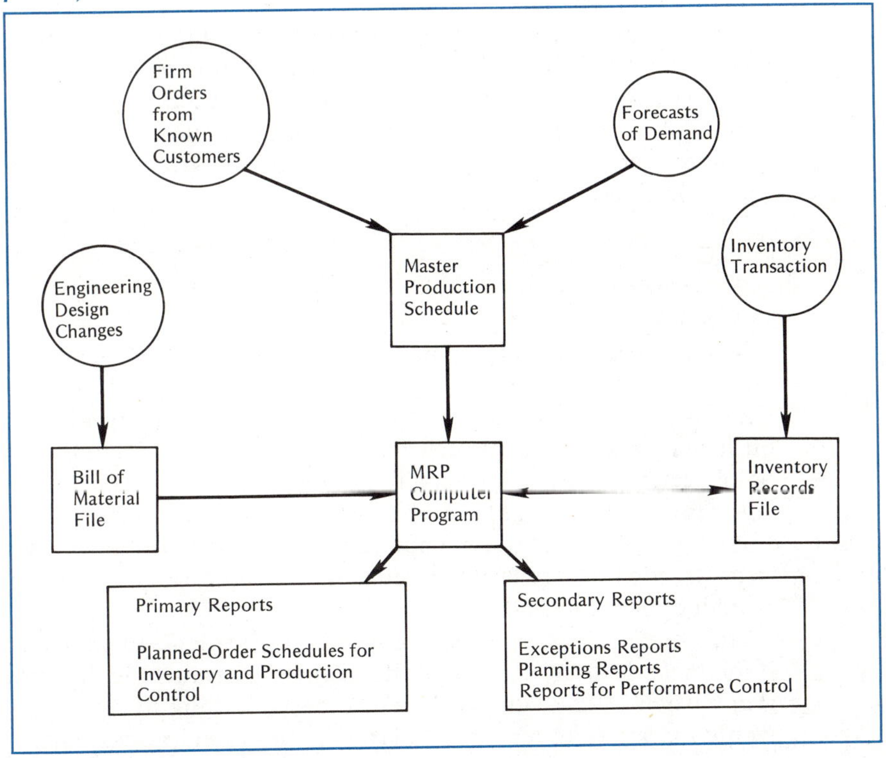

[1]An introductory discussion of MRP systems is available in Richard B. Chase, and Nicholas J. Aquilano, *Production and Operations Management,* rev. ed. (Homewood, Ill.: Irwin, 1977), Chapter 9.

[2]Ibid., p. 424.

indicates what goes into making the end items. The Master Production Schedule shows what end items are to be produced and when. The Inventory Records file maintains the current status of items carried in inventory. These inputs are processed by the MRP program to create the reports used in controlling dependent demand inventory items.

Items that experience independent demand are usually controlled by one of two methods. Both methods focus, however, upon the fundamental questions of how many items to order or produce at a time and when the orders should be placed. With the *fixed-order period* method, orders are placed at fixed points in time (for example, every two weeks), but the amount ordered varies. The *fixed-order quantity* method allows the timing of the placement of orders to vary, but the amount ordered is held constant. As an example of an inventory control model, we will later consider a fixed-order quantity model. In the model, attention will focus upon the *order quantity*, *Q*, the number of items ordered when an order is placed, and the *reorder point*, *R*, the number of items remaining when an order should be placed. In other words, an order is placed for *Q* items whenever the inventory balance drops to or below *R* items. The question is, what *Q* and *R* combination minimizes the costs of maintaining the item in inventory? No one answer can be given to this question, because it depends on a variety of factors that vary from situation to situation. However, a starting point is to consider the variety of costs typically associated with maintaining an item in inventory.

For convenience, all inventory costs can be grouped into one of the four following categories:

1. Carrying costs.
2. Ordering or setup costs.
3. Stockout costs.
4. Purchasing or production costs.

Carrying, or holding, *costs* are those associated with physically having the item on hand. Included in this category are warehousing, insurance, spoilage, theft, obsolescence, and tied-up capital costs.

Ordering costs include clerical costs associated with processing the order, shipping costs, and material handling costs once the order is received. When the items are produced rather than ordered for inventory, *setup costs* of preparing for a production run are incurred.

Stockout costs occur when the item is not available upon demand. If the item is for final sale to the consumer, the stockout costs include the foregone profits on that particular sale (unless the customer is willing to *back order*, or in other words, to wait), plus lost potential future sales when the customer shifts his or her business to a competitor. When the inventory item is for use in a production process rather than for final sale, stockouts disrupt production schedules and, hence, increase costs because of decreased production efficiency.

Purchasing costs are incurred when items are bought from a supplier. They represent what is paid for the items placed in inventory. If the items are produced rather than purchased by the organization, *production costs* are sustained instead.

Most inventory control systems are designed to minimize the sum of the carrying, ordering, stockout, and purchasing costs. One of the things that makes the inventory problem difficult, however, is that the carrying and ordering costs move in opposite directions with changes in the order quantity. Larger order quantities decrease the number of orders placed per time period and thus reduce the ordering costs. However, larger orders also increase the average inventory balance and, in doing so, increase carrying costs. Stockout costs tend to decrease with larger order quantities but generally are more closely related to the reorder point, rather than the order quantity decision. Purchasing costs are frequently *not incremental* to the analysis and can be excluded. That is to say, they do not vary with the decision alternatives that are available and, consequently, do not influence the analysis. An exception is when there are *quantity discounts* with orders of some specified minimum size. In that case, the purchase costs are incremental to the analysis and must be considered. The problem, then, is to find the order quantity Q and the reorder point R that minimize the sum of the carrying, ordering, stockout, and purchasing costs.

A Fixed-Order Quantity Model

Because of the frequency and well-defined nature of the inventory control problem, it was one of the first problems analyzed by the forerunners to today's management scientists. In fact, inventory control models were developed as early as 1915 by F. W. Harris. Today, a large number of models have been developed. These models are similar in that they are typically deterministic, make many assumptions about the real-world system they model, and are developed through traditional mathematical techniques such as differential calculus. The models differ from one another primarily in terms of the particular assumptions made about the real world.

As a representative example of an inventory model, we will consider a basic fixed-order quantity model. It is appropriate for situations in which the demand for the item is known with certainty (perfect knowledge) and is constant over time (no seasonal demand factors). Furthermore, the delivery, or resupply, time is also known with certainty, and there are no quantity discounts to consider. Although these are admittedly rather strong assumptions, they are typical of many inventory models.

Figure 15-2 depicts the usage and then resupply of the inventory item over time. At $t = 0$ an order for Q items arrives, resulting in an inventory balance of Q. This inventory is consumed at a constant, known rate over time. Eventually, the reorder point R is reached (at t_1) and an order is placed for Q more units. Because the delivery time is known with certainty, the reorder point can be set so that the last item remaining in inventory is used up just as the new order is received (at t_2). The arrival of the ordered items increases the inventory balance to Q units, and the process repeats itself.

Assuming a known demand D per unit of time, a carrying cost K_c per item per

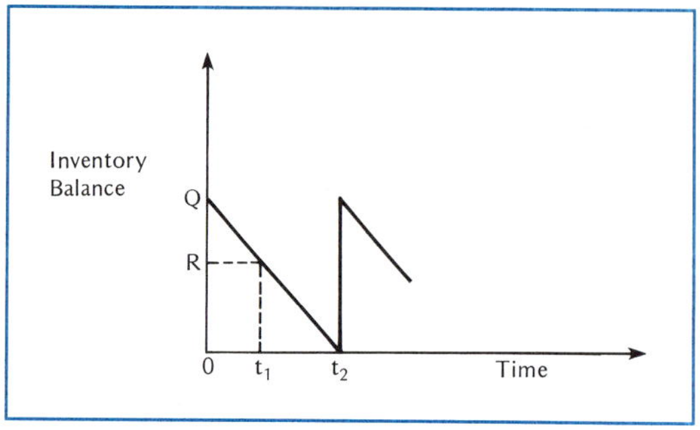

FIGURE 15-2. Amount in Inventory as a Function of Time.

unit of time, and an ordering cost K_o per order, it is possible to find the value of Q that minimizes the total inventory costs *TC*. There is no need to consider stockout costs, because the assumptions of certainty on demand and delivery time rule out the possibility of a shortage. Purchasing costs can also be excluded from the analysis, because there are no quantity discounts available.

We will first consider the *total carrying costs.* The greatest number of items ever in inventory is Q and the smallest is 0. Because demand is constant, the average inventory level is $\frac{Q + 0}{2}$, or Q/2. If K_c is the carrying cost per item, the total carrying cost for an average of Q/2 items must be

$$K_c\frac{Q}{2} \qquad [15\text{-}1]$$

If *D* is the demand per unit of time, and Q units are ordered at a time, *D*/Q is the number of orders placed per unit of time. When the cost per order is K_o, the *total ordering cost* is

$$K_o\frac{D}{Q} \qquad [15\text{-}2]$$

The *total incremental cost of inventory TC,* is the sum of the carrying and ordering costs:

$$TC = K_c\frac{Q}{2} + K_o\frac{D}{Q} \qquad [15\text{-}3]$$

In order to find the value of Q that minimizes *TC*, a first derivative of *TC* with respect to Q is taken.[3] This expression is then set equal to zero and solved for Q

[3]The mathematics of the analysis are $\frac{dTC}{dQ} = \frac{K_c}{2} - \frac{K_oD}{Q^2} = 0$. Solving for Q results in expression [15-4].

in order to find the value of Q that minimizes TC. The result is the formula shown in [15-4].

$$Q = \sqrt{\frac{2DK_o}{K_c}} \qquad [15\text{-}4]$$

The formula just developed can be used to determine the optimum number of items to order for inventory when the demand, carrying costs, and ordering costs are known and the assumptions underlying the model are satisfied. The following example illustrates the use of the model.

An Illustration

Gatewood Engineering Company forecasts an annual demand for 1,000 units of an item carried in inventory. Costs analyses indicate that the carrying costs are $4 per unit each year and that the ordering costs are $20 per order. These data can be inserted into expression [15–4] to find the optimal order quantity.

$$Q = \sqrt{\frac{2(20)(1000)}{4}}$$

$$= 100 \text{ units per order}$$

This order quantity would result in the following average annual incremental costs (using expression [15–3]):[4]

$$TC = \frac{4(100)}{2} + \frac{20(1{,}000)}{100}$$

$$= \$400$$

In order to determine the reorder point, it is only necessary to find the average usage of the item per week $\bar{d}$ and then multiply this figure by the number of weeks it takes for an order to be delivered L, the lead time. If the delivery time is 2 weeks after an order is placed, the demand is for 1,000 units per year, and the firm operates 52 weeks per year, the reorder point should be

$$R = \bar{d}L$$

$$R = \frac{1000}{52}(2)$$

$$\cong 40 \text{ units} \qquad [15\text{-}5]$$

[4]Purchase costs are not included. They are not incremental to the analysis, because in this example they do not vary with the order quantity decision.

Obviously, the assumptions that underlie the model that has just been developed and illustrated are seldom completely satisfied in the real world. However, there are a number of instances in which the assumptions are nearly enough satisfied and the model therefore produces optimum or near-optimum results. In cases when the real-world situation differs significantly from the model's assumptions, it is possible that models based upon the correct assumptions have previously been developed and can be used.[5] If neither of these approaches is viable, it is sometimes possible and appropriate to use the best model available and then apply a carefully worked out adjustment. For example, a safety stock is usually maintained by firms to adjust for the fact that demand and delivery time are not know with certainty. All of these approaches to inventory control are practiced in industry and typically produce satisfactory results.

PERT ANALYSIS

Organizations frequently undertake projects that have many interrelated activities. The military develops complex weapons systems. Contractors construct buildings and houses. The National Park Service develops parks for the public's enjoyment. Companies create new products. Local governments sponsor projects for the revitalization of downtown. Difficulties can occur, however, in planning and controlling activities in projects such as these. Fortunately, decision technology can be used to assist management in these endeavors. It is known as PERT (Program Evaluation and Review Technique), and its origins and functioning are described next.

In the late 1950s, PERT was developed by the U.S. Navy working in conjunction with several prime contractors for use in planning and controlling the Polaris missile project.[6] It has been estimated that the use of PERT on the Polaris project reduced project completion time by as much as two years. Since that early successful application, PERT has become almost a requirement of contract compliance for government prime contractors.

As has been suggested, PERT is applicable to many kinds of projects. In fact, it can be applied to any undertaking with component activities that must be planned, organized, and controlled. It is one of the simplest, yet most useful, of the management science methods. It must be stressed that PERT is as much a planning as a controlling technique. PERT is first employed to plan a project and

[5] See, for example, Richard J. Tersine, *Materials Management and Inventory Systems,* (New York: American Elsevier, 1976).

[6] At about the same time, CPM (Critical Path Method) was developed by DuPont for use in managing projects in the chemical processing industry. These project management methods have similarities and differences. Because the structure of the network is handled differently with the two methods, only one, PERT, is presented here in order to avoid confusion and because of space limitations.

then to control it. Convenience, as much as any other reason, has resulted in it being placed in the chapter on controlling models.

Steps in PERT Analysis

When using PERT, the basic steps are the same across various projects, and include the following:

1. Identify the *component activities* that must be performed.
2. Show the *sequencing* of the component activities in a *network*.
3. Perform an *analysis of the time* required to complete individual activities and the entire project.
4. *Improve upon the initial plan* through modifications.
5. *Control* the project.

Let us now explore these steps by considering an example. For our illustration, we will plan and control the development of an industrial park.

An Illustration

In recent years it has become common for communities to develop industrial parks. These parks are used to attract new industry and centrally locate existing companies. The local Chamber of Commerce often plays an important role in the development of an industrial park. Working in conjunction with local business and government leaders, the Chamber often provides the driving force behind the development of the park.

Component Activities. Table 15-1 presents the major activities involved in the development of an industrial park. The activities vary somewhat from

TABLE 15-1
Major Activities in the Development of an Industrial Park

a. Form a task force to study and work on the park.
b. Ascertain whether there is a need and sufficient interest in the park.
c. Seek required approvals for the park.
d. Determine the type of industry desired.
e. Select a site for the park.
f. Secure requisite financing for the park.
g. Purchase the site selected.
h. Perform required site improvements (roads, water, and so on).
i. Prospect for possible clients for the park.
j. Price locations in the park.
k. Sell the park locations.
l. Follow up with clients until the park is turned over to a permanent management group.

community to community, but our list has been judged by Chamber of Commerce professionals to be representative of what must be done.

Our list contains only major activities. However, these activities are usually also composed of component activities. In order to keep our example simple, the number of activities presented has been kept small. In practice, however, the activities would usually be more detailed and in greater number.

It should be noted that simply generating an agreed upon list of activities is an important first step. Commonly, there are differences of opinion as to what exactly is required, and getting these differences out in the open and resolved at an early date is helpful. As with most management science techniques, PERT forces planning.

Sequencing and the Network. After the major activities have been identified, their sequencing must be specified. For small projects, the simplest way to decide upon the sequencing is to turn directly to the preparation of a PERT network. A *network* shows all of the activities and their sequencing relative to other activities. Figure 15-3 shows a PERT network for the industrial park example.

At the far left of the network is a circle with the number 1 on the inside. All circles in a network are *events* and represent points in time. Our network starts with an event, because the project begins at some point in time.

Leading out of event 1 is an arrow that has been identified as activity *a* from Table 15-1. In a PERT network, *activities* are represented by arrows. Because all activities start and end at some point in time, activity *a* begins and ends with an event.

Also shown in Figure 15-3 are numbers within parentheses. These are time estimates and do not pertain to our current discussion. They are, however, important in the next of our five steps.

Upon completion of activity *a*, activities *b* and *c* begin simultaneously. By paralleling the performance of activities, the completion time for the entire

FIGURE 15-3. PERT Network for the Development of an Industrial Park.

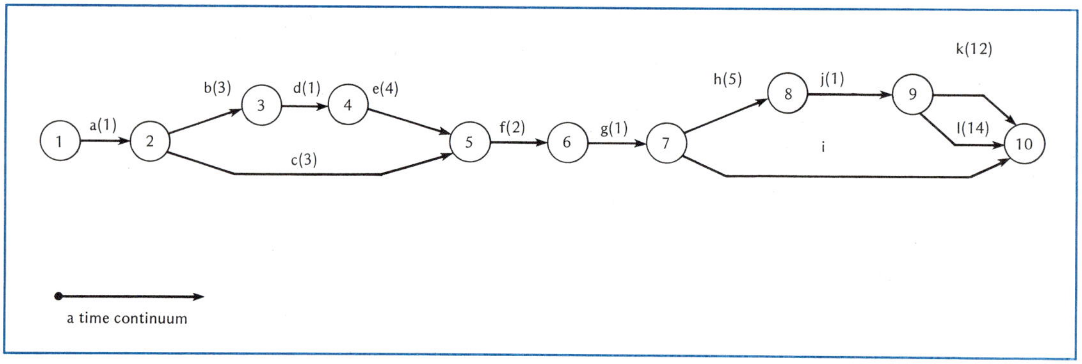

project can usually be reduced substantially. Activity *d* starts after *b* is completed, and *e* follows after *d*. Only after both *e* and *c* are completed can *f* begin. Multiple activities ending at the same event must all be completed before any activities begin from that event. Activity *g* follows *f* and is in turn followed by *h* and *i*. Activity *j* follows *h*, which is then followed by *k* and *l*. When *i*, *k*, and *l* have been performed, the development of the industrial park is completed.

The PERT network provides an excellent visual representation of the entire project. Its development requires careful thinking about the component activities and their sequencing. As mentioned previously, this forced planning is desirable.

Time Analysis. When time estimates are provided for how long it will take to complete each activity, it is possible to determine the expected completion time for the entire project.[7] Expected completion times for each activity in our illustration are included in parentheses in Figure 15-3. For example, it is thought that activity *a*, the formation of the task force, will take one month. The only activity that does not have an expected completion time is activity *i*, because the prospecting for clients will continue until the park is full. Therefore, its time is really determined by how long it will take to complete activities *h*, *j*, *k* and *l*.

Once the individual time estimates have been provided, it is possible to determine the *critical path*. The critical path can be thought of in two ways. First, from a time point of view, it is *the longest path through the network*. Second, it is the path that determines *the shortest time in which we can expect to complete the project*. These views are not conflicting, because the path that requires the longest time also controls the shortest time in which the project can be completed. Figure 15-3 has four possible paths (excluding paths through *i*, because it does not influence project completion time). These paths are indicated in Table 15-2, along with a summation of the individual expected completion times along each path.

From the analysis in Table 15-2, it can be seen that path *a-b-d-e-f-g-h-j-l* is the critical path, because it has an expected completion time of 32 months, which is longer than that of any other path. This path also dictates how long we should

TABLE 15-2
The Paths and Their Expected Completion Time

Paths	Times Along the Paths	Total Time
a-b-d-e-f-g-h-j-k	1+3+1+4+2+1+5+1+12	= 30 months
a-b-d-e-f-g-h-j-l	1+3+1+4+2+1+5+1+14	= 32 months
a-c-f-g-h-j-k	1+3+2+1+5+1+12	= 25 months
a-c-f-g-h-j-l	1+3+2+1+5+1+14	= 27 months

[7] PERT is presented here only in its deterministic form. Presentations of its probabilistic form are available in almost all introductory management science and production/operations management books. Cost considerations can also be included with PERT. Methods most commonly known as PERT/COST are used for this purpose. These and other variations on the basic PERT model are available in Chase and Aquilano, op. cit., Chapter 12.

expect the project to take, because all paths must be completed before the entire project is finished. If the Chamber of Commerce were to initiate the project today, it should expect the industrial park to have a completion date 32 months from now.

Improving Upon the Initial Plan. Our analysis of the project should not stop after the critical path has been identified. The potential exists for substantially improving upon the initial plan. Let us now consider how we might bring about this improvement.

There is sometimes the possibility of resequencing some of the activities that lie along the critical path. When this is possible, it can reduce the time along the critical path, resulting in a shorter expected project completion time. For example, it might be possible to perform activities *b* and *d* in parallel, rather than sequentially. This action would have the effect of reducing the time along the critical path by one month. Figure 15-4 illustrates this reduction.

Sometimes, of course, it is not possible to resequence activities. For example, if a project involves a sanding and a painting operation, it is not possible to perform them other than the sanding first and then the painting.

Time estimates for the activities are developed based upon initial assumptions about the resources that will be committed to each activity. In some instances, it is possible that additional resources can be obtained or that existing resources can be shifted in order to improve upon their utilization. For example, we might be able to shift personnel from activity *c* to *b* in order to reduce the expected time to complete *b*. Even if the time to complete *c* increases, the shift might be desirable. Figure 15-5 illustrates such a shift. In the revised plan, activity *b* now takes two rather than three months to complete. Activity *c* takes an additional month, but this does not matter because *c* is still not on the critical path, even with the changes in expected completion times. The net effect is a one-month reduction in the time along the critical path.

The reason the shift in Figure 15-5 is advantageous is that in the original plan, activity *c* contains five months of *slack* time. Slack is the amount of time an activity can slip or be delayed without it becoming part of the critical path. Because in the original plan activities *b-d-e* have an expected completion time of

FIGURE 15-4. Resequencing the Activities.

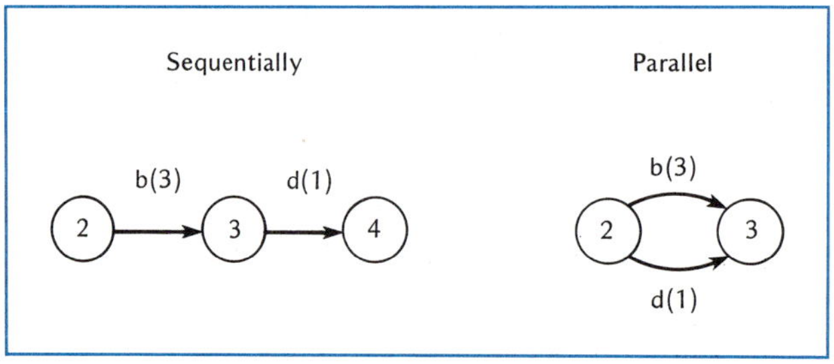

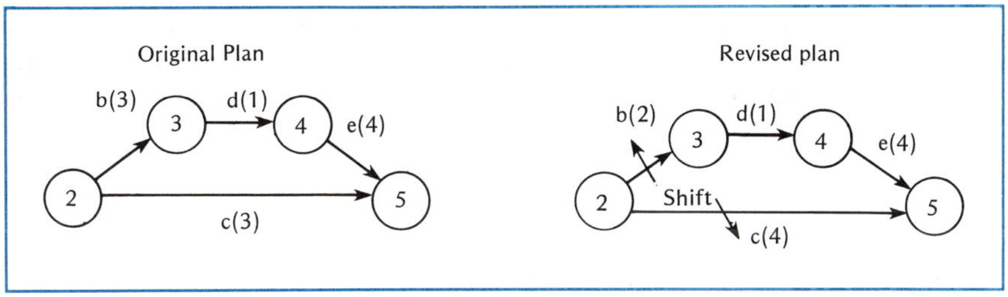

FIGURE 15-5. Shifting Organizational Resources.

$3+1+4 = 8$ months and activity *c* has a completion time of three months, there is five months of slack. In the revised plan, the slack associated with activity *c* is reduced to three months. This much slack suggests that perhaps even more resources might be shifted from *c* to other activities.

The PERT network is useful for investigating how to shorten the time to complete a project. Its role is at least equally important, however, in controlling the project once it is begun. Let us now explore the controlling aspects of PERT.

Controlling the Project. The obvious focus of attention for controlling the project is on the activities along the critical path. If there are delays in these activities, the completion of the entire project is delayed. Slippages of activities that are not on the critical path are less serious, if they do not then create a new critical path.

Suppose, for example, that the person in charge of activity *b* reports that it will take one month longer than expected to complete the activity. The project manager should view this development with some concern, because it will lengthen the time along the critical path. In this case, the network can possibly be used as a motivational device by showing the person in charge of activity *b* what the effect of the slippage will be. Sometimes with projects involving many persons and activities, it is difficult for personnel to comprehend the consequences of a slippage in a single activity. Once the consequences are understood, personnel may feel more responsible for meeting completion dates.

Just as the network reveals points for concern, it also shows where meeting completion dates is less critical. For example, a request for a slight extension of time to complete activity *c* might be approved, because *c* does not lie on the critical path.

Final Comments

The PERT material presented here has been limited to the basic model and how it can be used by managers. There is more about PERT that could be presented, but it is best left to courses in management science and production/operations management. In these courses, for example, you will most likely learn how to employ PERT as a probabilistic method of analysis, how to include cost considerations, and how to use packaged computer programs for analyzing projects with many activities.[8] However, for most practicing managers, it is the basic model that provides the greatest benefits.

SIMULATING HUMAN DECISION MAKING

Up to this point, the models presented have been standard management science models. We would like to close, however, with a somewhat unusual model. The type of model described is for simulating human decision making. Research has shown that it is possible to develop computerized models that duplicate the decisions made by managers in judgmental decision-making situations.[9] For our illustration, we will describe the development of a model for duplicating the decisions of a bank officer processing overdrafts (bad checks).[10] Although this is a model useful for controlling purposes, other models for simulating human decision might be used in planning.

Steps in Building the Model

Models for simulating human decision making must be custom built. It is possible, however, to identify a series of *steps* to follow when developing such a model. The steps are the following:

1. Gain an understanding of the information flows and the decisions that are made.
2. Generate a list of variables that might be used in the decision-making process.
3. Analyze the decision-making process by having the manager verbalize his or her thought processes while performing the activity under study.
4. Collect appropriate data for developing the model.
5. Develop the model for the decision-making process.
6. Test the model that has been built.
7. Repeat steps 3 through 6 until an appropriate model is developed.
8. Implement the model in the organization.

[8] A survey of available PERT packaged programs is provided by Ann B. Pushkin, and Jim Wynne, "A Survey of Computerized PERT/CPM Related Packages," *Review of Industrial Management and Textile Science*, (Fall, 1976), pp. 15–34.

[9] See, for example, Robert D. Smith, and Paul S. Greenlaw, "Simulation of a Psychological Decision Process in Personal Selection," *Management Science*, (April 1967), pp. 404–419, and Geoffrey P. E. Clarkson, *Portfolio Selection: A Simulation of Trust Investment* (Englewood Cliffs, N.J.: Prentice-Hall, 1962).

[10] Portions of this section are adapted from Hugh J. Watson, and H. William Vroman, "A Heuristic Model for Processing Overdrafts," *Journal of Bank Research*, (Autumn, 1972), pp. 186–188.

Let us now consider how these steps were followed in developing an actual model for processing overdrafts.

An Illustration

There are a number of approaches that have developed for handling overdrafts. A common way is to have a bank officer decide upon their final disposition. The bank officer decides which checks to immediately honor (pay), not honor (not pay), and which require a personal call to the depositor before a decision is made. Consequently, there are three decision alternatives.

Even relatively small banks receive up to several hundred bad checks a day. The bank officer who deals with these checks on a day-to-day basis develops a sensitivity to the appropriate disposition of any particular check. Some checks, because of the integrity of their writers, are honored routinely. Other checks, say from notoriously careless depositors, may not be paid. In other words, the bank officer accumulates a wealth of information about the bank's customers. In addition, he develops an efficient set of *heuristics* (rules-of-thumb) that define how he will probably act in a given situation. Any system that replaces the previous one should maintain the professional expertise accumulated by the bank officer over time.

The building of the model began with the bank's officer, Charles Burch, of the First National Bank of Athens, Georgia, working in conjunction with the model builders, listing those variables that were thought to be the most important in the decision-making process. The initial list contained 14 variables, including the dollar amount of the check, to whom the check was written, and the credit worthiness of the depositor. The initial list of variables even indicated that the bank officer was more likely to honor a check written by a University of Georgia coed than one written by a male student.

The next step in the model-building process was to observe Burch at work and record appropriate empirical data. It was found that a number of variables that were originally considered to be important actually were not and could be discarded. For example, it was learned that it did not matter whether the depositor was a male or female student.

After the data had been gathered, an initial model was built. Because the model was prepared based upon the collected data, it was not surprising that it accurately described the decisions made by Burch.

The analysts then collected more data to further test the model. During the testing process, it became clear that parts of the model had to be changed; for example, the need for a procedure for handling multiple overdrafts (several by the same person) became apparent. This process of data collection, model testing, and model revision was repeated until a model had been developed that closely described Burch's actions. The final testing of the model revealed that it correctly predicted his actions more than 95% of the time.

An analysis of the remaining 5% resulted in the conclusion that some of the factors responsible for the errors were inherent in the human variable—Burch. It was noticed that Burch became weary and distracted by customer calls toward the end of the day and tended to adopt a harsher attitude toward overdrafts. In this regard, the model was more internally consistent than the bank officer.

Even when the model was in error, the errors were not of the worst possible kind. There were no instances, for example, in which the model predicted that Burch would honor a check and he actually did not. The errors that occurred were of the type in which Burch decided to pay the check, whereas the model predicted that he would "hold and call."

The model that was finally used contained five variables. The *type of account*—regular or special—was one of the factors considered by Burch. Another variable was whether the *existing balance* was already negative, a consideration that was necessary for handling multiple overdrafts. Burch's subjective evaluation of the person's *general credit worthiness*—whether it was good, bad, or unknown—was also important. To the extent it was known, this factor included the depositor's past history of overdrafts, his place of residence in the city, property ownership, employment record, savings account balance, and so on. Another variable was the *magnitude of the overdraft compared to the current balance.* This consideration was quantified by dividing the difference between the check's amount and the account's balance by the account's balance (check − balance/balance). The final variable was the *amount of the check.* Overdrafts for small amounts are usually paid.

The model that contained the five variables was formulated as a *tree diagram.* The tree diagram shows all of the possible variable interactions and the resultant courses of action. Figure 15-6, for example, is one branch of the tree diagram (the tree diagram contains many similar branches). This branch shows that a check of $50.00 or less that is not a multiple overdraft and was written by a depositor with a good credit rating is paid by Burch.

The model developed for the First National Bank of Athens is probably appropriate only for that bank. Other bank officers might employ a different set of decision criteria in judging overdrafts, and even if the same variables are used, the tree diagram formulated would probably be different. This likelihood is not

FIGURE 15-6. Sample Branch of the Tree Diagram.

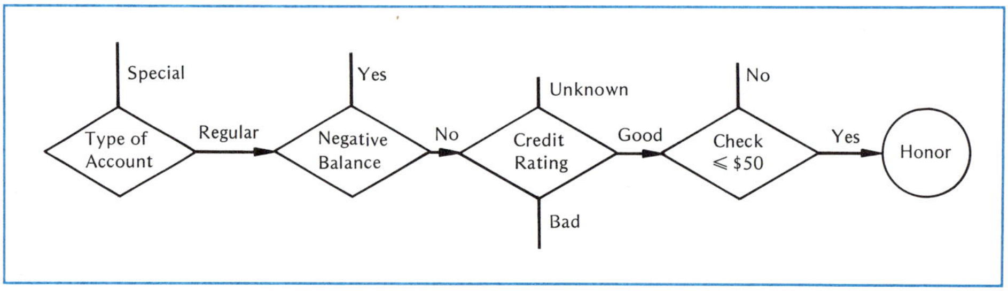

surprising, because people perceive things differently, operating conditions vary from bank to bank, and the implications of the social environment vary from community to community.

Computerization does not completely release Burch from the task of handling overdrafts. There are still some customers categorized as "hold and call" by the model, and these will have to be handled by Burch or some other official. In addition, regardless of how their checks are handled, there will be some customers who believe their overdrafts are the result of a unique situation and should be handled specially. Burch can treat these people in an unhurried manner, thus avoiding possible customer complaints of such bureaucratic dysfunctions as categorization and impersonality. Burch's psychological set is to treat customers as individuals. When he was alternating his overdraft task with customer relations, the mental chore of switching psychological sets was necessary. This is costly to the individual because it is tiring, and costly to the organization because, as time progresses, the switching becomes inconsistent.

The model developed for the bank was easily computerized. The equivalent of a week's overdrafts were processed in less than a minute. The only information required by the model that was not readily available in the bank's accounting system was the depositor's credit worthiness. Over time, this data could be added to each depositor's record. Until then, the unknown branch off of the credit worthiness variable permitted all overdrafts to be processed.

Potential Benefits

A modeling effort should not be undertaken unless there are potential benefits for the organization. This criterion certainly applies to models for simulating human decision making. The following list describes most of the benefits that might be derived:

1. Personnel might be freed for other activities.
2. Decisions might be made more quickly.
3. Money might be saved on the decision making activity.
4. Decision-making skills that are in short supply might be provided.[11]
5. Once decision-making behavior is duplicated, it might then be improved upon.
6. Decision making might be made more consistent.
7. The model might be used in training new personnel.

Any one application would probably not generate all of the benefits mentioned here, but some combination is likely for many routine, judgmental decision-

[11] This benefit is particularly applicable to the field of medicine; see Norman E. Betaque, and G. Anthony Gorry, "Automating Judgmental Decision Making for a Serious Medical Problem," *Management Science*, (April 1971), pp. 421–434.

making tasks. In our overdraft processing example, the benefits would include freeing personnel for other activities, making decisions more quickly, saving money, and improving decision-making consistency.

Conditions Conducive to Modeling

Not all decision-making situations lend themselves to models that simulate human decision making. Certain conditions are important if cost-effective models are to be developed. More specifically, most of the following conditions must exist if the possibility of developing a model that simulates human decision making is to be seriously considered:

1. Top-to-bottom managerial support.
2. A heavy commitment of organization resources being devoted to the decision-making task.
3. A computerized environment with many of the data inputs already contained in the organization's data base.
4. Lower paid personnel being able to encode most of the required data inputs.
5. The decision-making process being relatively stable over time.
6. The cost of a bad decision not being too great.

In our overdraft processing example, each of these conditions was satisfied to a reasonable extent.

Final Comments

The computerized model for processing overdrafts should provide some insight into the potential of the computer for affecting manager's jobs. Although there is considerable controversy over the extent to which the computer will assume managerial functions, there is no doubt that it will continue to have an increasing impact on them.

SUMMARY

Three useful controlling models were discussed in this chapter. The models selected for presentation—inventory control, PERT, and simulating human decision making—illustrate the wide variety of models that can be used in support of management's controlling responsibilities.

Inventories are common to almost all organizations. Depending upon whether the items experience dependent or independent demand, appropriate controlling techniques are used. Material Requirements Planning (MRP) systems are increasingly being used with dependent demand items. Either fixed-order period or fixed-order quantity methods are used with items that have independent demand. Fixed-order quantity models attempt to identify the optimal order quantity Q and reorder point R to use with an item. The optimal solution is the one that minimizes the sum of the carrying, ordering, stockout, and purchasing costs.

PERT is a method of analysis useful in planning and controlling large projects. A PERT network is prepared that visually shows the project's component activities and their sequencing. The critical path is the longest path through the network from a time point of view, and also indicates the shortest time in which to expect to complete the project. By rescheduling activities and shifting resources, it is often possible to reduce the project's completion time. Those activities that are on the critical path should be closely controlled.

Computerized models can be used to simulate human decision making. The models need to be custom-built, but there is a series of steps that can be followed. Models for simulating routine decision making can generate a variety of benefits. However, certain conditions should exist if the modeling effort is to be cost-effective. Models for simulating human decision making have the potential for having a significant impact upon management personnel and their job responsibilities.

Assignments

15-1. A university, like most organizations, must maintain inventories. Give some examples of the types of items that are held in a university's inventory.

15-2. Prepare a graph that has cost on the vertical axis and the order quantity Q on the horizontal axis. Sketch approximate curves for the following types of costs:
a. Total carrying costs.
b. Total ordering costs.
c. Total costs, the sum of parts *a* and *b*.

15-3. What are the assumptions that underlie the fixed-order quantity model presented in this chapter? Give examples of items that do and do not correspond with the underlying assumptions.

15-4. Give several examples not mentioned in the chapter in which PERT analysis might be applied.

15-5. What data inputs are required in performing PERT analysis? What difficulties might be encountered in obtaining the required inputs?

15-6. Getting up and going off to class is in a way a project.
a. Prepare a PERT network for this project.
b. Provide time estimates for the activities and identify the critical path.
c. Is there any way that you can shorten the time along the critical path?

15-7. Identify a routine, judgmental decision-making task that might be profitably simulated. What benefits might be derived from developing, computerizing, and implementing an appropriate model?

15-8. Not all types of decision-making activities can be simulated. Describe some types that do not lend themselves to modeling efforts.

Case 15-1

THE BAKERY HOUSE

The Bakery House is located in a large metropolitan area and provides local bakeries with a variety of products—breads, cakes, cookies, and so on. An important inventory item for The Bakery House is flour. On the average 200 pounds of flour are used per day. The Bakery House operates 250 days per year, which accounts for a lot of flour being used. The resupply time after an order has been placed is four working days and the cost of placing an order is $40. The cost per year of carrying a pound of flour in inventory is $0.40.

How many pounds of flour should The Bakery House purchase at a time? Assuming no safety stock, what should be the reorder point?

Case 15-2

CLASSIC ENTERPRISES

Bill Kirby, a recent business school graduate, has just gone to work for Classic Enterprises in its production department. One of his first assignments is to review the order quantity levels for some of the items carred in inventory. Bill discovers that for Part No. 23864 an order quantity of 500 units is being used, based upon a forecasted demand of 5,000 units per years, ordering costs of $25/order, and carrying costs of $1/item/year.

1. Verify, if you can, that the optimal order quantity is being used. After studying the inventory costs associated with part No. 23864, Bill concludes that ordering costs are actually running $49 rather than $25/order.
2. What order quantity should be used now that the correct costs have been identified?
3. How much will Bill's discovery save Classic Enterprises per year?

Case 15-3

ATHENS RECREATION DEPARTMENT

The Athens Recreation Department sponsors a variety of community recreation programs. A fairly new addition to the series of programs is a long distance race. Last year over 300 runners participated in the fall race, and this year's race promises to attract even more participants.

Alan Gibbs coordinates the race for the Athens Recreation Department and has identified the following major activities, their sequencing, and expected completion times.

Activity	Description	Must Follow	Time
A	Establish race distance	—	1 week
B	Identify course route	A	1
C	Clear course route with police	B	1
D	Map and measure course and prepare signs	C	2
E	Clear race date with race clearing house	A	1
F	Contact "name" runners	E	4
G	Develop race flyers	D&F	2
H	Print race flyers	G	2
I	Contact news media	H	1
J	Contact T-shirt sponsor	I	3
K	Develop T-shirt design	J	4
L	Obtain T-shirt bids	K	3
M	Award T-shirt contract	L	1
N	Arrange for medical assistance	I	1
O	Arrange for police escorts	N	2
P	Arrange to have course cleared	O	2
Q	Arrange for starters and timers	P	1
R	Put up signs	M&Q	1

1. Develop a PERT network for the race. How many weeks in advance of the race is it necessary to begin preparing for the race?

Case 15-4

SPACESHOT, INC.

Mr. Johnson, president of Spaceshot, Inc., calls you into his office early one morning to reveal some news. Spaceshot has just been awarded the contract for the design, testing, and production of the Saturn XII. The Saturn XII is the rocket that will enable the United States to be the first to land astronauts on the planet Mars.

As the head of the PERT department, you know that your department has a major task ahead, because the contract will require PERT. From discussions with other employees involved in the Saturn XII project, you gain some insight into the activities that have to be performed and the time required to complete these activities.

From discussions with Mr. Albert, head of circuit design, you obtain the following information:

Specifications for the circuit design must be completed and should take eight months. The actual performance of the initial circuit design will take 16 months. Temperature and vibration tests on the circuits should take two months. Circuit design revision and building will take eight months.

Mr. Ray, head of the vehicle department, gives you the following information:

The writing of specifications for the vehicle will take six months. The initial design for the vehicle will take 14 months, testing the vehicle design will take eight months, and vehicle design revision and production will consume six months.

Mr. Williams, chief of propulsion, adds the following:

The writing of specifications for the propulsion system will take seven months, followed by experimentation with different propulsion systems, which will require 18 months, the testing of the propulsion system should take six months, and the revisions and building of the propulsion system should take eight months.

Mr. Fitzgerald, head of systems integration, adds the following necessary information:

The writing of specifications is very important. In fact, none of the other activities can be undertaken until all of the specifications are completed.

After the circuits and vehicle have been built, the two are integrated. This activity should take four months. This part of the rocket, without the propulsion system, will be tested, taking about two months.

After this testing, the propulsion system will be integrated with the rest of the rocket, which should take two months.

1. Prepare a PERT network for the project.
2. Identify the critical path and the time along the critical path.
3. What effect would reducing the initial design for the vehicle by one month have on the project's expected completion time?

Case 15-5

WINSTON FEDERAL SAVING AND LOAN

Terri Farmer recently graduated from college with a degree in finance. She has now been working for Winston Federal S & L in the mortgage loan department for about three months. During this period of time she has gained an understanding of the loan granting process. Winston Federal S & L averages about eight requests for mortgage loans a week. With every loan request is a completed application form which contains information such as the person's name, address, income, place and length of employment, credit references, and so on. In response to an application, Winston Federal S & L obtains a credit report from the credit bureau and sends an appraiser out to appraise the property. All of this information is then provided to the executive loan committee which makes the final loan-granting decision.

In college Terri studied several decision-making tasks which had been computerized and she wonders whether the mortgage loan-granting decision might also be automated. What is the possibility of developing a model that simulates the loan committee's decisions? What is the practicality of such a model? Outline a procedure for developing a model.

Case 15-6

PEOPLES BANK OF WASHINGTON

A bank officer with the Peoples Bank of Washington spends a substantial portion of each working day processing charge card applications. He has expressed an interest in the possibility of computerizing his decision-making process. Based upon your discussions with him, it appears that three variables are of critical importance in the decision-making process: previous credit record—excellent, good, fair, or poor; income—over \$10,000, or under \$10,000; homeowner—yes or no. The bank officer has three decision alternatives available to him. He can issue no card, issue a card with a \$300 credit limit, or issue a card with a \$700 credit limit.

1. Using the following data, prepare a tree diagram that describes the bank officer's decision-making process.

Case	Previous Credit Record	Income	Homeowner	Decision
1	Fair	Over $10,000	Yes	Card—$300
2	Poor	Under $10,000	No	No Card
3	Fair	Over $10,000	No	Card—$300
4	Excellent	Over $10,000	Yes	Card—$700
5	Good	Under $10,000	No	Card—$300
6	Good	Over $10,000	Yes	Card—$700
7	Poor	Over $10,000	Yes	No Card
8	Fair	Under $10,000	No	No Card
9	Fair	Under $10,000	Yes	Card—$300
10	Good	Over $10,000	No	Card—$700
11	Excellent	Over $10,000	No	Card—$700
12	Excellent	Under $10,000	Yes	Card—$700
13	Good	Under $10,000	Yes	Card—$700
14	Excellent	Under $10,000	No	Card—$700

2. Using your tree diagram, determine what decisions would be made by the bank officer on the following charge card applicants.

Name	Previous Credit Record	Income	Homeowner
HALL	Good	Over $10,000	No
LEE	Poor	Over $10,000	No
CASE	Excellent	Under $10,000	Yes
HILL	Fair	Over $10,000	Yes
MIX	Fair	Under $10,000	Yes
PAGE	Good	Over $10,000	Yes

3. What benefits might accrue from computerizing and implementing the tree diagram model?
4. What difficulties might be encountered in operating the computerized model?

References

BUFFA, ELWOOD S. *Modern Production Management.* 5th ed. Santa Barbara, Calif.: Wiley/Hamilton, 1977.

CHASE, RICHARD B., AND NICHOLAS J. AQUILANO. *Production and Operations Management.* rev. ed. Homewood, Ill.: Richard D. Irwin, Inc., 1977.

DREYFUS, HUBERT L. *What Computers Can't Do: A Critique of Artificial Reason.* New York: Harper & Row, Publisher, 1972.

FEIGENBAUM, EDWARD A. AND JULIAN FELDMAN, eds. *Computers and Thought.* New York: McGraw-Hill Book Company, 1963.

LEVIN, RICHARD I., AND CHARLES A. KIRKPATRICK. *Planning and Control with PERT/CPM.* New York: McGraw-Hill, Book Company, 1966.

MEIER, ROBERT C., WILLIAM T. NEWELL, AND HAROLD L. PAZER. *Simulation in Business and Economics.* Englewood Cliffs, N.J.: Prentice-Hall, Inc., 1969.

MEINHART, WAYNE A. "Artificial Intelligence, Computer Simulation of Human Cognition and Social Processes, and Management Thought." *Academy of Management Journal.* (December 1966), pp. 294–307.

MODER, JOSEPH J., AND CECIL R. PHILLIPS. *Project Management with CPM and PERT.* New York: Van Nostrand Reinhold Company, 1964.

WATSON, HUGH J., TED F. ANTHONY, AND WILLIAM S. CROWDER. "A Heuristic Model for Law School Admissions Screening." *College and University.* (Spring 1973), pp. 195–204.

WIEST, JEROME D., AND FERDINAND K. LEVY. *A Management Guide to PERT/CPM.* 2nd. ed. Englewood Cliffs, N.J.: Prentice-Hall, Inc., 1977.

MAJOR GENERAL STEWART CANFIELD MEYER

General Meyer is currently the Army's Ballistic Missile Defense Program Manager at the Redstone Arsenal in Huntsville, Alabama. His military career includes duties in World War II, Korea, and Vietnam, with numerous decorations for service.

WILLIAM C. WALL, JR.

William C. Wall, Jr. has worked in project management with the Department of the Army for more than 20 years. He is currently the Deputy Project Manager, Ground Laser Designators Project Office, U.S. Army Missile Research and Development Command, Redstone Arsenal, Alabama. While working in Ballistic Missile Defense, he was responsible for the development, implementation, and operation of the SAFEGUARD Management Information System. Dr. Wall has served as a senior management advisor on numerous government ad hoc study groups and committees.

Executive Commentary
PERT in Ballistic Missile Defense (BMD)

The performance of the planning and controlling functions of management in complex, large-scale endeavors is perhaps the most challenging aspect of a program manager's job. It's where the action is and it requires that program managers be innovative, practical, and decisive. We are delighted to share our experiences in the use of planning and controlling techniques in ballistic missile defense by means of this executive commentary.

Background

Ballistic missile defense got its start in the United States in 1955 when the U.S. Army began looking at anti-missile feasibility in earnest. Such an undertaking was a staggering technical problem. Placed in perspective, an effective ballistic missile defense capability has been aptly described as "hitting a bullet with a bullet." Ballistic missile defense is also a formidable management challenge because of its technical complexity, intense public visibility, geographic dispersion of activity, and the large number of participants from both the private and public sectors.

Current ballistic missile defense activity is an outgrowth of work accomplished in the 1960s and early 1970s on the now defunct SAFEGUARD program and its predecessors. It was here that PERT was used with varying degrees of success.

PERT was first implemented in our research and development effort in the early 1960s. It was a contractual requirement with the prime development contractor. It was later applied to the production program in its infancy and to the site construction and activation tasks. We tried PERT for a number of years. It was useful in the site construction and activation work, but it did not prove to be effective over the long term in the research and development or production programs.

BMD Experience

BMD experience with *site construction and activation* was typical of many organizations. It was invaluable in determining all required activities, in establishing their precedent ordering, in identifying interfaces among all participants, and in developing the total management logic of the site construction and activation effort. The application was computerized, so we were able to summarize PERT input data into reports that provided executive overview of this portion of the program. Because of the ordered logic of the networks, however, we could also become very specific and pinpoint problem areas and isolate precise causes of schedule difficulties with relative ease.

PERT in the *prduction* program served a beneficial role in that the inherent discipline of the technique forced extremely detailed planning of the production program. It also facilitated the identification and maintainance of program and participating organization relationships and interfaces. Because production is a repetitive operation, PERT was not a useful tool for controlling the process, nor is it intended to be. However, it did serve as an effective planning tool for laying out the complete production flow process.

PERT was neither productive nor effective in our *research and development* program for several reasons. First, PERT was applied on top of an existing schedule control system at the prime development contractor facility. The contractor did not use PERT for internal control and it became a superimposed and ineffective method for formal reporting to the government. PERT created a double accounting system for schedule control, and it was used to record historical data rather than to manage the program. Also, insufficient attention was paid to maintaining a high degree of data fidelity. Resolution of data discrepancies required an inordinate amount of time and was costly. Submission of PERT data was more ritualistic than useful. Finally, PERT was a very expensive schedule control system, and its usefulness to the research and development program clearly did not merit the cost involved. The PERT networks from the research and development program were used to input summary data into the production and site construction programs, but alternate methods of reporting were substituted.

The Strengths and Weaknesses of PERT

Like any planning and controlling system, PERT has both strengths and weaknesses that aid the practitioner in deciding whether to use it or not. We have identified the most significant as we perceive them.

PERT is the epitome of integration between the planning and controlling functions because the same instrument is used for both. It is also a useful tool for forecasting impacts of known, potential, or "what if" schedule changes. Perhaps the greatest strength of PERT is not so much the technique itself as it is the conceptual discipline that its use imposes. It not only requires that all activities and events be identified, but the technique also demands that they be precedent sequenced.

On the other side of the coin, the largest, single limitation of PERT is its cost of implementation and operation. It is an expensive technique in a large program with many events and activities, and requires a large number of people in its operation. It also has a great deal of inertia against change. In other words, once established, a major change in schedule causes extensive turbulence in the PERT networks and the underlying data processing.

Taken on balance, PERT is a highly useful tool in the proper setting. Although it is expensive, the cost of not having it may be even higher. It is a potent tool in the search for order in complex endeavors.

Thoughts on Control Models in General

This account of actual PERT experience is illustrative of control models in general and leads to the following concluding thoughts. It must be remembered that control models, for all of their ingenuity of design, cannot be any better than the fidelity of the input data. Because conditions change over time, is necessary to update models on a continuing basis to ensure usefulness. Control models to be effective must be accepted by managers at all levels, and the behavioral implications must be understood and accommodated. Control models must be thought of in positive terms as beneficial aids to management. They must be developed rationally, implemented carefully, and operated diligently. This may require new management skills as control models achieve higher levels of maturity. As managers, we must understand and meet this exciting challenge.

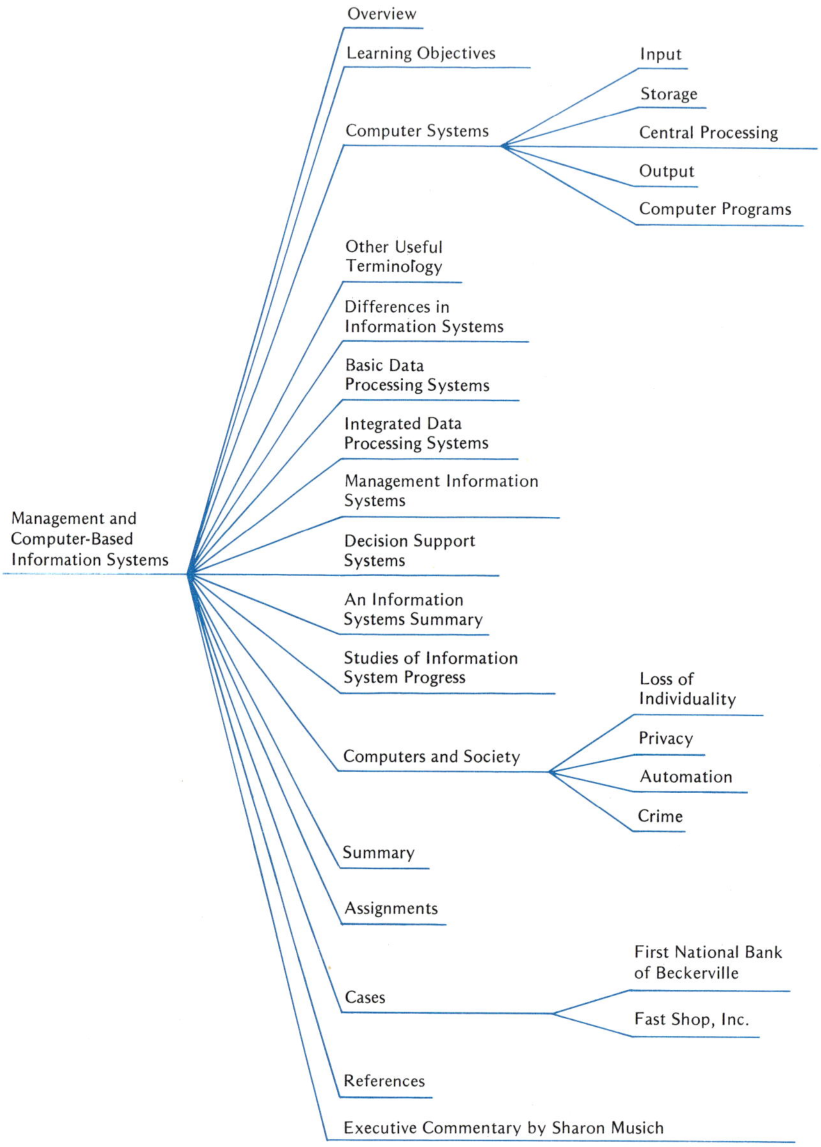
Management and Computer-Based Information Systems
Overview
Learning Objectives
Computer Systems
Input
Storage
Central Processing
Output
Computer Programs
Other Useful Terminology
Differences in Information Systems
Basic Data Processing Systems
Integrated Data Processing Systems
Management Information Systems
Decision Support Systems
An Information Systems Summary
Studies of Information System Progress
Computers and Society
Loss of Individuality
Privacy
Automation
Crime
Summary
Assignments
Cases
First National Bank of Beckerville
Fast Shop, Inc.
References
Executive Commentary by Sharon Musich

16

MANAGEMENT AND COMPUTER-BASED INFORMATION SYSTEMS

OVERVIEW

This chapter concludes our discussion of how decision technology is affecting management and organizations. Here we will focus attention on computers and computer-based information systems. There are relatively few organizations, especially larger ones, that have not been impacted by the computer.

Computers can be discussed from many perspectives—programming computers, designing computerized systems, operating the computer, and so on. Here, however, we will explore what managers should know if they are going to function effectively in an organization that has a computer.

As a starting point, it is necessary to have a general understanding as to what the components of a typical computer system are and the role that each component plays. Fortunately, this understanding can be gained without going into great technical detail. With this background, we can then meaningfully explore the differences in performance capabilities of various types of information systems. For example, information systems vary in the tasks they perform, the information they provide to management, their impact upon personnel and the organization, and other important areas of interest to students and practitioners of management.

LEARNING OBJECTIVES

This chapter is especially intended to help the student:

1. **Gain a managerial knowledge of computers and computer-based information systems.**
2. **Understand the components and functioning of a typical computer system.**
3. **Learn the characteristics and impacts of basic, integrated, management information, and decision support systems.**
4. **Be aware of the current status of information system development.**
5. **Understand the issues surrounding computers and society.**
6. **Learn, especially in the context of thinking about management, the meaning of the following concepts:**

computer system	**data base**
input	**integrated data base**
storage	**information**
central processing	**information system**
output	**basic data processing system**
computer program	**integrated data processing system**
hardware	**management information system**
software	**decision support system**
data	

COMPUTER SYSTEMS

From our previous discussion of systems in other chapters, you should understand that when we refer to *computer systems,* we are talking about more than the computer itself. Included, for example, are all the mechanisms for inputting and outputting from the computer. With most computer systems, we must also consider storage devices for maintaining the large files of data required by most organizations. All of these interrelated components comprise a computer system.

Figure 16-1 shows and identifies the skeletal outline of a typical computer system. The major components include input, storage, central processing, and output. It is useful to briefly describe the function served by each component.[1]

Input

Data can be input to the computer in a variety of ways. Punched cards can be read by a card reader, which converts the punched holes into electrical pulses that are communicated to the computer. Data can be entered from the keyboard of a

[1]The description is adapted from *The Computer Age* (White Plains, N.Y.: The IBM Corporation, 1976), p. 15.

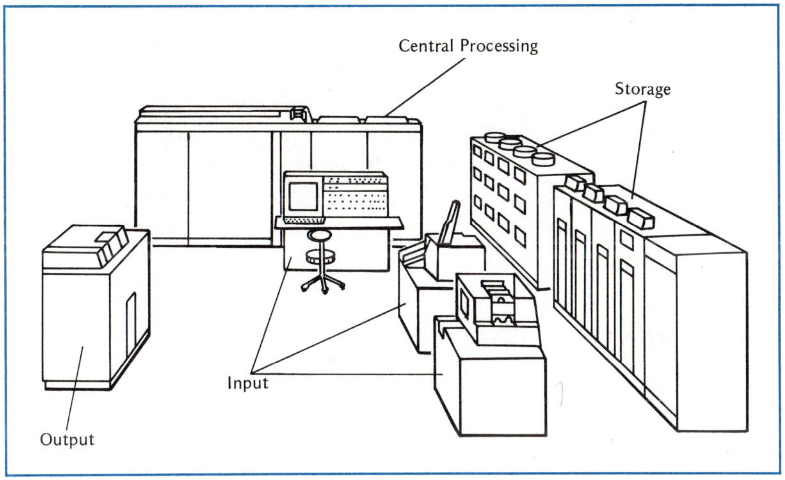

FIGURE 16-1. The Components of a Typical Computer System. (Source: Courtesy of the IBM Corporation.)

typewriter terminal similar to those used by bank tellers and airline reservation clerks. Have you ever noticed the oddly shaped numerals on the bottom of checks? They are printed in magnetic ink, later sensed, and converted into electronic signals for input to the computer. For some applications there is even voice input to computers.

Storage

Once data are entered, a place is needed for storage so that the data are readily available when needed. The most popular storage media in use today are magnetic tape and magnetic disk. These media store tremendous quantities of data that can be quickly retrieved from them when needed. Increasingly, organizations are committing to computer storage data that are vital to their continued existence. These centrally stored data are commonly referred to as the organization's *data base*.

Central Processing

Suppose that a company's payroll data are stored on magnetic disk. To prepare the payroll checks, each in the proper amount with the proper deductions, the data must first be transferred to central processing. It is here that the actual computing takes place. Using electronic arithmetic/logic circuits, the required computations are made. Once the computations are completed, the results are available for output.

Output

High-speed printers, activated by electronic impulses, can be used to print checks, invoices, tables, reports and other output. Or, managers can sit at a terminal, enter instructions and data, and receive a typewritten or video-displayed response in only seconds. Banks often provide time and temperature information based upon computerized systems. Special plotters are purchased as peripheral equipment with some computer systems in order to provide graphical output.

Computer Programs

A computer must be given instructions about how to process data—how to store it, where to store it, what logical and arithmetic operations are required, and how to output the results. This information is provided in a *computer program* that is written by a *computer programmer.* There are hundreds of computer programming languages that have been developed for use with computers. Some of the more popular ones are BASIC, FORTRAN, COBOL, PL/1, RPG, and APL. In the final analysis, however, these languages must be translated into the language that the computer understands. This language is known as *machine language.* Special programs known as *language translators* are used to translate the languages such as FORTRAN and COBOL into machine language.[2] Continuing efforts are being made to make programming languages more powerful in their capabilities and more like English in their structure.

OTHER USEFUL TERMINOLOGY

A distinction is made between computer hardware and software. *Computer hardware* includes all of the devices (electrical and mechanical) in a computer system. For example, card readers, tape drives, and terminals are all computer hardware. They are, so to speak, the nuts and bolts of the system. *Computer software,* on the other hand, are the programs that are run on the hardware and all of the supporting documentation for the programs. Computer software is run on computer hardware in order to transform data into information. *Information* is usually thought of as *data* that has been processed in some meaningful way. For example, summary statistics on accounts receivable or forecasts of future sales are all examples of information that results from processing data. Systems designed to process data into information are referred to as *information systems.* They include the data that are used, the software associated with the processing of the data, the hardware that is employed, personnel charged with the responsibility of designing, developing, operating, and managing the system, and the information that is provided to the end user. When the information system involves the use of

[2] "Language translator" is a generic term that encompasses assemblers, interpreters, and compilers.

a computer, it is commonly referred to as a *computer-based information system*. Not all information systems are computer-based, and not all need be, but they are becoming increasingly prevalent in the contemporary business world.

DIFFERENCES IN INFORMATION SYSTEMS

It is important to understand that information systems can vary tremendously. For example, the mini-computer system at your local McDonalds is at the heart of an information system. However, information systems found in the airlines industry bear little resemblance to a McDonalds' information system. Obviously, these systems differ in the tasks they perform. But there are many other differences in information systems, including the required financial commitment to hardware and software, personnel required to operate and manage the system, the nature of the information supplied to management, and the impact of the information system upon personnel and the organization. Because these are obvious concerns of management, it is important for managers to be able to conceptually differentiate among various types of information systems and understand the impacts typically associated with each type.

We will describe information systems in terms of various levels of performance. Although alternative classification schemes have been suggested, it is useful to our presentation to think of information systems in terms of *basic data processing systems, integrated data processing systems, management information systems,* and *decision support systems.*[3] These various information systems have been listed in ascending performance levels. We will discuss them in the same order and see the ways in which they build upon one another, yet also have considerably different characteristics. Along the way we will also comment on their impact upon personnel and the organization. Let us begin by considering basic data processing systems.

BASIC DATA PROCESSING SYSTEMS

In the mid-1950s when computers were first introduced for commercial purposes, *basic data processing systems* were all that existed. They were developed to automate routine business data processing applications such as preparing the payroll, accounts receivable accounting, sales order processing, inventory record keeping, and the like.[4] Basic data processing systems with their attendant speed,

[3]An interesting, alternative classification system is found in Frederic G. Withington, "Five Generations of Computers," *Harvard Business Review* (July-August 1974), pp. 99–108.

[4]A detailed description of the functioning of routine data processing applications is provided in Alan L. Eliason, and Kent D. Kitts, *Business Computer Systems and Applications* (Chicago: Science Research Associates, 1974).

Herman Hollerith

A significant contributor to the development of computers was Herman Hollerith. In 1887 he was hired by the Census Bureau to help process the 1890 census count. He developed the machine-readable card concept which he incorporated in his "census machine." He later developed many other card-oriented systems and the familiar Hollerith punched card is named after this important inventor.

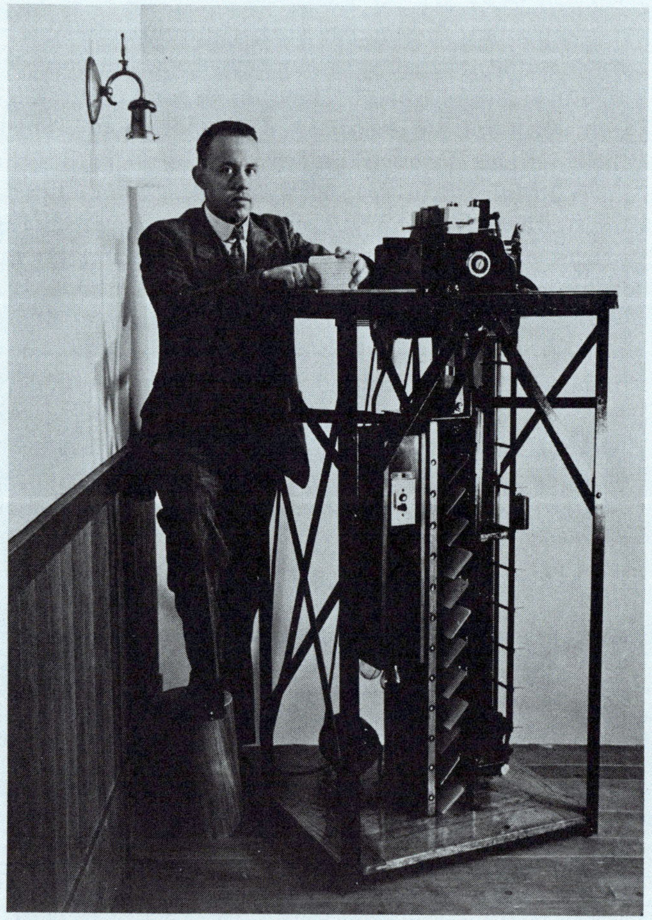

Source: Courtesy of the IBM Corporation

accuracy, and storage capacity replaced manual systems in many organizations.

Although larger organizations have tended to evolve to more sophisticated performance levels, it is interesting to note that the appearance of low-cost mini-computer systems have put computerized systems within the reach of many small businesses. Often, these small businesses are operating basic data processing systems.

Basic data processing systems tend to duplicate many of the features of their noncomputerized predecessors. A computer program is written that instructs the computer to perform the same types of logical and arithmetic operations that have been performed by hand. Data for each application are maintained separately. The system's functioning results in processed data and a limited set of summary reports. Typically, no management science models are integrated into the system.

Basic data processing systems have their greatest impact upon clerical personnel. Thomas Whisler found that skill changes for clerical personnel took place in 90% of the departments that were affected by the computer.[5] And in 70% of the cases, skill *increases* were demanded of clerical personnel.

Clerical personnel often find that their role in the previous manual system has been either eliminated or significantly modified. In some cases, they may discover that their services are no longer needed by the organization and they must seek employment elsewhere. In many instances, however, clerical personnel are given the opportunity to be retrained for positions that are created by the introduction of the computerized system. When management can handle change as an opportunity rather than a threat, some of the resistance to change may be eliminated.

Management is relatively unaffected by a basic data processing system. The summary reports do little to influence decision making. With the exception of those managers who have managerial responsibilities for the computerized system, job requirements remain basically the same.

A computerized system does create new positions. There are needs for computer operators, programmers, and systems analysts. Some of the more specialized positions must typically be filled from outside the organization. When computers were first introduced, there was a shortage of trained personnel that made staffing the data processing department difficult. Although there is still a shortage of computer specialists, the shortage is not nearly as great as it once was.

The introduction of a computerized system affects an organization's structure. Some departments are eliminated, new departments are created, and other departments have their roles significantly changed. The usual placement for a basic data processing system is in an accounting department. This positioning is natural because many of the applications are accounting-related. However, this placement becomes less desirable as the organization's information system needs progress to the point where higher performance levels are required.

INTERGRATED DATA PROCESSING SYSTEMS

Most organizations which begin with a basic data processing system eventually evolve to at least an *integrated data processing system*. The major enhancement over a basic system is the integration of the data base and the applications.

[5]Thomas L. Whisler, *The Impact of Computers on Organizations* (New York: Praeger, 1970), p. 140.

Consider first the integration of the data base. Rather than having a separate data file for every application, as with a basic data processing system, a common data base is created. This common data base is referred to as an *integrated data base.* Every application then draws from the integrated data base. This arrangement is efficient in that it eliminates the redundant storing of data. The data are stored only once in a standard format, and every application retrieves data as needed from the same data base.

An organization's *customer master file* is a good example of a shared file in an integrated data base. The file contains information such as the customers' name, mailing address, credit limit, and the like. It first comes into use when a customer's order is received. The file is updated to reflect any necessary changes (a new mailing address), or additions to the file (perhaps the order is from a new customer). The file is later used in preparing acknowledgement notices to send to customers, and in deciding which orders to accept (some customers' credit limit may have been exceeded). After an order has been filled, the customer must be sent an invoice, which requires yet another use of the customer master file for the mailing address. The same customer master file comes into play once more with the accounts receivable application. It is required in sending monthly billing statements.

An integrated data processing system also features integrated applications. The output from one application becomes an input to another. Consider the sales order processing, customer billing, and inventory control applications. An output from sales order processing is an accepted sales order file. This file is an input to both the customer billing and inventory control applications.

Another characteristic of many integrated data processing systems is the use of simple management science models. Built into the inventory control application, for example, can be simple demand forecasting models that provide input to economic order quantity formulas of the type shown in the previous chapter.

With an integrated data processing system, there is relatively little additional impact upon clerical personnel. Most of the impact was absorbed with the establishment of a basic data processing system. The effects upon management are also small. However, seeds are sown at this level of performance that ultimately have an effect on management as the information system continues to evolve to higher performance levels. One of these seeds is the integrated data base. Storing all of the organization's data in a central place makes it possible to perform analyses and generate reports that cut across functional areas. It is this sort of information that is often important to middle and top management.

Second, the introduction of management science models eventually has a managerial impact. For highly *structured* or *programmable* decision-making situations, it is possible for the computer to largely substitute for the manager. An example of this possibility was seen in the preceeding chapter with the model for simulating the bank officer's processing of overdrafts. However, the use of management science models typically does not result in the replacement of managers. Decision making is just one of management's functions. Furthermore, except for highly structured decisions, management science models only support rather than make decisions, because typically a number of factors need to be considered in arriving at a decision that do not lend themselves to quantification in a model.

The technology associated with the creation, operation, and maintenance of the integrated data base demands personnel with specialized skills. These people must typically be hired from outside the organization. At this point, the organization may also begin to employ systems analysts with the specific responsibility of serving as a go-between for the needs of the functional areas and the data processing department. The organization may also hire more personnel with management science skills.

With an integrated data processing system, only relatively minor impacts are felt by the organization, as compared to when the computerized system was first introduced. The most notable change is the possible relocation of the data processing department to a position of higher status and influence in the organization. The requirement for an integrated data base that cuts across organizational levels seems to require a positioning that is more equal to other functional areas in order to ensure cooperation.

MANAGEMENT INFORMATION SYSTEMS

Some people refer to any information system as a *management information system* (MIS). This usage of the term is not very precise, and in fact is even somewhat misleading. As we have seen, lower performance level information systems provide relatively little information of value to management.

When we are referring to a MIS, it is in reference to an information system with specific performance characteristics. It is the third of four performance levels that we are considering. Our conceptualization of a MIS follows that of Robert Head who suggests that it features: (1) an integrated data base, (2) a hierarchical information structure, and (3) a decision-support orientation; see Figure 16-2.[6]

The integration of the data base that was begun in an integrated data processing system is extended in a MIS. As is shown in Figure 16-2, data for many applications and from the various functional areas are maintained. In addition to internal data, *external* or *environmental* data are stored. These data are important in satisfying the information needs of the upper managerial levels, because such data describe the environment in which the firm operates.

A MIS is designed to satisfy the information needs of managers at different organizational levels and in the various functional areas. Obviously, great care must be taken in planning appropriate information flows in the light of the information needs of individual managers. Lower, middle, and top managers must

[6]Robert B. Head, "Management Information Systems: A Critical Appraisal," *Datamation* (May 1967), pp. 22–27.

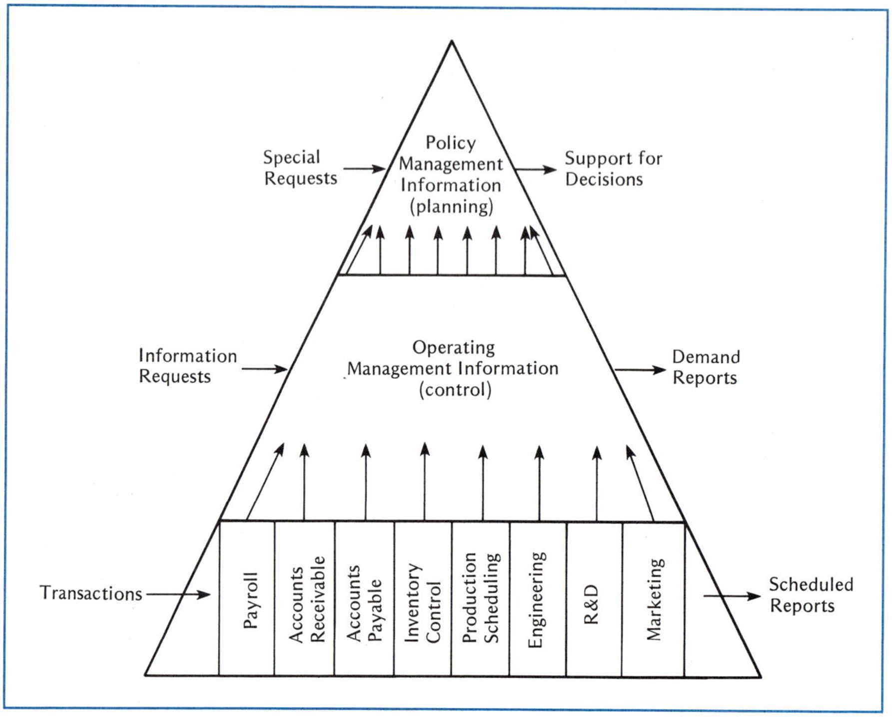

FIGURE 16-2. A Visual Conceptualization of a Management Information System. [Source: Robert B. Head, "Management Information Systems: A Critical Appraisal,"* Datamation *(May 1967), p. 23.]

be supplied with information that is appropriate for their organizational responsibilities.

In supporting decision making, a MIS must be able to supply information in a variety of ways. It provides, of course, summary reports on a scheduled basis. The system must also be able to generate *demand reports* in response to ad hoc information requests. The system should also permit users to *query the data base;* that is, explore the data base for specific information. The Berry's World cartoon on the next page provides a humorous commentary on the computer's ability to provide reports.

A MIS also contains an expanded number of management science models that are designed to support management's decision-making responsibilities. These models can very in scope from simple economic order quantity models to those that simulate the functioning of the organization in its environment.

An area of continued interest, speculation, and controversy revolves around the impact of MIS-type systems on management.[7] Definitive comments are still

[7]Starting the controversy were Harold J. Leavitt, and Thomas L. Whisler, "Management in the 1980s," *Havard Business Review* (November-December 1958), pp. 41–48.

An Interesting Illustration of the Ability of Information Systems to Generate Reports. (Reprinted by permission of NEA.)

difficult to make because of the difficulty of studying a variety of organizations and how they change over time in response to computer-based information systems. However, some general observations can be made.

High-performance information systems have had relatively little impact on the jobs of top managers.[8] However, several exceptions can be noted. First, when appropriate simulation models are available, they allow top executives to analyze the consequences of proposed strategic plans. Second, high-performance systems increase a top manager's ability to measure and evaluate performance. As one manager has said,

> *The availability of almost any sort of information I want makes it possible for me to know where to apply pressure, and/or how I ought to organize activities.*[9]

The extent to which a MIS affects middle or lower management positions depends upon the characteristics of the position.[10] When the job does *not* require the processing of large amounts of data, the impact of the computer is minor. Better information is available to support decision making and to measure and evaluate organizational performance, but the nature of the manager's job does not substantially change. However, when the job involves processing large amounts of quantitative data, the computer has more of an impact. Rational rather than intuitive decision making becomes increasingly possible, and the number of

[8] See, for example, "People Count More Than Computers," *Business Week* (May 4, 1974), p. 80.
[9] Charles W. Hofer, "Emerging EDP Pattern," *Harvard Business Review* (March-April 1970), p. 29.
[10] Hofer, ibid., p. 22.

managerial positions is sometimes slightly reduced as the computer assumes routine decision-making responsibilities.

Some lower- to middle-level managers experience an increase in their decision-making responsibilities. Backed by better, more complete information and increased analysis capabilities made available by management science models, upper-level management grants lower-level managers more decision-making authority.

It is still difficult to judge the impact that high-performance information systems are having on organizational structure. More time must pass before definitive statements can be made. However, Frederic G. Withington, a respected observer of the information systems scene, has observed that there will be "substantial redistributions of management functions in the organization. Most notably, procurement, transportation, personnel administration, cash management, and other logistic functions will be moved from the field to headquarters to achieve economies of scale available from applying specialist skills to the pooled needs of the entire organization."[11] Previously, these logistic functions had been decentralized because of the difficulty of bringing together all the required data. Now with geographically dispersed field locations being increasingly linked by computer networks, the data collection and analysis process has been facilitated, which permits more decisions to be made at an organization's headquarters.

By the time an organization's information system has reached the MIS stage, the data processing department has typically been positioned at a fairly high organizational level. The head of the data processing department may even carry a title such as vice-president for information systems.

DECISION SUPPORT SYSTEMS

Since the late 1960's, a special type of information system has begun to appear in organizations. These systems have been referred to by a variety of names such as strategic planning systems and management decision systems, but more recently the name *decision support system* has been used.[12] It is not altogether clear whether these systems should be categorized as a separate type of information system or whether they are a highly advanced MIS. For our purposes, however, because of their special characteristics, decision support systems (DSS) will be discussed as the fourth and highest level of information system performance.

In most organizations where a decision support system is found, a MIS has already been in operation for some time. Consequently, there already exists a strong computer hardware and software base and experienced personnel to

[11] Withington, op. cit., p. 103.

[12] See, for example, Michael S. Scott Morton, *Management Decision Systems* (Cambridge, Mass.: Harvard University Press, 1971), and William R. King, and David I. Cleland, "Decision and Information Systems for Strategic Planning," *Business Horizons* (April 1973), pp. 29–36.

develop the system. The DSS is created in order to provide more extensive decision-making support in a particular area. As examples, decision support systems are currently being used for production control,[13] marketing, service, and distribution simulations to aid in short-term forecasting,[14] and for asset allocations in banks.[15] Systems are also being developed, however, to support a wide variety of decisions. The IBM-sponsored GADS system is a general purpose system, which constructs and displays computerized maps for use in designing police force beats, planning urban growth, and delineating school district boundaries.[16]

A salient design feature of a DSS is the integration of management science models, an enhanced data base, and the decision maker into an effective decision-making system. Rather than generating a structured flow of reports that hopefully will support decision making, a DSS is activated only in response to the user's commands. Most commonly, the manager or an intermediary sits at a computer terminal with specific information needs, enters commands that access desired management science models and data, and interacts with the system until the desired information has been obtained.

The number, use, and complexity of models in a DSS depends upon the system's scope and purpose. The models can vary from simple statistical analysis routines for computing means and standard deviations to large linear programming models. Models for upper level, strategic types of decision making typically are designed to answer "what if" questions. The manager enters proposed courses of action to the model, and the model outputs a description of the consequences of these actions. For lower-level, more structured types of decisions, the model is more likely to output suggested optimizing solutions. The economic order quantity model presented in the previous chapter is illustrative of this type of model.

Most organizations that operate a sophisticated information system already maintain an abundance of internal, accounting-related data. Although such data are important to a DSS, many decision-making situations require additional data. For example, engineering data may be needed for certain production decisions. For strategic decision making, environmental data are often required. Consequently, an organization's data base typically has to be enhanced with additional data required by the intended purpose of the DSS. This enhanced data base is often referred to as a *decision support data base.*[17] Also needed is sophisticated computer software for entering, maintaining, and accessing the data.

[13] Scott Morton, ibid.

[14] Charlotte Seaberg, *On-Line Corporate Models: Tools for Managerial Decision Making at Xerox of Canada, Ltd.*, (Montreal, Canada: Xerox of Canada, Ltd.).

[15] James W. Bruce, "Management Reporting System: A New Marriage Between Management and Financial Data Through Management Science," *Interfaces* (Vol. 6, No. 1, Pt. 2, November, 1975), pp. 54–63.

[16] E.D. Carlsen, and J.A. Sutton, "A Case Study of Non-Programmer Interactive Problem Solving," (San Jose, Calif.: IBM Research Report RJ 1382, 1974).

[17] Ralph H. Sprague, Jr., and Hugh J. Watson, "A Decision Support System for Banks," *Omega: The International Journal of Management Science* (Vol. 4, No. 6, 1976), p. 657–671.

Until recently, the uncontested thinking has been that managers would begin using computer-based systems as soon as the systems became easier to use. The proponents of such thinking envisioned managers, such as shown in Figure 16-3, using a computer terminal to obtain information. This condition might still evolve; however, for more complex systems such as a DSS, the manager often uses the system through an information systems staff intermediary, especially when nonroutine analyses are required.[18] The point of this discussion is that the decision maker must be conceptualized as being part of the system. Unless the manager's information needs, the way in which the system will be used, and the

FIGURE 16-3. A User Operating a Computer Terminal. (Courtesy of Data General.)

[18]Suggesting the need for intermediaries is Peter G. W. Keen, "'Interactive' Computer Systems for Managers: A Modest Proposal," *Sloan Management Review* (Fall, 1976), pp. 1–17.

manager's individual preferences are taken into consideration during the design and development stages, it is unlikely that the system will be used to its fullest potential.

As has been suggested, a DSS is made up of data base, management science models, and decision maker subsystems. Figure 16-4 shows the components of the subsystems and the relationships among the subsystems. Notice that the data base subsystem on the left contains transaction data, other internal data, and external data. The management science models subsystem on the right contains models that support decision making at various organizational levels. The decision maker subsystem on the bottom contains the decision maker and the mechanisms through which the system is used.

The users of a DSS experience the greatest impact. They have analysis capabilities that were previously more limited or not as readily available. This added information tends to improve the quality of their decision making.

A DSS has little additional impact upon an organization over that of a MIS.

FIGURE 16-4. A Conceptual Model of a Decision Support System.

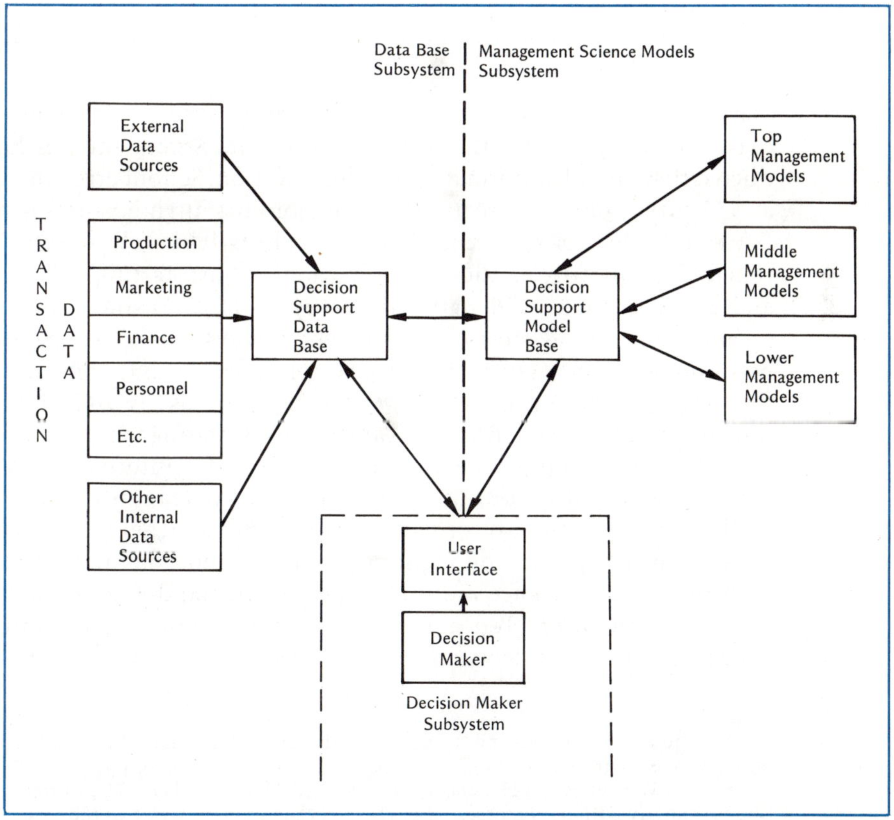

Most of the significant changes occur at earlier stages of evolution. A DSS does require, however, that management scientists, data processing specialists, and the end user work as a team in developing the system. In some cases, specialized skills may have to be brought in from outside the organization.

AN INFORMATION SYSTEM SUMMARY

Information systems have been categorized as being either basic data processing systems, integrated data processing systems, management information systems, or decision support systems. These systems have been discussed in terms of their characteristics and impacts upon personnel and upon the organization. This discussion is summarized in Table 16-1. At each higher performance level, only the incremental changes are shown.

STUDIES OF INFORMATION SYSTEM PROGRESS

Having discussed various types of information systems, it seems appropriate to consider how prevalent the different types are. Several studies have been conducted that provide information on this question. Schonberger and Buterbaugh in a 1975 survey of a cross section of 28 major Pittsburgh business firms found that "more than half of the firms claim to be 'heavily' involved with MIS, with the remainder reporting 'cautious' involvement or 'just starting.'"[19] Watson, Sprague, and Kroeber, in a 1976 national survey of large business and governmental organizations found most of the information systems to be operating at a high-performance level.[20] Using the same performance levels described in this chapter, the 153 responding organizations were categorized, as shown in Table 16-2. Notice the high percentage (65.3%) of organizations operating management information systems. These studies show that high-performance information systems are not developments of the future but, rather, are in operation today.

The movement to an information system with a higher performance capability does not just happen. The required resources and potential impacts associated with this type of change are such that they demand a considerable amount of managerial attention. Too much is at stake to completely delegate information system development decisions to data processing specialists.

[19]Richard J. Schonberger, and Terry L. Buterbaugh, "Management Information Systems in Pittsburgh Business Firms," *Pittsburgh Business Review* (Winter, 1976), pp. 1–4.

[20]Hugh J. Watson, Ralph H. Sprague, Jr., and Donald W. Kroeber, "The Current State of Information Systems Evolution," *Proceedings of the Eighth Annual Meeting of the American Institute for Division Sciences*, San Francisco, California, (November 1976), p. 332.

TABLE 16-1
Various Types of Information Systems, Their Characteristics, and Impacts upon Personnel and the Organization

	Basic Data Processing Systems	Integrated Data Processing Systems	Management Information Systems	Decision Support Systems
Characteristics	Performs routine data processing applications. Data for each application are stored separately. No management science models.	Data base and applications become integrated. Simple management science models are used.	Structured information flows to support decision making. Features an integrated data base, a hierarchial information structure, and a decision support orientation.	Provides information to support specific decision-making tasks. Features an integrated system of models, data base, and decision maker.
Impact upon Personnel and Organization	Biggest impact is upon clerical personnel. Positions are eliminated, changed, and created. Departments are eliminated, changed, and created.	Seeds are sown for later impact upon management. Data processing department may be moved from an accounting-related position to a higher-level organizational position.	Some structured decision-making tasks are assumed by the computer. Managerial positions requiring the processing of considerable amounts of quantitative data are affected. Some managers are given expanded decision-making responsibilities. Logistical functions become more centralized. The data processing department is typically positioned as an equal to the other major functional areas.	Better information for selected decisions. Little new impact upon the organization's structure.

Managers must play an active role in specifying their information needs. Computer specialists can identify what information is feasible from the existing system, but managers best understand what information is required to support their decision-making responsibilities. An unfortunately common occurrence is

TABLE 16-2
The Information System Performance Level of 153 Large Business and Governmental Organizations

Level	Number of Organizations	Percentage of Organizations
Basic Data Processing Systems	4	2.6%
Integrated Data Processing Systems	31	20.3
Management Information Systems	100	65.3
Decision Support Systems	18	11.8
	153	100.0%

for computer specialists to supply management with any information they believe might possibly be used. The consequence of this practice is too often "information indigestion," in which more information is supplied than can possibly be screened and assimilated. Russell Ackoff suggests that this a major problem with many information systems.[21] Managerial involvement in system development helps ensure that only meaningful information is provided.

COMPUTERS AND SOCIETY

As a closing topic for this chapter, it seems appropriate to briefly consider how computers and computer-based information systems are affecting society. Computers in recent years have increasingly become a concern of many different publics. It is important for managers to be aware of these concerns and to be prepared to accommodate them in appropriate ways. This discussion will consider the issues of loss of individuality, the invasion of privacy, fears of automation, and computer-related crime. Unfortunately, space permits only a brief commentary on these important issues.

Loss of Individuality

Computerized systems by their very nature treat human characteristics in a numerical manner. Furthermore, the computer's storage capacity and processing speed allow millions of records to be processed very quickly. In an environment

[21]Russell L. Ackoff, "Management Misinformation Systems," *Management Science* (December 1967), pp. B147–B156.

where only quantifiable aspects of a person are considered and a person is only a miniscule portion of the whole, it is not surprising that one often feels a loss of individuality.

Computer systems do not need to be as impersonal as they often are. The technology is such that computers can be programmed to identify important individual differences. For example, the model for processing overdrafts in Chapter 15 recognized the bank officer's evaluation of the depositor's general credit worthiness. This permitted some degree of subjectivity to influence the decisions that were made. More attention can and should be devoted to the human factor in systems design.

It should be emphasized that computers do much to improve the quality of life. Efficient airline reservation systems, convenient ticket outlets, and virtually error-free banking statements are just a few of the computer-based systems that make life simpler and more enjoyable.

Of course, the computer is just one of many factors that are making individuals feel less unique. Forces such as the weakening of family ties, living in large urban areas, and increased governmental intervention in people's lives all tend to make one feel adrift, out of control, and somewhat less important.

Privacy

An issue of considerable interest has been the computer's role in the invasion of individual privacy. Because of the quantity of data that can be permanently stored in a computer and the speed with which data can be accessed, more is easily known about an individual than ever before in man's history. Table 16-3 shows some of the data bases that are maintained by the federal government. Many local governments and private organizations also maintain extensive data bases on individuals.

It needs to be emphasized that the computer per se does not create privacy problems; it is only a facilitator. It is an organization's *policies* regarding the storage and use of data that create the "horror stories" reported by the news media. Because privacy problems emanate from human sources, they should also be solvable through man's efforts. Some progress is being made in this regard, but there is still much more that needs to be done.

At the national level, the most significant action to date has been the passing of the Privacy Act of 1974. This law is the result of a compromise privacy bill, but it does contain some significant provisions. A Privacy Protection Comission was established, although it has no enforcement power and a limited budget. This commission investigates government and private data processing systems and makes legislative recommendations on privacy to the Congress and the President. Other provisions of the Privacy Act of 1974 apply to all federal information systems, with certain exemptions for law enforcement, military, and civil service records. It allows individuals access to their files and permits them to obtain copies and to correct inaccuracies by mail. The legislation also requires federal agencies to

TABLE 16-3
The Main Data Banks Maintained by the Federal Government

Department of Health, Education and Welfare: 693 data systems with 1.3 billion personal records, including marital, financial, health, and other information on recipients of Social Security, social services, medicaid, medicare, and welfare benefits.

Treasury Department: 910 data systems with 853 million records that include files on taxpayers, foreign travelers, persons deemed by the secret service to be potentially harmful to the President, and dealers in alcohol, firearms, and explosives.

Justice Department: 175 data systems with 181 million records including information on criminals and criminal suspects, aliens, persons linked to organized crime, securities-laws violators, and "individuals who relate in any manner to official FBI investigations."

Defense Department: 2,219 data systems with 321 million records pertaining to service personnel and persons investigated for such thing as employment, security, or criminal activity.

Department of Transportation: 263 data systems with 25 million records, including information on pilots, aircraft and boat owners, and all motorists whose licenses have been withdrawn, suspended, or revoked by any state.

Department of Commerce: 95 data systems with 447 million records, primarily Census Bureau data, but including files on minority businessmen, merchant seamen, and others.

Department of Housing and Urban Development: 58 data systems with 27.2 million records, including data on applicants for housing assistance and federally guaranteed home loans.

Veterans Administration: 52 data systems with 156 million records, mostly on veterans and dependents now receiving benefits or who got them in the past.

Department of Labor: 97 data systems with 23 million records, many involving people in federally financed work and job-training programs.

Civil Service: 14 data systems with 103 million records, mostly dealing with government employees or applicants for government jobs.

Source: Reprinted from *U.S. News & World Report* (April 10, 1978), p. 45. Copyright 1978 U.S. News & World Report, Inc.

enforce standards of accuracy, relevance, completeness, and timeliness in using or transferring information to other agencies, and agencies are prohibited from selling mailing lists. Federal, state, and local governments are no longer allowed to withhold a right, benefit, or privilege because of refusal to disclose a social security number.

The Privacy Act of 1974 is a movement toward ensuring a measure of privacy in a computerized age, but much still needs to be done. Legislation regulating the private sector is still needed and will undoubtedly be forthcoming.

At the corporate level, one of the leaders in privacy issues and practices has been the IBM Corporation. Its management has sponsored numerous advertisements supporting important privacy principles. Its policies regarding the collection and use of data on their own employees surpass those of most other organizations.[22]

IBM's concern about an employee's privacy begins when one first applies for a position. The applicant supplies only data IBM believes important to the employment decision—name, address, previous employment, education, and a few

[22] An interview with Frank T. Carey, Chairman and Chief Executive Officer of IBM, on privacy policies at IBM is presented in "IBM's Guidelines to Employee Privacy," *Harvard Business Review* (September-October 1976), pp. 82–90.

other basic facts. The applicant's age is not required until after the decision to hire has been made. Only criminal convictions during the previous five years must be revealed. No personality or polygraph tests are used.

Once an applicant becomes an employee, care is still exercised about what data are collected and maintained. The focus is still upon storing only job-related data. As data become obsolete, they are purged from the employee's files. For example, IBM course grades and instructor's comments are kept for only three years.

Access to stored data is closely controlled. IBM employee identification numbers are used rather than social security numbers. This action is in response to growing national concern about social security numbers becoming a *de facto* universal identifier. Requests from outside organizations for data on employees are carefully handled; very little data are supplied to outsiders without written approval from the employee, unless required by law. Operating managers can see only job-related data about their subordinates. Some data, such as medical benefits, wage garnishments, payroll deductions, and the like are available only to the personnel and finance departments. An employee's file is almost completely open for the employee's review. There are exceptions, however. An employee is not allowed to see plans for possible salary and position advancements.

IBM makes an active attempt to communicate its privacy policies. They are covered in management training programs, and employees are encouraged to bring privacy infringements to the attention of management.

Automation

Automation can be thought of in many contexts, but we will consider it in terms of machines replacing the efforts of humans. The first significant appearance of automation was in the eighteenth and nineteenth centuries when the First Industrial Revolution saw machines replacing men and women in the work environment. More recently, a Second Industrial Revolution is taking place as machines assume the monitoring of other machines. This development is particularly evident in industries such as chemical processing in which entire systems are almost completely computer-controlled.

The fear of automation centers on unemployment, changed traditions and social customs, boredom resulting from excessive amounts of leisure time, and the like. Although all of these issues are of some importance to management, it is unemployment that management must most frequently address. Technological unemployment does occur, and management should strive to soften the impact on those affected.

On a larger scale, automation creates employment opportunities. New devices must be produced, sold, and operated. In a way, the problem of automation is how to handle the transition problem. Paul Einzig provides a good perspective on the automation issue.

> *Those who are opposed to automation for fear of technological unemployment do not realize that if their policy were followed, their country would be exposed to much*

more and intractable nontechnological unemployment. Automation is bound to proceed sooner or later, whether we like it or not. Our choice does not rest between automation and full employment but between prompt automation with the possibility of moderate temporary unemployment and delayed automation with the certainty of grave perennial unemployment, until our progress has caught up with that of our competitors.[23]

Crime

In the wake of the insurance industry's 1973 Equity Funding fraud in which millions of dollars were lost through bogus policies, there has been a growing concern on the part of management over computer-related crime.[24] Crimes of this type have been on the rise, are embarrassing to management, and are costly to the organization. Furthermore, if the crime is attributed to negligence, lack of adequate security, or failure to set up adequate auditing procedures, directors of companies can be held personally liable for damages under Section 11 of the Securities Act of 1933. Unfortunately, in many cases, management has allowed computer crimes to occur mainly because of ignorance and loose or nonexistent internal controls.

The story of Jerry Schneider and the Pacific Telephone and Telegraph (PTT) provides an interesting case in point.[25] Schneider was an excellent electronics technician and con man in his early twenties. He owned his own electronics company and because of poor disposal techniques by PTT was allowed to salvage PTT equipment from its supply center. In his excursions through PTT's garbage, Schneider also collected enough information to understand almost the entire PTT inventory ordering system. By receiving guided tours while posing as a free-lance reporter and paying for or conning information from ex-employees, Schneider was able to learn what he did not already know about the system. From a terminal at his business, Schneider was able to access and interact with the inventory ordering and control system. Schneider would order equipment, pick it up in an old telephone company truck, and take it to his business, where he would repackage the equipment to resemble refurbished Western Electric equipment. He then sold this equipment to his customers and, in some cases, sold it back to PTT after having deliberately ordered the equipment to pull its inventory balance down below the recorder point. Schneider was eventually caught after stealing $1.5 million in equipment. One of his ex-employees eventually told PTT about his boss's activities, which lead to his arrest. Today, Schneider is free after serving 40 days in jail, and now serves as a consultant to companies on how to prevent computer-related crime.

The interesting curiosity about computer-related crime is that it is usually the

[23] Paul Einzig, "Must Automation Bring Unemployment?" in *The World of the Computer,* John Diebold, ed. (New York: Random House, 1973), pp. 335–344.

[24] A description of the Equity Funding fraud is available in "On the Coast-to-Coast Trail of Equity Funding," *Business Week* (April 21, 1973), pp. 68–72.

[25] Donn B. Parker, *Crime by Computer* (New York: Charles Scribner's Sons, 1976).

result of weaknesses in human security precautions. In the Equity Funding insurance fraud mentioned previously, no internal auditor was employed by the company, and the financial auditors made no effort to check on the information that was received from the computer. Equity Funding made sure that no "Big 8" accounting firms audited them. It is interesting to note that Touche Ross' packaged auditing program, STRATA, uncovered 99% of the bogus policies on the first run and, with some modifications, also found the other 1%. Imparting to employees a concern about and an awareness of the possibility of computer-related crime is the single most important precautionary measure that management can take.

SUMMARY

A computer-based information system employs a computer to process data into information. These systems are having a significant impact on personnel, organizations, and society.

A computer system is made up of several components—input, storage, central processing, and output. An input unit is used to enter data and instructions encoded in a computer program. A storage unit maintains the vast quantities of data required by today's organizations. The actual logic and arithmetic operations are performed in the central processing unit. An output unit provides the output in a prespecified form.

An information system can be at one of several performance levels—basic data processing system, integrated data processing system, management information system (MIS), or decision support system (DSS). These systems have varying characteristics and impacts upon personnel and the organization.

A basic data processing system performs routine data processing applications with a separate data file maintained for each application. The system's biggest impact is upon clerical personnel and departments associated with the manual system being replaced.

An integrated data processing system sees at least a partial integration of the data base and the applications. Some simple management models are used to support decision making. Information that cuts across functional areas begins to be supplied. The data processing department may be moved higher in the organization's structure.

A MIS features an integrated data base, a hierarchial information structure, and a decision support orientation in serving management's information needs. Management is sometimes freed from highly structured decision-making responsibilities. Those decision-making tasks that involve the processing of large amounts of quantitative data are also affected. Some managers are given expanded decision-making authority. There is a tendency for logistic functions to become more centralized.

A DSS is used by a decision maker in support of a specific decision-making task. The system features models, an enhanced data base, and an integrated role for the decision maker. Such systems are a relatively recent development, but are providing more and better information to support decision making.

Several studies of information system progress have been made. They tend to show that most large organizations already have a relatively sophisticated information system. Management does have important responsibilities, however, in guiding an information system's evolution and identifying information system requirements.

Computer-based information systems are also affecting society. These impacts are seen in areas such as individualism, privacy, automation, and crime.

Assignments

16-1. What are the components of a typical computer system? Briefly describe the function served by each component.

16-2. Listed below are elements of computer hardware. Identify with what computer component(s) each element is associated.
a. Card reader.
b. Printer.
c. Magnetic disk.
d. Logic circuits.
e. Typewriter terminal.

16-3. Distinguish among the various information system performance levels.

16-4. Read the article by Frederic G. Withington, "Five Generations of Computers," *Harvard Business Review* (July-August 1974), pp. 99–108. Compare and contrast the performance levels identified by Withington with those presented in this chapter.

16-5. What are the characteristics of the various information system performance levels in terms of the following:
a. Applications.
b. Data base.
c. Information supplied to management.
d. Use of management science models.
e. Impact on personnel.
f. Impact on the organization.

16-6. Identify some of the clerical jobs that might be affected in a switch from a manual to a computerized system in a typical business organization.

16-7. Several advantages of moving to an integrated data base were cited in the text. What do you see as some of the possible disadvantages or problems in such a move? If you were a manager in a functional area, what would be your reaction to the suggestion of moving to an integrated data base?

16-8. Some people contend that as more English-like programming languages are developed, as computer terminals become more widespread and easier to use, and as managers become better trained and more experienced in data processing concepts, all managers, even top managers, will be using computers in support of their decision-making responsibilities. Do you see this possibility occurring?

16-9. Identify some of the things in your life that are computer-related and that make you feel less of an individual. From a cost-benefit point of view, are these things justifiable?

16-10. Social Security numbers have almost assumed the role of a universal identifier. List the various data banks that contain data on you and that key off of your social security number.

Case 16-1

FIRST NATIONAL BANK OF BECKERVILLE

The First National Bank of Beckerville is the only bank in the community of Beckerville, a small agricultural community in southern California. It is a small bank with only a few thousand depositors. Several years ago the bank purchased a medium-size computer system and automated routine banking functions such as payroll, customer checking and savings accounts, and personal loans. Most of the applications programs were purchased from software vendors and implemented by the bank's only systems analyst and programmer.

James Gordon, president of the bank, has just returned from a banking seminar where several bank officers described their banks' advanced information systems. One capability that especially impressed Mr. Gordon was a financial planning system in which a bank officer could sit at a terminal and access management science models and data and perform long-range cash budgeting. Mr. Gordon has returned to Beckerville excited about the prospect of developing such a system for his bank.

Assume that you are a close friend and advisor to Mr. Gordon. React to Mr. Gordon's enthusiasm for the new system. Consider the following in making your recommendation:

1. The hardware, software, and personnel required for the financial planning system.
2. The costs and benefits associated with moving to the new system.
3. The impact that the new system would have upon management and the organization.

Case 16-2

FAST SHOP, INC.

Fast Shop, Inc., is a convenience store chain located in the Northwest. The potential for employee theft in this type of business is always great, and Fast Shop has always taken extensive preventive measures. Any applicant for employment must provide considerable personal data and be willing to submit to pre-employment and regularly scheduled polygraph tests. Prior to employment, credit bureau and private investigator checks are also made.

Recently, prospective and current employees of Fast Shop have become increasingly critical of Fast Shop's investigating practices. A number of well-qualified employees have stopped working for Fast Shop because of what they consider to be an invasion of their privacy.

1. Identify the costs and benefits associated with Fast Shop's practices.
2. Should other than economic considerations be of importance?
3. Develop a recommended policy for Fast Shop.

References

ADAMS, CARL R. "How Management Users View Information Systems." *Decision Sciences* (Vol. 6, 1975), pp. 337–345.

ALTER, STEVEN L. "How Effective Managers Use Information Systems." *Harvard Business Review* (November-December 1976), p. 97–104.

ARGYRIS, CHRIS. "Management Information Systems: The Challenge to Rationality and Emotionality." *Management Science* (February 1971), pp. B-275–B-292.

GIBSON, CYRUS F., and RICHARD L. NOLAN. "Managing the Four States of EDP Growth." *Harvard Business Review* (January-February 1974), pp. 76–88.

HAMMOND, JOHN S. "Do's and Don'ts of Computer Models for Planning." *Harvard Business Review* (March-April 1974), pp. 110–123.

NAYLOR, THOMAS H. AND DANIEL R. GATTIS. "Corporate Planning Models." *California Management Review* (Summer 1976), pp. 69–78.

O'BRIEN, JAMES A. *Computers in Business Management.* Homewood, Ill.: Richard D. Irwin, Inc., 1975.

WATSON, HUGH, J., RALPH H. SPRAGUE, JR., AND DONALD W. KROEBER. "Computer Technology and Information System Performance." *MSU Business Topics* (Summer 1977), pp. 17–24.

WATSON, HUGH J. AND ARCHIE B. CARROLL. *Computers for Business: A Managerial Emphasis.* Revised edition. Dallas: Business Publications, Inc., 1980.

SHARON A. MUSICH
Manager, Operations Department,
Senior Management Staff,
Naval Air Norfolk Federal
Credit Union

Sharon A. Musich began her career with Naval Air Norfolk Federal Credit Union in 1965, joining the clerical staff of the five-person operation. As the credit union has grown and expanded, she has held the positions of Loan Processor, Supervisor of Cash & Accounting, Assistant to the Manager, and Loan Officer. In 1973, the credit union's prosperity necessitated an organization restructuring, and Ms. Musich then joined the Senior Management Staff. As Manager of the Operations Department, she has direct responsibility for 13 employees with principal duties of accounting, data processing, and central records for the credit union's 47,000 accounts and 90-employee staff.

Executive Commentary

The Credit Union and Data Processing—in Retrospect

Naval Air Norfolk Federal Credit Union is a nonprofit financial organization, chartered in 1959 under the rules and regulations of the National Credit Union Administration. It is owned and operated by its members for the benefit of all who belong. The purpose of the credit union is to promote thrift among its members by providing them convenient, systematic savings plans and by creating a quick, economical source of confidential credit. After expenses and legal reserves are met, all financial profits made by the credit union are returned to the members in the form of dividends and services.

Computerized data processing became a necessity for the credit union in 1969, when the process of posting transactions for its 5,500 accounts on a bookkeeping machine could not be accomplished in a timely manner. Additional matters of significant consideration were the increasing growth in existing services and the future increases in the types of services to be offered by the credit union.

At that time, a batch-input data processing system was implemented with the credit union purchasing processing time from a local service bureau—a type of business organization that provides data processing services for a fee. Batch input means that the vouchers representing the daily transactions are summarized by the staff and sent to the service bureau as input for computerized processing.

The conversion to a computerized data processing system for the maintenance of savings and loan accounts resulted in several changes. First, ledger records detailing account transaction history were replaced by computerized listings. Second, record keeping had to become more standardized. Third, only composite daily business transactions were recorded, which made account research more complex and less timely.

Member reaction to the implementation of the computerized data processing system was somewhat negative, because passbooks that were kept current as each transaction was made were exchanged for voucher receipts that did not reflect current balances. Furthermore, members received only periodic statements detailing account activity. Member resistance to the change was reduced by positive attitudes on the part of the credit union staff who had been educated in the reasons for the changes.

Although only one staff position, a bookkeeping machine operator, was eliminated as a result of the conversion, the functions of computing interest due on loans, dividends earned on savings, and the compiling of data for various reports (such as delinquent loans) were eliminated, which allowed the credit union to grow considerably and to expand some services without hiring additional employees.

By 1973, the credit union had increased its number of accounts to 19,000 and was contemplating opening an additional facility. A natural consequence of this expansion was the need to expand the data processing system. Operating additional offices required that all sites have access to current account information, primarily to prevent the occurrence of overdraws. This and the need for more extensive processing features prompted the credit union to convert to an "on-line, real-time" data processing system with the service bureau. In such a system, transactions are recorded as they occur, as opposed to being recorded in a batch as in a batch-input system. The credit union staff now assumed the responsibility for inputting data by using terminals placed in the office sites. This meant not only a major expenditure for the acquisition of terminals, but the creation of special training programs to enable the staff to handle the new functions accurately and expeditiously. These programs included off-site training at the service bureau prior to the actual conversion and a continual on-site plan for new employees.

Even though the new system required a transfer of responsibility of input functions to the staff, these additional functions were offset by improvements in efficiency through the elimination of functions such as the filling out of voucher receipts (now posted on the terminals) and the retrieval of account information from one central source. Also, because the new system provided as much as 20 times more information, managerial decision making and planning abilities were enhanced. More importantly, member confidence and service were greatly improved by the availability of instantaneous updating of accounts, immediate information on account status, and on-the-spot error adjustments.

There were two major problems created with the evolution to the on-line, real-time system. First, the accessibility to account information by most employees made the credit union more vulnerable to internal theft. Our main line of defense was to develop more stringent internal auditing procedures such as increasing dual-control of duties. The most difficult to deal with is system down-time—the time when the system is not operating as a result of system failure. Because the credit union is dependent on the system to access current account information so as to provide two of its primary services (savings withdrawals and loan add-ons) and because not providing these services seriously injures the credit union's reputation with its members, processing the transactions becomes difficult and risky when the system is down. The timelines of members transacting their business is impaired because the staff must resort to referencing computer printouts for balance information, versus immediate access when the system is operating. Also, because the computer printouts are generated only on a periodic basis, the balance information may not be current and an overdraw may occur. However, because system downtime generally occurs less than 2% of our operating hours, the difficulties incurred are far outweighed by the 98% of system up-time.

Although the credit union currently purchases its data processing time from a service bureau, it is aware that the economics of scale and the need for expanded computer features, particularly in the area of providing more support for management decision making and planning, will eventually dictate an in-house computer system.

CASES FOR PART V

Case V-1

SHERIDAN MOTOR COMPANY[1]

The Sheridan Motor Company manufactured two specialized models of trucks in a single plant. Manufacturing operations were grouped into four departments: metal stamping, engine assembly, Model 101 assembly, and Model 102 assembly. Monthly production capacity was limited by the number of machine hours available in each department, as indicated in Table 1. The Table also shows the amount of time each of the two models required for production in each department.

For example, if the metal stamping department worked only on 101's in a given month, it could produce stampings for 7,000/2.8 = 2,500 Model 101's. If, instead, it worked only on 102's, it could produce stampings for 7,000/2.0 = 3,500. Similarly, if the engine-assembly department worked only on 101's, it could assemble 4,080/1.2 = 3,400 engines; if it worked only on 102's, it could assemble 4,080/2.4 = 1,700. And if it assembled engines for 2,000 Model 101's, it would have enough capacity left over to assemble engines for (4,080 − 2,000 × 1.2)/2.4 = 700 Model 102's. Thus, the capacity restrictions in the four departments could be represented by the straight lines shown in Exhibit 1. Any production combination within the area bounded by the heavy portion of the lines was feasible from a capacity standpoint.

The prices to dealers of the two models, f.o.b. the Sheridan plant, were $2,100 for the Model 101 and $2,000 for Model 102. Sheridan followed the price leadership of one of the larger manufacturers in the industry.

As a result of a seller's market in 1953, Sheridan was able to sell as many trucks as it could produce. The production schedules it had followed during the first six months of the year resulted in a monthly output of 600 Model 101 trucks and 1,400 Model 102 trucks. At this level of production, both the Model-102-assembly and the engine-assembly departments were operating at capacity, but the metal-stamping department was operating at only 64% of capacity and the Model-101-assembly department was at only 27%. Standard costs at this level of production are given in Exhibit 2, and further details on overhead costs are given in Exhibit 3.

TABLE 1

Department	Monthly Capacity (machine hours)	Machine Hours Needed Per Truck	
		Model 101	Model 102
Metal Stamping	7000	2.8	2.0
Engine Assembly	4080	1.2	2.4
Model 101 Assembly	4500	2.0	—
Model 102 Assembly	4480	—	3.2

[1] Adapted from an example used by Robert Dorfman in "Mathematical or 'Linear' Programming: A Nonmathematical Approach," *American Economic Review*, December 1953.

This case was prepared as the basis for class discussion rather than to illustrate either effective or ineffective handling of an administration situation.

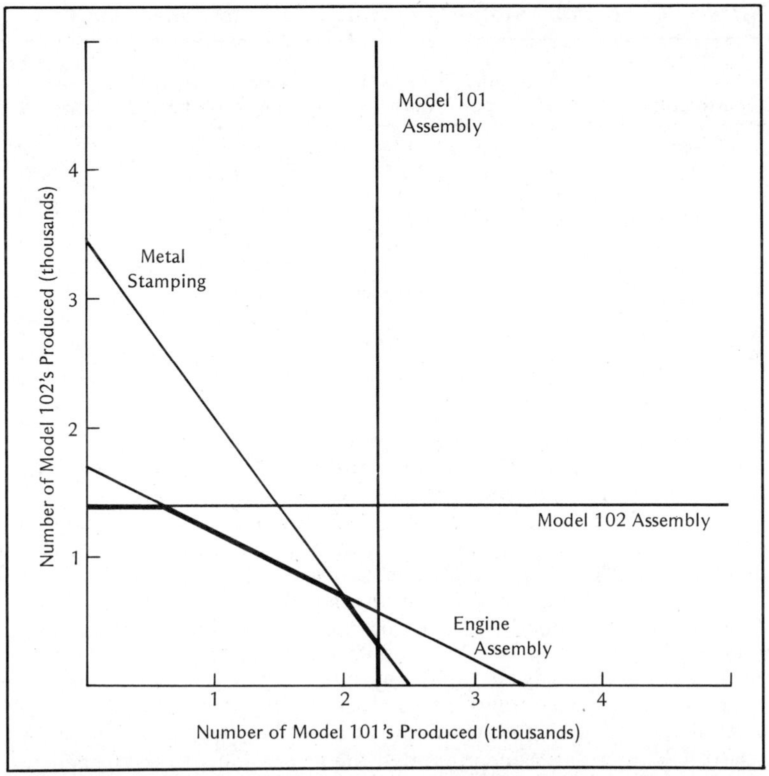

EXHIBIT 1. Sheridan Motor Company. Diagram Showing Production Possibilities.

At a monthly planning session of the company's executives in July 1953, dissatisfaction was expressed with the company's profit performance as reported in the six-month income statement just prepared (see Exhibit 4). The sales manager pointed out that it was impossible to sell the Model 101 truck to yield a profit and suggested that it be dropped from the line in order to improve overall profitability.

EXHIBIT 2. Sheridan Motor Company, Standard Costs of Two Truck Models

		Model 101		Model 102
Direct Materials		$1,200		$1,000
Direct Labor				
Metal Stamping	$ 40		$ 30	
Engine Assembly	60		120	
Final Assembly	100	200	75	225
Overhead*				
Metal Stamping	$204		$160	
Engine Assembly	130		250	
Final Assembly	400	734	179	589
Total		$2,134		$1,814

*See Exhibit 3

EXHIBIT 3. Sheridan Motor Company, Overhead Budget for 1953

Department	Total Overhead per Month*	Fixed Overhead per Month**	Variable Overhead/Unit	
			Model 101	Model 102
Metal Stamping	$ 347,000	$135,000	$120	$100
Engine Assembly	428,000	85,000	105	200
Model 101 Assembly	240,000	135,000	175	—
Model 102 Assembly	250,000	75,000	—	125
	$1,265,000	$430,000	$400	$425

*Based on planned 1953 production rate of 600 Model 101 trucks and 1,400 Model 102 trucks per month.
**Fixed overhead was distributed to models in proportion to degree of capacity utilization.

The controller objected to this suggestion. "The real trouble, Dick, is that we are trying to absorb the entire fixed overhead of the Model 101 assembly department with only a small number of units production. Actually these units are making a contribution to overhead, even though it's not adequate to cover fixed costs, and we'd be worse off without them. In fact, it seems to me quite possible that we'd be better off by *increasing* production of Model 101 trucks, cutting back, if necessary, on Model 102 production."

The production manager pointed out that there was another way in which output of Model 101 trucks could be stepped up that would not require a cutback in Model 102 production. This would be through purchase of engines from an outside supplier, thus relieving the present capacity problem in the engine assembly department. If this course of action were followed, Sheridan would probably furnish the supplier with the necessary materials but would reimburse him for his labor and overhead.

At this point, the president entered the discussion. He asked the controller, the sales manager, and the production manager to get together to consider the two questions raised by their comments and to report their recommendations to him the next day. The two questions were, (1) Assuming no change in present capacity and demand, what would be the most profitable product mix? (2) What was the maximum labor and overhead charge Sheridan could afford to pay for engines if it purchased them from an outside supplier?

Question

1. What would be your reply to the questions raised by the president?

EXHIBIT 4. Sheridan Motor Company, Income Statement for Six Months Ending June 30, 1953 (thousands of dollars)

Net Sales	$24,360
Cost of Goods Sold	22,920
Gross Margin	$ 1,440
Selling, Administrative, and General Expense	1,051
Net Income Before Taxes	$ 389
Taxes on Income	206
Net Income After Taxes	$ 183

Case V-2

KNIFE RIVER

On October 26, 1974, the Congress authorized the establishment of the Knife River Indian Villages National Historic Site in North Dakota. The site was established to preserve certain historic and archeological remnants of the culture and agricultural life-style of the Plains Indians. The Knife River Indian Villages comprise a cluster of archeological sites located largely on private farmlands where the Knife River empties into the Missouri. These villages are identified archeologically as follows: the Buchfink, Lower Hidatsa, Big Hidatsa, and Sakakawea villages (See Exhibit 1). These villages are all highly significant, both for their archeological content and for their relation to the history of the region. They are among the best surviving examples of aboriginal villages in the Missouri valley environment of the northern Great Plains.

The Buchfink site has been cultivated and has no visible surface remains, but archeologists believe that occupational remains exist intact below the plowzone. This site represents the earliest known occupation on the Knife River. The Lower Hidatsa, Big Hidatsa, and Sakakawea villages, being two to three centuries younger than the Buchfink site and spared modern cultivation, are all plainly visible. They consist of numerous circular depressions of varying widths, with indications of cache pits in and between the lodges (See Exhibit 2). The Sakakawea and Big Hidatsa villages exhibit the remains of fortified ditches. The villages range from approximately 5 to 23 acres in size. The village sites and such features as ancillary cemeteries, fortification remnants, and cache pits comprise the principal physical resources of the area.

These villages are outstanding historically, as well as archeologically, because of their associations with a succession of famous explorers, fur traders, scientific observers, artists, and other early travelers. Lewis and Clark visited these villages often during their stay at nearby Fort Mandan in 1804–1805. Sakakawea, the Indian woman who became a famous member of their expedition, lived here. Alexander Henry, David Thompson, John Bradbury, George Catlin, Prince Maxmilian, Carl Bodmer, and John James Audubon are among the notable river travelers to these villages.

The National Park Service's interest in preserving and interpreting the villages began in 1946, and it has grown steadily ever since. The Big Hidatsa village was registered as a national historic landmark in 1964. In 1967, a National Park Service planning team studied the villages, and the report that resulted recommended the establishment of a national historic site composed of the four villages.

The Missouri River Basin Archeological Salvage Program of 1946–1969 was a coordinated effort by the National Park Service, the Smithsonian Institution, and various state agencies to identify, excavate, and record historical and archeological sites that would be destroyed by dams and reservoirs created by the Corps of Engineers and the Bureau of Reclamation. Because the giant dams in the Dakotas—Fort Randall, Oahe, Big Bend, and Garrison—have now destroyed most of the known prehistoric villages along the Missouri River, a special survival value accrues to sites that remain unscathed. The largest number of archeological sites spared are scattered along 50 miles of the Missouri in North Dakota. Those at Knife River are located between the upper end of the Oahe Reservoir and Garrison dam.

The Knife River has changed its course over the years. Much of the riverbank within the authorized boundary of the villages is subject to continual erosion from the Knife River flow. The Sakakawea site is currently being eroded by the river. In order to preserve this site, the National Park Service planned a riverbank stabilization project to stop the

This case was prepared by Hugh J. Watson and Shirley A. Farmer, College of Business Administration, University of Georgia. Case materials were provided by Roy Slatkavitz of the National Park Service and "Knife River Indian Villages," Master Plan, United States Department of the Interior/National Park Service, (January 1978).

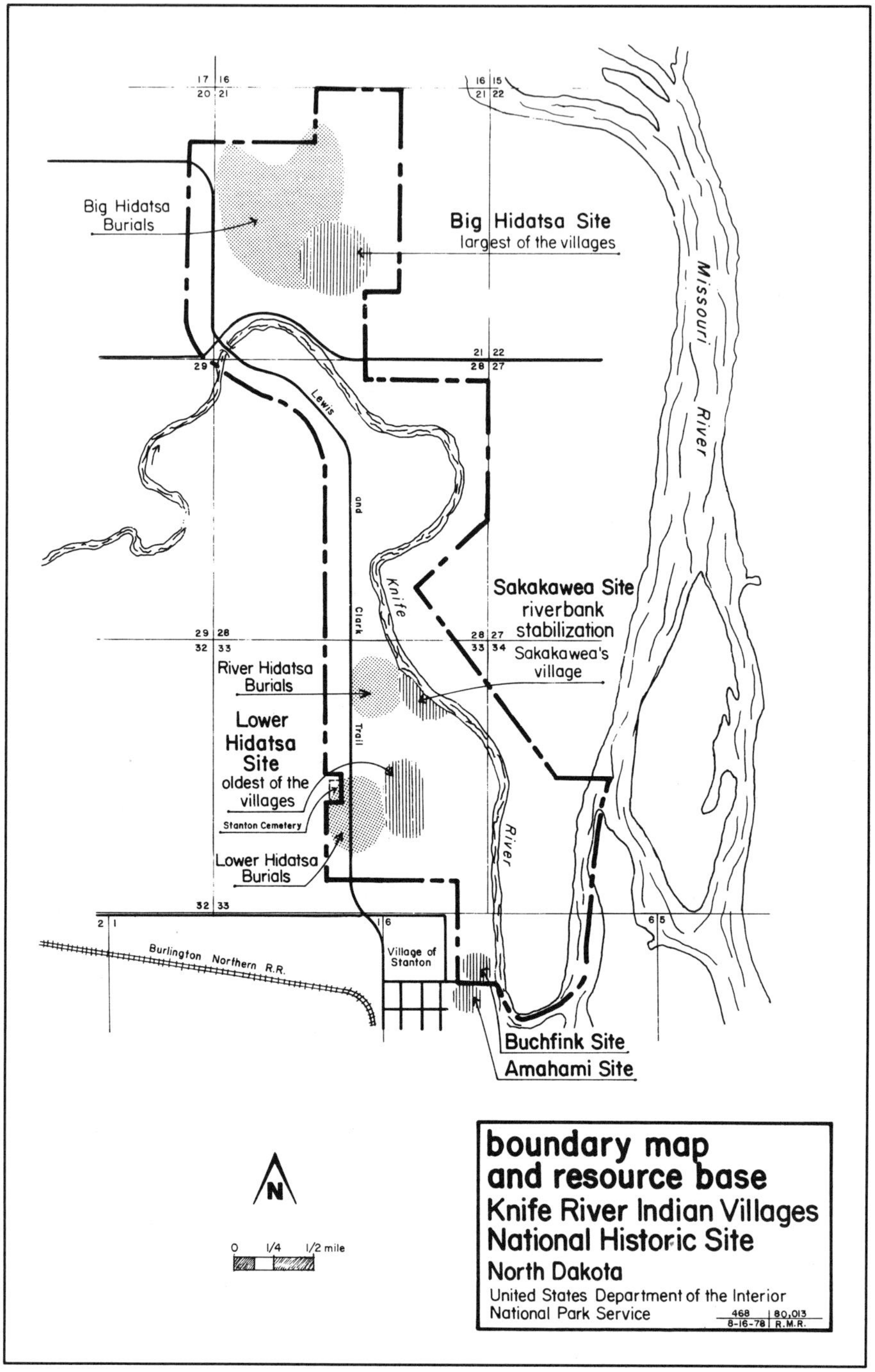
Big Hidatsa Burials
Big Hidatsa Site
largest of the villages
Missouri River
Lewis and Clark Trail
Knife River
Sakakawea Site
riverbank stabilization
Sakakawea's village
River Hidatsa Burials
Lower Hidatsa Site
oldest of the villages
Stanton Cemetery
Lower Hidatsa Burials
Burlington Northern R.R.
Village of Stanton
Buchfink Site
Amahami Site
N
0 1/4 1/2 mile
boundary map
and resource base
Knife River Indian Villages
National Historic Site
North Dakota
United States Department of the Interior
National Park Service
468 80,013
8-16-78 R.M.R.

EXHIBIT 1.

EXHIBIT 2. Knife River. Aerial Photograph of the Villages.

erosion of the riverbank. A total of 12 major activities comprise the riverbank stabilization project. These activities, their precedence relationships, and expected completion times are as follows:

Activity	Description	Must Follow	Expected Completion Time
A	Conduct field surveys of soil and water	—	4 weeks
B	Analyze alternative methods of protecting the riverbank	—	2
C	Determine the best method of protecting the riverbank	B	2
D	Prepare the project's preliminary design and cost estimates	A,C	4

Activity	Description	Must Follow	Expected Completion Time
E	Obtain approval of the preliminary design	D	4
F	Prepare specification and working drawings	D	3
G	Advertise request for bids	E,F	4
H	Award contract and have preconstruction conference	G	1
I	Contractor begins site preparation	H	2
J	Contractor installs stabilization materials	H	3
K	Review and suggest changes to contractor's work	I,J	1
L	Final acceptance of contractor's work	K	1

Questions

1. Prepare a PERT network for the riverbank stabilization project.
2. Identify the critical path and the expected time along the critical path.
3. What effect would a one-week delay in the advertising of requests for bids have on the expected project completion time?

EPILOGUE

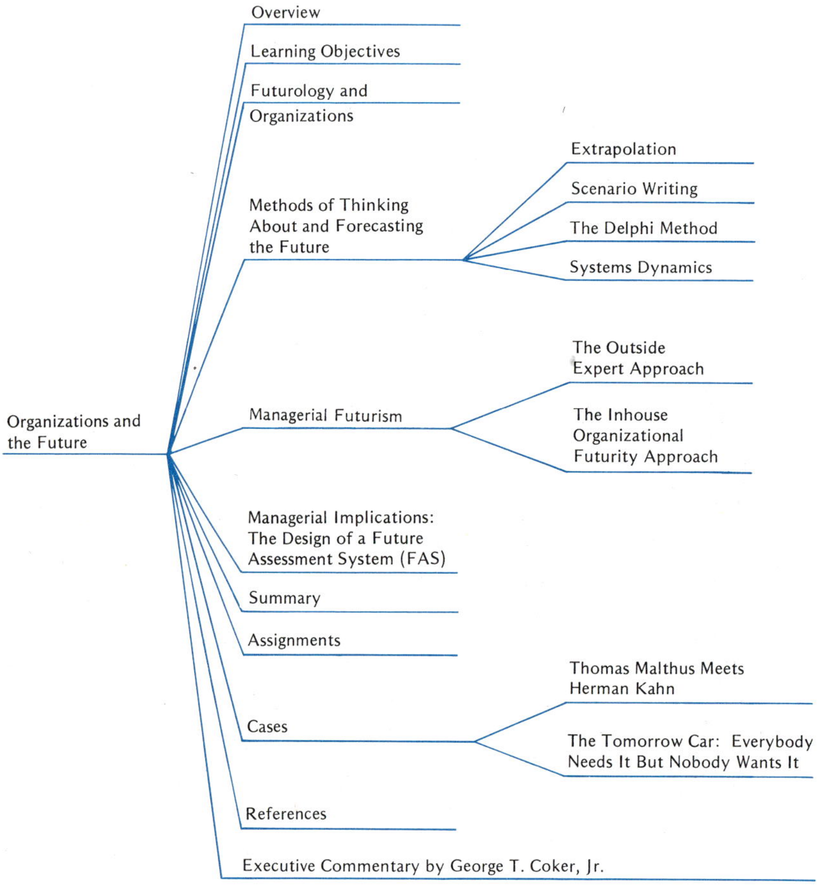
Organizations and the Future
Overview
Learning Objectives
Futurology and Organizations
Methods of Thinking About and Forecasting the Future
Extrapolation
Scenario Writing
The Delphi Method
Systems Dynamics
Managerial Futurism
The Outside Expert Approach
The Inhouse Organizational Futurity Approach
Managerial Implications: The Design of a Future Assessment System (FAS)
Summary
Assignments
Cases
Thomas Malthus Meets Herman Kahn
The Tomorrow Car: Everybody Needs It But Nobody Wants It
References
Executive Commentary by George T. Coker, Jr.

17

ORGANIZATIONS AND THE FUTURE

OVERVIEW

Most writings on the future of the organization and its management have traditionally centered on the internal aspects of the process of conceiving and managing an organization. For example, one finds considerable interest among management scholars and practitioners alike on the organizational structure of an enterprise and the way of living and working within such an organization. The usual questions raised and answered by management writers read something like, "Will the internal organizational structure be more hierarchical (bureaucratic), or will it be less hierarchical and more egalitarian?" "Will work in the factory and the office become more automated to the extent that more meaningful work will be done by R2D2s and C3POs, or will things revert to more jobs for humans and fewer machines?"

This focus on the internal workings of the organization stems from the conviction that an organization that is well-organized internally should be able to withstand any external disturbance. However, as it has been pointed out repeatedly in this book, successes and failures in the corporate world are more often than not attributed to drastic changes in the external environment and the organization's inability to change its structure and functions to accommodate to and profit from the change rather than to be destroyed by it. Thus, it appears that it is more appropriate to focus on the possible states of the external environment for the foreseeable future, and then to attempt to relate these possible developments to the changes in managerial philosophies and practices, which can ensure a smooth and profitable transition of the organizations into the future world.

In this final chapter of *Management: Making Organizations Perform,* an attempt will be made to prepare the student for some developments that are currently beginning to take shape and are bound to have some definite implications for the future manager or administrator. The underyling assumption of our approach to the study of the future and its implications for management is that *the fate of any given organization,* be it a business enterprise, a hospital, a university, a city, a state, or a nation, *depends as much on the changes in people's habits and attitudes and humanity's general way of living as it does on deliberate and rational managerial initiatives and organizational schemes.*[1] In addition to this philosophical assumption, it is also assumed that the newly developed discipline of *futurism or futurology* is a respectable addition to our scientific commonwealth.

For these reasons, the chapter begins with a brief review of Futurology and its usefulness for the future manager, and proceeds with some of the most important findings that the diverse schools of thought of futurology have been offering to the contemporary society for acceptance and verification. The overwhelming purpose of this chapter is not to explain to the student "everything you wanted to know about the future but were afraid to ask," but, rather, to whet the appetite and to make him or her sensitive to futuristic orientation.

LEARNING OBJECTIVES

This chapter is especially intended to help the student:

1. **Appreciate the importance of the future of management.**
2. **Become informed as to the degree of future orientation of other sectors of our society, such as its governmental and educational institutions and its intellectual forces.**
3. **Familiarize oneself with four of the major methods of thinking about and forecasting the future.**
4. **Learn how a manager can develop a sense of futurity by relating today's actions to their future consequences.**
5. **See how a rather simple system, the Future Assessment System**

[1]This "macro" orientation seems to be the latest development in corporate futurism. See, for example, the writings of Louis B. Lundborg, former Chairman of the Board, The Bank of America, *Future Without Shock: An Understanding of Vast Changes by One Who Believes in Human Choice and Responsibility* (New York: W. W. Norton & Co., Inc., 1974); his "Making A Living in the Third Century," *Saturday Review,* October 7, 1976, pp. 32, 38, 42; Project FORETHOUGHT, Shell Development Corporation; Irving Shapiro of DuPont Co.; and, of course, *The Futurist.* For a different approach, which might be termed "micro" because it focuses on the changes in the existing management technology, see W. J. Reddin, President of W. J. Reddin & Associates, Consultants, "Management Effectiveness in the 1980's," *Business Horizons,* August 1974, pp. 5–12. Mr. Reddin believes that "a good way to predict the future is to take a good look at what exists now: the present and future of management technology that impinges on managerial effectiveness, at the present and future of organization design and theory, desired managerial qualities, and management by objectives," p. 6.

(FAS), can help a manager keep an eye on some key emerging issues and how, by estimating their impact on the organization, the manager can derive ways of absorbing future shocks.

6. **Learn, especially in the context of thinking about management, the meaning of the following concepts:**

Futurology, futurism or futurity	**exponential growth**
extrapolation	**doubling time**
scenario writing	**trend analysis program (TAP)**
the delphi method	**environmental assessment**
systems dynamics	**future assessment**

FUTUROLOGY AND ORGANIZATIONS

People have always been interested in the future. This interest was not merely idle curiosity about the unknown, but also stemmed from a sincere desire to plan for contingencies that might upset otherwise sound plans. Thinking about the future is something that one engages in not only because it is pleasant (à la Thomas Jefferson: "I like the dreams of the future better than the history of the past"), but also because it is practical. In the history of futuristic thinking, one can sense two rather distinct schools of thought, so to speak, or two rather clearly identifiable streams of thinking. One includes people who believe that the future is in our hands and can be molded as we desire it; the other encompasses those who believe that because there is no way of knowing what the future is going to bring, we should not even try to prepare for it.

Human history is replete with examples of incidents exemplifying these two assumptions about the future. Over the history of human civilization, there have been both individuals and nations that have had a rather fixed idea of how the future ought to be and have accordingly devised some rather bizzare schemes to direct civilization toward that future. Although the "bad" examples of this kind of futuristic policy making are popularized, one should not forget that Adam Smith, Henry Ford, J. D. Rockefeller, and other great economic and industrial thinkers "knew" that the future of the Western world would be resting upon specialization, free economic activity, the automobile, and an energy system powered primarily by burning petroleum. The so-called free enterprise system, the automobile, and the super-automated oil refinery all stand as testimonials to the actions these individuals took to ensure the realization of their visions of a future world.

The lucky coincidence between prediction, or foresight, and reality is, of course, one of the two possible outcomes, the other being that the future might not turn out as expected. For every match between prediction and reality, there are many predictions that did not materialize. This lack of coincidence might be the result of complete inaction on the part of the predictor or of the inability of the predictor to act strongly and quickly enough to bring about the changes required or prescribed by the predictor's vision.

Today, there is a well-defined and respected discipline that deals exclusively with the study of the future. This discipline, known as futurology or futurism, may be defined as *the study of the possibilities of tomorrow and the efforts to convert these possibilities into preferred probabilities.*[2] It should be noted that futurology is concerned with both future possibilities or worlds and a set of societal and politico-economic changes that are necessary for converting these desirable possibilities into *preferred probabilities.* To that extent, contemporary futurism represents an *active* human involvement, rather than passive dreaming about the future along the lines of Aldous Huxley's *Brave New World* or George Orwell's *1984.* In both of the latter cases, the writers conceived of a future world that was much different than their contemporary worlds, but they did nothing directly to influence their political, economic, and business leaders to bring about their described worlds.

Contemporary futurism is the concern of one of the best-organized and most popular movements, known as *The World Future Society.* The World Future Society (WFS) is an international organization of futurists all over the world with some 31,000 members in 80 countries. The aims of the World Future Society are described on page 587.

The influence of the WFS on the United States and world educational, political, and business systems, as well as on life in general, has been extensive. In addition to the so-called future orientation of many curricula in high schools and in higher education, there are universities that offer undergraduate and graduate degrees in Future Studies.

In the political arena, leaders the world over are developing a tremendous interest in the future. The Congress of the United States recently intensified its efforts to identify emerging issues and pinpoint the potential long-term consequences of legislation. To help provide this foresight, the Congress has established several new organizations and given additional responsibilities to some old ones.

From modest beginnings in the mid-1960s, foresight in the Congress is becoming a significant component of the legislative process and is still gathering momentum. In recent years, the House of Representatives and the Senate have expanded their foresight organizations and required more foresight of their own committees. In addition, both Houses have studied and developed proposals for more foresight, including a Congressional Foresight Office, and have formed the Congressional Clearinghouse on the Future. The public statements of both President Jimmy Carter and Chief Justice Warren Burger also have reflected an interest in the use of futures information, indicating that foresight may spread

[2] Raymond E. Glos, Richard D. Steade, and James R. Lowry, *Business: Its Nature and Environment* (Cincinnati: South-Western Publishing Co., 1976), Chapter 29, pp. 570–588.

World Future Society

An Association for the Study of Alternative Futures

The Society is an association of people interested in future social and technological developments. It is chartered as a non-profit scientific and educational organization in Washington, D.C., and is recognized as tax-exempt by the U.S. Internal Revenue Service. The World Future Society is independent, non-political, and non-ideological.

The purpose of the World Future Society is to serve as an unbiased forum and clearinghouse for scientific and scholarly forecasts, investigations, and intellectual explorations of the future. The Society's objectives, as stated in its charter, are as follows:

1. To contribute to a reasoned awareness of the future and the importance of its study, without advocating particular ideologies or engaging in political activities.
2. To advance responsible and serious investigation of the future.
3. To promote the development and improvement of methodologies for the study of the future.
4. To increase public understanding of future-oriented activities and studies.
5. To facilitate communication and cooperation among organizations and individuals interested in studying or planning for the future.

Membership is open to anyone seriously interested in the future. Since its founding in 1966, the Society has grown to more than 31,000 members in over 80 countries. Most members are residents [of the United States], with growing numbers in Canada, Europe, Japan, and other countries. Members include many of the world's most distinguished scientists, scholars, business leaders, and government officials.

The Futurist, April 1978, p. 95

through the executive and judicial branches, following the early lead of the Congress.[3]

The business community is slowly but steadily moving toward enhancing the sense of futurity in the corporate world by encouraging executive decision makers to relate their present actions to future consequences. Wayne Boucher, secretary of the Futures Group, a research and consulting firm in Glastonbury, Connecticut, believes that more and more companies will be hiring futurists.

[3] Reno Renfro, "How Congress is Exploring the Future," *The Futurist*, April 1978, pp. 105–112. Also, Anne W. Cheatham, "Helping Congress to Cope with Tomorrow," *The Futurist*, April 1978, pp. 113–115.

MASTER OF SCIENCE IN

STUDIES of the FUTURE

at the University of Houston at Clear Lake City

The interdisciplinary graduate program in Studies of the Future -- the largest program of its kind -- helps prepare Master of Science degree candidates for futures-oriented careers in business and government.

Depending upon professional objectives, a student taking the 33 credit hour program may concentrate in urban, educational, corporate, governmental, environmental, or global aspects of futures studies.

The course of study can be completed with an internship in the practical application of futures thinking. Internships are available in agencies and firms in Houston, Washington, D.C., and elsewhere.

The participating faculty of eleven scholars from seven disciplines includes Ervin Laszlo (author of *A strategy for the Future* and the Club of Rome report, *Goals for Mankind)*, Jib Fowles (author of *Mass Advertising as Social Forecast* and editor of the *Handbook of Futures Research)*, and Christopher Dede (President, Educational Division, World Future Society).

For information and application, write: Chairman, Studies of the Future, University of Houston at Clear Lake City, 2700 Bay Area Boulevard, Houston, Texas 77058.

(Reprinted with permission from The Futurist, *April 1978.)*

"Times are perilous," Mr. Boucher says. "It's a crisis with a capital C for industry. And the changes will accelerate."[4]

Corporate planning departments of old are far from adequate today. Using economic data, marketing statistics, and a smattering of demographic information, they merely estimated the profit potential of new products over a future of no more than five years. As Mr. Boucher puts it: "They looked at birth rates without considering birth-control pills."[5]

Futurists, on the other hand, try to peer much farther into the future and to bring a host of social and political factors to bear on a number of corporate problems. Usually trained as economists or market researchers, they are apt to be voracious readers who have an ability to develop contacts and to spot trends. Their function, although not yet formally named at many companies, is beginning to be called social and political forecasting, environmental scanning, or early warning systems.

[4] Liz Roman Gallese, "More Companies Use Futurists to Discern What Is Lying Ahead," *The Wall Street Journal,* March 31, 1975, p. 1.
[5] Ibid.

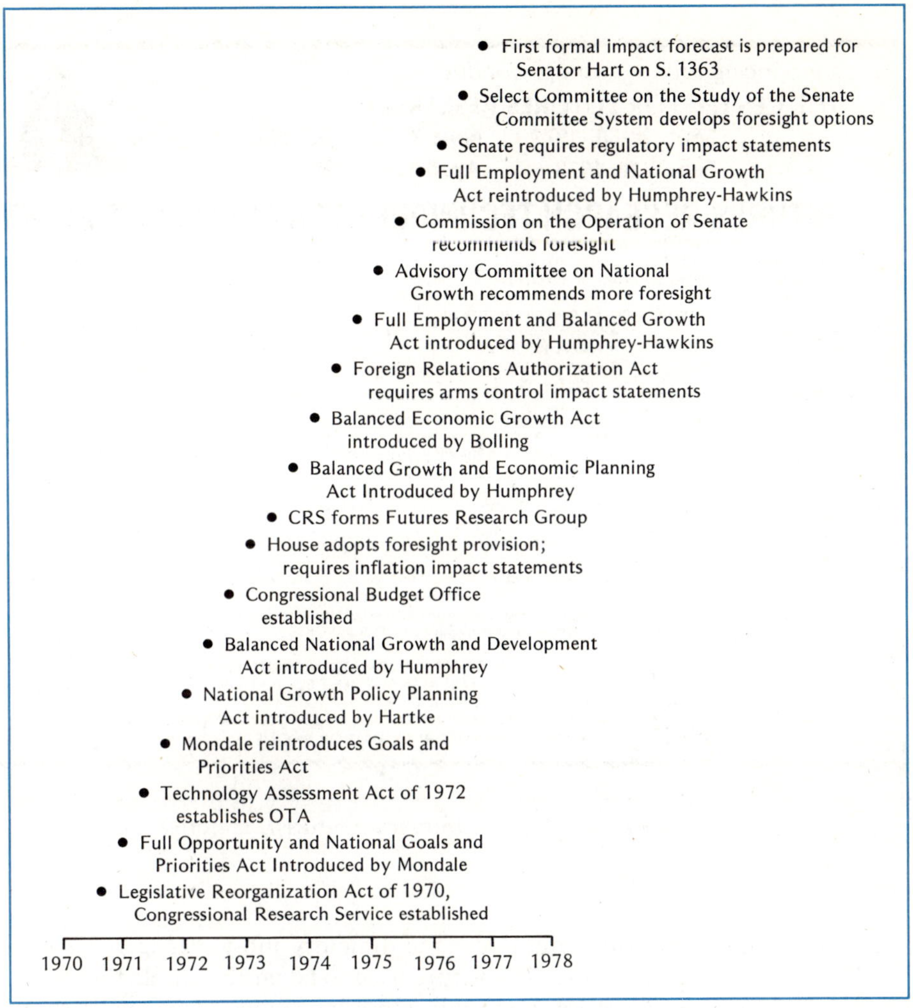

Recent Foresight-Related Developments in the Congress.

METHODS OF THINKING ABOUT AND FORECASTING THE FUTURE

Several years ago one of the authors of this book gave a talk in an Executive Development Program on the subject of the future. A month or so later one of the participants sent him a plaque with the inscription:

The trouble with our times is that the future is not what it used to be.—Valery announcing four workshops conducted by . . .

THE CENTER FOR FUTURES RESEARCH

Sept. 28-30, 1977 Nov. 30-Dec. 2, 1977

Feb. 8-10, 1978 April 12-14, 1978

FUTURES RESEARCH TECHNIQUES FOR CORPORATE PLANNERS

WHO SHOULD ATTEND?

This workshop is designed for experienced corporate planners who are generally familiar with publications such as *The Futurist*, and are seeking a more detailed familiarity with the techniques of futures research. Over 200 major corporations have sent representatives to earlier versions of this workshop including, for example, the following:

- General Electric
- General Motors
- Eastman Kodak
- IBM
- Atlantic Richfield
- Weyerhaueser
- Sears, Roebuck and Co.
- Prudential Insurance
- Westinghouse
- Monsanto
- Bank of America
- Bethlehem Steel

WHAT WILL BE COVERED?

- Gathering expert opinion
- Trend measurement and monitoring
- Technology assessment
- Process of futures analysis
- Futures modeling
- Presenting alternative futures
- Structuring alternatives
- Interactive cross-impact methods
- Case studies of futures research

WHO WILL INSTRUCT?

- Burt Nanus, Director of the Center for Futures Research, author of two books and more than 30 articles, and Chairman of the TIMS College on Planning
- Selwyn Enzer, Associate Director of the Center, formerly Senior Research Fellow at the Institute for the Future, and a leading methodology developer for over ten years.
- James O'Toole, author of five futures books including *Work in America, Energy and Social Change* and *Work and the Quality of Life*, and currently director of a study of the future of business/government relations.
- Paul Gray, an internationally noted operations researcher who has directed futures research efforts in systems engineering and transportation, author of several dozen technical papers and officer in both TIMS and ORSA.

FOR FURTHER INFORMATION, WRITE TO:
CENTER FOR MANAGEMENT EDUCATION
GRADUATE SCHOOL OF BUSINESS ADMINISTRATION
UNIVERSITY OF SOUTHERN CALIFORNIA
LOS ANGELES, CALIFORNIA 90007 OR PHONE (213) 741-2677

(Reprinted with permission from The Futurist, *October 1977.)*

This inscription epitomizes the difficulty most managers have when they contemplate the future. The future used to be rather simple for them. In general, the manager whose job was to do some long-range planning, such as financial and marketing forecasting, "knew" that the next few years would be much like the past few years with perhaps a few changes here and there. Overall, however, next year's sales would equal the past year's sales plus a certain percentage of increase, depending upon the increase of the population, customer's income, and so on. The future, in other words, belonged to the manager; he or she could do whatever was desirable.

By the middle of the 1960s, it began to become increasingly obvious that the future was not what it used to be. Because, as was pointed out earlier, population statistics were compiled and extrapolated without taking into consideration the birth control pill and society's changed attitude toward reproduction, "some 78 million hypothetical Americans and a hypothetical $177 billion in yearly Gross National Product appear simply to have vanished from American of the year

2000."[6] What actually happened? No natural or man-made disaster occurred. Was it a calculation error? Of course not. What actually happened is that the methods for both thinking about and forecasting the future were inadequate.

As disciplines of human inquiry mature, they develop sophisticated methods for contemplating and explaining the world around us with ever-greater accuracy and believability. Of the multitude of methods employed by futurists, the following four seem to be the most commonly used and most useful to future managers:[7]

1. Extrapolation.
2. Scenario writing.
3. The Delphi method.
4. Systems dynamics.

Extrapolation

Extrapolation (or trend analysis) is perhaps the oldest, simplest, and, under certain circumstances, the most useful technique or method for thinking about and forecasting the future. In its simplest form, according to the Random House Dictionary, extrapolation means "inferring the unknown from something which is known." In other words, one considers past experience to be a good guide for future expectations. Obviously, extrapolation requires that both the past and present have been perceived, studied, and understood accurately and that the movement from the present to the future point of interest will follow a certain path in accordance with a well-defined, well-documented, and tested "law."

Extrapolation is very often used to project or estimate the population of a given species, such as humans; or the quantity of total goods and services that will be produced by a given society by the year 2000; or, for that matter, the amount of money accruing to an initial investment. All of these examples refer to a well-known phenomenon of growth of a given quantity, be it people, money, resources, or fish. Let us assume that a person has the possibility of putting ten dollars a year under a mattress for future use. This person wants to know how much money he will have by the end of the tenth year. Obviously, he will have accumulated $100. Now, let us assume that the same person takes the $100 and

[6]Donald Moffit, *America Tomorrow* (Princeton, N.J.: Dow Jones Books, 1977), p. 8.

[7]The literature on the types or kinds of methods for studying the future or future forecasting is rather confusing. Both the nomenclature and the use of each technique or a combination of several techniques have been reported to be in a rather unclear state. For example, extrapolation is by some used synonomously with trend analysis, whereas for others the two terms are distinctly different. For an adequate explanation of six future research or studying methods, see Stuart Sandow, "The Pedagogy of Planning: Defining Sufficient Futures," *Futures,* December 1971, p. 328–334. For an empirical investigation of the frequency of use of forecasting techniques with an emphasis on social forecasting, see Kenneth Newgren, "Social Forecasting: An Overview of Current Business Practices," in Archie B. Carroll, Editor, *Managing Corporate Social Responsibility* (Boston, Mass.: Little, Brown, 1977).

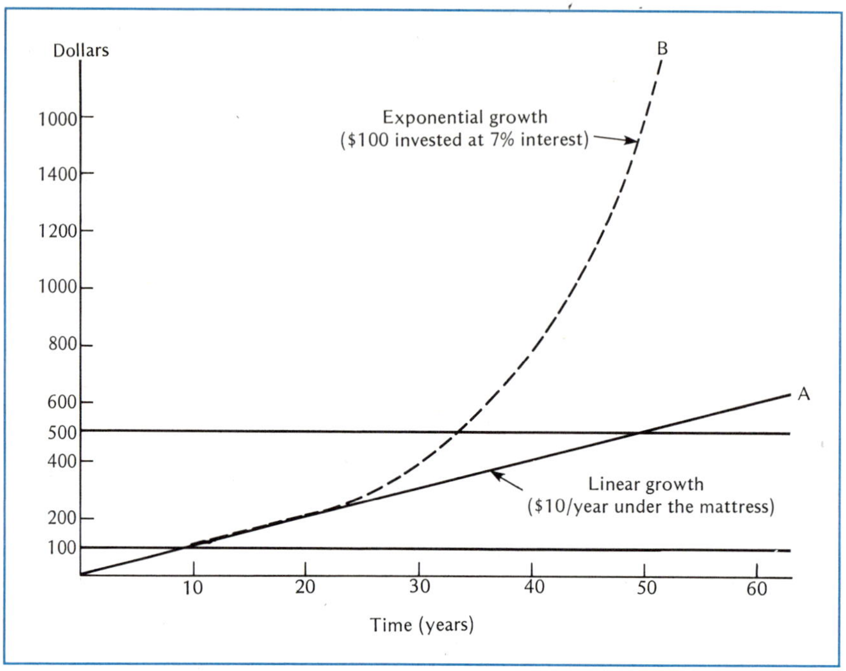

FIGURE 17-1. Linear and Exponential Growth.

instead of placing the money under the mattress, he deposits it in a bank as an initial one-time investment for which he is getting 7% annual interest. Now the question is, how much money will he have by the end of the tenth year? Figure 17-1 depicts both forms of growth.

Curve *A* in Figure 17-1 shows the case in which a miser puts ten dollars under the mattress every year. At the end of the tenth year the miser has accumulated $100, at the end of the twentieth year, $200, and so on, until the end of the fiftieth year when the wealth of the miser is $500. A look at Curve *B* of Figure 17-1 reveals that if the person invests an original sum of $100 at 7% interest and lets the interest accumulate, the principal investment will have doubled after ten years and will continue to double every ten years; at the end of the fiftieth year, the original $100 will have grown to $1,600. The kind of growth exhibited by *B* is called *exponential growth,* and it is defined as that kind of growth in which a given quantity increases by a constant percentage of the whole in a constant time period. In other words, each increment is kept and allowed to increase virtually forever at the same percentage as the initial quantity.

The mathematics of exponential growth is simple and is a convenient shorthand for a rather complicated process that can be found in many aspects of everyday life. Let us take a well-known problem that is at the forefront of societal concerns. That is the subject of population growth. For some people, population is growing too fast. For others, it is not growing fast enough. In any case, the manager who is interested in estimating the size of the population at some point in the future could do so by using the following formula and acquiring the appropriate data.

$$Nt = N_o e^{rt}$$

in which

N_o = Population now
N_t = Population in the future time (t)
e = Constant = 2.718
r = Rate of growth
t = Time

By putting the appropriate figures in this formula and then showing the results graphically, one will produce the curve exhibited in Figure 17-2.

The easiest way to think about future quantities of certain things is to think in terms of the number of years required for a given quantity to double, that is, the doubling time. See Table 17-1 for some examples of doubling times for different rates of growth.[8]

To determine the doubling time, one must set

$$\frac{N_t}{N_o} = 2$$

$$\frac{N_t}{N_o} = e^{rt}$$

$$2 = e^{rt}$$

Taking the natural logarithm for both sides gives

$$ln\ 2 = rt$$

$$\frac{ln\ 2}{r} = t$$

$$t = \frac{.6931}{r}$$

or the doubling time

[8] See, for example, Paul R. and Ann H. Ehrlich, *Population, Resources, Environment: Issues in Human Ecology* (San Francisco: W. H. Freeman), 1970. p. 10.

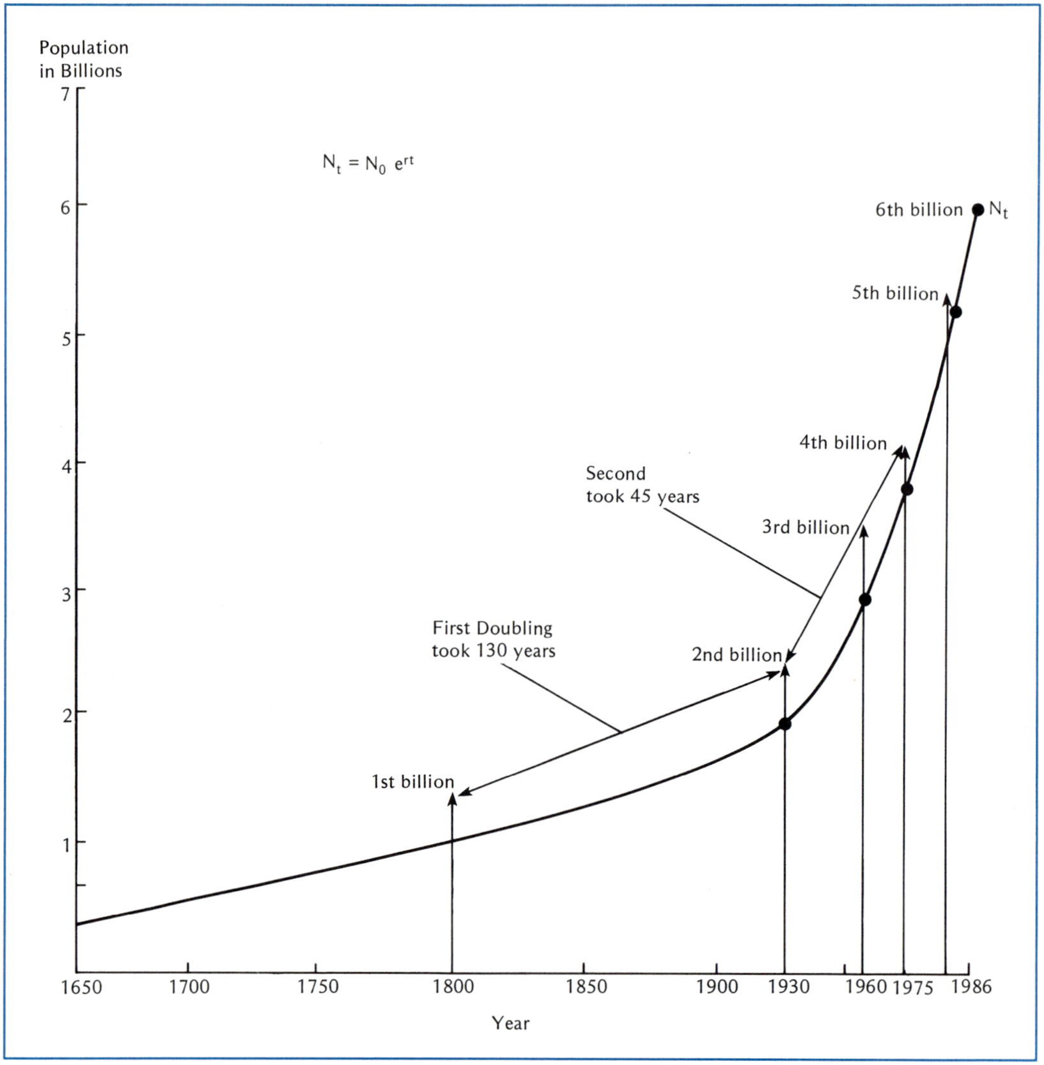

FIGURE 17-2. World Population Estimates.

$$t = \frac{70}{r}.$$

Let us call this the *Rule of Seventy:* to find the doubling time of an exponentially increasing or decreasing quantity, one divides Seventy (or .6931) by the rate of growth.

A look into Figures 17-2 and 17-3 reveals that the doubling time for both population and Gross National Product (GNP) has been cut to one third of the

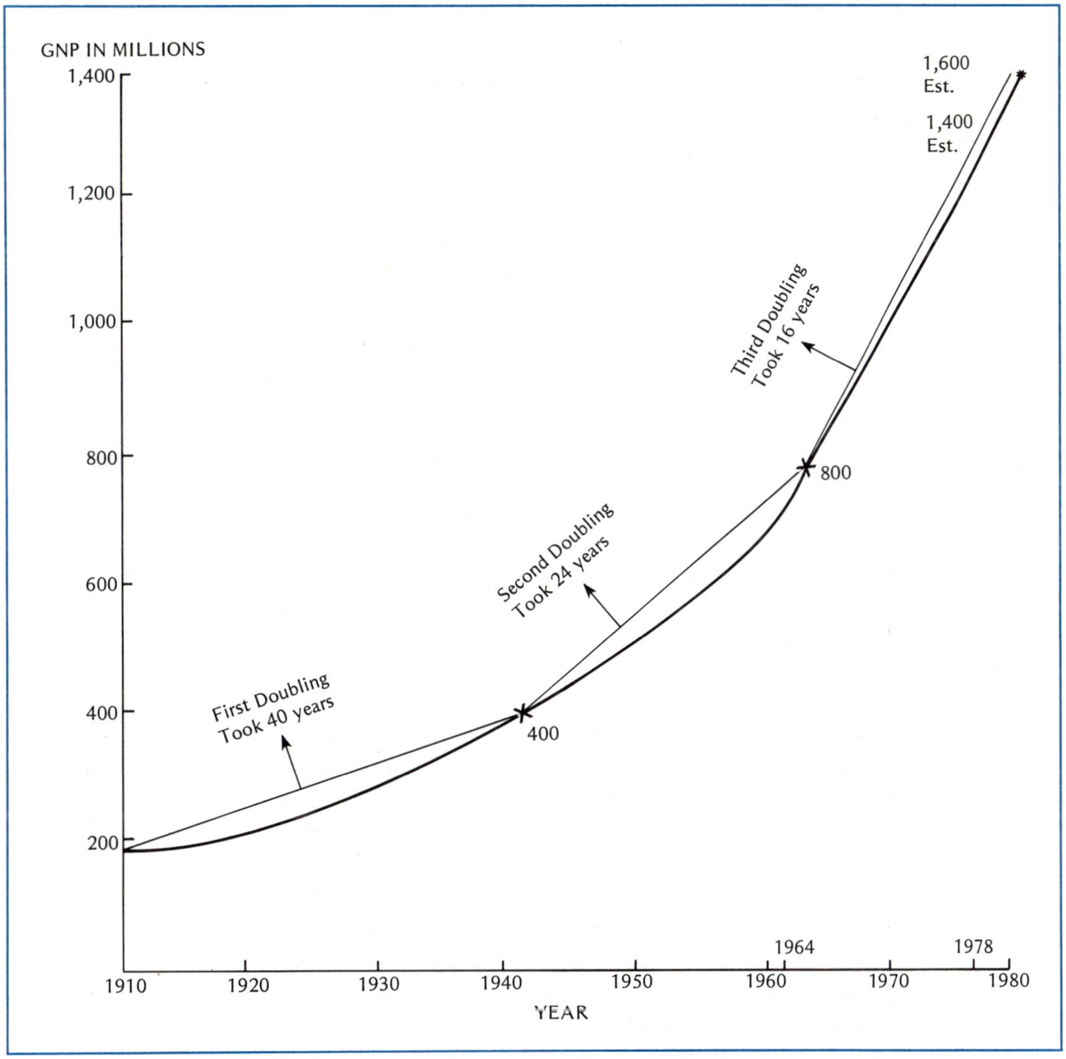

FIGURE 17-3. GNP: Total Outputs of Goods and Services in USA (1972 dollars to offset impact of inflation).

1900 rates. This is indeed one of the most insidious characteristics of exponential growth or decay. In later sections, we will return to some of the tremendous managerial implications of both exponential growth and decay processes.

Scenario Writing

Unlike extrapolation, which is almost as old as recorded civilization, scenario writing is the product of post-World War II futuristic thinking. Although no one

TABLE 17-1
Doubling Time

Growth rate (r) (% year year)	Doubling Time (t) year $t = \frac{70}{r}$
0.1	700
0.5	140
1.0	70
2.0	35
3.0	23
4.0	18
5.0	14
6.0	11.6
7.0	10
8.0	8.75
9.0	7.78
10.0	7

is sure of the exact origins of the technique, Herman Kahn is perhaps the man most people credit with its discovery and popularization during the 1950s while he was with RAND Corporation. The initial rationale for the development of scenario writing was the need to incorporate into the formal, rational, or analytic forecasting techniques a more intuitive set of assumptions and probable events to supplement and augment the validity of the analytic models. It must be clearly pointed out that scenario writing is a supplementary forecasting and futuristic thinking method, the introduction of which is justified on the grounds that the futures thinker desires to maximize the ability to grasp as much as of the *whole* as possible. Because analytic or explicit futuristic methods are constrained by the conditions of the formal symbolic system used (mathematics), scenarios that can be written in any natural language such as English, Japanese, or Greek provide for flexibility and for comprehensibility by the largest populace.

Scenarios are hypothetical sequences of events constructed for the purpose of focusing attention on causal processes and decision points;[9] or, alternatively, a scenario is a sequence of possible (but not necessarily highly probable) events and sociocultural choices.[10] Robert Ayres explains two main advantages of scenario writing.

1. Scenarios are an effective tool to counteract "carry-over" thinking, and to force the analyst (or policy maker) to look at cases other than the straightforward "surprise-free projections."
2. Scenarios are an antidote for concentrating exclusively on the forest and ignoring the trees: analysts who limit themselves to abstract generalizations may easily overlook crucial details and dynamics (because no single set seems especially

[9] Herman Kahn, and Anthony Wiener, *The Year 2000* (New York: Macmillan, 1967), p. 6.

[10] Mihaljo Mesarovic, and Edward Pastel, *Mankind at the Turning Point* (New York: Signet, 1974), p. 37.

worthy of attention) even though looking at some random specific cases can be quite hopeful.[11]

In order to illustrate how a scenario writing technique works, let us take a look at a recent study commissioned by the Ford Foundation. The project, entitled *Exploring Energy Choices,*[12] was designed to study the future of energy availability for the United States. The research team constructed three plausible but very different energy futures for the period through the year 2000. The alternative futures, or scenarios, are based on different assumptions made about the energy growth patterns our society might adopt for the years ahead, and the policies and consequences that each would entail. Of course, an infinite number of futures is possible, and it is unlikely that the real energy future of the United States will conform closely to any of the three scenarios. The scenrios are not predictions, but tools for rigorous thinking.

The first scenario, which is called *historical growth,* assumes that the use of energy will continue to grow much as it has in the past. It assumes that the nation will not deliberately impose any policies that might affect our ingrained habits of energy use but will make a strong effort to develop supplies at a rapid pace to match rising demand.

The *technical fix* scenario shares with *historical growth* a similar level and mix of goods and services. But it reflects a determined, conscious national effort to reduce demand for energy through the application of energy-saving technologies. Research so far has revealed that the slower rate of energy growth in *technical fix*—about half as high as *historical growth's*—permits more flexibility of energy supply but still provides for an adequate quality of life. Only one of the major domestic sources of energy—Rocky Mountain coal or shale, or nuclear power, or oil and gas—would have to be pushed hard to meet the energy growth rates of this scenario.

Zero energy growth is different. It represents a real break with our accustomed ways of doing things. Yet, it does not represent austerity. "It would give everyone in the United States more energy benefits in the year 2000 than he enjoys today, even enough to allow the less privileged to catch up to the comforts of the American Way of Life. It does not preclude economic growth."[13] This obviously requires the use of less energy-intensive equipment and methods of production and operations. Zero energy growth would emphasize durability, not disposability of goods. It would substitute for the idea that "more is better" the ethic that "enough is best."

All three scenarios share certain characteristics. They all assume household comforts and conveniences greater than today's; no one must live, because of energy scarcity, in a lightless shack or a sweltering tenement. Every American

[11]Quoted in Robert V. Ayres, *Technological Forecasting* (New York: McGraw-Hill, 1969), p. 143.

[12]*Exploring Energy Choices: A Preliminary Report of the Ford Foundation Energy Policy Project* (Washington, D.C.: Ford Foundation, 1974).

[13]Ibid., p. 40.

would have a warm home in winter, air-conditioning in hot climates, and a kitchen complete with appliances. He would still drive a car and have a job, although he might drive less or have a different job, depending on the scenario the nation follows.[14]

The Delphi Method

Another intuitive technique of thinking about and forecasting future events is the so-called Delphi Method, named after the Greek oracle of Delphi, situated some 70 miles north of Athens. The Delphi Method is usually referred to as a structured interaction among members of a group known as the "experts," who are either verbally, electronically (through a computer terminal) or through a questionnaire interrogated with regard to their expectations for a series of hypothetical futures.[15] The ultimate outcome of the Delphi method is a consensus of expert opinion concerning the possibility and timing of certain technological evidence. For example, the following question may be asked of a panel of experts: In what year (if ever) do you expect nuclear power to supply more than 10% of the electricity needs of the United States?

Delphi was developed by the RAND Corporation during the early 1960s. In its most common form, Delphi consists of rounds of a series of questionnaires, distributed by the investigator to the experts. The first round is a series of questions, the responses to which are then statistically compiled. The results of this first round are then fed back to the original panelists, who are asked to submit revised answers together with reasons for agreeing or disagreeing with the initial consensus. In the third (and most often the last) round, the procedure is repeated, often with additional discussion and debate. The ultimate outcome desired is always an expert consensus, which is arrived at after considerable arguing, clarifying and, sometimes, compromising.

An example of a Delphi Study will illustrate the general procedures employed.

Figure 17-4 shows a world population projection based on "naive" trend extrapolation and, beneath it, an envelope of projections obtained from a panel of experts interrogated separately by T. J. Gordon and Olaf Helmer.[16] The experts in this case clearly took account of the existing trend but almost unanimously agreed that the future rate of population growth would slow down for various reasons, notably the continuing invention and wider acceptance of birth control measures. The panel was also cognizant of contrary trends, such as a continued decline in the death rate as a result of medical progress, and the possibility (but not probability) of greater improvement in the technology of food production and distribution. The result is a balanced forecast in which the best information available has been utilized in a way that no simple model or statistical extrapolation could hope to duplicate.[17]

[14] Ibid, p. 42.
[15] Ayres, op. cit., p. 149.
[16] "Report on a Long-range Forecasting Study," *RAND Corp.*, September 1964, p. 2982.
[17] Ayres, op. cit., p. 150.

Four Types of Scenario

	Type of Scenario	Aim(s) of Scenario	Premises of Scenario	Procedures Used
Exploratory Scenarios	1. Tendential Scenario.	Seek to determine a possible future.	Suppose that 'heavy trends' are permanent and predominant.	Examine the continuation in the future of these trends and the mechanisms that explain them.
	2. Framework Scenario.	Try to delimit the space of range of possible futures.	Suppose that 'heavy trends' are permanent and predominant.	Make very varied (extreme) hypotheses concerning the evolution of these trends.
Anticipatory Scenarios	3. Normative Scenario.	Seek to produce an image of a future that is possible and 'desirable.'	Suppose that we can determine at the outset a range of possible objectives to achieve.	Make a synthesis of these objectives to achieve and relate this image of the present.
		Establish a procedure relating the future to the present.		
	4. Contrasted Scenario.	Outline a 'desirable' future located at the frontier of possibilities.	Suppose that we can determine at the outset a range of possible objectives to achieve relating to the objectives desired.	Make a synthesis of objectives to achieve and relate this image of the future to the present.

Peter Hall, *Europe 2000* (New York: Columbia University Press, 1977), p. 7.

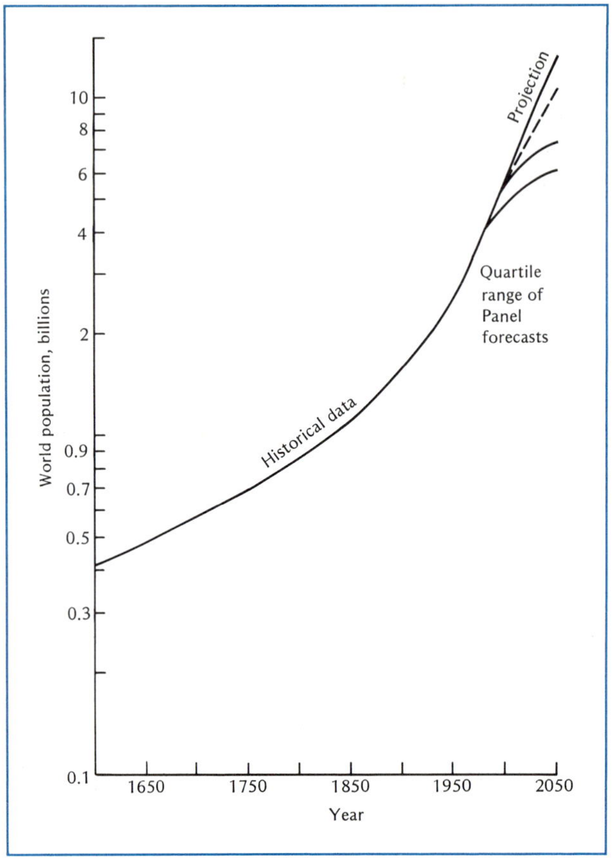

FIGURE 17-4. **Delphi Forecasts of Population (1960–2000).**

Systems Dynamics

All three previously explained futuristic techniques—extrapolation, Delphi method, and scenario writing—are characterized by their main preoccupation with a single issue, event, or phenomenon. As was shown, in extrapolation, a given quantity of a certain item is projected into some future time, following a predetermined path. Under the Delphi method, different possible paths of developments in a given area are eventually narrowed down to a few that constitute the most probable ones. A similar function is performed in the scenario writing method. In all these cases, little allowance is made for more than one phenomenon to be occurring, either simultaneously or sequentially.

Systems dynamics, as the name implies, focuses on a set of events, issues, or phenomena that are in continuous relation to each other and form a system. The logic of systems and the systems approach were explained in Chapter 3. Here, we concentrate on two of the most important applications of systems dynamics. The first example comes from the Massachusetts Institute of Technology (MIT) systems dynamics group, and the second, although more international in origin, is known as the Case Western Reserve Institute model. Both of these applications of the systems dynamics method for thinking about and even planning for the future have been commissioned by the Club of Rome, an international group of citizens concerned with the problems contemporary society faces on a global basis. The Club was formed in 1968 by Aurelio Peccei.[18]

The Limits to Growth. After considerable discussions through formal conferences and private gatherings, the Club of Rome decided in 1969 to commission Jay Forrester, Professor of Management at MIT, to develop a model that could be used to study how the world as a whole functions. The Volkswagen Foundation provided the initial funding. After several years of study, the MIT group, under the directorship of Donnela and Dennis Meadows, published the results of its work in a short paperback, entitled *The Limits to Growth.*[19] The book has sold more than 3 million copies and has sent shockwaves all over the world.

The method employed by the MIT group is a systems approach along the lines described in Chapters 3, 13, 14, 15, and 16 of this book. The entire world has been modeled as a system of five interacting variables: population, food production, industrial production, nonrenewable resources, and pollution. Figure 17-5 presents the conceptual model in a pictorial form. Each variable depends upon and affects the others. Each variable is defined in terms of both its *level,* or *state,* (meaning the absolute quantity of a given time), and its *rate,* or *flow* (meaning the degree of incoming and outgoing people, food, industrial capital, resources, and pollution). Figure 17-6 provides a partial example of these multiple feedback couplings.

The total computerized model is, of course, more complex than the portion depicted in Figure 17-6, but the basic structure is the same. Figure 17-7 shows the result of the first computer version of the world system under conditions similar to those that prevailed in 1970. As the figure shows, this so-called *standard run* indicates that the world will indeed collapse sometime around the year 2000. The reason for this collapse is the exhaustion of the nonrenewable resources (which will cause a decline in both food and industrial production), coupled with a tremendous increase in population. This twentieth-century, super-computerized team at MIT reached the same conclusion as was revealed by the Reverend Thomas Malthus more than a century ago when the availability of pencil and paper was considered a luxury.

[18]For an eloquent description of the history of the Club of Rome and the two reports we will describe here, see the autobiography of the founder of the Club, Aurelio Peccei, *The Human Quality* (Oxford: Pergamon Press, 1977).

[19]Donnela Meadows, Dennis Meadows, Jorgen Randers, and William Behsey, III, *The Limits to Growth* (New York: Signet, 1972).

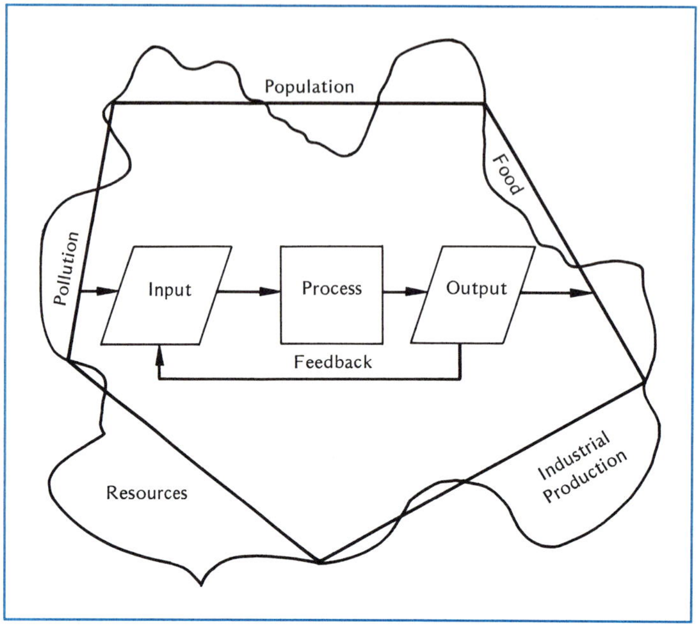

FIGURE 17-5. "The Limits to Growth" Conceptual Model.

Of course, there is no reason to believe that the conditions that prevailed until 1970 will continue in the future. New social and technological innovations might cause population to decline, as it did after 1970, and new resources might enable industrial and agricultural production to continue without excessive pollution. *The Limits to Growth* contains detailed explanations of attempts made by the group to account for such changes and their results. Figure 17-8 depicts the ultimate world model stabilized. There are no collapses in this model.

There is one condition that must be satisfied if this equilibrium is to occur. It is known as the "Double Zero Condition": Zero Population Growth (ZPG) and Zero Economic Growth (ZEG). In terms of the mechanics of the model, the situation depicted in Figure 17-8 will materialize only if

Birth Rates = Death Rates
(or Birth Rates − Death Rate = 0) (ZPG)
and New Investment = Depreciation
(or New Investment − Depreciation = 0) (ZEG)

This double zero condition for a world equilibrium earned the MIT study the name, the Doomsday Book.

Mankind at the Turning Point. Although a sizeable portion of the world's scientific community dismissed The Club of Rome's first report, *The*

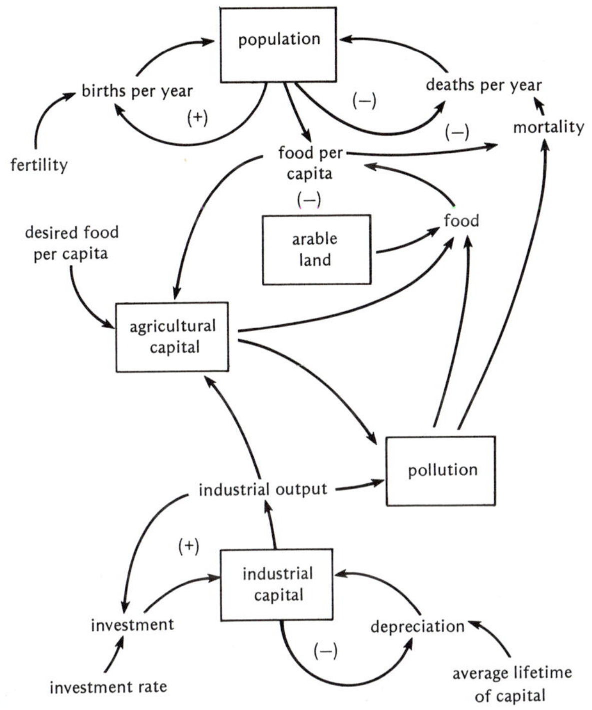

Some of the interconnections between population and industrial capital operate through agricultural capital, cultivated land, and pollution. Each arrow indicates a causal relationship, which may be immediate or delayed, large or small, positive or negative, depending on the assumptions included in each model run.

FIGURE 17-6. Feedback Loops of Population, Capital, Agriculture, and Pollution. (Source: Meadows, et. al.,* The Limits to Growth, *p. 106.)

Limits to Growth, as a most sophisticated neo-Malthusian attempt to create panic, some took it seriously but set out to prove that it was wrong. Still, many concerned scientists set out to remodel the world by carefully studying *The Limits* and by incorporating some of the valid criticisms levied against it. Mihaljo Meserovic from the Case Western Reserve Systems Institute (Cleveland, Ohio), and Edward Pestel from the Hannover Institute of Technology, in Hannover, West Germany, are two representatives of the last group who were commissioned by the Club of Rome to produce the second report to the Club, entitled *Mankind At The Turning Point.*[20]

[20] Mihaljo Meservoic, and Edward Pestel, *Mankind at the Turning Point* (New York: E. P. Dutton, 1974).

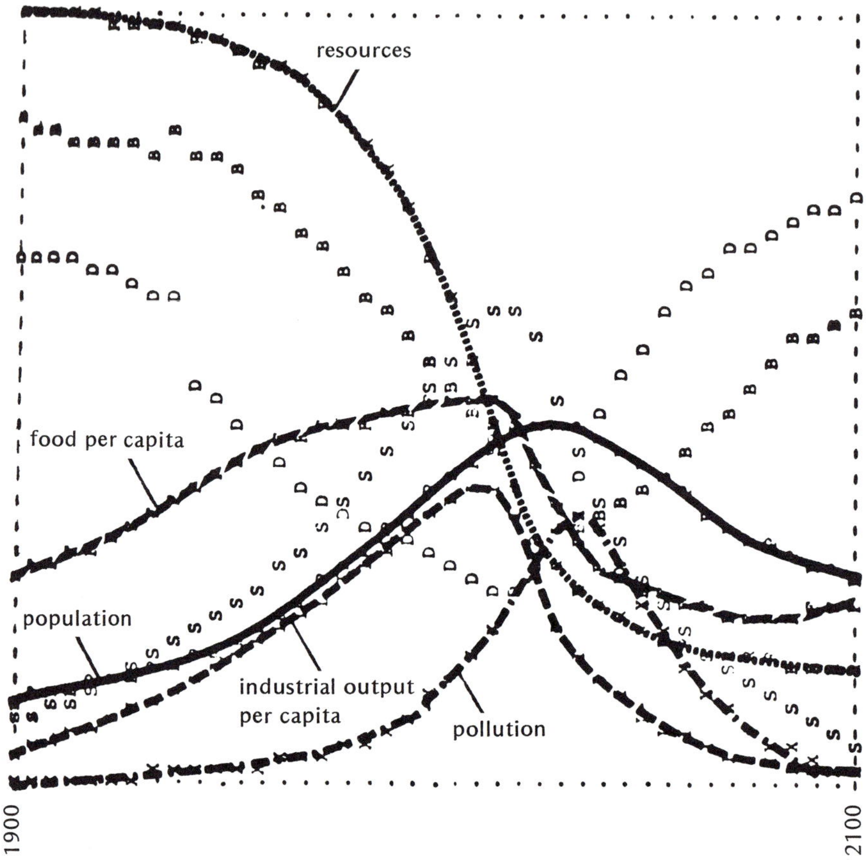

The "standard" world model run assumes no major change in the physical, economic, or social relationships that have historically governed the development of the world system. All variables plotted here follow historical values from 1900 to 1970. Food, industrial output, and population grow exponentially until the rapidly diminishing resource base forces a slowdown in industrial growth. Because of natural delays in the system, both population and pollution continue to increase for some time after the peak of industrialization. Population growth is finally halted by a rise in the death rate due to decreased food and medical services.

FIGURE 17-7. World Model Standard Run. (Source: Meadows, et. al, The Limits to Growth, *p. 129.)*

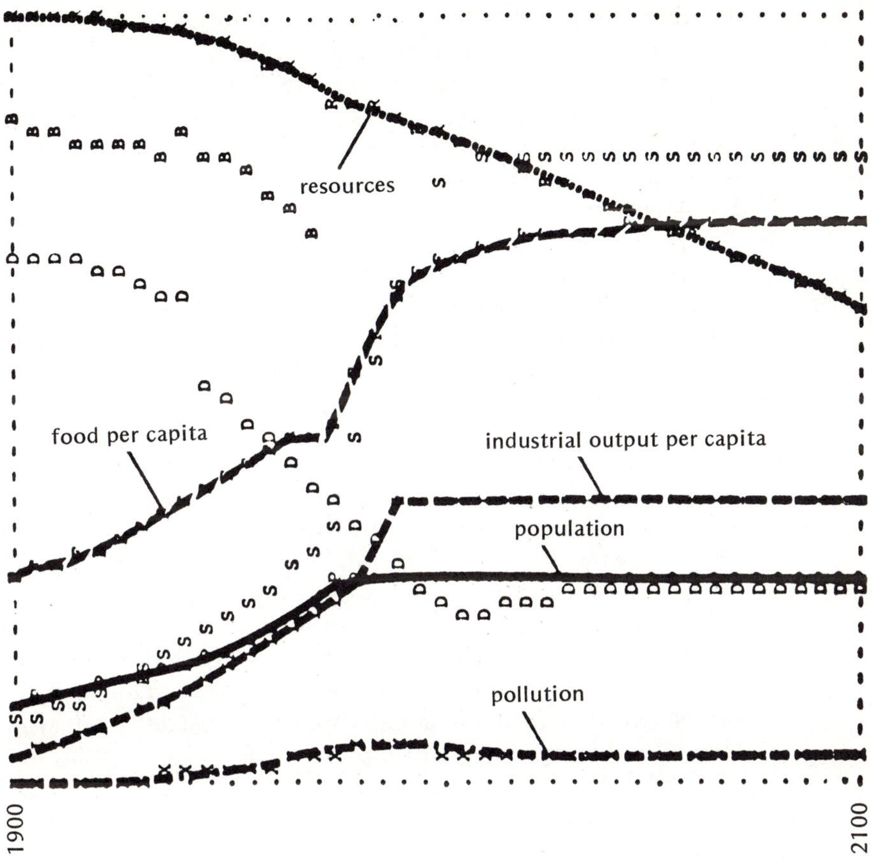

Technological policies are added to the growth-regulating policies of the previous run to produce an equilibrium state sustainable far into the future. Technological policies include resource recycling, pollution control devices, increased lifetime of all forms of capital, and methods to restore eroded and infertile soil. Value changes include increased emphasis on food and services rather than on industrial production. As in figure 45, births are set equal to deaths and industrial capital investment equal to capital depreciation. Equilibrium value of industrial output per capita is three times the 1970 world average.

FIGURE 17-8. Stabilized World Model I (Source: Meadows, et. al., The Limits to Growth, *p. 168.)*

Mankind, like *The Limits*, employs a systems approach, although of a slightly different nature. Also, like *The Limits*, it focuses on the long-term survival of humanity. Unlike *The Limits*, however, *Mankind* conceives of the world not as a homogeneous system, resembling the United States, but, instead, models the world as consisting primarily of 10 regions that can be grouped into four main "worlds": (1) the first, developed or industrialized world (Regions 1–4, North America, Western Europe, Japan, Australia, and South Africa); (2) the second, or centrally planned economies world (Regions 5 and 6, Russia and the rest of the Communist world); (3) the third world or resources-rich, less-developed countries (Latin American, the oil- and other new material-rich countries); and finally, (4) the fourth, or poor, world (Asia and Africa).

Looking at the world through *Mankind's* glasses does offer one some hope. There is no one gigantic and catastrophic collapse in the *Mankind's* crystal ball, but there are a series of regional collapses, known as *crises*. For example, the population crisis is mostly a third and fourth world collapse. The remedy? Zero population growth. Then there is the resources crisis that is mostly a first world collapse. The remedy? Organic growth, meaning a 1% to 2% per year economic growth (GNP increase) for the first world, coupled with a 6% to 7% growth per year for the third and fourth worlds, made possible by the transfer of wealth from the first to the third and fourth world (installation of factories, and so on in the third and fourth world, rather than in the first world).

One conclusion seems to emerge from both of these systems dynamics glimpses into the future: *the earth will not be able to sustain an ever-growing population that needs more food and demands more industrial goods while creating more human and industrial pollution.*

MANAGERIAL FUTURISM

How does the contemporary manager go about developing what William James referred to as a sense of futurity? In other words, *how do today's managers relate today's actions to their future consequences?* In this last section of the chapter, we offer two somewhat distinct and yet related approaches to the development and enlargement of a sense of *managerial futurity*. We do not subscribe to the popular philosophy that unless every manager becomes a trained futurist, organizations will collapse. What we believe is that because managerial actions have planned and unplanned immediate and future consequences, it behooves every modern manager to attempt to think carefully about the future consequences as much as he or she thinks about the immediate results of managerial actions.

It must be said at the outset that before managers decide what approach should be used, they must clarify for themselves their general viewpoint toward the future. For example, one must show alliance with or dissociation from the following statements:

I saw the future and it's rosy!
I saw the future and it doesn't work!
Posterity be damned! What has it done for me lately?
Let's enjoy the here and now.
The future is in my hands—as it always has been.
I never saw the future so I can't do anything about it.
Well, by then, I'll be long gone!

As a general rule, the manager must remember what the Greek philosopher Epicurus said about the future some 2,300 years ago.

Remember that the future is neither ours nor wholly not ours, so that we may neither count on it as sure to come nor abandon hope of it as certain not to be.

The Outside Expert Approach

One way to develop a sense of managerial futurity is to engage an outside individual or firm that specializes in future research. There are by now thousands of individuals, working alone or as members or associates of organizations (usually called think tanks, centers, institutes, or groups), who claim a competency in assessing an organization's future in general and the future consequences of an organization's actions or inactions in particular. These think tanks usually produce periodic research reports, either custom-made or general, regarding particular sets of events and their possible and probable impacts upon a given industry or firm.

In general, one can divide outside expert groups into two categories: those that specialize exclusively in futuristic research (such as Herman Kahn's The Hudson Institute, Stanford Research Institute, and The Center for Futures Research at The University of Southern California), and those institutions whose main purpose is to do research for a given group of organizations and which periodically center on the subject of future, (such as The American Management Association, The Conference Board, The Ford Foundation, and Brookings Institute).

The In-house Organizational Futurity Approach

Despite the conceptual elegance, simplicity, and practicality of the outside expert approach to developing a managerial sense of futurity, most organizations find it insufficient to deal with today's complexities and the accompanying uncertainty of their future environments. For this reason, more and more organizations develop their own future group. The *Wall Street Journal* has quoted James B. Webber, a director at Cambridge Research Institute, as saying that "as many as one out of five of the Fortune 500 companies now have employees who play the genie in a practical sense, keeping firms abreast so they don't get caught short."[21] The composition, mandate, status, importance, and decision-making capacity of the future groups that are to be found in organizations vary, but in general they are expected to perform the function of early warning systems to keep busy executives alert as to what is ahead in business and society. Space does not allow us here to provide a complete description of how these groups operate. Two examples are presented in the following boxes. Suffice it to say here that there is considerably more emphasis placed on sociocultural and demographic trends and less on economic projections.

MANAGERIAL IMPLICATIONS: THE DESIGN OF A FUTURE ASSESSMENT SYSTEM (FAS)

Irving S. Shapiro, Chairman of the Board, E.I. du Pont de Nemours and Company, concluded his address to the September 16, 1976 conference organized by The Conference Board as follows:

> *The future role of business in society will depend to a major extent on* how *business management proceeds as well as the results it achieves,* how *constructively it works with government to achieve public goals,* how *candidly it responds to inadvertent mistakes,* how carefully it handles new safety risks, *how* wisely it introduces new technology, *how* successfully it helps to solve job and economic growth problems, *how* responsibly it blends business goals with energy and environmental priorities, and *how* effectively it joins with other sectors of society to help solve recurring national and international problems.[22]

The basic philosophy underlying the system is to *identify* the major stakeholders of an organization, *assess their needs* and *desires* and, based upon this assessment, *make the necessary changes* in managerial philosophies and practices that will assure a maximum satisfaction of these needs and desires.[23] Operationally, the system depends heavily on (1) timely and accurate scanning of the organization's environment; (2) timely and accurate feeding to the organization's management of information pertaining to deviations between a desired position and an actual situation; and (3) timely, accurate, and appropriate corrective action designed to minimize the deviations.

Figure 17-9 provides a matrix-type of arrangement of a Future Assessment System (FAS). The rows of the matrix are reserved for the major emerging issues that appear to dominate the contemporary and, to some extent, the future scene.

[21] Liz Roman Gallese, op. cit., p. 2.

[22] Irving S. Shapiro, "An Industrialist's View," in *The Future Role of Business in Society* (New York: The Conference Board, 1977) p. 11.

[23] George Coker, "Alternative Futures for the Corporation," presented at the 22nd Annual North American Meeting of the Society for General Systems Research, February 18, 1978, Washington, D.C.

The Trend Analysis Program (TAP) of the American Council of Life Insurance

From among its member companies, the Council recruited volunteer "monitors," each of whom is assigned one of 60 carefully selected publications, ranging from the *Wall Street Journal* to *Rolling Stone* and from the *American Journal of Sociology* to *Technology Review.* This information universe is arbitrarily divided into four broad categories: science and technology, social sciences, business and economics, and politics and government. Each monitor is also assigned a subject area and reads his or her publication for articles that meet the following criteria:

1. The article should involve an idea or event that is indicative of either a trend or shift in the environment.
2. The implications to be drawn from the article should have some relation to the long-range concerns of both our society and the life insurance business.

The monitor prepares an abstract of any article that meets these criteria and then submits it to the Council. A Council staff group known as the Abstract Analysis Committee meets every other month for a day-long session to review the 80 to 100 abstracts submitted during the preceding two months and analyze their implications. A summary of each meeting is sent to a steering committee made up of a dozen senior executives from the membership. This committee meets three times a year to review the summaries, deliberate on staff recommendations for report contents, review drafts of reports, and, in general, oversee the program.

Arnold Brown, "How to Get the Jump on your Future," *Management Review* (June 1977) p. 45.

The columns of the matrix depict the organization and its environment. The manager gets a sense of futurity by looking at the issue and by inquiring about its relationship to the organization and its environment. The possible and probable relationships are measured in terms of both magnitude (size) and importance (significance).[24]

How does the manager determine what the emerging issues are? The answer is, by observing the world around the organization and inside the organization and by relating those observations to what the manager's job is all about. The seven issues in Figure 17-9 are chosen after careful reading about and observing the most significant changes in the American and most of the world societies. Some of these changes are depicted in the box taken from the front page of the December 1977 issue of *The Congressional Clearinghouse on the Future,* a

[24] A. G. Kefalas, "Managerial Futurity: Relating Today's Actions to Their Future Consequences," *Working Paper,* College of Business Administration, the University of Georgia, Athens, Georgia.

The Sun Company Environmental Assessment System

The Sun Company has assigned the responsibility for the long-range future of the corporation to the chairman and vice-chairman of the board of directors. One of the resource facilities that the vice-chairman has established is "Environmental Assessment." In this context, environment refers not to the air, water, and land but rather to the very general environment of economics, technology, politics, and society in which Sun operates today and will have to operate in the future.

The Environmental Assessment group consists of Sun's chief economist, a specialist in technological assessment, and a public issues consultant—all reporting to the vice-president of environmental assessment. The chief economist evaluates and forecasts the state of the economy; the technological assessment specialist covers technology and science, and the public issues consultant concentrates on politics and society. ("Politics" should be interpreted very broadly, running to the idea of "political climate" and the "science of the possible" rather than Republican/Democrat.)

Eric A. Weiss, "The Future Public Opinion of Business," *Management Review* (March 1978) p. 9.

publication designed to keep members of the U.S. Congress informed on future matters.[25]

Although the emerging issues chosen for this FAS may not apply to a specific organization, they are general enough to cover a wide spectrum of organizations. In general, an emerging issue is defined as a related set of widely discussed or publicized ideas, events, or viewpoints that are still in an evolving state (over which no definitive and final decision has been made), allowing for active participation by the affected parties.[26] All of the seven issues that appear in Figure 17-9 satisfy this definition. A brief example will suffice to explain the function of the FAS.

As can be seen from the closeup in Fig. 17-9 (example), there is usually (but not always) an inverse relationship between the magnitude (that is, the intensity of the emerging issue as measured by the percentage of time devoted to it by the media, legislators, and so on) and its impact upon an organization. In other words, although there appears to be "no issue" because neither the public at large nor legislators are talking about it, organizations are at the apex of their concern. For example, most people would agree that the "ecology issue" (pollution of air, water, and land by business) reached a climax in 1970 with the passage of the

[25] Americans Change, Special Report, *Business Week*, February 20, 1978, pp. 64–70. See also, Peter Schwartz, Peter Teige, and Willis W. Harmon, "In Search of Tomorrow," *The Futurist* (October 1977), pp. 269–273. Also, by the same authors, "Forty-one Future Problems," *The Futurist* (October 1977), pp. 273–278.

[26] The Conference Board has recently established an Emerging Issues System Program in its Management Research Division. *What's Next Congressional Clearinghouse on the Future*, Washington, May 1978, p. 2.

The Emerging Issues / The Organization and Its Environment	THE ENVIRONMENT: The General External Business Environment						THE ENVIRONMENT: The Immediate Ext. Bus. Env.			THE ORGANIZATION		
	Public	Government	Technology	Domestic Market	World Market	Ecology	Customers	Suppliers	Stock Holders	Inputs: —Money —Natural Resources —People	Process: —Management —Science —Technology	Output: —Goods —Services —Waste
The *Bedroom* Issue Storks vs Stocks (population)	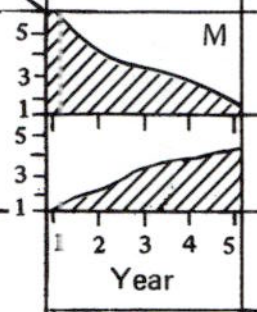											
The *Boardroom* Issue The Golden Goose vs. The Ecological Nest (Economic Growth)												
The *Conservation* Issue: Do More with less vs. Do Less with less												
The *Control* Issue: Manage the External Relations vs. Being Externally Managed (Regulations)												
The *Ethics* Issue: The Written Law vs. The Natural Harmony												
The *Size* Issue: Big is Best vs. Small is Beautiful												
The *Survival* Issue: Quantity of Output vs. Quality of Life												

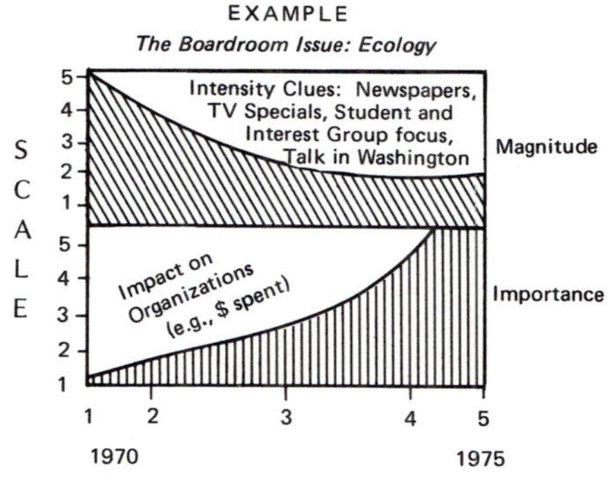

FIGURE 17-9. A Future Assessment System. (© Kefalas.)

WHAT'S NEXT?

CONGRESSIONAL CLEARINGHOUSE ON THE FUTURE

DECEMBER 1977 VOL. 2 NO. 6

HARRIS POLL FINDS SIGNIFICANT CHANGES IN AMERICANS

In late September, the results of a recent Harris poll of the American public were circulated to Democratic Members of the House of Representatives.

"Basically, our people are far more concerned with the quality of life and far less with the unlimited acquisition of more physical goods and products," remarked Mr. Harris. "These are radical findings by any measure, for they mean that the age of materialism as we have known it is going to be radically altered."

Selected findings are presented here. We think you will find them interesting.

Those polled said:

--by 73-23% that they want to participate in community decisions affecting their lives

--by 72-23% that they prefer to cooperate, rather than compete, with others

--by 86-9% that they want to experience life directly rather than watching it on TV

--by 84-13% that they welcome challenges to their creative abilities

--by 61-27% that they think modern technology has caused as many problems as benefits to people

--by 71-18% that they would prefer a clean environment to one which provides many jobs

--by 83-7% that the country would be better off if children were educated more to find their own inner satisfaction than to be a success and make a lot of money

--by 68-21% that economic growth falsely makes people want to acquire more possessions than to enjoy non-material experiences

--by 79-17% that it is more important to teach people to live with basic essentials than to reach higher standards of living

--by 77-15% that they prefer spending time getting to know each other as human beings, rather than speeding up our ability to communicate through technology

--by 63-29% that it is more important to learn to appreciate human values--as opposed to material values--than it is to find ways to create more jobs for producing more goods

--by 66-22% that they want more emphasis on breaking up big things and getting back to more humanized living than to develop bigger and more efficient ways of doing things.

National Environmental Protection Act and has simmered down since then. Its impact on organizations did not start to become visible until 1972–1973. By 1975, business concern was very high, whereas environmentalists were in a state of relative quiet.

There is no intention in this book to provide a complete "how-to-do-it" recipe for assessing and managing the future. The intentions are to emphasize that it is possible to assess the future and its impact on an organization, as well as to point out that managerial involvement in this process is necessary and rewarding.

SUMMARY

This chapter dealt with the subject of futurology, which was defined as the study of the possibilities of tomorrow and the efforts to convert these possibilities into preferred probabilitities. Thus, futurology is both an intellectual activity envisioning alternative worlds *as well as active attempts aiming at organizing society* and its institutions so that some of these alternative visions will materialize. It was pointed out in this chapter that most sectors of our society have developed well-organized efforts to "future sensitivize" their members. Particular mention was made of The World Future Society, The Master of Science in Studies of The Future Program at the University of Houston at Clear Lake City, The Congressional Clearinghouse on the Future, and The Center for Futures Research of The University of Southern California.

Thinking and organizing one's business with respect to the future has become a well-respected academic endeavor. In this chapter, four major future forecasting techniques were briefly explained. These techniques are: (1) extrapolation; (2) scenario writing; (3) the Delphi method; and (4) systems dynamics. There are innumerable methods of thinking about the future and forecasting its possible implications upon one's life and upon organizations. However, the preponderance of them are variations or combinations of the four major techniques described in this chapter.

The last part of the chapter touched on the subject of managerial futurism. Managers of organizations can develop a sense of futurity; that is to say, relate their today's actions to their future consequences by either employing an outside group that specializes in future studies or by developing their own organizational futurity-oriented management style. We recommend the latter approach. This approach requires that an organization develop (in addition to an organizational climate conducive to futuristic thinking) a Future Assessment System (FAS). This system monitors certain key issues, which we labeled "emerging issues," and assesses both their magnitude and the importance of their impact upon the organization and its environment.

Assignments

1. What is futurology?
2. How does the U.S. Congress explore the future?

3. What is extrapolation?
4. How does scenario writing differ from the Delphi method?
5. What is systems dynamics?
6. Briefly describe the three scenarios advanced in the Ford Foundation's study of Explaining Energy Choices.
7. Write a short description of *The Limits of Growth.*
8. How does *Mankind at the Turning Point* differ from *The Limits*?
9. How does a manager develop a sense of futurity?
10. What is a Future Assessment System?

Case 17-1

THOMAS MALTHUS MEETS HERMAN KAHN

Mike Mellon feels confused. It's almost noon and he has not been able to do any work. Just yesterday, he returned from New York City where he attended a one-day seminar on "The Future and Its Implications for Business." In the morning session, he listened to a forum of researchers presenting some very gloomy findings about the problems of the world and the inability of people, organizations, and the government to deal with them. Mike remembers vividly how a particular professor kept talking about the Reverend Thomas Malthus, who around 1800 presented a paper talking about how humanity was doomed because population increased at such a fast rate that sooner or later food would run out and people would begin to starve to death. The professor was making the case very colorfully by using charts representing the outputs of computer models that confirm Malthus' theory. It was a very bleak picture. First, the earth would run out of oil, then copper, then bauxite, and then one by one, most of the resources. Likewise, most of the major industries were shut down either because of a lack of the necessary inputs or because of too much pollution. "You see, ladies and gentlemen," said the professor, "it's simple. We must stop our population and our industry from growing, or else we will die."

In the afternoon session, a rather heavyset man entered the lecture hall. He must have been a well-known person, because most people began applauding as soon as he entered the room. Finally, the lady who was chairing the meeting took the microphone and announced, "Ladies and gentlemen, I'm proud to present to you Herman Kahn from the Hudson Institute. Mr. Kahn will present, so he says, a rather different view from the one you heard this morning."

Mr. Kahn's message was simple: "We've got where we are today thanks to a rather healthy growth in GNP and everything else, so why quit growth now? In the future we will continue to grow. The difference will be that we will grow differently and also slower. So cheer up and enjoy yourselves. However, I'd advise you to get ready, because your life and business will change considerably."

All of these thoughts were going through Mike Mellon's head. He feels that he, as president of General Infants, Inc., must do something. *Time, time is the problem.* He doesn't have the time. He would like to have something for the board meeting next week.

1. You have been called on as an outside expert. Write a scenario as to what the implications for General Infants will be under each of these two futures.

Case 17-2

THE TOMORROW CAR: EVERYBODY NEEDS IT BUT NOBODY WANTS IT

"I don't know, Ms. Jackson," said Mr. Alton, the president of WMW, the World Motor Works. "You've got it all wrong. You're supposed to think about designing, producing, and marketing a car that everybody wants. What is all this talk about committing 100 million dollars for a car that everybody needs but nobody wants?" "Well, sir," said Ms. Jackson, "it is like this." And Jackson went ahead to explain the merits of the new car. Mr. Alton was listening to Jackson, but he wasn't really hearing anything. He kept thinking "My God, what do they teach these kids in school nowadays?"

Jackson was about through when Mr. Alton noticed a sheet of paper pushed toward him. Among other things, the paper contained a list of forecasts, a sample of which looked like this:

	Years		
Items	1980	1990	2000
....	.....	.....	.....
Steel	$5/ton	$20/ton	$100/ton
Copper	$10/ton	$50/ton	$150/ton
Gasoline	70¢/gal	$1.50/gal	$5/gal
Lube oil	70¢/qt	$2.20/qt	$6/qt
....	....	.....	.....
....	....	.....	.....
....	....	.....	.....
Electricity	10¢/kwh	15¢/kwh	17¢/kwh
....	....	.....	.....

(Figures hypothetical)

"Wait a minute, Jackson. Where did you get those figures?" "You see, sir," said Jackson, "these figures came from the latest report on 'Industrial Outlook: The Next Two Decades.'" Jackson pushed a heavy, thick book to Mr. Alton. Mr. Alton took the book in his hands, turned to Ms. Jackson, and said, "Could you run that by me once again? You want us to build a car that will be different. It will be small and light, rather ugly in appearance, and will get 60 miles to a gallon? Am I reading you right?" "Well, sir," said Ms. Jackson, "that's one option. We could think of a scenario in which a rather nonconventional car could be built." "Listen," said Mr. Alton. "Tomorrow, I'm taking up the subject with the executive committee. Could you give me a one-page description of at least two scenarios?"

1. Assuming Ms. Jackson's role, write these two scenarios.

References

ACKOFF, RUSSELL. *Redesigning the Future: A Systems Approach to Social Problems.* New York: John Wiley & Sons, Inc., 1974.

BEER, STAFFORD. *Platform for Change.* New York: John Wiley & Sons, Inc., 1970.

BELL, DANIEL. *The Coming of Post-Industrial Society: A Venture in Social Forecasting.* New York: Basic Books, Inc., 1973.

BELL, DANIEL. *Toward the Year 2000: Work in Progress.* Boston: Beacon Press, 1967.

CARSON, RACHEL. *Silent Spring.* Greenwich, Conn.: Fawcett Publications, 1962.

GABOR, DENNIS. *Inventing the Future.* New York: Alfred A. Knopf, Inc., 1971.

GABOR, DENNIS. *The Mature Society.* London: Secker and Warberg, 1973.

HEIBRONER, ROBERT L. *The Limits of American Capitalism.* New York: Harper & Row, Publishers, 1965.

KAHN, HERMAN. *Thinking About the Unthinkable.* New York: Avon, 1962.

KAHN, HERMAN. *The Next 200 Years.* New York: William Morrow & Co., Inc., 1976.

KEFALAS, A. G. "The Future of the Corporation." *Proceedings,* Society for General Systems Research, 1978.

LASZLO, ERVIN, and others. *Goals for Mankind.* New York: E. P. Dutton & Co., Inc., 1977.

LASZLO ERVIN. *A Strategy for the Future.* New York: George Braziller, Inc., 1974.

LILLIAN, KAY W., ed. *The Future Role of Business in Society.* New York: The Conference Board, 1977.

LINSTONE, HAROLD, AND W. H. CLIVE SIMMONDS. *Future Research: New Directions.* Reading, Mass.: Addison-Wesley Publishing Co., Inc., 1977.

MCHALE, JOHN. *The Future of the Future.* New York: Ballantine Books, Inc., 1969.

America Tomorrow: Wall Street Journal Views. Princeton, N.J.: Dow Jones Books, 1977.

PALUSTEK, JOHN. *Business and Society: 1976–2000: An AMA Survey.* New York: American Management Associations, Inc., 1976.

TOFFLER, ALVIN. *Future Shock.* New York: Bantam Books, 1970.

GEORGE T. COKER, JR.
Staff Engineer, Shell Development Company, Houston, Texas

In his 25-year research and development career with Shell, George T. Coker, Jr.'s varied assignments in six different locations have necessitated working closely with the management of many industrial concerns. His political and civic affairs were highlighted by the 1967 selection as an Outstanding Young

Man of America. As an active futurist since 1972, he served as Education Chairman of the Bay Area Corporate Planners Association and created Project Forethought, an informal network of several hundred futures-oriented corporate planners. He has reported the activities of this network at IAPS, several PEI conferences, and the 1978 Society of General System Research meeting.

Executive Commentary

Futurism: A Tool for Resource Allocation

Let me begin this commentary by underscoring a statement made in this chapter: "The scenarios are not predictions but tools for rigorous thinking." This statement is not limited to scenarios but is equally applicable to all forecasting techniques, including some not mentioned by the authors, such as substitution theory, mission flow analysis, step function patterns, relevance tree analysis, and so on. Many have grappled with the practical application of futurism. This commentary suggests a technique for using futurism as an aid in the problem of resource allocation decisions either in your personal or professional life.

In managing resources, money, time, people, or equipment, either yours or those entrusted to you by others, success comes to those who wisely and efficiently allocate these limited resources. All resource allocation decisions are based on some view of the future. This view may be conscious or subconscious and, unfortunately, in most cases, it is based on the assumption that tomorrow will be like today but better for me because I am more intelligent than others. Applying futurism forces one out of the tomorrow-like-today dilemma that has caused many problems for corporations.

Classifying scenarios as just one of the many forecasting methods is a mistake. Scenarios are, in fact, a display method of integrating the data collected by other forecasting techniques. Obviously, from a given data base, an infinite number of scenarios can be constructed, and the data base can be derived from one or more forecasting techniques. For illustrative purposes, this discussion will be limited to using three scenarios: a most likely future and two boundary scenarios, a pessimistic and an optimistic one. A note of caution on the use of the terms *pessimistic* and *optimistic*. Remember these terms are in the eye of the beholder. What may be an optimistic future for you or your company might well be a pessimistic future for someone else. For example, electric cars would be an optimistic future for an electric company but most certainly a pessimistic one for a gasoline company.

The first question faced is the time frame selected for your futurism study. The general tendency is to forecast 5 years or, straining a bit, perhaps 10 years into the future. Utilizing this approach, one generally ends up with an extrapolation from today, because it's so difficult to see how things might change in so short a period of time. My advice is to leap forward 25, 30, or 50 years, and develop scenarios from a twenty-first-century vantage point. This will provide some insight as to the long-range impact of today's trends and events. For the twenty-first century, most likely, optimistic and pessimistic scenarios can be useful in resource allocation decisions.

Contrast your long-range plan with these scenarios. Are there opportunities and threats to the implementation of the long-range plan? Any opportunities or threats that would have a significant impact on the long-range plan should obviously be studied in more detail. After completing such studies, the long-range goals may necessitate some modification. Because the best "guesstimate" today is that the most likely future will evolve, the temptation is to allocate all available resources on this very shaky, at best, premise, completely ignoring the two boundary cases based on pessimism and optimism. You wouldn't bet all your net worth on one roll of the dice, or would you? Perhaps one should allocate resources by hedging the bet. To make the most use of the time and effort that went into the development of scenarios, set up a tracking system that outlines what has to happen today to reach each of the scenarios. Once one appreciates how each of the various futures might be reached from today, the impact of events as they unfold can be understood. This raises a very important point. Futurism and its integration into long-range planning is a dynamic process, continually changing as events occur.

Perhaps a wise use of resources would be to allocate some 75% or 80%, assuming that the most likely future will evolve. However, to hedge this bet, one might allocate 10% to 15% on the pessimistic case and the remaining 5% or 10% on the optimistic case. With the implementation of a monitoring system such as the future assessment system (FAS) suggested by the authors, one now understands the potential impact of emerging events that permits making, as it were, mid-course corrections. If a shift is noted toward either the pessimistic or the optimistic case, reallocate resources as indicated.

A final note that may be of some assistance in thinking about the future is to recognize in perhaps its most simplistic terms that basically four processes or elements will determine the future. These are the social, technological, economic, and political trends and events. Although many have in the past successfully based scenarios or images of the future on technological forecasting, recent experiences suggest that this is a poor choice. In my opinion, society will get and accept whatever technology it wants. Illustrating this departure from the past in that whatever technology is possible will happen is the literally billions of dollars that this assumption has caused the nuclear power industry and such industries as Boeing in the development of the SST. When viewing the futures, always keep in the back of your mind societal needs and desires.

One cannot predict the future, but by using some of the techniques suggested in this chapter and commentary, one can develop procedures to deal with the almost infinite futures that lie ahead, and it is hoped if the job is done right, wise decisions will be made on resource allocation.

INDEX